300

630/908

THE PRODIGIOUS MUSE

The Prodigious Muse

Women's Writing in Counter-Reformation Italy

Virginia Cox

The Johns Hopkins University Press
Baltimore

This book was brought to publication with the generous assistance of the Lila Acheson Wallace–Reader's Digest Publications Subsidy at Villa I Tatti.

© 2011 The Johns Hopkins University Press
All rights reserved. Published 2011
Printed in the United States of America on acid-free paper
9 8 7 6 5 4 3 2 1

The Johns Hopkins University Press
2715 North Charles Street
Baltimore, Maryland 21218-4363
www.press.jhu.edu

Library of Congress Cataloging-in-Publication Data

Cox, Virginia.
   The prodigious muse : women's writing in counter-reformation Italy / Virginia Cox.
       p. cm.
   Includes bibliographical references and index.
   ISBN-13: 978-1-4214-0032-7 (acid-free paper)
   ISBN-10: 1-4214-0032-4 (acid-free paper)
   1. Italian literature—Women authors—History and criticism. 2. Women and literature—Italy—History. I. Title.
   PQ4063.C685 2011
   850.9′92870945109032—dc22   2010048724

A catalog record for this book is available from the British Library.

Special discounts are available for bulk purchases of this book. For more information, please contact Special Sales at 410-516-6936 or specialsales@press.jhu.edu.

The Johns Hopkins University Press uses environmentally friendly book materials, including recycled text paper that is composed of at least 30 percent post-consumer waste, whenever possible.

CONTENTS

Acknowledgments vii
Introduction xi

CHAPTER ONE. CONTEXTS   1
1. The Female Writer in Context: Opportunities, Attitudes, Models   1
2. Women's Writing and the Counter-Reformation   19
3. Religious Writing in Post-Tridentine Italy: A Poetics of Conversion   32
4. Secular Writing in Post-Tridentine Italy: The New Sensualism and the Misogynist Turn   45

CHAPTER TWO: LYRIC VERSE   51
1. Women's Lyric Output, 1580–1630   51
2. *Pietosi affetti*: Spiritual Lyric and the Female Poet   55
3. The Dwindling Muse: Female-Authored Secular Lyric in Post-Tridentine Italy   76

CHAPTER THREE: DRAMA   87
1. Drama for the Doge: Moderata Fonte's *Le feste*   88
2. Arcadian Adventures: Women Writers and Pastoral Drama   92
3. The Challenge of Tragedy: Valeria Miani's *Celinda*   119

CHAPTER FOUR: SACRED NARRATIVE   129
1. Women Writers and the New Sacred Narrative   129
2. Refashioning the Gospels: New Testament Narrative in Moderata Fonte and Francesca Turina   131
3. Hagiographic Epic: Lucrezia Marinella's Lives of Saints Columba and Francis   141

4. Hagiographic Epic Remade: Marinella's Lives of Mary and Saint Catherine of Siena   151
5. A Medicean Sacred Epic: Maddalena Salvetti's *David perseguitato*   157

CHAPTER FIVE: SECULAR NARRATIVE   164
1. Women Writers and the Literature of Chivalry   165
2. Ideology and History in Female-Authored Chivalric Epic   169
3. Gender, Arms, and Love in Female-Authored Chivalric Fiction   177
4. The Fortunes of Female-Authored Chivalric Fiction   196
5. Beyond Chivalry: Lucrezia Marinella's Experiments in Mythological Epic and Pastoral Romance   197

CHAPTER SIX: DISCURSIVE PROSE   213
1. Output and Principal Trends   213
2. Authorizing Women: The Problem of *Docere*   219
3. Preachers in Print: Religious *Institutio* in Maddalena Campiglia and Chiara Matraini   227
4. Proclaiming Women's Worth: Fonte, Marinella, and the *Querelle des femmes*   236

CODA   250

Appendix: Italian Women Writers Active 1580–1635   253
Notes   271
Bibliography   371
Index   427

ACKNOWLEDGMENTS

This book draws on the twenty years or so of research that resulted in my 2008 book *Women's Writing in Italy, 1400–1650* (Johns Hopkins). In that sense, the acknowledgments for help and inspiration offered in that book are equally relevant here. In addition, however, this second book profited from a very intense period of research and writing in 2008 and especially 2009. It is to this more specific and targeted later period of research that the present acknowledgments relate.

The principal external institutional support from which I benefited during the period in question was from the Gladys Krieble Delmas Foundation and from the Lila Acheson Wallace Publications Fund of the Harvard Center for Italian Renaissance Studies, Villa I Tatti. A grant from the Delmas Foundation funded a research trip to Verona, Venice, and Treviso in October 2009 that produced much valuable material, including one of this book's foremost "discoveries," the manuscript of verse by the Venetian-born poet Lucia Colao discussed in chapter 2, which appears to have escaped any previous critical notice. A grant from the Lila Acheson Wallace Publications Fund helped subsidize the publication of the volume. It gave me particular pleasure to receive this support from Villa I Tatti since it was during my fellowship year at I Tatti in 1996–97 that I made my first acquaintance with many of the works discussed in this study, and first began to think through some of the historical issues that form its conceptual core. The Delmas Foundation was similarly implicated in the genesis of the project, in that it was with the assistance of a travel grant from the Foundation in 1991 that I conducted my first research on Lucrezia Marinella and Moderata Fonte, two of the dominant figures of this book.

Working in a field such as early modern women's writing is inevitably a peripatetic activity, given that many of the primary texts under discussion survive in small numbers or occasionally unique copies, which must be sought out in the sole library in which they are found. I was fortunate to be based between Florence and London in 2009 and so had access to those cities' exceptional library holdings, but even so, my work that year took me to more than twenty libraries and archives in thirteen different cities, in addition to the British Library and Florence's Biblioteca Nazionale Centrale. While I am grateful for the help I received in all the libraries in question, a few more particular debts of gratitude need to be mentioned. My research on Lucchesia Sbarra was vastly assisted by Mariarita Sonego, archivist at the Archivio di Stato of Conegliano, whose knowledge of the cultural and publishing history of late sixteenth and early seventeenth-century Conegliano was vital in directing my investigations. I am also grateful to Emilio Lippi, director of the Biblioteca Comunale of Treviso, for making the manuscript of Colao's *rime* available to me at a time when the Rare Book and Manuscript Room in the Library's Borgo Cavour section was closed, showing a flexibility for which Italian libraries are not always famed. Other libraries and archives in which I encountered exceptional helpfulness from staff include the Biblioteca Civica V. Joppi in Udine, the Biblioteca Angelo Mai in Bergamo, and the Archivio di Stato in Verona. In addition to the help I received in libraries I was able to visit in person, I am grateful to Angela Rogges, of the Biblioteca Provinciale Tommaso Stigliani in Matera, for helping procure a copy of Isabella Capece's rare *Consolatione dell'anima* and to Marco Mazzotti, of the Biblioteca Comunale Manfrediana in Faenza, for his kindness in sending me a copy of Felicia Rasponi's *Dialogo dell'eccellenza dello stato monacale* free of charge; I am also grateful to Alison Lefkovitz, of the University of Chicago Library, and Robert Betteridge, of the National Library of Scotland, for their help in answering bibliographical enquiries.

In addition to these institutional debts of gratitude, my thanks are also due to fellow scholars who were kind enough to share with me work not yet available in the public domain at the time I was completing the manuscript of this book. Valeria Finucci and Maria Galli Stampino sent me copies of the page proofs of their editions of, respectively, Valeria Miani's *Celinda* and Lucrezia Marinella's *L'Enrico;* Laura Lazzari shared with me the page proofs of her monograph on *L'Enrico;* and Eleonora Carinci and Katie Rees sent me electronic copies of their extremely valuable PhD dissertations, completed in 2009 and 2010. I would also like to thank Alison Smith, of Wagner College, for her invaluable advice on how to proceed in my archival research on Veneranda Bragadin in Verona and for allowing me to read her unpublished work on Ersilia Spolverini, as well as Lisa Sampson for reading and commenting on an early draft of the discussion of pastoral in chapter 3. Danielle Callegari, Shannon McHugh, and Paola Ugolini assisted my research by checking books I was unable to consult myself, and Valerie Hoagland and Shannon McHugh helped me inestimably in taking on the task of the index, a heroic labor in a book of this length.

The greatest personal debt I have incurred during my research for this book is to Paolo Bà, whose research on the figure of Francesca Turina has done so much to call critical attention to this remarkable poet in recent years. I have been corresponding with *professor* Bà since I had the pleasure of meeting him during a visit to the Archivio Bufalini in San Giustino in summer 2008. He has tolerated with exemplary patience my numerous e-mails requesting information regarding Turina and her associates, and he has kindly supplied me with transcriptions of several of Turina's unpublished sonnets, along with an inventory of the contents of an important unpublished manuscript of her verse. As I was writing this book, I began by acknowledging *professor* Bà in my notes for each individual transcription or detail for which I was indebted to him. I had to stop this practice, however, since these micro-acknowledgments were simply becoming too numerous; suffice it to say that all references in this book to unpublished material of Turina's may safely be assumed to originate from him.

This book is dedicated to the memory of Henry Y. K. Tom, my long-term editor at the Johns Hopkins University Press, of whose sudden death, shortly following his retirement, I was shocked and saddened to hear earlier this year. It is safe to say that neither the present book nor its predecessor would have existed without the breadth of vision and unfailing advocacy of scholarship that distinguished Henry as an editor. I count it as a privilege, as well as a pleasure, to have had the opportunity to work with him over the years.

INTRODUCTION

prodigious, *adj.* (and *int.*) and *adv.*
1. Of the nature of an omen; portentous. Now *rare*.
2. a. That causes wonder or amazement; marvellous, astonishing. Also in an unfavourable sense: appalling. . . .
   c. Of a person: exceptionally or precociously talented.
3. Unnatural, abnormal; freakish. Now *arch.* and *rare*.
4. Of great size, extent, amount, etc.; enormous, immense; extreme; prolific.

The material surveyed in this volume, the literary production of Italian women in the later sixteenth and early seventeenth centuries, chimes uncannily well with every sense of the adjective *prodigious* that the *Oxford English Dictionary* has contrived to define. This was a remarkable period in the history of early modern women's writing, unprecedented in the quantity and range of its output, not only within Italy but in Europe generally. The half-century from 1580 to 1630 saw the publication of more than sixty single-authored works by Italian women, with a particular concentration in the 1580s and 1590s.[1] These included an epic poem, the first by a woman; three pastoral dramas; a tragedy; a pastoral romance; two volumes of letters; nine narrative poems, secular and religious; and fourteen volumes of verse. By early modern standards this output was prodigious indeed, in terms of "size, extent, amount." By the same standards, it was also quite clearly "marvellous" and "astonishing," in the sense that it contradicted conventional notions of women's intellectual capacities and limitations. Women writers had been considered "wonders" since the time of their emergence in Italy within the humanistic culture of the fifteenth century. They were still routinely hailed as such in the vernacular literary culture of the early sixteenth century, despite their increasing familiarity as figures. A new sense of marvel may, however, be sensed in the latter part of the century, as women's ambitions expanded beyond the "feminine" reach of lyric into narrative and dramatic genres that had previously been men's province. At the same time, women were gaining an equally startling new prominence within the fields of musical and theatrical performance and the visual arts.[2]

The sense of marvel aroused by this body of writing by women is not limited to their contemporaries. It has the capacity to amaze us still today, not least because until very recently there was no real awareness of its existence. A hard-wired academic commonplace within Italian literary scholarship, still enduring in some circles, has it that female authors featured as a salient collective phenomenon in Italy for a period of only a few decades in the mid-sixteenth century. Articulated authoritatively by the great literary scholar Carlo Dionisotti in 1967, this view gained purchase from the long-standing tradition of regarding the Counter-Reformation in Italy as marking the end of the innovative and intellectually alive cultural moment conventionally designated by the term *Renaissance*.[3] In this view, beginning about 1560 Italy mutated into an increasingly closed and repressive culture, socially conservative in its attitudes and programmatically silencing of women. The notion that a quintessentially progressive and "Renaissance" phenomenon like women's writing might flourish in the era of the Counter-Reformation seemed so profoundly counterintuitive that few energies were directed at seeking it out. Even when two female-authored works from this period, Moderata Fonte's *Il merito delle donne* and Lucrezia Marinella's *La nobiltà et l'eccellenza delle donne*, began to be studied in the late 1970s, the situation did not change substantially.[4] The fact that these texts, both published in 1600, were protests against misogyny, one written in response to a lengthy vituperative tract on the "defects of women," did nothing to dispel the notion that the late sixteenth century in Italy was an unpropitious age for female intellectual endeavor. It is only in the past twenty years that serious work has begun to be done on women's writing in this period more generally, and the volume and range of this writing has been a genuine revelation—prodigiously so.

Two senses of *prodigious*, then, map very well on the body of literary production encompassed by this book. What of the third, "exceptionally or precociously talented"? None of the Italian female writers of this age come down to us with the canonical imprimatur of a Vittoria Colonna (c. 1490–1547) or a Gaspara Stampa (c. 1525–54), which makes direct comparison on grounds of "talent" even more problematic than such evaluative judgments generally are. Without entering into the question whether any of the female writers of the later period equaled the achievements of Colonna and Stampa, however, it may be safely asserted that quite a number wrote to a very high standard, manifesting the technical sophistication and control of register that qualified writers at the time as deserving of respect. More important to us today, several also show notable thematic originality and distinctiveness of voice. Two of the most accomplished Petrarchist poets of the mid-sixteenth century, Laura Battiferra (1523–89) and Chiara Matraini (1515–1604), were still active in this period and worked at a high literary level until their death. Among writers of younger generations, the works of Maddalena Campiglia (1553–95), Francesca Turina (1553–1641), Moderata Fonte (1555–92), Maddalena Salvetti (c. 1557–1610), Leonora Bernardi (1559–1616), Margherita Sarrocchi (c. 1560–1618), Isabella Andreini (1562–1604), Lucchesia Sbarra (1576–?1662), and Lucrezia Marinella (c. 1579–1653) are all amply deserving of study on literary grounds.[5] It is a striking token of just how invisible Italian women's writing of this period has traditionally been that Katharina M. Wilson's compendious, two-volume *Encyclopedia of Continental Women Writers*, of 1991, includes entries for only two of these nine writers, Andreini and Fonte, while Rinaldina Russell's 1994 *Italian Women Writers* adds only Marinella to this meager roll call.[6]

Besides the positive senses of *prodigious* reviewed above, the adjective's negative sense ("unnatural, abnormal, freakish"; "appalling") has a certain applicability to women's output in this period when viewed through the eyes of some of their less sympathetic male contemporaries. How "normal" was it for a woman like Margherita Sarrocchi to think herself equipped to embark on the project of an epic, "one of the greatest enterprises that the human intellect can undertake"?[7] How "natural" was it for a woman like Lucrezia Marinella to stage herself as a philosophical authority and talk breezily of "demolishing" Aristotle's theories of sex difference and gender roles?[8] While as late as about the 1620s male voices could still be found to champion women's intellectual aspirations in a way that elite Italian literary culture had done quite consistently since at least the 1530s, the mood began to turn from about the turn of the seventeenth century, with Sarrocchi in particular becoming the object of unprecedentedly vituperative comment from some of her male peers. As the Seicento progressed, the environment in which women writers operated became an increasingly treacherous and hostile one in which fewer and fewer women ventured to disseminate their literary works publicly, until, in the second half of the seventeenth century, the figure of the secular female writer virtually disappeared from the literary scene.[9] The half-century or so under discussion in the present book can thus be seen as constituting quite a distinct period within the history of early modern Italian women's writing, with a fairly precise beginning and endpoint. It was the moment when women's writing in Italy reached its highest point of confidence and assertiveness, but it was also the moment when its intrinsic "abnormality," within a society and culture still entirely dominated by men, began to undermine it from within.

This book represents the first attempt at a comprehensive study of the female-authored literature of this period in Italy. It expands on a chapter in my 2008 study *Women's Writing in Italy, 1400–1650*, which introduced this body of literature and pointed out its salient characteristics but did not discuss any individual texts in detail. In many respects, a project such as this may be seen as a little "previous," in that it attempts a survey at a time when not all of the individual texts have been properly studied (or, in many cases, studied at all) and when Italian literature of this period in general remains a woefully underexplored area. One of the legacies of the remarkable post-Risorgimento tradition of Italian literary historiography originating with Francesco de Sanctis (1817–83) has been an enduring unconcern with the literature of the later sixteenth century, especially the substantial proportion of that literature whose subject matter is religious. Early seventeenth-century writings that can be located under the stylistic rubric of baroque have been redeemed by the later twentieth-century interest in that movement, but this still leaves the half-century from 1560 to 1610 as an orphan period within Italian literary historiography, little studied with the exception of the titanic figures Torquato Tasso (1544–95) and Giambattista Marino (1569–1625) and a few lesser but still canonical figures, such as Giovanni Battista Guarini (1538–1612) and Gabriello Chiabrera (1552–1638). Other writers of this period who figure substantially in mainstream literary history tend to be "eccentric" figures such as Giordano Bruno (1548–1600) and Tommaso Campanella (1568–1639), impressive thinkers and writers, without doubt, but hardly among the most representative figures of the age.

The extent to which the religious literature of this era has been neglected is well demonstrated by the fact that no modern edition exists of works as important and influential in the period as Luigi Tansillo's narrative poem *Le lagrime di San Pietro* (1560/1585) or the religious lyrics of Gabriele Fiamma (c. 1533–85) and Angelo Grillo (1557–1629).[10] A traditional survey of Italian literary history such as the 1999 *Cambridge History of Italian Literature* contains only brief, dismissive mentions of Tansillo's *Lagrime* and of Grillo, while

Fiamma does not figure at all.¹¹ This critical neglect has had the surprising result, pointed out by Amedeo Quondam at the beginning of his groundbreaking 2005 survey of sixteenth-century *poesia spirituale e religiosa*, that musicologists are often better acquainted than literary scholars with the religious poetry of this age.¹²

The relative invisibility within the critical tradition of the vast majority of male-authored literary texts produced in Italy in the late sixteenth and early seventeenth centuries presents a serious impediment for anyone wishing to work on the female-authored literature of the period, especially the quite substantial portion of it that is religious in theme. As the mention of Quondam's study above suggests, the longstanding critical inattention to the religious literature of this period is finally beginning finally to dissipate: the first decade of the twenty-first century has produced more substantial scholarship in this area than did the twentieth century as a whole.¹³ Despite this remedial endeavor, however, the slightness of the critical tradition in this area is still debilitating. It is difficult to establish what, if anything, is distinctive in women's contribution to a given genre of writing if the norms of that genre as practiced by representative male authors remain underexplored. The problem is compounded by the fact that recent work in this area has tended to be conducted almost exclusively by Italian critics, working within a tradition in which attention to gender in the sense intended by Anglo-American scholarship is rare. Little work has been done to date on the representation of women in the gradually reemerging religious literature of this era, and still less on its construction of masculinity. Years, perhaps decades, are likely to be needed before a work such as the present one could be sensibly undertaken, if sense dictates that scholarly projects should wait until the requisite ancillary critical instruments are in place.

Nonetheless, difficult as it has been to work with confidence in this area, and provisional as this work's findings must necessarily be as a result, an overview of women's writing in the age of the Counter-Reformation in Italy seems a useful undertaking at the present juncture. Interest in the female-authored literature of this period is increasing rapidly within Anglo-American scholarship, fueled especially by the impressive energies of the University of Chicago Press's Other Voice in Early Modern Europe series of editions of early modern writings by women. In the past fifteen years, this series has made available ten texts written by Italian women during the period covered by this book, and two more editions are in preparation.¹⁴ However, critical attention to date has focused almost exclusively on secular literature by women in this period, and the vast majority of critical studies within this area have been on single authors and works.[15] There is a need for an overview that corrects the secular bias of the critical literature to date and reads the female-authored literature of the period comparatively and collectively, noting continuities across boundaries of genre and giving some sense of the broad developments of the age.

The need to bring the female-authored religious literature of this period into the critical fold deserves special emphasis, given that a distinguishing feature of the age was, precisely, secular women's strong investment in spiritual literature, a relative novelty in this period despite the important precedent of Vittoria Colonna. A high percentage of the most interesting Italian female writers of this period—Marinella, Campiglia, Fonte, Turina—wrote religious as well as secular literature, moving freely between the two in the course of their literary careers rather than, in the manner of Colonna, "converting" from one to the other. To read the secular female-authored literature of the period without the sacred is to risk an impoverished reading of these important authors and to introduce a hierarchy of preference quite remote from the values of the age. A parallel might be drawn with the *oeuvre* of Lavinia Fontana (1552–1614), the leading female painter of the age and recently the object of an important study by Caroline Murphy.[16] Fontana's output embraces worldly portraits of Bolognese scholars and society matrons, a handful of mythological paintings, and many religious works, ranging from large-scale altarpieces to jewel-like paintings on copper intended for private religious devotion. To consider Fontana's secular output without reference to the sacred would seem an absurdity in the field of art history. That the same is not true within Italian literary scholarship is a quirk of the tradition that deserves to be addressed.[17]

Although the prime target audience of this book is clearly those with an interest in Italian literature and culture, it should also prove of value to those working on other national traditions. While Italian women's writing has always been recognized as important as a precedent and point of comparison for women's writing in a tradition like the English, for example, an understanding of quite how rich it could prove as comparative material has been impeded in the past by the tendency to regard the Italian tradition as limited to verse, principally secular verse, and concentrated in the 1540s and 1550s, when women's writing in England had barely emerged. The writings under scrutiny in the present study were written and published at the same time that writers like Mary Sidney (1561–1621), Aemilia Lanyer (1569–1645), and Mary Wroth (1587–1651/53) were active in England, and the production of Italian women has much in common with theirs in terms of genre affiliations and poetic influences.[18] Rich possibilities for comparative analysis exist, for example, between Wroth's *Urania* and Marinella's *Arcadia felice,* between Wroth's *Love's Victory* and Italian female-authored pastoral drama, and between Lanyer's *Salve Deus Rex Judaeorum* and the narratives of Christ's life and passion by Fonte and Francesca Turina.[19] Similarly, an acquaintance with the gender polemics of the early seventeenth century in Italy, in which women for the first time participated as writers, can offer valuable comparative material for the debate triggered in England by Joseph Swetnam's *Arraignment of Lewd, Idle, Froward, and Unconstant Women* of 1615.[20]

What is true of England in this regard is perhaps even truer of France, given the close cultural ties in this period between France and Italy, particularly after the marriage of Maria de' Medici (1575–1642) to Henri IV in 1600. For France, more than for England, it is possible to document a direct knowledge of literary works by Italian women of this period. Isabella Andreini published a volume of verse in Paris in 1603, while on tour there with her acting troupe, the Gelosi, and her pastoral *Mirtilla* was translated twice into French, in 1599 and 1602, as was her *Lettere,* much later, in 1642.[21] The Latin hymns of Lorenza Strozzi (1514–91), originally published in 1588, received a second, Parisian edition in 1601, dedicated to the Italian-born queen, and there is evidence that they were translated into French and set to music at about the same time.[22] The work of other Italian women writers of this period was known indirectly through "famous women" books such as Hilarion de Coste's *Les eloges et les vies des reynes, des princesses, et des dames illustres en pieté, en courage, et en doctrine,* of 1647, which includes extensive biographies of Strozzi, Moderata Fonte, Tarquinia Molza (1542–1617), and Margherita Sarrocchi, the latter praised as the equal in her poetic talents of Petrarch, Ariosto, and Tasso.[23] Sarrocchi's high-profile role within Roman literary culture in the first decade of the seventeenth century should probably be considered a direct inspiration for the Parisian salon activities of the Roman-born Catherine de Vivonne, Marquise de Rambouillet (1588–1665), who was also acquainted with Andreini, as two sonnets in the latter's *Rime* of 1603 attest.[24] Several sources speak of Sarrocchi not only being a member of various literary academies but also hosting some form of academy in her home.[25]

After an initial contextualizing chapter, this book is organized by genres of writing: chapter 2 discusses lyric verse; chapter 3, drama; chapters 4 and 5, respectively, sacred and secular narrative; chapter 6, didactical and polemical prose. The comprehensiveness of coverage varies according to the volume of extant writings in the genre under discussion: chapter 4, for example, accords a reasonably full treatment to all works of sacred narrative produced by Italian women in this period, while chapters 2 and 6, covering more frequented genres of writing, are of necessity more selective in their coverage. Except occasionally in cases where a work is a genre unicum, I discuss related works comparatively rather than analyzing individual works separately. I do this partly because of considerations of space but also because one of the most useful tasks a survey like this can perform is to cut against the atomism inevitable in the early stages of collective research on a neglected area, when critical energies are largely directed toward the recuperation of individual works. Where thematic emphases are concerned, my analysis in successive chapters is unashamedly oriented toward issues of gender, in part as a means of supplying a continuity of argument that a book covering a series of diverse genres might easily lack. This is not, of course, intended to suggest that writings by women are of interest solely from the point of view of gender—far from it. It simply reflects the narrowing of focus inevitable in a work of this scope, whose every chapter might have afforded sufficient material for a book in itself.

Before proceeding with a summary of the separate chapters of this book, it might be useful first to bring out some of the most important general points to emerge from it. These are principally concentrated in chapter 1, though with exemplification and development in the chapters that follow.

The key point, which I have already made elsewhere but which is much more fully articulated here, is that contrary to received opinion, the Counter-Reformation had, initially at least, largely positive effects on the Italian tradition of women's writing. It is not a coincidence that the most "prodigious" phase in that tradition occurred at the time when Counter-Reformation religious initiatives were beginning to reshape Italian literature. In fact, counterintuitive as it may seem to those accustomed to viewing the Counter-Reformation as an intrinsically misogynistic movement, this very reshaping helped to make this such a propitious cultural moment for female writers. Far from being uniformly conservative in its attitudes toward women's intellectuality, as it is frequently represented, Counter-Reformation religious culture was quite often notably supportive, to the extent that most of the leading contributors to the profeminist side of the *querelle des femmes* in this period were clerics, as was the author of the first Italian biographical dictionary of *donne letterate*, which appeared in 1620.[26] The habits of interaction and support among female and male writers that had developed in the earlier part of the sixteenth century did not lapse after 1560; nor were they limited, on the male side, to laymen. A figure like the Genoese Benedictine Angelo Grillo, mentioned above as the author of one of the most influential collections of religious poetry of the age, numbered as many female writers among his extensive literary acquaintance as did figures such as Pietro Bembo (1470–1547) and Benedetto Varchi (1503–65). There were reasons for this. As I argue in chapter 1, the figure of the pious and refined female writer was one of considerable discursive utility to male clerical *letterati*, representing in many ways an ideal to which secular men might be encouraged to aspire. At a time when the church was engaged in a campaign to refashion Italian literature according to criteria of moral decency and piety, elite women, socialized from birth to precisely these virtues, formed a valuable exemplary literary cadre.

A further factor to consider in accounting for women's success as writers during the first half-century or so following the closure of the Council of Trent is that the new tradition of vernacular religious literature that took shape in this period offered an environment that in many ways was intrinsically more attractive for female writers than the secular literary tradition that had preceded it. One important consideration here was that religious writing offered fewer problems of decorum for women than did writing on most secular subjects, since it could be presented as an extension of culturally acceptable practices of devotion. Another was that religious literature was often more gender-egalitarian than secular literature in its representational norms. One of the most frequented character types of the period, for example, in narrative and drama but also in lyric, was the martyr saint, who represented an ideal of physical and spiritual fortitude and virility that was as likely to be embodied in a woman as it was in a man. The contrast with secular, martial epics, to which the martyr-saint narratives of this period quite self-consciously represent themselves as heir and corrective, could hardly be stronger. Similarly, religious lyric offered a subject position that women could occupy as easily as men, if not more so, unlike secular, amorous lyric, which, except perhaps in its most spiritualized, Neoplatonic variant, had always fitted slightly ill with feminine decorum. Given these attractions, it is anachronistic to present female writers' interest in religious subject matter in this period as something forced on them by the "spirit of the age," as one sometimes sees implied in modern criticism. Religious literature was a live and vibrant, self-reinventing sector of the literary market, in some ways more so than secular literature in the 1580s, before the new injection of energy it received from the baroque.

A last point that needs to be made here, connected with the previous, is that religious literature did not represent another world from secular literature in this period, as modern habits of criticism, in Italy at least, have tended to suggest. Counter-Reformation religious writers were intensely conscious of the continuing appeal that secular literature, especially Petrarchan love lyric and chivalric fiction, held for contemporary readers. It was widely recognized that it would be impossible to wean readers from this spiritually debilitating subject matter without attempting to rival the pleasures secular literature offered within a new spiritual context. As I argue in chapter 1, Counter-Reformation religious literature forged itself very self-consciously in dialectic with Petrarch and Ariosto, seeking to reverse-engineer their iconic texts in the interest of re-creating an equally compelling and seductive spiritual alternative. Poets like Gabriele Fiamma, following the pioneering work of Vittoria Colonna in the 1530s, used the model of the Petrarchan love lyric, combined with biblical and especially psalmic material, to craft a refined and affect-rich model of religious lyric that could present itself as heir to both Petrarch and David. Similarly, narrative poets like Felice Passero (c. 1570–1626) and Benedetto Dell'Uva (1530–?82) drew amply on epic topoi as they sought to weave some of Ariosto's magic into their narratives of martyrs and saints. One of the fascinations of this literature for the modern reader is, precisely, that of observing this process of spiritual *riscrittura,* as rich and intricate a process, in many ways, as the far more familiar phenomenon of classical imitation within the works of early sixteenth-century vernacular writers such as Ariosto himself. As in the case of vernacular imitation of the classics, this can sometimes work in unexpected ways, as when Moderata Fonte echoes Ariosto's description of the naked Angelica, chained to a rock, in a description of Mary Magdalene keeping vigil outside Christ's tomb in her 1592 *La resurrettione di Giesù Christo* or when Lucrezia Marinella uses Tasso's description of the duplicitous seductress Armida in characterizing a virgin martyr saint.[27]

While the bulk of chapter 1 is devoted to introducing these questions and tracing the effects of the Counter-Reformation on women's cultural activity, the first section of the chapter examines the social and cultural contexts of women's writing in this period more generally. Emphasized in this discussion is the degree to which the practice of women's writing had become normalized within the Italian literary tradition by the late sixteenth century, to the extent that it was not uncommon to find "respectable" women of the elite orchestrating a public career for themselves as published writers in a manner not unlike that of their male peers. A striking token of this normalization is the incidence of cloistered women who published literary works during their lifetime, a phenomenon that may be registered first in the 1570s and 1580s and encompassed some important works, such as Lorenza Strozzi's *Hymni*, whose reception in France I remarked on above. Among the points covered in this contextualizing discussion are the support and enablement female writers derived from their generally highly cultured family backgrounds, as well as the nature of the relationships they developed with cultural institutions such as literary academies. While relatively few women seem to have been invited to join academies, this cannot necessarily be taken as indicative of their exclusion from academic culture. One of the most fruitful and well-documented relationships between a female writer and a literary academy in this period, that between Maddalena Campiglia and the Accademia Olimpica in Vicenza in the late 1580s, seems to have been conducted without Campiglia's ever being formally inducted as a member.

Of the chapters involving women's relationship with various literary genres, chapters 2 and 4, on lyric poetry and religious narrative, venture into regions barely touched by criticism to date. Chapter 2 covers both religious and secularly themed verse, both printed works and manuscript sources. Poets featured include Laura Battiferra, Francesca Turina, Lucchesia Sbarra, Lucrezia Marinella, Maddalena Campiglia, Isabella Andreini, and Lucia Colao. Chapter 4 discusses Moderata Fonte's remarkable ottava rima poems on Christ's passion and resurrection (1582 and 1592), as well as a rosary-themed sonnet sequence by Turina (1595), four hagiographic works by Marinella (1595–1624), and an unfinished Old Testament epic by Maddalena Salvetti (1611). Chapter 3 surveys secular drama by women in this period, including Fonte's philosophical drama *Le feste* (1581) and Valeria Miani's tragedy *Celinda* (1611). The bulk of the chapter is given to a comparative analysis of five pastoral dramas written in the 1580s and 1590s: Barbara Torelli's *Partenia* (c. 1586), Andreini's *Mirtilla* (1588), Campiglia's *Flori* (1588), Miani's *Amorosa speranza* (published 1604), and an anonymous manuscript play in the Biblioteca Marciana (c. 1590–91), discussed here for the first time and conjecturally attributed to the Lucchese poet Leonora Bernardi. Chapter 5 discusses secular narrative works by women, starting with three chivalric poems, Fonte's romance *Il Floridoro* (1581) and two epics, Marinella's *L'Enrico, overo Bisanzio acquistato* (1635) and Margherita Sarrocchi's *La Scanderbeide* (1606/1623). The chapter concludes with a discussion of Marinella's pastoral romance *Arcadia felice* (1605) and her mythological poem *Amore innamorato, et impazzato* (1618), the latter curiously neglected by criticism but unquestionably one of Marinella's finest works. Chapter 6, finally, considers discursive prose writings by Italian women, tracing important developments such as the increased engagement of secular women with religious genres and the emergence of a new tradition of female-authored polemical writing from the turn of the seventeenth century. The second part of the chapter examines four sample texts, two religious and little studied, Campiglia's *Discorso sopra l'annonciatione* (1585) and Chiara Matraini's *Dialoghi spirituali* (1602), and two secular and among the best-known works by women in this period, Fonte's *Il merito delle donne* and Marinella's *La nobiltà et l'eccelenza delle donne*.

In view of the number of writers I attempt to cover in this book, I have made no attempt in the text to provide a biographical introduction to each at the moment of her introduction; rather, biographical and other information is given in the appendix. In addition to brief details of social status, geographic origins, family circumstances, and marital career, the appendix entry for each writer contains lists of her published and unpublished works and of her male and female literary contacts insofar as this is possible. This seems important both for the light it can shed on individual writers' cultural standing and for its value, collectively, as documentation of the extent of female writers' integration in Italian literary culture.

Where chronology is concerned, this volume focuses essentially on the half-century from 1580 to 1630, but these boundaries are not always applied strictly. Chapter 1's discussion of nuns' published work incorporates two works from the 1570s for the sake of completeness, and the discussion of pastoral in chapter 3 makes occasional mention of plays by Isabetta Coreglia (fl. 1628–50) published in 1634 and 1650. One work published after 1630 is given a more detailed discussion: Lucrezia Marinella's epic *L'Enrico, overo Bisanzio acquistato*, which is analyzed comparatively in chapter 5 with the two other female-authored chivalric poems of the age. The time period 1580–1630 was chosen as defining a coherent phase in the history of Italian women's writing, dominated by the activities of women born in the 1550s to the 1570s, members of the first generations to come to maturity in the aftermath of the Council of Trent and the last generations of women to profit, at least in their youth, from the philogynous attitudes that had dominated Italian elite culture throughout most of the sixteenth century, prior to the "misogynist turn" of the seventeenth. The writings of women like Margherita Costa (1600–1664) and Arcangela Tarabotti (1604–52), which began to appear in the 1630s and 1640s, contemporaneously with Marinella's late writings, are the products of a very different culture. Even if considerations of word count were not an issue, to incorporate works from this later period would have diluted the focus of the book.

Two further points that deserve to be glossed are my usage in respect of female writers' names and my use of the term *Counter-Reformation* in preference to alternatives such as *Catholic Reformation*, *Tridentine Reformation*, or the more generic and neutral *early modern Catholicism*.[28] Where the first is concerned, I have not aimed for consistency but use the form of a given writer's name that has become standard in modern Anglo-American critical usage, for example, the feminine form of Lucrezia Marinella's surname but the masculine form of, say, Margherita Sarrocchi's (rather than *Sarrocchia*, sometimes found at the time). Where no usage has yet established itself definitively, I tend to prefer the modern Italian practice of using the masculine form rather than the archaic practice of declining the surname to the feminine, revived by some recent American scholars.[29] Writers are generally referred to in the text, notes, and bibliography by their natal surname only rather than by their natal and married surnames, a common naming practice at the time. Writers' married surnames are only used as their primary identifiers in those rare cases where custom has dictated such usage: I refer to the Ferrarese poet Orsina Bertolaio Cavaletti (d. 1592), for example, as Orsina Cavaletti rather than Orsina Bertolaio.

Concerning the term *Counter-Reformation*, I use it in part simply because it has remained the dominant academic usage and also because to a great extent the revisionist impulses that led scholars to propose alternative usages no longer obtain. At least on its home territory of history of religion, the "black legend" of the Tridentine reform movement as purely reactive and repressive is in abeyance, and a strong recent tradition of scholarship examines post-Tridentine religious culture on its own terms, outside the perspective that would see it essentially in terms of rejection or negation, whether of northern European Protestantism or of Italy's own, home-grown pre-Tridentine movement of Catholic reform.[30] In a trajectory familiar from terms like *mannerism* and *baroque*, the term *Counter-Reformation* has completed, or is in the process of completing, a redemptive semantic journey from an original, pejorative meaning to a neutrally descriptive one. This is truer to date within the field of history than within literary history and criticism, where traces of outdated historical models persist. Rather than through terminological fine-tuning, however, this seems a problem best addressed through a form of scholarship that examines the literary products of the Counter-Reformation as far as possible on their own terms and without preconceptions. Needless to say, such is the aim of this book.

THE PRODIGIOUS MUSE

❧ CHAPTER ONE ❧
CONTEXTS

1. The Female Writer in Context: Opportunities, Attitudes, Models

Before proceeding to a consideration of what Italian women wrote in this period, we need first to take account of the context of their writing. What kind of women wrote in this period, and in what circumstances? To what extent were they integrated within the literary culture of the age? What kind of education did they receive, and to what extent were their families supportive of their literary ambitions? What relationship did they have with cultural institutions such as literary academies?[1]

I should begin by noting that by the late sixteenth century the tradition of women's writing in Italy already had considerable historical depth. Secular women had emerged as writers in the Latin humanism of the fifteenth century, and they had flourished after the reprise of the vernacular literary tradition, achieving a degree of visibility by the mid-sixteenth century that no alert vernacular reader could ignore.[2] Although for a variety of reasons the 1560s and 1570s saw a decline in women's published output, when women began to publish once again in the early 1580s, they did so with a recent and substantial tradition of female-authored literature behind them. Nor had this tradition been forgotten. The names, and often the biographies, of earlier women writers were available to their literary descendants through a variety of sources, ranging from "famous women" treatises such as Giuseppe Betussi's *Delle donne illustri* (1545; expanded 1596), to works on the cultural excellences of particular cities, to the encyclopedic *selve di varia erudizione* (lit. "forests of diverse learning") that so characterize the lower levels of polite literacy in this age.[3]

The period of interest to us here was exceptionally rich from this point of view, in that it saw the first specific collection of biographies of women writers, Francesco Agostino Della Chiesa's *Theatro delle donne letterate* (1620), as well as the vast, encyclopedic, multivolume set of dialogues by Cristoforo Bronzini, *Della dignità e nobiltà delle donne* (1624–32), which constitutes an extraordinary source for biographical information on female artists, writers, and musicians and "famous women" of all kinds.[4] Evidence also exists that in this period women themselves may have begun to add their voices to this celebratory biographical tradition, which had its roots in the Latin humanism of the fourteenth and fifteenth centuries. Pietro Paolo Ribera in 1609 speaks of Moderata Fonte (1555–92) having gathered "some trophies of ancient and modern women" that she was planning to insert in her *Il merito delle donne,* which was left unpublished at the time of her death.[5] In a different medium, Lavinia Fontana (1552–1614) is said by one eighteenth-century source to have painted a Parnassus of contemporary "famous women," perhaps similar to that later commissioned by Cardinal Mazarin from Giandomenico Romanelli in the 1640s in France.[6]

What this meant, of course, was that women writing in this period could do so from a relatively consolidated position, with an established tradition behind them. A late sixteenth-century Paduan writer like Valeria Miani (c. 1563?–after 1620) almost certainly will have known of her mid-century compatriot and predecessor Giulia Bigolina (fl. 1560) and quite probably also of the distant, fifteenth-century precedent of Maddalena Scrovegni (1356–1429).[7] Similarly, in neighboring Verona, Ersilia Spolverini (c. 1572–after 1597) is likely to have grown up hearing of the prodigious achievements of Isotta Nogarola (1418?–66) and Laura Brenzoni (c. 1460–1532).[8] More proximately, it seems likely that the cluster of women writers we find in Lucca in the late sixteenth and early seventeenth centuries, including Leonora Bernardi (1559–1616), Laura Guidiccioni (1550–99), Silvia Bendinelli (fl. 1587–95), and Isabetta Coreglia (fl. 1628–50), owed much to the precedent of Chiara Matraini (1515–1604), who had attained fame in that city in the 1550s and was still writing and publishing down to 1602.

Late sixteenth-century and early seventeenth-century women writers' awareness of their predecessors is attested in their work, both through explicit laudatory mention and through imitation. An interesting example of the first is a passage in Maddalena Campiglia's pastoral drama *Flori* (1588) in which the protagonist, an aspiring poet, cites as a role model an outstanding nymph-poet of a past generation, clearly identifiable in context as Vittoria Colonna (c. 1490–1547).[9] In a letter written in the same year, Campiglia (1553–95) speaks of "the divine Vittoria," along with the fifteenth-century Nogarola sisters and Veronica Gambara (1485–1550), as figures worthy of pictorial immortalization.[10] Veneranda Bragadin (c. 1566–after 1619), in the dedicatory letter to her *Rime* of 1619, includes Gambara, along with the more recent Fonte and the still living Lucrezia Marinella (c. 1579–1653), in a list of learned women, praising Gambara for having "given luster to the female sex with her divine works."[11] Marinella herself lists some modern women writers in the chapter on learned women in her *Nobiltà et l'eccellenza delle donne*, although her exemplification is generally classical, as it is elsewhere in the treatise.[12]

Where imitation is concerned, we find Francesca Turina (1553–1641) self-consciously reprising Colonna's poetry of widowhood in a sequence of poems for her dead husband published in 1595, which concludes with a madrigal praising Colonna for her "learned, angelic words" and her "lofty and famous verse."[13] Five years earlier, Maddalena Salvetti (c. 1557–1610) drew on the tradition of poetry in praise of Eleonora of Toledo (1522–62), Duchess of Florence, by Tullia d'Aragona and Laura Battiferra (1523–89) in the mid-century in her more elaborate monographic praise sequence for Eleonora's successor Christine de Lorraine (1565–1637).[14] More obliquely, we might see a consciousness of literary "maternal descent" in the representations we find in Margherita Sarrocchi (c. 1560–1618) and Lucrezia Marinella of female warriors in epic who have been inspired to their prowess by the model of warrior mothers or aunts.[15] This "Amazonian," rationalist pattern of maternal or quasi-maternal transmission goes against the more traditional, exceptionalist presentation of the female warrior in romance as a "marvel," her prowess explained by a fantastic educational backstory often featuring upbringing by a wizard or suckling by wild beasts.[16]

All this needs to be taken into account when considering the position and status of women writers in this period. Reservations over whether "respectable" women should expose themselves in public by publishing their writings appear to have been largely superseded in Italy by this point. The habit of celebrating women writers as the honor of their city or their age was sufficiently well entrenched to counteract the social prejudices against culturally active women that we find attested in the fifteenth century and in some more provincial settings in the sixteenth.[17] Even in Venice, which earlier in the century had proved distinctly unpropitious as a locus for elite women's writing, the emergence in this period of two native writers as celebrated as Fonte and Marinella suggests that something had changed.[18] One factor that probably contributed to the social normalization of the figure of the female poet in this period was the emergence, beginning in the mid-sixteenth century, of other female creative types, such as artists, professional or semiprofessional singers, composers, and actresses.[19] In a culture that increasingly accepted live public performance by women—even the controversial profession of acting attained a degree of respectability with the figure of Isabella Andreini (1562–1604)—the metaphorical self-exposure constituted by the circulation of a woman's writings must have begun to seem tame.

A striking illustration of the degree to which Italian culture had absorbed the novelty of the "learned woman" is the occasional incorporation of erudition and eloquence among the charms of the female love object in the erotic lyric of this era. The Venetian Giovanni Battista Leoni has a poem in his *Madrigali* (1602) praising the attractions of a lady who "bears Helicon in her mouth" and whose "fine and lovely verses" are so many "darts and arrows" directed at the lover.[20] More ambitiously, a sequence of *canzoni* by the Pugliese courtier-poet Muzio Sforza (1542–97) in his 1590 *Rime* imitating the three *canzoni sorelle* of Petrarch's *Rerum vulgarium fragmenta* transforms what in Petrarch had been a sequence in praise of Laura's eyes into an extended paean to his beloved's eloquent speech and the beauty of her song.[21] A remarkable feature of Sforza's *canzoni* is the way in which they fold the language of female intellectual prowess familiar from contemporary "defenses of women" into the construction of the poetic beloved. The lady's words, like those of Petrarch's Laura, still issue from between the "pearls and rubies" of her mouth, but they are given a new weight by Sforza's comparison of her eloquence to that of Sappho, Aspasia, and Cornelia.[22] More surprisingly, transcending the gender-specific, Sforza goes on to cite Orpheus, David, and Pericles as further exemplary analogs.[23] Elsewhere, the lady figures as a "new Minerva, wise and alert, virile, eloquent, charming, and chaste."[24] Her virility is further emphasized in Sforza's commentary to an earlier *canzone* in which he describes her as "a virago of the kind Hippocrates calls a 'bull-woman' [*Taura*]," noting that Platonists speak of such women as inciting men particularly to love.[25]

More prosaic exemplification of the extent to which the figure of the female writer had become normalized by the later sixteenth century may be had by comparing the social backgrounds and publishing practices of women writing in this period with those of their mid-sixteenth-century predecessors. In the earlier period, we find relatively few women publishing single-authored books, and fewer still claiming full ownership of such books by putting their name to the dedicatory letter. More common is the pattern found in the first two books of Laura Terracina's *Rime* (1548 and 1549) or in Tullia d'Aragona's *Rime* and *Dialogo* (both 1547), where a male associate presents himself as having taken the initiative of persuading the modestly reluctant author into print.[26] Those women whose names we do find figuring on the title pages of books tend to be of a less exalted social background than most female writers in this period, at least if we exclude Vittoria Colonna, whose work was extensively published, but without her consent. Respectable married women of the elite in this period certainly did write poetry and circulate it in manuscript, but they tended to be chary of publication, other than in the most socially selective contexts. One senses that a perceived social-moral dividing line for women in this period fell not between writing and not writing, nor indeed between circulating and not circulating one's work, but between the elite, socially controlled medium of manuscript circulation and the more promiscuous availability of print.[27]

The pattern in the later sixteenth century differs quite distinctly in this respect. A highly visible phenomenon in this later period is that of the "respectable" gentlewoman writer happy to circulate her writing through the press and to take ownership of her authorial self-presentation. The only real precedents for this among mid-century female writers were Laura Battiferra and Laura Terracina in her works published after 1549. Well-known examples of the type in the period we are interested in here are Fonte and Marinella, the former the daughter of a lawyer, the latter that of a prominent medic, and both members of the peculiarly Venetian status group of *cittadini*, who were excluded from holding political office but otherwise comparable to the lower ranks of the patriciate in terms of wealth, education, and social prestige.[28] Comparable examples in the mainland Veneto are Issicratea Monte (1564–84/85), of Rovigo, and Valeria Miani, of Padua, both, like Fonte, the daughters of lawyers, though Monte in particular seems to have come from a less wealthy background.[29] Meanwhile, figures such as Maddalena Campiglia, of Vicenza, and Lucchesia Sbarra (1576–?1662), of Conegliano, offer examples of noblewomen happy to see their works appear in print. Further south, in central Italy, high-status women who saw their works printed include the

Florentine patrician nun Lorenza Strozzi (1514–91), her compatriot Maddalena Salvetti, again from a Florentine patrician background, and the Umbrian noblewoman Francesca Turina, daughter of a *condottiere* endowed with various fiefdoms by the French crown and descended through her mother from the counts of Carpegna. Less exalted by birth but still impressively well connected within aristocratic circles was the Neapolitan though Rome-based Margherita Sarrocchi.

Most of these women published under their own name, with only Fonte adopting a pseudonym, and all but Sbarra and Sarrocchi signed the dedicatory letters of their works.[30] Some, like Campiglia, Marinella, and Sarrocchi, showed themselves hardly less professional in their attitude toward their writings than a figure like the actress Isabella Andreini. Sarrocchi's letters attest to the care she devoted to the encomiastic opportunities offered by the epic she was writing: she left key passages of the poem unwritten while she deliberated on which acquaintances and patrons she wished to honor in print.[31] Campiglia was sufficiently concerned about her claims to public ownership of her writings to speak in the preface to her eclogue *Calisa* (1589) of having rushed out a printed edition of the poem because she feared that an unrevised copy stolen from her might be published without her permission.[32] This represents a remarkable shift from the perspective of Colonna, who allowed her verse to be pirated for years without bringing out an authorized edition. A letter from Torquato Tasso (1544–95) thanking Campiglia for a copy of her pastoral *Flori* shows her to have been active in the postpublication promotion of her work.[33] Similar epistolary evidence attests to Francesca Turina's involvement in circulating copies of her *Rime spirituali sopra i misterii del santissimo rosario* and Moderata Fonte's in disseminating her dramatic texts.[34]

As an example of the degree of professionalism some women writers attained in the period we are interested in here, it is illuminating to consider the case of Lucrezia Marinella, who reflects to a particularly marked degree the developments just discussed. Marinella was the most prolific female writer of her age and the most diverse in the range of genres she attempted: besides verse and prose hagiography, her favored genre, her published works include a mythological-allegorical epic, a pastoral romance, a historical *poema eroico*, a polemical treatise, and a volume of religious verse. With only one exception, she signed the dedicatory letters to her works, and she pursued an ambitious strategy with regard to her dedications: among those receiving her works were two grand duchesses of Tuscany, two duchesses of Mantua, two doges, and a pope.[35] Her correspondence in the 1620s with the Medici courtier Cristoforo Bronzini (c. 1560–1640), who had offered to serve as broker for her literary courtship of the Medici, shows the seriousness with which she pursued such contacts, and there is evidence that she was successful in attracting favorable responses from patrons in the form of recognition and gifts.[36] Although Marinella was a wealthy woman who had no need to write for a living, there is also some evidence that she occasionally wrote to commission from publishers. One famous instance is her 1600 treatise *La nobiltà et l'eccellenza delle donne,* which appears to have been written to a deadline at the request of the publisher Giovanni Battista Ciotti (c. 1560–after 1625). Another publisher, Barezzo Barezzi, commissioned Marinella in 1606 to compose a series of allegories and *argomenti* for a new edition of Luigi Tansillo's *Le lagrime di San Pietro.*[37] In many ways, Marinella's modus operandi as a writer is striking precisely because it so resembles that of a male writer of similar social status. While she is exceptional in some regards—few female writers of the time were quite so assertive in their authorial self-presentation, for example—Marinella was not so different in her practice and ambition from figures like Fonte, Campiglia, Sarrocchi, and Andreini as to be unrepresentative of the trends of the age.

One particularly striking piece of evidence of the relative normalization of print publication for women in this period is that for the first time nuns began to countenance publication of their works. Convents had long constituted important loci of cultural production for women, but the writings of nuns had tended to remain in manuscript, to be published in rare cases by their acolytes after their death.[38] This pattern prevailed, with very few exceptions, in the fifteenth and early sixteenth centuries and reestablished itself in the later seventeenth.[39]

For a period of about eighty years, however, from the 1570s to the 1650s, we encounter quite a number of nuns publishing their own work during their lifetime, of whom the Venetian Benedictine Arcangela Tarabotti (1604–52) is only the most famous and prolific.[40] The appearance of verse by the Bolognese Dominican Girolama Castellani in two anthologies of the 1550s may have helped inspire this trend, as may also, conceivably, the publications of the French nun Anne de Marquets (d. 1588) in the 1560s.[41] Limiting ourselves to single-authored texts, in the 1570s we find a dialogue on the excellence of convent life published in Bologna in 1572 by the Benedictine Felicia Rasponi of Ravenna (1523–79) and a verse prayer to the Virgin by the Bolognese Clarissan Eugenia Calcina published, again in Bologna, in 1576.[42] The 1580s saw the publication in Vicenza of a treatise on the celebration of holy office by the Dominican Osanna Pigafetta of Vicenza, as well as Lorenza Strozzi's 1588 *Hymni*, already mentioned.[43] To these may be added the four-volume *Opere* (1588 and 1602) of the Genoese Lateran canoness Battista Vernazza, by far the most substantial and intellectually ambitious work by an Italian cloistered woman in this period. Vernazza died in 1587, the year before the first three volumes of the *Opere* were published, but she had sanctioned the publication of her writings, and the edition was in preparation at the time of her death.[44] Further publications by living nuns during the period covered by this book are a life of Santa Grata of Bergamo published by the Bergamasque Benedictine Flavia Grumelli in 1595; an oration delivered by the Vicentine Clarissan Beatrice Gatti on the occasion of her *monacazione* in 1604; a history of the miraculous icon of the Virgin held at the sanctuary of the Monte della Guardia in Bologna, published in 1617 by the Bolognese Dominican Diodata Malvasia (c. 1533–after 1617); and a volume of spiritual verse, *La Calliope religiosa* (1623), published by the Bolognese Lateran canoness Semidea Poggi (1560s?–after 1637).[45] A further possible example is a *sacra rappresentazione* on the life of Saint Cecilia by the Umbrian Benedictine Cherubina Venturelli, which is recorded as first published in Macerata in 1612, although the first edition to survive dates from 1631.[46]

In addition to these single-authored works, we find nuns occasionally figuring in the print record as contributors to poetic anthologies. The main instances here are the Palermitan Onofria Bonanno, who appears in the *Rime degli Accademici Accesi*, of 1571; the Pavian Augustinian Laura Beatrice Cappello, who figures in Stefano Guazzo's dialogue-anthology *La ghirlanda della Contessa Angela Bianca Beccaria*, of 1595; and the Bolognese Dominican Febronia Pannolini, verse by whom is found in anthologies of 1600 and 1601, the first in praise of the cardinal, literary patron, and papal nephew Cinzio Aldobrandini (1551–1610), the second celebrating the Marian icon whose history Diodata Malvasia would later trace in her 1617 work.[47] Later, an otherwise unidentifiable "Suor Damiana" is among the contributors to a Venetian collection in praise of the actress Maria Malloni (1599–after 1627) published in

1613, while a poem by Semidea Poggi appears in a 1632 volume in praise of the Bolognese painter Guido Reni (1575–1642).[48]

Given this evidence, there seems some justification for questioning the conclusions of Elisabetta Graziosi, who represents convent writers as largely invisible within the arena of printed literature, especially after the advent of the Counter-Reformation.[49] While it is true that, as Graziosi has noted, the extreme rarity of many of the publications cited here argues for low initial print runs and limited distribution, this is not true of the works of Strozzi, Malvasia, and Vernazza, of which relatively high numbers of copies survive.[50] Nor can the other indicators of "weak authoriality" that Graziosi cites as characteristic of nuns' literary production, such as a tendency to anonymity and extreme authorial self-deprecation, be said to be universal.[51] It is noteworthy that of the cloistered women who published single-authored works in this period, all but Vernazza signed their own dedicatory letters, while of nuns who appear in anthologies, with the rule-proving exception of "Suor Damiana," all appear in a fully identifiable guise. Nor should we attribute too much weight to the gestures of modesty we find quite routinely in nuns' self-presentation as authors, which are in any case not greatly out of line with the authorial self-staging of their secular peers. Even a writer as ostensibly self-deprecating as Lorenza Strozzi, who describes herself as a "worm" and compares her writings to the babbling of an infant, still manages an oblique self-compliment when she speaks of having been reluctantly persuaded into publishing her *Hymni* by "the counsel and urgings of most illustrious men."[52] Later nun writers were sometimes quite forthright about their literary ambitions: an eighteenth-century source credits Semidea Poggi with a published collection of verse entitled *Desideri di Parnaso*.[53]

One interesting point about nuns' published work in this period is that it provides evidence of their continuing contacts with the secular world, even during the age of more restrictive claustration introduced by the Council of Trent. Tarabotti's *Lettere*, of 1650, provides the most striking example of this, but not the only one. The printed works of Rasponi, Malvasia, and Poggi contain laudatory prefatory or concluding verse by lay *letterati* from their cities, and Poggi's is dedicated to a layman, the Vicentine noble Onorio Capra, identified as a benefactor of her family.[54] Something of a high point of worldliness in nuns' publications is represented by the encomiastic madrigals by Laura Beatrice Cappello included in Guazzo's *Ghirlanda della Contessa Angela*

Bianca Beccaria, where they are given a particular salience, having been chosen to open and close the collection. Cappello's closing madrigal offers up as an homage to Countess Beccaria the hair (*capelli*, a pun on her name) that she had cut when she entered the convent, an interesting symbolic recuperation of an emblem of secular feminine identity that she had ritually renounced in her retreat from the world.[55] Cappello had professed in 1561, and her acquaintance with the newly fashionable form of the literary madrigal must certainly date from the period of her life in the convent, a notable point in that most madrigals circulating in the early 1590s were still secular, and generally amorous, in subject matter.[56] Cappello's contacts with secular literary culture are also attested by the published verse addressed to her by Guazzo and by Giovanni Battista Massarengo (1569–c. 1596). One of Guazzo's madrigals to her is even incongruously couched in the idiom of Petrarchan love.[57]

In conclusion, it seems safe to assume that by the later sixteenth and early seventeenth centuries the circulation and print publication of literary works by women had become a sufficiently accepted phenomenon in Italy that even the involvement of nuns did not arouse any particular moral concern. It hardly needs to be pointed out how significantly the Italian experience differs in this respect from the English, where print publication by elite women in this period was virtually unknown.[58] The social backgrounds of nuns who published in this period are comparable with those of the upper ranks of secular female writers of this period: Rasponi, Bonanno, Pigafetta, Strozzi, Malvasia, Poggi, and Grumelli were all from prominent noble families within their respective cities, while Cappello was the daughter of a Venetian patrician and a noblewoman from the Brescian family of the Martinengo, and Gatti was the daughter of a physician, from a background not dissimilar to that of Lucrezia Marinella.[59] Connections between literary nuns and secular female writers are not difficult to trace, allowing us to speculate that nuns may have been inspired to circulate and publish their writings by the example of their secular peers. Flavia Grumelli was the daughter of Isotta Brembati (c. 1530–86), a secular female poet of some renown, while Onofria Bonnano was the sister of the secular female poets Laura and Marta Bonnano, who appear in the same anthology that she does.[60] Cappello was almost certainly acquainted, personally or by reputation, with the secular Pavian noblewoman-poet Alda Torelli Lunati, verse by whom appears in Lodovico Domenichi's anthology of female-authored verse of 1559, and we can also probably assume an acquaintance between Osanna Pigafetta and Maddalena Campiglia.[61] Further research on convent writings in this period will doubtless bring other such relationships to light.

To what extent did families condone women's literary aspirations and encourage their literary activities? The answer is obviously a complex one and varies from case to case. One point that it is useful to underline here is how often, as we have just seen in the case of Grumelli, women writers came from a literary background.[62] At the most exalted end of the spectrum, two female poets of the period that interests us here, Laura Guidiccioni and Tarquinia Molza (1542–1617), came from families that had produced two of the most celebrated Petrarchist poets of the first half of the Cinquecento, Giovanni Guidiccioni (1480–1551) and Francesco Maria Molza (1489–1544). Guidiccioni's brother Cristoforo (1538–82) was also a *letterato* of some note. Other writers who benefited from a distinguished intellectual background were Lorenza Strozzi, whose brother, Ciriaco Strozzi (1504–65), taught philosophy and Greek literature at Pisa; Vittoria Galli (fl. 1588–94), of Urbino, daughter of the courtier-poet Antonio Galli (1510–61); Lucrezia Della Valle (d. 1622), niece of the Calabrian erudite Sertorio Quattromani (1541–1603); and Margherita Sarrocchi, raised as ward to the cardinal and Vatican librarian Guglielmo Sirleto (1514–85). At a slightly less exalted level, Lucrezia Marinella was the daughter of a physician and *letterato*, Giovanni Marinelli (d. before 1593), and sister to another, Curzio Marinelli (d. 1624). Setting aside Guidiccioni and Galli, for whom the evidence is inconclusive, all these women were unusually learned by the standards of their sex and seem to have received an initial (i.e., pre-university) education comparable to that of a young man of their status. Sarrocchi, whose education is unusually well documented, was tutored in mathematics by Luca Valerio (1552–1618), destined to become one of the outstanding Italian mathematicians of his age, while her tutor for literary subjects was Rinaldo Corso (1525–82), distinguished as a grammarian and literary critic.[63] All these writers were familiar with Latin, most notably Strozzi, whose *Hymni* is the most important collection of Latin verse produced by a woman in early modern Italy, while Molza is also said to have studied Greek and Hebrew. Molza, Marinella, and Sarrocchi all displayed interests in philosophical and scientific fields well beyond women's normal purview at the time.[64]

The examples just cited are exceptional for the level of educational attainment of the women concerned, but the same general patterns may be observed elsewhere. Lucchesia Sbarra was the sister of Pulzio Sbarra (1560–1626), founder of two literary academies and an active sponsor of drama, while, at a lower social level, Silvia Bendinelli, of Lucca, was the daughter of a soldier turned schoolmaster, Antonio Bendinelli (1515–75), and sister of the Latin poet Scipione Bendinelli.[65] The sisters Fabrizia (fl. 1587–90) and Innocenza Carrari (1561–1618), of Treviso, and the aristocratic Udinese poet Lucella di Zucco (fl. 1590–1601) appear in poetic anthologies alongside brothers who also wrote verse.[66] In these instances, the connection between women's literary ambitions and their propitious family background may only be inferred, but a better-documented case is that of Moderata Fonte, whose biography, by her uncle by marriage, the historian Giovanni Niccolò Doglioni (1548–1629), credits her lawyer step-grandfather Prospero Saraceni with encouraging her early studies and particularly her interest in poetry and himself with having recognized the exceptional character of her talent and exerted himself to reveal it to the world.[67] Among female writers of this period for whom we have some biographical information, it is actually quite difficult to find one who did not come from a literary background, except perhaps Francesca Turina, who in one autobiographical poem laments having had her childhood energies directed to the "spindle and the needle" rather than "spending her years in the fine studies of Pallas."[68] Turina's representation of her upbringing differs interestingly from the depiction of a young noblewoman's education that we find in Lucchesia Sbarra's, the only other female poet of the era to write of her early life. Sbarra portrays herself in a sonnet as having spent her adolescence happily absorbed in reading Virgil and Homer, "those who sang of Turnus and Ajax."[69]

One interesting question, when we consider these questions of context and education, is the degree to which women, rather than simply having their literary ambitions facilitated by their family contexts, may sometimes have been actively groomed by their families for cultural stardom. Sirleto's choice of Rinaldo Corso as Sarrocchi's tutor is suggestive in this sense, in that Corso was closely associated with the two most iconic female writers of the century, Vittoria Colonna and Veronica Gambara: he wrote a commentary on Colonna commissioned by Veronca Gambara and a biography of Gambara after her death.[70]

Two less well known but intriguing cases in which a degree of domestic engineering may be suspected are those of Caterina, or Catella, Marchesi (c. 1585–after 1623), of Udine, who figures in a number of local anthologies in the 1590s, and Isabella Cervoni (c. 1576–after 1600), of Colle Val d'Elsa, near Siena, a more committed writer, who published a number of independent short works in the same decade and was admitted to the Pavian Accademia degli Affidati sometime before 1599.[71] Both Marchesi and Cervoni were remarkably precocious, the first appearing in a volume of *poeti udinesi* put together by her tutor, Giacomo Bratteolo, in 1597, when she was only 12 years old, the second figuring for the first time in the manuscript record with a *canzone* sent to Grand Duchess Christine of Lorraine in 1590, when Cervoni was 13 or 14.[72] Cervoni was the daughter of the Medicean occasional poet Giovanni Cervoni (fl. 1574–1607), who appears almost to have crafted Isabella in his own image: the two wrote largely in the same genre and published with the same publishers, although Isabella, perhaps by virtue of the "novelty" of her sex, appears to have attracted the greater attention.[73] Intriguingly, a Giovanni Cervoni of Colle di Val d'Elsa, probably Isabella's father, appears as the profeminist spokesman in Giovanni David Tomagni's *querelle* dialogue, *Dell'eccellenza de l'huomo sopra quella della donna*, of 1565, where he speaks with great warmth of women's intellectual potential and condemns as an abuse the refusal of most men to countenance educating their daughters as they might.[74] Although it is wise not to assume that the views expressed by speakers in sixteenth-century dialogues necessarily reflect those speakers' actual opinions, it is certainly tempting to make some such equation in this case.[75] Interesting particularly in this light are the speeches Tomagni gives to Cervoni condemning the unenlightened attitude toward female learning of his Colle compatriot, the humanist chancellor of Florence Bartolomeo Scala (1430–97), whom he accuses of having burned the entire *oeuvre* of his famous daughter Alessandra (1475–1506) out of jealousy at her intellectual superiority, "so that no one would say that a woman had outshone a man or a daughter her father."[76]

Regardless of the accuracy of Cervoni's, or Tomagni's, anecdote relative to Scala, it is undoubtedly of interest in considering Isabella Cervoni's emergence as a writer that a local and well-remembered role model existed for her in the person of Alessandra Scala. Such a role model also features quite prominently in the case of Catella Marchesi, in a manner that reminds us of the centrality patterns of parochial emulation had in the history of women's writing in this period. Marchesi was the daughter of a wealthy and cultured, though non-noble, couple, Antonio Marchesi and Lidia Sasso Marchesi, the first the dedicatee of Muzio Sforza's 1590 *Rime*, discussed above, the second of the 1597 volume in which Catella made her debut as a poet. Lidia was the sister of Andrea Sasso, who also featured prominently as a poet in the latter volume, and clearly Lidia herself had a reputation for learning: Sforza praises her in a *canzone* for "abandoning the needle and the skirt" to devote herself to reading, while his dedicatory letter to Antonio Marchesi speaks of Lidia's *studiolo* as equipped with "copious, well-chosen, and most beautiful books."[77] The dedicatory letter to the 1597 volume by Giacomo Bratteolo describes at some length the care with which Catella was being educated: after elementary schooling in the Clarissan convent of Santa Chiara, under the aegis of the aristocratic nun Gabriela Colloredo, she was being tutored at home by Bratteolo himself in "vernacular and Latin letters."[78] Bratteolo's ambition for his pupil, presumably espoused by her parents, is clearly stated in a sonnet addressed to her in the volume: he hopes to see her "shine on a par" with the local, Friulian cultural heroine Irene di Spilimbergo (1538–59), whose premature death had been mourned in one of the most remarkable poetic mausolea of the age.[79] Four years later, in another poetic anthology, Bratteolo was able to congratulate himself on the success of his pupil's education, this time celebrating the marriage of the 16-year-old Caterina, as he now refers to her, to the local nobleman Count Giulio della Torre (d. 1623).[80] The volume is distinctive among such epithalamic collections in the emphasis it places on the bride's literary distinction, which is given as much weight in the poems addressed to her as more conventional qualifications, such as beauty and virtue.[81]

After this promising start, Caterina Marchesi seems to have more or less disappeared from the literary scene after her marriage, in a manner recalling patterns some scholars have noted as paradigmatic of early modern women's literary trajectory.[82] Moderata Fonte and Lucrezia Marinella are sometimes cited as examples of this pattern, in that both, after an energetic publishing career in their early to mid-twenties, experienced a long hiatus in their literary production following marriages in, respectively, 1583 and 1607. There is certainly a degree of truth in this, though it needs to be noted that this hiatus was, precisely, a hiatus rather than a disappearance: Fonte had resumed writing on an ambitious scale by the time of her death in 1592, while Marinella published a significantly revised and expanded version of her 1602 *Vita di Maria Vergine* in 1617, followed by a new major work in 1618.[83] Both women also maintained a certain public profile during their "career break" through the production of occasional verse.[84]

Other women who figured publicly as writers during the years of their marriage—setting aside Isabella Andreini, who, as a professional actress, might be counted an exception—include Laura Battiferra, Maddalena Salvetti, Laura Guidiccioni, Margherita Sarrocchi, Orsina Cavaletti (d. 1592), Barbara Torelli of Parma (1546–after 1602), and Veneranda Bragadin of Verona. Instances are not difficult to cite of husbands who were supportive of their wives' literary talents, even aside from a remarkable case such as that of the Dalmatian philosopher and *letterato* Niccolò Vito di Gozze (Nikola Vitov Gučetić) (1549–1610), whose 1585 *Discorso sopra le metheore d'Aristotile* is prefaced by a lengthy dedicatory letter by his wife, Maria Gondola (Mara Gundilić), arguing that women were intellectually superior to men.[85] Both Battiferra's husband and Salvetti's acted as their wives' literary executors, in Salvetti's case publishing a posthumous volume of her writings, in Battiferra's preparing one for publication.[86] Moderata Fonte's husband, Filippo Zorzi (1558–98), a lawyer, contributed a prefatory sonnet to one of her works and composed an epitaph for her emphasizing her literary attainments over her domestic merits as a wife.[87]

Within the courts, such supportive marriages seem to have been especially frequent: we find Ercole and Orsina Cavaletti as a "poetic couple" in Ferrara in the 1580s, appearing jointly in this guise in Tasso's dialogue *La Cavaletta overo de la poesia toscana*, while, in Florence, Orazio Lucchesini appears to have conducted his court career more or less in the shadow of his talented wife, Laura Guidiccioni.[88] Muzio Manfredi and Ippolita Benigni presented themselves as a creative couple to the extent of sharing an academic name: he was "il Fermo" in the Innominati of Parma, she "la Ferma" in the Insensati of Perugia and the Affidati of Pavia.[89] Even in cases where women apparently were not active as writers during the time of their marriage, we should not assume that this reflected social or spousal disapproval of their literary aspirations. Francesca Turina does not appear in the printed record as a writer until she was in her early forties, in 1595, twelve years after the death of her husband. In a letter from her husband in 1578, however, written during an absence from home, he asks her to send him "any fine sonnet or *ottava*" she has written, suggesting that the Petrarchizing verse narrative of this period of her marriage finally published in 1628 was composed and perhaps circulated at the time.[90]

More than the fact of marriage, it was probably the size of a woman's family that determined the likelihood of her continuing her writing career after marriage. Of the most prominent Italian early modern women writers, many either were childless (Vittoria Colonna, Laura Battiferra, Maddalena Campiglia, Margherita Sarrocchi) or appear to have had just one or two children (Veronica Gambara, Chiara Matraini, Maddalena Salvetti, Lucchesia Sbarra, Lucrezia Marinella). Although women with larger families who continued to write are not unknown, they do appear to be exceptional. It is perhaps relevant to note that of the principal examples in the period examined here, Isabella Andreini, Moderata Fonte, and Veronica Franco (1546–91) all died in their thirties and forties, Andreini and Fonte in childbirth, while the mean age at death of the eleven writers listed above is, by contrast, somewhere in the mid-sixties.[91]

A final question: to what extent can women be said to have been a part of the literary culture of their cities? It is safe to say that from the outset women in this period, even the most privileged, were at a disadvantage in comparison with men because of their lesser freedom of movement and the constraints on their social interaction. Perhaps most crucially, with few exceptions they tended to be excluded from formal membership in literary academies, which, outside the universities, were undoubtedly the most important loci for cultural interaction in this period. Even among the relatively few cases of women offered academy membership, it is not clear whether they participated in meetings in person. Some exceptions may be noted. Margherita Sarrocchi's participation in meetings of the Roman Accademia degli Umoristi is well documented, although the reputation she gained in some circles for overbearingness suggests that her participation did not meet with universal approval.[92] According to one seventeenth-century source, Tarquinia Molza, a member of the Accademia degli Innominati of Parma, spoke eloquently in academic settings, while another late source speaks of Orsina Cavaletti having distinguished herself in an extraordinary, Carnival-time meeting of the Accademia Ferrarese in 1570 by arguing against one of fifty theses Torquato Tasso was defending on the philosophy of love.[93] These were rare cases, however. Within their closed sessions, as opposed to extraordinary events open to the public, academies functioned as male clubs, and women could not easily have participated without causing etiquette problems and social unease.

Despite these limitations, it does seem clear that many female writers benefited directly or indirectly from the cultural stimulus of academic culture. Some were actually granted membership. Besides Sarrocchi's membership in the Umoristi and Molza's in the Innominati, noted above, two well-documented cases from this period are Isabella Andreini's and Isabella Cervoni's membership in two Pavian academies, the Intenti and the Affidati. It is an intriguing conjunction, suggestive of the kind of inter-academy rivalry that seems to have motivated the near-simultaneous election of Laura Battiferra and Virginia Salvi to the academies of the Intronati and the Travagliati in Siena in the 1560s.[94] The Affidati appear to have elected at least one other female member, Ippolita Benigni, who was also a member of the Insensati of Perugia, probably along with Francesca Turina.[95] Other well-attested cases of academy membership for women are those of Innocenza and Fabrizia Carrari of Treviso, who identify themselves in print as members of the Accademia degli Erranti of Ceneda, and Isabella Pallavicino Lupi, Marchioness of Soragna (c. 1545–1623), founder and member of the Accademia degli Illuminati in Farnese, where her son-in-law, Mario Farnese, ruled.[96] Less well-documented instances include those of Issicratea Monte, in the Concordi of Rovigo; Domicilla and Silvia Silvi, in the Elevati of Reggio Emilia; Isabella Sori, in the Immobili of Alessandria; and Lucrezia Della Valle, in the Accademia Cosentina, in her hometown of Cosenza.[97] The early seventeenth century also saw the first cases of women being admitted to artistic academies. It has been conjectured that Lavinia Fontana may have joined the Roman Accademia di San Luca in 1609, while Artemisia Gentileschi was admitted to the Florentine Accademia del Disegno in 1616.[98]

Besides the kind of formal association with academies implied by membership, we can identify other, less "official" but often quite rich and productive interactions between female writers and their local academies. One particularly interesting case is the relationship between Maddalena Campiglia and the Accademia Olimpica of Vicenza. There is no direct evidence that Campiglia was ever formally elected to the Olimpici, but her connections with the academy seem to have been quite close. She speaks in the dedicatory letter to her *Flori* of feedback on the play received from the academy's secretary, Paolo Chiappino (1538?–93), and sonnets by a number of Olimpici accompany the work, as they did her *Discorso sopra l'annonciatione della beata Vergine*, published three years earlier.[99] Campiglia also appears to have contributed to an event organized by the academy on at least one occasion. In a letter of 1588 to Francesco Melchiori (1528–90) she speaks of a madrigal she wrote for a planned visit to Vicenza by Isabella Pallavicino Lupi. Campiglia mentions that the poem was set to music, adding that "these things were prepared in the Academy."[100] At the height of her brief but meteoric literary career, Campiglia seems to have become a kind of figurehead for Vicentine literary culture, aided by her novelty value as one of the first published female playwrights in Italy and the aristocratic cachet that facilitated her interaction with foreign literary grandees such as the Mantuan Curzio Gonzaga (1536–99), a relative by marriage, who seems to have entrusted Campiglia with the management of his literary affairs in the 1590s.[101] The question of whether Campiglia formally belonged to the Olimpici becomes in this case something of a red herring; certainly, she was associated with it to the degree that her fame could be seen as contributing to its luster. Another prestigious literary acquaintance, the aristocratic Genoese poet Angelo Grillo (1557–1629), compliments her in a sonnet by speaking of Vicenza's sons as "deserving truly to call themselves Olympians" on her account.[102]

It is not clear at the current state of research how typical Campiglia's relationship with her local literary community was; few female writers of the period have enjoyed such a strong modern biographical tradition.[103] Other women who appear to have had close contacts with their local literary academies, whether or not they were members, include Barbara Torelli, with the Innominati of Parma; Issicratea Monte, with the Pastori Fratteggiani of Fratta Polesine; and Valeria Miani, with the Ricovrati of Padua, an academy that later in the seventeenth century would prove exceptional for its openness to women.[104] It would also be interesting to know more of Lucchesia Sbarra's relationship with her brother Pulzio's two academies, the Accademia degli Scolari Incamminati (1587–90), notable for its public educational program, and the Accademia degli Aspiranti (founded 1603).[105] On a less provincial level, an interesting case of a distanced but productive relationship between a female writer and an academy is that between Lucrezia Marinella and the Accademia Veneziana (the second of that name, founded in 1593). Marinella's brother Curzio was a member of the academy, as was Lucio Scarano, the dedicatee of Marinella's *La nobiltà et l'eccellenza delle donne,* whom she thanks in her dedicatory letter for praising her work in a public lecture, perhaps in an academic context.[106] The academy's founder, Boncio Leoni, like Curzio Marinelli a medic and *letterato,* contributed a sonnet to Marinella's first published work, *La Colomba sacra* (1595), which came out with Giovanni Battista Ciotti, publisher to the academy from 1594. As noted earlier, *La nobiltà et l'eccellenza delle donne* seems to have been produced under commission from Ciotti, and it has been suggested that Marinella was writing as a semiauthorized spokeswoman for the academy.[107] If she was, this would be a further, striking illustration of how close such semidetached relationships could be.

2. Women's Writing and the Counter-Reformation

What, in all this, of the Counter-Reformation? To what extent did this movement affect women's cultural life and their possibilities as writers in this period? To what degree did it reshape gender attitudes, and especially attitudes toward women's access to culture?

One thing that needs to be stated quite clearly from the outset is that the Counter-Reformation was not responsible for introducing any concerted global policy of female subordination beyond what women had been used to in the past. Certainly, elements of Tridentine policy did impact directly on the lives of women, especially those in religious orders, who found themselves subjected to a new, notably stricter regime of claustration at the same time that the powers of abbesses were being progressively encroached upon by the male-run ecclesiastical authorities.[108] There seems little doubt that these measures were experienced by many nuns at the time as oppressive: numerous female religious communities resisted them, although others embraced the new stringency with zeal.[109] The negative effects of this development were, however, much exacerbated in this period by shifts in nubility patterns among the Italian elite that resulted in a notable increase in the number of nuns, many without a religious vocation.[110] This cannot in itself be laid at the door of the Catholic Church, although it is true that the church colluded with the secular elite by providing "warehousing" for these unmarriageable girls.[111] It must also be recalled that although it was certainly applied with far greater stringency after Trent, the impulse toward a stricter enclosure and invigilation of convents dates back further, at least to the reform initiatives of the early decades of the sixteenth century.[112] In this sense, developments in the later sixteenth century may be seen as simply continuing a trend.

Another concrete area in which Tridentine regulations affected women's lives was marriage.[113] Rather than an individual compact between a man and woman that could theoretically be sealed outside any institutional framework, through Tridentine regulation marriage came under the control of the ecclesiastical establishment, which ruled marriages that had not been formally celebrated in church invalid. This institutionalization of marriage has sometimes been presented as a development oppressive of women, in that it strengthened patriarchal control by outlawing clandestine marriage, while at the same time Tridentine moralism drew a new and stricter line between marriage, as the sole socially acceptable state for a sexually active woman, and looser arrangements such as concubinage, which previously had enjoyed a degree of informal social acceptance. Recent studies of marriage practices among the elite of Venice in the seventeenth century, however, tend to suggest that the moral imperatives of the Counter-Reformation church were only effective to the extent that they accorded with families' social and economic interests. It also appears that the enforcement of Tridentine decrees allowed quite a degree of flexibility. Certainly, concubinage did not disappear as a social practice after Trent, nor were extramarital relationships necessarily regarded with opprobrium; on the contrary, they arguably acquired an enhanced social role in the seventeenth century given the reduced nubility among the elite.[114]

More generally, social and religious historians of the past two decades or so have begun to distance themselves from the traditional view that saw the Counter-Reformation as uniformly oppressive of women, proposing instead a more nuanced view.[115] Even truisms such as the one that saw the moral rigorism of the papacy as having banished prostitution from Rome in the later sixteenth century or driven it to the margins of society are questioned in a work such as Tessa Storey's *Carnal Commerce in Counter-Reformation Rome*, which is consistent with much recent work in seeing continuities in this period where traditional scholarship had tended to posit a sharp disjunction.[116] This revisionist impulse has even begun to extend to areas previously considered paradigmatic for the detrimental effects of Tridentine reforms on women, such as the imposition of *clausura* on convents. Important in this regard is the 2005 volume *I monasteri femminili come centri di cultura tra Rinascimento e Barocco*, edited by Gianna Pomata and Gabriella Zarri, whose essays collectively suggest that the stricter imposition of claustration did not necessarily reduce nuns' connections with lay society or convents' presence within the broader culture of their cities as drastically as has often been understood. The discussion above on convent writers' engagement with the press provides further evidence on this score.

Beyond the question of women's concrete social position, how true is it that the Counter-Reformation sponsored an ideological renaissance of misogyny, as has very often been suggested? It is certainly true that sexual morality figured significantly as a concern within the project of ecclesiastical reform put in place by the Council of Trent. It is also true that the rhetoric associated with this moral reform often posited women as agents of temptation, witting or otherwise. This was in large part the logic of the drive to conventual claustration, as well as of the reorganization of church and confessional space pioneered by Carlo Borromeo in Milan.[117] Obviously, the notion of female sexuality as a dangerous force demanding strict social discipline was hardly new or specific to Counter-Reformation Italy, but it did attain a particular cultural purchase at this time. This had implications for thinking on women's education, obviously a subject of particular importance for this book. The curial secretary and future cardinal Silvio Antoniano (1540–1603), in his much-published *Dell'educatione christiana dei figliuoli,* of 1584, speaks with disapprobation of parents who educate their daughters to the same level as their sons, allowing them to indulge in studies such as poetry and rhetoric. Still more dangerous, writes Antoniano, is the habit of allowing these young girls to display their eloquence in public in the presence of men. Antoniano's unease is clearly motivated predominantly by concerns of sexual decorum, but he also manifests an undertow of distaste at the notion of women's empowerment through education, warning of the vanity educated women are prone to and the danger of their contravening the Pauline dictum against women teaching or having authority over men.[118] The same arguments would be adduced sixty years later in the Jesuit Giovanni Domenico Ottonelli's *La pericolosa conversatione con le donne, o poco modeste, o ritirate, o cantatrici, o accademiche* (1646), which devotes a lengthy chapter to arguing against the dangers for men of attending social events at which educated women *(accademiche)* are present: not only will the speaking woman's feminine charms represent an intolerable assault on her male listeners' senses but these listeners, in participating, will be complicit in a breach of the God-given discursive order dictated by Paul.[119]

It would not be difficult to conclude from evidence of this kind that Counter-Reformation thinkers were solidly opposed to women's intellectual cultivation in a manner that contrasts quite sharply with the relative openness of earlier secular humanistic thought.[120] If we move beyond the evidence of prescriptive literature, however, this clear dichotomy begins immediately to crumble. Even Antoniano and Ottonelli are less absolute on the subject than they are sometimes represented to be. Antoniano, who had corresponded poetically in his youth with Laura Battiferra and was no doubt aware of the exceptional education his Curia colleague Guglielmo Sirleto had given to his ward Margherita Sarrocchi, allows at the end of his stern discussion of women's education that some exceptions may legitimately be made.[121] Ottonelli cites Sarrocchi as a counterexample to his fears of the corrupting effects of *accademiche,* noting that the gatherings she herself hosted in Rome were remarkable for the strictness of their mores.[122] The very fact that a figure like Sarrocchi could emerge precisely in Rome and under the tutelage of a cardinal should itself warn us not to draw hasty conclusions about Counter-Reformation clerics' attitudes toward women's education. In practice, in fact, it is no easier to generalize about the gender attitudes of "Counter-Reformation thinkers" than it is to generalize about those of "Italian humanists" a century earlier. A particular attitude toward women did not prevail in either of these cultural movements. On the contrary, there was a broad spectrum of gender attitudes in both, varying according to individuals' cultural and social background, life trajectory, patronage situation, and intellectual sympathies. As in the case of humanism, we are more likely to find profeminist views among Counter-Reformation clerics with close ties to the world of the secular courts, in which a reputation for gallantry was socially advantageous, and relationships with female patrons often had a key role in male intellectuals' strategies for social advancement.

An interesting example of a profeminist cleric in the period is the aristocratic Piedmontese priest Francesco Agostino Della Chiesa, whom we have already encountered as the author of the first systematic compendium of biographies of women writers, the baroquely entitled *Theatro delle donne letterate* of 1620. The *Theatro* is prefaced by a polemical *Discorso* on women's superiority to men that positions itself at the more politicized end of the spectrum of profeminist views of the era, arguing that women's subordination represents a form of tyranny rather than natural justice.[123] At the time he published these two works, Della Chiesa was already a priest, having taken orders soon after his legal studies in Turin and Rome. The *Theatro* was dedicated to Margherita of Savoy (1589–1655), daughter of an infanta of Spain and later appointed queen of Portugal, while its author's later advancement owed much to another prominent woman of the Savoyard dynasty, the long-term regent Maria Cristina of France (1606–63). Della Chiesa ended his career as bishop of Saluzzo, a post to which he was elected in spite of some murmurings concerning the "inappropriate" profeminism of his youth.[124]

Della Chiesa offers a good example of the way in which the choice of a religious career did not preclude the public espousal of profeminist sentiments, in the early Seicento in Italy. While he ironically remarks at the beginning of his treatise that because he was a priest, his "profession should be to flee women's company rather than to praise them," the offhandedness of the comment suggests that he had no serious qualms on this score.[125] Nor can we see the *Theatro* and the *Discorso* as a secular diversion on the part of a man of less than whole-hearted vocation. On the contrary, in the *Theatro*, while giving due respect to secular and classical female writers, Della Chiesa manifests his greatest enthusiasm for those who deployed their learning to religious ends. One of the interesting features of the *Theatro*, in fact, is the strong case it implicitly makes for female learning as conducive to devotion, in conscious polemic with the view that saw "letters" as corrupting for women and ignorance as their best protection against sin.[126] Although Della Chiesa's profeminist sympathies were clearly motivated by patronage concerns, it would be reductive to see these as his sole motivations. He was not the first in his family to celebrate the achievements of women; indeed, one of his cited sources is an unpublished twelve-book treatise on the nobility of women by his uncle Francesco Scipione della Chiesa, a Cistercian monk who attained the status of vicar-general of his order before his early death in 1578.[127] His own family circle included cultured women: the *Theatro* has an entry for his sister, Francesca Benedetta della Chiesa, a nun at the Cistercian convent of Rifreddo in Saluzzo and author of a "most beautiful discourse" on the pleasures of convent life, which her brother refers to intriguingly as not "yet" given to the press.[128]

The extent to which family and civic tradition inflected male religious attitudes toward female intellectuality is interestingly illustrated, in an earlier generation, in the figure of the Genoese Benedictine Angelo Grillo, already encountered as a literary contact of Maddalena Campiglia's. Grillo's mother was a Spinola, possibly related to Genoa's first female poet of note in the mid-sixteenth century, Maria Spinola. Two other female Spinola poets figure among Grillo's poetic correspondents: Livia, the wife of his cousin Alessandro, also a poet, and Laura, probably a relative of Grillo's.[129] During Grillo's youth Genoa was also home to the painter Sofonisba Anguissola (c. 1532–1625), as well as to the Lateran canoness Battista Vernazza, the most remarkable female devotional writer of the age. The city could also boast one of the great fifteenth-century female mystics in Saint Catherine of Genoa

(Caterina Fieschi Adorno [1447–1510]), who had been Vernazza's godmother and mentor.

These experiences may have contributed to Grillo's seemingly remarkable openness toward female poets and creative artists generally. Besides sonnet exchanges with Campiglia, the Spinolas, and the Lucchese poet Leonora Bernardi, his *Rime* of 1589 contains sonnets in praise of Anguissola, the singer Laura Peverara (1555–1601), and the otherwise unknown Genoese lutenist Pentisilea Ferri, as well as a laudatory poem by the Ferrarese poet Orsina Cavaletti.[130] Grillo's *Lettere* further document his relationships with Bernardi, to whom he was particularly close; with the Florentine composer Francesca Caccini (1587–1641), to whom he sent madrigal texts for musical setting; and with Lavinia Fontana, whose portrait of him he praises enthusiastically in a 1606 letter to his brother, contrasting her genius with that of many male painters who had attempted to capture his likeness but "only succeeded in depicting their own inadequacy."[131] We also see him offering literary encouragement to an aspiring female writer who had contacted him, the otherwise unknown Angela Lurago of Como, perhaps consciously echoing a similar letter of Pietro Bembo's addressed to Ippolita Clara (1487–1550).[132] Never in Grillo's writings do we sense any diffidence regarding the propriety of female education or literary aspiration; on the contrary, in the letter to Lurago we find him speaking with humanistically inflected admiration of the prowess of the women of antiquity who "emulated the achievements of Heroes" and lamenting that the modern age had produced so few women capable of equaling their fame.[133] In addition to showing himself supportive to living female writers and creative artists, Grillo was also responsive to the tradition of female mystic writing, represented in his own age by Battista Vernazza. Suggestive in this regard is the sonnet in his 1608 *Christo flagellato* addressed to Saint Bridget of Sweden (1303–73), to whose "famed great volume" (chiaro alto volume), probably her *Rivelationes*, he attributes the inspiration of his own work.[134]

The patterns we observe in the case of Grillo are also apparent in, for example, that of his contemporary Bernardino Baldi (1553–1617), abbot of the Gonzaga satellite court of Guastalla from 1585 to 1609 and later in the service of the Duke of Urbino. Though from a less prominent family than Grillo's, Baldi too was of noble birth and seems to have moved effortlessly within secular courtly society. Intellectually he was far more eclectic: his works include technical and mathematical treatises and historical works, as well as sacred and secular vernacular lyrics.[135] Baldi's Urbino background clearly acquainted him with the phenomenon of the female writer, most famously in the form of Laura Battiferra, whom he proudly touts in his *Encomio della patria* (1603) as one of the literary glories of her age.[136] Another Urbinate female poet mentioned in the *Encomio* was the noblewoman Vittoria Galli, dedicatee of Baldi's 1590 *Rime varie,* and a third, Minerva Bartoli (1562–1602), was among the many addresses of the vast collection of vernacular epigrams left unpublished at his death.[137]

It is possible that Baldi's own family circle, like Grillo's, may have offered examples of educated women. His mother, Virginia Montanari Baldi, of Pesaro, is probably both the "Virginia Montanara" praised by Cristoforo Bronzini for her mastery of Latin and Tuscan and the "Virginia Baldi" included by Cornelio Lanci (d. c. 1600) in a list of female poets in a treatise of 1590.[138] An unpublished treatise of the 1580s by Baldi addressed to his nun sister Leonora, in which he contrasts the pleasures of monastic over secular life for women, envisages the reading matter of nuns in notably ambitious terms, embracing patristic and scholastic theologians such as Jerome, Ambrose, Augustine, and Gerson, as well as more conventional material such as saints' lives.[139] Beyond his compatriots Galli and Bartoli, Baldi's female literary acquaintance included Maddalena Campiglia, whom he praises in one eclogue for "having drunk the nectar of the Muses along with her mother's milk"; Barbara Torelli, for whose pastoral *Partenia* he contributed a prefatory sonnet; and Tarquinia Molza and the French religious poet Gabrielle Coignard (1550–86), both of whom were among the addresses of his epigrams.[140]

Besides their engagement with female writers, worldly religious writers such as Baldi and Grillo also frequently selected noblewomen as dedicatees of their works. Baldi, for example, dedicated his *Corona dell'anno* (1589) to Vittoria Doria Gonzaga (1569–1618), consort of his employer, Ferrante II Gonzaga (1563–1630), while Grillo dedicated the second edition of his *Lagrime del penitente* (1594) to Giovanna Doria Colonna (d. 1620), the second part of his *Essequie di Giesù Christo* (1610) to Orsina Peretti Sforza, Marchioness of Caravaggio, and three of the successive editions of his principal verse collection, *Pietosi affetti* (1595, 1601, 1613), to Vittoria Doria Gonzaga, Livia Feltria della Rovere, and the Bergamasque noblewoman-poet Paola Solza Rota, respectively.[141]

As these case studies show, one should not assume hostility toward female writers on the part of Counter-Reformation male clerical intellectuals. On the contrary, it is worth entertaining the hypothesis that at least some clerics may have actively welcomed women as cowriters. In an age that was actively, even evangelically, seeking to harmonize the demands of literary pleasure and moral and religious edification, women, schooled as they were to values of piety and "honesty," may well have appeared to be among the writers best accommodated to the demands of the age. The logic of this becomes very clear if we look at a writer like Maddalena Campiglia, who, as we have seen, was an acquaintance of both Grillo and Baldi and whose wide network of literary contacts included numerous other men of the church.[142] Although modern critical attention has centered largely on the remarkable treatment of issues of gender and sexuality in Campiglia's pastoral *Flori*, it was as a religious writer that Campiglia first came to attention, with her 1585 *Discorso sopra l'annonciatione della beata Vergine*. Her last work, now lost, probably a narrative poem or *tragedia sacra*, was on the life and presumably the martyrdom of Saint Barbara.[143] Even *Flori*, though secular in theme, was consistent with the general tendency of Counter-Reformation moral prescriptions in its Neoplatonic and antisensualist treatment of its central love relationship. Similar points could be made about other female writers among Grillo's and Baldi's acquaintances, such as Barbara Torelli, whose *Partenia* is even more morally austere in its treatment of love than Campiglia's *Flori*.[144] It is easy to see how women like Campiglia and Torelli might have represented to their male religious literary admirers a kind of moral vanguard within literature, taking on traditionally "lascivious" genres such as pastoral drama and converting them to more edifying ends. Contradictory though this seems from the perspective of conventional Italian literary historiography, female authors were probably *less* marginalized and *less* "other" within the purified Counter-Reformation literary landscape of the late sixteenth century than they had been in the "freer" world of early sixteenth-century literature. To preach celibacy within the sensual, prelapsarian world of Arcadia would have seemed an eccentricity half a century earlier. In the late 1580s, when Campiglia and Torelli were writing, such "feminine" propriety made a new cultural sense.

If this was the case even where essentially secular literary projects such as *Partenia* and *Flori* were concerned, the female-authored religious literature of the age was even less morally contentious. Scrutinizing the paratexts of editions of such works, we not infrequently find evidence of collaboration between female writers and male clerics, sometimes considerably exceeding the level of commitment implied by a prefatory sonnet. The aristocratic Brescian

Benedictine Gregorio Ducchi (d. 1591) contributed an effusive afterword to Campiglia's *Discorso*, praising her as a "most ardent spirit, whose mind converses always . . . with the heavenly," as well as a sonnet counterposing her writings to those of "profane pens" who devote their energies to singing of arms and love.[145] Chiara Matraini's *Vita e laude della beatissima Vergine* (1590) is accompanied by a series of annotations by the Neapolitan Augustinian canon Giuseppe Mozzagrugno, noted as a preacher and religious writer, and Mozzagrugno and his fellow Augustinian Alessandro Bovio also contributed two prefatory sonnets to the collection. These are cases of works published under women's own aegis being adorned and legitimated by male-authored paratexts, but instances may also be cited of female-authored religious works that were published at male clerics' behest. Battista Vernazza's 1588 *Opere* was published through the agency of her order, following a complex process of ecclesiastical scrutiny, while a collection of meditations by the young Neapolitan noblewoman Isabella Capece (1569–90) was published posthumously in 1595 by her confessor, Pietro Cola Pagano.[146]

Examples such as this demonstrate how misleading it is to speak of the shift in the cultural climate introduced by the Counter-Reformation as universally detrimental to women's intellectual pretensions. The religious and moral turn that occurred so markedly in Italian literature in this period served in many ways to shift the center of literary gravity onto more classically feminine terrain. Religious literature and the kind of expurgated secular literature that flanked it in this period proved a congenial habitat for women, and numerous male authors associated with the reformed literature of the Counter-Reformation welcomed the opportunity to associate themselves with female writers. For the more worldly among them, this was a way to establish their courtly credentials, a form of cultural shorthand long established in Italian literature.[147] At the same time, it also offered an opportunity to display their commitment to the particular form of "simple," emotive, quasi-instinctual religiosity that women within this culture were regarded as embodying par excellence and that made a figure like Mary Magdalene a privileged spiritual role model for both sexes in this period. An interesting document of this discursive construction is Ducchi's afterword to Campiglia's *Discorso*, in which he represents Campiglia's art as an emanation of her personal faith and proposes her explicitly as a model for intellectuals of both sexes, who may learn from her how best to spend their time, to the edification and benefit of their fellow man.[148] Similarly, Angelo Grillo, in a sonnet in his 1589 *Rime* addressed to Vittoria Malaspina, Marchioness of Fosdinovo, contrasts Malaspina's spontaneous and powerful emotional response in reading a poem of his on Christ's passion with his own relative weakness of affect in writing it. The female reader here offers a standard of piety to which the male poet can only hope to aspire.[149]

Within this frame of reference, a clear "career path" was implicitly mapped out for the culturally attuned female writer, one embodied in an exemplary manner by Lucrezia Marinella, even if the modern focus on Marinella's feminist treatise *La nobiltà et l'eccellenza delle donne* has until very recently tended to obscure this fact. Marinella began her career with two exquisitely "Counter-Reformation" *poemetti sacri* in ottava rima recounting the lives of the *beata* Columba of Sens (1595) and Saint Francis of Assisi (1597); she followed them in 1602 with the far more ambitious *Vita di Maria Vergine imperatrice dell'universo*, combining lives of the Virgin in both ottava rima and prose, and in 1603 with a collection of religious lyrics *(Rime sacre)*. The last three works mentioned were among Marinella's most successful works in terms of republication. The *Vita di Maria Vergine* was reprinted in 1604, 1610, and 1617, the third time accompanied by a new series of lives of the apostles, while the *Vita di San Francesco* was republished in 1605 and 1606, the second time in a multi-authored volume of works in praise of Saint Francis edited by the Franciscan Fra Silvestro da Poppi.[150] Extracts from the *Rime sacre* were published in a probably unauthorized edition in 1605 by the Bergamasque publisher Comin Ventura, who in 1606 also brought out an edition of Marinella's *Vita di Maria Vergine*, again with no sign of authorial involvement.[151] It was quite possible for the Augustinian Giacomo Alberici to present Marinella in 1605 purely as a religious writer, ignoring her activity as a feminist polemicist in *La nobiltà et l'eccellenza delle donne*.[152] His perspective was probably not unusual; in the same year, in his introduction to her secular *Arcadia felice*, the publisher Giambattista Ciotti lists her spiritual works before proceeding to *La nobiltà et l'eccellenza delle donne*, which he describes, perhaps with a little distance, as written under the impulse of "the truth, and the love each of us bears toward our own sex."[153]

The species of compact between women writers and sympathetic male clerics argued for here finds its most striking exemplification in the dynamics of the early seventeenth-century *querelle des femmes*. The long-simmering debate on women's status and moral character was revived at the end of the Cinquecento in Italy with a series of local debates in the Veneto before "going national" in 1599 following the publication in Venice of Giuseppe Passi's *I donneschi difetti*.[154] This was the context of Marinella's *La nobiltà et l'eccellenza delle donne*, which is constructed as a direct response to Passi (1569–c. 1620), and the new topicality of gender issues in these years may have prompted the posthumous publication of Fonte's *Il merito delle donne*. The two decades or so following the publication of Passi's and Marinella's treatises saw a fairly intense rhythm of publication of treatises for and against women, the latter a novelty with regard to the Cinquecento, when overt misogyny was rarely expressed within mainstream literary culture.[155]

There was a further novelty regarding the personae of the dispute: not only did women participate, for the first time in Italy, as combatants and not merely spectators but the male "defenders of women" who lined up beside them included three priests, a canon, and a friar.[156] Two, both priests, have already been discussed: Francesco Agostino Della Chiesa and Cristoforo Bronzini.[157] The others were Francesco Caruso (1505–93), bishop of Sulmona, who published a *Dialogo della nobiltà delle donne* in Naples in 1592; the Lateran canon Pietro Paolo Ribera, author of the grandiosely entitled *Le glorie immortali de' trionfi et heroiche imprese d'ottocento quarantacinque donne illustri antiche e moderne dotate di conditioni e scienze segnalate*, published in Venice in 1609; and the Augustinian friar Lucrezio Bursati, or Borsati, author of the dialogue *La vittoria delle donne*, which came out in the same city in 1621.[158] This represents a genuine novelty in the period, in that the authors of pro-feminist *querelle* texts had, to this point, been almost exclusively laymen.[159] This development is the more striking in that the majority of authors of misogynist works in this period were laymen: besides Passi, examples here are Anton Maria Spelta (1559–1632), who includes a chapter on women's "madness" in his *La saggia pazzia, fonte d'allegrezze* (1607), and the Paduan *medic-letterato* Giovanni Battista Barbo, author of a misogynist verse satire, *L'oracolo*, composed and circulated before 1613, which elicited a polemical response from Veneranda Bragadin.[160]

Although Ribera's, Bursati's, and Della Chiesa's works vary considerably in character and scope, all explicitly present themselves as intended to combat contemporary misogynist writers, described by Della Chiesa as "rabid dogs" with mouths "full of venom."[161] Ribera, the most florid and eccentric of the three, consistently assimilates misogyny to heresy, comparing misogynists to "Lutherans" at one point and condemning them as worse than "[Theodor] Beza in Geneva or the Rabbi in the Ghetto of the Jews."[162] In the analytic (as opposed to the exemplificative) portions of their treatises, Ribera, Bursati, and Della Chiesa draw extensively on the humanistic profeminist tradition, culminating in Lucrezia Marinella's *La nobiltà et l'eccellenza delle donne*, of which all three writers show themselves to be aware.[163] A clue to the motives of these writers is offered by the fact that all present women as representing an ideal from which men might profitably learn. Bursati is the most explicit on this point, having his feminist speaker Gaudenzio Moreschi, clearly identified as the spokesman of the author, state that "women's decorousness, manners, refinement, and good customs give to men the true and just rule, the correct norm for living in the world in a civilized manner and with reputation."[164] Della Chiesa similarly urges those men who waste their energies in vituperating women to consider women's "generosity, nobility, prudence, temperance, and sagacity" and to contrast it with the "baseness, ignobility, imprudence, intemperance, madness, cowardice, cruelty, and harshness of most modern men."[165] Finally, Ribera, in a list of reasons why women may be considered superior to men, leans heavily on arguments from morality, maintaining that "woman is more devoted and assiduous in the service of God; she is more compassionate in all that regards the needs of her neighbors; and she offends God less through grave sins, such as murder, blasphemy, perjury, sects, seditions, treacheries, and heresies."[166]

Here, perhaps, ultimately, we can locate the positive discursive utility that women represented for some Counter-Reformation thinkers: they could serve as a model for a feminized ethos of piety, continence, and containment, now felt to have a new relevance for men. As has often been noted, the conduct norms fashioned by Renaissance humanism were heavily gender-dichotomized in comparison with the medieval monastic behavioral codes that preceded them.[167] Effectively, they displaced onto the feminine what had previously been unisex monastic ideals of chastity, humility, and obedience, while reinventing for the masculine a more active and power-oriented classicizing ethos that licensed a degree of aggression and pride in the name of fortitude and minimized celibacy as a virtue of any relevance to men.

The Counter-Reformation represented something of a reversal of this trend, seeking to reinstitute a distinctively Christian model of masculinity, a development consummately illustrated by Tasso's *Gerusalemme liberata*, which represents its "pagan" warriors as quasi-parodic epitomes of classical heroic masculinity, while fashioning for its Christian knights, in particular Goffredo, a more sober and tempered ethos. To an extent this process may be seen as one of feminization, or refeminization, of the masculine, but one that takes as its point of reference a particular, exalted vision of femininity, not the feminine in general but the heroic and virile ideal of femininity embodied by biblical heroines such as Judith and Esther or virgin martyrs such as Cecilia, Lucy, or Catherine of Alexandria, themselves heirs to the classical heroines extolled by humanism, such as Artemisia, Zenobia, and Lucretia. Especially in its religious variant, this ideal of heroic femininity functioned admirably as an ethical model adaptable to both sexes; Giacinto Branchi, in his 1642 *Giuditta trionfante,* provocatively describes Judith as "the type of the true Christian knight."[168] While secular humanism had extolled women for assimilating themselves to men, Counter-Reformation culture was as likely to reverse this equation, praising women as role models for men to follow. "What have women not done in the way of the spirit?" Angelo Grillo exclaims in a letter after hearing of the widowed poet Leonora Bernardi's resolve to retire to a convent. "There is no reading matter that moves me more than that of holy women, who have left the way behind them for us to follow."[169]

It was not just in Counter-Reformation Italy that women were recognized as figureheads of faith and living reproaches to men in their piety. The attitude of an English Catholic of the period such as Richard Crashaw (1613–49) is similar in its privileging of femininity. "Can a woman be so strong in her faith?" Crashaw asked regarding the Canaanite woman in a Latin epigram of his youth. "Now I believe that faith [*fides*] is feminine more than in simply a grammatical sense."[170] This notion that faith and the moral imperatives that derive from it gender as feminine more immediately than as masculine was widespread within Catholic culture in this period, to the extent that anti-Catholic polemicists consistently used Catholicism's "effeminacy," most iconically realized in what was perceived as its Mariolatry, as one of the most persistent topoi in their vituperative language.[171] The modern Italian historiographical notion of the Counter-Reformation as intrinsically misogynistic does not map in any easy way onto the evidence of gender attitudes in this period and accords ill with the most thoughtful recent scholarship on this subject within other national contexts. Studies of French literary and religious culture in the late sixteenth and early seventeenth centuries have described this period as witnessing a "feminization of devotion," a formula that may be applied as accurately to a poet like Grillo as to Saint François de Sales.[172] Until Italian literary historiography is prepared to reexamine the commonplace of the Counter-Reformation as a misogynist era with a critical eye, not only the gender history of this period but also its cultural and religious history generally will remain only partially understood.

3. Religious Writing in Post-Tridentine Italy: A Poetics of Conversion

The later sixteenth century was a time of extraordinary literary ferment in Italy, as writers and theorists strove to forge a new sacred literary tradition on a par with the secular vernacular tradition of the earlier part of the century. Stylistically, the same period witnessed a gradual and complex process of transition from the classicizing ideals of clarity, naturalism, rationality, and balance that had dominated the first half of the century and the poetics of the "extraordinary," the extreme, and the self-consciously artificial that would come to maturity with the age of the baroque. Despite the introduction of censorship, which curbed writers' freedom of expression in some key fields, it is a travesty to present this period as one in which creativity was stifled: rather, it was a period of reinvention, reappropriation, redirection, of a dissolution of old paradigms and a gestation of new ones.[173] It saw the birth of a newly militant Catholic literature of religious conquest and, at the same time, the emergence of a new vein of classicizing sensuality in lyric. Dismissed for much of the twentieth century as little more than a coda to the High Renaissance, the late sixteenth century is a period of literary history that is now, rightly, beginning to attract new critical attention. It offers a compelling field of study, particularly for those with an interest in the ideological dimension of literature and in the dynamics of cultural change.[174]

My discussion here begins with what may be seen as the central literary development of this period: the emergence, in theory and practice, of a new ideal of sacred literature, framed quite self-consciously as a corrective to the previous, secular tradition. A good starting point is the preface to Gabriele Fiamma's 1570 *Rime spirituali*, which contains an exceptionally lucid consideration of how vernacular literature, and specifically lyric poetry, might remodel itself to meet the era's spiritual demands.[175] Fiamma (c. 1533–85) begins by lamenting that Tuscan literary education in his day should be entrusted to a reading of Boccaccio and Petrarch, authors who, while they may be safely enjoyed by mature minds, represent a moral danger to the impressionable young. Fiamma offers his own religious verse as an innocuous alternative that will allow young readers to develop their appreciation of poetic style without risking moral corruption.

This is all modest enough, but in the course of the preface Fiamma unveils a much broader ambition: no less than to "return" (ritornare) poetry to its original vocation, the praise of the divine, from which it has been perverted to serve secular and idolatrous ends such as erotic love and the adulation of princes.[176] In his account of the origins and history of poetry Fiamma draws on the Neoplatonic syncretic tradition popularized by Ficino, citing as representative of poetry's initial, divine inspiration both the songs of legendary Greek *vates* such as Orpheus, Linus, and Musaeus and the canticle tradition of the Old Testament, culminating in the insuperable poetry of the psalms.[177] To find its way back to the path it has abandoned, modern vernacular poetry needs to recoup the lessons of David, who takes the place Fiamma's fellow Venetian Pietro Bembo (1503–65) had allocated to Petrarch, as supreme stylistic model, capable of serving as a textbook in the use of "ornaments, figure, tropes, and beauties of language."[178] The Bembist substrate of Fiamma's poetics is apparent in his identification of the stylistic essence of the psalms as residing in their *grave leggiadria* (grave charm), a supple and faintly oxymoronic combination of qualities close to the balance of *gravità* and *piacevolezza* that Bembo had identified in his *Prose della volgar lingua* as Petrarch's supreme achievement.[179]

As this deft use of Bembo indicates, Fiamma positions himself tactfully with regard to the secular poetic tradition whose demise he is advocating. Zealots capable of calling for Petrarch to be banned as a "ringleader and teacher of filthy lusts" were not absent in this period, and Fiamma himself was capable of stern language: for example, he refers to the dominance of erotic subject matter in the modern lyric tradition as a "great and almost intolerable error."[180] A noted preacher as well as a poet, however, Fiamma was too rhetorically astute not to recognize the strategic utility of conciliatory language in arguing a difficult case. He treats Petrarch with great respect, describing him as "worthy of every praise that may be offered to a rare and singular intellect" and lauding him for his achievement in polishing the vernacular and bringing it to the summit of stylistic perfection.[181] Fiamma does not even unequivocally condemn the erotic content of Petrarch's *rime*, given the sublimated character of the love they describe; although they are dangerous reading for the young, he acknowledges that mature readers may profit from Petrarch's lessons in "Platonic and philosophical love."[182] Fiamma's practice as a poet also attests to his sedulous imitation of Petrarch, even if he downplays this in the commentary that accompanies his *Rime spirituali*, instead emphasizing his biblical and other religious sources.[183] The new religious poetry Fiamma seeks to craft in the volume is one that builds on the strengths of the existing, secular, vernacular tradition, while converting—or reconverting—it to uses more consonant with humanity's ultimate ends. This is a poetics of conversion, both in the religious sense of a spiritual transformation and in the more banal and material sense of adapting a structure originally for one use to another.[184] The model proposed is essentially the Augustinian one of an appropriation of "Egyptian gold" for sacred uses, though here the gold to be plundered is not the classical tradition but the modern trove of vernacular, secular eloquence represented quintessentially by Petrarch.[185]

Although Fiamma was exceptional in the theoretical finesse with which he articulated the claims of religious lyric, there was no absolute novelty in his project of returning vernacular verse to its divine roots.[186] The roots of Fiamma's poetics of conversion may be found in Petrarch himself, in his great final *canzone*, which systematically reapplies the praise style he evolved for Laura in the sacred context of a hymn to the Virgin. The consonance between this poem and Counter-Reformation poetic ideals is reflected in the exceptional *fortuna* it enjoyed in the period: it was the subject of three independent commentaries, by Pietro Caponsacchi (1577), Giovanni Angelo Lottini (1595) and Celso Cittadini (1604), as well as being set numerous times to music, most notably, in this period, by Palestrina (1581).[187] Among Cinquecento writers, the possibility of a conversion of Petrarch's erotic language to spiritual ends had already become an object of keen interest, at least from the 1530s and 1540s. Besides awkward pastiches such as Girolamo Malipiero's *Petrarca spirituale* (1536), which "translates" Petrarch's poems directly into religious lyrics, preserving their rhyme words, this same impulse produced sublime results in the *Rime spirituali* of Vittoria Colonna, whose pioneering role as "the first to write with dignity on religious subjects in vernacular lyric" Fiamma acknowledges in his dedicatory letter.[188] Colonna's religious verse was first published as a discrete collection in 1546 by Vincenzo Valgrisi, whose preface to this edition preface anticipates in several respects Fiamma's theoretical discourse in his preface to the *Rime spirituali*.[189] Precedents may also be cited for Fiamma's alertness to the psalms as potential models for a new vernacular religious poetry. A similar impulse is found in a number of poets of the 1550s and 1560s, such as Laura Battiferra, Bernardo Tasso (1493–1569), and Antonio Minturno (1500–1574), all of whom produced collections of Petrarchizing psalm translations. A popular anthology of vernacular psalm versions appeared in Venice two years prior to Fiamma's publication of his *Rime*.[190]

Despite all these precedents, however, it is not too much of a distortion to present Fiamma as a pioneer in the field of vernacular religious lyric; in statistical terms, certainly, it was beginning in the 1580s that this thematic subsection of the lyric tradition saw its most explosive growth.[191] This is apparent most immediately in the number of monographic volumes of *rime spirituali* or *sacre* published in the period, but to have a true sense of the scale of the phenomenon it is necessary also to take into account the mounting space given to religious lyrics within thematically miscellaneous verse collections, especially as the custom of dividing such collections into subsections containing amorous, occasional, and spiritual verse became entrenched.[192] While the authors of most monographic collections of spiritual verse were clerics, such as Fiamma himself or Angelo Grillo, an important role in the development of the tradition was also played by lay poets such as Torquato Tasso and Giovanni Battista Marino (1569–1625), who occupy a dominant place within the anthologies of religious verse that appeared with increasing frequency in the early Seicento.[193] The rise of *rime spirituali* as a subgenre within literature was accompanied in music by the increasing prominence of the *madrigale spirituale*, which used spiritual lyrics as its texts and shared with its literary co-genre a profound concern with the role of the emotions (*affetti*) in faith.[194] Eloquent in this last regard is the title of Grillo's principal verse collection, *Pietosi affetti*; still more so, that of a 1587 collection by the Trevisan composer and poet Giuseppe Policreti (d. 1623), *I vivi interni affetti del core*.

An interesting feature of this "converted" vernacular lyric tradition in the present context is its incorporation of women as authors, at a theoretical as well as a practical level. Fiamma's account of the origins of poetry in the divinely inspired song of the *prisci poetae*, pagan and Hebrew, derives from a tradition initiated by Christian Neoplatonists such as Marsilio Ficino (1433–99). Fiamma initiates with regard to the tradition, however, in positing the Hebrew tradition as bigendered: among the eleven biblical figures he names who praised God in verse and hence stand as the ultimate prototypes for the modern lyric poet are four women, Judith, Deborah, Miriam, sister of Moses, and the Virgin Mary.[195] Of these biblical *prisci poetae*, Miriam is, together with

Moses, the earliest; hence women are located at the origin of poetry understood in its pristine sense, as the articulation of God's praise.[196] Although Fiamma's reconstruction is faithful to scriptural evidence, his emphatic positioning of women within the earliest poetic tradition may also reflect his awareness of the contribution of modern female spiritual poets like Colonna and Laura Battiferra, with the latter of whom he had corresponded in his youth.[197] Fiamma himself experiments with a female poetic voice at points in the *Rime spirituali*, perhaps most interestingly in a politically inflected *canzone* written in the voice of Margaret of Parma (1522–86) during her tenure as regent of the Netherlands. Margaret is portrayed in the poem as giving thanks to God in the manner of Deborah or Judith following her suppression of Protestant rebels in the Netherlands in 1566–67.[198]

A further sense of the way in which the new religious poetics might offer a place for the female poet may be had from the brief statement of poetic principles in Francesca Turina's interesting dedicatory letter to her *Rime spirituali sopra i misterii del santissimo rosario* (1595), addressed to Pope Clement VIII (Ippolito Aldobrandini [1536–1605]).[199] In this letter Turina adopts much familiar feminine rhetoric of self-abasement, describing her work as composed with the "artless thread of womanly manufacture" and making up "the simplest of cloth."[200] She is quite assertive, nonetheless, in justifying her writing, which she casts as the fulfillment of humankind's natural and universal duty to praise God; in fact, her dedication starts with the statement that "it is the duty of every tongue, according to its capacity and worth, to praise and glorify the Lord, so that this whole universe seems to me nothing other than a concert of voices ordained by divine pleasure for the giving up of praise."[201] Recognizing in herself, as a divine gift, a "very powerful inclination to poetry," she has channeled her literary "vein" between the banks of religious piety, finding the poetic water deriving from secular sources "either bitter or without taste."[202] From this religious perspective, the "womanly" lack of poetic artifice Turina acknowledges may be turned from an artistic defect into a strength: if, as she asserts, "poetry is not born here on earth, but rained down from heaven," then it is proper that it be clothed not in "meretricious adornments" but in the "vestments of matronly chastity."[203] Turina's metaphorical language perhaps intentionally echoes a passage in Fiamma's commentary on his *Rime spirituali* in which he calibrates the level of rhetorical elaboration appropriate in spiritual verse as that which might grace a "chaste matron," rather than a "shameless young girl."[204] Used by a female poet, however, this language demands a more literal reading than it had in its original context; by defining matronly simplicity and modesty as the proper dress of spiritual verse, Turina is implicitly making space within the religious Parnassus for an actual matron-poet like herself.

While the poetics of conversion was first articulated and seen operative within the field of lyric poetry, traditionally the privileged locus for innovation within the Italian literary tradition, it would not be long before the same tendencies became apparent in the narrative literature of the age. The key works here are the *Gerusalemme liberata* of Torquato Tasso, completed in its original version by 1575, and Luigi Tansillo's *Le lagrime di San Pietro*, circulating in incomplete forms in print from 1560 and in a fuller version from 1585.[205] Tasso's poem sets out quite self-consciously to revise the popular formula of chivalric romance, embodied most successfully in Lodovico Ariosto's *Orlando furioso* (1532), by assimilating it formally to the unity and grandeur of classical martial epics like the *Iliad* and the *Aeneid*, while injecting it with a new spirit of militant Christianity consonant with the tenor of the age. Tansillo's solution is quite different, though he retains the verse form of ottava rima, which had established itself definitively, after Ariosto, as the preferred meter for vernacular narrative. In place of Tasso's chivalric though religiously charged subject matter—the conquest of Jerusalem in the First Crusade—Tansillo turns to the Bible for his subject, recounting Peter's rejection of Christ following his arrest and his subsequent protracted repentance. *Le lagrime di San Pietro* recalls earlier sixteenth-century experiments in Christian epic, such as Iacopo Sannazaro's *De partu virginis* (1526) and the *Christiad* (1535) of Girolamo Vida, but draws also on the more popular penitential-meditative tradition of envisioning the Passion through a concerted exercise in imaginative empathy with its protagonists.[206]

Both the *Gerusalemme liberata* and the *Lagrime di San Pietro* were immensely influential, not least in demonstrating the popular appeal of religious subject matter, whether in the carefully edulcorated form we see in Tasso's *Liberata*, where it is combined with the traditional delights of chivalric poetry, not excluding the erotic, or in the purer formula of Tansillo's *Lagrime di San Pietro*, whose principal concession to readerly *delectatio* resides in the vividness of its narrative and the fluency and polish of its style.[207] Beginning in the 1580s and 1590s, the energies that had been devoted earlier in the century to reworkings of Carolingian subject matter were directed increasingly toward religious narrative, whether this took the form of the Tassesque Christian *poema eroico*, often adapted to biblical or hagiographic, rather than historical, subject matter, or the more introspective and meditative *Lagrime* model pioneered by Tansillo.[208] The latter rapidly developed as a distinctive tradition, centering most often on biblical (or quasi-biblical) figures such as Mary Magdalene and the Virgin, although sometimes, in its less narrative and more lyric variants, it centered on the "tears" of an individual, everyman sinner; an example of the latter, much published in the 1590s, often with Tansillo, is Grillo's psalm-inspired *Lagrime del penitente*.[209] The extent to which the new genres of religious narrative had established themselves by the late 1580s and 1590s is reflected in Tasso's reworking of the *Liberata* as the *Gerusalemme conquistata*, which was far more decided than the *Liberata* in its Christian commitments and less inclined to dalliance with secular modes.[210]

This conversional turn in Italian narrative in the latter decades of the Cinquecento is interestingly glossed in the dedicatory letter to the Friulian lay poet Erasmo di Valvasone's *Angeleida* (1590), an epyllion on the rebellion of the angels against God sometimes cited among the precedents for Milton's *Paradise Lost*.[211] Like Fiamma, Valvasone (1528–93) locates the origins of poetry and its core vocation in the praise of God and regards its later deviation into the erotic in particular as a straying from the true path. The lessons of Homer, however, and more especially those of Virgil, teach that poetry may perform a useful role in readers' moral and political education, giving imaginative reality to the truths often obscured by the "subtle and recondite disputes of philosophers."[212] The task now is to extend poetry's educational remit from moral and political philosophy to Christian doctrine, conveying in an intelligible and pleasurable form the lessons that readers struggle to absorb in the rebarbative language of Scotus or Aquinas.

Valvasone represents this task as already in process in lyric, noting the popular success of "the sonnets and *canzoni* of some worthy men of our age who have decided to leave behind amorous inventions . . . and chosen instead religious and moral subject matter."[213] Epic poetry, he suggests, should now follow this lead, especially when Tasso in his *Liberata* has shown the way with a poem that is "if not sacred at least pious."[214] There is no reason why "religious histories elegantly related in verse" should be any less appealing to Christian readers than "the marvels of knight errants," especially if these religious poems go beyond the still largely secular matter of Tasso to engage directly with "the miraculous works of God and the merits of his glorious saints."[215] Vida and Sannazaro had showed the way earlier in the century in the *Christiad* and the *De partu virginis*. Now it was time for vernacular narrative literature to recoup this tradition in a more accessible vein.

A point to note in Valvasone's proposal for a new religious epic literature is the emulative relationship he posits between it and the secular, chivalric literature it is to replace. Just as religious lyricists like Fiamma sought to show that sacred lyric was not only superior to amorous poetry in the dignity of its subject matter but could also rival it in respect of *delectatio,* so authors of religious narrative sought to win readers seduced by the pleasures of chivalric literature by showing that they could compete on the same ground.[216] A good example of this neochivalric strain in the religious narrative of the time is the self-consciously revisionary *Vita di San Placido* (1589), by the Benedictine Felice Passero (c. 1570–1626), a friend and coreligionist of Grillo's and a literary acquaintance of Maddalena Campiglia's.[217] Passero presents himself in a prefatory sonnet as a poetic convert who has turned to the writing of "sacred history" after much time spent trifling with less worthy objects.[218] His expiatory work is a five-canto life in ottava rima of "Saint Placidus," a composite of two figures, an early aristocratic acolyte of Saint Benedict and a Sicilian martyr-saint of the sixth century.[219] Placidus is initially described in Passero's poem in distinctly chivalric terms, as a "warrior [*guerriero*], as wise as he was courageous and strong," while of his father, Tertullus, Passero notes that "it was difficult to judge well whether he was a greater saint or a greater knight [*cavaliero*]."[220] Born to "a most ancient family," Placido "prize[s] nought but true honor from his cradle"; the only difference between him and the chivalric hero he resembles is that his *imprese* will consist of self-conquest rather than the conquest of external foes.[221]

Passero relates Placido's adventures in an ornate and polished style that clearly aspires to Valvasone's criterion of "elegance" (leggiadria). The poem is strewn with such familiar epic devices as the visionary prediction, connecting the history related to the present day, and the ekphrastic description of a series of "miraculous" reliefs decorating a building (here depicting, however, not classical mythological scenes but the seven days of Creation).[222] Natural beauty is celebrated with the requisite lyricism, especially in the scene of Saint Benedict's first arrival at Montecassino, which is cast in the guise of a Polizianesque or Ariostan *locus amoenus,* complete with references to the classical gods.[223] Passero even succeeds in incorporating extended passages describing the physical charms of his protagonists, first Placido, whose youthful beauty is said to exceed that of Adonis or Narcissus, and later his sister Flavia, who is destined to be martyred alongside him.[224] Flavia's description, an extended Petrarchan *blazon,* is peculiarly incongruous as a piece of poetic "conversion," in that details of it echo quite closely Ariosto's description of the seductive *maga* Alcina, a famous set piece of the genre.[225] Passero's attentiveness to readers' demand for "delight" is matched by other religious narrative poets of the period: the index to Sebastiano Castelletti's *La trionfatrice Cristina* (1594), for example, flags such poetic pleasures as a "beautifully described steed," as well as descriptions of dawn and of night adorned with "most beautiful metaphors."[226]

A similar trajectory to the one we have seen in lyric poetry and narrative literature may also be observed to an extent in drama, where sacred subject matter began to be introduced from the 1560s and appeared with increasing frequency from about the 1580s. Religiously themed drama was nothing new, of course, but the previous tradition had taken the medieval form of the *sacra rappresentazione*. The novelty in this period was the combination of sacred subject matter with the neoclassical formal norms that the modern secular traditions of comedy and tragedy had respected since their inception earlier in the sixteenth century, notably the use of the classical five-act structure, the observation of the Aristotelian unities, and, in the case of tragedy, the banishment of violent action from the stage.[227] Sacred tragedy *(tragedia spirituale)* characteristically took as its theme the lives of saints and martyrs, with a preference for the female virgin martyr. Representative examples are *La trionfatrice Cristina* by the Palermitan Gaspare Licco (1549–1619), performed in Palermo in the 1570s and printed several times in the Veneto from 1584, and *Giustina, reina di Padova* (1605), by the Paduan Cortese Cortesi (1550–1617), the latter containing in its preface an interesting theoretical defense of the genre.[228] Many works of the period described as *rappresentazioni*, including most of the plays collected in Giovanni Battista Ciotti's anthology *Corona overo ghirlanda di candidi gigli di virginità e di sanguigne rose di martirii*, of 1606, might in fact be more accurately described, in formal terms, as *tragedie spirituali*.

Tragedia spirituale's comic counterpart, *commedia spirituale*, was less constrained in terms of subject matter than tragedy and could embrace invented subjects as well as biblical stories such as that of the prodigal son.[229] One extraordinary confection by the Sienese priest Ercolano Ercolani (1561–1604), entitled *Rappresentazione eremitica spirituale*, uses the quintessential comic devices of twins and cross-dressing to construct a drama of mistaken identity and "deviant" erotic attraction, which nevertheless ends not with marriage or sexual consummation but with the four protagonists' separate retreat to a hermitical life.[230] Another of Ercolani's comedies, *Eliodoro*, concerns two pairs of noble siblings, one in each case a flawless physical specimen and destined to marriage, the other a hunchback and destined to the convent. The comedy arises from the fact that the marriage-destined pair both have a strong religious vocation, while their impaired siblings are correspondingly lacking in vocation and devote their considerable energies to reversing their fathers' plans. Ercolani's ingenious plot allows the audience the classic pleasures of comedy, including the transgressive delight of seeing patriarchs' plans thwarted by an alliance of minors and servants. At the same time, however, it glamorizes religious vocation and critiques the elite social practice of consigning the less marriageable of one's daughters and sons to God. In his preface to *Eliodoro* Ercolani describes the play as "part spiritual, part worldly," in a manner accommodated to an audience that might be assumed to be similarly divided into two "factions" (schiere), one of "men over-attached to the world," the other of "persons who aspire to Paradise."[231] Within the theatrical mainstream, the same principles seem to inform a play like Giovanni Battista Andreini's five-act *sacra rappresentazione*, *La Maddalena*, performed for the wedding of Ferdinando Gonzaga and Caterina de' Medici in 1617. This indulges the viewer with three acts of comic and erotic diversion before moving on to the serious matter of Mary Magdalene's conversion and penitence, with which the play ends.[232]

By the early Seicento, then, the conversion of vernacular literature augured by Erasmo di Valvasone a decade earlier was fully in process: both narrative and, to a lesser extent, drama had followed lyric verse in reinventing itself in new, religious forms. Female authors participated in this process with some enthusiasm. Moderata Fonte, Lucrezia Marinella, Francesca Turina, and Maddalena Salvetti wrote biblical and hagiographic poems, and Marinella and Margherita Sarrocchi authored Tassesque chivalric-religious epics. In drama, Cherubina Venturelli's *Rappresentazione di Santa Cecilia* is effectively a *tragedia spirituale*, while Maddalena Campiglia's lost "tragic song" on Saint Barbara may well have been a work in this genre.[233] We also find women featuring quite frequently as dedicatees of religious narrative and dramatic works, as they did of religious lyric.[234]

This point deserves underlining, as studies of the representation of women in secular works of this period sometimes give the impression that this was an era of encroaching misogyny within Italian literature, with little to offer women either as readers or as writers. Critics have noted that Tasso's *Gerusalemme liberata*, the most intensively studied work of the period, places its female characters almost universally on the side of the "pagans," whereas Ariosto gives a prominent role to the Christian female warrior Bradamante and balances his demonized enchantress Alcina with the benign *maghe* Logistilla and Melissa. Especially telling is the contrast between the fates of the two poems' principal martial heroines: while Bradamante ends Ariosto's poem marrying her beloved Ruggiero, Clorinda dies gorily at the hand of her unwitting Christian lover, Tancredi, reviving in a more emphatic and sexualized form what had already been a topos in classical epic, the death of the female warrior at the hands of a male.[235] The other two most widely studied male-authored works of the period, both pastoral plays—Tasso's *Aminta* (1581) and Guarini's *Pastor fido* (1590)—do not prove a great deal more heartening in their representation of women. Even setting aside the voyeuristically rendered rape scene at the heart of Tasso's *Aminta*, which reduces the initially self-willed nymph Silvia to a passive and fetishized object of desire, the female characters in the two pastorals tend toward the meekly passive (Guarini's Amarilli) or the forceful and morally compromised (Tasso's Dafne, Guarini's Corisca).[236] The persistence of unequivocally admirable female figures tends to be realized in this period most frequently within secular literature in drama and particularly in the *commedia erudita*, where Louise Clubb has noted the popularity of the motif she labels "woman as wonder."[237]

This picture changes notably when one looks at religious literature. Women feature very prominently as protagonists in the religious narrative and drama of the period, often in contexts intended to foreground their moral exemplarity, not simply as a pattern for their sex but as a human ideal *tout court*. This was a novelty especially in the case of epic, which in its secular variant had traditionally privileged heroic masculinity as its theme. The female protagonists of the *poemi* and the *poemetti sacri* of the era vary from New Testament figures like the Virgin and Mary Magdalene to Old Testament heroines like Judith and Esther, to virgin martyrs like Saints Catherine of Alexandria, Cecilia, and Agatha. First established in practice, the choice of a woman as epic protagonist was defended theoretically by the Rome-based Veronese poet Bartolomeo Tortoletti (c. 1560–c. 1648) in his *Juditha vindicata*, of 1628.[238] The virtues the new female epic heroines exemplified varied, but all were readable as strongly affirmative of women's nobility and dignity within the value system of the day. "Defenses of women" of the era cite the virgin martyrs as icons of fortitude alongside favored humanistic classical exempla like the Amazons and Semiramis. "He who cannot see what women are capable of, in body and soul, by looking at the martyrs of the Holy Church . . . is blinder than a mole," wrote the medic Scipione Mercurio (1540–1615) in an interesting profeminist text of 1596 that includes one of the earliest mentions of Lucrezia Marinella in print.[239] For Mercurio, Catherine of Alexandria, in her dispute with the philosophers, demonstrates women's capacity to outstrip men intellectually, while in their capacity to withstand suffering the girl martyrs overshadow the Roman heroes Regulus and Mucius Scaevola and the Athenian Codrus, all prepared to suffer torment and death for their countries.[240] Similarly, we see the publisher of Lucrezia Marinella's *La nobiltà et l'eccellenza delle donne*, Giovanni Battista Ciotti, in his dedicatory letter to a 1606 collection of martyrdom tragedies remarking to his female dedicatee that "if one considers with what constancy so many virgins shed their blood for the faith, those who denigrate the female sex stand reproached with good reason."[241]

As the new heroine of the era, the virgin martyr may in many ways be seen as the "spiritual" heir to the female warrior of chivalric romance. This relationship is less intuitive to us today than it was for readers at the time, used to making an equation between literal combat and the spiritual militancy of the saints; even a saint as pacific as Francis was consistently cast in this period as a "general" or a warrior of God.[242] Some of the topoi familiar from depictions of the female warrior transfer directly to the virgin martyr. Both are beautiful but careless of their beauty, intent instead on their "profession" of chivalry or faith. Both are superhuman in their fortitude, routinely startling their male antagonists by their effortless transcendence of the weakness of their sex. In Passero's *Vita di San Placido*, for example, the tyrant Mamuca, having assumed that Flavia would break more easily under torture, being a woman, becomes speechless with astonishment when he observes her remarkable powers of resistance.[243] The scene reproduces precisely in a spiritual key the standard chivalric episode in which the female warrior is taunted before a fight by a contemptuous male antagonist who rapidly learns the error of his ways.[244] Seen from this perspective, the scene early in Tasso's *Gerusalemme liberata* in which Clorinda rescues the would-be Christian martyr Sofronia when she is on the point of being burned as a willing scapegoat to save her fellow believers from retribution from the "pagan" tyrant Aladino resonates profoundly within the literary history of the period.²⁴⁵ We see here a face-to-face encounter between two literary archetypes of heroic femininity, one classical-chivalric, the other Christian; one, from the point of view of the new converted literature, backward looking, the other the way of the future. It is symbolic of this, as much as anything, that Clorinda ends the poem defeated on her own martial terms, though redeemed by her death-bed conversion, while Sofronia exits the poem in triumph after her memorable cameo appearance.

Once we incorporate spiritual writings into our consideration of gender in late sixteenth- and early seventeenth-century Italian literature, then, the age emerges as less clearly one of hardening misogyny than it is often considered to be. Aside from witnessing an interesting refashioning of the female heroic, this period was equally interesting in its refashioning of the male, again most apparent when we contrast the religious narrative of the age with the chivalric literature it sought to rewrite. Passero's San Placido offers a good example again here, his very name a proclamation of the "placidity" of his ethos. Brave and resolute as his sister when faced with martyrdom, Placido's characterization is in other respects quite notably "feminine": in an account of his monastic training under Saint Benedict, for example, we are told that "of all the virtues he learned, or that he brought with him from his mother's cradle, obedience was that which most enflamed his soul and which he preferred to all others."²⁴⁶ Tasso's Goffredo, the most familiar religious epic hero of the period, is still in some sense a compromise hero, possessed of the traditional martial qualifications of the classical epic hero, especially of the "pious" Virgilian model. The male heroes of the true sacred literature of the age are formed in a quite different, pacifist mold. The Franciscan Agostino Gallucci underlines this in his sacred *riscrittura* of the *Liberata*, the 1618 *San Francesco, overo Gerusalemme celeste acquistata,* which polemically substitutes in its first stanza for Tasso's description of Goffredo's heroism ("much did he achieve . . . much did he suffer") a more radical formula, removing the element of action in favor of a double dose of Christ-like *passio:* "much did he endure . . . much did he suffer."²⁴⁷

An effect of this shift within the converted epic of the Counter-Reformation from a "heroics of action" to a "heroics of endurance" was to bring the sexes into a far greater convergence than had been the case in the previous, secular tradition.²⁴⁸ Setting aside the figure of the female knight, always destined to exceptionalism, secular chivalric literature was intrinsically dichotomizing in its treatment of gender, with men essentially figuring on the "arms" side of

Ariosto's *armi/amori* equation and women on that of "love." In Counter-Reformation hagiographic narrative this gender differentiation was much diminished. While it is true that the construction of the hero was still inflected by gender—one only has to think of the importance virginity assumed in Counter-Reformation accounts of female martyrdom—something much closer to equivalence had been reached.

4. Secular Writing in Post-Tridentine Italy: The New Sensualism and the Misogynist Turn

One of the more remarkable documents of the Counter-Reformation drive to poetic conversion is Agostino De Cupiti's twelve-canto ottava rima epic, *Il poeta illuminato*, published in Vico Equense, near Naples, about 1599.[249] De Cupiti's poem, which expands on a much briefer version already present in his *Rime spirituali* of 1593, develops on a narrative plane the motif of the poet-convert, exploited in this period by quite a number of writers in crafting their authorial personae.[250] De Cupiti recounts in this poem the tale of a "lascivious" secular poet whose conscience is awakened when he is visited in a dream by an angel who convinces him of the iniquity of his ways and leads him through an extensive purgative penitential trajectory. The message of the poem is trenchantly expressed in the opening stanzas:

> Dio solo cantar si deve . . . ;
> E gli Heroi santi, e gli altri cari sui;
> E degno è chi nol fà d'eterno pianto,
> Che sol per Dio lodar trovossi il canto.[251]

[God alone should be sung, and his sainted Heroes and those dear to him. He who ignores this is worthy of eternal lamentation, for song was found solely to praise God.]

This is the religious poetics we saw expressed almost three decades earlier by Fiamma, now carried to new extremes of moral absolutism: secular verse, especially amorous verse, is not only misguided but an abomination that will lead its practitioner to hell.

The vehemence of De Cupiti's condemnation of lascivious literature in *Il poeta illuminato* contrasts interestingly with the less emphatic tones of Gabriele Fiamma thirty years earlier. Although this may simply reflect differences in individual temperament and intellectual style, or between the cultural climate of Venice in the 1570s and that of Naples in the 1590s, it is worth considering the possibility that De Cupiti's fiercer tone might be a reaction to the character of erotic lyric in his day. The last decades of the sixteenth century saw a marked shift within the Italian tradition of love lyric, from the decorous and sublimated Neoplatonic erotics of Petrarchism to something more sensual and less "honest." This trend was already beginning to be apparent in the love poetry of Tasso, written mainly in the 1560s and 1570s, and it would attain more uninhibited levels in the erotic verse of Marino and his followers shortly after the turn of the century.[252] The poets of the new age did not limit themselves to extolling the beauty of a lady's hair and eyes, but lingered sensually as well on descriptions of her breasts, a new and popular poetic topos of the era. Nor was the poet content with enjoying this beauty through the Neoplatonically condoned senses of sight and hearing: a further topos described the rapture of given or stolen kisses, often transparently synecdochic of further sexual pleasures. De Cupiti was not the only religious poet to protest in these years at the degree of "paganizing" license in which secular poets were prepared to indulge. A letter from Angelo Grillo to Bernardino Baldi datable to between 1608 and 1611 congratulates the latter warmly on a poem attacking the shamelessness of modern poets, under the "sweet laughter" of whose "soft verses one drinks the tears of eternal damnation."[253] Another letter of Grillo's, probably datable to the same period, warns that "he who spreads his pages with lascivious verse sows seeds of death in others' hearts."[254]

If it seems odd that this new sensuality should be finding its way into the lyric tradition at precisely the height of the Counter-Reformation drive for a return to poetry's religious roots, the two developments are probably best seen in a relation of dialectic complementarity rather than one of genuine opposition. Within the early sixteenth-century tradition of Petrarchism codified by Bembo, the tradition of erotic lyric had been sublimated into a form of Neoplatonic spiritual quest, and the lady into a kind of spiritual guide, à la Beatrice, contemplation of whose ethereal beauty could lead the virtuous poet to God. The rise of Petrarchizing religious verse from the 1530s and 1540s on began to threaten the cultural logic of this tradition of spiritualized love poetry by making available attractive poetic options for an unmediated expression of the poet's quest for God. Telling in this respect is Fiamma's condemnation of Petrarch as reading matter for the susceptible young and his call for a redirection of vernacular poetry from the love of women, however "honest," to the love of God. An unintended consequence of this trend was arguably to free erotic verse, now uncoupled from its Petrarchan spiritual vocation, for a new, more worldly career of untrammeled eroticism, taking its cue as much from the sensuality of the Roman elegists as from the medieval Italian tradition. Ironically, in this sense, however assiduously the church attempted to police "obscenity" in literature, the increased sensuality of mannerist and baroque lyric may be seen as a reflection of the Counter-Reformation moral turn within literature, as much so as more obvious offspring such as the tradition of spiritual verse.[255]

This development is important from the point of view of the present volume, as it has a clear bearing on the literary position of women. Early sixteenth-century Petrarchism had proved hospitable to women as writers and readers precisely on account of its Neoplatonic high-mindedness, which had allowed even the most "decent" of women to speak of love without compromising their social position. Nor was a female authorial position too difficult to craft using the persona of the poetic *donna* as configured in the tradition. Laura and her sixteenth-century descendents were impeccable in their morals and "honest" in the emotions they inspired in their admirers. They aroused love as much for the beauty of their intellect, their soul, and their "wise words" (parolette accorte) as for their conventionalized golden hair and white skin. In many ways, the female Petrarchist voice of the early sixteenth century may be seen as the poetic *donna* incarnate.[256] She was welcomed as an interlocutor by male poets precisely in this guise, as a figure to whom "honest" poems might be addressed, expressing a spiritualized love that was validating on an ethical level (as well as, frequently, a social one, given the high social status of many female poets in these years).

The more sensual tradition of lyric poetry gathering momentum in the late sixteenth century offered less space in this regard for a female voice. As the *donna* of poetry became more patently an object of sexual fantasy, the figure of the respectable female poet became of less use to her secular male peers in fashioning their poetic personae. The practice of poetic correspondence with women, which had played such a crucial role in ensuring women's visibility in the 1540s and 1550s and even in the 1580s and 1590s, began to dwindle from about the turn of the century, living on mainly in provincial settings. The substantial collection of poems addressed to Marino that forms an appendix to the 1629 edition of his *La lira* contains a contribution by only one woman,

Francesca Turina, while the correspondence section contains only an early exchange with Margherita Sarrocchi, dating from prior to Marino's emergence to national fame with his *Rime* of 1602. Poets of the school of Marino were more likely to choose their objections of adoration from the ranks of singers and actresses, who were more socially accessible than most female poets and more amenable to sensualized description. These were not poems intended to solicit a response, or at least not one that took the form of a sonnet: where the baroque poetic *donna* was vocal, she was a "siren," not a rational interlocutor.

While female writers' gradual marginalization within baroque secular literary culture was to an extent structurally determined—they simply did not "fit" in the way they had within Petrarchism—it would be hard to deny that this marginalization also had an ideological component. A resurgent misogyny is clearly detectable from the very late sixteenth century, as noted above, a trend epitomized by Giuseppe Passi's *I donneschi difetti*, of 1599, with its interminable recitation of women's flaws. Intellectual vanity was posited among these from the outset. Passi rails against "ignorant" women who set themselves up as savants and public speakers, failing to reflect that "the true ornament of women is silence and few words."[257] His follower Antonio Maria Spelta is similarly damning of women who attempt to transcend their natural and endearing "foolishness" (scempiezza), daring instead to position themselves as literary authorities capable of passing judgment on the productions of men.[258] Traiano Boccalini (1556–1613), meanwhile, in a famous passage in his *Ragguagli di Parnaso*, ridicules the sixteenth-century practice of mixed literary interaction, imagining a scenario in which a group of august Cinquecento lady poets are invited to participate in the Accademia degli Intronati of Siena but are then ejected by Apollo after their poetic intercourse with the academicians begins to take the "inevitable" sexual turn.[259] This last line of attack was a particularly devastating one, given how relatively fragile the cultural persona of the female poet remained and how vulnerable she was in particular to the accusation that her learning gave her a propensity to sexual vice or at least laid her open to would-be seducers. The impact of Boccalini's satire was compounded in the seventeenth century by the fact that his work circulated most commonly accompanied by an *aggiunta* by the Modenese poet Girolamo Briani (1581–1646) that pursues the original's misogynistic satire in a more heavy-handed vein. Briani's forty-ninth *ragguaglio*, for example, shows a group of *poetesse* attempting unjustly to usurp a place in Parnassus, to the outrage of the censors, who are shocked that "in an academy of such great prestige and dignity that the famous Ariosto and the great Torquato Tasso had to labor for their entry, the female sex, created only to study the *Priapeia*, should have been so honorably received."[260]

I have examined the causes of this misogynistic turn in seventeenth-century Italian literary culture elsewhere in some detail, and it is not necessary to repeat the analysis here.[261] What is important to recall here is the result: that the ambient conditions of women's writing became considerably less favorable beginning about 1600, with the result that it declined progressively as a practice, especially after about 1650.[262] During the first three decades of the Seicento, the period that interests us here, the principal evidence we see of the change in the cultural climate is the increasing number of writings by women that are polemical in character, responding either to *ad hominem* attacks on them or to attacks against women as a whole. Examples from the first three decades of the century are Lucrezia Marinella's and Bianca Naldi's refutations of Passi, Margherita Sarrocchi's public falling out with Marino, Veneranda Bragadin's polemic with Giovanni Battista Barbo, Sara Copio Sullam's self-defenses against attacks by Baldassare Bonifaccio and Numidio Paluzzi, and Isabella Sori's defenses of women directed against an unnamed antagonist. Later, in the 1640s, with two exceptions, Arcangela Tarabotti's entire *oeuvre* consists entirely of polemical texts.[263]

The period covered in the present book is, then, a contradictory moment in the history of Italian women's engagement with literary culture, one that saw both the height of their integration and the beginning of their banishment to the margins. That these two competing developments may be seen in such close and dramatic conjunction is probably more than a coincidence: the passages from Passi and Spelta quoted above suggest that some male *letterati* at least felt threatened by the advances that women had made in the intellectual sphere.

As much as against female writers themselves, their attackers were likely protesting against the cultural constructions that had allowed them to flourish: on the one hand, what appeared to them the tiresomely predictable poetic culture of Petrarchism, with its stylized reverence for women as a conduit to the divine; on the other, those strains within Counter-Reformation religious culture that positioned women as idealized role models for men on account of their piety and their obedience to the ethical dictates of the church. If, as suggested earlier in this chapter, elements within the church exalted the feminine quite systematically in the interest of an attempted remaking of masculine secular ethos, it is not difficult to see that this may have provoked resentment on the part of some of the laymen to whom this message was addressed. We should at least entertain the possibility that the hostility some male secular authors in this period directed toward women, as well as the trend toward aggressive displays of sexuality in literature, such as we find in Marino, should be read as a refracted expression of *insofferenza* toward the feminized ethos of humility, chastity, and obedience the renewed church was attempting to demand from its sons. Suggestive in this regard is the coincidence of misogyny and explicit eroticism with anticlericalism in the elite literary culture of Venice, especially following the formation of the Accademia degli Incogniti, which became a powerful sponsor of both trends.[264]

※ CHAPTER TWO ※
LYRIC VERSE

1. Women's Lyric Output, 1580–1630

One area in which women writers in the later sixteenth and seventeenth centuries cannot be said to have equaled their early sixteenth-century predecessors was the production of lyric poetry. The decades from 1530 to 1560 saw female poets' first entry into the world of print in Italy, and their impact was very considerable: with Vittoria Colonna, they produced one of the finest poets of the age and an instantly canonical figure; with the Neapolitan Laura Terracina, a bestselling author, her *Rime* of 1548 going through nine editions over the following seventeen years.[1] By the late sixteenth century, female poets no longer represented such a striking editorial novelty, and the market conditions that had sustained the great outpouring of vernacular literature in the middle decades of the century were no longer in place.[2] No female poet of the period we are looking at here attained anything like the standing of Colonna or the popularity of Terracina, although some enjoyed a reasonable degree of recognition, with Isabella Andreini's verse, in particular, being widely anthologized and eliciting numerous musical settings.[3]

Despite the lesser impact and historical importance of this later moment of women's lyric production, the output of female poets in the later sixteenth and early seventeenth centuries is undoubtedly deserving of greater critical attention than it has been accorded until now.[4] Although lyric was no longer as central in women's literary production as it had been in the mid-sixteenth century, it remained important. The period 1580–1630 saw the publication of fourteen single-authored volumes of verse by ten separate female authors, as well as nine slighter pamphlet publications containing single poems or small clusters of verse.[5] For only five of these twenty-three works is there any secondary literature to speak of, and there are complete modern editions of only three.[6] As in the earlier, mid-century period, moreover, the poetry contained in such single-authored collections is only part of a far larger whole including verse published in anthologies or remaining in manuscript.[7] Especially when we take this less visible production into account, we have a considerable body of work here, some of it of remarkable interest. Two of the most accomplished female poets active in the 1550s, Laura Battiferra and Chiara Matraini, continued to write lyric verse of high quality until their death, in 1589 and 1604, respectively, while of the new poets of the age, Andreini, Maddalena Salvetti, Lorenza Strozzi, Lucrezia Marinella, Francesca Turina, and Lucchesia Sbarra in particular produced bodies of verse that merit study on both literary and cultural-historical grounds.

Before we examine women's literary production in this period, an outline of the principal developments in the Italian lyric tradition at this time may be useful. The last quarter of the sixteenth century was a moment of transition within Italian lyric, as the long-dominant idiom of Petrarchism, codified by Pietro Bembo in the early decades of the century, entered into crisis.[8] While lexically Petrarch remained the basis for the poetic language of the period, the metrical dominance of the Petrarchan forms of sonnet and *canzone* began to be challenged by the rise of the madrigal: the 1598 *Rime* of Battista Guarini (1538–1612), one of the leading exponents of the form, contains 107 sonnets to 150 madrigals, and collections composed entirely of madrigals were not uncommon in the 1590s and early 1600s.[9] In the organization of verse collections, the unified Petrarchan model of the love *canzoniere* had fallen almost entirely out of favor by this point, replaced for the most part by collections organized by theme, with amorous verse segregated from spiritual, moral, and correspondence verse, and/or by metrical form.[10] Regarding thematics, the most important development was the rise of religious verse, in many ways the most vibrant and energized lyric subtradition of the period.[11] An important development here was the conversion to spiritual uses of the light, pointed, witty, madrigalesque mode first developed in an amorous context by poets such as Tasso and Guarini in Ferrara. The key figure here was Angelo Grillo, the dominant figure in religious lyric at the turn of the century and an important influence on the development of the baroque style.[12] The tradition of love lyric, meanwhile, was in the process of reinventing itself in the manner described at the end of the last chapter, leaving behind its weighty, spiritualized Neoplatonic-Petrarchan heritage for something more sensual and profane. A further, more minor thematic development, deserving of mention in this context since it would prove important for female poets, was the increased space given in verse collections to domestic affections as opposed to the traditional Petrarchan theme of extramarital erotic love. Representative works here include the sequence in the Piedmontese poet Giuliano Goselini's 1574 *Rime* mourning the death of his son and that in the 1600 *Rime* of the Venetian Orsatto Giustinian (1538–1603) celebrating his long marriage to Candiana de' Garzoni.[13]

One quite marked stylistic development in the late sixteenth century was a taste for overtly displayed artifice and intricate wordplay, sometimes labeled as mannerism, a tendency associated especially with the Venetian school of Domenico Venier (1517–82) and Luigi Groto (1541–85).[14] This trend toward the elaborate and self-consciously "artificial" and striking became more pronounced after the turn of the century, especially following the publication in 1602 of the *Rime* of Giambattista Marino, the most brilliant exponent of the baroque style. Awareness increased in the early years of the Seicento that popular taste had definitively shifted from the relative sobriety and chastity of classic Petrarchism to something more flamboyant and capricious: Francesco Visdomini in 1609 complained of "monstrous sonnets" filled with "high-sounding words," "outrageous metaphors," and "senses so obscure that we cannot understand them ourselves."[15] Thematically, baroque caprice manifested itself especially in amorous verse, with an increase in verse keyed to particular narrative occasions (the lady hunting or fishing or snowballing or wearing particular garments or items or jewelry) and in verse to beauties outside the narrow range of womanly perfection prescribed by Petrarchism (the older woman, the ethnically diverse woman, the brunette).[16]

Lyric verse by women in this period broadly mirrors these more general developments, with certain significant deviations. With very few exceptions, women in this period refrained from writing love poetry, concentrating instead on religious and occasional verse. This represents a notable difference from the early and mid-sixteenth century, which saw a significant tradition of erotic verse by women. Where women did write love lyric in this period, they generally adopted a male voice, an expedient earlier utilized by Laura Terracina and Gaspara Stampa (c. 1525–54).[17] The only substantial body of female-authored love poetry written in the quasi-autobiographical Petrarchan mode that survives from this period is that of Francesca Turina, who followed the marital tradition of love lyric initiated by Vittoria Colonna, although there is evidence that Lucrezia Della Valle wrote a Neoplatonic love *canzoniere*, now lost.[18] While one cause of this relinquishment of love as theme may have been the stricter moral climate introduced into literature by the Counter-Reformation, another was the shift within the male-authored tradition of erotic lyric toward more sensual modes, which were difficult to accommodate within a "decent" female voice. An indication of this is offered by the erotic verse of Isabella Andreini, who produced the most substantial collection by any female poet of the period and who was the only female poet to venture very far into the sensual territory being mapped out by her male peers. Andreini writes love poetry in both a male and a female voice, but her more sensual mode is limited to her male-voiced verse, while her female-voiced lyrics remain within the more decorous erotics of Petrarchism.

Although the virtual elimination of erotic love as an acceptable theme for female-authored lyric represented a restriction on female poets' creative freedom, it was not an especially onerous one in context, nor one they were alone in suffering. Male clerics too—a substantial body of writers in this period—were similarly prevented by decorum from participating in the tradition of erotic lyric, a rule-proving exception being Grillo, who appears to have written love lyrics under the pseudonym Livio Celiano in his youth.[19] As we might expect, religious verse makes up a very substantial part of women's lyric output in this period. So does occasional verse, with a particularly interesting cluster of work in praise of Medici women, including an extraordinary quasi-erotic *canzoniere* addressed to Grand Duchess Christine of Lorraine by Maddalena Salvetti.[20] We also find women participating in the newer tradition of domestic Petrarchism noted above: Lucchesia Sbarra has a sequence of poems mourning the death of her infant son, while Francesca Turina, in one of the most remarkable female-authored poetic works of the era, wrote an entire autobiographical *canzoniere* recounting her life from her girlhood, through her marriage and widowhood, into old age, covering events such as the birth and childhood of her sons and grandsons and the death of one son.[21]

In stylistic terms, for reasons I have examined more fully elsewhere, women tended on the whole to be relatively conservative, preferring the "candor and clarity" of Petrarchism to the extravagances of the baroque.[22] The principal exceptions are Lucrezia Marinella's 1603 *Rime sacre* and Lucchesia Sbarra's 1610 *Rime*, both of which show a marked influence from Marino, in Marinella's case an extremely precocious one.[23] Even the choice of the term *sacre* for Marinella's title, rather than the more traditional *spirituali*, may reflect the influence of Marino, who had opted for that term. The baroque influence in Sbarra's case is limited to style; she remains metrically faithful to the sonnet form. Marinella's *Rime sacre*, by contrast, has a distinctly contemporary and post-Petrarchan flavor in its organization, comprising as it does two metrically segregated sequences of sonnets and madrigals, followed by a narrative poem in ottava rima, which elsewhere is her meter of choice. Similarly post-Petrarchan in its metrical choices, though much vaster in scale, is Isabella Andreini's *Rime* of 1601, which contains 190 sonnets to 115 madrigals, as well as numerous other metrical forms, including some, such as the *scherzo*, of recent invention.[24] The collection contains a sonnet exchange with the Genoese poet Gabriello Chiabrera (1552–1638), who had showcased the metrical novelty of the *scherzo* in his *Maniere de' versi toscani* (1599), prefaced by an important manifesto on the need for metrical innovation within what he perceived as the ossified Petrarchan tradition.[25]

Although Andreini and Marinella were unusual in the thoroughness of their embrace of post-Petrarchan trends, they were not alone among female poets in showing an awareness of contemporary developments. Orsina Cavaletti, author of a small but accomplished *canzoniere* of ten sonnets and eighteen madrigals, first published in the influential 1587 anthology *Rime di diversi celebri poeti dell'età nostra*, was among the earliest adopters of the madrigal mode as it evolved at the court of Ferrara. More unexpectedly, we find Chiara Matraini experimenting extensively with the madrigal in the verse she incorporated in her last two religious prose works, the *Breve discorso sopra la vita e laude della beatissima Vergine* (1590) and the *Dialoghi spirituali* (1602), an impressive tribute to her openness to new influences in her later years (she was 75 in 1590, 87 in 1602).[26] Matraini's younger contemporary Laura Battiferra shows a similar openness to post-Petrarchan stylistic influences in her late spiritual verse. She and Lucia Colao were the only female poets of this period to attempt the hypermannerist form of the *sonetto continuo*, a sonnet using only two rhyme words in continual alternation. One of Battiferra's essays in this form still more virtuosically uses both rhyme words together in each line.[27]

2. *Pietosi affetti*: Spiritual Lyric and the Female Poet

Besides Marinella's *Rime sacre*, mentioned above, only two verse collections of this period authored by women, both nuns, are devoted exclusively to spiritual verse: Lorenza Strozzi's *Hymni* (1588), important as the only published Latin verse collection by an Italian woman in the entire early modern period, and Semidea Poggi's *La Calliope religiosa* (1623).[28] Francesca Turina's *Rime spirituali sopra i misterii del santissimo rosario* (1595) is also principally spiritual, as the title suggests, though it contains a short appendix of amorous verse.[29] This relatively meager list does not begin to give an idea of the extent of women's engagement with spiritual lyric in this period, however. Besides the works by the four authors just noted, we have substantial collections of religious verse from this period by Laura Battiferra, Chiara Matraini, Isabetta Coreglia, Lucia Colao, and Battista Vernazza; lesser but not negligible clusters by Maddalena Salvetti, Isabella Andreini, and Veneranda Bragadin; and high-quality individual lyrics by Moderata Fonte, Maddalena Campiglia, Livia Spinola, and Leonora Bernardi.[30] Of the principal female poets of this period, only Isabella Cervoni, Orsina Cavaletti, and Lucchesia Sbarra left no surviving religious poetry, although Cavaletti's and Sbarra's verse includes interesting examples of the subgenre of occasional verse comprising laudatory verse addressed to nuns.[31]

There are numerous reasons why devotional verse proved a congenial genre of writing for women in this period. One very powerful one was the existence of precedent. Here, unusually, rather than a genre of writing established by male authors in which women belatedly sought to negotiate themselves a place, we have one in which a woman, Vittoria Colonna, was widely acknowledged to have had a founding role. Colonna's standing remained high in the period we are interested in here, despite her close association during her lifetime with the Italian reform movement. Far from her being "forgotten" by the late Cinquecento, as a recent study claims, there are grounds for thinking that her religious verse in particular came to enjoy a new currency with the Counter-Reformation.[32] A new edition of her *Rime spirituali* was published in 1586, the first since 1560, and several musical settings of poems by her are known from the 1580s.[33] Tasso praises her "lofty intellect," "splendid eloquence," and "divine poetry" in his 1582 *Discorso della virtù feminile e donnesca*, while, outside a gender-specific context, we find her cited by Gabriele Fiamma as the founder of the tradition of vernacular religious lyric and by Agostino De Cupiti and Giovanni Giovenale Ancina (1545–1604) as one of its leading exponents.[34] More generally, Ancina also places Colonna among the greatest poets of the vernacular tradition, along with Petrarch, Della Casa, Sannazaro, Giovanni Guidiccioni, Francesco Maria Molza, Tansillo, and Tasso.[35] One reason for Colonna's continuing appeal in this period is perhaps suggested by Francesco Agostino Della Chiesa's praise of her verse in his *Theatro delle donne letterate* as richer than any other Tuscan poet's in the "grandeur and beauty of its fluent *concetti*."[36] Della Chiesa's use of the key baroque poetic term *concetti* here perhaps implies a particular appreciation of Colonna's sometimes bold poetic imagery, exemplified in the much-imitated opening sonnet of her *Rime spirituali*, which speaks of the poet's desire to write with Christ's blood for her ink and the nails of his torment for her pens.[37]

A further attraction of religious lyric for women was that unlike love poetry, this was a genuinely bigendered literary field, without particular exclusion zones for female writers. In both erotic and spiritual lyric, a broad thematic division can be made between a more subjective vein, exploring the poet's affective experience, and a more objective vein, characteristically taking an epideictic form: praise of the beauty of the love object in the case of love lyric, praise of saints and other sacred persons within the tradition of *rime spirituali*. Within the tradition of erotic verse, women had been practically limited to the subjective, while the language of erotic description had been largely closed to them for reasons of decorum. This was not the case in the tradition of religious lyric, where subjective and objective modes of poetry lay equally within women's reach. Even the religious subgenre that maps perhaps most closely onto the erotic *descriptio* of Petrarchism, the lingering, often eroticized contemplation of Christ's crucified body, was equally available to female and male poets as an acceptable form of poetic devotion. Indeed, especially in verse on this theme, it is not uncommon to find male religious poets of the era adopting a feminized voice, following the mystic tradition that configured the human soul as bride to Christ's bridegroom; a madrigal of Grillo's, for example, addresses the crucified Christ as "my wounded bridegroom" (mio piagato sposo).[38] Generally, the gendering of poetic voice and poetic object were more fluid in religious lyric than in love lyric, creating space quite easily for the participation of female authors. It is quite common, for example, to find male-authored poetry written in a female voice, most usually that of Mary Magdalene or the Virgin. Grillo's *Essequie di Giesu Christo Nazareno* (1608), for example, is written almost entirely in the Virgin's voice.[39]

Of the dedicated collections of religious verse produced by women in this period, those most deserving of critical attention are undoubtedly Marinella's *Rime sacre* and Strozzi's *Hymni*. If we except a series of ottava rima versions of the seven penitential psalms contained in her 1643 *Vittorie di Francesco il serafico,* Marinella's *Rime sacre* constitutes the only sustained exercise in lyric poetry by this important and prolific writer.[40] The collection seems to have been inspired by a request Marinella received in 1602 for a contribution to a planned verse collection to celebrate the miraculous icon of the Madonna located in the sanctuary of the Monte della Guardia in Bologna, which had already been the subject of an anthology published the previous year, to which Chiara Matraini, Tarquinia Molza, and Febronia Pannolini had contributed.[41] Traces of this project, which fell through, are apparent in the *Rime sacre,* which contains a narrative poem recounting the history of the icon as well as a series of sonnets to the icon; to its supposed author, Saint Luke; to the Monte della Guardia and its nun custodians; and to the city of Bologna.[42]

Perhaps as a result of this messy genesis, the *Rime sacre* has a slightly halfhearted air: the volume seems to have been published in a small print run, to judge from the surviving number of copies, and is the only one of Marinella's published works for which she did not write the dedicatory letter.[43] Nonetheless, the verse is of high quality, and it seems to have enjoyed quite a degree of recognition in the years after its publication: poems from it were anthologized in two collections, and the Bergamasque publisher Comin Ventura published a selection in a separate volume, presumably unauthorized, in 1605.[44] The full, 1603 version of the text contains a sequence of thirty-six sonnets, followed by a shorter one of twenty-four madrigals, concluding with a dialogue poem and the Monte della Guardia narrative in ottava rima, which is divided into three parts comprising a total of eighty-three stanzas. The sonnet sequence is dominated thematically by sections on Christ's life and passion (seven sonnets) and in praise of the Virgin and various saints (three and fifteen sonnets, respectively). Much less space is devoted to more introspective, first-person penitential-meditative sonnets. The proportions of the madrigal sequence are similar, with hagiographic material again dominant (eleven sonnets, with a further four to the Virgin).

Lorenza Strozzi's *In singula totius anni solemnia hymni,* first published in Florence in 1588, stands outside the tradition of vernacular devotional lyric, connecting instead with the humanistic tradition of classically inflected hymnography that would culminate, thirty years later, in the revision of the Roman breviary commissioned by Pope Urban VIII.[45] Strozzi draws on Horace's odes as her prime model in the collection, while her extensive use of Sapphic meter encouraged a reading of her as the Christian Sappho, an invitation taken up with enthusiasm by admirers of her work such as Janus Nicius Erythraeus (1577–1647), who develops a lengthy comparison between the lewdness of Sappho's inspiration and the purity and sublimity of Suor Lorenza's.[46] Strozzi was a nun at the Dominican convent of San Niccolò in Prato, and it is likely that she originally wrote her hymns for performance during divine office in the convent. The meters she uses, even those that are classical in origin, had all been used in medieval hymnography, with the result that her texts could be sung to familiar tunes, a point underlined by a note in the second edition of the collection, published in Paris in 1601.[47]

Strozzi's *Hymni,* which is dedicated to the bishop of Pistoia, Lattanzio Lattanzi (d. 1587), is composed of 104 hymns keyed thematically to Christian feasts, arranged in chronological order from the Circumcision (1 January) to the feast of Saint Sylvester (31 December). Most were important within the liturgical calendar generally, but a degree of particularization is apparent; thus we find hymns to the Florentine saints Antoninus, Zenobius, and Reparata, the last concluding with a plea to the saint to watch over the city's Medici rulers, while Saint Nicholas and Saint Dominic are identified in the headings as, respectively, *patronus noster* and *pater noster.*[48] The classicizing elegance of Strozzi's compositions, together with the energetic promotional campaign undertaken on her behalf posthumously by her Paris-based nephew, Zaccaria Monti, ensured a significant seventeenth-century fortune for her hymns. Monti oversaw the 1601 Paris edition, which he dedicated to Maria de' Medici, and he is probably either the author or the instigator of an anonymous Latin *Vita* of Strozzi that appeared in Paris in 1610.[49] There is some evidence that the hymns were translated into French and set to music by Jacques Mauduit (1557–1627).[50]

Beyond the printed tradition, two female-authored collections of spiritual verse surviving only in manuscript deserve notice: the "Rime spirituali" section of the manuscript of Laura Battiferra's collected verse held in the Biblioteca Casanatense in Rome and a manuscript of mainly religious verse by the Venetian Lucia Colao in the Biblioteca Civica of Treviso.[51] Of the two, Battiferra's manuscript is the more finished. It was clearly put together with a view toward publication, probably by Battiferra's husband, Bartolomeo Ammanati, in the years immediately following her death in 1589. Had it been published, it would certainly have constituted the most important female-authored verse collection of the age. The collection is divided into two parts, the first secular, the second sacred, and incorporates the texts of Battiferra's two earlier published works, *Il primo libro delle opere toscane* (1560) and *Sette salmi penitentiali* (1564), along with much previously unpublished verse. In the case of the "Rime spirituali," as the second section is headed, the previously unpublished poems number more than fifty, including a fragment of religious epic in ottava rima.[52] While little of this religious verse can be precisely dated, it is likely that much dates from the 1580s and thus falls into the temporal remit of this study. Of the few datable sonnets, one addresses Claudio Acquaviva (1543–1615), superior general of the Jesuits from 1580, while another records the death of Pope Gregory XIII in 1585.[53]

Although less notable than Battiferra's in terms of its literary quality, Lucia Colao's verse collection in the Biblioteca Comunale in Treviso holds considerable interest as a rare contribution by a female author to the practice of poetic conversion at its most literal level, that composed by the religious *contrafactum* of a secular source text. The Treviso manuscript is a working manuscript with no indication of date, but a manuscript of Colao's verse that Luisa Bergalli consulted in the early eighteenth century, presumably a finished copy prepared for presentation, allows us to date the collection to 1578–87.[54] The collection, a substantial one—the Treviso manuscript includes about forty *canzoni* and eighty sonnets, some in two or three different redactions— was dedicated in Bergalli's manuscript to Bianca Cappello (1548–87), the Venetian-born wife of Francesco I de' Medici, Grand Duke of Tuscany (1541–87), whom Moderata Fonte had chosen in these same years as the dedicatee of her chivalric romance, *Il Floridoro*.[55]

Colao's *rime* may be placed within the tradition of religious poetic *riscrittura* initiated in the 1530s by her Venetian compatriot Girolamo Malipiero (1480–c. 1547) with his *Petrarca spirituale* and continued in her own age by writers such as Crisippo Selva of Parma (1546–c. 1630), who published a spiritualized version of Tasso's *rime amorose* in 1611.[56] The practice involves a literal, poem-by-poem overwriting of the chosen poet's verses, maintaining the same meter and rhyme words but substituting a new religious subject matter for the original's profane themes. Thus, in Colao, Petrarch's sonnet of erotic reminiscence, *Erano i capei d'or a l'aura sparsi* (sonnet 90), becomes the penitential *Quanti lamenti vani a l'aura sparsi*, while sonnet 20, *Vergognando talor ch'ancor si taccia*, on the poet's incapacity to express Laura's beauty in verse, is transformed into *Sì mi sprona il desir, che più non taccia*, a similarly themed meditation on the Virgin's ineffability as subject.[57] Within the formal constraints of the exercise she has set herself, Colao succeeds surprisingly well in producing *contrafacta* that have some independent life as poems. Unlike Malipiero, who recasts Petrarch in an impersonal and sententious form, Colao retains the subjective and confessional character of the original, crafting an image of the poet that is consistent with Petrarch's proemial sonnet as an ex-victim of love now repentant of her ways. That there was an element of truth in this, at a literary if not an autobiographical level, is attested by the presence in the Treviso manuscript of a handful of amorous sonnets independent of Petrarchan subtexts, presumably reflecting an earlier poetic moment in Colao's career, prior to her shift to a conversional mode.[58]

Of the female religious poets of this period, the most faithful heirs to the tradition of Vittoria Colonna in thematic terms are Laura Battiferra and Francesca Turina, both of whom follow Colonna in privileging the subjective model of devotional lyric over the objective.[59] Although Colonna was important in broadening the range of religious lyric to include poems in praise of the Virgin and saints and marking the feasts of the liturgical year, the vast majority of her *rime spirituali* are introspective in character, whether penitential, following the Petrachan model, or more optimistically self-exhortatory, as in those sonnets where the poet augurs or even "sees" in a mystical ecstasy her future spiritual union with God. Of these two modes in Colonna, both Battiferra and Turina lean toward the penitential, which was far the more common generally within the poetic culture of their age, although some echo may be found in Battiferra's spiritual verse of Colonna's distinctive jubilant mystical afflatus.[60] Both Battiferra and Turina lived to a relatively advanced age for the era—Battiferra died at 66, while Turina published her *Rime* at 77— and Turina's verse in particular makes frequent reference to her aging and her anticipation of a fast-approaching death.[61] Both poets take up a key theme of Colonna's, the plea for an accretion of faith capable of breaking through the barrier that separates the poet from God, and both draw on Colonna's powerful and violent imagery of breaking, melting, and burning in envisioning how this spiritual self-transcendence might take place. In a particularly Colonnesque sonnet, *Vorrei Signor che con il tuo flagello,* Battiferra calls for divine "flagellation," while in another, *Qual hor ch'io miro il gran figliuol di Dio,* she augurs a reduction of her heart to "burning fire" (foco ardente) to purge it so that it may better receive Christ's love.[62] Turina, meanwhile, in her sonnet *Amor cui non capisce humano ingegno* draws on the more sexual vein of imagery found occasionally in Colonna, calling on divine Love to pierce her with the gold of his arrows and "melt her ice" in his fire.[63]

Besides Colonna and, more distantly, Petrarch, Battiferra's penitential verse in particular owes much to the tradition of vernacular psalm translation that did so much to enrich Italian devotional verse in the 1560s and 1570s, to which she had contributed with her *Sette salmi penitentiali*. In addition to her psalm translations, conducted in an idiom drawing richly on Petrarch and Dante, Battiferra's *Sette salmi* contained a short sequence of nine independent penitential sonnets, all later incorporated into the Casanatense manuscript. This mingling of psalm translations and original verse is suggestive of what Gabriele Fiamma states explicitly in the preface to his *Rime spirituali*, discussed in chapter 1: that a "reformed" vernacular tradition of verse must look beyond Petrarch to David to revivify poetry's original religious vocation. Battiferra's religious verse presents itself in the *Sette salmi*, in the manner of Colonna's, as palinodic in respect to her earlier, secular lyrics. In the sonnet she later chose as the opening poem for the "Rime spirituali" section of the Casanatense manuscript, *Ecco Signore (e n'è ben tempo omai)*, she speaks of her "changed style" (cangiato stile), while in the complex and brilliant *Verace Apollo, a cui ben vero amore*, she reappropriates to sacred ends the governing Apollo-Daphne myth of Petrarch's *Rerum vulgarium fragmenta*, using it to describe the relationship between the desiring, pursuing Christ-Apollo and her sinfully resistant fleeing soul.[64]

In general, female-authored penitential sonnets like Battiferra's and Turina's are unexplicit about the nature of the sins for which the poet is repenting, although Lucia Colao and Isabella Andreini follow the classic male Petrarchan model in identifying their errancy as love.[65] An exception of great interest is constituted by two penitential sonnets by Semidea Poggi that refer to a more particular experience, namely, a revulsion from convent life that made her "consider the cloister as a prison" and "consume months and years raving vainly" as a result.[66] These quotations are from the more explicit of the two sonnets, *Signor, qual vita fu quella in ch'io vissi?* In another, *Mie colpe, e voi varii pensieri erranti*, the poet speaks only more generically of her "faults and errant thoughts."[67] In both sonnets, the poet locates her moment of errancy in the past, during what she describes in the second as a "long winter within the enemy fortress, between danger and error."[68] In the latter sonnet, however, she still portrays her inner enemy forces as strong enough to pose a threat to her spiritual well-being: *Mie colpe, e voi varii pensieri erranti* is cast as a psychomachia, in which the poet's reason challenges her sinful thoughts to battle and contrasts her internal "clash of arms" with the calm of the "sacred hymns" intoned around her.[69] Though in a more discreet register, these two sonnets of Poggi's anticipate the writings of Arcangela Tarabotti in their candid attention to the problem of involuntary claustration. Poggi may have written more in this vein, presumably destroyed: she refers in *Signor, qual vita fu quella in ch'io vissi* to writings from the period of her spiritual crisis, apparently dramatic in tone.[70]

The tercets of Poggi's *Signor, qual vita fu quella in ch'io vissi* show the poet dissolving her anguish by contemplating Christ's passion and finding hope in the thought that one drop of his blood can wash her sin-stained soul "pure and white."[71] The theme of penitence in devotional lyric generally was profoundly bound up with that of reflection on Christ's passion, to the extent that the two are virtually inseparable: not only does the sinner's hope of salvation derive from Christ's torment, as in Poggi's sonnet just cited, but his or her sin is also the cause of that torment, so that reflection on the Passion serves both as an engine of penitence and as a protection from the sin of despair. Angelo Grillo, a particular devotee of this species of Christocentric penitential poetry, speaks of it as inspired by "the Muses of Calvary" (le muse del Calvario); Calvary here implicitly becomes the new Parnassus, and the crucified Christ its Apollo.[72] This whole tradition of verse very obviously reflects the kind of devotional meditative practice we find systematized in authors such as Ignatius Loyola (1491–1556) and Luis de Granada (1504–88), whose writings enjoyed vast circulation in the period. The meditative program of Loyola's *Exercitia spiritualia* (1548) and Granada's *Libro de oración y meditación* (1554) combine structured reflection on Christ's passion and on the sins of the penitent, encouraging precisely the form of integrated meditation on sin and redemption we find in a poem such as Tasso's 1590 *canzone Alma inferma e dolente* or, in a very different vein, Grillo's protobaroque *Capitolo al Crocifisso* (1587).[73]

Within the female-authored religious lyric of the period, the work that most closely approximates to this kind of extended poetic meditation on sin in the context of Christ's passion is the impressive seven-stanza *canzone S'angelico pensier, puro intelletto*, which Moderata Fonte published in appendix to her 1582 narrative poem, *La passione di Christo*. The poem holds considerable interest as Fonte's only surviving religious lyric. Fonte's *canzone* anticipates Grillo in the self-consciousness of its conversional poetics, devoting its first two stanzas to the metapoetic problem of how to speak of what lies beyond the compass of human thought. Her solution, like his—and like Vittoria Colonna's in the proemial sonnet to her *Rime spirituali*—is to find Parnassus in the "tremendous Cross," her Muses in the weeping angels of the Passion, and her poetic fount in Christ's blood.[74] The following five stanzas ponder the theological mystery of the Incarnation and elliptically evoke the story of the Passion from Christ's prayer in the garden of Gethsemane to his entombment and descent into limbo. This narrative is plotted against a recurring meditation on human sin, both in general and as embodied in the poet herself. These two strands in the poem are brought together in the dramatic *congedo*, which begs the buried Christ at the moment of his descent into Limbo to entomb the poet's sin and draw her soul from "the limbo of unworthy thoughts" so that she may ascend with him to heaven.[75] The boldness of this closing conceit looks forward to later, baroque developments, while Fonte's occasional dalliance with virtuosic wordplay in the *canzone* reflects trends in late Cinquecento Venetian lyric, most apparent in a poet like Domenico Venier.[76]

Fonte's *S'angelico pensier, puro intelletto* stands at the ratiocinative and intellectual end of the spectrum of Christocentric penitential verse. Far more visceral is a poem like Laura Battiferra's sonnet *Questo foco sì ardente e questa fiamma*, one the finest of her late religious lyrics and one of a significant number of poems by her in this thematic vein. In addition to Vittoria Colonna, Battiferra's Christocentric verse may reflect the influence of Michelangelo, whose poetry, although not printed until 1623, she may well have seen in manuscript.[77] *Questo foco sì ardente e questa fiamma* explores a frequent topos within this subgenre of poetry, exploited almost to obsession by Grillo: the desire to empathize with Christ's suffering to the point of quasi-stigmatic incorporation. The quatrains speak of the poet being consumed by the fire of love exhaled from the crucified Christ's breast and pierced to the heart by the lance that ran through him, while the tercets describe her being "wounded by [his] wounds," "nailed by [his] nails," and crowned by his crown of thorns.[78] This experience of fusion is given an erotic inflection by an allusion to the "sweetness" of the poet's empathetic pain and the use of the Dantean rhymes *dramma* and *fiamma*, which occur in an erotic context in *Purgatorio*, as well as, more explicitly, in the closing lines, which speak of Christ as the "immortal Lover who binds the soul to him by such fast knots."[79] An interesting feature of sonnet's spiritual erotics is how little they correspond to the culturally privileged heterosexual model of male-female penetration. Penetration is almost ubiquitous in the sonnet's imagining of ecstaticized pain, from the lovingly dwelt-on lance of the second quatrain to the wounding wounds, piercing thorns, and nailing nails of the first tercet. Aside from the first quatrain's fire, however, which communicates itself from Christ's breast to the poet's, this penetration does not lend itself to being read as male-female. Instead, it invests the male and female protagonists of the poem, Christ and the poet, equally: the bodies of both are portrayed as similarly vulnerable and perforable; indeed, it is on this perforability that their identification rests. Similar emphases are found in a poem like Francesca Turina's on the instruments of the Passion, *Spine pungenti, e voi spietati chiodi:* "You, cruel Lance, which pierced the breast of my Lord, today wound my heart."[80]

After Christ, no religious figure loomed larger in Counter-Reformation devotional verse than the Virgin. Marian lyrics occupied an important role in virtually every spiritual *canzoniere*, with some poets manifesting a particular devotion to her. Vittoria Colonna's 1546 *Rime spirituali* contains a sequence of eleven sonnets to the Virgin, Ferrante Carafa's *Dell'Austria* a sequence of thirty-one.[81] In the period with which we are primarily concerned here, important bodies of Marian verse were composed by Tasso, Grillo, and Marino, while monographic lyric collections devoted to the Virgin were published by poets such as Aurelio Corbellini (1562–1648) and Giovanni Giovenale Ancina, the latter with musical settings.[82] Mary even had her own epics, with Lucillo Martinengo's twenty-five-book *Vita di nostra signora, la gloriosa vergine Maria* (1595) and Ridolfo Campeggi's sixteen-canto *Le lagrime di Maria Vergine* (1617), as well as Lucrezia Marinella's smaller-scale, four-canto *Vita di Maria Vergine imperatrice dell'universo* (1602).[83] While theology was clear on the point that Mary's status, however sublime, could not approach that of the Creator, popular and elite religious tended to elevate her to a role almost of coprotagonist in salvation. Emblematic in this sense are two *sonetti continui* in Carafa that play on the names of Christ and Mary, positioning the words *Cristo* and *Maria* with perfect symmetry and equal weight in each line.[84] A sonnet by Battista Vernazza goes as far as to address Mary as a "most powerful Goddess" (potentissima Iddia), while a madrigal by Francesca Turina strikingly describes her as "the right hand of God."[85]

The most substantial body of published female-authored Marian verse from this period is by Chiara Matraini, whose late religious writings, especially her *Breve discorso sopra la vita e laude della beatissima Vergine*, of 1590, contain a rich seam of poetry on this theme.[86] Matraini seems to have attained a degree of recognition as a poetic devotee of the Virgin: she was invited to contribute to an anthology in 1601 in praise of the icon of the Virgin at the sanctuary of the Monte della Guardia in Bologna, and Francesco Agostino Della Chiesa's entry for her in his *Teatro delle donne letterate* emphasizes her devotion to the Virgin and praises as "leggiadrissimi" (most beautiful) the Marian sonnets of the *Breve discorso*.[87] Other female poets of this period whose published and unpublished writings include substantial numbers of poems to the Virgin include Lucrezia Marinella, Veneranda Bragadin, Francesca Turina, Laura Battiferra, and Lucia Colao.[88] We also have interesting individual Marian poems by Livia Spinola, Semidea Poggi, Diodata Malvasia, and Leonora Bernardi, the latter of whom was hailed by Angelo Grillo in a much-published sonnet as the Virgin's own poet of choice.[89]

In purely quantitative terms, it would be difficult to claim that Marian verse held a more significant place within the devotional lyrics of female poets of this era than it did among those of male poets. Together with other verse addressed to female religious figures, however, it did perform a particular, authorizing function within female-authored religious *canzonieri*, offering an exemplary model of women's capacity for faith to set against the imperfect poetic "I" and, more generally, recalling the dignity accorded to women in Catholic theology and devotional practice. In addition, we sometimes find female-authored Marian verse of this period speaking a more explicit language of profeminist vindication, citing Mary's role in redeeming the female sex from the moral slur under which it had fallen through Eve's sin. This vision of Mary as generally dignifying womankind is noteworthy, given that it has sometimes been argued that Mary's exceptionality to the laws of nature, as virgin and mother, rendered her an implicit reproach to women in general, who remained fatally compromised by the taint of sexuality that she, "alone of all her sex," had escaped.[90] There is little evidence for this in the Marian writings of sixteenth- and early seventeenth-century women, which tend quite consistently to position Mary as ennobling of women generally. "Happy the female sex," wrote Isabella Capece, "for having among its number such an Empress of Heaven and Earth."[91] Even Maddalena Campiglia, whose 1585 *Discorso sopra l'annonciatione* uses the Virgin's modesty, humility, and silence as sticks with which to beat the moral errancies of contemporary women, nonetheless speaks of Mary's having "aggrandized and ennobled our sex."[92]

The tendency to posit the Virgin as generally dignifying of women is developed most programmatically, within the lyric tradition, in an unpublished sonnet by Francesca Turina, *Io non da vil fango hebbi i natali*. As explained by the title that accompanies it, "The Female Sex Narrates its Prerogatives and

Power: Sonnet on the Annunciation," the poem demands to be read as voiced by a personified *sesso femminile*, reflecting on the theological status of women from the Creation to the Incarnation, passing through Eve's role in the Fall.[93] The first quatrain of the poem draws on the feminist reading of Genesis popularized by Agrippa's *De nobilitate et praecellentia foeminei sexus*, whereby women's superiority to men was established through the fact of Eve's creation, not from "vile mud," but from the nobler matter of Adam's rib.[94] The second quatrain counterposes Eve's role in the Fall (lines 5–6) with Mary's corrective role in redemption (lines 7–8): if the female sex closed the portals of heaven to mankind, it will also be instrumental in throwing them open again.[95] The Annunciation, in this perspective, marks not only the beginning of the earthly narrative of the spiritual redemption of humanity but also that of the restoration of the *sesso femminile* to the pristine dignity intended for it by God. The first tercet of Turina's sonnet narrates the event in self-consciously epic style ("Plummeting from starry Olympus to the basest sands . . . a sublime Angel comes to proclaim it"), while the second in more analytic tones emphasizes its place within God's providential plan.[96] Compacted and elliptical in its expression to the point of obscurity, especially in the quatrains, the poem opens up in its final tercet, concluding with an elegantly turned conceit: "From the sea [*mar*] of Maria rises my Sun."[97]

The same intriguing intersection between Marian theology and *querelle* discourses on the dignity of women that we find in Turina's sonnet is also apparent in Leonora Bernardi's fine *canzone Se pur sù ne li stellanti chiostri*. Unlike Turina's sonnet, for which there is no evidence of circulation, Bernardi's *canzone* achieved a certain degree of fame in its own day. In addition to an initial, anthology publication in 1591, it was reprinted in a Marian treatise by the Lucchese religious writer Cesare Franciotti (1557–1627), first published in 1616, while a nineteenth-century source speaks of its also having been printed independently in Venice in 1610.[98] The *canzone* was also the subject of the laudatory sonnet by Grillo mentioned above, a significant tribute, given his fame as a religious poet at the time.

Se pur sù ne li stellanti chiostri consists of eight ten-line stanzas and a *congedo* and falls essentially into three sections: a *captatio benevolentiae* and invocation to the sacred Muse (stanzas 1–2), the latter closely modeled on the incipit of Tasso's *Gerusalemme liberata*; a passage in celebration of the Virgin (stanzas 3–5), comparing her to a series of classical and biblical feminine exempla; and a final section (stanzas 6–8) pleading for her salvific intervention in the poet's care-ridden life. Of particular interest for us here are the central epideictic stanzas, which sequentially compare the Virgin to the vestal virgin Tuccia and the Old Testament heroines Judith and Esther. The use of Judith and Esther as typological exempla for the Virgin is relatively straightforward and predictable: as Judith slew Holofernes, so Mary defeats the devil through her role in the incarnation of Christ; as Esther intervened with her husband to save her people, so Mary, another queen, intervenes for the faithful before God in her triune role as mother, daughter, and spouse.[99] The use to which the Tuccia example is put is less expected and more original: where the Roman vestal had proved her chastity against a false accusation by carrying water in a sieve from the Tiber, so Mary "purges the world of Eve's infamy," redeeming the world as an instrument of God.[100] The use of a secular example of female virtue in this otherwise sacred context is interesting, since it invites us to read the biblical exempla of feminine excellence cited in a profeminist key, as celebratory of women's natural capacity for virtue, rather than, for example, as proof of God's power in transforming "weak vessels" into providential agents of grace.[101] Bernardi's strategy here recalls that of a contemporary *querelle* treatise like Pietro Paolo Ribera's *Le glorie immortali de' trionfi et heroiche imprese d'ottocento quarantacinque donne illustri antiche e moderne*, which lines up classical pagan examples along with Christian saints as evidence of women's capacity for excellence in all fields.

While the cult of Mary can hardly be described as a localized phenomenon in Italy, it is intriguing that two of her most acclaimed female poetic devotees in late sixteenth-century Italy, Chiara Matraini and Leonora Bernardi, were from Lucca. The Tuscan city was a particular focus of Marian devotion at this time, following a miracle in 1588 that drew vast numbers of pilgrims; in addition, 1574 saw the foundation there of the Marian-inspired teaching order known as the Chierici Regolari della Madre di Dio, recognized by Clement VIII in 1595.[102] It seems safe to speculate that under these circumstances Marian verse took on a particular patriotic resonance for Lucchese poets. Indeed, conventional though the imagery is in itself, Matraini's particular emphasis on the Virgin's "luminousness" in the poems of her *Breve discorso sopra la vita e laude della beatissima Vergine* may have been intended to reinforce the pun on *luce* (light) and *Lucca* (Lucca) found in one of the prefatory sonnets, a pun that also embraces the author via her onomastic *senhal*: *chiara* (bright).[103]

It is perhaps also possible to detect similar patriotic inflections in the case of the Venetian Lucrezia Marinella, who gives a prominent role to Mary in her *Rime sacre*. Marinella had dedicated her *Vita di Maria Vergine imperatrice dell'universo*, published in the previous year, 1602, to the doge and the senate of Venice, in a gesture that alludes to the extraordinary place Mary held within the Venetian republic's political mythology.[104] Venice dated its foundation to the day of the feast of the Annunciation and identified itself politically as a "virgin city," never conquered or invaded, an image whose potency for Venetians increased in the sixteenth century, after the near loss of this virginity in the disastrous aftermath of the Battle of Agnadello in 1508.[105] It seems significant in this context that the first Marian poem of Marinella's collection, and perhaps the most striking, *Di glorie oggi, di gemme, e di splendori,* should be on the Assumption, the most triumphalist of Marian themes and the subject of Titian's great 1517 altarpiece in the Franciscan Church of the Frari, a visual reference likely to have been familiar to Marinella, whose Franciscan sympathies are clear from her writings.[106] Marinella's sonnet, which was to prove the most anthologized of her poems, portrays the event as a kind of cosmic *son et lumière,* taking place in a shower of light and flower petals, with the surrounding air booming, the sea leaping to the heavens, and the earth exploding in flowers. Mary is here at her most imperial, crowned with "glories and jewels and splendors."[107] While the political overtones of the image remain entirely implicit, the sonnet anticipates in some sense the scene in Marinella's later epic, *L'Enrico,* in which a hermit recounts his vision of Mary granting Venice her own gift of immaculate conception ("bearing sons, you will yet remain a chaste virgin"), as well as empire ("the grave burden of the scepter of Italy, indeed of the world").[108]

The lushness of Marinella's language in the sonnet just discussed, while particularly suited to its exuberant subject matter, is characteristic, more generally, of the poems in her *Rime sacre* dedicated to female religious figures. These are quite numerous; indeed, the prominence of the place female sanctity is given in the collection is one of its most distinctive features. Poems on female saints, excluding the Virgin, account for seventeen of the collection's sixty-one poems. Together with the eight poems to the Virgin, they make up twenty-five in total, about four-tenths of the whole. Female saints outnumber male saints in the *Rime sacre* by nine to seven: along with Mary Magdalene, Marinella addresses poems to Catherine of Siena, Catherine of Alexandria, Agnes, Ursula, Lucy, Euphemia, and Columba, as well as the eccentric Saint Marina, who spent the majority of her existence in male dress, disguised as a monk.[109] The proportions are strikingly different from those we find in a contemporary anthology of religious lyric such as Eugenio Petrelli's *Nuovo concerto di rime sacre*, whose section devoted to hagiographic lyric includes poems addressed to nineteen male saints and only seven female saints and places the male saints before the female, an order reversed in Marinella.[110] Petrelli's proportions coincide more or less with those of Vittoria Colonna, with poems to seven male saints and two female saints, and Lorenza Strozzi, with poems to more than fifty male saints and only seventeen female.[111] Of female poets, only Francesca Turina, in an unpublished hagiographic sequence, comes closer to Marinella's proportions, with ten male saints to six female.[112] Marinella's interest in the poetry of female sanctity is also attested by a manuscript in the Biblioteca Civica of Padua, undated but presumably dating from after her marriage in 1607, when she moved to her Paduan husband's home city. The manuscript contains writings in praise of the blessed Beatrice d'Este (c. 1200–1226), who retired at the end of her life to a hermitage near Padua, including four sonnets by Marinella in an idiom close to that of the *Rime sacre*.[113]

Marinella's poems to female saints take to a very marked extreme the general tendency of her devotional lyrics toward the visual and the decorative; one respect in which she reflects the poetic trends of her age is in her attraction to ekphrasis as a form.[114] Sanctity is characteristically manifested in her female—though not her male—protagonists by an extreme of physical beauty, conceived in classicizing and Petrarchizing terms. The face of Saint Catherine of Siena, as she weeps at Christ's passion in the moment of her receipt of the stigmata, is compared to a "pure white rose or the finest ivory, strewn with bright, crystalline drops," while, later, her skin is compared to "snow or pure milk," on which her wounds flower like "vermilion roses or bleeding stars."[115] Saint Ursula in glory is a "gleaming pearl," a "candid lily," a "wondrous sun," while Beatrice d'Este is compared to a "proud Rose ... gilded and pearled" by the coming of dawn.[116] The Virgin is equally beautiful, her blushing at the Annunciation compared to "rosy Dawn as she comes laughing from the golden heavens, strewing nectar and flowers from her breast and her hair."[117] One madrigal explicitly assimilates her to Venus, hailing her as "beautiful mother of Love."[118] While there is nothing especially novel about this aestheticization of female religious figures within the literary as well as the pictorial tradition, it gains a particular interest in Marinella's case when we consider the emphasis she places on women's beauty in her treatise *La nobiltà et l'eccellenza delle donne,* where the supposed greater beauty of the female sex figures prominently as an argument for its spiritual and moral superiority over the male sex.[119] Within this Neoplatonic perspective, the beauty of the female saints of the *Rime sacre* is clearly more than an accidental property: their physical flawlessness is the visible manifestation of the sublimity of their souls.

In Marinella's general portrayal of female sanctity in the *Rime* a particular emphasis is given to the figure of the female martyr: while only one of her seven male saints, the protomartyr Saint Stephen, falls into this category, fully six of her nine female saints do. In privileging female martyrs as protagonists of her *Rime,* Marinella is distinctive among female poets of the era, although a precedent exists in a fine sonnet by Colonna addressed to Saint Catherine of Alexandria.[120] Among the six female saints in Francesca Turina's unpublished sequence, for example, only two martyrs are found.[121] In the lyrics of the *Rime sacre* the individual narrative details of the saints' martyrdom are barely alluded to. Instead, Marinella's martyr poems work epideictically, collectively constructing a radiant image of a female spiritual excellence effortlessly transcendent of all mortal fear and weakness, the "invincible and divine fortitude" she attributes to Catherine of Alexandria in the madrigal *O felice regina.*[122] The theme interests her poetically as well, as allowing her to explore the paradoxical coexistence in the martyr of "fire and ice," ardor and chastity. This conceit is worked to its limits in the poem to Saint Agnes, which contains nine uses of *ardere,* "to burn," and its cognates and which opens with the line "You burn in the ice of chastity, you burn with love."[123] The language of the poem is notably sensual, especially toward the end of the second quatrain, when God, watching the spectacle of Agnes's martyrdom from on high, sends down to her "sorrowing senses happy sweetnesses of celestial ardor"; in the tercet that follows, Agnes lights heaven itself with her ardor, and the two burn in a mutual conflagration of love.[124] The madrigal to Catherine of Alexandria mentioned above, *O felice regina,* makes similar use of the topos of the burning virgin, placing "ardente affetto" (ardent love) in juxtaposed rhyme with "pudico petto" (chaste breast).[125] The madrigal ends with an image from the legend of Catherine that revisits the chromatics of the fire/ice dichotomy, showing "white milk" flowing from the neck of the beheaded martyr in place of blood.[126]

Marinella's tendency toward stylistic opulence in her poems describing female religious figures is sufficiently consistent for the rare exceptions to be quite revealing. One is her sequence of poems on the figure of Mary Magdalene, which tend toward a certain austerity of diction: while Magdalene is credited in one sonnet with "living Suns" for eyes and "alabaster limbs," she is aestheticized to a far lesser degree than we find in Marinella's poems on Catherine of Siena or Ursula or the Virgin.[127] This is noteworthy in that the poetic tradition so often used Mary Magdalene's famous beauty as an opportunity for *descriptio pulchritudinis*. Among female-authored works, an example of this probably known to Marinella was Moderata Fonte's ottava rima poem *La resurrettione di Giesu Cristo,* which contains an extended, Petrarchizing description of Magdalene's beauty.[128] Marinella quite decidedly resists this option in the *Rime sacre*, associating Magdalene's beauty with her youthful sinful transgressions and rejecting it as a theme appropriate for elaboration in a sacred context, in a manner that perhaps constituted a critique of the practice of worldlier poets. A sonnet describing the life of penitence that medieval legend attributed to Mary Magdalene after Christ's ascension opens with an aestheticizing incipit reminiscent of Petrarch and Bembo ("The beautiful Magdalene has loosed her golden locks to wave in the breeze") but rapidly reneges on this approach for something much starker ("she hates herself, tears her hair, beats her breast").[129] The message seems clear: the pleasures of poetic beauty are to be kept for the expression of transcendent, unflawed sanctity of the kind embodied in the Virgin and in virgin martyrs such as Ursula. Mary Magdalene, the epitome of human error redeemed by penitence, may be celebrated for her spiritual merits, but in a different, less exuberant language; the heights of poetic ornament must be kept for the impeccable and, specifically, the virginal, for Marinella seemingly the true locus of sanctity. At times in her Magdalene poems Marinella comes close to a demonization of beauty—her protagonist is portrayed, in her preconversion days, as a "nest of infernal monsters"—although, true to her Neoplatonic sympathies, she takes care to remind us that the beauty Magdalene abused was "still a gift from God."[130]

If Mary Magdalene presents something of a problem within Marinella's essentially epideictic, externalizing verse, she held a central place within more subjective traditions of devotional lyric, where the human frailty that diminishes her with Marinella as a poetic subject made her a valuable touchstone and role model for the poetic "I." Of female religious figures, Magdalene occupies a place in devotional lyric in this period second only to that of the Virgin among both male and female poets.[131] Among female poets, she is arguably on a par with the Virgin in terms of the richness and variety of the poetic responses she elicits. Her very accessibility as a figure encouraged imaginative identification, along with awe and devotion, while the richness of the narrative material associated with her added to her attraction as a poetic subject: besides the biblical (or quasi-biblical) episodes of her conversion and anointing of Christ's feet, her presence at the Passion, and her vision of the risen Christ in the garden, legend had added the episode of her later life as a penitent and mystic, invoked by Marinella in the sonnet just examined.[132] Vittoria Colonna devotes two sonnets in her *Rime spirituali* to Mary Magdalene, speaking in one quite explicitly of Magdalene as role model and exemplar: "I mirror and polish myself in her beautiful example."[133] Other poets reference the earlier, preconversion Magdalene as a mirror of their own sinfulness and an aspirational model in their hopes for divine mercy. This is the theme, for example, of a sonnet of Maddalena Campiglia's, *Signor se per amor, per pianger molto,* in which a Good Friday meditation on Christ's passion is crosshatched with reflection on the grace accorded to the errant Mary Magdalene, concluding with a prayer that Christ listen to the plea of "another Maddalena"—the poet—and similarly grant her pardon for her sins.[134] The onomastic association alluded to here seems to have weighed heavily with Campiglia, whose meager surviving lyric production contains two other sonnets on Mary Magdalene and whom we find addressed by Muzio Sforza in a sonnet of compliment as a "true Magdalene" in her closeness to God.[135]

Besides Mary Magdalene's role as a "mirror of lovely penitence" (Campiglia), a further aspect of the saint that attracted both female and male poets was her particularly close relationship with Christ, which cultural tradition, if not dogma, had long treated as quasi-erotic.[136] Christocentric piety in this period often took markedly erotic forms, and in this sense too Magdalene could act as "mirror" for the worshipper and a conduit of desire. Here was a woman who had enjoyed physical contact with the adult Christ in the episode of the washing and anointing of his feet and to whom he had chosen to reveal himself before all others after his resurrection, in a scene that must have appeared all the more intimate in a society in which unmarried men and women could not decently meet together unchaperoned. The episode of Mary Magdalene's washing of Christ's feet occurs quite frequently in the female-authored poetry of the era.[137] Campiglia narrates it dramatically and in detail in an unpublished sonnet, *Ecco la Maddalena ai piedi santi,* notable for the sensuality of its language in describing the central action:

> Chiede perdon pentita e in caldo humore
> Tutta par che si sfaccia, e con tremanti
> Gesti lava felice quelle piante.[138]

[She asks pardon, penitent, and in warm liquid seems entirely to melt, and with trembling gestures she happily washes those feet.]

A notable stylistic feature in the sonnet is its insistent enjambment, which goes so far in the case of "con tremanti / Gesti" as to cross the normally impermeable boundary between octave and sestet, a metrical "error" that contributes to the air of breathless intensity that characterizes these lines.[139]

Francesca Turina is perhaps the female poet in this period who engages most closely and imaginatively with the figure of Mary Magdalene. Magdalene appears in her usual roles in the narrative of Christ's life, passion, and resurrection in Turina's 1595 *Rime spirituali,* and an ottava rima narrative poem in her 1628 *Rime* recounts Christ's apparition to her in the garden.[140] It is within the lyric poetry included in the latter volume, however, that Turina's most striking Magdalene-themed poetry occurs. Like Campiglia's, Turina's poet identifies strongly with the saint in her role as sinner and penitent: she exhorts herself in one sonnet to follow the "great-souled, amorous Magdalene" in spending her late years in repentance after a youth given over to the world.[141] Again like Campiglia's poet, Turina's enters with close imaginative engagement into the narrative of Magdalene's intimacy with Christ: the same sonnet opens with a quatrain in which she figures herself, Magdalene-like, bathing Christ's feet in the tears of her "liquefied heart."[142] What is novel in Turina is the extent of this imaginative compenetration: as in this sonnet, rather than empathetically representing the saint's narrative, she sometimes has the poet inhabit this narrative herself.

The most striking instance of this occurs within an interesting sequence of poems set in a wild mountain landscape that is perhaps that of Gattara, in the western Marche, near the Tuscan border, where Turina had spent her youth.[143] These poems of hermitage make up a distinct group within Turina's *rime sacre,* unified by the protoromantic theme of the closeness to God inspired by nature. In the second, entitled *Rivolgimento a Dio,* she speaks of her thoughts in this retreat as "direct journeys to God."[144] In the same poem, she speaks of the divine light "revealing its most secret arcana here with its immense rays," and one of the features of these poems is the occurrence in three of them of divine fantasies or visions.[145] Gattara's proximity to Saint

Francis's retreat at La Verna, where he received the stigmata, may have partially informed these imaginings, although they may also be read as sacralized versions of the rural erotic dream visions Petrarch portrays in a poem like *canzone* 129, *Di pensier in pensier, di monte in monte*, similarly set in a landscape of "high mountains" and "wild woods."[146] Mary Magdalene appears in all three of Turina's vision poems, twice explicitly and once at the level of suggestion. In one, Magdalene figures along with the Virgin, Christ, and John in a vision of the Lamentation, "making the caves echo with their laments."[147] In another, she appears alone, in her late guise as a penitent, while the poet makes her way through a bleak landscape of "steep remote hills and desert wastes":

> Tosto alla vista mi figuro avante
> in quella alpestre grotta Maddalena
> ascosa fra' i suoi crin fino alle piante.
> E volta al Ciel la faccia alma, e serena
> chiamar piangendo il suo celeste amante
> che tal gioia può 'l cor capire a pena.[148]

> [At once I figure before my eyes in that mountain cave Magdalene, hidden to her feet in her long locks, as she turns her lovely and serene face to heaven and weeping calls on her divine lover. Such joy a heart can hardly hold.]

In the final poem, *O se mentre dal volgo m'allontano*, the poet imagines encountering Christ himself in her solitary wanderings, "in the manner that he showed himself to others, as an earthly pilgrim, when he returned from death."[149] In this last fantasy, she is more than simply a spectator of the heavenly scene: she prostrates herself "weeping with love" and wishing to "kiss his beloved feet a thousand times."[150] While the initial pilgrim scenario recalls Christ's appearance on the road to Emmaus, the poet's response is that of Mary Magdalene to Christ's earlier postresurrection appearance in the garden, familiar from the visual tradition of noli me tangere. Reinforcing this, the rhyme words in the tercets closely echo those of Turina's sonnet on the penitent Magdalene quoted above: that poem's *avante-piante-amante* becomes here *davante-piante-amante*, with the close of the penultimate line particularly close in both cases ("celeste amante" and "cortese amante"). The poet here, then, in a mystical transformation, effectively *becomes* Mary Magdalene, in the saint's most theologically significant and affectively charged moment.

The exercise of imaginative empathy, fundamental in devotional lyric, could hardly be more vividly expressed.

3. The Dwindling Muse: Female-Authored Secular Lyric in Post-Tridentine Italy

Female-authored secular lyric production in the late sixteenth and early seventeenth centuries offers a less consistent and unified panorama than women's sacred production, to the extent that it hardly makes sense to speak of a tradition. This is especially the case after the very early seventeenth century. Within the essentially late-Petrarchan secular lyric production of the 1580s and 1590s, women continued in the role of "integrated minority," which they had enjoyed since at least the mid-sixteenth century, with Isabella Andreini emerging as something of a figurehead toward the end of this period. After this, as the stylistic shift to the baroque took effect, women played an increasingly marginal role in the secular lyric tradition, although this does not lessen the interest of some of their output, Lucchesia Sbarra's *Rime* of 1610 and Francesca Turina's of 1628 being notable cases in point.

Of the secular single-authored verse collections authored by Italian women in this period, the most interesting from the point of view of structure and conception are Maddalena Salvetti's *Rime toscane*, of 1590, and Isabella Andreini's 1601 *Rime*. Both may be seen, in their different ways, as responses to the impasse at which women now found themselves with respect to love poetry and more generally as reflections of the disintegration of the Petrarchan tradition in these years. Salvetti's volume reprises the mid-century Florentine tradition of verse collections dedicated to the reigning Medici consort: where Tullia d'Aragona in 1547 and Laura Battiferra in 1560 had dedicated volumes to Eleonora de Toledo, Salvetti dedicated hers to Christine of Lorraine, who had married Ferdinando I de' Medici (1549–1609) the previous year.[151] While d'Aragona's and Battiferra's collections had, however, been miscellaneous collections, merely prefaced by a sequence of poems in praise of the Medici, Salvetti's is monographic: an entire sequence of ninety-nine poems (seventy-one sonnets, twenty-two madrigals, six *canzoni*) in praise of Grand Duchess Christine, followed by a shorter sequence of forty-six poems (thirty-two sonnets, twelve madrigals, two *canzoni*) in praise of her spouse.[152] The Christine sequence is without question the more interesting and original of the two: rather than straight encomiastic verse, it takes the form of a Neoplatonizing Petrarchan love *canzoniere* addressed to the grand duchess, reworking the tradition of erotic verse as it had developed through the century, from Bembo to Della Casa to Tasso, but adapting it to nonamorous ends.[153]

Salvetti was not the first female poet to use the language of love to praise a female patron: a famous early instance was a sequence of sonnets by the Sienese poet Laudomia Forteguerri (1515–c. 1555), addressed to Margaret of Austria, another Medici consort, while a more contemporary use of the device may be found in Maddalena Campiglia's 1589 pastoral eclogue *Calisa,* in praise of Isabella Pallavicino Lupi.[154] Prior to Salvetti, however, no poet had produced an entire *canzoniere* in this idiom; nor had any deployed it with such programmatic revisionary intent. Salvetti's precise point of reference in the *Rime toscane* is the Neoplatonic tradition of love lyric that had cast the lady in the role of quasi-angelic spiritual guide. While within erotic lyric proper this idealizing tradition was rapidly falling out of fashion at the time of her writing, redeployed as a metaphor for the relationship between a divinely appointed Christian monarch and her subjects, it acquired a new purchase and sense.

Andreini's 1601 *Rime* offers a very different response than Salvetti's to the breakdown of the Petrarchan tradition of love poetry, dramatically abandoning one of the central premises of that tradition, its identification of the poetic "I" with the author. The proemial sonnet of the classic Petrarchan love *canzoniere* had traditionally presented the verse that would follow as an account of the poet's experience, offered to the world as an exemplum of the vanity, or, more rarely, of the pleasures, of love. Andreini's, by contrast, identifies her love poetry as an extension of her acting: a projection of "feigned ardors," "false sorrows," "false delights," such as those she impersonated on stage.[155] The *trouvaille* is a brilliant one, the more so for its witty reversal of Tasso's emphasis on the veracity of the experiences described in his *Rime amorose,* the first line of whose proemial sonnet reads "True were these joys and these sorrows" (Vere fur queste gioie e questi ardori).[156] Rather than a testament of experience, nominally to be measured by the yardstick of truth, love lyric in Andreini becomes purely ludic, pure performance, a development she underlines by writing love lyrics in both male and female voices.[157] In practice, the histrionic model of love lyric Andreini adopts licences her to experiment with sensual erotic idioms too risqué for a woman to adopt without some such distancing device. One *scherzo, Movea dolce un zefiretto,* describes a dawn vision of a naked beauty, focusing with particular voyeuristic rapture on the loveliness of her breasts.[158] Other poems speak of kisses given or "stolen" from the beloved, an established subgenre of the age.[159]

Andreini was not the only female poet of the day to experiment with love lyric by adopting the expedient of a male voice. A handful of male-voiced love poems by Orsina Cavaletti appeared in anthologies from 1587 on, and a few more, perhaps inspired by Cavaletti's, are found in Moderata Fonte's *Il merito delle donne*, where they are attributed to her poet-speaker Corinna.[160] The most substantial body of such verse after Andreini's is the twenty-two love sonnets found in a sequence in Lucchesia Sbarra's 1610 *Rime*, written in an extravagant and sometimes whimsical, baroque-inflected idiom: one poem shows the beloved ineffectually fishing, while the "golden net" of her hair trawls in an unwanted catch of lovers, while others describe the lover being gnawed by an "amorous woodworm" or entangled in the "Gordian knots" of the lady's extravagantly dressed hair.[161] Sbarra's engagement with love lyric is particularly intriguing given her close association with the noble family of the Collalto, to which Gaspara Stampa's beloved, the soldier and literary patron Collaltino da Collalto (1523–69), had belonged.[162] Also worth noting is her connection with theatrical culture through her brother Pulzio Sbarra's activity as a patron of drama; this, as much as the precedent of Andreini, may have led to her adoption of the intrinsically histrionic device of poetic impersonation.[163] As we might expect, Sbarra's love lyrics are less overtly sensual than Andreini's, remaining for the most part within the limits of Petrarchan erotics, whereby the most that the poet hopes for from his lady is an emotional acknowledgment of his love. Sensual overtones are lent to her verse, however, through her allusions to the more risqué reaches of classical mythology. One sonnet opens with an image of Europa carried off by her "bestial lover," while another refers to Diana in her role as moon goddess as "she whom Endymion clasps naked."[164] Other allusions are to Jupiter's rape of Danae in the form of a shower of gold and Vulcan's catching of Mars and Venus *in flagrante* in a net.[165]

Although Sbarra's ventriloquized love lyrics are not without interest, far the most original sequence of poems in her *Rime* are those mourning the death of her infant son, Giovanni Battista Coderta, who died sometime before 1607.[166] Sbarra's poetry of maternal loss may to an extent be located within a tradition of parental mourning verse, represented in the late sixteenth century by poets such as Giuliano Goselini (1525–87) and Orazio Lupi (b. c. 1556).[167] Local, Veneto examples that may have been known to Sbarra were Giovanni Antonio

Gelmi, of Verona, and Bartolomeo Burchelati (1548–1632), of Treviso, who published volumes of funerary verse on the deaths of their sons, in 1588 and 1599, respectively.[168] Sbarra is distinctive within this tradition in that she does not locate her grieving within a domestic and familial context. There is no mention of her husband, for example, as comourner, although this may be because he died shortly after his son.[169] Sixteenth-century mourning poetry for family members and close friends allies itself for the most part with the tradition of occasional verse and may be seen as an intimate counterpart to the much vaster category of verse mourning the deaths of public figures, local or national.[170] Sbarra's verse for her son approximates instead to the Petrarchan, erotic tradition of mourning poetry, less controlled in its grief and less socially embedded. Her use of myth is indicative here: while a poet like Goselini employs mythological embellishment relatively decoratively and superficially in his mourning poetry for his son, Sbarra uses myth to create an irrational, hyperbolic space in which the monstrosity of her loss can play out.[171] Another difference between Sbarra and the majority of poets who addressed the death of a child is the relatively slight role that Christian religious consolation plays in her verse. While two sonnets attempt self-consolation through a vision of her son's beatitude in heaven, even within the compass of the poems this consolation falters.[172] For the most part, Sbarra's focus is terrestrial, and the grief she portrays is without remedy or mitigation, to the extent that she confesses in one poem to an attempted suicide.[173] Others end with stark statements of her inconsolability: "Against my weeping, I hope for no remedy but weeping"; "I did not, shall not, do wish for help."[174]

A good example of Sbarra's poetry of mourning is the sonnet *Prestami i draghi, o Dea, prestami i pini,* which carries her characteristic stylistic extravagance to remarkable dramatic extremes. The sonnet fuses two mythological narratives of parental and erotic loss, that of Ceres's hunt for Proserpine, alluded to in the first quatrain, and that of the death of Adonis after his departure from his lover Venus, which supplants the Ceres myth in the second quatrain and dominates the remainder of the poem. The transition between the two myths is handled in a manner so oblique as initially to jeopardize comprehension: line 6 of the sonnet has the poet suddenly contemplating an unexplained wild boar and fearing that she "recognizes her blood on its lips."[175] It is only in the tercets, when Adonis is named, that we can make sense of what we have heard. The poem's obliquity is enhanced by the volatile quality of the relationship between the poetic "io" and her mythological archetypes. In the first myth adduced, Ceres, addressed as "tu," remains quite distinct from the poet, although an analogy exists between them as mothers driven to near madness by the loss of a child. In the second, by contrast, the persona of the poet coincides with that of the anguished Venus to the point that they effectively fuse. In the tercets, the bereaved mother watches the face of her dying son dissolving into an anemone, like Adonis in the myth, the only difference being in their color—purple in the myth, where Adonis dies by violence, white in the sonnet, evocative of the illness by which Giovanni Battista in reality presumably died.[176] In its allusiveness and ellipticism, the sonnet has an oddly protomodernist character: in a manner quite alien from Petrarchism, which characteristically expresses extreme emotion in a rationally controlled manner, it is prepared to tear at the fabric of discursive logic to express the violence of the emotional experience described.

Aside from Sbarra, two other female poets of this period participated in this poetry of domestic affections: Veneranda Bragadin and Francesca Turina. Bragadin's 1619 *Rime* contains four elegiac sonnets on the deaths of her mother and husband, which are among the strongest productions of this generally uninspired poet, as well as a curious accusatory sonnet arraigning the medic she considered responsible for her husband's death.[177] Turina's commitment to this thematic is far more substantial; indeed, a sequence of poems devoted to her life and domestic travails makes up one of the four principal segments of her 1628 *Rime*, together with a collection of religious verse and two substantial encomiastic sequences, devoted principally to the Colonna and Barberini families.[178]

The structure of Turina's sequence of autobiographical verse retains a distant resemblance to that of the Petrarchan narrative *canzoniere* from which it descends, and it is perhaps possible to see the first nucleus of the project in a series of poems close to Petrarch thematically, namely, those describing her husband's long absence during the early years of their marriage, in the 1570s, which transmute to a marital context the classically Petrarchan themes of amorous yearning and competing hope and fear.[179] What is novel, however, in Turina's autobiographical *rime* is her chronological and thematic expansion of her narrative. Rather than starting with the moment of her *innamoramento*, she pursues her story back to her childhood and adolescence, and rather than focusing exclusively on love, she embraces far more varied experiences, including motherhood, grandmotherhood, the death of a child, the death of a friend, geographic displacements, and the experience of aging. The result is a work of remarkable interest that demands to be located within the early history of autobiography as a genre, as well as of lyric verse. It seems extraordinary, given its interest, that until very recently this sequence of poetry had attracted serious attention only from critics local to Turina's native Città di Castello, even if Croce's favorable comments on her simplicity and sincerity won her a somewhat fossilized place in twentieth-century anthologies.[180]

One problematic feature of Turina's autobiographical verse as it appears in the 1628 Città di Castello edition of her *Rime* is the unlinear manner in which it is presented. An initial autobiographical sequence grows organically from Turina's encomiastic verses in praise of the Colonna of Paliano, with whom she lived during the period 1614–22 as companion to the duchess, Lucrezia Tomacelli, and perhaps also as tutor to the daughters of the family, including Anna Colonna (1601–58), the dedicatee of the volume.[181] The Colonna sequence concludes with a series of sonnets recounting the poet's anguish at the death of Lucrezia, which, preceded as they are by more formal occasional poems, effect a notable shift in the emotional tenor of the collection.[182] The poems on Lucrezia's death are followed by a sonnet recalling the murder of Turina's younger son, Ottavio, in 1623, and then by others that recount the much earlier death of her husband, her arrival at the Colonna household, and her return to San Giustino, where she had lived with her husband, to visit his tomb after Lucrezia's death.[183] Following this "private" sequence, the collection plunges once more into occasional verse, this time mainly addressed to the papal Barberini family, into which Anna Colonna had married, before embarking more formally on a chronologically ordered autobiographical narrative that opens with a proemial sonnet entitled *Principio dello stato dell'autore* (The beginning of the author's condition).[184] The narrative traces the poet's life from her orphaned infancy, through her marriage to Giulio Bufalini and the birth of their two sons and her widowhood, to Ottavio's death and her consolation in her grandsons. (In a manner profoundly revealing of the social attitudes of the period, Turina's daughter, Camilla [b. 1579], who survived into adulthood and married, is entirely absent from the narrative.)[185]

Within this rich body of verse—the second sequence alone amounts to about one hundred sonnets—some of the most remarkable lyrics are the series recording the poet's adolescence in the Umbrian home of her maternal uncle, Count Pietro di Carpegna.[186] Thematically these are almost without precedent within the tradition of female-authored Italian verse, a rare exception being a sonnet by Lucchesia Sbarra, *Vent'anni vissi in libertade, e in pace*, which speaks nostalgically of her carefree youth as a time when she "truly lived and knew she was alive."[187]

One especially interesting feature of Turina's poems of adolescence is the distinctive persona the poet crafts for herself, drawing on the imaginative worlds of pastoral and epic, as well as that of Petrarchan lyric, which provides the incipit for her most anthologized sonnet, *Cara, fida, secreta cameretta*.[188] Turina portrays her adolescent self as melancholy, solitary, and studious but also, more unexpectedly, as athletic and intrepid: in one poem we see her spurring an "agile steed" across mountainous terrain, careless of danger; in another, hunting, Diana-like, with a bow; in a third, imitating Virgil's fleet-footed Camilla in footraces against the *pastorelle* of the district.[189] Whether these sonnets have any basis in fact hardly matters; what they demonstrate very interestingly is the degree to which fictional stereotypes of the heroic woman inflected the imaginative self-identities of educated women of the time.[190] A striking feature of Turina's self-portrait is the element of competitiveness and will to dominance it incorporates: the equestrian sonnet lays great emphasis on the young horsewoman's mastering of her "bold and proud" mount, while the race sonnet concludes with a description of the laurel of victory as "that which the heart most desires."[191] Elsewhere Turina shows herself intensely proud of the military prowess of her *condottiere* father, Giovanni Turini (d. 1554), of whose "power [*dominio*], wealth, deeds, and honor" she boasts in the first line of her proemial sonnet, before recounting how following his death she was compelled to leave his house along with her mother.[192] The notion of exile from a place of belonging, established in this first sonnet, continues to inform Turina's verse throughout the narrative: her marriage is presented as a restoration to the Edenic state of plenitude from which her early orphanhood had expelled her, while her husband's death, like her father's, exposes her once more to a life of displacement. The loss and recuperation of *dominio*, in both a material and a moral sense, is one of the prime unifying themes of the sequence.

Besides her sonnets of adolescence, another remarkable thematic subgroup of Turina's autobiographical poems is that dealing with motherhood and her relationship with her sons. While one sonnet on the birth of her first son, Giulio (1576–1642), welcomes him in "official" terms, speaking of her hope that he will revive the glories of his ancestors, a second, more characteristic sonnet revels in a far more spontaneous and private emotional pleasure in maternity. The poem opens with an outpouring of endearments— "lifeblood of my heart, apple of my eye, dearest little thing"—and goes on to speak of the poet's delight in breast-feeding her son and singing him to sleep.[193] Similar poems later in the sequence address her infant grandsons, that to the son of her murdered second son, Ottavio, gaining particular emotional charge from its placement immediately after a sequence on Ottavio's death.[194] As with Turina's sonnets of adolescence, it is difficult to think of parallels for these verses in the literature of this period. Thematically they are certainly unique, and it is not easy to think of parallels within the elite poetic tradition in terms of register and language, other than perhaps Turina's own, similarly fond treatment of the infancy of Christ in this book and in her *Rime spirituali sopra i misterii del santissimo rosario*.[195] Especially striking, given the unreciprocated character of the loves classically sung by Petrarchism, is the emphasis in these poems on physical intimacy and mutual communication of affection: a sonnet to Giulio's son Giovanni has the poet "melting and dissolving" as her baby grandson reaches out to her or looks at her with his "beautiful calm eyes."[196]

Though quite remote from each other in style, Turina's autobiographical verse and Sbarra's sequence on the death of her son are comparable in certain regards: both are distinctive and original in a manner that may perhaps be connected with their authors' relative marginalization. Neither Turina nor Sbarra may be described as marginalized in an absolute sense, in that both received encouragement from their immediate environment. Sbarra came from a literary family, while Turina engaged in extensive poetic correspondence with local and less local literary figures and appears to have been a member of at least one literary academy.[197] Both were writing, however, at a time when women no longer performed the kind of structural role within the Italian lyric tradition that they had for a period in the sixteenth century, with Petrarchism. By 1610, female-authored lyric verse was already becoming an oddity; by 1628, even more so. Sbarra betrays something of a consciousness of this in an occasional sonnet published in 1615 in a volume otherwise containing only the work of male poets; she describes herself there as a "scavenging female" come to loot herself some fame in the company of men.[198] Ironically, it may have been this relative marginalization that allowed her, like Turina, the freedom to write outside their tradition. While nothing particular was to be gained by attempting to be "one of the boys," nothing was to be lost by relinquishing this aim.

A last body of writing by Italian female poets in this period deserving of discussion is that celebrating prominent women. In its basic dynamic, this body of writing offers an interesting point of comparison with religious verse celebrating the Virgin or other outstanding female figures from the history of Christianity; in both, celebration of an exemplary female figure often functions as a vindication of the female sex as a whole. The formula is made quite explicit in a sonnet by Maddalena Campiglia addressed to Isabella Pallavicino, which motivates the poet's praise of her subject's "divine visage" and "magnanimous and heroic heart," noting that "if my sex is today held in esteem, it is solely on your account."[199] Similarly, Valeria Miani in a dedicatory letter to Eleonora de' Medici Gonzaga, Duchess of Mantua (1567–1611), speaks of the female sex as "marvelously illuminated" by her dedicatee's "brilliant sun."[200] As we would expect, most female-female encomiastic literature of this period derives from court contexts, although some examples are found within the Venetian cultural sphere, notably Moderata Fonte's series of sonnets to Venetian patrician brides, found in the closing pages of her dialogue *Il merito delle donne*, and various poems by female poets of the *terraferma* in praise of the wives of Venetian officials sent to govern their hometowns.[201] Elsewhere we find verse by Orsina Cavaletti to ladies of the Este family and by Veneranda Bragadin to ladies of the Gonzaga, while Francesca Turina's published and unpublished writings offer numerous examples of encomia addressed to ladies of the great baronial and papal dynasties of Rome.[202]

Far the richest environment for this kind of writing, however, was the Medici court in Tuscany, especially after the arrival of the French princess Christine of Lorraine. In addition to Maddalena Salvetti's *Rime toscane*, already mentioned, Isabella Andreini and Isabella Cervoni both wrote verse for Christine, as well as for Christine's niece by marriage Maria de' Medici, married in 1600 to Henri IV of France.[203] Turina's unpublished verse also includes poems to Maria de' Medici, as well as to Christine's daughter-in-law Maria Maddalena d'Austria, consort of Cosimo II (1590–1621), and to other, later Medici women.[204]

Within this Medicean literature, Cervoni's 1600 *canzone* to Maria de' Medici is particularly interesting for the explicitness of the profeminist conclusions it draws from its subject's excellence. By the time she composed this *canzone*, which was published along with two others, one to Henri and one jointly to the couple, the 24-year-old Cervoni was already a veteran Medici encomiast, having begun her career with a *canzone* on the birth of Cosimo II de' Medici in 1590.[205] In her *canzone* to Maria, Cervoni draws liberally on the tradition of the *querelle des femmes*, comparing her subject to Minerva and Cornelia in her learning, to Zenobia in her governmental skills, and to Lucretia in her chastity.[206] Especially interesting are the two stanzas praising women's political contribution, and specifically the role of ruler-consorts in counseling their husbands, citing examples from Augustus's wife Livia to Pompey's Cornelia and Trajan's Plotina, and concluding with an admonition against the "false judgment" (giudizio fallace) that prompts men to rate women's intelligence as lesser than their own.[207] Cervoni strengthens her argument on an *ad hominem* level by citing several exempla of Christian consorts who guided their pagan husbands to the true faith, suggesting an implicit parallel with Maria's potential role in increasing her formerly Protestant husband's adherence to Catholicism. (In 1597 Cervoni had published two *canzoni* celebrating Henri's conversion and benediction by the pope).[208]

Although she is less explicit than Cervoni, Maddalena Salvetti shows herself similarly alert in her *Rime toscane* to the profeminist possibilities implicit in the act of praise for a female subject. Especially revealing on this score is the sonnet *Alma felice e gloriosa Donna*, which juxtaposes the figure of Christine of Lorraine, described in the quatrains in all her numinous splendor, with that of the poet, depicted in the tercets as a worshipful acolyte who hopes, by means of praise for her patron, to win poetic immortality for herself.[209] The two figures are as carefully differentiated in terms of dignity and scale as the sacred subject and donor in a medieval altarpiece, yet a parallel exists between them as exceptional women: if Christine was sent by God Neoplatonically to illuminate the dark world and to support "lovely Hesperia" (la bella Esperia) like a column, the poet similarly depicts herself as destined by heaven for the poetic vocation from which she hopes to win fame. Neither is touched by the inferiority their culture conventionally attributed to women: Christine's transcendence of women's purported imperfection is self-evident, while the poet speaks proudly of herself as "shunning the base offices" of her sex.[210]

The profeminist tenor of Salvetti's sonnet is reinforced by its echoes of sonnets by other female poets in praise of famous women, notably Veronica

Gambara's *O de la nostra etade unica gloria*, an encomium of Vittoria Colonna, and Laura Battiferra's *Lassa nel tuo partire, ahi lassa, in quante*, mourning the death of Eleonora of Toledo.[211] Battiferra's sonnet similarly juxtaposes the figures of patron and poet, using the transition between octave and sestet to articulate the double portrait, and it similarly defines the poet's vocation in terms of a transcendence of conventional gender roles.[212] In both cases, the poet's fame is made dependent on her relationship with her powerful female patron: Battiferra laments that her inspiration must wither without the vivifying influence of her "Muse and Lady," while Salvetti speaks of her chances of poetic immortality as depending on Christine's harboring her "in the shadow of her veil."[213] Christine's role as living emblem of the possibility of feminine power is underlined with special emphasis in Salvetti, who opens and closes the octave she devotes to the grand duchess on the rich rhyme of *Donna* and *s'indonna*, a device that serves to root the word *donna* etymologically in notions of power and dignity, in a manner that would have leapt to the eye of contemporary readers primed in the debates of the *querelle des femmes*.[214] The same wordplay is used to similarly gender-conscious effect in a Marian poem by Chiara Matraini included in her 1602 *Dialoghi spirituali*, in a manner that underlines the rhetorical parallels existing between praises of "great ladies" in secular and spiritual verse.[215]

❧ CHAPTER THREE ❧
DRAMA

The body of secular and sacred lyric discussed in the previous chapter has many claims to novelty at the level of detail, but in other respects it continues the tradition of female-authored writing of the earlier sixteenth century. Far more novel as a development of the later Cinquecento is the emergence of women as writers of narrative works and secular drama. This was not entirely without precedent: a rich tradition of female-authored sacred drama had flourished in Italy, especially in the convents, since at least the fifteenth century, and we know of a scattering of narrative works by women prior to 1580, notably a romance and a lost *novella* collection from the 1550s by the Paduan Giulia Bigolina.[1] There is, however, nothing in the preceding tradition to compare to the extraordinary outpouring of narrative and dramatic works that appeared from the 1580s: in addition to several lost but documented works, we have seven surviving secular plays by Italian women from the period 1580–1630, all but two published during the authors' lifetime, and twelve published secular and religious narrative works, including two epics.[2] There was no parallel for this output in Europe in this period in terms of scale, despite precedents such as Beatriz Bernal's chivalric romance *Don Cristalián de Espana* (1545), Marguerite de Navarre's *Heptameron* (first published in 1558), and, if they are indeed the work of a woman, *Angoisses doulouereuses* (1538) and *Songe* (1541), by "Hélisenne de Crenne."[3] In England, for example, only three plays by women survive from the half-century following 1580 (Mary Sidney's *Antonie* [1592], Elizabeth Cary's *Tragedy of Mariam* [1613], and Mary Wroth's *Love's Victory* [1620s]), together with three narrative works (Margaret Tyler's *Mirrour of Princely Deeds and Knighthood* [1578], Anne Dowriche's *French History* [1587], and Wroth's *Urania* [1621]).[4]

The expansion of literary genres attempted by Italian women in this period speaks very clearly to their increasing confidence and their relatively high level of integration within literary culture. Women's core genre in the first half of the sixteenth century, lyric poetry, could be defensively presented as mere scribblings, "scattered rhymes," written purely to wile away time or provide an outlet for emotion. The composition of a romance, a play, or a *novella* collection, not to mention an epic poem, was far less easy to present as a private or casual diversion, since the scale of such works implied a sustained intellectual engagement over time. These were also genres in which modern women were quite consciously breaking new ground with respect to their classical antecedents: while female lyric poets could look to distinguished classical precedents such as Sappho and Corinna, no dramatic or narrative writings by female authors were known from the ancient world, with the exception of the Virgilian and Homeric centos of Proba and Eudocia.[5] The "prodigiousness" of women's literary attainments was hence more than usually clear in the field of fictional writing and drama, especially where ambitious genres such as the *poema eroico* are concerned. It is perhaps not surprising, then, that Margherita Sarrocchi, the first Italian woman to attempt an epic in the early seventeenth century, was also the first female writer to excite notable hostility among her male peers.[6]

1. Drama for the Doge: Moderata Fonte's *Le feste*

The first surviving secular dramatic work by a female Italian writer is a brief philosophical-encomiastic *rappresentazione* by Moderata Fonte performed before Doge Niccolò Da Ponte (1491–1585) on Saint Stephen's Day in 1581.[7] The piece, about 350 lines in the printed edition, appears to have been intended for a performance combining declamation and singing. It belonged to a genre of performance texts commissioned for similar occasions in Venice from about 1570, a genre Doge Da Ponte had been active in fostering. The genre would develop under subsequent doges, reaching a new level of complexity and ambition under Marino Grimani (1532–1605), who became doge in 1595.[8] Although *Le feste* is the only dramatic piece of this kind that was published under Fonte's name, she probably also authored some of the anonymous *rappresentazioni* that survive from the period: her generally reliable biographer Giovanni Niccolò Doglioni speaks of her having written other, anonymously published *rappresentazioni* performed before more than one doge.[9] In any case, the existence of *Le feste* is eloquent testimony to the level of public recognition attained by this time by the 26-year-old poet, who had earlier that year made her publishing debut with the chivalric romance *Tredici canti del Floridoro*. Although we know the names of relatively few of the authors of such pieces, a sonnet of Celio Magno's thanking the acting company who performed a play of his at the Saint Stephen's Day *festa* in 1585 shows that the authors included prestigious names: Magno was, at the time, following the death of Domenico Venier three years earlier, probably the most celebrated Venetian poet of his day.[10]

Although Fonte is the only female author who we know was involved in writing a dramatic text for this kind of performance occasion in Venice, some precedent for her involvement in such a state occasion is offered by Issicratea Monte's authorship of three congratulatory orations in the late 1570s, addressed to Doge Da Ponte and his predecessor, Sebastiano Venier (c. 1496–1578). Monte performed at least one of these in the presence of Doge Venier.[11] This was certainly an event of which Fonte was aware, as she contributed a prefatory sonnet to the printed edition of Monte's performed oration, praising Monte as a "new Minerva."[12] The two probably came to know each other through a mutual literary acquaintance, the dramatist Luigi Groto, who, in a letter to Monte of 12 January 1583, mentions Fonte's sending him a performance text that may have been *Le feste*.[13] Besides this oratorical precedent, it seems likely that Fonte was acquainted in her childhood with the tradition of female-authored convent drama: Doglioni's *Vita* explicitly mentions her participation in dramatic *rappresentazioni* at the convent of Santa Marta as a child.[14]

Although undoubtedly slight and ephemeral, *Le feste* is not without interest, both for its philosophical self-positioning and its attention to gender.[15] The play opens with a prologue by the Year coming to a close *(L'Anno)*, who ushers in as a last gift to his listeners the eponymous choruses of "The Feasts" (Le Feste). The Feasts' celebration of the holiday spirit prepares for the introduction of the figure of an Epicurean, who speaks with warmth of "pleasures and delights" as man's "supreme happiness and supreme good."[16] The Epicurean's position is countered by a Stoic, who maintains the superior claim of virtue over pleasure, flattering Da Ponte and his senate by presenting himself as speaking in Virtue's own home. The two philosophers then embark on a dispute, interrupted by the arrival of the Erythraean sibyl, who has arrived to pay seasonal homage to the doge. The philosophers agree to have her arbitrate between their positions, which they restate. The sibyl then delivers the sentence, adjudging neither right and proposing instead a *via di mezzo* whereby material goods are not despised, as the Stoic advocates, and the pursuit of wisdom and virtue is not mocked, which is the inclination of the Epicurean. She concludes by pointing the two philosophers forward to the truer *festa* that Christians may aspire to in heaven and referring to the role she had played in prophesying the advent of Christ.[17]

The structure of a contest between two male figures adjudicated by a female had a certain literary tradition, the most accessible instance perhaps being Petrarch's *canzone* 360, which stages a forensic debate between the poet and Love before the tribunal of Reason.[18] Fonte's choice of a sibyl, rather than an allegorical figure such as Reason, Truth, or Wisdom, is significant with respect to this figure's authorizing role: for sixteenth-century readers, the sibyls were not mythological figures but historical archetypes of the learned woman, and they are found cited as such in countless lists of classical *donne illustri* compiled from the fifteenth century on. In 1576, five years before Fonte's *Feste* was performed, Chiara Matraini ordered the completion of an altarpiece that she had commissioned in her hometown of Lucca, portraying the Tiburtine sibyl prophesying the advent of Christianity to the emperor Augustus.[19] The sibyls are mentioned by Fonte in her brief list of classical women who excelled in letters in *Il merito delle donne,* while Lucrezia Marinella includes them in the equivalent listing in *La nobiltà et l'eccellenza delle donne* (1600), terming them "most learned women" (donne dottissime).[20]

In *Le feste* the sibyl appropriately represents a spiritualized *sapientia* capable of silencing the earthly *scientia* of classical philosophy. At the same time, however, the philosophical position she defends is a distinctly worldly, essentially Peripatetic one: she argues that if the Epicurean is at fault for not giving a higher place in his scheme to virtue and wisdom, the Stoic is wrong in failing to acknowledge the harmlessness of material pleasures if moderately indulged. The relaxed attitude toward "honest pleasure" that *Le feste* evinces might be explained as a concession to the holiday context of its performance, but it is consistent with the tenor of Fonte's later dialogue, *Il merito delle donne*, whose female interlocutors speak with gusto of the delights of hunting and the pleasures of the table, even—contrary to the prescriptions of most conduct manuals for women—acknowledging their enjoyment of good wine.[21] Fonte's worldliness in this regard contrasts sharply with the extreme asceticism of her younger contemporary Lucrezia Marinella, whose Platonizing *Rivolgimento amoroso verso la somma bellezza* (1597) recommends that the body be "despised and hated . . . as a rotting corpse and dark tomb of the soul."[22]

Among the formal qualities of Fonte's play, worthy of note is the sprightliness with which she handles what could easily have become something more ponderous: the figure of the Epicurean in particular, comically characterized and licensed to insult his opponent with more freedom than the graver Stoic, offers Fonte an opportunity for satirical freedom that looks forward to the lighter moments of *Il merito delle donne*. Especially effective is the Epicurean's baiting of the Stoic as specter at the feast and "portrait of melancholy" ('l ritratto de la malinconia), as he has just been defined:

> mi maraviglio
> come tra i piacer nostri entrato sei.
> Certo io credea ch'in qualche grotta or fossi
> a contemplar la stoica scienza,
> ch'insegna altrui, come, tra vivi, uom viva
> peggio che morto, senza alcun ristoro.[23]

[I marvel at how you have intruded in our pleasures. I thought you would be in some cave, contemplating that Stoic science that teaches us how, among the living, a man may live worse than the dead, devoid of all recreation.]

Another formal merit of the play is that it is effectively constructed, within the limits of the genre, with the philosophical dispute between Stoic and Epicurean subtly inflected by the musical interventions of the choruses, which tend to favor—even on the page and presumably more in performance—a worldly and morally flexible solution.[24] The Stoic's delight at the arrival of the sibyl suggests his confidence that she will award him the victory, as does the perfunctory nature of his pleading, giving an element of surprise to her eventual judgment that neither position is right, and neither wrong. Another strength of *Le feste* is Fonte's adept handling of forensic rhetoric, an area of contemporary rhetorical culture that she would have been aware of growing up in legal circles in Venice and one that she has her speakers discuss knowledgeably in *Il merito delle donne*.[25] *Il merito* itself, structured as an adversarial debate, draws richly on this same rhetorical tradition. In this sense, *Le feste*—and perhaps the other *rappresentazioni* Doglioni attributes to Fonte—may be seen as anticipatory of *Il merito*, which distinguishes itself from many contemporary literary dialogues precisely through its lively handling of debate.

2. Arcadian Adventures: Women Writers and Pastoral Drama

About a year before Fonte's *Feste* was performed before Doge Da Ponte, the first printed editions began to appear of Torquato Tasso's pastoral *Aminta*, one of the most popular dramatic works of the century and the play that, more than any other, served to establish the modern courtly *divertissement* of pastoral drama as a third theatrical genre, capable of standing alongside the venerable classical genres of comedy and tragedy.[26] Increasingly, from the 1580s on, pastoral dramas poured from the Italian presses, in a vogue later given new impetus by the 1590 publication of Giovanni Battista Guarini's *Pastor fido*.[27] In a famous treatise on theater written in 1598 the poet and theatrical director Angelo Ingegneri could speak within acceptable limits of hyperbole of "a good thousand pastorals" (ben mille pastorali) having been composed in Italy over the previous decades.[28] The appeal of the pastoral within the theatrical culture of the age was strong; unlike tragedy, it was tonally suited to celebratory occasions such as weddings and Carnival, while it had the advantage over comedy of moral decency *(onestà)* and its elevated subject matter. It was also relatively cheap to stage, in that it did not demand the kind of ambitious perspectival stage set that had become conventional in the traditional dramatic genres. Pastoral also held much appeal as a literary exercise, especially after Tasso demonstrated in the *Aminta* the poetic heights of which it was capable. Many of Ingegneri's thousand plays were never actually staged, being at most publicly read in a literary academy or court.[29]

The emergence of pastoral as a theatrical genre is important for the history of women's writing in Italy, since this effectively secured women's entrée into secular theatrical composition. One tragedy by a woman survives from the period of interest to us here, Valeria Miani's *Celinda* (1611), discussed below. The first printed comedy by a woman, Margherita Costa's *Li buffoni*, would not appear until 1641.[30] Pastoral, by contrast, proved notably popular with women. Seven pastoral plays by early modern Italian women survive, five written in the 1580s and early 1590s, when the genre was at the height of its vogue. The first in terms of composition is probably Barbara Torelli's *Partenia* (c. 1586), unpublished at the time and surviving only in manuscript.[31] The first to appear in print were Isabella Andreini's *Mirtilla* and Maddalena Campiglia's *Flori*, both published in 1588.[32] Two other female-authored pastorals date from the 1590s, an anonymous "Tragicomedia pastorale," surviving in a manuscript in the Biblioteca Marciana in Venice, datable from internal evidence to the early 1590s, and Valeria Miani's *Amorosa speranza,* published in 1604, though apparently completed by 1598.[33] The remaining two works, Isabetta Coreglia's *Dori* (1634) and *Erindo il fido* (1650), date from a later moment, when pastoral was less culturally central. To these seven surviving pastorals we should add three lost pastoral sketches—not full, five-act dramas —that Laura Guidiccioni wrote for the Medici court in the 1590s in collaboration with the composer Emilio de' Cavalieri (c. 1550–1602).[34] Various sources also credit Guidiccioni's Lucchese contemporary Leonora Bernardi with one or more pastoral dramas, one of which is probably identifiable with the Marciana "Tragicomedia pastorale." The author of that play is said on the title page to be "a gentlewoman from Lucca" and is identified by a name in code, "Xqcbcfm Hqxmllm," compatible with a version of Bernardi's name, "Leonora Belatta," that we find in printed sources of the time.[35] In the discussion that follows, I assume Bernardi's authorship of the play, although this is a matter of conjecture, not fact.

The reasons for the appeal of pastoral drama to women are quite numerous.[36] First, and perhaps key, was the "honesty" of its subject matter, by comparison with comedy, a feature pointed to by an early theorist of the genre, Angelo Ingegneri, in his *Della poesia rappresentativa,* of 1598, when he remarks that pastorals "admit the figures of virgins and honest women on to the stage, as is not permitted in comedy," and "give space to noble sentiments, not unfitting to tragedy itself."[37] Although the plots of pastoral dramas centered on love, as did comedies, the love theme was characteristically treated in a decorous Petrarchan manner, with well-bred shepherds soulfully wooing chaste nymphs and displays of overt sexuality generally limited to marginal figures such as satyrs. Arcadian convention, moreover, allowed nymphs, though in many respects transparent figures for contemporary upper-class women, a freedom of movement, speech, and sociability with males that the more "realist," urban settings of comedy denied.

The "decency" of pastoral drama increased over the 1580s and 1590s, as what had originally been an ephemeral and unregulated form of court entertainment was drawn into the literary system and laboriously codified as a genre. Iconic in this regard is the dialogue between the notoriously libertine first-act chorus of Tasso's *Aminta* and the corrective that Guarini inserted in his *Pastor fido,* arguing for the pleasure of love only when sanctified by marriage.[38] By 1602 the playwright Muzio Manfredi (1535–1609) was able to present his play *Il contrasto amoroso* to the Duchess of Guastalla, Vittoria

Doria Gonzaga, as ideal reading matter for respectable upper-class women on the grounds that it contained "more than one of those things in which respected noblewomen and court ladies and princesses of your estate like to take delight: [things] entirely modest and reputable and consistent with chaste behavior and the edification of chaste and well-behaved matrons and good and prudent virgins."[39] Interestingly, Manfredi recommends the work as suitable not simply for reading but for a possible performance by the duchess's ladies-in-waiting, who could happily cover the parts, the only male character being a young shepherd, who might equally well be played by a girl.[40] This is not the only evidence we have that noblewomen occasionally acted in private amateur court performances of pastorals. One famous case involves a performance of Ingegneri's *Danza di Venere* at Soragna, near Parma, in 1583, in which the lead role was performed by the 13-year-old daughter of Dowager Marchioness Isabella Pallavicino Lupi, one of the dedicatees of Campiglia's *Flori*.[41]

Pastoral was suited to a feminine authorial ethos not only because of its decency but also because of its modest standing within the literary hierarchy, determined both by the perceived baseness of its rustic subject matter and by the novelty of the form and hence its lack of a distinguished classical tradition of the kind that comedy and tragedy could boast. This was important, especially considering that the pastorals of Torelli, Andreini, and Campiglia were among women's earliest ventures beyond the realm of lyric poetry. Female poets had already begun to experiment with the pastoral mode in verse as early as the 1550s, laying the groundwork for their engagement with pastoral drama. The first woman to engage with pastoral eclogue appears to have been Laura Battiferra, two of whose eclogues survive, although only one appeared in print in her lifetime. Battiferra's published eclogue figures the author, as "Dafne," in conversation with Leonora Cibo Vitelli, "Europa."[42] Battiferra's second surviving eclogue, unpublished at the time but clearly circulated, since a song from it was set by Alessandro Striggio (c. 1536–92), portrays Dafne as poet-nymph singing the pleasures of the Tuscan countryside in the presence of a mixed group of friends.[43] Outside the genre of eclogue, Battiferra engaged in correspondence verse with her Florentine circle of male poets under the name Dafne, while Gaspara Stampa adopted the pastoral name Anassilla in her 1554 *Rime*. Although Tullia d'Aragona did not use a pastoral pseudonym in her verse, an eclogue by her admirer Girolamo Muzio published in her 1547 *Rime* portrays her as the poet-nymph Tirennia, carving her "lofty loves" on the surrounding trees and competing in song with the shepherds of her age.[44] Texts such as these all helped establish the nymph-bard as a figure in Arcadian imaginary, in a manner that reflected the place women had come to assume within the contemporary Petrarchan tradition. The female pastoral dramatists of the 1580s exploited this new tradition to authorize their work, with Campiglia, Andreini, and Torelli all including representations of nymph-poets in their dramas, in each case under their own pastoral name.[45]

Besides this literary tradition, women also helped forge the stage language of pastoral drama in the theater, both as actresses in scripted plays and, perhaps more intriguingly, as improvisers. It is telling in this regard that one of the earliest female authors of pastoral drama was a professional actress, Andreini. The first actresses for whose performances we have some documentation, active in the 1560s, are credited with extending the range of the *commedia dell'arte* from its traditional, comic and farcical base to include "high" roles such as that of the *innamorata*, acted without masks and featuring elevated sentiment and an elegant Petrarchizing language. Early actresses on this model, such as Vincenza Armani (d. 1569), were clearly literate and drew on literary sources in crafting their performances, in a manner prefigured by singer-poets such as Gaspara Stampa, known to have performed her own texts to music.[46] Armani is credited by her biographer Adriano Valerini with having been "the first to introduce pastorals on stage," meaning, presumably, that she was the first to introduce pastoral performances within the improvised, *commedia dell'arte* tradition.[47] Although Armani, like Andreini, played both male and female parts, a significant proportion of her energies were probably devoted to nymph roles. Like later, second-generation figures such as Andreini and her rival, Vittoria Piissimi, we may assume that Armani did much to shape court audiences' collective imagining of the nymph figure's presence, language, and affect.[48]

While Andreini's engagement with pastoral drama as a written form may obviously be seen as deriving from her activity as an actress, in order to understand Torelli's and Campiglia's experiments with the genre a consideration of their immediate literary context is useful. In the 1580s both Parma and Vicenza were noted for their traditions of drama. In the first half of the decade, Vicenza's Accademia Olimpica erected a magnificent theater, the Teatro Olimpico, inaugurated in 1585 with a performance of Sophocles's *Oedipus Rex* in vernacular translation. Parma was also active as a center for theatrical production, as were nearby smaller courts such as Soragna and Guastalla, while Parma's Accademia degli Innominati was important in sponsoring dramatic writing and fostering theoretical debate on the forms drama should take. It is certainly more than a coincidence that two of the earliest female pastoralists came from cities so culturally invested in drama, and it is worth considering the possibility that both *Partenia* and *Flori* should be seen as in some sense academic initiatives, even if there is no decisive evidence that either Campiglia or Torelli was formally a member of the academy in question. Campiglia's relations with the Olimpici were discussed in chapter 1. In Torelli's case, the most immediate evidence of a relationship is the presence of four Innominati among the twelve poets who contributed encomiastic poems to the play, although Laura Riccò has also noted correspondences between Torelli's dramaturgical practice and the dramatic theory of the academy.[49] It is even conceivable that Campiglia's play was promoted by the Olimpici in emulation of the Innominati: if Parma had its Torelli, then Vicenza had every reason to welcome the prospect of a female pastoralist of its own.

Perhaps partly as a result of such local academic agendas, the earliest female-authored pastorals, those dating from the 1580s, all attained a fairly high degree of cultural visibility. We should not be misled by the fact that Torelli's *Partenia* remained unpublished. This was not an unusual fate in this period for works by aristocratic writers and does not mean that the play did not circulate.[50] Muzio Manfredi, who praised *Partenia* in his *Cento madrigali* (1587) as the most beautiful pastoral yet written, seems to have been especially active in promoting Torelli's play.[51] A letter of 1587 shows him recommending *Partenia* for performance at the wedding of Ferrante II Gonzaga, Duke of Guastalla, while in a letter dated 1591 he speaks of having sent a copy of *Partenia* to the ruler of Savoy, Carlo Emanuele I (1562–1630).[52] Another admirer of the play was Angelo Ingegneri, who in *Della poesia rappresentativa* ranks *Partenia* as one of the finest pastorals written to date in Italy, putting it in a class with Tasso's *Aminta* and Guarini's *Pastor fido*.[53] Campiglia's *Flori* also seems to have won her a considerable degree of fame and could boast some distinguished admirers: Angelo Grillo and Curzio Gonzaga wrote sonnets in praise of the play that were published in the 1589 and 1591 editions of their *rime*, while Tasso himself, to whom Campiglia sent a copy of her play, responded with a letter of praise.[54] Andreini's *Mirtilla*, meanwhile, proved a considerable publishing success, buoyed by the author's extraordinary fame as an actress; the play went through nine editions between 1588 and 1605 and was translated twice into French, in 1599 and 1602.[55]

Of the other two Italian female-authored pastorals that survive from this period, Valeria Miani's *Amorosa speranza* and Bernardi's *Tragicomedia pastorale*, neither attained the attention that the plays of Andreini, Campiglia, and Torelli received. Miani's play was published in her home city of Padua with a modest complement of anonymous prefatory verse but does not seem to have attained wider notice. Although there is some internal evidence that the play was performed, this was probably a small-scale, amateur production in a villa near Padua.[56] Bernardi's *Tragicomedia* also seems to have been performed, probably also in an amateur performance, but in a socially much grander setting than *Amorosa speranza;* the prologue indicates that it was acted before Ferdinando I de' Medici and Christine de Lorraine at the Medici villa in Fiesole, probably in the spring of 1591.[57] Bernardi may have owed this honor to her family connection with the Medici: she was goddaughter to Francesco de' Medici, and she was named for his and Ferdinando's mother, Eleonora of Toledo.[58] It should also be recalled that a precedent existed for the performance of female-authored dramatic texts at the Medici court, in that two of Laura Guidiccioni's *pastorelle per musica—Il satiro* and *La disperazione di Fileno*—had been performed there the previous year.[59]

In the discussion of Italian female-authored pastoral drama that follows I concentrate on the five pastorals composed in the 1580s and 1590s, those of Torelli, Campiglia, Andreini, Bernardi, and Miani, although I occasionally make comparative reference to the later pastorals of Isabetta Coreglia. Despite superficial similarities, the five plays discussed are notably different in their structure and tone. Of the five writers, Torelli, Campiglia, and Bernardi were the highest in social standing, and their plays, probably in part for this reason, are more decorous and edifying than Miani's or Andreini's, eschewing the comic possibilities of pastoral for its "higher," spiritual and moral-didactic potential. Besides the authors' status, a further factor to consider is the early date of composition of the three plays in question. Miani, probably writing about a decade later, may have felt freer to experiment with comic modes, which had been legitimized for female authors by the precedent of Andreini. With respect to plot structure, Torelli's *Partenia* is quite distinct from the other four plays, and indeed unusual within the history of the development of Italian pastoral after *Aminta*, in that it follows Tasso's "tragic" model of a single, unified plot. The plays of Campiglia, Andreini, and Miani more closely follow current practice in employing a more complex structure, deriving from comedy, featuring interwoven parallel love stories thematizing the ironies of conflicting desires. Bernardi's play is a little harder to place within this schema, but it is closer to Torelli's than to Campiglia's. It remixes the tragicomic love plot of *Aminta* but complicates the scenario by doubling Tasso's single pair of protagonists into two couples and allocating a portion of the original plot to each couple.

Brief plot summaries of the five plays will be helpful before we proceed. Torelli's play portrays its young heroine, Partenia, as caught between two suitors, Tirsi and Leucippo, to the latter of whom she is promised in marriage by her father, while the former has tricked her into promising herself to him by a solemn vow in Diana's temple.[60] Apprised of her situation by a prophetic dream of a vengeful Diana, Partenia is torn between the duties of obedience to her father and observance to her vow. Tirsi too is rent with guilt and falls down, apparently dead from grief, on hearing which Partenia also collapses lifeless. Meanwhile, the dilemma of Partenia's inadvertent double betrothal is resolved when Leucippo is revealed to be her long-lost brother. When we learn subsequently that Tirsi and Partenia have been resuscitated by the medically skilled nymph Talia, earlier introduced as Partenia's friend and the faithful lover of Coridone, the way is opened for the revived heroine to wed her betrothed, thus safely fulfilling her vow.

As noted above, Bernardi's *Tragicomedia* centers on the tragicomic loves of two interlinked couples.[61] When the play opens, Clorilli and Filemone, once happily in love, have been estranged for two years, since Filemone consented to a marriage proposed to him by his father with another nymph, Dalinda. Meanwhile, Dalinda, who mysteriously disappeared the night before her arranged marriage, is revealed in the course of the play to have eloped with her beloved, Clorilli's brother Fillinio. In fact, however, the two failed to meet that night, and both believe, or fear—in a plot motif borrowed from *Aminta*—that the other has been killed by a bear. In the third act, Fillinio returns from two years of grieving errancy and is seen by Filemone being embraced by Clorilli. Failing to recognize Fillinio as her brother, Filemone assumes that he is a new lover. In a frenzy of jealousy and erotic despair, he flings himself off a cliff in an Aminta-like suicide attempt. As in *Aminta*, the tragedy is resolved when Filemone is discovered to have survived his fall and is reconciled with the now-repentant Clorilli. Meanwhile, Dalinda has reappeared, having spent the past two years with the priestess Lidia, who dissuaded her from suicide during her initial anguish at learning of the supposed death of Fillinio. A secondary character, Coribante, informs her that her lover is alive, and the play ends with the prospect of their joyous reunion.

Both Torelli's and Bernardi's plays proclaim fidelity to the model of *Aminta* in their central use of the motif of the false suicide, a plot device also featuring in Ariosto's story of Ariodante and Ginevra, an important subtext for Bernardi in particular.[62] The other three female-authored plays of the period are more independent of this paradigm, although Tasso remains an important influence in each case. Of the three, Campiglia's *Flori* has the most complex plot, involving no fewer than four interlinked love stories, as well as two parallel agnitions.[63] Campiglia's play opens dramatically with its eponymous heroine driven mad by grief following the death of her beloved fellow nymph Amaranta. At the same time, the shepherd Androgeo is mad with unrequited love for Flori. A ritual sacrifice has been arranged in the pastoral community to petition the gods to restore the sanity of the two sufferers, and an oracle has foretold that the sacrifice will be successful but that Flori will fall in love with the first man she sees upon recovery of her sanity. The man in question turns out to be Alessi, a passing pilgrim who is himself afflicted by grief following the death of a former love.

Besides this main plot, subsidiary plots concern the love of Flori's friend Licori for Androgeo and the love of another nymph, Urania, for the fickle Serrano, whose machinations to win the love of Flori occupy much of the first half of the play. In the later part of the play, a further, more "comic" plot is introduced, that of the love of Serrano's servant, Leggiadro, for his master's sister, Gelinda. This plot is resolved when Leggiadro is revealed to be, along with Androgeo, one of the two lost sons of the wealthy Tirsi, who has earlier been encountered lamenting his double loss. Androgeo, meanwhile, having recovered from his madness, has been persuaded without too much difficulty to transfer his love from Flori to the faithful Licori, while Serrano, disappointed in his scheming, proves equally happy to settle for Urania.

Though less energetically plotted than Campiglia's play, and lacking the complicating element of mistaken identity and agnition, Andreini's *Mirtilla* similarly presents us with an initial tangle of conflicting desires that is ultimately resolved through changes of heart.[64] Mirtilla and Filli are rivals for Uranio, who himself is unrequitedly in love with the hardhearted Ardelia. At the same time, Igilio loves Filli, who is unable to return his love. Ardelia is punished for her obduracy by suffering the fate of Narcissus and falling in love with herself—a new motif in pastoral, though anticipated in part by Tasso in the figure of Silvia—before ultimately repenting and resolving to return the faithful Uranio's love.[65] Meanwhile, Filli has been similarly brought round by Igilio's devotion, which leads him by act 5 to the point of suicide. Mirtilla settles for a third shepherd, Tirsi, who, having started the play a confirmed bachelor, now reveals himself a late convert to love. *Mirtilla*'s somewhat perfunctory plot serves predominantly as an ad hoc structure on which to hang a series of poetic excursuses, such as Uranio's extended Petrarchizing description of Ardelia's charms in act 1 or Tirsi's eulogy of the joys of hunting in act 4, and semiautonomous action scenes, such as the one in act 3, in which Filli outwits a lustful satyr by pretending to reciprocate his love and then tricking him into allowing himself to be tied to a tree. More than a unified drama, *Mirtilla* may almost be seen as a series of sketches, clearly reflecting Andreini's background as a practitioner of the *commedia dell'arte*.[66]

Valeria Miani's *Amorosa speranza* differs from the plays of Torelli, Campiglia, and Andreini in not deriving its title from the name of its heroine. In practice, however, Miani focuses very sharply on the dilemmas of a single female protagonist, Venelia, far more so, in fact, than Andreini, whose titular character, Mirtilla, is not especially dominant as a figure within the play.[67] Miani's Venelia differs interestingly from the stereotypical nymph in that she is not a virgin votary of Diana but an abandoned wife or mistress: prior to the beginning of the action of the play, she has been seduced and deserted by Damone, who fled Arcadia after "plucking her virginal flower."[68] During the play, she is pursued by two shepherds, the classically "noble" Alliseo, formerly betrothed to her friend Fulgenzia, and the more aggressive Isandro, who suborns her farm servant, Bassano, to aid in his seduction attempts. Another nymph, Tirenia, is in love with Alliseo and tries to destroy Venelia's chances with him by telling him of her sullied past. In the course of the plot, Isandro rescues Tirenia from a satyr, and the two fall in love, simplifying the love convolutions. Venelia then tricks Alliseo by extracting a promise from him to grant her a favor when he is on the point of killing himself out of love for her. The promise is that he honor his vow to marry Fulgenzia, a proposition to which he reluctantly accedes. The play ends with a deus ex machina in the form of the priest Lucrino, who ushers back a Damone rendered penitent by the will of the gods. The requisite multiple marriage ensues, and Venelia pardons her errant herdsman Bassano.

Of the five plays, it is, predictably, Andreini's *Mirtilla*, written by a practicing actress, that is most theatrical in character, although Miani follows Andreini in her inclusion of elements of action, most notably in the scenes involving Tirenia and the satyr. Of the two plays closest to the prototype of Tasso's *Aminta*, Torelli's *Partenia* adheres more strictly to Tasso's rigorously undramatic model in that all of its action is narrated, rather than directly represented, and its principal lovers are never brought together on stage. Bernardi's *Tragicomedia* is less austere in this respect, including a scene where Fillinio saves Clorilli from a satyr, and bringing one of her two pairs of lovers, Filemone and Clorilli, together in a dramatic confrontational scene.[69] Campiglia's *Flori* also incorporates some elements of action, principally in the staging of the ritual sacrifice that results in Flori's cure, and the scenes in the first act featuring the two mad characters, Androgeo and Flori, would have had dramatic potential in performance. As Campiglia herself confesses, however, the length of many of *Flori*'s speeches might be seen as excessive in a piece genuinely intended for staging, while the convoluted character of the plot would also be more of a deterrent in performance than it is on the page.[70]

Where thematics are concerned, perhaps the clearest way to bring out the differences in character among the five plays under discussion is to compare their approach to the key pastoral thematic concern, erotic love. The most sensual of the plays, as we might expect given its authorship, is Andreini's *Mirtilla*, which, in keeping with the mainstream of male-authored pastoral, tends to the celebration of love as a natural and irresistible force. When characters resist love, this is presented as misguided: Ardelia's initial resistance to Uranio's love is portrayed as narcissistic, and Tirsi's resistance to love in general is identified as perverse. By the end of the play, both have recognized their errors and succumbed to the universal power of eros. Key to Tirsi's conversion is a speech in act 4 by a character introduced for this purpose, Coridone, who speaks rapturously of the pleasures of love, seen as the apex of human pleasure and the fulfillment of an immutable natural law.[71] Coridone's monologue marks the climax of a series of set-piece speeches extolling various human pleasures in what clearly appears to be an ascending order of nobility: the comic goatherd Gorgo praises gluttony in act 3; Tirsi, the pleasures of hunting in act 4; and finally Coridone, the pleasures of wealth and intellectual activity, followed by love. In addition to valorizing love, Andreini's teasing scale of human pleasures—which is entirely secular, it will be noted—also valorizes women: whereas the love-skeptical Tirsi had extolled the self-sufficient pleasures of hunting, Coridone admonishes him, saying that "he who flees woman also flees the most valuable and noble part of himself" and that "man can no more live without woman than woman can sustain her frail life without man."[72] Coridone continues by alluding to the sensual pleasures of love in language that, while discreet, is quite explicit in its evocation of physical intimacy, speaking of lovers' experiencing a "superhuman sweetness" as they breathe "fiery sighs" into each other's mouths.[73] The passage clearly registered as sufficiently steamy with one of the French translators of the text for him (or her) partially to censor these lines, along with an earlier reference in Coridone's speech to an amorous nymph "removing," or perhaps just "lifting," the clothes of the shepherd lying in her lap to allow him the relief of a cool breeze.[74]

Predictably, Torelli's and Campiglia's plays are notably more modest than Andreini's in their treatment of sex and desire. *Partenia* opens with its eponymous heroine yielding to the wishes of her father, Ergasto, in agreeing to marry, while making no secret of her preference for preserving "my so beloved virginity" (la tanto cara mia virginitate).[75] While this is not the only perspective present in the play—an older nymph, Talia, performs a more "honest" version of the role of Tasso's Dafne in *Aminta*, urging Partenia to give up her resistance to love—we are clearly in a rather different world here than the Venusian one of *Mirtilla*, where all the principal nymphs, with the exception of Ardelia, begin the play as desiring subjects. Nymphs resistant to love were a common feature of pastoral drama, but they generally succumb willingly to their lovers' determined wooing by the end of the play. *Partenia* is different, in that its heroine remains "virginal through and through" during the whole course of the play.[76] Even her name derives from the Greek *parthenos*, "virgin." Although the work ends, conventionally, with Partenia's marriage to Tirsi, Coridone underlines that she is consenting to marriage not because she loves her prospective husband but simply on account of her vow.[77] Partenia's ironclad chastity is repeatedly underlined in act 4, scene 2, when Ergasto first suggests the idea of marriage to Leucippo and attempts to win Partenia over by painting her prospective bridegroom as "courteous, charming, and handsome."[78] Partenia pronounces herself entirely indifferent to such considerations, to the point of not even wanting to know what such qualities might signify in a man. Her sole interest in assenting to marriage, as she makes clear, lies in the satisfaction of obedience to her father. Her submissiveness elicits a response of delight on his part: "Blessed be all the pains I have suffered for your sake."[79]

This foregrounding of Partenia's relationship with her father differentiates Torelli's play from those of Andreini and Campiglia, in which the protagonists are largely portrayed as free to make their own marital choices, without the pressure of parental authority. Partenia's stance of filial obedience is so emphatically underlined in the play that Lisa Sampson has suggested a prototype for it in the Annunciate Virgin's submission before God.[80] In *Partenia* we are close to the Christianized and moralized pastoral world of Guarini's *Pastor fido*, in which an immutable divine providence governs the protagonists' lives and transgressions against the gods are severely punished. Political authority too is present in Torelli's play, though it is not as oppressive as it is in Guarini's. The play is set not in Arcadia but in the Farnese villa of Collecchio, and the "great shepherd" Ottinio—Ottavio Farnese (1524–86)—is praised in the opening scene for his cultivation of the surrounding lands.[81] In its moralizing "domestication" of the pastoral scene, Torelli's play is consistent with general trends in the genre in the last decades of the sixteenth century; indeed, it has recently been suggested that in its treatment of love *Partenia* may be seen one of the most consistent expressions of the reformist literary program espoused by the Accademia degli Innominati, centered on a Christian rereading of the classical and neoclassical "science of love" that had informed earlier pastoral literature.[82] The extreme chastity of *Partenia* is evidently due in part to constraints of authorial decorum: a noblewoman like Torelli was less free to write of sensual love than an actress like Andreini had she so wished. The play also, however, exemplifies the way in which the moralizing trends of Counter-Reformation literature were in many ways beneficial to female authors; as Ingegneri's enthusiastic response demonstrates, *Partenia*'s moral austerity placed it in some respects in the literary avant-garde.[83]

Campiglia's *Flori*, though closer in tone to *Partenia* than to Andreini's *Mirtilla*, may be seen as standing somewhere between them in its depiction of love. Unlike *Partenia*, which follows the Tassesque convention of not showing lovers together on the stage, *Flori* is happy to stage scenes of courtship, and two of the play's love stories, those featuring Licori and Androgeo and Serrano and Urania, are developed in a manner reasonably close to the pastoral norm. Radically different, however, and quite distinctive within the spectrum of sixteenth-century pastoral generally, is Campiglia's treatment of the successive amours of her protagonist Flori, who is shown stricken with love first for her companion Amaranta, whose death has driven her to madness, and then for the shepherd Alessi, with whom she had been destined to fall in love, as she recovers her sanity.

As hardly needs to be noted, the initial motif of a love between women is quite novel within sixteenth-century literature. While same-sex attraction between women had been explored in drama and narrative previously, it had tended to be within contexts of mistaken identity, as when Ariosto's Fiordispina falls in love with the female knight Bradamante, believing her to be a man.[84] An example of this within female-authored literature is found in Giulia Bigolina's mid-century romance *Urania*, in which a young woman, Emilia, falls passionately in love with the eponymous protagonist while the latter is disguised as a youth.[85] Even where this model is not followed and a woman is shown to be attracted to a woman or girl not disguised by male clothing, the object of attraction tends to be revealed in the course of the narrative or drama as a young male in female dress.[86] Flori's love for Amaranta, by contrast, is motivated by no such identity confusion. The two nymphs are presented as having known each other from childhood; this is female-female desire in an unmediated form. Nor does there seem much justification within the text for Laura Riccò's reading of Flori's attraction to Amaranta as representing a pure, Neoplatonic desire for "a disembodied, divine beauty," its chastity guaranteed by the sex of the object.[87] While *Flori*'s treatment of desire is as "honest" as we might expect from a writer in Campiglia's position, there is a clear differentiation within the play between Flori's love for Amaranta, represented as terrestrial and corporeally focused, and her more fully spiritualized love for Alessi, the inception of which is made to coincide with her passage from mental sickness to health. The opening scenes of the play show the mad Flori haunting Amaranta's tomb in a manner that aptly symbolizes the deluded state of the earthbound lover in Neoplatonic theory. The message is underlined by the priest Damone, who pityingly reproaches her for having "delighted too much in mortal beauty."[88]

The "revolutionary" character of Campiglia's play is not limited to this unwonted portrayal of a love between women.[89] Flori's second love, for the shepherd-poet Alessi, is similarly disruptive of the norms of the genre. Flori's second *innamoramento* coincides miraculously with her restoration to sanity, following a ritual sacrifice enacted by the pastoral community under the aegis of the priest Damone. At first, the development seems to be ideologically recuperative, with Flori's recovery of her reason coinciding with her restoration to heterosexual "normality" in a ceremony that also celebrates her return to social and confessional integration after a period of marginality and abjection. Things are not so simple, however. As a key scene between Flori and her companion Licori (5.1) reveals, rather than seeing her future as lying in the customary feminine path of marriage, Flori intends to pursue a radical alternative, preserving her virginity and her vows to Diana but conjoining herself with Alessi in a Neoplatonic spiritual union that her bemused interlocutor acknowledges as unique. The scene revises the traditional episode within pastoral in which an older female companion persuades a younger nymph devoted to celibacy of the virtues of love. In *Flori*, Licori takes the role of Talia in Torelli's *Partenia*, urging Flori to abandon the "sterility" of her present freedoms for the emotional and sensual plenitude of marriage and motherhood. Crucially, however, in Campiglia's play Licori's persuasion fails. Not only does Flori remain unpersuaded herself but she succeeds in persuading Alessi to accept her extraordinary proposal and unite with her in chaste partnership as a fellow votary of Diana. In classic Neoplatonic mode, this form of spiritual union is proposed as a nobler alternative to the more earthbound loves of sensual lovers, and Flori ends the play with her *sui generis* solution approved by society and the gods. Although it is cast in the customary neoclassical, paganizing language of pastoral, it is not too difficult to glimpse Christian templates behind Flori's ideal of a celibate spiritual "marriage," notably in the sexless relationship of Mary and Joseph, praised at length by Campiglia in her *Discorso sopra l'annonciatione*.[90]

One factor that needs to be considered in assessing Campiglia's extraordinary treatment of the love theme in *Flori* is her own situation at the time of writing. After the failure of her brief marriage in 1576 to a Vicentine nobleman, Dionisio Colzè, Campiglia had been living as, effectively, a single woman, "in a manner," as one contemporary noted, "quite different from the usual custom of women, to the amazement of all."[91] There is much within the text and outside it to condone a reading of Flori as a figure for the author, not least the fact that "Flori" was the pastoral name used by contemporary poets in her circle to refer to Campiglia, just as Isabella Pallavicino Lupi went by the name "Calisa"; Barbara Torelli, "Talia"; and Muzio Manfredi, "Edreo."[92] Within the play, Flori is clearly presented as a poet, like Campiglia, as is her lover Alessi, whom some textual hints indicate may be a figure for Torquato Tasso.[93] In act 1 Licori recalls Flori's contempt for traditional feminine roles and her ambition instead to excel in literary pursuits, inspired by the precedent of a legendary nymph poet whose description as "VITTORIOSA e DIVA" permits us to identify her as Vittoria Colonna in pastoral guise.[94] Flori's literary ambitions are also foregrounded in a scene in act 5, where she is portrayed as having rejected maternity as her natural feminine destiny, arguing instead that she would be content to see her sole "offspring . . . the things created by [my] divine and rare intellect."[95] In passages such as these, we are clearly intended to make a connection between Flori's intellectual aspirations and her singular life choices, both facets of what Licori characterizes at one point as her tendency "always to race after the impossible."[96] Among other things, then, the play demands to be read as an idealized recasting of Campiglia's own anomalous marital circumstances, which are heroically reworked here as an exemplary vocational choice, enabling her literary career.

Partenia and *Flori* are quite distinctive within the tradition of Italian pastoral in their programmatically unsensual treatment of love. With a play like Miani's *Amorosa speranza,* we return to an erotic world more comparable to Andreini's *Mirtilla,* in that no character starts or ends the play resistant to love or accepting of it only in a sublimated form. As we might expect given her "respectable" status, Miani is less sensual than Andreini in her treatment of the pleasures of love, which, in any case, do not feature particularly saliently in the play by comparison with its pains. The most distinctive feature of the play is the complexity of the emotional situation of its sexually mature heroine, Venelia, who has been abandoned by one man, Damone, and appears to be attracted to two others, Alliseo, ex-suitor of Fulgenzia, and Lucrino, now a priest of Diana. While Damone is absent for most of the play, we see Venelia in emotionally fraught scenes with Alliseo, whose advances she resists out of a sense of honor, and with Lucrino, with whom her relationship appears to be passionate and mutual, if necessarily platonic.[97] The complexity of Venelia's affairs gives *Amorosa speranza* considerable interest, not least because it is so unwonted. Given the strictness of sexual decorum for upper-class women in this period, female authors inevitably tend to play safe in matters of sexual morality; this is a very rare case of a woman in an "irregular" sexual situation being given sympathetic attention in a female-authored narrative or dramatic work.[98] Especially striking, given the preponderantly monogamous —or serial-monogamous—nature of erotic bonds in pastoral, is Venelia's attraction to multiple suitors, captured at one point by her rival Tirenia, who characterizes her as having a "bipartite heart."[99]

The particularity of the love quadrangle sketched around the figure of Venelia in *Amorosa speranza*, along with the author's references in her dedicatory letter to her own "troubled thoughts" and "vexatious cares of the soul," has led Françoise Decroisette to propose that the play should be read as autobiographical.[100] While Decroisette's reasoning is unpersuasive, the possibility cannot be excluded that Miani's plot contains some kind of *à clef* element. The priest Lucrino seems to be identified quite precisely at one point as a Venetian patrician, and Venelia's situation shows intriguing similarities to that of the Trevisan poet Fabrizia Carrari as recounted in an eclogue of 1590, where she complains of her abandonment by a male figure, presumably her husband, to whom she refers using the pastoral name Damone.[101] Since Treviso is only about twenty-five miles from Padua, and fairly close connections existed between the literary circles of the two towns, it does not seem unlikely that Miani would have known of Carrari's story. Whatever the play's possible biographical substrate, however, we also need to bear in mind the tendency within Italian literature in general in this period toward an ever-greater complexity and intricacy of love intrigues, with Guidobaldo Bonarelli's controversial portrayal of a nymph torn between two loves in his *Filli di Sciro* (1607) a notable instance within pastoral drama.[102] Where *Amorosa speranza* is concerned, it must be noted that the emotional complexity generated by the multiple love plots compromises the moral and sentimental logic of the play's genre-mandated happy ending. Venelia ends the play reunited with her treacherous husband, a mere scene after her rapturous reencounter with Lucrino, while Fulgenzia finds herself wedded to a man who loves another and who would apparently have preferred death to marriage with her.

The final play under consideration, Bernardi's *Tragicomedia*, makes an interesting comparison with both *Amorosa speranza* and *Partenia* in its treatment of love. It shares with Miani's play a willingness to engage dramatically with a socially aberrant erotic situation, in this case that of Dalinda, whom we see prepared to defy her father when he attempts to arrange a marriage for her and to elope with her lover instead. Although Bernardi orchestrates events in such a way as to preclude the lovers' physical consummation of the secret marriage they are planning, Dalinda's behavior is clearly morally questionable by the standards of the day. This is underlined by the comment of a sympathetic minor character, Coribante, who describes her elopement as "mad" and "insane."[103] It is noteworthy, in the light of this, that Dalinda is accorded a happy outcome, ending the play on the point of marriage to her beloved

Fillinio, in a manner that implicitly condones her filial disobedience as justified by her fidelity to love. This moral is, indeed, explicitly spelled out in the opening scene in an interesting speech by Fillinio's father, Alfisbeo, who, unaware of his son's part in Dalinda's disappearance, reproaches her father, Alcone, for his harshness in attempting to impose his will on his daughter, when she has made her resistance to the prospect of marriage with Filemone quite clear. It is tempting to read this episode in Bernardi as a polemical response to the episode in Torelli's *Partenia* in which Partenia cedes meekly to a marriage imposed on her by her father. "In all other things, children are subject to their parents," Alfisbeo states, in a *sententia* marked as such in the margin, "but in this, God and Nature have conceded to them liberty to find the match that pleasure and attraction dictate."[104] Dalinda's willingness to assert this primal liberty is contrasted in the play with the filial docility of Filemone, who is punished for his readiness, when faced by the same dilemma, to cede to his father's mandate. His culpability is the greater in that it may be assumed that, as a young man, he is less subject to his father's authority than a young woman might be. As he reproaches himself at one point, "What power could your old father's will have exerted if your own blind will had not bent to another's desire?"[105]

Striking though the detail of Dalinda's resistance to her father's marriage proposals is, the love story about her and Fillinio is otherwise unremarkable, and the two are given little psychological depth. Far more complex and interesting is Bernardi's development of the relationship between Clorilli and Filemone, marked by an extreme hostility on her part that cedes to love only at the end. Bernardi takes her template here from *Aminta*'s similarly dissonant relationship between Silvia and Aminta, but she introduces two significant novelties to Tasso's scenario. First, she considerably complicates her female protagonist's history and character by making Clorilli the betrayed ex-lover of Filemone rather than simply an oblivious object of desire to him, in a manner that helps motivate both her obduracy toward him during the course of the play and her passionate change of heart at the end. Similarly, Filemone is a more complex figure than Aminta, fluctuating between self-justification and despairing self-reproach.

The second major novelty Bernardi introduces into *Aminta*'s love plot is to equip Clorilli not with a single advice-giving female friend, as in Tasso, but two, ideologically opposed ones. While Armilla takes the role of Tasso's Dafne, urging Clorilli to take pity on her languishing lover, another nymph, Licasta, advises her that she is well shot of him, arguing from men's universal duplicity in matters of love. Although the outcome of the play proves Licasta's thesis wrong, in that Filemone shows himself to be an Aminta-like paragon of devotion, her misandrist diatribes, reminiscent of those given to Corinna and Leonora in Moderata Fonte's exactly contemporaneous *Il merito delle donne*, nonetheless constitute a memorable rhetorical tour de force. Striking especially is the lengthy reported speech comparing men's instability and treacherousness to those of a raging sea, attributed to the extradramatic character of Cellia, a figure clearly based on the Ferrarese princess Marfisa d'Este (1553?–1608).[106] Cellia's speech deftly gender-reverses the stereotype of women's mutability, describing men as "a new Proteus," "firm and constant only in their inconstancy."[107] It is intriguing that this same theme of men's unreliability in love features prominently in the recently discovered 1582 Ferrarese pastoral entertainment *Martel d'amore*, scripted by Guarini, in which Marfisa d'Este performed as a member of Margherita Gonzaga's *balletto delle donne*.[108]

Although erotic love is the thematic focus of all five of our pastorals, other affective relationships are not neglected. *Flori*, in particular, pays close attention to the relationship between its two principal female characters, Flori and Licori, who appear together in lengthy and prominent scenes in acts 1, 3, and 5.[109] The two are notably supportive: in act 1 we see Licori faithfully accompanying Flori as she wanders in her love-madness, while in act 5 we see Flori, returned to sanity, engineering Licori's union with her beloved, Androgeo. The loyalty of this female bond is emphasized at the beginning of act 2, where two scenes show Licori and Androgeo's friend Serrano confronted with the classic dilemma of a "duel between friendship and love."[110] More specifically, both Licori and Serrano find themselves love rivals to their friends at a time when these friends are incapacitated by madness and unable to help themselves. Serrano ignobly responds to this challenge by deciding to pursue his own interest at the expense of Androgeo, while Licori struggles successfully with her feelings, concluding that "he little deserves the name of friend who, pretending to serve others, in fact pursues only his own good."[111] This appropriation of the language of perfect friendship in the context of a relationship between women should probably be seen as consciously revisionist, given that the classical and humanistic tradition of *amicitia* had tended to reserve this most morally distinguished of relationships to males. An interesting parallel is offered by an episode in Curzio Gonzaga's chivalric romance, *Il fido amante* (1582), which imitates Virgil's story of Nisus and Euryalus—a *locus classicus* of the literature of male *amicitia*—but places two female characters, Virginia and Costanza, in the roles of Virgil's ill-starred soldier friends.[112] This was a work certainly known to Campiglia, who contributed *argomenti* to its second, 1591 edition. Gonzaga underlines his gender revisionism by comparing his two heroines to other classical exempla of devoted male friends.[113]

While Campiglia is unusual in the self-consciousness with which she approaches the gendering of friendship, she is not alone in placing a supportive female relationship at the heart of her play. Both Valeria Miani and Isabetta Coreglia pick up Campiglia's motif of the nymph who reluctantly finds herself a successful love rival to a female friend whose interests she has at heart. All three plays end with the less-favored friend (Campiglia's Licori, Miani's Fulgenzia, the Corilla of Coreglia's *Dori*) united with her beloved through the offices of her friend. In Andreini's *Mirtilla*, meanwhile, we see the rivalry between Mirtilla and Filli for the love of Uranio amicably resolved when the two nymphs vow friendship irrespective of the outcome of their love.[114] This general rule of supportiveness finds a sole exception in the case of the malicious Tirennia in Miani, who shows herself happy to blacken Venelia's reputation in pursuit of Alliseo's love.

Besides female friendship, another interesting thematic aspect of Campiglia's and Andreini's plays, and to a lesser extent Torelli's, is their use of pastoral fiction to celebrate female artistic creativity. Shepherds in pastoral poetry had traditionally had "song" as one of their primary pastimes, and Renaissance pastoral plays such as *Aminta* featured shepherd-poets who stood as thinly veiled figures for their authors. Torelli, Andreini, and Campiglia all translate this motif into the feminine. Campiglia's characterization of Flori as poet has already been discussed, as has her probable status as a figure for the author. Torelli's *Partenia* contains a parallel figure in the nymph Talia, a secondary character. Again, as in the case of Campiglia/Flori, the name coincides with Torelli's own pastoral *nom de plume*.[115] Talia is figured as poet in one scene in the drama (3.1), where we see her inscribing on a tree the tragic tale of the love of the shepherd Lice, encountered earlier in the play mourning his dead beloved (1.4). Talia, like Tasso's Erminia in the *Gerusalemme liberata*, is also portrayed as acquainted with the science of healing, a knowledge that becomes crucial to the plot when she resuscitates the near-dead Tirsi and

Partenia.[116] Another, later poet-nymph in female-authored pastoral drama is Nerina in Isabetta Coreglia's *Dori* (1634), who shares with Campiglia's Flori her attachment to a celibate life: in one scene she is figured as having abandoned love to enjoy "dear liberty in the shadow of the laurel."[117]

In the plays of Torelli and Campiglia, female creativity is figured for the most part in literary terms, although Campiglia incorporates a compliment to two female musical *virtuose* associated with the Accademia Olimpica, and she has Flori and Alessi lead their companions in singing rounds of compliments to her patrons in the last act.[118] Andreini goes much further in portraying her lead nymphs in the guise of performers when, in one of *Mirtilla*'s most striking scenes, she has the love rivals Mirtilla and Filli engage in a singing contest modeled on that in Virgil's third eclogue between Menalcas and Damoetas.[119] The wit and brilliance of the scene is already apparent on the page, but the contest's display of female virtuosity must have been greatly enhanced in performance, especially if, as has been conjectured, the two roles were played by Andreini and her fellow actress Vittoria Piissimi, translating into the fiction of a love rivalry the two women's rivalry in their art.[120] Besides its dramatic function within the play, the scene contributes vitally to Andreini's self-positioning in *Mirtilla* as both actress and poet, as heir to the "high" tradition of Virgil and simultaneously as a matchless exponent of a modern improvisatory performance tradition. Although the exchanges between Mirtilla and Filli are obviously scripted, the dramatic fiction obviously demands that we perceive them as improvised; as in Virgil, written poetry presents itself in the guise of spontaneous "song." In *Mirtilla*, however, a further dimension is added to the scene by the fact that Andreini is herself a celebrated improviser: literate poet and Arcadian nymph-singer here miraculously coincide.

In addition to her creativity, another interesting characteristic of the nymph figure as crafted in female-authored pastoral drama is the forcefulness and self-assertion that frequently describe her. Torelli is an exception in this regard, portraying Partenia as a traditionally feminine figure, defined by her deference to paternal authority and expressing her strength of mind through the conventionally feminine virtues of self-abnegation and endurance in the face of suffering. As noted above, Bernardi's more assertive Dalinda may perhaps be read as a direct critical response to this representation. Like Bernardi, Campiglia, Andreini, and Miani tend toward active and "virile" models for their nymph characters, although their emphases differ, and a distinction may usefully be made, especially in Campiglia and Andreini, between leading figures such as Flori and Filli and minor characters such as the narcissistic Urania and Ardelia, who are cast in a more conventionally feminine mold.

Andreini's Filli is seen at her most obviously empowered in a scene in act 3 in which she foils the attack of a satyr intent on assailing her virtue and takes a playfully sadistic revenge on him: feigning a reciprocal attraction to him, she binds his hands on the pretext that she wishes to kiss him without fear of being crushed by his embrace and then takes the opportunity to tear his beard while apparently raising herself to his height to kiss him and makes him consume bitter aloe disguised as breath-freshening herbs.[121] A similar episode is found in Miani's *Amorosa speranza*, although there the nymph-satyr encounter is spread over two scenes. In the first, the nymph Tirenia tricks the aged satyr Elliodoro into climbing a tree to recover a lost arrow for her, then ties his feet to a branch "for security" and leaves him to his fate. In a later scene, Elliodoro seeks revenge on Tirenia, but she is rescued by a band of shepherds, whose leader, Isandro, her future lover, then binds Elliodoro and leaves him in her hands.[122] Tirenia takes the opportunity for revenge that is reminiscent of Andreini's Filli, though with the element of symbolic castration already implicit in Filli's beard-plucking still more emphatic: besides cutting off Elliodoro's beard entirely, Tirenia also tears off a horn.[123]

As critics have noted, Andreini's and Miani's handling of these scenes are particularly interesting when compared with preceding versions of the satyr-nymph encounter in male-authored pastoral literature.[124] This is especially clear when the point of comparison is the relevant scene in Tasso's *Aminta*, which has the nymph Silvia trapped by a satyr, stripped naked, and tied to a tree, finally to be rescued from her threatened rape by Aminta. For a figure first encountered as a fearless huntress whose greatest pleasure is "fighting strong beasts to the ground," there is an undoubted element of misogynistic *contrapasso* in this reduction of Silvia to the state of quiveringly naked sexual prey.[125] Viewed against Tasso's model, Andreini's rewriting of the nymph-satyr relationship is clearly transformative in a profeminist sense, emphasizing not the nymph's vulnerability but her quick-wittedness and capacity to master brute strength by intelligence, a lesson that Andreini's physical grace and agility would doubtless have made still more compelling on stage. Miani's version also has Tirenia initially handling the satyr herself, and even though in the later reprise of the scene she is saved by a shepherd, the element of sexual humiliation of the nymph so central to Tasso's treatment of the episode is absent.

Interesting though Andreini's and Miani's versions of the nymph-satyr scene are, however, it would be inaccurate to represent their solutions as unique within the genre tradition. Nymphs are found tricking satyrs who attempt to assault them in what is often considered the earliest prototype for pastoral drama, Agostino Beccari's *Il sacrificio* (1555), which had been revived for performance in 1587 and received a new print edition in Ferrara in the same year.[126] Beccari's version of the device is particularly close to Miani's, in that he shows a nymph, Stellinia, first tricking the satyr and then being tricked by him and captured, only to be rescued by a shepherd.[127] Another likely source for Miani is Francesco Contarini's *Fida ninfa*, published in her hometown of Padua in 1598, a telling coincidence here being that Miani, like Contarini, supplies her satyr with a satyress wife.[128] Aside from Beccari and Contarini, other male-authored plays that show nymphs tricking satyrs include Leone de' Sommi's *Irifile* (c. 1570) and Guarini's *Pastor fido*, both probably known to Andreini when she was writing *Mirtilla* even though they were unpublished at the time.[129] What seems most novel in Andreini and Miani is the emphasis they place on the satyr's physical humiliation by the nymph, a detail that in Andreini seems to derive directly from the *commedia d'arte* tradition of physical farce.[130] Although the tone and treatment are quite different, the gendered dynamic of the victim turned avenger recalls that of Ariosto's Marganorre story—famously adapted for performance by the actress Flaminia Romana in the 1560s—in which the regime of a misogynist tyrant is overturned by his female victims.[131] Miani's emphasis on the satyr's advanced age brings her version close, as well, to the classic comedic stereotype of the humiliation of the *senex* who presumes to fall in love.[132]

The kind of broad physical comedy Andreini and Miani wring from their satyr episodes has no place in the decorous universe of Campiglia, Torelli, and Bernardi, and it is perhaps unsurprising that none of the three authors makes a great deal of the *de rigueur* satyr scene. Torelli is the most extreme in this regard, keeping her satyr figure, Cromi, to two solo scenes, in which he meditates assaults on Partenia that are thwarted in the event by her flight.[133] Both Campiglia and Bernardi, by contrast, do feature scenes staging attacks on their heroines. These are relatively brief, however, and only in Bernardi is the satyr's sexual intent made explicit, in an ironic monologue in which he justifies his intended rape of Clorilli with reference to the precedent of Jove: "Is this not the way of great men?"[134]

In both Bernardi and Campiglia the resolution of the satyr scene follows the damsel-in-distress model familiar from *Aminta*, in which the threatened nymph is rescued by a shepherd, whether her spurned lover (following Tasso, Campiglia gives the role to Androgeo) or her long-lost brother (Bernardi uses the device to introduce Fillinio for the first time). This motif of the gallant male hero rescuing the female clearly aligns with conventional stereotypes of male strength and female weakness, but the conventionality of these authors' handling of this particular scene cannot be regarded as representative of their construction of gender identities as a whole. For example, Campiglia's Flori reveals her virility as a character in her intellectual domination of the events of the play following her recovery of her sanity in act 3. Striking in particular in this regard are the long scenes in act 5 in which we see her dictating the terms not only of her own Neoplatonic union with Alessi but also of Androgeo's marriage to Licori.[135] Noteworthy here are the relative passivity of both male figures and the freedom with which the female characters make their decisions: while Licori defers her formal consent until she has received the approval of her father, Melampo, it is Flori whom we see on stage in practice arranging the match at the request of her friend.[136] A further interesting feature of these scenes is the equality of the love relationship outside marriage that Flori establishes with Alessi: if she defers to him fondly as her "king" and "leader," he quickly reverses the compliment and hails her as his "queen."[137]

The play of strength and virility between the sexes is developed in an especially interesting way by Leonora Bernardi in her *Tragicomedia*, which is unusual within female-authored pastoral in the degree of its imaginative investment in its male protagonist, Filemone. Bernardi imitates from *Aminta*, though in a less sexualized context, the notion of love as a testing ground for manhood. Just as Tasso's Tirsi urges Aminta to show himself "a man, a bold man" by taking his sexual opportunity with Silvia, Bernardi's more decorous erotic counselor figure, Coribante, upbraids Filemone for his "unvirile" lachrymosity and advises that if he cannot win Clorilli's love, he should return her disdain with disdain and hence recover his lost "manliness and strength."[138] Masculinity is here defined as emotional self-mastery and self-sufficiency, while dependency and subjection figure as marks of effeminacy. Ironically, by this measure the character in the play who best fits the moral profile of masculinity is Clorilli, who has responded to Filemone's earlier rejection in precisely the "virile" manner recommended by Coribante. First plunged into despair by his abandonment, as we learn from her own confession, she later exchanges this for a stance of scorn, which she clearly experiences as empowering: she speaks at one point of "recovering her original freedom," something Coribante vainly urges Filemone to embrace.[139]

Bernardi's dialectical characterization of Filemone and Clorilli through their different responses to the experience of erotic rejection demands to be placed in the context of the fashionable late sixteenth-century lyric motif of "amorous scorn." This had notable currency within musical madrigal culture in the 1580s, featuring in two madrigal anthologies, *I lieti amanti* (1586) and *Sdegnosi ardori* (1587), the latter comprising settings of a famous poetic exchange between Guarini and Tasso in the voice of two parting lovers expressing mutual indifference and disdain.[140] Anger as a response to amorous rejection offered poets a refreshing alternative to the more hackneyed Petrarchizing reactions of despair and abjection, allowing an energized portrayal of the newly freed lover, "happy outside the amorous bind."[141]

Sdegno as a response to rejection in love tended to be gendered as masculine, and the theme was sometimes developed in an implicitly misogynistic manner. Francesco Bracciolini's pastoral *Amoroso sdegno,* for example, first published in 1597 but written about 1590–91, shows a recalcitrant nymph, Clori, brought to heel by a display of righteous anger from her previously docile and adoring lover, Acrisio. Acrisio's love counselor, Urania, advises him on this subterfuge, arguing essentially from women's irrationality in love.[142] Bernardi's development of the motif is revisionist, in that it attributes the conventionally male position to her female protagonist, while showing her male protagonist incapable of maintaining a response of *amoroso sdegno* even when he believes himself to have been displaced by a rival.[143] In one of the ironies in which the play abounds, moreover, it is Filemone's despised "feminine" affect of hapless subjection to love that is ultimately vindicated, while Clorilli's "virile" scorn almost leads her to drive her faithful lover to his death, to her eternal guilt and despair. The basic emotional plot here is that of *Aminta,* Bernardi's model, in which Aminta's similar invincible devotion to Silvia is similarly rewarded, but Bernardi's reconfiguring of the Silvia character in Clorilli gives her treatment of the theme greater complexity and depth.

In addition to their pastoral dramas, Maddalena Campiglia and Isabella Andreini both also experimented with the related genre of pastoral eclogue, pioneered for women writers by Laura Battiferra. Campiglia's eclogue, *Calisa*, published in 1589 in two slightly different versions, celebrates the marriage of Giovanni Paolo Meli-Lupi (1571–1642), son of Isabella Pallavicino Lupi, with the Paduan noblewoman Beatrice Obizzi (d. 1590).[144] Despite its brevity, *Calisa* is a work of considerable interest, and one that has attracted quite a degree of critical attention, especially for its treatment of the theme of female-female desire. *Calisa* is structured as a dialogue between two figures, Flori (Campiglia) and Edreo (Muzio Manfredi). It opens with Edreo alone, speaking of his displeasure with his friend Flori over a series of love lyrics that she has carved on trees in praise of a female love object. He then announces that he has resolved to use his powers of persuasion to talk her out of her "vain and unhappy love," which he characterizes as against nature.[145] Flori appears, rapt in thought, and admits to her anomalous love ("I know that I, a woman, love a woman"), defending herself with reference to the irresistible power of Eros; eventually, however, she identifies the object of her desire as "Calisa," the pastoral name of Isabella Pallavicino.[146] This explanation seems to assuage Edreo's concerns, and the poem concludes with the two amicably singing of the forthcoming wedding of Calisa's son.

One detail in *Calisa* that deserves notice is that it attests to a body of lyric verse by Campiglia that has not come down to us, which seems from the evidence here to have celebrated Isabella Pallavicino using the language of pastoralized Petrarchan love.[147] Unusually for such verse addressed to a patron, there is a hint in *Calisa* that the poetic relationship may have been reciprocal, in that there is an allusion to a reply poem from Calisa.[148] Another interesting feature of *Calisa* is the insouciant manner in which Campiglia negotiates the scandal that her depiction of female-female desire in *Flori* appears to have occasioned in her literary circle. Traces of this may be found in the laudatory sonnets that accompanied the play in an appendix: Prospero Cattaneo expresses surprise at this "strange, contrary, and unwonted turn of nature," while Manfredi himself warns that "no woman feels for a woman what Flori felt for Amaranta."[149]

One way of reading *Calisa* within this context is as a palinode to the Flori-Amaranta episode in *Flori*, domesticating the play's courageous depiction of same-sex desire between women by re-presenting it in a more socially acceptable guise, as a metaphor for Campiglia's literary courtship of Pallavicino. This would be to deny, however, the teasing quality of the eclogue, which shows Flori deliberately stoking Edreo's moral outrage before offering him the palliative of the identification of her beloved. Similarly, at a metaliterary level, by encouraging an identification between the author and her homonym within the play, Campiglia teases her contemporary readership by inviting speculation about her sexuality at the same time that she appears to be reassuringly "explaining away" her deployment of the language of female-female desire. The high-mindedness and occasional solemnity of a work like *Flori* should not be allowed to obscure the more playful components in Campiglia's literary persona. Unusually for a female poet, she participated in the comic tradition of dialect verse that thrived in the Veneto in this period, and more remarkably still, especially for a woman in her precarious social position, she was happy in 1592 to sign the dedicatory letter to Curzio Gonzaga's distinctly scurrilous comedy *Gli Inganni*.[150] Despite its blandly courtly encomiastic surface, there is a provocative quality to *Calisa,* a proud reassertion of the "singularity" and defiance of convention that were such key elements in Campiglia's poetic persona and that find emblematic expression in the Vicenza edition of the poem in an engraving of a phoenix, a species unto itself.[151]

Isabella Andreini's nine pastoral eclogues, published in her *Rime* of 1601, depart entirely from the autobiographical *à clef* model exemplified by Campiglia and, before her, Battiferra. Andreini's eclogues are purely fictional exercises, showcasing her fluency of invention and skills in dramatic ventriloquism. They vary in form, with some effectively dramatic monologues— Coridone's lament over his frustrated love for Nigella in eclogue 5 *(Nigella)* and the shepherd-poet Mopso's similarly disgruntled complaint about the "ungrateful" Clori in eclogue 6 *(Clori)*—and others more dialogic, such as the spirited love combat in eclogue 2 *(Amaranta)* between the enamored Selvaggio and the unresponsive Amaranta. The latter is of interest in relation to pastoral drama for its staging of the classic character type of a nymph recalcitrant to love and devoted instead to her "dear liberty" and the thrills of the hunt. Especially witty here is Andreini's attribution to Amaranta of a speech on the fugacity of female beauty, generally employed in pastoral drama as an argument in persuading nymphs to abandon their resistance to love but here adduced by Amaranta as a reason for embracing chastity, as more enduring than love.[152]

Also of thematic interest, specifically in relation to *Mirtilla*, is the lyric eclogue 8 *(Mirtillo)*, a hymn to the power of love, viewed in quasi-Lucretian terms as the motive power of the created universe.[153] The poem might almost be read as a philosophically inflected gloss on the celebratory and sensually accepting conception of love that informs the earlier drama. In structural terms, it is interesting to note that several of Andreini's more dialogic eclogues include elements of described or implied action, which suggests that they may have been composed as short performance texts, to be inserted as *intermezzi* within longer dramas. *Amaranta* ends with the female speaker fleeing, pursued by her importunate lover, while eclogue 3 *(Incantesimo)* stages a scene of love magic, and the longer eclogue 9 *(Galatea)* constitutes a virtual miniature pastoral drama, complete with the attempted suicide of a lovesick shepherd and his rescue.[154]

A pastoral eclogue by a far less well known female author deserves brief mention in conclusion: Fabrizia Carrari's *Zefiro torna, e la stagion novella*, published in a 1590 collection of verse published in her hometown of Treviso in praise of Count Antonio Collalto on the occasion of his election to the prestigious administrative post of collateral-general of the Venetian army.[155] Carrari's eclogue is on the *à clef* model practiced by Battiferra and Campiglia, in which the author figures herself among the speakers. Here Carrari figures under her academic name, "Boscareccia," itself a statement of her allegiance to the pastoral mode, in that *boschereccio* (lit. "of the woods") was a virtual synonym of *pastorale* in literary terms. Boscareccia's interlocutors, Florinda and Filiria, are also figured as poets, as is a fourth female poet-nymph, Amaranta, clearly from Treviso or its region, in that she is described as having sung Collalto's virtues "on the left bank of this river" (presumably the Sile).[156] If we can assume that these names too conceal the identities of real figures, Carrari's eclogue attests intriguingly to a community of female poets seemingly relatively well integrated in the local male literary culture: Boscareccia speaks familiarly of a male shepherd-poet, Coridone, and makes reference to the Accademia degli Cospiranti, of which Carrari's brother Silvestro was a member.[157] Published two years after Campiglia's *Flori* in nearby Vicenza and not long before the composition of Miani's *Amorosa speranza* in nearby Padua, Carrari's eclogue offers further testimony both to the exceptional environment the mainland Veneto constituted for women's writing in this period and to the way in which the imaginative world of pastoral enabled the construction of female writerly identities in these years.[158] As noted above, it may also supply a key to an *à clef* reading of Miani's play, in that Boscareccia refers lamentingly at the opening of the poem to her Venelia-like abandonment by "Damone."[159]

3. The Challenge of Tragedy: Valeria Miani's *Celinda*

When Valeria Miani published what was to prove the sole tragedy by an Italian woman of the early modern period in Padua in 1611, almost a quarter-century had passed since the pastorals of Campiglia and Andreini placed female-authored secular drama on public view. Miani's boldness in making the transition from pastoral to tragedy should not be underestimated. Pastoral could be modestly, if disingenuously, figured as a simple, rustic form and hence suitable to a writer unsure of her talents. Tragedy, by contrast, was, along with epic, one of the noblest of genres, dealing exclusively with the deeds of kings and heroes and heir to a distinguished classical tradition. The framing of Miani's tragedy, *Celinda,* also suggests an enhanced degree of self-assurance compared with her earlier *Amorosa speranza*. While the pastoral's dedicatee was a private Paduan gentlewoman, Marietta Descalzi Uberti (d. 1642), and the play was prefaced merely by three poems by anonymous authors, the tragedy was dedicated to the Duchess of Mantua, Eleonora de' Medici Gonzaga, and was accompanied by poems by seven named authors, including, intriguingly, the Genoese poet Gaspare Murtola (1570–?1624), famed for his polemics with, and attempted assassination of, Marino.[160] While Miani's chorus of poetic admirers does not have quite the mass of the team of twenty-seven celebrants Maddalena Campiglia had summoned in 1588 to accompany her *Flori,* her showing in *Celinda* was still an impressive one, especially in terms of geographic range. Besides Murtola, the contributors include two other Rome-based *letterati,* Fabio Leonida and Arrigo Falconio, the latter a friend and correspondent of Marino's, the former a neo-Latin poet who would later attain some fame within the literary entourage of Urban VIII.[161] A further contributor, "il Cavalier Vanni," is probably the Sienese painter Francesco Vanni (1563–1610), who spent significant portions of his career in Rome and was made a papal knight by Pope Clement VIII.[162]

Although *Celinda* is the only surviving tragedy by a woman of this period, it may not have been the only one written. A sonnet by Angelo Grillo records a late work by Maddalena Campiglia on the theme of Saint Barbara, which he describes as a "tragico carme."[163] If this was, as seems likely, a *tragedia spirituale,* then it is a relevant precedent for Miani, whose hometown, Padua, was only about twenty miles from Campiglia's Vicenza and whose *Amorosa speranza* shows an awareness of Campiglia's *Flori.* More generally, the first decade of the Seicento represents something of a high point in women's engagement with previously "male" genres: Lucrezia Marinella published the first female-authored pastoral romance, *Arcadia felice*, in 1605, and a pirated edition of Margherita Sarrocchi's epic *La Scanderbeide* appeared in 1606. Although there is evidence that Miani was already working on her tragedy by 1598, it is possible that these precedents emboldened her to publish *Celinda* and her publisher, Francesco Bolzetta, to take it on. That Miani and Bolzetta knew of *Arcadia felice* seems very likely, given that Marinella was living in Padua from 1607.[164] The fact that *Celinda* and *Arcadia felice* share a dedicatee, Eleonora de' Medici Gonzaga, seems suggestive on this score. It seems quite likely, as well, that Miani knew of Sarrocchi's epic, given the Roman contacts attested by the prefatory poems to *Celinda*. Both Leonida and Falconio moved in the circles of the Accademia deglia Umoristi, to which Sarrocchi belonged.[165]

At the time of *Celinda*'s appearance the genre of tragedy enjoyed a curious status in Italy.[166] As a literary genre, it was flourishing, having received new impetus in the 1570s and 1580s from the work of playwrights such as Luigi Groto (*Dalida* [1572] and *Hadriana* [1578]) and Torquato Tasso (*Torrismondo* [1587]). Between 1590 and 1611, when *Celinda* was published, about sixty new tragedies were published in Italy, mainly still secular and classicizing in their subject matter, though a dozen or so were within the newer, Counter-Reformation tradition of the *tragedia spirituale*.[167] In Miani's Padua, famous within the history of the genre in Italy for Sperone Speroni's controversial incest tragedy, *Canace* (1542), the principal tragedians active in the period were Claudio Forzatè (1550–1610), author of the tragedy *Recinda*, first published in 1592 and reprinted in 1609 following a revival for performance, and Cortese Cortesi, author of *Giustina*, a *tragedia spirituale*.[168] Even though tragedy was flourishing on the page, however, its place in performance culture was languishing, according to the analysis of the drama theorist Angelo Ingegneri, in part because of the intrinsic melancholy of the spectacle, which deterred "the eye desirous of delight" and was perceived by some as an ill augury, and in part because of the extreme costliness of mounting a spectacle that sought to represent the grandeur of a royal palace on stage.[169] Pastoral could rival tragedy in the elevation of its language and sentiments, while undercutting it significantly in terms of cost. From the first decade of the seventeenth century, moreover, the new genre of the *dramma per musica* competed with both pastoral and tragedy for princely sponsors' attention. Tragedy thus remained something of an orphan within Italian dramatic culture and perhaps to a degree within literary culture, in which, despite the achievements of dramatists such as Speroni, Tasso, Lodovico Dolce (1508–68), Giambattista Giraldi Cinzio (1504–73), and Pomponio Torelli (1539–1608), the genre was not felt yet to have attained the heights it had reached in the classical world. Ingegneri relates in the preface to his own tragedy, *Tomiri* (1607), an allegory devised by a Tuscan wit in which the various literary genres, figured as ladies at a dance, are invited to stand up by various "suitors." Satire accepts the hand of Ariosto, epic that of Tasso, lyric that of Petrarch, and so on. Tragedy, however, remains seated, an appropriate Italian *principe azzurro* not having yet come.[170]

Perhaps in part because of this somewhat ambiguous status, in the last two decades of the sixteenth century tragedy in Italy became increasingly porous to influences from other genres, particularly pastoral and romance. Love featured increasingly as central to tragic plots, and the setting of tragedy frequently migrated from its traditional locus in classical Greece or Rome to more exotic "romance" locations in Scandinavia, North Africa, or the East.[171] At the same time, wholly invented plots increased in popularity, challenging the dominance of the plots from myth or classical history that Aristotelian purists preferred. This romanticization of tragedy may in part have been a concession to the perceived tastes of a feminine audience, to which Italian tragedy tended to reach out, in any case, through its marked preference for female protagonists.[172] It may have been this, in part, that encouraged Valeria Miani in her engagement with the genre. Certainly, *Celinda* fits precisely the model of the early seventeenth-century *romanzo tragediato* in terms of subject matter (invented), setting (temporally remote and geographically exotic), and plot (vicissitudes occasioned by love).[173]

The plot of *Celinda* is as follows: Autilio, son of Fulco, king of Persia, has fallen in love from afar with Celinda, princess of Lydia. To be close to his love, he has come to Ephesus in the guise of a female slave, "Lucinia," and contrived to have himself sold into Celinda's service. Celinda, attracted to "Lucinia," engages in erotic play with her, in the course of which Autilio reveals his masculine identity. The two become lovers, and at the opening of the play, Celinda is already pregnant with his child. Meanwhile, apprised by an oracle that his son is being held in Lydia, Fulco has led a vast Persian army to the gates of Ephesus, threatening war if Celinda's father, Cubo, does not release him. Having allowed a search, Cubo is disinclined to make further compromises, and the two nations appear set on a path to war. At the beginning of act 2, Cubo unexpectedly reveals his own love for Lucinia-Autilio, whom he intends to marry and make his queen. "Lucinia" succeeds in temporizing and begs him to allow her to prove her merit by fighting, Amazon-style, at his side. Cubo permits this after she proves her fighting skills by defeating a Spartan suitor of Celinda's in a joust. The war commences at the beginning of act 4, and Celinda, in despair, is narrowly prevented from committing suicide. She is heartened when the Lydian captain Alcandro brings back two high-ranking Persian prisoners whom Autilio-Lucinia has defeated in battle. Act 5, however, predictably brings disaster when a messenger brings word of the defeat of the Lydian army and the fatal wounding of Autilio-Lucinia at the hands of his father. The dying man is brought back to the palace, where, as Celinda mourns over him, a Persian envoy brings a grisly tribute of war from King Fulco in the form of Cubo's severed head, heart, and hands. Fulco then arrives to seek his son, only to find him close to death. Penitent, he announces his intent to cede Lydia to Celinda and to recognize her unborn child as heir to his own kingdom. Despite this concession, however, and in denial of Autilio's own dying wishes, Celinda shows herself intent on following her lover to the grave, and the play ends with an account of her suicide.

As we might expect given the highly codified character of tragedy as a genre in Italy, much in Miani's play is dictated by tradition. *Celinda* opens, as was conventional in later sixteenth- and early seventeenth-century works, with a scene spoken by a vengeful ghost, in this case that of Autilio's abandoned fiancée, Eusina, who killed herself in grief after his departure from Persia.[174] Celinda is paired, as was conventional, with a nurse figure, to whom she confides her troubles; while Cubo is paired with a wise counselor, whose advice he ignores.[175] As was standard in Italian tragedies, following classical norms, most action takes place offstage and is conveyed through narration. The "Senecan" taste for gore so apparent in the tragedy of the era is indulged in the episode of Fulco's gift to Cubo's daughter of his severed and gouged remains. The treatment of the tragic business is less distinctive than the romance backstory of the love of Autilio and Celinda, particularly the treatment of their early relationship and the development and consummation of their love. This is narrated by Celinda to her nurse in a scene of remarkable vividness and emotional intensity, certainly the strongest in the play.[176]

Despite the originality of certain details, precedents did exist within contemporary tragedy for Miani's Autilio plot. The romance motifs of *amour de loin* and the disguised lover are found, for example, in Leonoro Verlato's *Rodopeia* (1582), which has its royal hero feign the persona of a gardener to be close to his royal beloved.[177] Cross-dressing had been introduced into tragedy as early as Giraldi Cinzio's chivalrously themed *Arrenopia* (1563) and was used as a device in a number of late sixteenth-century plays, such as Gabriele Zinani's *Almerigo* (1590) and Niccolò degli Angeli's *Arsinoe* (1594).[178] Generally, however, the cross-dressing character was a young woman, as in the two plays just cited, rather than a young man, as in *Celinda*. Miani's most likely source for the plot device of the transvestite boy who seduces a woman in his adopted household is a *novella* by Agnolo Firenzuola (1493–1543) included in his *Prose* (1548) and his *Ragionamenti* (1552).[179] The *novella* tells of a young man, Fulvio, who disguises himself as a servant girl to gain access to his beloved Lavinia's house, where he subsequently becomes an object of desire to Lavinia's husband. The plot coincides quite closely with Miani's, and the likelihood of an influence is increased by the similarity of the assumed names of the young men in the two cases: Lucia in Firenzuola, Lucinia in Miani.

One interesting feature of Miani's Autilio plot is the way in which it is used to explore, though obliquely, the theme of female-female sexual desire. Celinda's confession of her love to her nurse makes clear that her sexual interest in Lucinia was aroused when she believed her to be a young woman. Indeed, it is precisely her physical seduction attempt on her slave, and particularly her repeated attempts to fondle her breasts, that makes it impossible for the timid and respectful Autilio to continue to hide his identity. Miani's venture into the territory of female-female desire in *Celinda* obviously invites comparison with Maddalena Campiglia's more direct but less sexualized treatment of the same theme two decades earlier in *Flori*. Both are unusual within the general conspectus of treatments of female-female desire in Italian Renaissance literature in that the desire in question is not based on one protagonist's having mistaken the other for a man.[180] Especially striking in Miani's version is the pervasive aura of gender ambiguity surrounding the figure of Lucinia-Autilio, even though we are informed of his biological sex from the start of the play. We first encounter Autilio as a boy masquerading as a girl, but beginning in act 3, when he cuts his hair and dons armor, we see him instead as a boy masquerading as a girl enacting the "masculine" role of knight. Celinda frequently refers to him as Lucinia, even in soliloquy, and compares him admiringly to the Amazons and Bellona after watching him joust. His looks too are feminine, to the extent that the incongruously lyrical Lydian general Alcandro rhapsodizes that his "lovely face revealed the beauties of Venus among the horrors of Mars."[181]

Aside from this play across boundaries of sex difference and heteronormativity, Celinda's story is of interest within Italian female-authored fiction and drama as a rare case of a sympathetic portrayal of a woman in a sexually irregular position. In this it invites comparison with Miani's portrayal of her heroine Venelia in *Amorosa speranza* as a seduced and abandoned wife or mistress. Celinda is in a similar position, although her lover, unlike Venelia's, is faithful: she speaks of Autilio as her husband, and they have clearly pledged an informal troth, yet she nevertheless suffers shame at the thought of her "amorous crime" and is acutely aware of its implications for her honor.[182] That Miani twice chose to place at the center of a play such a relatively audacious sexual scenario is one of her greatest sources of interest as a writer. Her choice in *Celinda* is particularly interesting when we consider that such subject matter was not forced on her by her choice of genre. Although Renaissance tragedy plots were often driven by illicit sex, this was not a compulsory feature of the genre, and with the rise of the *tragedia sacra* in the late sixteenth century it had become still easier to avoid. The heroines of the spiritual tragedies of the early Seicento frequently were virtuous Old Testament heroines such as Judith or, still more frequently, early Christian virgin martyrs. Padua offered a recent successful example in Cortesi's *Giustina*, which told the story of a legendary fourth-century virgin martyr who was the city's patron saint. It may be that rather than having been forced onto the difficult ground of illicit sex by her ambition to write a tragedy, Miani chose to write a tragedy at least in part because of the opportunity it offered to deal with such material within a context that allowed for moral complexity in its handling, while offering the safety net of a punitive ending that saw social propriety in some sense restored.

Even by the standards of its genre, which are alien in many respects to modern tastes, Miani's *Celinda* cannot be said to be an artistic success. In addition to the lapses in verisimilitude presented by Cubo's decision to make a slave girl his queen and by Lucinia's revelation of her hitherto unsuspected warrior prowess, there are quite grave structural problems. *Celinda* loses tragic momentum in acts 2 and 3, occupied by the dramatically inert subplot of Cubo's love for Lucinia, while the Aristotelian requisite of unity of place precludes development of the character of King Fulco, potentially the most compelling tragic figure of the play. Perhaps more crucially, the human decisions that lead to the disaster of the dénouement seem significantly undermotivated, something fact that the play's sporadic references to fate and the will of the gods do not do a great deal to redress. Autilio and Celinda seem prepared to let their two nations go to war essentially out of fear of exposing a sexual shame that was due, in any case, shortly to come to light through her pregnancy.[183] Both are of the same royal status and unmarried, and there seems no suggestion of a preexisting feud between their dynasties that would have prevented their marriage in the event of a confession. We are not in the fully star-crossed territory of couples such as Boccaccio's Ghismonda and Guiscardo or Luigi da Porto's Romeo and Giulietta, both of whom had served as the inspiration for late sixteenth-century tragedies that may well have been among Miani's sources.[184] Celinda's suicide is also morally problematic, compared with the clearer-cut cases of Giulietta's and Ghismonda's, since in killing herself she is also killing her and Autilio's unborn child, against the express wishes of her dead lover. Nor is the future she and her child face if they live one of shame or servitude, since Fulco has agreed to restore her to rule.[185]

The question of Celinda's seemingly under- or ill-motivated suicide is worth pursuing, since it can lead us to some interesting considerations. On one level, of course, her death is mandated by the moral logic whereby a sexually transgressive woman must be punished for her transgression, if only for didactic-exemplary reasons. To allow Celinda to end the play alive and free, if traumatized by the deaths of her father and husband, may have appeared to Miani morally unacceptable on this score. Beyond this, however, Miani appears to be using the character of Celinda in the play to dismantle the classicizing tragic character type of the strong woman whose moral strength is displayed in suicide.[186] Celinda's suicide seems rather to be motivated by the weakness that is her most salient character trait throughout the play. In the course of the piece, we see Celinda upbraided by her nurse, by her father, and ultimately by Autilio himself on his deathbed for her failure to live up to the ideal of magnanimity that Miani's culture admired in women of her high status.[187] The timorousness and despondency with she meets danger, typically "feminine" traits, would be acceptable in a woman of the people, but in a princess and a tragic protagonist they are shameful. As Tasso argues in his 1580s *Discorso della virtù femminile e donnesca,* women of high status participated in the male, rather than the female, system of virtues and could thus decorously display the same moral virility as their male peers.[188] Celinda throughout the play refuses this rhetoric of *virtù donnesca*, to use Tasso's term. It is her acknowledged lack of strength—she refers at one point to her "weak heart"—that seems eventually to motivate her suicide, when Autilio has urged her, in a stoically inflected speech, to steel herself to life without him.[189] In this regard, despite its apparent conventionality, *Celinda* may be seen as a revisionist work, implicitly critiquing the classicizing morality so widespread in Renaissance tragedy that had glorified suicide—a sin in Christian terms—as a heroic moral choice.[190]

Can *Celinda* also be read as revisionist in terms of gender, specifically in regard to the Renaissance ideal of the *femme forte*? That certainly seems to be a possibility that we should consider, however accustomed we are as modern readers to seeking feminist messages in female-authored texts. The self-declaredly weak Celinda is paired in the play with a conventional image of virile femininity in Lucinia, who defies Aristotelian gender norms and humiliates male adversaries in the classic manner of the Renaissance female knight.[191] Here, however, Lucinia's seemingly miraculous virility is of course explained by her biological maleness, to which we are privy from the start of the play. Female writers such as Moderata Fonte had used the figure of the female knight ideologically to argue for women's capacity, given the appropriate educational opportunities, to match the achievements of men.[192] At least with respect to the key physical and moral attribute of fortitude, Miani's *Celinda* seems implicitly to argue the opposite: where a woman appears in the fiction of the play to manifest the fortitude of a warrior, this turns out to be an optical illusion, while the "true" woman at the heart of the play is neither physically strong nor possessed of fortitude in the psychological or moral sense. The gender attitudes in *Celinda* are perhaps best seen as the product of an age in which the *bien-pensant* profeminism that had triumphed in the polite literature of the sixteenth century was under new threat from a resurgent misogyny. Most female authors of the period remained faithful to profeminist positions, but this was not an immutable law.[193]

Ultimately, perhaps, what *Celinda* demonstrates is simply the difficulty that the figure of the sexually transgressive woman represented for female authors of this period. A male author such as Boccaccio could admiringly portray a forthright sexualized heroine such as Ghismonda without censure. Even a Counter-Reformation male author such as Pomponio Torelli, in his more attenuated portrayal of Ghismonda in *Tancredi* (1597), still portrays her quite explicitly as an exemplum of the heights to which "female valor" might attain.[194] For female authors attentive to their extraliterary reputation, such imaginative identification with a "sullied" woman was far more problematic, except in the special case of Mary Magdalene, the depth of whose penitence for her past transgressions absolved her. To figure strength in a sexually transgressive woman, in particular, is likely to have been especially problematic; interestingly, Miani's Celinda at one point makes a connection between the loss of her virginity and the loss of her "regal spirit."[195] Most of the strong women who people Italian female-authored fiction in this period are implicitly or explicitly virgins, from Risamante in Moderata Fonte's *Tredici canti del Floridoro* to Columba and Erato in Lucrezia Marinella's *La Colomba sacra* and *Arcadia felice* to Rosmonda in Margherita Sarrocchi's *Scanderbeide* and Flori in Maddalena Campiglia's play of that name. Miani's Celinda is in many respects an interesting figure as a rare case of a sympathetically treated sexualized heroine, yet there are limits to Miani's sympathy, and it is difficult not to feel that these limits are ideologically defined. In one rather remarkable speech, Miani's otherwise proper heroine speaks with wistful envy of the sexual freedom that can be enjoyed by a woman of the people, whose heart is not gnawed continually by the "woodworm" (tarlo) of concern for her honor.[196] Celinda's phrase here, "S'ella vuol tutto lice" (If she wants, all is permitted), echoes Tasso's notorious libertine formula in *Aminta*, "S'ei piace, ei lice" (If it pleases, it is permitted), which in turns echoes Dante's damning words, said of Semiramis, in the *Inferno*, "libito fé licito in sua legge" (what she desired she condoned in law).[197] At first appearance simply a romantic young girl who has yielded to an adored lover, Celinda acquires in this passage a more morally equivocal quality by the standards of the day, which makes her dispatch at the end of the play something more than simply the observance of a trite genre norm.

Given the infrequent performance of tragedies in this period, we are probably safe in assuming that Miani wrote *Celinda* without any thought of its being staged. Perhaps because of her previous presumed involvement in the staging of her pastoral *Amorosa speranza*, however, *Celinda* has a relatively high level of what Jonas Barish has termed *hypothetical stageability*: it is conceived, that is, for performance, even if it was primarily intended to be read.[198] Compared with many tragedies of the period, *Celinda* is relatively unprolix in its speeches, the only real exceptions being narrative speeches such as Celinda's account of her seduction of Lucinia in act 1, scene 3, and Alcandro's admiring narration of Lucinia's military prowess in act 4, scene 7. By contrast, an extended passage of *stickomythia*, or rapid-fire dialogue, enlivens Lucinia's encounter with Cubo in act 2, scene 4. While onstage action is strictly limited, following tragic convention, some degree of spectacle is provided by scenes such as the carrying in of the wounded Lucinia and the delivery to Celinda and Lucinia of Cubo's remains.[199] Lucinia's transformation across the first three acts from decorative lady-in-waiting to shorn-haired warrior could also potentially have had a certain theatrical impact, underlined by a scene in act 3 when Cubo, breaking in on a conversation between Celinda and the armor-clad Lucinia, is shocked to see his daughter ostensibly (and, ironically, of course, in actuality) in a position of intimacy with a man.

※ CHAPTER FOUR ※
SACRED NARRATIVE

1. Women Writers and the New Sacred Narrative

The works discussed in this chapter form part of a vast and critically underinvestigated body of religious narrative produced in Italy in the late sixteenth and early seventeenth centuries, mainly in the dominant narrative meter of ottava rima. This corpus of writings encompassed numerous, often overlapping genres and subgenres: verse hagiography, retellings of biblical narratives, religious epics such as Tasso's *Il mondo creato; lagrime* poems dramatizing the penitence of Saints Peter and Mary Magdalene or the sorrows of Christ or the Virgin, and rosary-themed collections combining narratives of Christ's life, passion, and resurrection with lyric and meditational excursuses.[1] Religious poetry of this kind was not new in the Counter-Reformation, and older works, some written as early as the fourteenth century, continued to circulate alongside newly produced ones.[2] Several factors, however, lent distinctiveness to the production of this era: new genres arose, such as the *lagrime* poem, which had its root in Luigi Tansillo's *Le lagrime di San Pietro*, while older ones, such as hagiographic verse narratives, reposed themselves in a stylistically refashioned, Petrarchist or post-Petrarchist guise. The religious narrative production of this era, moreover, was characteristically informed by a self-conscious mission of poetic "conversion," often presenting itself quite explicitly as revisionist with respect to earlier secular narrative devoted to "arms and love."

This body of literature is important for the study of women's writing in this period, since sacred narrative, like sacred lyric, was a genre of writing in which women could feel relatively at home. Aside from the general suitability of devout subject matter for women, notable precedents existed for female writers of religious narrative: distantly, the late antique poets Proba and Eudocia, authors of centos on the life of Christ based on, respectively, Virgil and Homer and, more proximately, Lucrezia Tornabuoni de' Medici (1425–82), whose ottava rima religious narratives, though unpublished, were known by reputation in this period.[3] Women in the late sixteenth and early seventeenth centuries embraced the new models of sacred literature with enthusiasm: besides the eight works discussed in this chapter, we know of two lost works and one planned but left unfinished at the author's death.[4] This was an area of literature in which female poets were working in the vanguard; we are very far here from the familiar scenario, well exemplified with Valeria Miani's *Celinda*, in which a female writer belatedly engages with a genre whose conventions have long since been codified by men. The thrust to produce a modern, sophisticated model of religious narrative, taking on the lessons of Ariosto and Tasso, was one that had barely begun in the early 1580s, when the first of the works discussed here was published, and it was still gathering momentum in the 1590s, when four more of these works appeared.

Women's involvement in the formative processes of the new religious narrative is well captured in the creative relationship between Francesca Turina and her Città di Castello compatriot Capoleone Ghelfucci (1541–1600), who worked simultaneously in the 1590s on two rosary-themed works, her 1595 *Rime spirituali sopra i misterii del santissimo rosario*, discussed below, and his *Il rosario della Madonna*, published posthumously in 1600. An unpublished poem of Ghelfucci's credits Turina with inspiring him to write his highly successful religious epic, and manuscript evidence shows that his original intent was to dedicate his work to her.[5] Ghelfucci, in turn, appears to have acted as Turina's poetic mentor, aiding her in the stylistic revision of her work.

The eight works discussed in this chapter are divided into three groups according to their subject matter. The first group, discussed in section 2, comprises works recounting Christ's life and passion and relying on the Gospels as their principal sources. These are Turina's *Rime spirituali*, just mentioned, and Moderata Fonte's *La passione di Christo* (1582) and *La resurrettione di Giesu Christo* (1592). The second group, discussed in sections 3 and 4, is devoted to hagiography and covers a number of verse and prose works by Lucrezia Marinella, ranging in time from her first published work, *La Colomba sacra* (1595) to her *De' gesti heroici e della vita meravigliosa della serafica S[anta] Caterina* (1624). Finally, section 5 discusses the only surviving female-authored work based on Old Testament material, Maddalena Salvetti's *David perseguitato* (1611), published posthumously as a three-canto fragment but evidently conceived as a full-scale epic work.

2. Refashioning the Gospels: New Testament Narrative in Moderata Fonte and Francesca Turina

A fundamental distinction to be made among the poems discussed here regards subject matter: that of Fonte, Turina, and Salvetti is drawn from the Bible, while Marinella's is mainly drawn from hagiographic tradition. The distinction was a crucial one in the late sixteenth century. While hagiography was a relatively safe field, vernacular poetic versions of the Bible were theologically sensitive, coming under scrutiny for the same reason that biblical translations did: a concern that they might encourage unlettered and "unauthorized" readers to engage critically with biblical texts. Vernacular texts drawing their inspiration from the Bible became the object of Inquisitional suspicion beginning about the 1570s, with a volume such as Gabriele Fiamma's *Rime spirituali*, for example, banned on account of the psalm adaptations it contained.[6] A complete ban on vernacular poetic reworkings of the Bible was introduced in 1596, only four years after Fonte's *Resurrettione* was published, although the ban was rescinded nine years later, in 1605, when the rule was limited to direct *volgarizzazioni* of the sacred text.[7]

Like other sixteenth-century retellings of Christ's life, passion, and resurrection, Fonte's two poems discussed here show a certain liberty in their handling of the theme.[8] The essential narrative derives from the Gospels, but the selection of episodes is her own, as are the pacing and emphases, and she elaborates quite freely on the bare narration of the Gospels, enriching it in particular, *lagrime* style, with lyric-meditational excursuses focalized through figures such as Mary Magdalene and the Virgin. Following two brief prefatory episodes of Peter's denial of Christ and Judas's suicide, the *Passione di Christo* tells the story of Christ's trial at the hands of Pilate and his torture, crucifixion, and death. It concludes with his deposition from the Cross at the hands of Nicodemus and Joseph of Arimathea. Fonte draws eclectically on the Gospels for secondary detail, using Matthew, for example, for the eccentric detail of Pilate's wife's dream, Luke for Christ's address to the "daughters of Jerusalem," and John for Christ's entrusting his mother to "the disciple whom he loved."[9]

Non-biblical episodes include long tacit monologues attributed to the Virgin and Mary Magdalene as they watch Christ carrying the Cross and a lamentation of the Virgin following Christ's death.[10]

The *Resurrettione di Giesu Christo,* picking up the narrative of the *Passione,* tells of the various appearances of the risen Christ to his followers in the days before his ascension, combining its narrative with lyric digressions on, for example, the grief of the Virgin and the penitence of Peter.[11] The episodes are told, in sequence, of the three Marys' visit to the sepulcher (Mark 16:1); Mary Magdalene's encounter with the risen Christ in the garden (John 20:11–18); Christ's meeting with Cleopas and Luke on the road to Emmaeus (Luke 24:13–35); his appearance to the disciples, with the exception of Thomas, in Jerusalem (John 20:19–24); the episode of Thomas's doubts (John 20:24–28); Christ's appearance to the disciples while fishing in the Sea of Galilee, with his instruction to Peter to "feed my sheep" (John 21:1–23); and finally his appearance to the disciples and a crowd of about five hundred in Galilee (I Corinthians 15:6). The poem concludes with a description of the Ascension.

Although written ten years apart, there are obviously strong continuities between Fonte's *Passione* and *Resurrettione,* to the extent that the long title of the latter—*La resurrettione di Giesu Christo nostro signore, che segue alla Santissima Passione descritta in ottava rima da Moderata Fonte*—presents the new text as a sequel to the earlier. These continuities are underlined by structural parallels, whose presence cannot be explained solely by the ordering of events in Fonte's Gospel sources: the *Passione*'s early scene of Peter's denial of Christ, for example, is balanced by the *Resurrettione*'s scene of his penitence, while the *Passione*'s closing lamentation by the Virgin has continuities with the *Resurrettione*'s opening meditation by the same figure.[12] This said, however, there is a marked difference between the two poems in scope and ambition, as well as, predictably, in mood and tone. The *Resurrettione* is 152 stanzas long to the *Passione*'s 115, and whereas the former is composed in the fluent and conversational "mediocre" style also employed in the *Floridoro,* Fonte aims at times in the *Resurrettione* for a more elaborate and self-consciously elevated diction, reminiscent more of the Tasso of *Gerusalemme liberata* than of Ariosto or Tansillo. Similarly, while the *Passione* launches directly into its narrative, the *Resurrettione* opens with a resonant four-stanza exordium announcing the theme of the poem. Although the structure of both poems is inevitably episodic, the *Resurrettione* has a greater thematic unity, deriving from its focus on the question of faith. In the course of the poem we see a sequence of figures successively struggling to comprehend the miraculous fact of Christ's resurrection, weighing the evidence of their senses against the apparent rational illogic of his transcendence of death. This gives the poem a more philosophical character than the *Passione* has and also lends it a self-referential dimension, in that the issues of belief lying at the poem's theological heart are also key to the poetics of devotional narrative of this kind, which seeks to evoke the supernatural with such verisimilitude and sensory vividness as to occasion the reader's suspension of disbelief.

Besides these internal differences, there are also quite significant differences in the framing of the *Passione* and the *Resurrettione*. Both are prefaced by an authorial dedicatory letters, the first to Doge Niccolò da Ponte, the second to the Piedmontese noblewoman Margherita Langosca Parpaglia, Countess of Bastia and wife of the ambassador of Savoy.[13] The *Resurrettione* letter is considerably longer and more fulsome and is couched in a notably courtly and ceremonious register, hailing the dedicatee as not simply a "most miraculous Lady" (mirabilissima Donna) but a "most glorious terrestrial Goddess" (gloriosissima Dea in terra).[14] In addition to this dedicatory letter, the *Resurrettione* is prefaced by a sonnet on the mystery of the Resurrection by Fonte's husband, Filippo Zorzi, here introduced, however, without any reference to his relationship to the poet. The *Passione*, by contrast, has no prefatory verse, though it concludes with a seven-stanza penitential *canzone*, which has the effect of framing the preceding narrative as a personal spiritual exercise analogous to Vittoria Colonna's *Pianto sopra la passione di Christo* (1556).[15] Overall, the effect of the *Passione* is more austere and introspective, that of the *Resurrettione* more worldly. While the intrinsic sobriety of the subject matter was obviously a consideration here, another factor is likely to have been Fonte's growing maturity and ambition. We should not forget that the composition of the later poem presumably coincided with that of Fonte's major late work, *Il merito delle donne*.

Of particular interest in the *Passione* and the *Resurrettione* are those passages where Fonte elaborates most freely on her Gospel sources, perhaps especially those concerning her female "principals," the Virgin and Mary Magdalene. The Virgin appears twice in the *Passione di Christo*, first on the road to Golgotha, where she laments over her son's suffering, and later, more briefly, after his death, where we see her grieving and lamenting beneath the Cross.[16] In the *Resurrettione* she appears at the beginning of the poem, mourning "in a solitary cell" and meditating on the theological meaning of Christ's death and resurrection.[17] Mary Magdalene features in the *Passione* on the road to Golgotha, her reflections following those of the Virgin, while in the *Resurrettione* she plays a leading role as the first witness of the Resurrection.[18]

As was frequent in the meditative tradition, the Virgin and Mary Magdalene, along with Peter, serve as the principal conduits for pathos in the two poems, serving through their emotional responses to the events depicted to prompt and channel the reader's own response. Both also call attention to the theological meaning and devotional function of the narrative. Mary Magdalene, in the *Passione,* meditates with bitter shame on her culpability as a sinner in causing Christ's death, a theme also developed in Fonte's closing *canzone* and clearly intended to prompt the reader to similar penitential reflections. In the *Resurrettione*'s narrative of gradually unfolding miraculous revelation both the Virgin and Magdalene play important roles, the former as an archetype of faith and the sole character initially capable of looking beyond Christ's death to his future glory, the latter as recipient, in the noli me tangere scene, of a revelation of a "new love" (novo amore) capable of transcending the realm of the human and "apparent" in which figures such as Thomas and Cleopas are still mired.[19] This evidence of women's capacity for faith lends a calculated irony to the misogynistic reaction of some of the disciples in the *Resurrettione,* who dismiss the three Marys, when they tell of Christ's resurrection, as "foolish and trivial women" undeserving of credence.[20] Women are valorized in Fonte's poem precisely for the "credulity" of which misogynists had traditionally accused them, recast in positive terms as a capacity to transcend the limits of reason through faith. Even among the demonized Jews of the *Passione* —Fonte shares the anti-Semitism that was an increasingly marked feature of Venetian culture at the time when she was writing—the "daughters of Zion" who pity Christ and provoke his sorrowing prophecy of their future sufferings are treated with more sympathy than their male peers.[21]

Mary Magdalene's portrayal in these two religious poems of Fonte's is deserving of particular attention, not least because it is here that we can see Fonte's devotional poetry most creatively intersecting with secular traditions. In keeping with tradition, Magdalene's beauty is foregrounded in both poems, along with her past sin and passionate repentance. The *Passione* shows her reflecting bitterly on her past vanity as she watches the torture and degradation of Christ's "chaste and virgin body," condemning the beauty of which she had once been so proud as an instrument of sensual entrapment.[22] As in many contemporary *lagrime* poems focused on the figure of Mary Magdalene, there is an element of penitence at work here on a metapoetic level: rejected, implicitly, along with Magdalene's beauty is the poetic culture of Renaissance Petrarchism, with its Neoplatonically inspired deification of female beauty, now seen, despite its pretensions to "honesty," as a lightly disguised incitement to lust. Fonte characterizes Magdalene's beauty in Petrarchan terms, describing her "beautiful curling golden locks" and "milk-white skin" at her first appearance, before having Magdalene herself apostrophize her "evil tresses" and "vain and insidious eyes."[23] There is clearly a degree of misogyny at work in the topos of Magdalene's excoriation of her beauty. Although she functioned on one level within the religious culture of the age simply as a type for the sinner, male or female, the emphasis on her sexuality and beauty has the effect of implicitly gendering sexual temptation as feminine and demonizing the female body as a locus of sin. Although Fonte does not go as far in this demonization as did some writers of the time, such as Camillo Camilli, who, in his *Lagrime di Maria Maddalena* (1592), has Magdalene describe her eyes as "tombs of filth and stench" (sepolcri d'immondizia, e di fetore),[24] we are still very clearly within a discursive tradition that associated femininity with vanity, sensuality, and corruption.

Far more original and poetically interesting than her essentially conventional treatment of the topos of Magdalene's beauty in *La passione di Christo* is Fonte's revisiting of this commonplace in her *Resurrettione*. The episode of the poem centered on Magdalene deals with her miraculous encounter with the risen Christ, a moment that confers on her considerable theological dignity, as the first witness to his resurrection. The bare facts of Fonte's narrative here are drawn from the Gospel of John: in succession, we see the two angels at the tomb asking her why she is weeping; Christ's appearance to her and her initial error in believing him to be the gardener; her moment of recognition; and his instruction to her not to touch him, the noli me tangere familiar from art. Completely novel with respect to Fonte's scriptural source, however, is the long, lush descriptive passage with which she prefaces the episode, evoking Magdalene's beauty and sorrow as she sits mourning in the garden immediately prior to Christ's appearance.[25] This passage stages Magdalene as beauteous tragic spectacle, with the invisible Christ watching his "sweet beloved" weep and listening to her "sweet laments."[26] Fonte draws extensively in this passage on Petrarch's descriptions of Laura, especially in the incipit, which portrays the golden-haired young woman in a garden, surrounded by flowers and a "flower" herself.[27] Especially evoked perhaps is the sequence at poems

155–58 of the *Rerum vulgarium fragmenta*, where the poet watches Laura weeping over an unspecified bereavement, which similarly foreground her mourning as tragic spectacle through the device of voyeurism, in this case the poet's.[28] Fonte's text reads:

> Partonsi gli altri ella in quell' orto resta
> Quasi un bel fior, che solo a sè simigli.
> Sparso ha 'l thesor de la dorata testa,
> Che ondeggia vago su i nativi gigli.
> Par che il terren sotto il bel piè si vesta
> D' herbe, e di fior, più verdi, e più vermigli,
> Et che il girar de l' una, e l' altra stella
> A' sassi, a' sterpi dia senso, e favella.
>
> Par che ogni ramo, ogni arbore, ogni foglia
> Col pianto suo mova a pietade e a riso,
> Et che ogni herbetta appalesar le voglia
> Il miracol gentil con muto aviso.
> Benche vezzosa ella di cor si doglia
> Ride ogni cosa inanzi al suo bel viso,
> Ma giace ella con fredde, immote membra
> E mira il caro sasso, e un sasso sembra.[29]

[The others leave; she stays in that garden, like a lovely flower that has no like. She has loosed the treasure of her golden hair, which wafts across the native lilies of her face. It seems as though the ground under her lovely foot springs with a greener grass and more crimson flowers and that the movements of her starry eyes give sense and language to every stone and twig.

It seems as though each branch, each tree, each leaf is moved to pity and laughter at her weeping and that each blade of grass is mutely seeking to apprise her of the noble miracle. Although she is grieving from her very heart, all else laughs before her lovely face, but she lies with cold and motionless limbs. She gazes on the dear stone and seems a stone herself.]

While the Petrarchan subtexts of this passage are perhaps to be expected, more surprising is the Ariostan echo introduced in the last line cited, which sees the grieving Magdalene gazing on the "dear stone" of Christ's tomb and transformed in appearance herself into a stone.[30] The line closely echoes a famous passage in canto 10 of the *Orlando furioso,* in which Ariosto describes the Dutch princess Olimpia, abandoned on the seashore by her faithless lover, Bireno, as "petrified" by grief.[31] In the stanza that follows those just quoted, Fonte echoes similarly closely Ariosto's description of his antiheroine, Angelica, tied naked to a rock waiting to be devoured by a sea monster. Ariosto compares Angelica to a statue, revealed as living only by the movement of her hair in the breeze and the tracks of her tears. Similarly, only the wafting hair and falling tears of Fonte's Magdalene reveal her as more alive than the stone on which she sits.[32]

One feature of particular interest in this passage is the manner in which it "recuperates" and spiritually resemanticizes the erotic imagery of its sources. Fonte's Ariostan allusions map her Magdalene onto the literary archetypes of the Ovidian abandoned heroine (Olimpia) and the Andromeda-like chained maiden (Angelica). Both acquire new levels of meaning when applied to a figure like Mary Magdalene, often regarded as the spiritual archetype of the sinful but repentant soul, here portrayed moments before her vision of the resurrected Christ assures her of her spiritual salvation. It is relevant to recall here that Neoplatonic allegorical readings of the Perseus-Andromeda myth traditionally interpreted the episode as alluding to Christ's "rescuing" of the soul from the spiritual death of sin.[33] Although she is portrayed in an eroticized manner, the "innocence" of Magdalene's sexuality is stressed. Where Petrarch had described Laura's golden tresses as the "nets" (reti) that entrapped him in a sinful erotic obsession, here Magdalene's become "holy" nets ("reti di caste alme, pudiche"), evocative less of demonic entrapment than of the spiritual "fishing" that Christ defines in Mark 1:17 as the future task of his disciples Simon and Andrew.[34] By contrast with *La passione di Christo,* where Magdalene's physical beauty is vilified, here it is implicitly offered up to us, in Neoplatonic fashion, as a signifier of her spiritual dignity. We would perhaps be unwise to read too much into this shift in the representation of Mary Magdalene between Fonte's *Passione* and her *Resurrettione,* which is probably largely explicable by the difference in the subject matter and tenor of the two works. It is interesting, however, that the positive cast given to Magdalene's beauty in the *Resurrettione* is consistent with Fonte's positive treatment of women's beauty in her dialogue *Il merito delle donne,* where her speaker Corinna argues strongly for self-adornment as an innocuous form of self-expression for women rather than a means of entrapping men.[35]

Fonte's two religious poems are for the most part relatively objective in their narration and do not address the reader directly, although the first-person meditational *canzone* at the end of the *Passione* serves to relate the Gospel story to the author's own spiritual experience and hence, more implicitly, to the reader's. Francesca Turina's narration of the same story in her *Rime spirituali sopra i misterii del santissimo rosario* is far more directive and evangelical in soliciting our response.[36] In a manner that is consistent with the conventions of the genre, Turina constructs her rosary text not as a simple narration but as part narration, part spiritual exercise; this is an implicitly interactional text that might be used by a reader to structure her own devotional practice.[37] Turina's sonnet sequence starts with an injunction to her "idle Soul" to "awake and arise," and the poet subsequently makes frequent interjections in the narrative to place herself in the scene, to solicit spiritual reactions, or to admonish herself for insufficiencies of response.[38] "Soul, this is no time to sleep!" reads the sonnet on the Agony in the Garden. "Come with Christ into the garden to keep vigil."[39] The tenor of the poet's interventions varies. At times she urges herself to become more than a spectator and to assist the holy actors in their practical needs.[40] At other times her interjections are more moral-didactic in character, especially, though not exclusively, in the "Doloroso" section, when she reproaches herself unceasingly for her hardness of heart in being able to witness Christ's passion without tears.[41]

Following the conventions of rosary-themed works generally, Turina's *Rime spirituali sopra i misterii del santissimo rosario* is divided into three sections: "Gaudioso" (Joyous), "Doloroso" (Sorrowful), and "Glorioso" (Glorious). The first recounts the Annunciation and Christ's birth and life down to his betrayal by Judas; the second, his passion and death; and the third, his resurrection and ascension, followed by the Virgin's assumption and coronation. While the narration as a whole is conducted in sonnets, metrical variety is supplied by the inclusion of two ottava rima poems, *Pianto della Madonna* and *Della gloria del Paradiso*, at the end of the "Doloroso" and "Gaudioso" sections. The work is an ambitious one, on a different scale from Fonte's modestly dimensioned Gospel narratives: the three sonnet sequences contain, between them, 127 sonnets, while the ottava rima poems are, respectively, 20 and 25 stanzas long.[42] The dedication of the work is also ambitious: it is addressed to Pope Clement VIII, whose *stemma* appears on the frontispiece of the work.[43]

Despite the importance of its reflective and meditational element, much of the poetic energy of Turina's *Rime spirituali sopra i misterii del santissimo rosario* is devoted to narration. Unlike the majority of writers of rosary texts, who limited themselves to the fifteen canonical mysteries associated with the rosary, Turina ranges much more broadly across Christ's life for her narrative material, encompassing, for example, in the long "Gaudioso" section episodes such as the Massacre of the Innocents, Christ's Baptism, and the Sermon on the Mount. There is also an extensive subsection describing Christ's miracles, signaled by a prefatory sonnet pointing to the testifying power of these "most wondrous signs."[44] Like Fonte, Turina blends episodes drawn from various Gospels, but unlike Fonte, she also includes some nonscriptural material. One surprising scene has Christ appearing to the Virgin in the immediate wake of his resurrection, accompanied by the spirits released by the harrowing of hell.[45]

Turina succeeds surprisingly well in co-opting the seemingly unpromising meter of the sonnet to the task of narration.[46] She often uses simpler rhyme schemes than were common in the lyric sonnet, frequently rhyming her quatrains or tercets on alternate lines, so that the sonnet comes closer to a more conventionally narrative meter such as ottava rima.[47] This lends fluency to the narration, as does her use, for the most part, of a clear and simple diction and a relatively linear syntax, with few inversions. Variety is attained within thematically unified sections of the narration by modulations in the construction of each sonnet unit and by shifts in the relation in each between narrative and declamatory or reflective elements. Some sonnets are strictly narrative, a few are purely reflective, but the majority are made up of a mixture: narration in the quatrains may be followed by an exclamation of self-reproach or an exhortation to empathy in the tercets, or a sonnet may begin with an exhortation or expression of affect before going on to narrate the action to which it relates. Turina's confidence in her readers' familiarity with her narrative material enables her occasionally to experiment with dramatic and elliptical modes of narration. The miracles of Christ's cure of the centurion's servant and his exorcism of the daughter of the Canaanite woman, for example, are narrated in sonnets that open *in medias res* with the cry of the afflicted person: "My servant is lying ill" in the first case, "Have pity on me: a foul evil spirit is slaying my daughter" in the second.[48] A further source of variety is stylistic: occasionally Turina abandons her usual plain style and indulges in a passage of lyric description, as when she prefaces her account of the Resurrection with a classicizing evocation of the coming of dawn or manneristically dwells on the rain of jewel-like drops of blood sweated by Christ during the Agony in the Garden.[49]

As we saw in chapter 1, Turina's dedicatory letter to the *Rime spirituali* makes the claim that a poetry that recognizes its divine source and mission should clothe itself not in "meretricious adornments" but in the "vestments of matronly chastity."[50] The remark is interesting not least for its gendered metaphorical language. The notion that sacred poetry required an idiom of "holy and devout simplicity," widespread in Turina's culture, allowed her to make a virtue of the "feminine" artlessness and facility of her style.[51] The simplicity of the poetic language she deploys in the *Rime spirituali* corresponds to the ingenuousness of her poet persona, whose focus in her reliving of her sacred narrative is consistently on the human drama of the events narrated rather than their theological significance and whose response flows through channels of affective empathy rather than intellectual analysis.

This immediate and emotive quality in Turina's poetry is perhaps most apparent in the twelve-sonnet segment of her narration of Christ's nativity and infancy, which is also perhaps the most interesting part of the poem from the point of view of gender. What is most striking in the sequence is the amount of poetic space Turina dedicates simply to a dotingly tender contemplation of the charms of the baby Jesus and an evocation of the delight he arouses in those around him, especially his mother. Two sonnets are devoted entirely to the Virgin's enrapturement with her child, and two others are devoted in large part to the wondering delight he arouses in the Magi and in the aged Simeon, who holds the baby in his "trembling arms" and is overwhelmed by "sweetness and affection."[52] The poet too is entranced and volunteers herself in one sonnet to help Mary tend to the baby, "rocking the cradle, lighting the little fire; warming his swaddling clothes, and preparing his baths."[53] While the infant Jesus's divinity obviously subtends the narrative, it is not brought particularly insistently to the reader's attention. Turina's emphasis in the sequence falls very squarely on what is human and shared. The language of the infancy sonnets is particularly affective and tender, marked by the presence of *vezzeggiativi* ("amorosetto infante," "caro pargoletto") recalling the autobiographical poetry of maternity included in her 1628 *Rime*.[54] While adult male figures (Joseph, Simeon, the Magi) feature in the sequence, the experiences described and the language describing them are for the most part markedly feminine, a point Turina underlines at the end of her first sonnet on the Virgin's love for her child when she describes this as apt matter for her "feminine cithara."[55]

Needless to say, the feminine model of narration Turina crafts for herself in the *Rime spirituali* was not the only option for female poets in this period. A sharply contrasting approach is offered by Lucrezia Marinella's narration of Christ's nativity in the ottava rima *Vita di Maria Vergine*, published in 1602. Marinella's narration is conducted in an unwaveringly epic style, quite remote from Turina's simplicity of syntax and diction, and her emphasis falls almost entirely on the theological moment of the event rather than on the emotions of her protagonists. Marinella omits the encounter with Simeon from which Turina wrings such pathos and devotes little time to evoking the human charm of the divine infant. The Virgin's feelings toward her baby are barely explored except in the statement, "She loves him as a son, prays to him as a God, and honors him as a Father."[56] In the prose version published alongside the ottava rima *vita*, even this tepid passing mention of maternal feeling is omitted, in favor of the "reverence of a Daughter, the charity of a Bride, and the humility of a Servant."[57] Turina's and Marinella's radically different treatments of this same narrative material offer two models of poetic decorum, one solemn, elevated, and "public," the other self-consciously humble and plain. Both modes of writing had a place in the religious literature of the age, and both were equally available to women, even if Marinella's higher level of education is likely to have had some bearing on her choice.

3. Hagiographic Epic: Lucrezia Marinella's Lives of Saints Columba and Francis

One of the most unexpected developments in Turina's *Rime spirituali* occurs in the final section ("Glorioso"), when Christ, consigning the papal role to Peter, digresses to predict the future glorious pontificate of the work's dedicatee, Clement VIII. A further encomiastic moment is found in the closing ottava rima poem, *Le glorie del Paradiso*, where, in the space reserved in heaven for the blessed yet to die, a conspicuous throne of topaz and alabaster is seen reserved for the Aldobrandini pope.[58] Turina was not alone among the religious poets of the age in finding space in her narratives for encomiastic digression, which was sometimes even directed at secular patrons; Agostino De Cupiti, for example, incorporates several passages of praise for Caterina d'Austria, Duchess of Savoy, in his *Caterina martirizzata* (1593).[59] The employment of such classically epic devices in religious narrative poems in this period reveals the extent to which these poets regarded their works as heirs, as well as correctives, to secular epic and chivalric romance. This comes through very clearly in the preface (by Fra Lodovico Malfitani) to Giovanni Domenico Montefuscoli's narrative rosary poem *Grandezze del verbo ristrette ne' misteri del rosario* (1593), which explicitly likens the literary pleasures of Montefuscoli's epic to those of the more familiar poetry of "arms and love" (cose d'armi e d'amori).[60]

Lucrezia Marinella was the female writer of this era who participated most significantly in the Counter-Reformation's drive to convert epic to religious purposes, perhaps building on Moderata Fonte's foray into an epic stylistic register at points in her *Resurrettione di Christo*. Rather than writing Gospel narrative, as did Fonte, Marinella wisely opted, for the most part, for less controversial, hagiographic material, although her popular *Vita di Maria Vergine*, of 1602, and the series of lives of the Apostles that she added to the third edition of that work in 1617 take her closer to Fonte's domain. Marinella's two earliest hagiographic works, discussed here, were published in 1595 and 1597, when she was about 16 and 18 years old.[61] They are united by their use of verse, specifically ottava rima, and by their self-conscious crafting as epics, if on a miniature scale (*La Colomba sacra* and *Vita del serafico, et glorioso S[an] Francesco* are, respectively, four and three cantos long).[62] Marinella followed this model as well in her *Vita di Maria Vergine*, but she accompanied the verse *vita* with an alternative, prose version. This signaled a turning point in her hagiographic output, in that her future writings in this genre, down to her 1648 *Holocausto d'amore della vergine Santa Giustina*, are all written in prose.

In choosing the form of the verse epyllion for her two debut works, Marinella was fully in line with literary trends in this period. Besides Agostino De Cupiti's *Caterina martirizzata*, mentioned above, representative hagiographic epics of the late 1580s and 1590s include Felice Passero's *Vita di San Placido*, discussed in chapter 1, Lucillo Martinengo's *Vita di Santa Margherita detta Pelagia*, of 1590, and Sebastiano Castelletti's *La trionfatrice Cecilia*, of 1594.[63] An earlier example, certainly known to Marinella, was the Calabrian Marco Filippi's popular *Vita di Santa Caterina vergine e martire*, first published in 1562.[64] We might add to these single-protagonist poems Benedetto Dell'Uva's popular anthology *Le vergini prudenti*, of 1582, which encompasses short ottava rima lives of Saints Agatha, Lucy, Agnes, Justina, and Catherine of Alexandria.[65] These works varied in scale: Passero's and Castelletti's were comparable to Marinella's *Colomba sacra*, with five and three cantos, respectively, while Martinengo's had ten, Filippi's thirteen, and De Cupiti's a fully epic twenty.[66] The authorship of the works was predominantly clerical, as was the case with so much of the religious literature of the period: Passero, Dell'Uva, and Martinengo were Benedictines, while Castelletti was a Dominican, and De Cupiti, a Franciscan.[67] Secular authorship of such poems was not, however, unknown, even excepting the case of Marinella: Filippi was a layman, and Tasso turned to this genre at the very end of his life, in 1594, embarking on what seems to have been intended as an epic-scaled life of Saint Benedict, of which only the opening seven stanzas remain.[68]

Not surprisingly, hagiographic epic was considered appropriate reading matter for women, and a number of works in the genre were dedicated to them (including, of those mentioned in the previous paragraph, those of Dell'Uva, De Cupiti, Martinengo, and Castelletti).[69] Marinella was consistent with this trend—though also, more generally, with the dedicatory practices of later sixteenth-century female writers—in choosing aristocratic women as the dedicatees of her first two works: she dedicated *La Colomba sacra* to Margherita Gonzaga d'Este, Duchess of Ferrara (1564–1618), and the *Vita di San Francesco* to Christine of Lorraine, Grand Duchess of Tuscany.[70] Both works are presented with a certain style, particularly the *Vita di San Francesco*, which has two full-page engravings, as well as more local decorative features, such as ornamented initials and friezes marking the opening of each canto.[71] *La Colomba sacra* has four prefatory sonnets, by poets and intellectuals of a certain weight in the city; the *Vita di San Francesco*, two, including one by the patrician poet Orsatto Giustinian, one of the most prestigious Venetian *letterati* of the day.[72] These are ambitious works for a beginning writer, showing Marinella's determination to insert herself into a prestigious male literary tradition. It is notable that while she makes the standard gestures toward authorial modesty in her dedicatory letters, speaking of her "crude and low style" in the first and the "baseness and weakness" of her intellect in the other, in neither does she mention her sex as a disabling factor, as was common in women's presentation of their works.[73] A phrase in the dedicatory letter to Christine of Lorraine suggests, rather, a desire to measure herself against the heights of the vernacular tradition. Marinella speaks there of her initial feelings of bashfulness at the thought of addressing her work to the ruler of a land (Tuscany) that had produced "the most divine and most noble of poets."[74] The tone is one of modesty, but the effect is assertive, given that Marinella clearly got over these qualms.

Marinella offers no reason in either of her dedicatory letters for her choice of these particular saints as protagonists of her poems. Francis, of course, hardly needs explanation, given his towering position in religious history and his popularity as a subject of literature and art. His life had already been the subject of ottava rima poems by Lodovico da Filicaia (*Leggenda, overo vita di San Francecso* [1549]) and Giacomo Garibbi da Porto San Maurizo (*Il serafico San Francesco* [1595]), and it would later inspire a full-scale Tassesque epic by Agostino Gallucci, *San Francesco, overo Gerusalemme celeste acquistata* (1618). Marinella's personal dedication to Francis and to the Franciscan movement is also apparent in her 1603 *Rime sacre* and her second, prose life of Francis (1643).[75] The choice of the relatively obscure third-century Hispano-French virgin martyr Saint Columba of Sens is less easy to explain. Although Columba had some following in Italy—she was the titular saint of Rimini cathedral—there seems to have been no particular devotional reason for Marinella's choice. It seems more likely that the appeal of Columba's story to Marinella lay in its intrinsic narrative interest and in the allegorical potential suggested by the heroine's name, "Dove," which recalls the traditional imagery of the Holy Spirit and makes her story not simply one of a single, heroic maiden but one of the triumph of Christianity as a whole.[76]

Though similar in scale, meter, and epic intent, *La Colomba sacra* and *La vita di San Francesco* are nonetheless quite different poems.[77] *La Colomba sacra* is strong on action, descriptive color, and the physical "marvelous," and it is structured around the conflict between two powerfully characterized antagonists, Columba herself and Emperor Aurelian (AD 270–75), the agent of her persecution and death. The first canto recounts Aurelian's initial, nonviolent attempts to persuade Columba to renounce her faith, and the fourth recounts her martyrdom by beheading. The second and third are devoted to Columba's escape, through divine aid, from two previous assaults by the emperor, first a punitive rape, from which she is protected by a she-bear, then an attempt to burn her alive, from which she is saved by a heaven-sent downpour. *La vita di San Francesco* is notably more austere in its narrative pleasures, a manner not entirely dictated by the different character of the source material. Marinella excludes some of the more picturesque incidents of Francis's legend, such as his domestication of the wolf of Gubbio and his preaching to the birds, and she is relatively sparing in her treatment of potentially "embellishable" episodes, such as Francis's voyage to the East and his preaching before the sultan.[78] Her focus is preponderantly on internal, rather than external, action, especially in the second half of the poem: Francis's penitence, his fasting and self-mortification, and his mysticism, culminating in his stigmatizing union with Christ. Where *La Colomba sacra* remains quite close to the model of secular epic, not least in its agonistic structure, pitting saint against emperor, *La vita di San Francesco* is more thoroughly "converted," more entirely a narrative of the spirit. Francis's only struggle in the poem is with the flesh and the devil, and this is essentially dispatched in eleven stanzas in canto 1.[79] One of the most distinctive features of the *poema sacro* in general was its inclusion of "descriptions of devotions and contemplations," as one reader put it—prayers, visions, ecstasies, penitential reflections, and devotional meditations of all kinds.[80] We find a number of such passages in *La Colomba sacra*, but they are balanced by a reasonably copious dose of action. In *La vita di San Francesco* these introspective elements dominate the poem as a whole.[81]

Read against the genre backdrop of epic, *La Colomba sacra* and *La vita di Santa Francesco* are interesting for their refashioning of the figure of the epic hero. Columba is a young woman; Francis, a programmatically nonaggressive man. Both are at a considerable distance from the martial ideal configured in Virgil's Aeneas or even the Christianized version of that ideal represented by Tasso's Goffredo. Marinella underlines the revisionist character of her relationship with traditions of secular epic at the beginning of the *Vita di San Francesco*, when she rejects the inspiration of Calliope, Muse of epic ("You who sing to the sound of arms the fearful aspect of cruel Mars"), placing her poem instead under the inspirational aegis of Francis himself.[82] This does not prevent Marinella from implicitly casting her protagonist as heir to the epic heroes of history. The poem opens in Virgilian style with "I sing the great man" (Canto il grand'huomo), and Francis is described, using the langage of epic, as "most dauntless hero" (invitissimo heroe), "new champion" (novello campione), and "sweet warrior victor" (dolce . . . vincitor guerriero).[83] The semiclad, self-starved saint, reduced by the end of his life to little more than a living skeleton, makes an incongruous match with the godlike armed warriors of secular epic, but it is this very incongruity that underlines the radical character of the genre's conversion.

Similarly, in *La Colomba sacra* Marinella makes much of the power reversal that occurs during the course of the poem between the young female saint and the emperor, whom we first see in the full panoply of his masculine authority, dressed in regal purple and "with a venerable aspect shining forth, beyond anything one might see in a normal man."[84] Like Francis, Columba is described as a warrior ("guerriera di Christo"), and her magnanimity in the face of her persecutor is emphasized.[85] Toward the beginning of the poem, in a scene that implicitly assimilates Aurelian to Virgil's defeated warrior Turnus, the harpy Alecto goads him, saying that Columba is a "base female for whom the spindle would be too great a burden."[86] By the end of the work, Aurelian is forced to describe himself as defeated, even as he orders Columba's physical beheading. Unable to meet her eye, he declares:

> costei guidate, ch'io son vinto;
> Vinto è già il vincitor, mie illustri prove
> Ella ha scemato, e il mio valor estinto.[87]

[Take her (to her death), for I am defeated; the victor is now beaten. She has diminished my illustrious deeds and extinguished my valor.]

At the level of allegory, as Aurelian's speech goes on to make explicit, this defeat has an epochal significance. It signifies the victory of Christianity, and the Christian values symbolized by the "dove" Columba, over the pagan values symbolized by Aurelian's Roman "eagle," a victory underlined by Aurelian's distinctly "unaquiline" inability to look Columba in the eye.[88] At a metaliterary level, Aurelian's defeat may be read as announcing the defeat of the classical ideal of an epic of might by the Christian ideal of an epic of endurance.

Marinella's construction of Columba as epic heroine is conducted quite consciously in dialectic with existing literary archetypes of female fortitude and valor. The story of Aurelian's mortal combat with Columba is prefaced by a brief account of the emperor's defeat of Zenobia, queen of Palmyra (AD 270–72), described as a "great lady" (gran donna) and an "illustrious and magnanimous Queen" (illustre e magnanima Reina).[89] This implicitly stages Columba as Christian successor to the classical ideal of the Amazonian female warrior —Homer's Penthesilea, Virgil's Camilla—reworked to great success in the Renaissance as the female knight of chivalric romance. The most obvious literary prototype of Marinella's Columba, as of the Counter-Reformation literary virgin martyr in general, is Tasso's protomartyr Sofronia, in the *Gerusalemme liberata*.[90] At times, however, she also draws more immediately on the warrior-woman type, both explicitly (as we have seen, she is referred to as a "guerriera di Christo") and implicitly (the scene of her loosing her golden hair on the way to her martyrdom recalls the poetic topos of the female knight releasing her hair as she removes her helmet).[91]

In addition to drawing on these positive epic archetypes of female valor, Marinella also draws, far more unexpectedly, on a negative female type from the chivalric epic in crafting the figure of Columba. As Columba makes her way to meet Aurelian in the opening canto, her beauty is described in a stanza that imitates very closely, to the point of borrowing three rhyme words, an equivalent stanza in Tasso describing the demonic enchantress Armida as she progresses through the crusader camp in the guise of a bashful damsel seeking chivalric assistance from Goffredo and his knights. Marinella's stanza reads as follows:

> La chioma d'oro, che se stessa in onde
> Dolcemente rincrespa, è d'arte priva:
> Tien gli occhi in atto honesto, e i rai nasconde,
> Onde il foco d'amor dolce deriva:
> Nel candor del bel viso si confonde
> Rosa, che i gigli in bel purpureo avviva
> Le belle labia, anzi il rubin ardente
> Cela il più bel Thesor de l'Oriente.[92]

[Her golden hair, which of itself sweetly curls in waves, is arranged without art. She keeps her eyes modestly downcast, hiding those beams from which the sweet fire of love is born. In the whiteness of her lovely face a rose is mingled, which lights up the lilies with fine crimson. Her beautiful lips, rather her burning ruby, conceals the loveliest treasures of the East.]

Tasso's stanza reads:

> Fa nove crespe l'aura al crin disciolto,
> che natura per sé rincrespa in onde;
> stassi l'avaro sguardo in sé raccolto,
> e i tesori d'amore e i suoi nasconde.
> Dolce color di rose in quel bel volto
> fra l'avorio si sparge e si confonde,
> ma ne la bocca, onde esce aura amorosa,
> sola rosseggia e semplice la rosa.[93]

[Her loosed hair, which Nature by itself curls in waves, is whisked by the breeze into new curls. Her avaricious glance is contained in itself and conceals Love's treasure and her own. A sweet color of roses in that lovely face mixes and mingles with the ivory; but in her mouth, from which an amorous air breathes, the rose stands alone in its redness.]

Marinella was not the only writer of the period to attempt to co-opt to religious ends the ravishing and sensual descriptive language Tasso had evolved for Armida in the *Liberata*.[94] Marinella's use of her Tassesque material here is particularly subtle, however. At an obvious level, it serves to underline the contrast between Armida's calculated artifice and Columba's transparency. Armida casts herself as a modest maiden for the purposes of her mission, and the speech she delivers before Goffredo is a tissue of self-serving lies. Columba, by contrast, actually embodies the chaste and modest ethos that Armida was feigning, and her words before Aurelian are fearless declarations of truth. At a more subtle level, however, the relationship between Marinella's heroine and Tasso's archvillainess is not wholly antithetical. Both are powerful figures, which their feminine beauty disguises, hiding, in Tasso's words, a "grey-haired wisdom" (canuto senno) and "virile heart" (cor virile) beneath their blonde hair and "soft appearance" (tenere sembianze).[95] Both are also empowered by supernatural forces, whether demonic (Armida) or divine (Columba), a parallel underlined when the frustrated Aurelian, seeing Columba miraculously escape his attempts to harm her, rails against her as an "evil enchantress" (incantatrice rea) and a "false witch" (falsa maga).[96] Aurelian's misreading of Columba's powers calls attention to Marinella's use of the Tassesque formula of the Christian *meraviglioso*, which allowed the traditional romance delights of magical enchantments to be incorporated into a reformed Christian epic. Her Christian reconfiguration of the literary type of the "evil enchantress" may also, however, be read as implicitly revisionary of Tasso, especially given the tendency within the *Liberata* to associate the feminine with the demonic and libidinous. Marinella's "frail warrior" is Armida reformed, as powerful and as beautiful as Tasso's enchantress but as chaste as Armida is sultry and as firmly in the forefront of God's victorious spiritual militia as Armida is in the routed pagan ranks.[97]

The description of Columba's Armida-like beauty cited in the previous paragraph is a good example of the kind of decorative material that Marinella employs in her first religious epic but austerely eschews in her second. One likely reason for the focus on female, rather than male, saints in religious epic in this period was the opportunity their legends offered for the traditional poetic exercise of *descriptio pulchritudinis*, and even, at times—though Marinella eschews this possibility—for some continuing limited place for the poetry of love.[98] Francis's story offered little scope for such embellishment opportunities. On the contrary, in the third canto, Marinella regales us instead with a kind of contra-blazon in the form of a description of the saint's emaciated and self-mortified body, which in its fascinated precision perhaps bears some trace of an acquaintance with contemporary anatomy culture on the part of this doctor's daughter:

> Egl'ha in due lunghe cave gli occhi accolti,
> Pallido e scarno il venerabil viso.
> . . . .
> Magro è così ch'ogn'osso par diviso.
> E le viscere sue tra gl'ossi molti
> Nel cavo ventre di veder ti è aviso,
> E tal magrezza a gli occhi altrui dipinge
> Come l'ossa Natura annoda, e stringe.[99]

> [His eyes are buried in two deep hollows, and his venerable face is pale and fleshless. . . . He is so thin that each bone appears distinctly, and you can almost see his entrails amid the many bones in his hollow abdomen. Such thinness paints to the eyes how Nature knots and knits our bones.]

Decorative passages are strictly limited in *La vita di San Francesco*, with even the inevitable descriptions of dawn confined to a few lines and the sole female figure to appear, Francis's follower and fellow saint Clare of Assisi, described with relatively little reference to her physical beauty other than generic mentions of her golden hair and white skin. A more rhetorically elaborated stanza describing the beauty of Mary Magdalene as she embraces the Cross in a dream of Francis's recounted in canto 2 turns out to be a borrowing from a parallel passage in *La Colomba sacra*, where its Petrarchan conceits are more in tune with the stylistic decorum of the piece.[100] Marinella's relative descriptive austerity is even apparent in her treatment of the episode of the stigmata, which appealed to baroque religious poets partly on the grounds of the scope it offered for spectacular visual effects and metaphorical acrobatics. The episode is dispatched in five stanzas in Marinella's poem, one of which is mainly given over to setting the scene, and the language in which she describes the miracle is relatively simple and unadorned.

Marinella focuses her poetic energies in *La vita di San Francesco* less on the external happenings of Francis's life and more on his interior, spiritual experience. This brings the poem close at times to contemporary lyric-meditational genres such as that of the *lagrime* poem. Counter-Reformation religious culture tended in general to underplay the social and communal dimensions of Francis's mission and to recast the saint as a hermit. Marinella is perfectly in line with this trend, in a manner that perhaps reflects her particular sympathy for the originally hermitical Capuchin branch of the Franciscan order: although she gives some space in the first two cantos to accounts of Francis's evangelism and his foundation of the Franciscan order, the bulk of the poem is given over to his solitary experiences of penitence and mysticism in the stark retreat of La Verna.[101] An extended passage in canto 1, especially close to contemporary *lagrime* poems, shows Francis meditating on sin and death with the aid of a skull and a crucifix in the manner of Jerome, while an even longer passage at the end of canto 2 recounts Francis's reimagining of Christ's passion and crucifixion, first through a conscious meditation and then again through a dream.[102] Canto 3, while laying more stress on physical happenings, such as Francis's self-inflicted protracted "martyrdom" and death, still contains quite lengthy passages of internal spiritual monologue, as well as further visions and "affects."[103] *La vita di San Francesco* and the *Discorso del rivolgimento amoroso, verso la somma bellezza*, which Marinella published in tandem with it in 1597, together constitute an exemplified disquisition on asceticism as a route to union with God, with Francis's life and spiritual progress serving as an aspirational model for the Christian reader's own trajectory.[104] More than a straight narration in some ways, *La vita di San Francesco* has rather the character of an incitement to "spiritual exercise," a feature of the poem that assimilates it to Francesca Turina's *Rime spirituali sopra i misterii del santissimo rosario*, which is in other respects a very different work.[105]

One notable consequence of Marinella's deemphasizing of Francis's role as spiritual leader and her privileging instead of his solitary meditative practice is that this makes him a more accessible role model for Christian readers of both sexes. Mysticism and asceticism were practices at which women had traditionally excelled on a par with men, and a female saint, Catherine of Siena—the subject of a later hagiographic work by Marinella—had even equaled Francis's in his supreme spiritual accolade, the receipt of the stigmata. The bigendered character of the spiritual ideal delineated in *La vita di San Francesco* is underlined when, at the end of the poem, Marinella names her brother Angelico and her sister, Diamantina, as modern exemplars of the Franciscan ideal of ascetic piety.[106] Diamantina, a married laywoman, is less obviously qualified to be cited in this context than Angelico, a Servite friar, and it is hard not to suspect that her presence is motivated in part by the desire to underline the relevance of Francis's lesson to both sexes. Also functional in this sense is the brief appearance in the poem of Mary Magdalene, who figures in Francis's dream vision in her role as mourner at the Crucifixion but whom readers would also have known in her later incarnation as Jerome-like hermit-penitent, a popular subject in the literature and art of the period and one with which Marinella herself would engage in her revised *Vita di Maria Vergine* of 1617.[107]

4. Hagiographic Epic Remade: Marinella's Lives of Mary and Saint Catherine of Siena

Two later hagiographic works of Marinella's fall within the chronological remit of this study: her *Vita di Maria Vergine imperatrice dell'universo*, of 1602, and her *De' gesti heroici e della vita meravigliosa della serafica S[anta] Caterina da Siena*, of 1624. The first of these works, originally dedicated to the doge and senate of Venice, was one of Marinella's most popular productions, appearing in later editions in 1604, 1610, and 1617, the last significantly expanded and revised.[108] It contains two separate texts, one in prose and one in verse, both divided into four segments (books or cantos) in the 1602 version. In the 1617 version, the verse text is expanded to seven cantos and incorporates material dealing with Mary Magdalene's later life, making it in a sense almost a joint life of the two outstanding female protagonists of Christ's story.[109]

As we might expect, in her account of Mary's life Marinella fleshes out the meager Gospel record with material drawn from the vast body of apocryphal material that had accumulated around the figure of the Virgin in late antiquity and the Middle Ages. The prose version of the *Vita* is particularly liberal in this regard, including, for example, the entire backstory of the Virgin's miraculous conception by Joachim and Anna, familiar from the Golden Legend and from Giotto's Arena Chapel, as well as less familiar details such as the miraculous excision and subsequent miraculous restoration of the hands of a priest who attempted to interfere with the Virgin's burial.[110] Marinella shows some ostensible concern for historical accuracy, including a prefatory essay listing sources ranging from the Gospels and patristic writings to modern biographies such as those of Marcantonio Sabellico (c. 1436–1506) and Silvano Razzi (1527–1611). Rather than an accurate account of her source material, however, this list is best read as an exercise in intellectual self-positioning. Marinella concentrates where she can on impeccable *auctores*, such as Jerome, while omitting her more questionable sources, which, as Eleonora Carinci has recently shown, included Pietro Aretino's *Vita di Maria Vergine* (1539), a work that had been officially banned for more than forty years at the time of her writing, along with the remainder of Aretino's writings.[111] The evidence Carinci cites shows Marinella's dependence on Aretino to have been extensive, perhaps even sufficiently to account for the accusation of plagiarism leveled against her, to which Giambattista Ciotti alludes in his preface to her *Arcadia felice*.[112]

Marinella opens her verse *vita* in a characteristically assertive mode by vaunting her authorship of *La Columba sacra* and *La vita di San Francesco:*

> Quella son io, ch'a l'aura in versi trasse
> Già di Sacra Colomba i gran martiri,
> E quella io son, ch 'n rima pria cantasse
> Del Serafico Heroe gli alti desiri.[113]

[That woman am I, who fetched the great torments of the Holy Columba into the light of day through her verses. That woman am I who first sang in verse of the sublime desires of the Seraphic Hero.]

At least in its original 1602 version, *La vita di Maria Vergine* resembles these earlier religious epics of Marinella's in format and scale. Of the two, it more closely resembles *La Colomba sacra* in its privileging of narrative action and in the greater emphasis given to descriptive and quasi-lyrical elements, although Mary is accorded quite extensive meditative-contemplative passages, especially in the account of Christ's passion. The principal novelty of *La vita di Maria Vergine* is its more self-consciously elevated and classicizing style, perhaps influenced in part by the existence of a precedent such as Iacopo Sannazaro's *De partu Verginis*, which had acquired a new currency during the post-Tridentine period, or from a more recent work such as Lucillo Martinengo's epic-scaled *Della vita di nostra signora, la gloriosa vergine Maria* (1595), compared in its dedicatory letter to Tasso's *Gerusalemme liberata*.[114] Classicizing language is frequent, such as "Diva" (goddess) for Mary, "Olimpo" for heaven, "Numi" (divine presences) for angels; when the Magi take leave of the Virgin and the Christ child, they are described as "Heroi" taking leave of their "Duce."[115] Extended epic similes and lingering descriptions of dawn and night, complete with references to Apollo and Aurora, contribute to the classicizing decorum of the poem, as do passages such as the Tassesque description of the birth of the Virgin as the restoration of a golden age in which the "rough trunks dripped with honey" and "the Hydras relinquished their venom," while Etna opened to release the anger and frustration of the "fierce King of the sempiternal horrors."[116]

It is not merely in the verse *Vita di Maria Vergine* that we see Marinella striving consciously for sublimity. The language of the prose *vita* is equally sumptuous and recherché, a stylistic choice that Marinella justifies in an interesting preface to the reader, one of the most ambitious literary-theoretical statements by a female writer in this period.[117] Marinella defends her use of a prose that approximates to poetry in its lyricism and rhetorical elaboration precisely on the grounds of *convenientia* to the subject matter and protagonists:

> Le azioni, che hanno del grande, del magnifico, e del divino, e che trapassano le operazioni umane, ricercano un modo di dire grande e mirabile, molto diverso da quello, che si usa nel raccontar quelle azioni, che picciole, umili e basse sono. E più si ricerca lo stile diverso, quando che tali azioni dipendono da persone, che eccedono per l'eccellenza della lor natura gli uomini e gli eroi.[118]
>
> [Actions that have the qualities of greatness, magnificence, and divinity, and that surpass human attainments, demand a manner of speech that is grand and miraculous, very different from that which is required to recount actions that are petty, humble, and base. And this different style is required all the more when such actions are performed by persons who exceed both men and heroes through the excellence of their nature.]

The words "exceed both men and heroes" require underlining here. What is called for in describing the life of the Empress of the Universe is not merely an epic style but one that transcends even epic in its sublimity, to "reach the very height of the summit of eloquence," as Marinella modestly claims of her own prose.[119] The choice of prose as a medium for the life, alongside verse, may have been attractive precisely for this reason: while epic style in verse was highly codified and hence difficult to transcend, epic style in prose, especially in the vernacular, had been less consistently cultivated and so offered greater room for "improvement." Marinella constructs an interesting line of descent for what she terms a "poetic *elocutio*" in prose, tracing it ultimately to the Greek sophist Gorgias, whom Aristotle had criticized in his *Rhetoric* precisely for speaking as a poet rather than as an orator. Besides Gorgias, Marinella claims as her classical stylistic ancestors Isocrates and Plato in Greek and Apuleius in Latin, following these with a pair of vernacular *auctores*, the Boccaccio of works such as *Fiammetta* and the orator Giulio Camillo (1479– 1544), whose *Lettera del rivolgimento dell'huomo a Dio* she had used as a source in her *Discorso del rivolgimento amoroso, verso la somma bellezza*.[120]

Despite the very specific, exceptionalist justification she cites for it in the *Vita di Maria Vergine,* in practice the grand prose style Marinella evolved for this work became the basic currency for her prose writings of the following decades, both secular *(Arcadia felice)* and spiritual *(De' gesti heroici e della vita meravigliosa della serafica S[anta] Caterina da Siena)*. The latter work was Marinella's first reprise of hagiographic writing since *La vita di Maria Vergine,* with the exception of the new lives of the Apostles that she published with the 1617 edition of her Marian opus and the digression on Mary Magdalene that she inserted in her verse life of the Virgin in the 1610 and 1617 editions.[121] *De' gesti heroici* is the second of Marinella's works to be dedicated to a grand duchess of Tuscany, after *La vita di San Francesco,* dedicated to Christine of Lorraine; this time the recipient was Maria Maddalena of Austria, widow of Cosimo II, and coregent of Tuscany with Christine at the time of Marinella's writing.[122] Unusually for Marinella, the work was clearly designed from the outset with a particular patron in mind. The fifth book of *De' gesti heroici* has Catherine experiencing a divinely sent vision of the triumph of the Medici dynasty, imagined theatrically as a procession, accompanied by the full imperial panoply of "spoils, arches, triumphal chariots, devices, and trophies."[123] We also see the saint prophetically praying at the moment of her death for the protection of her homeland by its future Medici rulers, "most just leaders and sublime heroes," who will "govern with compassion and love not simply beautiful Florence and Tuscany, but the world."[124] It may even have been to an extent as a result of patronage considerations that Marinella chose a Tuscan saint for her protagonist in the first place, although Catherine clearly also appealed to her as a subject for less opportunistic reasons: along with Francis, she features as one of the only nonmartyred saints in a prophetic vision accorded to the Virgin in Marinella's 1610 prose *Vita di Maria Vergine,* and she is the subject of four sonnets—more than any other saint—in Marinella's 1603 *Rime sacre*.[125]

The element of courtliness conferred on *De' gesti heroici* by its dynastic encomia and by its exceptionally lush and decorative prose style sits oddly with the asceticism of the subject matter, which recalls the *Vita di San Franceso* and the *Discorso del rivolgimento* in its emphasis on the abnegation of the body. The relaxed pace of the work—comprising six books and more than three hundred pages, it is considerably longer than any previous hagiographic work of Marinella's—allows for a gruesomely minute and protracted account of Catherine's physical self-mortification, far beyond anything found in *La vita di San Francesco*. A contributory factor here is undoubtedly also Catherine's sex, which qualifies her by default for construction as a Petrarchan beauty and lends an aestheticizing and eroticizing dimension to the account of her self-martyrdom that doubtless enhanced its poetic appeal to contemporary readers. Marinella's descriptions of Catherine's self-flagellation, like her early, less developed treatment of the same theme in her Magdalene digression in the 1610 and 1617 *Vita di Maria Vergine*, are cast in Petrarchizing language and play with the same color contrasts traditional in Petrarchism, essentially white, gold, and red or purple. Here, however, the "ruby" element is provided not by the lips or blushing cheeks but by the blood drawn through the women's self-excoriation, which spills across the white of their naked flesh like roses among lilies or scatters over their golden hair like purple enamel on gold.[126] The spiritual redeployment of secular poetic motifs is here carried to a point of absurdity on a literal level; it is unlikely that the program of self-starvation and self-mortification Marinella describes would produce quite such decorative effects. It finds justification, however, within the higher logic of Marinella's ascetic brand of Christianity, as a physical expression of the spiritual beauty of such gestures of contempt for the body. Within a literary context, Marinella's aestheticizing treatment of blood has precedents in the religious lyrics of the period, which develop the motif of the bleeding of the crucified Christ to similarly ornamental effect.

One interesting feature of *De' gesti heroici* where its narrative content is concerned is that it is one of the very few fictional works by a female author in this period to represent a mother-daughter relationship in any detail. Father-daughter relationships feature in a number of female-authored works, most notably Barbara Torelli's *Partenia*, Leonora Bernardi's *Tragicomedia*, Valeria

Miani's *Celinda*, and Margherita Sarrocchi's *Scanderbeide*, while female characters are represented as intellectual heirs to distinguished fathers in Marinella's *Arcadia felice* and *L'Enrico*.[127] Mother-son relationships, though less frequent, do occur in this literature, even aside from the obvious case of Marian writings, an interesting case being that of Venus and Cupid in Marinella's *Amore innamorato, et impazzato*.[128] Mother-daughter relationships, by contrast, are curiously absent from Italian women's writings in this period, to the extent that even Francesca Turina, who writes movingly of her relationships with her sons in her lyric poetry, makes no mention of her daughter.[129]

Marinella's inclusion of a mother-daughter relationship in *De' gesti heroici* was forced on her to a degree by her sources, which speak of Catherine's mother, Lapa, as a worldly woman intent on her daughter's marriage and hence an initial obstacle in the saint's path. Marinella, however, greatly expands Lapa's role, at one point making her, prompted by a demon, Catherine's principal antagonist in her spiritual mission.[130] Lapa's maternal love for her daughter is presented as sinful and "carnal" in character—her adoration of Catherine is frequently compared to that of a lover—and her obtuseness to her daughter's calling is contrasted to her husband Giacomo's more spiritually creditable stance of submission to God's will.[131] Despite the moral condemnation that surrounds her, however, Lapa is not caricatured or portrayed without sympathy; her suffering at the sight of her daughter's self-violence is vividly rendered, and her attempts to dissuade Catherine from her penitential practices are eloquently portrayed.[132] It might even be argued that the struggle between the strong-willed Lapa and the stronger-willed Catherine forms the emotional core of the *vita*, displacing the love story that nominally lies at the heart of it, between the Virgin of Siena and Christ.

Both the *Vita di Maria Vergine* and *De' gesti heroici* are of interest for their exploration of women's potential for spiritual authority. Mary, whose education Marinella describes as taking place in an institution closing resembling an elite convent of her own day, is portrayed as remarkably precocious in her understanding of scripture, astounding not merely her schoolmates but trained priests themselves by her insight into the sacred texts.[133] Both Mary and Catherine are portrayed as teaching their girlish companions, and both later take a teaching role also in relation to men, Mary following Christ's death, when she is portrayed in an evangelizing role not dissimilar to that of the Apostles, Catherine when God directs her, following a long period of retreat, to use her spiritual influence within the world.[134] Both women are, of course, portrayed as vessels or mediums of God's wisdom rather than figures of independent intellectual authority. This is especially the case with Catherine, who, consistent with the sources, is portrayed as illiterate until she is granted the gift of literacy by divine fiat.[135] This does not, however, prevent her from equaling "a Paul, a Dionysius, a John, a Dominic" in her role as communicator of sacred truth, nor does it keep her from serving in her preaching activity as an outstanding "fisher of souls."[136]

Marinella's representation of Mary as effectively a "thirteenth apostle" and of Catherine as a preacher is worth underlining, given the evangelizing role she herself assumes as a religious writer, perhaps especially her openly didactic *Discorso del rivolgimento*. Especially striking, perhaps, is the degree of intellectual prowess and spiritual leadership she attributes to the Virgin. While Catherine's life could scarcely be described without making some reference to her extraordinary public evangelizing mission, this was certainly not the case with Mary, for whose teaching role not a shred of scriptural authority exists. To craft Mary as quasi-apostle was not a default position for her biographers, and it is not a choice that we may regard as standard even among her female biographers: of Marinella's female predecessors in this field, only Vittoria Colonna is similarly emphatic regarding Mary's teaching role.[137]

5. A Medicean Sacred Epic: Maddalena Salvetti's *David perseguitato*

In addition to saints' lives and New Testament material, the third main category of narrative subject matter employed by religious poets of this era derived from the Old Testament. The most prestigious subtradition within this tradition of Old Testament narrative poetry was the hexameronic, recounting the story from Genesis of God's creation of the world, and the most famous example is Tasso's *Il mondo creato*, published posthumously in 1607.[138] Narrative epics centering on human heroic subject matter from the Old Testament were less frequent, despite the popularity of this material within *sacre rappresentazioni*, although a noteworthy example was offered by the *Ester* (1615) of the Genoese poet Ansaldo Cebà (1565–1622), well known within studies of Seicento women's writing for the enthusiastic response it elicited from the Venetian Jewish poet Sara Copio.[139] An interesting earlier example is the 1561 *Vita di Giuseppe*, by the *poligrafo* Lodovico Dolce, better known for his secular chivalric romances, such as *Il Sacripante* (1536). Among female writers, we have evidence for two projects for Old Testament epics, both Florentine and both unfinished. The manuscript in the Biblioteca Casanatense in Rome that preserves Laura Battiferra's late writings ends with fragments of the first canto of an ottava rima poem recounting the story of Anna and Phenenna from the beginning of the book of Samuel, presumably written toward the end of Battiferra's life, in the late 1580s.[140] More substantially, three cantos remain of an epic by Maddalena Salvetti based on the story of Saul's persecution of David, apparently prepared by the author for publication before her death in 1610 and published posthumously by her widower, Zanobi Accaiuoli, the following year.[141]

While it is difficult to gauge from Battiferra's untitled fragment the scale of the epic poem she intended to write, it is clear from the published opening cantos that Salvetti's *David perseguitato, o vero fuggitivo* was planned as a substantial work. The cantos that survive, comprising 289 stanzas, barely begin to tell the biblical story told in 1 Samuel 19, breaking off shortly after the dramatic episode of David's escape from Saul's palace, assisted by his wife Michal ("Micole"). Salvetti's dedicatory letter, to Maria Maddalena d'Austria, Grand Duchess of Tuscany, informs us that she intended the poem to continue on to include Saul's death and David's ascent to the throne.[142] As the letter also makes clear, Salvetti intended to complicate her main plot with a secondary, fictional plot concerning the love and eventual marriage between Italo, son of the legendary ancient king of Italy, Tarracone, and the Amazon princess Pantasilea, daughter of Marpesia, legendary foundress of Ephesus.[143] Salvetti provides no justification in her dedicatory letter for this mingling of biblical and nonbiblical elements other than to claim that the poem's subplots were fully integrated with the main action, as Aristotelian epic theory demanded, and, less tenably, that they were "founded on some true history."[144] Cebà, justifying similar fictional embellishments in his *La Reina Ester*, simply pleads a Tassesque poetic license: "poetry would lose the name of poetry if it did not spin fables around history."[145] Without stating this formally, writers may have considered Old Testament material more forgiving than New Testament material on this score. In Cebà's case, at least, this confidence proved unjustified, however: *Ester*'s infidelity to scripture led, in the event, to its being placed on the Index of Prohibited Books.[146]

Salvetti's choice of ancient Italian material for her chivalric subplot in *David perseguitato* was clearly motivated by patriotic and dynastic concerns. As her dedicatory letter already announces, the plot's romantic protagonists,

Italo and Pantasilea, are the distant ancestors of the Medici family, to which Maria Maddalena's husband, Cosimo II, belonged. This device allows for the inclusion of an extensive passage in praise of the Medici in canto 3 of the poem, levered in, as was traditional in epic, through an ekphrasis, in this case describing a series of gold and silver relief panels representing the glories of the Medici, as presciently revealed to King Tarracone by the Tiburtine sybil.[147]

In figuring the legendary founders of her patron's family as two young lovers originally on opposite sides in a martial conflict, Salvetti locates herself within the grand tradition of dynastic romance and epic that extended back through Ariosto and Boiardo to Virgil's *Aeneid*. Within this tradition, she follows the modern vernacular model in making her female dynastic ancestress a warrior like her husband, rather than, as in Virgil, simply a beautiful and chaste young princess. Salvetti may have been aware of Moderata Fonte's chivalric romance, *Il Floridoro* (1581), dedicated to an earlier grand duchess of Tuscany, Bianca Cappello, which similarly features a female knight, Risamante, as the Medici's dynastic foundress.[148] More proximately, the final redaction of Francesco Bracciolini's *Croce racquistata* (1611) gives the same dynastic role to the warrior woman Erinta, who serves implicitly in the poem as a heroizing fictional prototype of Maria Maddalena.[149] There is evidence that it was the grand duchess herself who, in a meeting in 1609, encouraged Bracciolini (1566–1645) to recast his poem as a Medicean dynastic epic, and it is possible that Salvetti, who was effectively a court poet, was responding to similar patronal demands.[150] An accomplished horsewoman and huntress and a scion of the greatest political dynasty in Europe, Maria Maddalena would be described in the 1620s by Cristoforo Bronzini as "a new Amazon in Tuscany."[151] Although she did not employ images of Amazons in her own political self-fashioning, for example, in the pictorial scheme at her Villa at Poggio Imperiale, analogous figures were depicted there, such as the ancient queens Artemisia and Semiramis, the latter famed for her prowess in warfare.[152]

It should also be borne in mind when accounting for Salvetti's apparently incongruous combination of Old Testament narrative with fictional ancient Italian chivalric material that an influential historiographical tradition in Florence had long posited a connection between ancient Hebraic and pre-Roman Italian culture. A key figure in this tradition was the forger Annius di Viterbo (d. 1502), whose pseudoantique writings constructed a prestigious proto-Hebraic genealogy for Etruscan civilization, presenting Etruria as founded by Noah's grandson Comerus or, in an alternate version, by

Noah himself. This had important linguistic consequences, in that the Tuscan tongue could be presented not as a corruption of Latin but rather as a descendent of Noah's ancient Aramaic, parent language of both Etruscan and Hebrew. This linguistic theory was developed with great energy in the 1540s by intellectuals in the circles of Cosimo I de' Medici, notably Giambattista Gelli (1498–1563) and Pierfrancesco Giambullari (1495–1555). At the same time, Old Testament motifs came to be increasingly deployed in the propaganda of the Medici dynasty, a famous example being the iconography of Bronzino's chapel for Eleonora of Toledo in the Palazzo Vecchio in the early 1540s.[153] Annius's ideas had been partially discredited by the time of Salvetti's writing, and she does not herself opt for his Tuscan foundation myth, preferring instead a fusion of the medieval legend of the origins of Fiesole at the hands of the hero Atlas and Aristotle's account in the *Politics* of the legendary Lucanian king Italus, from whom the Italian peninsula took its name.[154] Nonetheless, the cultural habit of positing a relationship between Old Testament and Etruscan history must have facilitated Salvetti's mingling of the two in her epic and lent plausibility, for her readers, to her positing of an alliance between Tarracone and Saul.

David perseguitato opens portentously, positioning the story it is to tell within the great sweep of providential history. Salvetti recounts in sequence the Fall, God's decision to redeem humankind through Christ's incarnation, and the devil's anger at the prospect and his resolve to compromise God's plan by seeking the death of David as ancestor to the Virgin. Her subplot of the dynastic romance of Italo and Pantasilea does not explicitly participate in the same providential scheme, but the integration of the two plots helps to imply a connection, as does the detail that the future glories of the Medici family are predicted to Tarracone by the Tiburtine sybil, who would also later, as Salvetti recalls, be responsible for predicting the advent of Christ to Augustus.[155] In its meshing of dynastic celebration and sacred narrative, Salvetti's *David perseguitato* recalls Lucrezia Marinella's *De' gesti heroici*, also dedicated to Maria Maddalena, which, as we have seen, imports praises of the Medici into a vision sent to Saint Catherine by God. The association of dynastic power and divine will was of course nothing new; on the contrary, it is practically a universal trope of monarchic political propaganda. The converted epic forms of the Counter-Reformation, however, found new ways to articulate this "truth."

What is most likely to interest the modern reader in Salvetti's *David* is that this poem offers a rare case of a dynastic epic written by a woman for a female dedicatee and consciously tooled for that purpose. The principal points of comparison here are Moderata Fonte's *Floridoro* (although Fonte dedicates her work jointly to Bianca Cappello and Francesco I de' Medici, her husband) and Barbara Tigliamocchi's later *Ascanio errante* (1640), dedicated to Maria Maddalena d'Austria's daughter-in-law, Vittoria della Rovere. As hardly needs to be noted, a remarkable feature of this microtradition is that all three of these works are dedicated to dynastic consorts of the Medici family, a reflection of the extraordinary prominence of Medici women in female cultural patronage in general in this period.[156] On the evidence of the fragment published, Salvetti's work represents something of a high point in the feminization of the genre. The titular hero, David, occupies only one canto of the three published, and we see him weak, young, and imprisoned, dependent on the help of a woman for his survival. Furthermore, as we have seen, his importance in providential history is presented in terms of his role as a distant ancestor to the Virgin. Within the dynastic subplot of the poem, Salvetti gives far less salience to Italo than she does to Pantasilea: while the former is introduced only briefly, in canto 3, with generic allusions to his beauty and valor, Pantasilea and her Amazon entourage merit a lengthy and glittering set-piece description in canto 2 that constitutes without doubt the most striking passage of the poem as it stands.[157] Clad in scarlet and gold with plumed helmets on splendidly caparisoned horses, Pantasilea's troops constitute a battery of concentrated feminine power. They are compared to the bow-wielding nymphs of Diana, whose militant chastity they share, while their leader is compared to Homer's armed Venus when she intervenes to fight alongside the doomed Trojans, a premonition, perhaps, of the similar rout that ultimately awaits the powerful Philistine army she has joined.[158]

The significance of Salvetti's decision to make her dynastic heroine not the classical "freelance" chivalric *guerriera* but an Amazon princess deserves to be underlined. This negates the exceptionalist character conventionally attributed to the warrior woman in chivalric romance, where she tends to figure as a sole, gender-defying heroine, or at most as one of a pair, for example, Ariosto's Bradamante and Marfisa or Tasso's Clorinda and Gildippe. Unsurprisingly, Amazonian women, seen as a collective, tend to fare less well in chivalric romance than the more "recuperable" figure of the single *guerriera*; typical in this regard is Ariosto, whose sympathetic treatment of Bradamante and Marfisa contrasts with his satirical portrayal of the *femine omicide* of cantos 19–20.[159] Given the unfinished state of Salvetti's poem, we have no certainty regarding the fate awaiting Pantasilea and her entourage, but the Amazon princess's destiny as cofounder of the Medici augurs well for at least her own personal survival and success. Rather than a threat to be suppressed, the figure of the Amazon here appears to be held up as an object for admiration, in a manner that reflects the particular circumstances of the Medici dynasty at the time of Salvetti's writing. One distinctive feature of the polity of the Amazons in myth is its matrilinear character: it emblematizes the capacity of leadership qualities to pass through the feminine line. This had a peculiar relevance to the Medici family under the reigns of Ferdinando I and Cosimo II. Christine of Lorraine, Ferdinand's wife and Cosimo's mother, was a Medici not only by marriage but by maternal descent from Caterina de' Medici, queen of France (1519–89), who was a descendent of the original, legendary Medici line stemming back to Cosimo il Vecchio (1369–1464). Ferdinando himself, by contrast, descended through his father, Cosimo I, from a minor branch of the family; thus, it was only through his marriage to Christine that the grand-ducal line was fully reconnected with the past glories of the Medici, including their two early sixteenth-century popes.[160] Few regimes in this period had as much reason to be open to the idea that princely *virtù* could descend through the feminine, as well as the masculine, line. It is also relevant here that the current grand duchess, Maria Maddalena d'Austria, was a Hapsburg and hence capable of endowing her offspring with the cachet of imperial blood.

The prominence of women within the Medici dynasty, as well as, perhaps, Salvetti's own gendered perspective as author, is reflected in the salience given to women within the genealogical encomium of the family in canto 3. Salvetti offers an interesting contrast here to Moderata Fonte, who had given a far more traditionally "patriarchal" narrative of the same dynasty in the equivalent passage of her *Floridoro*, and to Francesco Bracciolini, whose account of the Medici lineage again focuses for the most part on its men.[161] From the time of Cosimo I, Salvetti's account gives approximately equal billing to the dukes and their duchesses, giving an octave to both Cosimo and Eleonora of Toledo; two lines each to Francesco I and his first consort, Giovanna d'Austria (1547–78); an octave and a half and an octave, respectively, to Ferdinand I and Christine of Lorraine; and four octaves and three and a half octaves, respectively, to Cosimo II and Maria Maddalena d'Austria.[162] Christine returns later, in a second, female-dominated list, following a description of her grandmother Caterina de' Medici, the latter described as a "vast and deep sea of lofty prudence," the former as "a virile soul in a woman's dress."¹⁶³ This "matrilinear" moment, even if presented as clearly secondary to the patriarchal sequence of the dukes and their consorts, is sufficiently unusual in a genealogical encomium of this period to merit attention. Following her praise of Caterina and Christine, Salvetti goes on to praise the murdered Isabella de' Medici (1542–76), daughter of Cosimo I and Eleonora de Toledo, followed by her son and daughter, Virginio Orsini (1572–1615) and Leonora Orsini Sforza (d. 1634), a gesture that, again, appears to emphasize the capacity of Medicean greatness to convey itself through the feminine line.¹⁶⁴

※ CHAPTER FIVE ※
SECULAR NARRATIVE

The period covered by this book, 1580–1635, saw the publication of five works of secular narrative by women in Italy. Three are by Lucrezia Marinella: the pastoral romance *Arcadia felice* (1605), the mythological-allegorical poem *Amore innamorato, et impazzato* (1618), and the epic *L'Enrico, overo Bisanzio acquistato* (1635). The other two works are Moderata Fonte's unfinished chivalric romance, *Tredici canti del Floridoro* (1581), and Margherita Sarrocchi's epic *La Scanderbeide*, published in a partial version in 1606 and in a complete, revised version in 1623. To these may be added an unpublished work, Francesca Turina's romance "Il Florio," recently discovered in manuscript in her husband's family archives in San Giustino, while sources mention epics undertaken by Isabella Andreini and Veronica Franco; whether these were completed or merely started we cannot know.[1] Together, the surviving works make up a substantial body of literature, especially when we consider the scale of the works involved, which is quite different from that of the sacred narratives discussed in chapter 4. Turina's massive "Florio" comprises thirty-one cantos, Marinella's *L'Enrico* twenty-seven, and Sarrocchi's *Scanderbeide* twenty-three, while even the shorter *Floridoro* and *Amore innamorato, et impazzato* have, respectively, thirteen and ten.

The discussion that follows is divided into two main parts, the first discussing the three chivalric works *(Il Floridoro, La Scanderbeide, L'Enrico)*, the second, *Amore innamorato, et impazzato* and *Arcadia felice*. For reasons of space, the discussion is limited to those works published in the period, although "Il Florio" also merits critical attention.

1. Women Writers and the Literature of Chivalry

Although they are assimilable based on their chivalric subject matter, the three poems discussed in this section cannot be unproblematically described as belonging to the same genre. Fonte's *Floridoro*, the earliest of the three works by a quarter-century, falls squarely into the genre of romance as practiced by Ariosto in the *Orlando furioso*, while Sarrocchi's *La Scanderbeide* and Marinella's *L'Enrico* form part of the newer tradition of the classicizing Christian epic as pioneered by Tasso in the *Gerusalemme liberata*, which was published in its first complete edition in the same year, 1581, that Fonte's *Floriodoro* appeared.[2] The genre distinction invests both subject matter (purely invented in Fonte, historically based in Sarrocchi and Marinella) and plot structure (multiple in Fonte, with a series of equally ranking storylines "interlaced"; unitary in Sarrocchi and Marinella, with all subplots, or *episodi*, carefully subordinated to, and integrated with, the main plot).

Chivalric literature had always been immensely popular with female readers in Italy, as throughout Europe, despite the disapproval of moralists, who saw it as unsuitable for women. The bestselling female-authored work of the sixteenth century, Laura Terracina's *Discorso sopra tutti li primi canti d'Orlando furioso* (1550), was a verse commentary/reflection on the *Orlando furioso*, and one of the earliest recorded theatrical performances by an Italian actress, in the 1560s, was an adaptation of an episode from the same poem.[3] Women also had a rather limited history as authors of romances before 1580. In Italy, *Il Meschino, overo il Guerrino*, an adaptation of a fifteenth-century romance, appeared in 1560 with an attribution, since contested, to Tullia d'Aragona, while in Spain Beatriz Bernal published her *Don Cristalián de Espana* anonymously in 1545, and in England Margaret Tyler published her *Mirrour of Princely Deedes and Knighthood*, a translation of a Spanish romance, in 1578.[4]

Despite this hinterland, however, we should not underestimate the novelty represented by the works discussed in this present chapter, the first original works of chivalric fiction published by women of their own volition and under their own name. The two principal themes of chivalric literature, love and war, were both, for different reasons, problematic for women. War seemed intrinsically incongruous as matter for the feminine pen, as trenchantly articulated by the much-translated Spanish educationalist Juan Luis Vives (1493–1540), who opined that "that soul cannot be very chaste that occupies itself with thoughts of steel, or of muscles and male strength."[5] Love, in the frequently sensual and lascivious form it took within the Ariostan tradition, was equally suspect; it may be significant that the only Italian woman to have a chivalric romance attributed to her before 1580 was a courtesan, d'Aragona.

As with other genres of writing, however, a moralizing trend began to be felt within chivalric literature in the post-Tridentine era, facilitating women's engagement with this literature both as readers and writers. A good example of the new model of "honest" romance is Curzio Gonzaga's *Il fido amante* (The faithful lover), first published in 1582, whose pastoralizing title already anticipates the "honesty" of its treatment of love.[6] This was clearly a work women were happy to associate themselves with publicly: its 1591 edition contains a series of verse *argomenti* composed by Maddalena Campiglia, and Lucrezia Marinella approvingly cites its heroic female protagonist in her *La nobiltà et l'eccellenza delle donne*.[7] As a result of this cultural shift, it was no longer as daring a gesture for a woman to publish a chivalric romance in 1580, when Fonte's *Floridoro* appeared, as it would have been in 1540 or 1550. Nonetheless, Fonte's gesture was in its context quite "prodigious," a fact well captured in Giovanni Niccolò Doglioni's prefatory sonnet, which speaks with wonderment at the fact that "a sheltered virgin, closed between narrow walls," should sing so expertly of love, warfare, and strange lands.[8]

Besides the incongruity of the subject matter, another factor made the thought of women tackling this kind of chivalric narrative particularly striking: these were works of a literary ambition and scale that seemed to require a particular virility to attain. This was especially the case with the Tassesque *poema eroico*, which positioned itself very consciously as heir to the great classical epic tradition of Homer and Virgil. While opponents of romance could present it as a corrupt and, in some sense, feminized genre—diffuse, structurally errant, dominated by love at the expense of martial glory—this accusation could not be made against the reborn epic of Tasso, which sets out precisely to remasculinize epic and return it to the gravitas and structural stringency of the Homeric and Virgilian model. That a woman should even attempt what was universally regarded as the greatest challenge the practice of letters had to offer seemed remarkable, even unbelievable, to early seventeenth-century readers. The anonymous author of the dedicatory letter to the first, unauthorized edition of Sarrocchi's *La Scanderbeide*, in 1606, names as his motive in publishing the text a desire to vindicate Sarrocchi's authorship in the face of widespread skepticism that a woman could compose such a work.[9] Similarly, the Neapolitan writer Giulio Cesare Capaccio confesses in an encomium of Sarrocchi how difficult he would have found it to credit her achievement had he not witnessed the power of her intellect at first hand.[10] A sense of marvel also clings to the account of Sarrocchi's epic in the 1642 biography by Janus Nicius Erythraeus, which speaks of her "distinctly virile audacity" (audacia plane virilis) and notes with wonderment the complete absence of precedent in the classical world for a feat of this kind.[11] As I have argued elsewhere, the hostility that Sarrocchi encountered from male writers such as Marino and Tommaso Stigliani (1573–1651) can probably be accounted for largely by this sense of her having overstepped a mark that previous female writers had respected.[12] Stigliani dismisses La Scanderbeide in a work of 1625 as fit only for wrapping fish.

As we might expect, Fonte's *Floridoro* is the least martial of the three poems and the most fabulous in its subject matter. The poem is set in a fantastic, medievalized version of ancient Greece, a fairly popular choice of setting for romance when it departed from the Carolingian setting of the Orlando cycle. Unlike poems with a Carolingian setting, *Il Floridoro* does not posit a great collective martial struggle against which the "errancies" of individual heroes and heroines may be measured, although by the end of the thirteen cantos, where the printed version of the poem breaks off, trouble is beginning to brew between Greeks and "barbarians," which may have been intended to provide such a structure for the whole.[13] As it stands, in the 1581 edition, the poem represents something of an extreme of the tendency toward dispersiveness that contemporary Aristotelian critics found so unconscionable in romance. While the title privileges as hero the young knight Floridoro, whom we see falling in love with the beautiful Celsidora, daughter of Cleardo, king of Greece, equal weight is given to two other plot threads, whose connection with the Floridoro plot remains unclear at the close of the poem: the rivalry between the warrior princess Risamante and her twin sister, Biondaura, coheirs to the kingdom of Armenia, and the adventures of the Italian knights Silano and Clarido in their sojourn with the *maga* Circetta, the daughter of Circe and Ulysses. Still other plots are left hanging, presumably to be picked up later, one concerning the beautiful daughter of the king of Egypt, Raggiadora, falsely accused of murder, another concerning the Lydian beauty Lucimena, imprisoned in the Castle of Fear (Castello della Paura), to the despair of her faithful husband, Nicobaldo.[14] These various plots are combined using the medieval device of *entrelacement* familiar from Boiardo and Ariosto, whereby multiple narrative threads are artfully woven together. Given the unfinished state of the *Floridoro* as we have it, we have no way of assessing how structured Fonte's plan for her poem actually was, although it is perhaps telling that, rather than to Ariosto's preferred structural metaphor of a tapestry, she compares her work to a garland, stringing together flowers of different colors, an image that implies a rather looser narratorial control.[15]

In contrast to Fonte, both Sarrocchi and Marinella conform to Tasso's formula for historical subject matter quite precisely, choosing episodes from history sufficiently recent and well documented to ensure the reader's credence yet sufficiently distant to permit of discreet fictional embellishment.[16] Marinella's *L'Enrico* is especially close to Tasso's model in the *Liberata*, in that its narrative is drawn from crusading history. The crusade in question is, however, the fourth, rather than the first, and the episode chosen is of more local, Venetian significance. Marinella's poem describes the siege and capture of Byzantium by the Catholic crusading armies on their way east under the leadership—in Marinella's version—of Doge Enrico Dandolo (c. 1107–1205), an emblematic event in the history of Venice's acquisition of a maritime empire and hence its rise to "great power" status.[17] Sarrocchi's subject matter is less parochial, though still not devoid of a regional inflection. *La Scanderbeide* recounts the prowess of the Albanian hero Gjergj Kastrioti, or Scanderbeg (Iskender Bey) (1405–68), whose striking though short-lived victories against the Ottomans in his native land made him an icon of the postcrusades Christian warrior on a par with the leaders of the Christian victory at Lepanto.[18] Scanderbeg's story had a particular appeal in the Kingdom of Naples, where his family had settled in the late fifteenth century, and Sarrocchi's Neapolitan ancestry may have been a factor in her choice. She was not the first Italian poet to attempt an epic on the theme, having been preceded in the sixteenth century by the Pugliese Scipione de' Monti (d. 1583), whose poem on the subject is lost, and the Piedmontese Baldassare Scaramelli, who published two cantos of a poem on the theme in 1585.[19] Marinella was similarly preceded in her choice of subject matter by the Friulian Scipione Di Manzano's truncated *I tre primi canti del Dandolo* (1594) and by the Paduan-based Venetian playwright Francesco Contarini's tragedy *L'Isaccio* (1615).[20] A more immediate inspiration for her poem, which she was already working on by 1624, may have been the inset episode recounting the conquest of Byzantium in Camillo Pancetti's 1622 *Venetia libera*, which, along with Giulio Strozzi's *Venetia edificata*, first published in 1621, was one of the most substantial epics prior to *L'Enrico* to be based on Venetian historical themes.[21]

Of the three works under discussion here, the only one whose process of composition we can track with some accuracy is Sarrocchi's *Scanderbeide*, a rare case within the female-authored literature of this period of a work that we can observe *in fieri* rather than simply in its finished form. As noted above, a purportedly unauthorized partial edition of *La Scanderbeide* appeared in 1606, and Sarrocchi thus had some evidence of reception to go on while revising the poem.[22] She also submitted the unpublished revised text for scrutiny to literary advisers, following a practice well established among male authors, most famously Tasso. We see her anxiously soliciting the opinion, in particular, of Galileo, with whom she was acquainted through her ex-tutor and friend, the mathematician Luca Valerio, who doubtless also acted as a reader.[23]

Sarrocchi's letters to Galileo bespeak a dedicated pursuit of literary excellence and an unwillingness to settle for the patronizing "marvel" the writings of women could so easily occasion; she urges him to scrutinize her work "with an enemy eye" and speaks of her intent, if it does not meet with his approval, of "committing it rather to Vulcan than the sun."[24] As Sarrocchi's and Valerio's letters attest, during the later stages of her composition of the poem she was preoccupied with whom to choose as a dedicatee and which families to honor by the inclusion of heroic "ancestors" among Scanderbeg's Italian auxiliaries.[25] The professionalism of her attitude is notable in this respect; the years of hard labor she had poured into the project were clearly an investment she intended to make pay. After considerable hesitation, Sarrocchi appears to have settled for Giulia d'Este (1588–1645), daughter of the Duke of Modena and a descendent of the Medici through her mother, as well as of Ariosto's and Tasso's patrons, the Este, through her father. Fonte, meanwhile, jointly dedicated her *Floridoro* to Francesco I de' Medici and his Venetian-born wife, Bianca Cappello, and Marinella dedicated her *L'Enrico* to the doge and senate of Venice, a particularly apt choice in that the doge, Francesco Erizzo (1566–1646), had crusading credentials himself, having led the Venetian forces at the siege of Gradisca during the Uskok War of 1615–17.

2. Ideology and History in Female-Authored Chivalric Epic

Both Sarrocchi's and Marinella's works, though not Fonte's, may be seen in broad terms as part of the barrage of ideologically charged literature in this period that sought to recast Christian Europe's essentially losing battle against Ottoman encroachment in a more optimistic and self-flattering light. Whether they looked back to the genuine and substantial gains of the crusading period or the more nugatory victories of later centuries, these epics of religious conflict tended to take predictably Manichean and triumphalist form, portraying the battles between Christians and "infidels" in the guise of primordial struggles between the forces of good and evil, often complete with direct interventions by God and the devil, which answered readerly demands for a supernatural element in epic. Tasso's *Liberata* provides a strong model for this form of moral-religious structuring, attributing the initial successes of the "pagan" side to the machinations of the devil and the upturn of the crusaders' fortunes to a "new order" decided by God. Tasso's innovations were eagerly seized on by his Seicento followers, who often exceeded the model in the scope they allowed to supernatural agency: in Scipione Errico's *Babilonia distrutta* (1624) a scheming pagan enchantress is personally killed by the archangel Michael and transported, body and soul, straight to hell.[26]

Marinella's and Sarrocchi's poems conform to this ideological stereotype to interestingly differing extents. Although Marinella's *L'Enrico* is eccentric in portraying a war not between Christians and Muslims but between Western and Orthodox Christians, it is entirely conventional in its demonization of "the enemy": the Byzantine Greeks are described at one point as "this infidel people that despises Christ's Pastor, enemies to the Heavens and noxious to Man."[27] It is almost a surprise at one point in the poem to see the Greeks take the field carrying an icon of the Madonna (the Nikopeia, looted by the Venetians and now in San Marco); prior to this, the principal religious artifact we have seen venerated by the Greeks is a statue of Minerva, and their religious practices too, such as the politically motivated sacrifice of virgins, take us back to classical Greek mythology rather than to medieval Greek culture.[28] Sympathetic individual characters are not lacking on the Byzantine side, as they had not been on the Muslim side in Tasso's *Liberata*. Marinella invites sympathy especially for female figures such as the warrior Meandra, the archer Emilia, and the young noblewoman Areta, fated to see her husband perish in battle.[29] Byzantine males portrayed sympathetically tend to be those allied with these women, such as Meandra's nephew Ardelio and Areta's husband, Corradino.

Countering these more ecumenical portrayals, it is not difficult to point to demonized figures of males, in particular, on the Greek side: the cruel emperor Alessio, based on the historical figure of Alexius III Angelus (c. 1153–1211) and portrayed in a manner reminiscent of Tasso's tyrant Aladino; the titanic Hyrcanian warrior Oronte, the equivalent of Ariosto's Rodomonte or Tasso's Argante; and the luridly depicted wizard Esone, the counterpart of Tasso's Ismeno.[30] Equally devilish but less type-cast is Alessio's low-born sidekick Mirtillo, based historically on the figure of Alexius Ducas Murtzuphlus (d. 1204); although "murderous and cruel" in his ambition, he is partly humanized by his love for Alessio's adoptive daughter Eudocia (Eudocia Angelina [d. c. 1211]), which Marinella portrays not as political calculation but as a genuine, if convenient, reciprocal passion.[31]

Very different is the portrayal of religious conflict we find in Sarrocchi's *Scanderbeide*, which is remarkable for the period for its relatively nuanced handling of the theme.[32] This has partly to do with the nature of Sarrocchi's subject matter. Unlike the relatively clear-cut invasion scenario envisaged by crusading epics such as the *Liberata*, the Balkan-war situation portrayed by Sarrocchi is intrinsically more complex and internecine. Legend related that Scanderbeg himself, though of Christian ancestry, was brought up at the court of the sultan, and it is verifiable that he fought in the army of Murad II before breaking with the Ottomans after their defeat by the Hungarians at Nis.[33] The 1606 version of the poem includes as a character a Christian woman married to a Muslim, and both the 1606 and 1623 versions show numerous characters converting in the course of the poem, most spectacularly, in the 1623 version, Rosmonda, the sultan's daughter and commander in chief.[34]

In such a relatively fluid situation, quasi-essentialist distinctions between good Christians and evil "pagans" become difficult, and indeed Sarrocchi distributes moral goodness with a fairly even hand. Even some of the Ottoman soldiers who remain unconverted at the end of the poem, such as Orcano and Driarasso, are portrayed as honorable and humane men, while the most consistently reprehensible character is the poem is a Christian, the Iago-like Mauro, whose failed treacheries against Scanderbeg occupy much of the central portion of the poem.[35] Gestures of sympathy across the religious divide are not uncommon in the poem, even outside the field of romantic love, where we find them most commonly in epic: following a raid on the city, Scanderbeg orders Turkish prisoners to be treated humanely and their dead given a decent burial.[36] Demonic agency is practically absent from the poem, and there is no sign of the usual axis *mago*; the sole appearance of magic in the 1623 version of the poem is a brief, wizard-conjured storm at sea, which the papal nuncio, Giuliano Cesarini, quickly puts to rest with his prayers.[37]

The relative moral even-handedness of *La Scanderbeide* is apparent most clearly in its earlier, 1606 redaction, where it may have been sufficiently marked to strike early readers of the poem as a flaw.[38] In the 1606 redaction, much space is devoted to the narration of Scanderbeg's original seizure of power in Krujë, which Sarrocchi portrays, following her historical sources, as the result of a stratagem. In the early sixteenth-century Latin biography by Marinus Barletius, from which most subsequent accounts derive, Scanderbeg ambushes an Ottoman official and forces him to forge documents appointing Scanderbeg governor of the city. The official is then summarily executed to preserve secrecy, and his followers massacred almost to a man.[39] Sarrocchi softens the story by having the official, Comite, initially imprisoned and killed only when he attempts escape. She is also careful to attribute the massacre of Comite's men to Scanderbeg's unruly followers rather than to the hero himself.[40] Still, the Machiavellian means Scanderbeg employs in this case accord rather ill with his character as exemplary Christian hero and lend force to the sultan's later taunt that the Christians are capable of winning victories only while "protected by night or treason."[41] While there are structural reasons why Sarrocchi may have thought it opportune to cut much of the narrative of the taking of Krujë in her revision of the poem, one motive may well have been to enhance the poem's moral clarity by increasing the ethical distance between Christians and "pagans," in particular to burnish the character of her hero, whom epic theory demanded should exemplify virtue in the highest conceivable degree.[42] In the 1623 redaction, the shadowy episode of Scanderbeg's seizure of power in Krujë is swiftly glossed over and forms part of a narration by Scanderbeg's ambassador, Svarte, to predictably mitigating effect.[43]

This moral "stiffening" of the poem in the 1623 redaction is also apparent in the language Sarrocchi uses in speaking of Islam. The later version occasionally introduces pejorative terms such as *false* or *lying* where the language of the 1606 version had been neutral.[44] Nonetheless, by the standards of the era, even the 1623 version of the poem is remarkably sparing in its demonization of the "pagans," even gesturing on occasion to the possibility of a more ecumenical position. The most striking instance of this occurs in canto 7, during an account of a delicate truce negotiation that Scanderbeg is attempting to conduct with the sultan through his ambassador Artecino. The success of the talks is jeopardized when Artecino's loose-cannon servant, Romidone, takes the chance to preach a spontaneous evangelizing sermon to the enemy troops, exalting Christianity and heaping insults on the followers of Islam as a "foolish and base mob."[45] Artecino defuses the situation by assuring his Turkish audience that Romidone's "mad zeal" does not represent the position of Scanderbeg, as he has presumptuously claimed; rather, Scanderbeg speaks with the greatest respect of the Islamic religion and of the sultan himself.[46] Even allowing for the circumstantial motives dictating Artecino's emollient language, it is difficult not to read this as a self-distancing on Sarrocchi's part from at least the shriller registers of the militant Catholicism of her day.

It is ironic that Sarrocchi, raised in the heart of Counter-Reformation Rome, should show herself less strident in her religious ideology than Marinella, a citizen of the republic that the papacy had excoriated in the interdict crisis of 1605–6 for its lamentable tradition of relative tolerance of other faiths. It is possible that the hard-line position Marinella assumes in her poem should be seen as compensatory; certainly, she seems intent in her poem on showing Venice to be capable of spearheading an assault on religious alterity as relentless as any that might be orchestrated by Rome.

Despite the conventionality of much of its religious rhetoric, however, it would be mistaken to present *L'Enrico* as ideologically simplistic, especially where its nationalistic and imperialistic themes are concerned. On the contrary, Marinella's epic manifests a curious ambivalence with regard to its celebratory mission. It is true that the problematic character of the crusading army's decision to assail a Christian power instead of pursuing its war against the "infidel" is never acknowledged in the poem. It would be impossible to guess from reading *L'Enrico* that at the time of the events recounted in the poem the crusaders had already been excommunicated by the reigning pope, Innocent III (c. 1160–1216), for their earlier attack on the Christian city of Zara.[47] At points in the poem, however, a shred of skepticism is allowed to surface concerning the crusaders' motives, which are nominally those of justice and retrospective loyalty to an ally (the young rightful emperor, Alexius IV, whom the crusaders had helped put on the throne following Alexius III's usurpation, was murdered after their departure by Murtzuphlus).[48] Prior to their first assault on the city, the Latin foot soldiers are presented as "weary of repose and avid for booty," keenly aware of "how much wealth the ancient city harbors within its noble threshold."[49] Although this motive is quickly disavowed and replaced by a nobler call for just vengeance, it finds echo in a later passage portraying a council of elders in the stricken Byzantium forlornly discussing whether they should attempt to buy off the crusaders' "vast greed" and "evil thirst for gold."[50] This skeptical reading of the crusaders' motives accords with the judgment on the episode of most modern historians, even if

Thomas Madden, in a recent study, has reemphasized the less mercenary motives at play.[51]

Besides these hints of ambivalence concerning the motives of the Fourth Crusade, there seem to be occasional hints in Marinella's poem of a more generalized dissonance with the entire epic project of the glorification of war. The most obvious focus for this is in the parallel stories of Clelia and Lucillo in canto 15 and Corradino and Areta in cantos 17–18, young couples, on opposing sides, in which the husband dies tragically, having been drawn into the war through a sense of duty and a desire for glory, while the wife is left a hapless victim.[52] The former story, based on Ovid's tale of Halcyon and Ceyx, with input from Ariosto's of Bradamante and Fiordiligi, is particularly poignant, in that the young husband Lucillo dies in a storm at sea after setting out from Cyprus to accompany the Venetian hero Venier without even an attempt at the martial glory for which he has sacrificed his love. The narrative voice, while acknowledging the young man's nobility, is insistent in representing him as misguided in his choice to privilege his "ambitious yearning for honor" over the love of his young wife.[53] More tellingly, the narrative does not entirely condone the conventionally heroic desire of Venier himself, temporarily sequestered from battle after a shipwreck by the *maga* Erina, to get back to the fray. A metaphor glossing his moment of choice compares him to a man in a state of delirium who "despises that which is most salutary to his health."[54] Indeed, unlike his namesake, Sebastiano Venier, general of Lepanto, who survived his brush with the infidel to become doge of Venice in 1577, Marinella's Venier is returned to the battlefield by Erina only to perish at Emilia's hand.[55]

That these episodes all feature a woman who, like those in the *Heroides*, articulates the case for peace over war might encourage us to interpret Marinella's hints at critical distance from the martial spirit of epic as reflecting her status as a woman.[56] While there may be some truth in this, other factors also need to be taken into account, not least the intrinsic false consciousness stemming from the project of celebrating Venice's imperial and martial triumphs at a time when the Venetian maritime empire had been largely lost to the Ottomans and shortly after the humiliation of Venice's military defeat in the War of the Mantuan Succession (1628–31).[57] Also to be considered is the ascetic cast of Marinella's spirituality, which leads her in the majority of her works to figure heroism in the form of a rejection of the temptations of the world, including power and secular glory. It is perhaps telling in this regard that her next work after *L'Enrico*—*Le vittorie di Francesco il serafico, li passi gloriosi della diva Chiara*—was a reprise of the story of Saint Francis, subject of one of the earliest of her hagiographic works.

Marinella's discomfort with her self-imposed role as secular epic poet is most apparent in a rather extraordinary ekphrastic episode in canto 7 of *L'Enrico*, in which the *maga* Erina explicates to her guest Venier a series of sculptures and paintings representing Venetian history from the time of the city's foundation.[58] The episode is quite closely modeled on one in the closing cantos of Fonte's *Floridoro*, which also features a *maga*, Circetta in this case delivering an extended lesson on Venetian history through the medium of ekphrasis before a marveling male audience. Both Fonte and Marinella start their narrations with Venice's foundation at the time of the fifth-century barbarian invasions that put an end to the Roman Empire, preparing the ground for a celebration of Venice as the "new Rome."[59] Both subsequently trace the medieval rise of the city and its imperial expansion, and both progress to an extended description of the Battle of Lepanto, treated as a showcase for their skills in the key epic field of *enargeia*, the graphic visual evocation of action.[60] These similarities aside, however, Fonte's and Marinella's narrations are extraordinarily different in character. Fonte's is more conventional and celebratory, stressing the traditional theme of the city as bastion of liberty, ruled by leaders of "rare intellect."[61] Venice's acquisitions of territory are sedulously underlined, while its losses are carefully omitted, and a Veronese-esque allegory at the opening of the sequence figures Venice as a beautiful and queenly young woman holding an olive branch, surrounded by allegorical figures symbolizing glory, victory, triumph, and fame.[62]

The account of Venice's glories that Marinella gives to Erina in *L'Enrico* is far less untroubledly idealizing. Compared with Fonte's narration, which covers the whole of Venetian history, though selectively, in chronological order, Marinella's traces the city's history down to the late fourteenth century in a chronologically disordered manner, focusing on a series of particular dogeships, then curiously breaks off, as a mysterious cloud arises to engulf the images that follow, to resume only with the account of Lepanto.[63] Like Fonte, Marinella is selective, but unlike Fonte, she seems to focus almost by preference on less savory episodes in Venetian history, such as the murders of Doges Orso Ipato (d. 742) and Obelerio Antenori, the deposition and blinding of Teodato Ipato in 756 and the death in exile of Giovanni Galbaio, doge from 787 to 804, and Otto Orseolo, doge from 1009 to 1026, expelled from the city by an enemy faction. Rather than Fonte's city of peace and plenty, medieval Venice emerges in Marinella's ekphrasis as a place of factional strife and political disorder, its citizens "ferocious" and ungrateful, prone to turn on their leaders "like a snake."[64] Among the doges who emerge best in Marinella's list are those, such as Pietro I (d. 978) and Pietro II Orseolo (d. 1109), who relinquished worldly power before the end of their lives and ended their days in religious retreat.[65] Needless to say, this was not a version of Venetian history that Venetians generally liked to tell themselves.

Equally problematic in conventional encomiastic terms is the modern portion of Marinella's ekphrasis, centering on the Battle of Lepanto. Marinella's account of the battle itself is conventionally heroic and predictably demonizing of the enemy, notably more so than that of Fonte, who finds a moment of compassion for the doomed Turkish troops as they perish in the waves. This moment of Christian triumphalism is, however, followed immediately by the sobering counterweight of an account of the death of Marcantonio Bragadin (1523–71), the Venetian commander shockingly flayed alive following the surrender of Famagosta, some six weeks prior to the Christian victory at Lepanto. Marinella's account of Bradagin's "martyrdom" takes her back into her literary comfort zone of hagiographic epic; in an affect-rich scene, she portrays him "immobile and silent, most dauntless of Heroes, among torments and suffering," with a martyr's crown being prepared for him in heaven, to which his soul will fly like a "new star."[66]

Taken as a whole, then, Marinella's reprise of Moderata Fonte's ekphrastic encomium of Venice has almost the opposite effect to that generally intended by such encomia. More than the praise of a triumphant and inspirational city, we have something more like an argument for retreating from civic life altogether; rather than a litany of Venice's successes, we have a mixed account of its successes and failures, climaxing with the torture of one of its citizens by an enemy power in the wake of its greatest imperial loss.[67] Compounding the irony of Marinella's ambivalent ekphrasis is the fact that the palace in which the images of Venice's glories are displayed is home to the descendents of the tenth-century doge Pietro IV Candiano, suspected by his citizens of intending to usurp power for his family and hacked to death with his young son as they tried to escape the Ducal Palace, to which his pursuers had set fire. In Marinella's version, Candiano is saved by a wizard and whisked off with his son to a magic island, where they found a line of contemplative magi from which her Erina descends. The decision to resuscitate fictionally and give a second chance to a figure of such equivocal historical status seems odd, given the nationalistic-celebratory tone of the poem as a whole. Even odder is Marinella's reference to him at one point as "the exiled king" (il re sbandito), an epithet that squares ill with the republican sentiments one might expect a poem celebrating Venice to espouse.[68]

Marinella was clearly disappointed with the reception of *L'Enrico* by the leaders of the Venetian state, to whom it was dedicated, a disappointment perhaps expressed in the dedication of her subsequent *Vittorie di Francesco il serafico* (1643) to the republic's sworn enemy, Pope Urban VIII.[69] Given the ideological dissonances of the work, however, it is difficult to think that the doge and the senate would have been entirely satisfied with *L'Enrico* if they deigned to read it. Venice and its history do not exactly emerge burnished from this perplexing poem, whatever the intention of the author may have been.

3. Gender, Arms, and Love in Female-Authored Chivalric Fiction

One reason why chivalric romance in its Ariostan formula appealed strongly to women was without doubt the innovative quality of its representation of women, and especially its creation of the figure of the female knight, one of the most fascinating and distinctive new literary types of the age.[70] Building on the precedent of Matteo Maria Boiardo's *Orlando innamorato* (1483–95), Ariosto includes two female knights in the *Orlando furioso*: the Christian Bradamante, the protagonist of the poem's principal love story, destined with her husband, Ruggiero, to found the dynasty of Ariosto's patrons, the Este; and the slighter but striking figure of Marfisa, Ruggiero's sister, who, like him, starts the poem a pagan but converts by the end. Especially in the final, 1532 version of the poem, Ariosto draws out the profeminist implications of the *guerriera* figure overtly, arguing in two canto proems for women's capacity to equal men in their achievements if given the opportunity and citing as a modern archetype of female virility Vittoria Colonna, who was emerging in these years as a poet of note.[71]

In the wake of Ariosto, the figure of the *guerriera* enjoyed an immense literary vogue and became a ubiquitous figure in chivalric romance; Curzio Gonzaga's *Il fido amante,* for example, has three warrior women in its cast, including the invincible Ippolita/Vittoria, object of the eponymous hero's exemplarily faithful love. Tasso's revision of Ariosto in the *Gerusalemme liberata* brought about a shift in the representation of the *guerriera*, which tended from this point to revert to the classical, Virgilian model, according to which the warrior woman fights on the enemy side and perishes at the hands of a man. In the *Liberata* is the fate of both the "pagan" Clorinda, who perishes at the hand of Tancredi, and the Christian Gildippe, mown down in the final battle, along with her husband, Odoardo, by Solimano.[72] Popular as this Virgilian-Tassesque model proved, however, this more punitive figuration of the *guerriera* did not entirely displace the Ariostan model. As we saw in chapter 4, one of the most successful chivalric epics of the early Seicento, Francesco Bracciolini's *La croce racquistata* (1611), features a Christian warrior woman on the Bradamante model who survives the poem to become the foundress of the Medici dynasty, while Giovanni Leone Sempronio's *Il Boemondo* (1651), a reworking of the *Liberata*, gives a similar dynastic role to Tasso's Gildippe.[73] Even Tasso's earliest imitator, Camillo Camilli, did not follow the gender logic of his model: his *Cinque canti* (1583), intended as a continuation of the *Liberata* and often published with Tasso's poem in the late sixteenth and early seventeenth centuries, gives Goffredo a warrior sister, Idetta, who survives to the end of the poem intact.[74]

As we might expect, the three female chivalric authors discussed in this chapter embraced the figure of the female knight with enthusiasm, as did Maddalena Salvetti in her *David*, discussed in chapter 4.[75] Fonte has a single female warrior, Risamante, but gives her a prominence at least equal to that of her titular hero, Floridoro, with whom she shares the genealogical destiny of founding the Medici dynasty. Sarrocchi features two female warriors in *La Scanderbeide,* both initially on the enemy side but, like Marfisa, eventually converting. One is a classic female-knight figure, the sultan's daughter, Rosmonda, like Bradamante also the protagonist of an important cross-faith love story; the other, a more original type, Silveria, an archeress discovered living wild on Mount Olympus and recruited to the Ottoman army by Rosmonda. Marinella reproduces this Sarrocchian model in her own two enemy *guerriere*, the knight Meandra and the archeress Emilia. She differs from Sarrocchi, however, in having neither of these Byzantine warrior heroines convert in the poem. Instead, she includes a Latin knight, Claudia, as Meandra's opposite number.

While the portrayals we find of warrior women in female-authored chivalric texts owe much to the previous, male-authored tradition, there is also much that is novel. As might be expected, all three of our authors follow Ariosto in crafting the female knight as exemplary of women's capacity for heroic attainment generally and in making an explicit or implicit connection between the prowess at arms displayed by the *guerriera* and the prowess in letters displayed by the female writer. Fonte does this in the same manner as Ariosto, spelling out in the authorial proem to a canto the lesson of Risamante, namely, that given the same education as men, women would have the capacity to equal them in any field to which they turned their hand.[76] The device of the authorial proem was not one available to Sarrocchi and Marinella, who follow the classical and Tassesque model of the self-effacing narrator, but Marinella nonetheless underlines the significance of the female knight when she introduces the figure of Claudia, noting that she is living proof that "custom and not nature placed timorousness in one sex and valor in the other."[77] All three writers take some relish in having their female warriors defeat men in combat, sometimes after suffering gendered taunts from their opponents, who were misled by their sex into underestimating their prowesss.[78] It is notable in this regard that of the three female-crafted *guerriere* who die in battle, Sarrocchi's Silveria and Marinella's Claudia and Meandra, none falls at the hands of a man, even though this had, post-Tasso, become almost the default destiny for *guerriere* in Italian epic.[79] Sarrocchi develops this motif of female superiority at arms in a striking episode, probably modeled on a scene in Marinella's *Arcadia felice,* in which Silveria defeats and humiliates a series of male opponents in an athletic tournament in the Ottoman camp.[80] The episode seems clearly self-referential, as is underlined by the rancorous and violent response of Silveria's defeated competitors, which parallels the hostility Sarrocchi's literary ambitions aroused in certain of her most prominent male peers.

Perhaps the most interesting of the *guerriere* figures in female-authored epic, and certainly the most fully realized, are Fonte's Risamante and Sarrocchi's Rosmonda, both modeled to a significant extent on Ariosto's Bradamante but departing from the archetype in interesting ways. Risamante's most obvious departure from the model of Bradamante is her lack of a love object. Bradamante is in love with Ruggiero from the opening of the *Furioso* and spends much of the poem pursuing her errant lover. Risamante remains unattached throughout the portion of the *Floridoro* that was published, even if we know from dynastic prophecies that she is destined eventually to marry an unnamed king of Cyprus, apparently poised to enter the poem as a protagonist shortly after the published portion ends.[81] This plot decision allows Fonte to combine in a single figure the self-sufficiency Ariosto gives to his unattached Marfisa and the gravitas that accrues to Bradamante through her genealogical destiny as foundress of a great dynasty.[82] Risamante also gains, by comparison with Ariosto's Bradamante, through her virtually unchallenged status as exemplar of martial excellence within the poem. Bradamante is only one among many prominent warriors in the *Furioso*, no more successful as a knight than figures such as Ruggiero or Brandimarte and by some measures considerably less so.[83] In *Il Floridoro*, by contrast, it is Risamante who almost singlehandedly exemplifies the martial and moral qualities of the ideal knight in the poem. Although Floridoro makes a promising debut as a knight in a tournament midway through the poem, he is younger and less experienced than Risamante.

The finesse with which Fonte builds on and adapts her Ariostan archetype is especially apparent in the scene toward the beginning of the poem in which Risamante's destiny as foundress of the Medici dynasty is revealed by an unnamed "beautiful fairy" (bella fata) in the symbolic locus of a womblike cave.[84] The episode is closely modeled on the equivalent scene in the *Orlando furioso*, in which Bradamante receives a similar revelation from the fairy Melissa, again situated in a cave. Given the closeness of Fonte's imitation of Ariosto, the novelties that she introduces into her version of the episode are interesting. First, she eliminates the element of patriarchal oversight supplied in the Ariostan narrative by the figure of the dead Merlin, whose tomb, which harbors the wizard's still-living spirit, dominates the space in which Melissa delivers her revelation. As is clear, indeed, in Ariosto, the prophecy is Merlin's, and Melissa delivers it only under license. A second significant shift concerns the relative weight given to the originating spouses in the foundation of the dynasty. Although Ariosto had revised his own model, Virgil, in giving the genealogical revelation to the female of the pair rather than the male, his account of the origins of the Este remains firmly patrilinear. The immediate offspring of Bradamante and her husband, Ruggiero, will be a son, Ruggierino, whom Melissa describes to Bradamante as being "conceived in you by the seed of Ruggiero," a male-centered notion of the role of the sexes in generation that reflects the influence of Aristotelian theory.[85] Risamante, by contrast, as the *fata* informs her, will give birth to a daughter, Salarisa, "conceived by you" though fathered by the king of Cyprus.[86] The same egalitarian generative theory is later iterated by the *maga* Circetta in speaking of her parents, Circe and Ulysses: "by the one and the other I was conceived."[87]

Besides these revisions, Fonte also significantly departs from her Ariostan source in her initial narrative framing of the episode. Ariosto introduces Bradamante into Merlin's cavern by having her unceremoniously pushed into its well-like entry by the villain Pinabello. Fonte, by contrast, constructs for Risamante a more resonant and dignified entry: she is invited into the cavern by a mysterious female voice immediately after defeating in combat a vicious snake or dragon that had attacked her as she was resting in a meadow.[88] The voice turns out to be that of the adulterous queen of Phrygia, who has been sheltering in the cavern with her young son to escape the potentially murderous vengeance of her husband. The snake, as we learn from the queen, was created by the fairy of the cavern both as protection and to signal the eventual end of the queen's enforced concealment; she has destined it to die at the precise moment when the queen's husband dies and its guardian function becomes obsolete.[89]

This curious frame story lends considerable depth and complexity to the scene that follows, that of the fairy's revelation of Risamante's maternal destiny. One striking feature of the episode is the implicit association it creates between the snake guardian of the cavern and the queen's husband, figured as the embodiment of a patriarchal society that punitively controls women's sexuality and reproductive capacity. It seems telling in this regard that the dragon is represented simultaneously as protection and physical threat. Equally striking is that Risamante's induction into her future maternal career takes place in the presence of a woman represented as the devoted mother to a child born and nurtured outside the licit marital-reproductive economy. The grand dynastic lineage the fairy reels out for Risamante tells one story of maternity— that told in the corresponding passage of Ariosto—in which women figure as conduits for bloodlines through which power and wealth are transmitted. The figure of the adulterous queen and her beautiful androgynous young son, raised in a fairy cavern quite apart from society, tells another; here, maternity is recouped as a private, affective experience conducted, in this instance, in a purely matriarchal space.

Besides serving as a preamble to the scene in the cavern, Fonte's scene of Risamante's combat with the dragon is also of independent interest. Most obviously, the narration recalls the famous legend of Saint George, with a female figure this time cast in the role of dragon slayer. This allusion would have had particular resonance in Venice, given that George was one of the city's patron saints. A further image it may have conjured for contemporary readers was that of the Virgin Mary crushing the head of the serpent, an allegory of Mary's role in the incarnation, through which she was considered to have "crushed the devil" by rescuing humanity from its spiritual death following the Fall. Besides these religious allusions, a further level of meaning accrues to the episode through the classical literary references that Fonte introduces into her narration, notably her emphatic comparison of Risamante's battle with the serpent to that waged against a similar beast by the Phoenician hero Cadmus prior to his founding of Thebes, an episode known principally from its narration by Ovid in book 3 of the *Metamorphoses*.[90] The comparison is particularly interesting in this context, as the serpent fought by Cadmus is sacred to Mars, the god of war, while Cadmus himself enjoys the protection of the goddess Minerva. The episode may thus be seen as opposing a raw, hypermasculine, aggressive furor with a more tempered and androgynous model of fortitude associated with wisdom (it is perhaps worth recalling that Cadmus was famed, under Minerva's guidance, for introducing the art of writing to Greece).

Like Risamante, Sarrocchi's Rosmonda to an extent may be seen as a reworking of Bradamante, although Sarrocchi, writing after Tasso, clearly also had in mind the alternate model represented by Clorinda. Like Bradamante and Clorinda, Rosmonda is the protagonist of a cross-faith love story, in her case with Scanderbeg's nephew Vaconte, one of the principal warriors of the Christian camp.[91] Her story resembles Bradamante's in that she ends the poem happily married to her lover and sharing the same faith; however, their stories differ in that in Sarrocchi it is the female of the pair who converts. A further difference is that Rosmonda does not undergo the "normalization" to which Bradamante is subject in the final cantos of the *Furioso*, where we see her relinquish her armor for female dress. Like a less tragic version of Tasso's Christian warrior couple Odoardo and Gildippe, Rosmonda and Vaconte fight side by side in the climactic battle of the poem. Sarrocchi's portrayal of the love between Vaconte and Rosmonda is consistent with the post-Ariostan romance trend toward an idealizing treatment of love. Where Ruggiero torments Bradamante with jealousy and shows himself susceptible to the charms of Alcina and Angelica, Vaconte is entirely devoted in his passion. He is the subordinate figure of the pair for a substantial segment of the poem, captured by Rosmonda on the battlefield and spending an extended period of time as her prisoner, in an interesting cross-gendered adaptation of Tasso's motif of Erminia as "prisoner of love."[92] While his position is that of Tasso's Tancredi and Rinaldo, reduced to a position of erotic subjugation to a woman of the enemy religion, we are left in no serious doubt that this enthrallment will ultimately prove benign.[93] The connection between eros and moral errancy, so potent in Tasso, is broken in *La Scanderbeide*. Erotic captivation by a woman figures in Sarrocchi's poem as a means of self-realization for the Christian warrior, rather than a shameful effeminization, as it is figured in the *Gerusalemme liberata*.

Besides the figure of the female warrior, another romantic female character type that we find interestingly reconfigured in female-authored works is the dangerous enchantress who lures the hero temporarily from the path of duty, a type deriving ultimately from Homer's Circe and memorably developed by Ariosto and Tasso in the figures of Alcina and Armida. Both Fonte and, following her, Marinella have versions of this episode that differ very significantly from the male-authored norm of such episodes; the enchantress figures they craft are desexualized and do not represent a particular threat to the men who fall under their power. Fonte plays with the stereotype of the sinister enchantress before disabusing us: her Circetta first appears to us through the half-seduced, half-suspicious eyes of the knights Silano and Clarido, lately shipwrecked on her island, as they watch her lead a knight prisoner to her magic wood and transform him into a tree.[94] The sinister initial impression created by this scene is, however, quickly dispersed when we learn that Circetta is compelled to this witchery herself by an enchantment put in place by her mother and destined to remain in place until it can be broken by a knight whose valor is equal to that of Ulysses, who will then become master of the island.[95] Circetta subsequently proves to be an innocuous host to her Italian visitors, suffering herself from an incipient passion for Silano, who leads her on in the hope of gaining her assistance in breaking the spell and winning the kingdom even though his heart is engaged elsewhere.[96] As the narrative breaks off, Circetta seems about to repeat the fate of her mother, which is narrated by her daughter to the two *cavalieri*. Fonte's development of the Homeric story has Circe seduced and abandoned by Ulysses, left to slake her anger with an impotent posthumous revenge on his homeland of Ithaca, where the episode is set.[97]

The figure of Circetta is of particular interest when set against the Ariostan archetype of Alcina, on whose magical island in the *Furioso* Fonte's enchanted Ithaca seems to be largely modeled.[98] Much of the scene setting is similar in the two episodes. Circetta's gleaming crystalline palace recalls Alcina's golden one, and there are parallels in Ariosto both for the horde of wild beasts that assail the warriors and are dispelled by a word of Circetta's and for the sumptuous feast at which she entertains her guests. More tellingly, we see parallels in Circetta for two of Alcina's more sinister attributes, obviously deriving from the Homeric archetype: her agelessness, conferred on her by her mother, and her ability to transform men into plants.[99] Circetta differs radically from her archetype, however, in that rather than being portrayed as a practiced seductress, she is portrayed as an innocent young girl, clearly destined to be the deceived in love, rather than the deceiver. This transformation short-circuits the allegorical logic of the Ariostan episode, which makes the seductive Alcina an image of the illusory and morally dangerous charms of sensual pleasure, a false lure graphically revealed as such when the seemingly youthful enchantress is unveiled to her horrified victim, Ruggiero, in her true colors, as a repellent old hag. By devolving the role of deceptive seducer onto the male figures in this episode (Ulysses, Silano), Fonte disrupts the baleful allegorical connection between femininity, sex, and magic that pertains in the Ariostan archetype of her story and that also largely informs Tasso's reworking of the story in his narrative of Armida.[100] The distance she has traveled from the classic model of the evil enchantress is illustrated by the fact that she allocates to Circetta the role of ekphrastically outlining the glories of her homeland, a task usually reserved in romance and epic to authoritative and morally positive figures.

If Fonte's Circetta revises the figure of Alcina, Marinella's Erina similarly revises that of Armida. Both have the same structural role, in that both temporarily detain a crucial warrior on the Latin side, although Erina proves ultimately closer to the model of Circe, in that she ultimately speeds the warrior on his way.[101] Like Circe and Fonte's Circetta, Erina is the ruler of a magical island, to which the Venetian warrior Venier washes up, Ulysses-like, after a shipwreck. Like Armida or Circe, Erina offers the hero respite within a feminine world of pleasure, ease, and safety, which he ultimately rejects in the interest of duty. Erina differs very sharply from such literary predecessors, however, in that the detaining pleasures that she offers are not sexual. While she seems attracted to Venier when he first arrives and experiences a brief bout of Dido-like insomnia fretting about his imminent departure, she is promptly informed by her father's ghost in a dream that the Venetian warrior is a distant cousin and so immediately sublimates her attraction into "consanguinary love."[102] The activities she proposes to distract Venier from his lust for glory are conspicuously "honest": hunting, music, and the scientific contemplation of nature. In allegorical terms, rather than the lure of the senses, Erina seems to represent the appeal of the virtuous contemplative over the virtuous active life.[103] This is not a *maga* who is going to turn men into beasts, fish, or trees in the manner of Circe, Armida, or Alcina; Erina's "magic" is closer to the natural-philosophical model of Tasso's benign Mago d'Ascalona than to the darker brand of sorcery represented in the poem by the Greek *mago* Esone.

The Erina episode in Marinella appears to be very clearly framed as revisionary with regard to the allegorical tradition within epic that represents femininity as coterminous with sensual abasement and as an impediment to male heroic achievement. Oddly, however, we find Marinella entirely happy to engage with this allegorical construct in another episode in the poem, in which the Latin army, in the midst of battle, is afflicted with a collective illusion visited upon its members by the wizard Esone. The illusion takes the form of a horde of phantasmagoric temptresses decked out in the full sensual weaponry of the lascivious *donzelle* of Armida's island, their demonic nature concealed behind an appearance of beauty ("behind angelic faces, strange Acheronian forms").[104] These *larve* successfully emasculate the previously dominant Latin forces, plunging them into an erotic trance sufficiently powerful to resist all Enrico's calls to order. The army is forced to retreat in disorder, its rear guard savaged by the Greeks. The allegorical sense of the episode is entirely transparent and corresponds to that of the equivalent episode in Tasso: for all its attractions, sensual indulgence is the work of the devil and can only result in opprobrium and shame. What is surprising is that Marinella seems willing to represent the lure of the senses so emphatically as feminine and sexual, rather than opting for less gendered visions of sensual enticement that might have been available to her, such as entrancement by music. Although in her *De' gesti heroici e della vita meravigliosa della serafica S[anta] Caterina di Siena* Marinella had included scenes in which the young Saint Catherine is similarly tempted by male sensual *larve*, in the *L'Enrico* episode the only female warrior present, Claudia, suffers a delusion with no sexual component, seemingly constituted simply by an irrational fear.[105]

While this is clearly designed to protect Marinella's virgin knight from uncomfortable imputations of unchastity, it also has the effect of soldering traditional metaphorical associations of femininity with the lure of the flesh.

Another moment when *L'Enrico* veers close to the misogynistic discourse so entrenched within the male-authored tradition of epic is an episode in canto 18 in which the Byzantines discuss whether the women of the city should be evacuated in the face of the threatened Latin attack. Of the two principal speakers, one, Aristide, advocates evacuation, describing women as a "useless weight" (inutil peso) on the city, while the other, Costanzo, defends women's valor and patriotism, citing the cases of the Sabine women and, anachronistically, Joan of Arc.[106] The two are quite sharply differentiated in terms of ethos, with Costanzo portrayed as a smooth-tongued "lover of women and friend to ease" and Aristide (whose name recalls that of the fifth-century Athenian statesman famed for his attachment to justice) as "learned and grave."[107] Following a classic misogynistic topos shortly to be dramatically instantiated in the episode of Esone's enchantment, Aristide's speech portrays "the slow and soft sex" as sapping of male valor and disabling of martial prowess.[108] While it might be argued that Marinella intends the scene ironically—the contribution of the women of Byzantium to the defense of the city later in the poem retrospectively nuances Aristide's apparent ideological victory—the negative characterization of the profeminist Costanzo seems too pointed to ignore.[109] *L'Enrico*'s ambivalence in terms of gender ideology relative to the fairly clear-cut profeminism of *Il Floridoro* and *La Scanderbeide* is interesting given the late date of the work's composition. Marinella's treatment of gender is comparable to that of younger female writers such as Margherita Costa and Barbara Tigliamochi (fl. 1640), who show themselves considerably less resistant than most earlier female writers to the adoption of misogynist tropes.[110]

If Marinella may be distinguished from Fonte and Sarrocchi in her representation of the feminine, she may also be distinguished from them in her representation of masculinity. Marinella is the most conventional on this score, in the sense that her male figures map comfortably onto well-established character types.[111] Fonte, by contrast, departs quite notably from literary convention on this score, to the extent that one can speak of her challenging chivalric norms of masculinity at least as much as, or more than, she does those of femininity.

One very radical shift is the relatively slight weight *Il Floridoro* places on fortitude and virility as defining constituents of masculinity. This can be seen most clearly in two minor characters who, while deficient in terms of conventional masculine credentials, are presented as sympathetic figures: the knight Nicobaldo, who seeks Risamante's help in rescuing his adored wife, Lucimena, from an enchantment; and the king of the Pygmies, who we see similarly seeking help from the emperor of Byzantium in saving his beloved Raggiadora, princess of Egypt, from a false accusation of murder.[112] Neither figure is in a position himself to assist his lady in her troubles. Nicobaldo is under an enchantment that subjects him to an extreme fear when he attempts to approach the castle in which Lucimena is held, while the king of the Pygmies is impeded by the injustice of nature, which "has not given [him] strength equal to [his] spirit."[113] Neither man rates fully as a "man" by the conventional standards of epic, which admits as morally acceptable noncombatant males only the occasional saintly hermit or *mago*.

Aside from his fear problem—perhaps forgivable, since supernaturally induced—Nicobaldo is further feminized by details of his backstory, which casts him in sequence as the timorous son of an authoritative father who attempts to impose an unwanted marriage on him and as an unwilling love object to a sexually assertive *maga* attracted by his beauty.[114] The king of the Pygmies, meanwhile, is presented in strikingly feminized terms: physically extremely beautiful—he is compared to Cupid at one point—he presents his plea at Byzantium in a highly emotive manner, choking with tears and barely able to speak.[115] Both men are placed in a position familiar to women in the period, that of lacking the capacity to fight for their own ends without assistance. Tellingly, indeed, in a proem following the tale of the Pygmy king's plea to Risamante, Fonte speaks of her own gratitude to the lawyers who are assisting her, as a helpless orphan, in an inheritance case.[116]

As we might expect, Fonte's eponymous hero, Floridoro, has stronger claims to virility than does Nicobaldo or the king of the Pygmies: he is unquestionably valiant and cuts a dashing figure on the jousting ground, where he is described as the flower of the knights there in the splendor of his bearing and the gravity and hauteur of his looks.[117] However, it would be difficult to class Floridoro as wholly masculine. Sixteen years old when we first encounter him, he is described as angelically beautiful, with the curling golden locks and white skin of the Petrarchan *donna*. Until he speaks, we are told, it would be easy to mistake him for a "beautiful and noble young girl."[118] Even when we see him later in the poem riding into a tournament from which he will emerge victorious, an aura of femininity clings round him: he dresses in the white armor Tasso gives to his female knight Clorinda in token of her chastity, and his assumed name, Biancador, with its similar emphasis on purity, comes from a feminine, rather than a masculine, onomastic canon.[119]

Femininity of appearance and extreme youth were not entirely unknown as characteristics of the epic hero. Tasso's Rinaldo is barely older than Floridoro and equally fetching in his looks: one glance at him sleeping is sufficient to dissuade Armida from her murderous intent. Unlike Floridoro, however, Rinaldo is already a fully formed warrior, though still an adolescent. Where Fonte's initial description of Floridoro has him looking like "the image of Love," the equivalent passage in Tasso has Rinaldo appear like "Love when he uncovers his face, Mars when he fights."[120] In character terms too Floridoro's youthfulness plays out differently from Rinaldo's. Rinaldo's youthful flaws, impetuous wrath and sexual incontinence, are distinctly masculine and serve to assimilate him to classical archetypes of virility such as Achilles and Aeneas. Floridoro is very different, less fiery than Rinaldo and more timorous and respectful of authority, sometimes closer to a child than to the classic boy-hero type represented by Rinaldo.

Especially telling in this regard is the contrast between the two young heroes' relationship with the adoptive mothers who have raised them. Tasso takes care in his opening canto to underline that Rinaldo, despite his youth, has put the feminized realm of childhood entirely behind him. He was raised, we learn, in the household of Countess Matilda of Tuscany (1046–1115), but left this quasi-maternal figure before the age of 15 to seek glory in battle, in what the text describes as a "most noble flight."[121] Floridoro's relationship with his foster mother, by contrast, comes to the narrative forefront when he receives a false report that she is fatally ill.[122] His distress is described in some detail, as are his reminiscences of her maternal caresses. While the episode helps establish Floridoro's sensibility and *pietas*, it detracts from his masculinity, understood as self-sufficiency. Indeed, he is portrayed here in notably feminized terms, petitioning the king for compassionate leave from court "in the sweetest soft voice."[123]

A feature that Floridoro has in common with the lesser figures Nicobaldo and the king of the Pygmies is that he excels in the strength and purity of his love for his lady. This, more than the possession of physical valor, seems to be the essential discriminant in Fonte between "good" and "bad" male characters. The most negative of her male figures are offenders against the codes of love rather than those of martial chivalry: the would-be rapists Amandriano and Acreonte, both thwarted in their plans by the intervention of sympathetic male figures; Lideo, who frames Raggiadora for murder when she fails to respond to his love; even, at a lesser level of iniquity, Silano, who cynically encourages Circetta's love for pragmatic ends.[124] The story of the vain Acreonte's planned assault on Celsidea, foiled by the bashful but brave Floridoro, serves as a paradigm of the poem's moral values in this regard. There are echoes in the episode of the plot of Tasso's pastoral *Aminta,* where the similarly characterized Aminta rescues Silvia from attack by a satyr. Whether or not we may conjecture an influence—Tasso's play had been in circulation in manuscript since its first performance in 1573, although it was not published until 1581—the analogy with a pastoral plot is telling. Despite its impeccably chivalric cast list, Fonte's romance moves in value terms on the territory of pastoral, where fidelity and "honesty" in love rank as at least equal with valor in establishing male characters' credentials.

In pastoralizing chivalric romance Fonte is not entirely out of line with tendencies we may observe in male-authored romances such as Curzio Gonzaga's *Il fido amante,* whose male protagonist equals Fonte's in his devotion to his lady and which aligns with pastoral, as well, in casting its heroine as a votary of Diana, like a pastoral nymph.[125] Where Fonte is more radical is in deemphasizing military prowess, still an important component of masculinity in a poet like Gonzaga. Virility of the aggressive, monster-killing variety continues to play a role in *Il Floridoro,* but it is a female figure, Risamante, who best embodies it. Floridoro, meanwhile, despite his creditable performance at the joust, remains a hero more of sentiment than of action.

The tendency to an alternative scale of masculine values that we see so markedly in Fonte is also apparent to a degree in Sarrocchi's *Scanderbeide,* though she works much more closely with existing chivalric types in crafting her principal male figures. Besides Vaconte, whose characterization has already been discussed, we can point to the figure of Scanderbeg himself, who stands in an interestingly revisionist relationship to his Tassesque prototype, the Christian crusading general Goffredo. Scanderbeg is possessed of the same superhuman fortitude as Goffredo and, at least in the 1623 redaction of the poem, the same morally impeccable character. Despite his moral exemplarity, however, Scanderbeg remains a less monolithic character than Goffredo, or than Marinella's look-alike, Enrico.[126] As a Christian by ancestry and a Muslim by adoption, Scanderbeg is closer in some ways to Tasso's Clorinda than to his

Goffredo: less fixed in his identity, more doubting and complex. Like Clorinda in the *Liberata*, he is even seen on one occasion assuming disguised armor for a night expedition, an episode of some irony, given that the disguise he adopts, that of the leader of the Janissaries, Ferratte, is in effect a reprise of his identity prior to his conversion.[127] This relative mobility of identity lends Scanderbeg a feminine aspect quite remote from Tasso's characterization of the male hero; disguise in the *Liberata* is a device restricted to women (Erminia, Clorinda) or to members of the noncombatant squire class (Vafrino).

A further feature of Scanderbeg's characterization that serves to temper his masculinity by comparison with Goffredo's is connected to the situation in which he finds himself. The plot of the *Gerusalemme liberata*, like that of Marinella's *L'Enrico*, centers on the besieging and defeat of an enemy city. The model is that of Homer's *Iliad*, the archetype of such crusading poems. Sarrocchi's *favola* precisely reverses this pattern, at least in the 1623 version, where the narrative centers on Sultan Murad II's ill-fated siege of Scanderbeg's stronghold, Krujë. In Sarrocchi it is the Christians who are penned in their claustrophobic citadel, awaiting attack, while the Ottomans under the sultan are camped beneath its walls.

This shift quite radically alters the implicit gender politics of the poem from the outset, in that it cuts against the convention whereby victory over the "effeminate" infidel is figured in terms of forcible breach and penetration of the city, underlined in the *Liberata* by discreet references to the literal rapes that accompanied the taking of the city. In *La Scanderbeide*, although they perpetrate a number of successful raids on the enemy camp, the Christian heroes are essentially seen in a "feminine" position of passivity and defensiveness, a position underlined by a threatening scene in which the Ottomans break through the defenses of the city and are only with great difficulty forced back.[128] This has consequences for Scanderbeg's characterization on a more literal level, in that it positions him as the protector of a civilian community including women and children, as opposed to Goffredo, whom we see purely in the guise of a leader of men. More generally, he figures as less hermetically masculine than Goffredo or Enrico, less sealed from any contaminating association with the feminine. Besides the women of Krujë, whom we see him defending on the occasion of the Ottoman raid, he has a wife, the Sofronia-like Dori, whom he saves from an abduction attempt in the first canto of the poem, and a sister, Dianora, mother of the warrior Vaconte, a descendent of the Julio-Claudians and crafted as a Christian version of the type of the noble

Roman matron.[129] These women feature in the poem as active contributors to its Christian mission rather than as distractions from it, as women tend to figure in Tasso: it is during his rescue of his Christian future wife, Dori, that Scanderbeg feels the first stirrings of a desire to return to his original faith, while Dianora's prayers to the Virgin later elicit the first direct divine intervention in the plot.[130]

Before leaving the question of gender in female-authored chivalric poems, it may be useful to look briefly at their treatment of love. There is little to say about this in connection with Fonte's *Floridoro*, other than what has already been said concerning the prominence of erotic fidelity as a valorizing characteristic of masculinity. The loves of the *Floridoro* are largely conventional and idealized, without particular distinguishing features, although Fonte's sympathetic attention to the sexually transgressive queen of Phrygia should be noted as unusual within the conspectus of female-authored literature at this time.

Marinella, by contrast, distinguishes herself among epic poets of the period in the remarkably limited place she gives to the erotic in her poem. Unusually, no romantic narratives attach to any of her three warrior women, and the same is essentially true of the principal male warriors on both sides. On the Greek side, the only love story is that between Mirtillo and Eudocia, ending with Mirtillo's flight and death and Eudocia's rapid and disconcerting deterioration into a raving, Medea-like witch figure.[131] Among the principal Latin warriors, a romantic history is only sketched for the handsome Giacinto, who falls in love with the virtuous Greek princess Idilia after rescuing her from Esone. After a promising start, however, the lovers are separated, and the story disappears from the narrative, to reappear only briefly and illusorily when a demonic simulacrum of Idilia puts Giacinto off his martial stride.[132] Love is relegated essentially to the subplots, to the pathetic but circumscribed narratives of Clelia and Lucillo and of Corradino and Areta; both couples are already married at the start of their respective episodes, and so these are not romances in a conventional sense.

Marinella's virtual elimination of love as a theme from her epic may to an extent reflect concerns of decorum, although it should be noted that she is as anomalous among female writers of fiction in this regard as she is among male. It might be tempting to see this trait in her poem as connected with the fidelity to Homer she claims among its merits in her prefatory letter: contemporary theorists occasionally contrasted Homer's sternly military focus in the

Iliad with the decadent romance digressions of the moderns.¹³³ It needs to be kept in mind, however, when assessing *L'Enrico* that the same resistance to eroticism may be found in Marinella's other secular writings. As we shall see, *Arcadia felice*, her pastoral romance, is equally distinctive on this score.

If Marinella marginalizes love as a theme in *L'Enrico*, the same cannot be said for Margherita Sarrocchi, whose *Scanderbeide* gives the cross-battlefield love between Rosmonda and Vaconte a very prominent role in its narrative. Another love story given a certain salience within the poem, though in a subplot, is the *novella*-like romance of Pallante and Flora, two young lovers raised as siblings and believing themselves to be so but racked by a fierce mutual attraction. A notable feature of this latter story, especially in the 1606 redaction, is the relative sensuality with which it is treated. A scene in which the two lovers lie awake at night in their separate rooms, thinking of each other, makes it clear that the "Neoplatonic" senses of sight and sound do not satisfy them and that they are driven to a more physical consummation by an "unbridled desire" (sfrenato desir).¹³⁴

Even more overtly sexual is a love story in the 1606 edition of the poem that tells of the adulterous affair between Scanderbeg's handsome but unscrupulous lieutenant Serano and the beautiful *maga* Calidora, born a Christian but lapsed, whom Serano induces to betray the Ottoman governor of Krujë to further Scanderbeg's political ends. The story is omitted from the 1623 version of the poem, which, as we have seen, cuts the entire murky tale of Scanderbeg's taking of Krujë. This may have been a strategically wise choice by the standards of contemporary epic, given the moral ambiguity that attaches not only to Serano in the episode but also, to an extent, to Scanderbeg himself.¹³⁵ To a modern eye, however, it is an artistic loss, as the Calidora-Serano episode constitutes one of the most vividly imagined episodes in the poem, as well as one of the most psychologically complex. The growth of Calidora's Dido-like passion is well described, as are Serano's increasingly conflicted feelings, as sexual intimacy, Christian guilt, and a growing sense of the depth of his victim's love for him nuance his original, cynically exploitative stance.¹³⁶ The sympathy Sarrocchi brings to her portrayal of Calidora is remarkable, given that she is not merely an adulteress but also a witch and a renegade to her faith. As a sympathetic depiction of a sexually transgressive woman by a "respectable" female writer, it ranks with Valeria Miani's portrayal of the eponymous heroine of her *Celinda* and Moderata Fonte's of the adulterous queen of Phrygia in *Il Floridoro*, though it is much fuller than the latter of these and arguably more coherent than the former. Without being sexually explicit in terms of physical description, Sarrocchi's account is quite forthright about the bodily nature of her characters' lust. Prior to the consummation of their relationship, Calidora is described as racked by desire almost to the point of swooning: "a subtle fire burns through her bones . . . bathed in a moist, icy sweat, all strength fails her ears and her tongue."[137] Later, after their parting, we find Serano afflicted with erotic dreams of a naked Calidora that touch him with a "flaming hand of burning iron."[138]

It would be difficult to claim that the 1623 version of Sarrocchi's poem was the equal of the 1606 version in its sexual frankness. The Calidora story is dropped, and the Pallante-Flora story suffers a degree of self-censorship, attributing desirous nocturnal meditations to Pallante alone, rather than to both lovers, as in 1606.[139] The chief new love story introduced into the poem, that of Rosmonda and Vaconte, though interesting in many respects, is relatively conventional in the chastity of its treatment. Even so, Sarrocchi remains reasonably robust in her evocations of physical desire by comparison with the majority of female writers at the time: even Vaconte is allowed a moment of lasciviousness on his first encounter with Rosmonda, when, in the manner of Tasso's crusaders ogling Armida on her arrival to petition Goffredo in canto 4 of the *Liberata*, he imagines the beauty of her body under its armor.[140]

Especially interesting is Sarrocchi's depiction of masculine beauty in the poem, which extends beyond the golden locks and pink-and-white complexions to which a writer like Moderata Fonte demurely confines herself to include references to the body. Her description of Vaconte, for example, descends from his handsome face and blond hair to survey his "broad shoulders," "full chest," "lean flank," "muscular arm," and "sinewy hand."[141] Vaconte's description is presented objectively, but on another occasion we see a similar corporealized description of male beauty focalized through a desiring female gaze, when a minor character, Sofia, interestingly characterized as a philosopher and poet, nostalgically recalls her youthful erotic interest in the Turkish knight Ariodeno, whom she meets again later in life.[142] Speaking to the still enamored Ariodeno, whom she always virtuously repulsed despite her desire, Sofia confesses her past pleasure in admiring his prowess at tournaments and, perhaps still more, in watching him remove his armor afterwards, "damp with sweat" and standing apart from the crowd.[143] It is difficult to think of a parallel for this scene of female-male erotic voyeurism in the female-authored literature of the period, other than possibly the more etherealized scene early in Maddalena Campiglia's *Flori* in which Licori observes the sleeping Androgeo, dwelling on his mouth and fantasizing about the possibility of a kiss.[144]

Besides the Calidora-Serano episode, another, much briefer episode that appears in the 1606 version of the poem but is cut from the 1623 version deserves mention for its audacity. Describing a night raid by Christian forces on the Ottoman camp—a familiar topos in epic—Sarrocchi includes a vignette in which a young male lover of the Ottoman standard-bearer Varadino is killed by the Christian convert Sinano, whom Varadino then slaughters in revenge.[145] The scene is modeled on that of the death of Lesbino in the *Liberata*, avenged with equal violence by Solimano, who abandons his leadership of his troops in the process. Tasso is relatively discreet about Solimano's relationship with Lesbino, leaving us to infer it from his emotion at the boy's death and the description of Lesbino as "his" (suo).[146] Sarrocchi is notably more explicit, portraying Varadino in bed with his lover at the time of the attack, with the sleeping boy's hand, which his attacker will hack off in a form of symbolic castration, resting on the warrior's "ebony chest."[147] Of interest here is that the relationship is treated almost entirely without opprobrium, even though Sarrocchi must have been aware of the delicacy of the subject; the 1623 version of the poem heterosexualizes the episode, transforming the boy into a devoted, camp-following wife.[148] A further hint at a homosexual relationship within the Ottoman camp, one that is retained in the 1623 version, is the relationship between Pallante's father, Sabalio, and his close friend Saladino.[149] Again, this is mentioned quite neutrally, with no indication of authorial disapproval.

Much less explicit, but perhaps manifesting a similar openness on Sarrocchi's part to the possibility of same-sex attraction, this time between women, is the striking episode of Rosmonda's first encounter with Silveria, found in both the 1606 and 1623 versions of the poem. The episode constitutes a romancelike digression, taking place outside the closely defined, "real" geography of the plains before Krujë. Specifically, it is located on the slopes of Mount Olympus, where Silveria lives outside society as a huntress. We first hear of Silveria through an old woman who accosts Rosmonda and petitions her for justice, telling the princess of her two sons' murder at the hands of a wild woman ("better, a beast").[150] The introduction leads us to expect a grotesque female other, serving to define Rosmonda's culturally acceptable virility by contrast. In fact, what we see is a kind of classicizing noble savage, not far from the Arcadian stereotype of the man-shunning nymph. Sarrocchi depicts the encounter between the two women with remarkable *enargeia*, exploiting their physical and sartorial differences to particular effect. Both are described in detail, Rosmonda as she rides up the mountain on her richly caparisoned charger, glittering with arms, and Silveria as she comes out to meet her, dressed in a leopard skin and wielding a bow. While Rosmonda's looks are characterized in terms of the predictable Petrarchan canon that had characterized female knights since Bradamante, Silveria is a notably less conventional figure. She is described as athletic, lithe of limb and strong to the point of virility, with suntanned skin rather than the obligatory whiteness that serves to symbolize the chastity of the Petrarchan heroine and provides an arena for her blushes.[151] She radiates a physical energy and kineticism quite remote from conventional lyric descriptions of female beauty, which tend to the static and pictorial; even her eyes are differentiated from the usual starlike eyes of the lyric beauty by their more material characterization as "large" (grandi).[152]

Sarrocchi's portrayal in Silveria of a "nonstandard" beauty may be seen partly as a reflection of baroque trends in lyric, which increasingly privileged noncanonical female types.[153] In context, however, the physical contrast between Silveria and Rosmonda serves to intensify the palpable frisson of attraction at their encounter. Meeting suddenly on the mountainside, the two women stare at each other for a moment in stupor. While Silveria remembers herself sufficiently to venture a greeting, Rosmonda remains staring over the course of a second octave, wondering at Silveria's "unimagined beauty and daring" and her fascinating androgyny, "virile beauty with a feminine face."[154] The meeting has the unmistakable air of a *coup de foudre*, and its erotic resonances are developed in the following sequence, when Silveria shows Rosmonda the garden she has cultivated on the mountain. This is characterized fully according to the conventions of the "gardens of Venus" that generally feature as loci of seduction in romance.[155] Unsurprisingly, Sarrocchi does not pursue the narrative possibility of a love story between her two heroines; instead she supplies Rosmonda with a heterosexual love interest in the form of Vaconte, leaving Silveria in the enduring "wildness" of her self-chosen chastity, determined never to submit to a man. Nonetheless, the scene of their first meeting deserves notice as the most erotically charged scene between women in the female-authored literature of this period, with the more complex exception of Valeria Miani's description of the seduction of "Lucinia" by

Celinda in the play of that name.[156] It might even be speculated that Silveria's unassimilable queerness as a character motivates the spectacularly bizarre end that Sarrocchi concocts for her story: she is crushed to death in the final battle by the falling body of a war elephant she has killed and expires aesthetically in Rosmonda's arms.[157]

4. The Fortunes of Female-Authored Chivalric Fiction

In a passage in Marinella's *L'Enrico* in which Erina and Venier contemplate the marvels of Venice in the course of a set-piece world tour on the enchantress's magic chariot, Marinella takes the opportunity to insert a prophetic authorial self-portrait in the guise of a "lovely Siren" who will rise from Venice's waves.[158] The passage is remarkable for its forthright self-praise, untinged by any "feminine" scruples of modesty: Marinella portrays herself as an exceptional figure, courted by the Muses, crowned by Apollo, and "stupefying the world with her words."[159] Perhaps especially interesting is the claim she makes for herself that this siren will be "perhaps more worthy than any other."[160] The gender of the pronoun *(altra)* makes it clear that her point of comparison in this boast is other women, rather than "others" as a whole.

Marinella's claim to have outstripped female "others" in her poetic prowess is most probably to be read with reference in particular to Sarrocchi and to Fonte, the latter of whom had included a similar though far more modest two-octave self-portrait in *Il Floridoro*.[161] That Marinella knew of Sarrocchi's poem seems almost certain, given that she was in close contact with the Rome-based Cristoforo Bronzini at about the time of *La Scanderbeide*'s second publication, in 1623, and was familiar with his *Della dignità, e nobilità delle donne*, which gives Sarrocchi extraordinary prominence in its listing of famous women.[162] It may be significant in this regard that we first hear of Marinella's ambition to write an epic poem of her own in a work of 1624.[163] Rinaldina Russell has argued for a substantial influence of *La Scanderbeide* on *L'Enrico*, perhaps most apparent in Marinella's pairing of a knight and a "wild" archer as her two principal female characters on the enemy side.[164] Marinella also borrowed from Fonte, most notably in the Venier-Erina episode, which draws quite extensively on Fonte's Circetta episode, especially for its desexualization of the *maga* figure and the attribution to her of an important passage of patriotic ekphrasis.

Despite the emulative anxiety Marinella displays in proclaiming her superiority to her two predecessors in *L'Enrico*, her poem enjoyed the least contemporary critical success of the three poems we discussed here. Fonte's *Floridoro* won not only admiring mentions from "defenders of women" such as Bronzini, Cornelio Lanci, and Francesco Agostino Della Chiesa but also, more unexpectedly, a remarkable encomium in the "Istoria delle vite de' poeti italiani," of Alessandro Zilioli (d. 1650), who lauds it particularly for its style, which he presents as sublimely combining the virtues of Ariosto and Tasso.[165] Sarrocchi's *Scanderbeide*, although it aroused the scorn of Marino and Stigliani, was widely praised by others among her contemporaries; even the poisonous Janus Nicius Erythraeus, who does his best to destroy her character in his biography, admits her epic to be a remarkable achievement.[166] Marinella, publishing within a considerably less auspicious climate for women's writing, had the disappointment of seeing the epic from which she had already been predicting a "durable and great honor" eleven years before its completion effectively disappear without a trace.[167] I know of no favorable comments on *L'Enrico* in print other than Marinella's own self-promotions, and although there is evidence that she continued to expand her epic after its publication, no second edition appeared.[168] This disappointment may have contributed to the bitterness of tone of Marinella's 1645 *Essortationi*, which counsel women not to follow her in aspiring to literary glory but to content themselves instead with conventional roles.[169]

5. Beyond Chivalry: Lucrezia Marinella's Experiments in Mythological Epic and Pastoral Romance

Prior to *L'Enrico*, Marinella had published two works of secular fiction: the pastoral romance *Arcadia felice* and the mythological-allegorical poem *Amore innamorato, et impazzato*. The two works bookended the decade of suspension, or near suspension, of literary activity that followed Marinella's marriage to Girolamo Vacca in 1607: *Arcadia felice* was the last independent work she published before her marriage, *Amore innamorato, et impazzato* the first new work after her resumption of literary engagement with the revised *Vita di Maria Vergine*, of 1617.[170] Both works were dedicated to duchesses of Mantua who were Medicis by birth and hence heirs to a family noteworthy for its support of female literary activity: *Arcadia felice* to Eleonora de' Medici Gonzaga, later the dedicatee of Valeria Miani's *Celinda*, and *Amore innamorato, et impazzato* to Caterina de' Medici Gonzaga, later the dedicatee of Veneranda

Bragadin's 1519 *Rime*.[171] Both works of remarkable confidence and verve, they mark Marinella's graduation to large-scale narrative works from the miniature hagiographic epics with which she had made her debut in the 1590s. *Arcadia felice* has four substantial parts—more than three hundred pages in its printed edition—and *Amore innamorato, et impazzato* comprises ten cantos and "almost a thousand stanzas," as Marinella would later boast.[172] Together, the two works serve as a showcase for Marinella's skills as a writer of artistic prose and of stylistically elevated verse. *Amore innamorato, et impazzato* is written in her favored verse form, ottava rima, *Arcadia felice* mainly in the lush, poetic prose style she had first essayed in her 1602 *Vita di Maria Vergine*, though with some interpolated poems, as was customary in pastoral romance.[173] Both works represent new departures for a female writer in terms of genre, a fact that was probably not fortuitous, given the competitive attitude attested by Marinella's later remark in *L'Enrico* about outdoing "ogni altra" in her field. Noteworthy in particular is her engagement in *Arcadia felice* with a genre such as pastoral romance. Italian pastoral romance was not only traditionally male-authored but also distinctly male-centered in its cast list and gender ideology by comparison with its sister genre, pastoral drama, which, as we saw in chapter 3, had already attracted female authors in some numbers by the time Marinella began to write.

The main plot of *Arcadia felice* (to the extent that this highly episodic work may be said to possess one) concerns a fictional retreat to Arcadia by the emperor Diocletian following his abdication in 305.[174] The first of the book's four parts recounts the emperor's arrival in Arcadia and the elaborate welcome celebrations to greet him. The second part dramatizes the games held to celebrate his arrival, before deviating into a picaresque subplot regarding the origins of one of the victorious athletes, Ersilio, who is revealed as a young woman in disguise. The third part, though probably the most dispersive, centers toward the end on Diocletian's visit to the magical garden of the wizard Erimeno. We are also introduced here to the unhappy love story of the shepherd-poet Corimbo. The fourth part initially recounts the voyage of Diocletian and his companions to the mountain palace of the prophetic nymph Erato, who instructs Corimbo on the magic art that will free him of his love. The end of part 4 recounts the miraculous reappearance of the lost son of the shepherd Opilio, Fileno, whose picaresque tale of kidnapping and piracy brings the romance to an end.

As the work's modern editor, Françoise Lavocat, has noted, *Arcadia felice* represents a novelty within the tradition of Italian pastoral romance in the diversity and eclecticism of the source materials it draws on. Within other literary traditions, such as those of Spain, France, and England, this eclecticism would not be remarkable. At least since the time of Jorge de Montemayor's *Siete libros de la Diana* (1559) a contamination had been apparent between the humanistic lyric-descriptive tradition of pastoral novel represented most notably by Jacopo Sannazaro's *Arcadia* (1502) and more narratively oriented forms stemming from alternative traditions such as the Hellenistic novel, the chivalric romance, and the Boccaccian *novella-romanzo*.[175] The fusion model of pastoral romance developed by Montemayor proved immensely productive in the late sixteenth and early seventeenth centuries, with later important examples including Philip Sidney's *Arcadia* (1590) and Honoré d'Urfé's *Astrée* (1607–10). In Italy, however, despite the availability of Montemayor's *Diana*, editions of which were published in Venice in 1568, 1574, and 1585, this model never took root.[176] Far the dominant genre of Arcadian literature in Italy in this period was pastoral drama, which did manifest the eclecticism we see outside Italy in pastoral romance, freely fusing elements drawn from eclogue, comedy, and romance. The pastoral novel was less frequented as a genre and remained close to the revered model of Sannazaro, largely abjuring narrative action and plot complexity and describing a relatively static pastoral world of games and singing contests, inhabited by shepherds and sages.[177] The romance elements in Marinella's *Arcadia felice* are mainly concentrated in the semiautonomous stories that conclude the second and fourth parts of the novel (Ersilio-Ersilia, Fileno), although the figure of Diocletian himself is hardly a conventional Arcadian figure, and the captive Indian prince Ismaele, a member of the emperor's retinue, also seems an intruder from the world of romance.[178] This romance input extends the geographic boundaries of Marinella's novel beyond Arcadia to embrace Epirus, Naples, North Africa, and the Eastern Mediterranean, and it extends the cast list to include pirates (Fileno), anachronistic quasi-Moorish potentates (Agazelle), and peripatetic cross-dressing princesses (Ersilio-Ersilia).

If the presence of a substantial romance element in *Arcadia felice* serves to assimilate the work to the mainstream, European tradition of pastoral romance, a feature that serves to differentiate it from this tradition is its resistance to erotic love as a theme. In this regard, Marinella is substantially faithful to the Italian tradition of the pastoral novel initiated by Sannazaro, which includes love in its plot only at the level of *antefatto:* the hero of *Arcadia,* Sincero, suffering from the "malady" of an unrequited love at the opening of the novel, spends the course of it pursuing a cure. It may have been in part this antierotic bias that attracted Marinella to pastoral romance, rather than the more obvious and fashionable genre of pastoral drama, which inescapably placed love intrigue at the heart of its plot. Like Sannazaro's *Arcadia, Arcadia felice* features the cure of a lovesick shepherd (Corimbo) as one of its narrative threads, although the more complex plotting of Marinella's work diminishes the centrality of this theme to the whole. For the rest, love does not feature, even in the case of a classically romance subplot such as that concerning the cross-dressing princess Ersilia, for which genre tradition would lead us to expect an erotic resolution.[179] An intriguing situation is created when Ersilia is denounced to the judicial authorities for attempting to seduce two nymphs with the promise of marriage, but this device seems to serve purely as a means of bringing about the revelation of her true sex and as a pretext for introducing her picaresque backstory.[180] After she wins her exculpation by proving herself a woman and hence "harmless," the story is dropped. None of the other female characters in the work are given the least hint of a love story, unless we count Iele, the young shepherdess who is the recipient of Corimbo's unwelcome attentions and who, in her only direct appearance in the book, announces her intention to renounce love and marriage and remain a chaste votary of Diana.[181] The theme of the rejection of marriage by a woman had a certain voguishness among female writers of the period, featuring prominently in Maddalena Campiglia's *Flori* and Moderata Fonte's *Il merito delle donne.* In *Arcadia felice,* however, it has a particular emblematic force within a work so determinedly antierotic in its stance.

As we have seen in the case of *L'Enrico,* Marinella's resistance to the erotic is not limited to *Arcadia felice;* on the contrary, it is a hallmark of her secular narrative output and one of her numerous claims to distinctiveness among the female writers of her day. Marinella's most sustained antierotic statement —a virtual manifesto—is *Amore innamorato, et impazzato.* Paradoxically, however, this is also Marinella's most sensual and erotically charged work. As the first half of its title indicates, Marinella's poem is essentially an adaptation of the Cupid-Psyche myth as originally told by Apuleius, an author she had praised in her preface to *La vita di Maria Vergine* for the "sweetness and eloquence" of his prose.[182] The adaptation is a particularly free one, however. Love does not merely fall in love with a mortal woman, as is the case in

Apuleius; he is rejected by this beloved, Ersilia, and driven to a state of madness, from which he is only rescued by an intervention on the part of Jove. Apuleius is amusingly combined here as source with Ariosto's *Orlando furioso*, which portrays Orlando's descent into madness as the result of his love for Angelica, building on Boiardo's *Orlando innamorato*, which had first defied tradition by portraying the great Orlando in love. Marinella's witty conflation of chivalric and classical sources is already announced in her title, which echoes that of an earlier Apuleius adaptation, Antonio Minturno's 1559 *Amore innamorato*, while at the same time evoking the progression from love to frenzy recorded in the *Innamorato-Furioso* sequence.[183]

At the time of Marinella's writing, the myth of Cupid and Psyche was already immensely well established as a subject for vernacular poetry in Italy; a recent study lists nine versions of the myth published between 1491 and 1623.[184] Of these works, besides Minturno's, Marinella certainly knew at least the most recent at her time of writing, the Mantuan poet Ercole Udine's popular *La Psiche*. This had first been published in 1599 in Venice by Marinella's publisher of the time, Giambattista Ciotti, and it was dedicated to Eleonora de' Medici Gonzaga, dedicatee of *Arcadia felice*.[185] Udine's poem offered a model for Marinella in its scale, its epic treatment of the subject, and its accompaniment of the text by a prefatory allegory, contributed in Udine's case by Angelo Grillo. Marinella doubles the allegorical dose by including a more detailed, scene-by-scene allegory at the beginning of each canto as well.

Given this weight of tradition, Marinella's *Amore innamorato, et impazzato*'s insouciantly ameliorative approach to its source material is striking. This is underlined in the publisher's preface to Marinella's 1624 *De' gesti heroici*, where it is proudly stated that the plot of *Amore innamorato, et impazzato* was "of much finer invention than Apuleius's *Psyche*."[186] Marinella's claims to innovation are fully supported, at least in the realm of *inventio*, where she shows a notable freedom and ingenuity. Aside from her core innovation of having Cupid go mad, we see her in canto 7 supplying a metamorphosis myth for the iris, one of the few flowers to have escaped one in Ovid, when she has Cupid fulminate his mortal rival for Ersilia, Iridio, with a thunderbolt stolen from Jove.[187] Similarly, in canto 10 we see her providing a classical backstory for the romance motif, used by both Boiardo and Ariosto, of the twin springs in the Ardennes whose waters produce, respectively, love and erotic repulsion in those who drink from them. These, Marinella explains, were both sacred to Diana and productive of a chaste aversion to love until Cupid cured his love madness by bathing in one of them, leaving it ever after miraculously tinctured with erotic power.[188] This is an invention of particular wit and pointedness, especially given the traditional metaphorical associations between springs and poetic inspiration and between springs and sources in the literary sense.[189] By inventing a causal explanation for what Ariosto cites as given, Marinella effectively constructs herself as "source" to one of her principal poetic sources. Even given the remarkable confidence that had characterized her as a poet from her debut, this is clearly a gesture of some weight.

One obvious consequence of the Ariostan twist Marinella gives to the Cupid-Psyche myth in *Amore innamorato, et impazzato* is to convert its vision of erotic love from an essentially idealizing and positive one to a negative one. Love figures in the poem not as a spiritually elevating experience—a frequent reading of the myth in the Renaissance was as an allegory of God's love for the human soul—but as a base and degrading one.[190] Cupid is reduced during the course of the poem to a state of extreme abjection, rampaging over the land like the mad Orlando and leaving a train of destruction in his wake. Marinella spells out the poem's meaning in her prefatory allegorical discourse, glossing the figure of Cupid as representing the desiring *(concupiscibile)* faculty of the soul, and Ersilia as representing the rational *(ragionevole)*. Thus, in Ersilia's repulses of Cupid we see reason rejecting the blandishments of the senses, while Cupid's ultimate defeat at the hands of Jove signifies the victory of the divine intellect over the powers of sensual desire.

This is highly conventional moral doctrine; indeed, in its main outlines Marinella's allegory is modeled on Tasso's allegory of the *Gerusalemme liberata*, from which she had already liberally borrowed in her annotations to Luigi Tansillo's *Lagrime di San Pietro*, of 1606.[191] What is more surprising in *Amore innamorato, et impazzato* is that, as in the *Liberata* itself, the presence of a moral superstructure rigorously condemnatory of sensuality does not exclude a degree of indulgence in the poetry of the senses; on the contrary, in some sense, it legitimizes it. *Amore innamorato, et impazzato* is unusual for a female-authored work of this period in its classical setting and inspiration and in its allusions to a "pagan" poetics of untrammeled sensuality and immersion in the material world. The second half of canto 1, one of the passages of the poem most faithful to Apuleius, describes the palace and garden of Venus, the former adorned with images of the loves of gods and mortals, described in an extended ekphrasis; it then describes the arrival of Venus, borne across the sea in her shell chariot accompanied by Nereids and Tritons, to find her son Cupid asleep in her garden. The passage, and the poem as a whole, aims for the maximum of stylistic gorgeousness: description dominates over action, and the whole is clothed in the kind of florid and decorative style Tasso characterizes as "lyric."[192] Its principal characters, Venus, Cupid, and Ersilia, are all characterized by extreme physical beauty, revisited throughout the poem in a series of set-piece *descriptiones pulchritudinis*.[193] Actual scenes of sexual dalliance aside, few of the topoi of sensual poetry are omitted. Marinella even finds room in the poem for a quite audacious scene of erotic voyeurism when Cupid spies on the naked Ersilia as she bathes in a fountain, frothing with lust in the bushes as he watches. Here the distance between the allegorical and literal senses of the poem seem stretched almost to the breaking point: Marinella's allegory suggests that we read the figure of the naked bathing nymph as signifying "the Christian soul, who throws aside the vestments of worldly pleasure to bathe in the purity of the river of perfect penitence."[194]

It is an impressive measure of Marinella's confidence by this stage of her career that she was inspired to experiment, however cautiously, with the poetry of the senses. It probably also reflects her status as a married woman; it is not clear that she would have risked such a venture as an unmarried girl. What she is clearly attempting to do in the poem is create a space for herself within the fast-trending baroque tradition of sensual and erotic poetry, which characteristically drew on pastoral or on classical mythology for its subject matter. It is worth recalling that *Amore innamorato, et impazzato* preceded by only five years the publication of Marino's mythological epic *Adone* (1623), generally considered the masterpiece of this tradition.[195] Participation in this trend was obviously problematic for female writers, given the constraints of gender decorum that weighed on "respectable" women, yet nonparticipation effectively excluded them from one of the most vital literary arenas of the day.

Besides the negative valence it gives to love, a further consequence of the novel narrative twist Marinella gives to the Cupid-Psyche myth in her poem regards gender. Cupid in Apuleius's text is a mysterious numinous figure who lent himself quite easily to Christian allegorization as divine *caritas*. Psyche, meanwhile, though essentially a sympathetic figure, is flawed by an insatiable "feminine" curiosity reminiscent of Pandora or Eve. Marinella reverses the moral hierarchy of dignity between the two equivalent figures in her poem: Cupid reverts here essentially to his stereotype as a mischievous boy, ultimately lapsing after his madness into a more sinister and violent persona. Ersilia, meanwhile, is characterized as a self-consistent and morally exemplary figure, in keeping with her allegorical significance as reason. Her type is essentially the familiar one of the nymph votary of Diana, disdainful of love and dedicated to the pursuit of honor, although there are also traces in her makeup of the Laura of Petrarch's *Triumph of Chastity:* in one scene, like Laura there, she physically battles with Cupid and breaks his bow.[196]

In reducing Cupid from a heroic to an antiheroic figure, Marinella is following her second source text, Ariosto's *Orlando furioso,* or perhaps more accurately the dual assault on the Orlando character constituted by the *Furioso* and Boiardo's *Orlando innamorato.* Here too, however, Marinella is distinctly revisionist in terms of gender in her treatment of her source material. The Orlando-Angelica story in Boiardo and Ariosto lends itself to interpretation as an archetypal tale of a great man brought down by a woman. Angelica is manipulative and flirtatious, in Boiardo in particular, enjoying her power over her numerous admirers; she is also, though resisting Orlando, not immune from the lure of the flesh, as her erotic capitulation to the handsome Medoro shows. Marinella's Ersilia, by contrast, shows no sensual weakness and has no moral culpability whatever for the downfall of Cupid. Despite an initial flicker of interest, inspired by his extreme beauty, she subsequently shows herself adamantly resistant to the god's advances, fleeing whenever he attempts to speak to her and ultimately resorting to violence when he pursues her too hard.[197] The story of the relationship between the two is essentially that of a powerful male's quest for dominance successfully resisted by an apparently weaker female, a storyline already essayed in Marinella's *Colomba sacra,* where Columba heroically resists all the torments the emperor Aurelian can inflict on her. The parallel is underlined in the text when Cupid, pursuing Ersilia, is compared at one point to an eagle, and she to a dove.[198]

Further to this, the very idea of having Ersilia allegorically embody the faculty of reason and Cupid that of concupiscence is in itself a significant gesture in terms of gender ideology. While the medieval allegorical exegetic tradition of the Cupid-Psyche myth had seen Psyche as representing the rational soul, this was within a construct that positioned Cupid as the higher power of God. To align Cupid with the lower, sense-oriented faculties of the soul, and Ersilia with the higher, was a provocative gesture, given the centrality within orthodox Aristotelian gender thinking of the notion of women's rational deficiency and greater vulnerability to the lure of the senses. That it should be read as polemical in this regard seems likely at a time when the relation of the sexes was the subject, once again, of live and caustic debate.

Sometime before 1613, Giovanni Battista Barbo, a native of Padua, Marinella's home after she married, circulated a misogynistic poem, *L'oracolo, overo invettiva contra le donne*, which triggered a polemic with the Verona-based Veneranda Bragadin. In 1614 a letter purportedly by a Sicilian woman, Bianca Naldi, was published in Vicenza attacking Giuseppe Passi's notorious misogynistic treatise *I donneschi diffetti*, and Passi's treatise itself was reprinted in Venice in 1618.[199] Although it would be reductionist to read *Amore innamorato, et impazzato* simply as a profeminist statement, this is certainly a context we should take into account.

The profeminist tenor of *Amore innamorato, et impazzato* becomes still more apparent if we look beyond the poem's main protagonists. The figure of Venus in Apuleius is quite frequently played for laughs, as the archetypal baleful mother-in-law, touchy about her age and gnawed with jealousy toward the unfortunate Psyche. Marinella rejects this characterization, deflecting most of the poem's comic impulse onto the figure of Cupid and preserving Venus as a dignified figure, consistently motivated more by maternal solicitude than by antagonism toward her mortal "rival." Important too for the poem's gender configuration with respect to its source is Marinella's omission of the harpylike figures of Psyche's sisters, whose malice leads Amor at one point to exclaim against their "troublesome sex."[200] In the allegorical tradition of Apuleius, these figures were traditionally interpreted as representing the lower faculties of the soul. Female figures emerge almost universally well in *Amore innamorato, et impazzato*; this is even true of the shades of women damned for succumbing to lust whom Cupid encounters on a set-piece visit to hell, where much of the poem's comic business takes place. These "victims of Love," led by Dido, are allowed a Bacchante-like revenge on the divinity who brought about their downfall: they beat him and tie him to a myrtle, where Venus, coming to find him, subjects him to further, maternal chastisement in the form of a beating with rose branches.[201] The episode might be read as a riposte to Ariosto, who turns a similar scene of Dantean infernal parody in the *Furioso* to misogynistic ends.[202] More generally, Marinella's profeminist mythography in *Amore innamorato, et impazzato* may perhaps be seen as an answer to Barbo, the first part of whose *Oracolo* spins a misogynist yarn in which Jove places woman on earth as a punishment to man in the wake of Prometheus's transgression.[203]

Amore innamorato, et impazzato is a love story of sorts, though a notably one-sided and perverse one. This dictates the character of its gender representations, which take their cue from erotic prototypes even as they revise them. *Arcadia felice* is a rare case of an early modern work with a mixed cast list in which erotic desire barely figures as a driver of plot. The principal interest of the work from a gender point of view lies in Marinella's elaboration of a series of female figures embodying prowess of various kinds within a nonerotic context, not a particularly common phenomenon within Italian literature in this period, with the exception of the female knights of chivalric romance. *Arcadia felice* has three such figures: the bard Licori, or Canente; the cross-dressing athlete Ersilia; and the prophet and enchantress Erato, the latter interesting as well for her context, a kind of female intellectual community devoted to contemplative and natural-philosophical pursuits. When seen against the background of the Italian tradition of pastoral novel, the prominence given to female figures in *Arcadia felice* is a distinctive departure. Few aspects of the work so clearly illustrate Marinella's debt to romance.[204]

Arcadia felice's most obvious challenge to gender orthodoxy is constituted by the story of Ersilia, developed in part 2.[205] Ersilia is first introduced to the reader under the guise of her assumed male persona, Ersilio, who comes to the fore of the narrative during a description of the pastoral games held to honor Diocletian shortly after his arrival. The setting is significant. Games were a familiar and highly codified topos of the pastoral novel, originally appropriated by Sannazaro from classical epic.[206] Marinella has them structured by the Arcadian elders as a ritualized enactment of social and gender order, echoing the similarly demonstrative function of the procession to greet Diocletian in part 1. In the procession, the display populace is organized initially by age and secondarily by gender: a group of angelic young boys leads, followed by separate groups of handsome youths and white-robed maidens, with a party of distinguished male elders in the rear.[207] In the games, where youth rules, the division is by gender alone: first, the young men of the land display their speed and strength in a series of finely socially gradated contests; then the event is brought to an end by a gracefully choreographed dance by a "chorus of virginal nymphs."[208]

The irony of all this neat underlining of gender difference and complementarity is revealed at the end of book 1, when one of the stars of the games, Ersilio, victor of the archery and running contests, reveals himself to be female. The dynamic is precisely that of the tournament at the beginning of Moderata Fonte's *Floridoro*, won by a mystery knight who reveals himself after his victory as the female knight Risamante. Marinella takes the *meraviglia* effect on the reader to new heights in her imitation, however, with respect both to Fonte and to Fonte's own likely source, Ariosto. Rather than using the now-familiar trope of the unidentified champion, perhaps a pointer to gender indeterminacy for habitual readers of romance, she introduces Ersilio without ambiguity, as a named and identified male figure, effectively deceiving the reader rather than simply withholding information.[209]

Another example of the "sex-transcending woman" in *Arcadia felice* is Licori, the leader of the contingent of beautiful young nymphs that appear in Diocletian's welcome procession. Licori is represented to us as possessed of not only remarkable beauty but outstanding talents as a poet and singer. She is chosen to perform a song of greeting to the emperor, presumably in preference to other, male shepherd-poets whom we encounter in the course of the poem.[210] As a nymph famed for her poetic and musical talents, Licori bears some resemblance to figures in female-authored pastoral drama, such as Maddalena Campiglia's Flori, Barbara Torelli's Talia, and Isabella Andreini's Filli. Like those figures, Marinella's Licori may be seen generally as a celebratory embodiment of female creativity and more specifically as an idealized authorial self-portrait (Marinella's skill at music, as well as her literary gifts, was remarked on by contemporary observers).[211] What is novel and of interest in Licori is the institutional role she assumes as Arcadia's poetic ambassador or laureate, deputed by the government to greet the emperor. This is probably best read as wistfully aspirational on Marinella's part, though we should not forget the habit within Venice and the cities of the Veneto of occasionally having female orators greet prominent foreign visitors as representatives of their city.[212] A second figure of a female bard, Altea, appears in Marinella's later *L'Enrico*, as part of the entourage of the enchantress Erina. Like Licori, she is given a degree of prominence, and a song of hers is recorded in full.[213]

Like Altea, the Erina of *L'Enrico* is herself a second visitation of a female archetype first essayed by Marinella in *Arcadia felice*: the prophetess-enchantress, last descendent of a distinguished male line, living in a space apart, within a community of nymphs. The resemblance between Erina and the Erato of *Arcadia felice* is strong, yet both bear the traces of a genre-specific literary inheritance. Erina, as we have seen, derives from the figure of the sexualized enchantress of male-authored epic and romance (Circe, Alcina, Armida), with some input from Moderata Fonte's virginal and virtuous Circetta. Erato, by contrast, descends from the alternative, desexualized line of literary *maghi* found in pastoral romance, male in the Sannazarian archetype Enareto but already feminized in Montemayor in the figure of Felicia, the archetype of the Melissea of Mary Wroth's *Urania* (1621), the other female-authored pastoral romance of the age.[214] The function of this figure is in some sense antithetical to that of the seductive *maga* of chivalric romance, in that instead of inciting the hero to erotic temptation, he or she is sought out precisely to aid a lovesick hero on his road back to psychological and emotional integrity.

Although a precedent exists in Montemayor for a female figure in this role, Marinella's innovation deserves to be emphasized within an Italian context. Sannazaro had paired his suave and dignified Enareto with a contrastive female witch figure given a distinctly "black" coloring, as a night-flying, necromantic disciple of Circe and Medea, one of whose powers is "drawing down the stars from the heavens dripping with live blood."[215] Supernatural powers are here clearly gender-differentiated, in a manner hardly flattering to women. Marinella effectively reverses the pattern found in Sannazaro, keeping her "blackest," necromantic scene for an all-male episode early in the pilgrimage to Erato's kingdom, when Ismaele calls up the spirit of the archwizard Osimandro, ancestor to Erato, who instructs them on the arcana necessary to guarantee safe entry to the well-guarded domain of the nymph.[216]

As the mention of the Osimandro ceremony suggests, the episode of the pilgrimage to Erato's kingdom is a complex one, involving a number of initiatory stages. Besides the lovesick Corimbo, the party that makes its way to consult the nymph includes Diocletian himself, Ismaele, the retired Roman senator Tiberio, and the shepherd Opilio, whose recovery of his lost son, Fileno, constitutes the book's closing narrative. The first mention of Erato occurs in part 3, during Diocletian's visit to the magic garden of a renowned male wizard, Emireno, who tells him of Erato's distant kingdom and instructs him in the rites required to summon the shade of Osimandro. After their departure from Osimandro, the party must proceed up a high mountain circled by a river and a magic wood filled with strange signs and portents. Aspects of the approach to Erato's kingdom, which is fruitful and springlike though reached through a snow belt, recall the approach to Armida's garden in the *Gerusalemme liberata*, while the detail of the party having to equip itself with the herb moly to protect against enchantment is taken from Homer's account of Odysseus's encounter with Circe.[217]

Together with Erato's name, which echoes that of the classical Muse of love lyric, these allusions seem to hint at a possible erotic dimension to the magic kingdom to which Diocletian and his fellow initiates finally gain access. This is quickly dispersed, however, when the party encounters, as the first denizens of the place, a team of white-clad nymphs led by the Dianaesque Armilla, Erato's cousin. This is a realm of chastity, where female energies are devoted not to seduction but to virtuous intellectual pursuits and where even the *de rigueur* paradisiacal garden is inhabited by ermines, traditional symbols of purity, rather than by the customary love-possessed birds and beasts.[218] Specifically, as we learn from Armilla, who shows the visiting party around the garden following Erato's prophetic interlude, she and Erato spend their time contemplating the wonders of nature, with a special focus on meteorology and cosmology. The same protoscientific emphasis characterizes the realm of Erina in *L'Enrico*, where we see the bard Altea singing of the mysteries of nature. Rather than Venus, the tutelary deity of Erato's realm is Apollo, physically present in the form of a miraculous alabaster statue, holding a zither from which water pours forth, perfectly imitating the sound of the instrument in its course.[219] The god's prophetic and oracular associations are obviously of particular relevance in context, but his association with poetry is also not to be discounted. The feminized realm of unencumbered intellectual activity that Marinella depicts in Erato's kingdom may clearly be read as an ideal locus for her own poetic creativity, an alternative Parnassus, a connection made even clearer in the case of Erina's realm in *L'Enrico* with the episode of Altea's song.[220]

An interesting detail in the Erato episode is Armilla's account of a visionary journey once undertaken by the prophetess, guided by her father, Ciberione, through the infernal and celestial realms. The other world that unfolds itself to the "wise vates," as Erato is referred to here, is of interest from a gender perspective: while the underworld is populated by the expected chthonic deities and monsters (Minos, Pluto, Cerberus, Rhadamanthus, the Gorgons), Olympus is peopled by an all-female cast of gods, specifically Diana, Berecynthia (Cybele), and Ceres.[221] This points up a more general feature of Marinella's *Arcadia felice*, namely, that despite occasional mentions of male gods like Jove and Apollo, the dominant role in Arcadia's religious culture seems to be played by Diana, who has effectively usurped the theological center here, to the detriment of traditional pastoral deities such as Pan.[222] All the "clerical" figures portrayed in the romance—the unnamed "High Priest" who arraigns Ersilio at the end of part 2, the priest Entello, who recounts his tale of disappointed love in part 3, and the hermit and ex-political assassin Albino, of part 4—are explicitly said to be ministers of Diana, and the goddess herself appears indirectly in Entello's dramatic account.[223] To an extent, as the work's modern editor has argued, this may be seen as a classicizing transcription of the contemporary cult of the Virgin. Suggestive in this regard is the reference in the Entello episode to a virgin dedicated to Diana from her birth, who intercedes to help a relative through her prayers to the goddess—a very clear Arcadian transcription of a nun.[224] It is nonetheless worth noting that the Diana of *Arcadia felice* is the autonomous focus of a quasi-monotheistic cult and hence in a quite different position from the Virgin. Indeed, at times she takes on some of the attributes of the Christian God, notably his three-personed nature; the hermit Albino is described as "minister of the rites of the Triform Diana."[225] Technically the term *triform* is justified by Diana's role as goddess of the skies, the earth, and the underworld (in her persona as Hecate), but the trinitarian overtones in this phrasing are difficult to ignore.[226]

The present analysis has centered to this point on the aspects of *Arcadia felice* that are of particular interest from the point of view of gender, but much else deserves scrutiny in this complex, ambitious, and original work. Perhaps especially interesting is the oblique discourse on political power set in train by the curious motif of a Roman emperor retiring to Arcadia.[227] At an obvious level, this is interpretable as an exemplum of a creditable voluntary relinquishment of power, a theme foregrounded in an ekphrasis at the end of part 1 representing men such as Cincinnatus and Curius Dentatus, who wisely withdrew from the corrupting influences of power and wealth to spend their declining years literally and metaphorically cultivating their garden. The moral dangers represented by a "consuming desire for rule" are reflected in the Ersilia subplot, which features a classic wicked uncle whose aspiration to power leads him treacherously to murder Ersilia's mother, dowager ruler of Epirus, and to attempt to murder Ersilia herself.[228] Diocletian seems, according to this perspective, to reflect a human ideal of temperance and rational moderation, and he is generally treated as such in the romance. Marinella describes him at one point as "he who curbed the untamed peoples with his potent and moderate hand."[229] This idealizing discourse is not unchallenged, however. Despite his smiling rejection of the governance of Arcadia, offered to him by the elders of the land on his arrival, Diocletian later shows himself at times inclined to assume an unelected power there: we see him twice in the romance, in the cases of Ersilia and Fileno, taking up the role of autocratic dispenser of justice.[230] At another point, Marinella alludes discreetly to the "moderate" Diocletian's immoderate past as a persecutor of Christians, when a flattering ekphrasis in Erato's palace recording his triumphs as emperor ends with a prophetic sequence celebrating the victories of his ex-protégé and successor Constantine, concluding with Constantine kneeling at the feet of Pope Sylvester after his conversion to Christianity.[231] Diocletian is evidently disconcerted by the prophecy, which leaves him at the same time disbelieving and irate.

Arcadia felice is also interesting for the scientific knowledge that Marinella displays in the episodes set in the magic kingdoms of Emireno and Erato. The first of these is especially spectacular, featuring a series of thaumaturgical wonders, including a hydraulically operated automatic harp and machines simulating birdsong and the clamor of battle, and featuring also an automaton-shepherd capable of singing and playing a lyre.[232] The machines were probably inspired by Hero of Alexandria's *Pneumatics*, available in the vernacular from 1589, and reflect the fascination with "natural magic" that swept Italy and Europe in the late sixteenth and seventeenth centuries.[233] Another mechanical wonder is found in the realm of Erato, in the form of the animated statue of Apollo mentioned earlier. Here too Armilla describes the meteorological and cosmological studies she and Erato pursue from their mountain "observatory," culminating in a brief disquisition on the Milky Way that contradicts Aristotle's interpretation of the phenomenon as resulting from an exhalation of vapors from neighboring stars.[234] The representation of the wizard of romance in the guise of a master of natural magic was not a novelty; this was essentially Tasso's characterization of the Christian *mago* d'Ascalona in the *Gerusalemme liberata*. To give this role to a female *maga*, however, as Marinella does here and in her *L'Enrico*, was a novelty, and a significant one, given that the impulse to understand and to master and control nature was one that her culture tended to gender as male. Marinella's positioning of a statue of Apollo in the kingdom of Erato associates her own scientific writing in *Arcadia felice* with the *maga*'s studies of nature. Indeed, this automaton-Apollo, his hydraulic lyre gushing water like a high-tech Aganippe, serves as an ingenious metaphor for the increasingly prestigious literary discourse of science, soon to be taken to new heights by Galileo, who was teaching at Padua University at this time.

This kind of display of scientific knowledge was not entirely new in a female writer at the time of Marinella's writing. The self-described *speziala* (pharmacist) Camilla Erculiani had published two letter-essays on scientific issues in Padua in 1584, and Moderata Fonte had incorporated a series of disquisitions on natural philosophy into the second book of her *Il merito delle donne*.[235] Nonetheless, Marinella's scientific interests, manifested especially in *Arcadia felice* and in the Erina episode of *L'Enrico*, are an important and distinctive element in her intellectual profile, recalling her descent from the medic and polymath Giovanni Marinelli, from whose library she doubtless profited in this regard. It is probably no coincidence that both Erato and Erina are portrayed as having been taught what they knew of the arcana of nature by their fathers, Cibarione and Fileno, respectively.[236]

A feature of *Arcadia felice* and *Amore innamorato, et impazzato* that is worth underlining in conclusion is the prominence in both works of humor. This deserves comment not least because Marinella elsewhere tends toward high solemnity in her writings, as befitted her largely sacred subject matter. The humor in *Amore innamorato, et impazzato* is concentrated principally in the episode of Cupid's trip to the underworld, where we see his presence inspiring unwonted "sweet cares and amorous affects" in the hearts of its fiendish inhabitants; Megaera, for example, falls for Cerberus, and the two are happily united in love.[237] A little earlier, Cupid bribes his way across the Acheron by promising Charon the love of the fair nymph Eurinia, fulfilling his promise by placing Eurinia under a delusion that makes the hideous old ferryman appear a radiantly beautiful young man, a sly twist on the romance topos that had ancient gnarled witches like Ariosto's Alcina disguise themselves through magic as young beauties to take advantage of deluded male lusts.[238] In this poem the comedy is essentially one of *inventio*, but in *Arcadia felice* Marinella also essays linguistic comedy, as when she has two rustic grotesques, Dameta and Rustico, engage in a song contest parodying the familiar classical pastoral topos of the contest between shepherds. The *contrasto* is cast in the archaic verse form *versi sdruccioli*, favored by Sannazaro, and Marinella exploits the form's jagged rhythms to evoke her speakers' rusticity of speech without having recourse to dialect.[239] The main humor of the exchange lies in the protagonists' delusion that they are handsome and irresistible to women. As the narratorial voice notes of Rustico, he figures himself a Cupid or Adonis even though "in the whole of Arcadia there was no uglier face."[240] While this is hardly an original joke—the satyrs of pastoral drama similarly arouse laughter through their self-flattering delusions—Marinella's humor here seems pointed when placed alongside her similarly phrased diatribes against male vanity in *La nobiltà et l'eccelenza delle donne*.[241]

❦ CHAPTER SIX ❦
DISCURSIVE PROSE

1. Output and Principal Trends

The concluding chapter of this book surveys what may be broadly termed discursive prose writings by women, including treatises, dialogues, "meditations," volumes of letters, and polemical tracts. This was a field of literary activity in which female writers emerged strongly in the last decades of the sixteenth century by comparison with earlier eras, although their emergence was not as novel and unprecedented in this case as it was in secular fiction and drama. Religious writings by female religious writers, both tertiaries and nuns, had held a place in Italian literary culture since the early fifteenth century, and some, like the writings of Catherine of Siena, Catherine of Genoa, and Catherine of Bologna, retained a strong presence in print culture well into the sixteenth.[1] Again from the early fifteenth century, discursive writings by secular female Latinists such as Isotta Nogarola had circulated fairly extensively in manuscript; these were well known indirectly in the sixteenth century through mentions in "famous women" treatises, although they had only a minimal presence in print.[2] A few vernacular prose works by secular women had appeared in print in the middle decades of the sixteenth century, notably Tullia d'Aragona's *Dialogo dell'infinità d'amore* (1547), Vittoria Colonna's *Litere alla duchessa d'Amalfi* (1544) and *Pianto sopra la passione di Christo* (1556), and Chiara Matraini's *Oratione dell'arte della guerra* (1555) and *Oratione d'Isocrate a Demonico* (1556).[3] We might add to these the 1563 printed edition of Nogarola's dialogue on the relative gravity of the sins of Adam and Eve, originally composed in the early 1440s, and perhaps also the volume of letters published under the name of Lucrezia Gonzaga in 1552, although in the case of the latter work a degree of collaborative authorship with the work's supposed editor, Ortensio Lando, is assumed.[4]

If there is nothing new in absolute terms about the body of literature surveyed in this chapter, certain novelties can nonetheless be identified. One, the most striking, is the sheer volume of writings by women in this category published in this period, some twenty-six works in all, several very substantial in size. Other notable trends in this period are a new willingness on the part of nuns to publish their writings, a greater engagement with religious thematics on the part of secular women writers, and a new willingness on the part of women to participate in polemical debate.

The phenomenon of the cloistered woman who published her work during her lifetime has already been discussed in chapter 1. Works by nuns published between 1580 and 1630 falling into the category defined by this chapter are, in chronological order, Osanna Pigafetta's *Trattato detto direttorio delle hore canoniche* (1586), Battista Vernazza's *Opere* (1588 and 1602), Flavia Grumelli's *Vita di Santa Grata* (1596), Beatrice Gatti's *Oratione . . . nel suo entrar nel Monasterio d'Araceli* (1604), and Diodata Malvasia's *La venuta e i progressi miracolosi della s[antissi]ma Madonna dipinta da S[an] Luca posta sul Monte della Guardia* (1617).[5] While Grumelli's text might seem from its title to fall more naturally into the category of religious narrative rather than discursive writing, her actual account of Saint Grata's life takes up only the initial thirteen pages of the volume, the remaining twenty-eight being given over to a series of *discorsi* drawing out the moral lessons of this exemplary life. The works just listed differ notably in ambition and scale, ranging from Pigafetta's modest manual on the performance of the divine offices, addressed primarily to an audience of her fellow nuns and printed within her own convent, to Vernazza's vast, four-volume collected meditations, sponsored as a figurehead publication by her order, the Lateran Canons, following scrutiny by a high-powered theological committee appointed by Carlo Borromeo.[6] While Vernazza's works were published after her death, with her prior consent and collaboration, Pigafetta, Grumelli, and Malvasia all published their works during their lifetime, Pigafetta and Grumelli in a relatively self-effacing style, Malvasia in a more worldly and self-assertive one (her *Istoria* features an engraved frontispiece, a series of prefatory lyrics, including two madrigals in praise of the author, and an authorial preface that cites Xenophon, Plautus, Euripides, Plutarch, and Seneca, as well as, more predictably, Aquinas).[7]

Of the other principal novelties noted as characteristic of this period, secular women's increased involvement in the production of discursive religious works may be dated to 1581, when Chiara Matraini published a volume of *Meditationi spirituali* that would prove the first of four religious prose works this prolific author produced in the last twenty years of her long life. Precedents were available to Matraini in the form of Vittoria Colonna's *Litere* and *Pianto* and Laura Battiferra's *argomenti* to the psalm translations of her *Sette salmi penitentiali* of 1564.[8] These are all relatively small-scale works, however, Colonna's, for example, presenting themselves as private musings intended at most for a manuscript audience. Matraini's *Meditationi*, a ninety-page treatise clearly written for publication, represents a departure in this sense. Matraini's other three religious works are a psalm commentary (*Considerationi sopra i sette salmi penitentiali* [1586]), a life of the Virgin (*Breve discorso sopra la vita e laude della beatissima Vergine e madre del figliuol di Dio* [1590]), and a curious eclectic work incorporating a set of religious dialogues and a dream-vision narrative (*Dialoghi spirituali* [1602]).[9] Of these, the life of the Virgin proved the most successful in publishing terms, being reprinted several times in the Veneto down to the end of the seventeenth century after its initial printing in Matraini's hometown of Lucca.[10] Besides Matraini's *Meditationi* and psalm commentary, the 1580s also saw the publication in Vicenza of Maddalena Campiglia's *Discorso sopra l'annonciatione della beata Vergine*. The coincidence in place and time with Osanna Pigafetta's *Trattato*, which came out in Vicenza the following year, is quite notable, and it may be that the initiative of the secular author inspired the editorial activity of the cloistered woman.[11] In 1595 a vast compendium of spiritual meditations by the Neapolitan Isabella Capece was brought out by her confessor following her premature death under the title *Consolatione dell'anima*. This was the only single-authored work by a woman to be published south of Rome between Laura Terracina's death in the late 1570s and Antonio Bulifon's publication of editions of Terracina's and Vittoria Colonna's *rime* in 1692. In 1597, in more predictable geographic territory, Lucrezia Marinella published alongside her *Vita del serafico, et glorioso San Francesco* a *Discorso del rivolgimento amoroso, verso la somma bellezza*, essentially a Christian-ascetic manifesto, though cast in philosophical and, specifically, Neoplatonic-hermetic terms.[12]

Besides these religious works, secular women in this period also distinctly increased their output of secular discursive prose writings by comparison with the earlier years of the century. Veronica Franco's 1580 *Lettere familiari* was the first securely attributable volume of letters to be published by a woman.[13] This was followed by Chiara Matraini's *Lettere*, which she published alongside the revised version of her *Rime* in 1595 and 1597.[14] Two further letter collections, both published posthumously, are Battista Vernazza's, of 1602, and Isabella Andreini's, of 1607, although Andreini's is of problematic authorship, its dedicatory letter at least having been written under Andreini's name by her husband, Francesco.[15] Other secular discursive prose works by women in this period taking the form of letters include Camilla Erculiani's *Lettere di philosophia naturale* (1584), the earliest sustained published exercise in natural-philosophical writing by an Italian woman if we except Isabella Cortese's perhaps apocryphal *Secreti* (1561) and the Dalmatian Maria Gondola's brief letter-treatise arguing for the dignity of the female sex, published with the *Discorsi sopra le metheore d'Aristotile* of her husband, Niccolò Vito di Gozze, in 1585.[16] The Piedmontese Isabella Sori's conduct text *Ammaestramenti e ricordi circa a' buoni costumi, che deve insegnare una ben creata madre ad una figlia*, published in Pavia in 1628, is also cast in epistolary form, as a series of twelve letters from a mother to her daughter.[17]

Another genre of prose writing that we encounter with a certain frequency in women's writing in this period is the oration. As with the letter collection, this may be seen as a vernacular reprise of a fifteenth-century Latin tradition, most famously represented by figures such as Isotta Nogarola and Cassandra Fedele, the latter of whom, after debuting as an orator in the 1480s, survived long enough into the following century to be invited by the Venetian government to address the Polish queen Bona Sforza (1494–1557) during a state visit to Venice in 1556, when Fedele was about 90 years old.[18] In the later sixteenth century, probably inspired by this late-life feat of Fedele's, as well as by records of her public oratory of the 1480s and 1490s, we find two Veneto women writing vernacular orations for public occasions. Issicratea Monte, of Rovigo, published orations of congratulation to Sebastiano Venier and Niccolò da Ponte on their election to the Venetian dogeship in 1577 and 1578 and to Empress Maria of Austria (1528–1603) on her passage through Venetian territory in 1581, and an oration by Ersilia Spolverini, of Verona, to the Venetian noblewoman Chiara Cornaro, wife of the departing governor of the city, was published in 1596.[19] Spolverini's oration appears to have been delivered by the author at a farewell ceremony for Cornaro attended by the female elite of Verona, and at least one of Monte's dogal speeches was performed by the author before the Collegio of Venice, the highest council of state.[20] Also apparently delivered, this time in a religious context, was Beatrice Gatti's 1604 oration celebrating her admission as a nun into the convent of Santa Maria d'Araceli in Vicenza.[21]

Very different from the examples just discussed is the only oration by a non-Veneto woman published in this period, Isabella Cervoni's 1598 *Orazione . . . al santissimo . . . Papa Clemente ottavo sopra l'impresa di Ferrara*, whose length (28 pages) and close argumentation preclude the possibility that it was intended for delivery. Cervoni's *Orazione* is also distinctive in that it is cast in the form of a deliberative, rather than a demonstrative, speech. As the title suggests, Cervoni's oration sets out to counsel Clement on the matter of the Ferrarese succession, which had come to a head in 1598 after the death without issue of Alfonso II d'Este. It is a conceit of remarkable boldness, even though the work in fact resolves itself into an encomium of Clement's successful handling of the crisis. Cervoni's oration, unusual within women's writing in this period for the familiarity it displays with history and political theory, is followed by a political *canzone* addressed to the rulers of Europe, again deliberative and exhortative in tone.[22]

With the exception of Franco's and Andreini's *Lettere*, most of the works cited in the previous two paragraphs are relatively modest in scale. Even Cervoni's *Orazione*, by far the most ambitious of her published works, is only about forty pages long, including the *canzone*. This period also saw the publication, however, of two very substantial secular works of discursive prose by women: Moderata Fonte's two-book dialogue, *Il merito delle donne*, probably composed shortly prior to her death in 1592 but published posthumously in 1600, and Lucrezia Marinella's *La nobiltà et l'eccellenza delle donne*, published first in 1600 and then, in a substantially revised and expanded version, in 1601.[23] Both are works of exceptional interest and have attracted more critical attention than any other secular prose works by Italian women of this period with the exception of Franco's *Lettere*. Fonte's *Il merito* must be considered as standing somewhere between the categories of discursive prose and fiction, for its setting is far more vividly realized than those of other female-authored dialogues of this period, such as Tullia d'Aragona's *Dialogo dell'infinità d'amore* or Chiara Matraini's *Dialoghi spirituali*, and its representation of its speakers, a group of idealized female Venetian noblewomen varying in age and marital status, is of remarkable interest as the only fictional work we have from this period of an elite female circle portrayed from within. Marinella's *La nobiltà* is, by contrast, a straight academic treatise, arguing the case for women's excellence and, more originally, men's vices in a virtuoso display of rhetorical acuity and historical erudition of the type that participation in the *querelle des femmes* traditionally demanded. The work made a powerful impact, winning Marinella a national audience, and became one of the most celebrated female-authored works of the age.

One respect in which Marinella's *La nobiltà* is important within the history of Italian women's writing is that it may be seen as initiating a new trend toward polemic, and especially gender-related polemic, on women's part. Women had participated in the Italian tradition of the *querelle des femmes* prior to Marinella: in addition to Moderata Fonte and Maria Gondola, one could cite here a letter of Laura Cereta's, an unpublished dialogue by Giulia Bigolina, a *capitolo* of Veronica Franco's, and a handful of *proemi* by Laura Terracina.[24] What was new in Marinella was not simply the length and systematic character of her treatise but also her willingness to engage in a sustained polemical argument against specific male authorities. The treatise was initially composed as a rebuttal to Giuseppe Passi's misogynistic treatise *I donneschi diffetti*, of 1599, while the 1601 redaction adds an appendix of "demolitions" of previous misogynist thinkers, including Aristotle, Boccaccio, and Torquato Tasso.[25] A woman taking on and battling with named male antagonists in this way, even if the majority were dead at the time of her writing, was a novel and exhilarating spectacle, the more so since Marinella showed herself equal to the satirical bravura such polemical writing required. Of Italian female writers, only Veronica Franco, in her 1575 *Rime*, had similarly engaged in such *ad hominem* battles, and she had been more discreet: Franco does not name her antagonists, and only those within her literary circle would have been able to identify the men addressed.[26]

The Marinella-Passi dispute awakened a taste for male-female polemic that we can see developing over the following two decades, particularly in Venice and the Veneto, and that would reach its peak with the remarkable series of polemical works published by the Venetian nun Arcangela Tarabotti beginning in 1644. During the period that concerns us here, perhaps the most striking instance of this polemical trend was the debate that exploded between the Veronese poet Veneranda Bragadin and the Paduan satirist Giovanni Battista Barbo in about 1613–14, after Bragadin wrote a sonnet objecting to Barbo's misogynistic poem *L'oracolo*. Barbo replied with a hostile *capitolo* impugning Bragadin's honor, and she replied with a prose *discorso* composed in a spirit of out-and-out invective, accusing her opponent, among other things, of senility, effeminacy, and frequentation of low-grade prostitutes for lack of other erotic options.[27] The texts of the Bragadin-Barbo debate were published in Vicenza in 1614, and it was probably as a result of the public interest awakened by this controversy that a Vicentine publisher and bookseller in the same year published a letter that he purportedly had received from a gentlewoman of Palermo, Bianca Naldi, responding to the arguments of Passi's *Donneschi diffetti*, of which he had sent her a copy.[28] Two other polemical works by women were published before 1630. The Venetian Jewish writer Sara Copio (c. 1600–1641) published a polemical *Manifesto*, written in response to a letter by the Rovigan priest and jurist Baldassarre Bonifaccio that had accused her of questioning the immortality of the soul.[29] Finally, within the field of gender-themed polemic, Isabella Sori wrote a series of "defenses," published alongside her 1628 *Ammaestramenti*, defending herself and her sex against what we can infer was an *ad hominem* misogynist attack.[30]

2. Authorizing Women: The Problem of *Docere*

Even the brief descriptions supplied above will have made it clear that we are dealing here with an extremely diverse set of writings, ranging in subject matter from natural philosophy to theology to history to the upbringing of children and in form from unembellished devotional tracts to works of quite notable literary pretension. Generalization across this range of writings would be for the most part unfruitful, but one central feature common to all of them deserves consideration: all, to differing extents and in different manners, position their authors as authorities, capable of transmitting information or opinion that the very act of publication implicitly defines as useful to others. All, in other words, aspire to instruct the reader, however modestly that aspiration is veiled. The only real exceptions are works such as the laudatory orations of Issicratea Monte and Ersilia Spolverini and Veneranda Bragadin's invective against Barbo. Here, the underlying rhetorical genre is epideictic (praise or blame) rather than deliberative (the rhetoric of counsel, the core didactic genre).

This assumption of an authoritative role serves rhetorically to differentiate the writings grouped here under the rubric of discursive prose from the poetic and fictional works discussed in preceding chapters. The distinction is not absolute: it was a tenet of the literature of this period that fictional works should be edifying as well as "delightful," and quite strong moral-didactic impulses may be detected, for example, in works such as Campiglia's *Flori* and Torelli's *Partenia*, not to mention works of spiritual narrative such as Marinella's *La Colomba sacra* and *Vita di San Francesco*, the latter of which contain extensive passages of moral and spiritual instruction in the form of directly reported sermons by the saint. Still, there is a perceptible qualitative difference between the kind of didactic claim made by a work such as the *Vita di San Francesco* and that made by the *Discorso del rivolgimento amoroso verso la somma bellezza*, which Marinella published alongside it. The first presents an exemplary Christian life in a "delightful" and "moving" manner, calculated to encourage the reader to embrace the values it embodies. In the second, the young Marinella, still an adolescent, assumes a directly instructional role, adducing an impressive array of philosophical authorities to argue her Neoplatonizing case that spiritual ascent must start from a rejection of the body.

While the effortless air of intellectual entitlement Marinella displays in the *Rivolgimento* does little to suggest it, this assumption of authority on the part of a woman was far from uncontroversial in the culture of her day. Women might creditably teach their children in their earliest years, and nuns were widely engaged in the instruction of young girls of elite family, but beyond these circumscribed roles quite strong prejudices existed regarding women's assuming a teaching role, in particular women's teaching men. This was held to be not simply indecorous but actually morally and spiritually transgressive, in that it contradicted the Apostle Paul's explicit stipulation that "I suffer not a woman to teach, nor to usurp authority over the man."[31] Paul's injunction was quite frequently adduced in this period as an argument against women's assuming an instructional role, sometimes supported by the canon-law dictum "let not a woman, however learned and holy, presume to teach men in public."[32] The fullest and most strident discussion of the issue is found in a treatise of 1646 by the Jesuit Giovanni Domenico Ottonelli (1584–1670), which goes as far as to say that ever since Eve's original false counsel in Eden, "whenever a woman has set herself up to teach, she has generally been an instrument of the devil, an architect of fraud, a forger of deceptions, a mistress of lies and errors."[33] Besides these theologically based objections, satirists such as Giuseppe Passi and Antonio Maria Spelta were quick to ridicule the arrogance of intellectually aspirant women who dared profess learning in public, setting themselves up as "so many Platos and Aristotles, or, better, so many Thomases and Augustines."[34]

In attacking the "teaching woman," a figure like Ottonelli was clearly thinking primarily of oral situations, in which questions of sexual decorum might come into play. As he luridly puts it, "The words of a woman are live flames of lascivious ardor that often burn the hearts of their listeners."[35] Written contexts of instruction were less potentially inflammable, and we should not assume that the same reaction of opprobrium would necessarily apply in such cases. In practice, the notion of a woman imparting instruction to or disputing with a man was not invariably regarded as morally distasteful, especially within religious culture, where a woman might be considered a vessel of divine truth. Besides obvious examples such as Catherine of Siena and Catherine of Alexandria, it is not difficult to find other instances of female saints and *beate* whose mission included an intellectual and instructional component. Interesting in this regard is a text like Serafino Razzi's life of Saint Melania the Younger (c. 383–439), which lays much emphasis on the saint's advanced scriptural and philosophical erudition and has her disputing with philosophers, as well as acting as salvific spiritual mentor to her husband, "doing quite the contrary of Eve."[36] Other important authorizing figures for the female sage were the sibyls; as we have seen, Moderata Fonte placed a sibyl on stage adjudicating a dispute between philosophers in *Le feste*, and Chiara Matraini had depicted a sibyl in an altarpiece in Lucca.[37]

Besides these cases of women who exercised a *magisterium* rooted wholly or in part in a divinely infused *sapientia*, examples were also available at the time of women who had taught on the basis of a rationally acquired *scientia*. In his *Glorie immortali . . . d'ottocento quarantacinque donne*, Pietro Paolo Ribera includes a short section on female lecturers from the Neoplatonist philosopher Hypatia of Alexandria (d. AD 415) to Dorotea Bocchi and Novella Bolognese, who purportedly taught medicine and law at the University of Bologna in the fourteenth and early fifteenth centuries.[38] Francesco Agostino Della Chiesa is similarly open to the figure of the teaching woman in his *Theatro delle donne letterate*, which includes, for example, an approving entry on the classical figure of Leontion, who was reputed to have publicly disputed with Aristotle's disciple Theophrastus, earning her the opprobrium of Boccaccio in *De claris mulieribus*, where he reproaches her for her "feminine temerity" in this regard.[39] Della Chiesa also addresses the question of women's didactic role in the theoretical *Discorso della preminenza e perfettione del sesso donnesco*, which prefaces the *Theatro*. He argues that women are excluded from teaching publicly not because of any lack of ability but simply because of the inappropriate sexual attention they would inspire in their male listeners. If it were not for this, he contends, women would "teach in no less sound and learned a manner than the greatest and most eloquent orators in history."[40]

Della Chiesa even seems prepared to countenance the notion of women teaching in a formal religious context, despite the Pauline proscription: he refers to his *Theatro* for examples of women who have not only "taught in public universities before many most excellent doctors" but "preached in the most frequented churches in Rome and other cities of Europe in the presence of princes, cardinals, and the Pope himself."[41] While it is hard to judge how widely the liberal attitudes of figures such as Ribera and Della Chiesa were shared, they do suggest that Ottonelli's hard-line position was not the only one available, even for clerics. Remarkably, Cristoforo Bronzini records two invitations supposedly issued to Margherita Sarrocchi to take up university lecturing posts, in Palermo and Bologna, though there is no independent evidence of this.[42]

A number of strategies can be identified on the part of female writers of didactic texts for negotiating the social sensitivities surrounding the issue of women teaching. One very basic one, utilized in both secular and religious contexts, was to define the audience addressed as female. Whether a fiction or not, this avoided the indecorum of a woman overtly positioning herself in authority over men. A good example among religious writings is Flavia Grumelli's *Vita di Santa Grata*, dedicated to the nuns of her convent. This work reproduces in print a social situation no reader of the period could think other than admirable: a pious abbess instructing the nuns in her charge in matters of faith. A secular example, more complex, is the second book of Moderata Fonte's *Il merito delle donne*, which represents a series of informal lessons, primarily on natural history but also shading into dietology and areas of medical practice, delivered by a well-educated young Venetian noblewoman, Corinna, to an audience of her peers. In both works, to differing degrees, the fiction of an all-female audience mitigates the writer's assumption of a magisterial role that some would find indecorous, Grumelli in the field of morality, Fonte, more controversially, in that of natural science. This does not, however, mean that Grumelli or Fonte conceived of her actual readership as exclusively female; on the contrary, there are indications in both works that a broader, mixed audience was envisaged. It is noteworthy in this regard that both works incorporate quite lengthy, directly reported speeches addressed by women to men, in Grumelli's case an exhortation by Santa Grata to her father, enjoining him successfully to convert to Christianity, in Fonte's a staged oration by one of her speakers, Leonora, to an imagined audience of men, pleading the case for better treatment of women.[43] It is not difficult to see an element of authorial self-portraiture in these notably eloquent women. Grata is later explicitly accorded an apostolic role in relation to her pagan fellow citizens: "she taught and demonstrated the Christian religion through both her words and her deeds."[44]

Another strategy available to women for legitimizing didactic discourse was that of claiming divine inspiration. We see this used on occasion by male presenters of female-authored texts to account for the apparent anomaly of a "mere woman" having written works worthy of a reader's attention. The Neapolitan *letterato* Francesco de Pietri (1575–?1645), in his preface to Isabella Capece's *Consolatione dell'anima*, explains to readers skeptical of a young woman's ability to write a work of this kind that it is not so improbable, when one considers the holiness of the young author's life and her diligence in the study of scripture, that God in his omnipotence should have infused into her "spirit and energy" sufficient to achieve such a thing.[45] Similarly, Dionigi da Piacenza, introducing Battista Vernazza's 1588 *Opere spirituali*, notes that the piety of Vernazza's writings is such that they appear "to have been composed more through supernatural illumination and the constant use of prayer than through human industry or any other form of study."[46] More emphatically, in the dedicatory letter to the fourth volume of Vernazza's writings, published in 1602, da Piacenza notes as a remarkable feature of the modern age the appearance of female theologians such as Vernazza but attributes this to divine intervention, women being by nature more "fragile" than men and less capable of study.[47]

Besides these sometimes patronizing uses of the topos of divine inspiration in male-authored paratexts to female-authored texts, we also find female authors themselves sometimes deploying this same topos to offset the impression of arrogance or presumption that might otherwise be conveyed by their assuming a didactic role. A very clear example of this is the dedicatory letter to Chiara Matraini's *Considerationi sopra i sette salmi*, of 1586, where Matraini speaks of her initial reluctance to embark on the task of composing a commentary on the psalms despite being urged to it by "respectable and most learned persons," on the grounds that this seemed to her "a major and difficult enterprise . . . more suited to great and elevated intellects than to a simple Woman, ill-versed in the Mysteries of the Holy Scriptures."[48] Matraini finally resolved to accept the task, "perhaps inspired by God," with the consideration that even if she could not "ascend with my intellect to that point to which some extremely rare and speculative intellects had attained," she could nonetheless hope to benefit her fellow Christians by urging them to penitence, following the example of the prophet in her text.[49]

Matraini's reference to divine inspiration is hardly surprising in the context of a religious treatise, but we find the same argument employed, less predictably, in Isabella Cervoni's *Orazione* to Pope Clement VIII. Cervoni's text offers one of the most outstanding examples in this period of what the Boccaccio of *De claris mulieribus* might term *feminine temerity*, in that it sets out, at least ostensibly, to instruct the reigning pope on how to conduct his political business, even though Cervoni is careful to underline that she is telling Clement nothing that he does not already know.[50] Cervoni underlines the audacity of her project in her *captatio benevolentiae:* "What will the world say when it hears my words on this so lofty subject? A subject so remote from the nature and quality of a simple young virgin? Will it not be amazed that . . . I should dare to speak, and in the deliberative genre, and before a Pope?"[51] Her self-defense starts from the ostensibly self-effacing position that God frequently chooses weak vessels as mouthpieces for his truths, citing the biblical "Out of the mouths of babes and sucklings thou hast perfected praise."[52] Besides this self-presentation as divine vessel, however, Cervoni also on occasion appeals to more rational sources of authority, speaking of her close study of history, well exemplified in the exemplificatory portions of the oration, and the intellectual gifts nature has bestowed on her.[53] The *Orazione* ultimately reveals itself to be a bold pitch for papal patronage on the part of its young author. Cervoni concludes by noting wistfully that should such support be forthcoming, she would hope to make such progress in her studies that it would be clear that nature had not given her such talents in vain.[54]

Another authorizing strategy deployed quite often in the presentation of female-authored works to the public is the use of one or more male figures as guarantors of the quality of the work. In one extreme case this intervention amounts to coauthorship: the preface to Isabella Capece's posthumous *Consolatione dell'anima* make it clear that the treatise was not only scrutinized by Isabella's confessor, Pietro Cola Pagano, but also "enriched and adorned with many new *concetti*" in order to ensure its "fame and immortality."[55] Less interventionist is the contribution of Giuseppe Mozzagrugno to Chiara Matraini's *Breve discorso sopra la vita e laude della beatissima Vergine*, which comprises two prefatory sonnets and a set of *annotationi* presented in appendix to the work.[56] Although one of the text's few modern readers, Maria Pia Paoli, interprets Mozzagrugno's prominent presence in the book as essentially repressive—an externally imposed male policing of a female-authored discourse that could not have been allowed to stand alone[57]—there seems to be no particular reason why we should consider it as such. By 1590 Matraini had already published two religious treatises without any such male editorial mediation, and nothing suggests that it should have been seen as more necessary in this instance than in those. An alternative way of reading Mozzagrugno's annotations is as an honorific addition to the treatise, perhaps contributed at Matraini's own request. Similar points could be made regarding the numerous authorizing male paratexts that frame the printed edition of Battista Vernazza's *Opere,* collectively documenting the complex process of theological ratification to which Vernazza's writings were subjected. While these may be read as expressive of a religious culture that countenanced female spiritual teaching only within a tightly controlled patriarchal context, it is also true that the various framing texts have the effect of underlining Vernazza's dignity as a spiritual authority. We are very far here from the stereotypical Counter-Reformation position that dismissed women as fitted intellectually only to listen in silence to the teachings of men.

Moving back to religious works published under women's own aegis, perhaps the most striking example we have from this period of this authorizing use of male mediatory figures is Maddalena Campiglia's *Discorso sopra l'annonciatione*. The work is prefaced by a short essay by the Vicentine lay *letterato* Vespasiano Giuliani in praise of the author and followed by another, by the Benedictine Gregorio Ducchi. An appendix follows, separately numbered, with encomiastic poems by seventeen mostly lay authors, all male aside from one unidentified woman, including figures of the status of Luigi Groto, Muzio Sforza, and Angelo Ingegneri, as well as, ironically, Giovanni Battista Barbo, who would later author the misogynist satire that aroused Veneranda Bragadin's ire.[58] Together with Campiglia's own dedicatory letter, to Vittoria Trissino della Frattina (d. 1612), these paratexts serve to fashion the novel literary figure of the female lay religious writer, pitched as an author who might be read with profit not only by women but also by men. Ducchi's afterword speaks of the treatise as "spiritual nourishment" and as "milk" proffered to the reader by "this kindest of Mothers"—feminine language, clearly, but describing what was traditionally conceived of as a masculine role, that of teacher and spiritual guide.[59] Similarly, Giuliani, in his preface, praises Campiglia for procuring through her writings both utility to her fellow men and honor to her country.[60] Campiglia's verse encomiasts present her alternately as vessel for divine inspiration and skilled writer, with Muzio Sforza, for example, figuring her as "new Sappho," "new Sibyl," and Mary Magdalene–like "secretary" of divine truth.[61]

One final self-authorizing strategy on the part of a female writer may be noted: reference to an authoritative female figure. We see this very clearly illustrated in the *captatio benevolentiae* of Beatrice Gatti's 1604 oration celebrating her monacation in the Vicentine convent of Santa Maria d'Araceli, which, though primarily demonstrative, contains a didactic, sermonizing element in its arguments for the superiority of the cloistered life. Having noted, in a rather perfunctory manner, that speaking in public at such a young age might be supposed to induce "some fear" (qualche spavento) in her, Gatti goes on to recall the example of Catherine of Alexandria, on whose feast day, 25 November, she was speaking. Catherine is proposed as an inspirational model to any woman who might be daunted at the prospect of public speaking, in that she offers an example of a woman "endowed with all the eloquence and knowledge and prudence that was scattered among the sages of Greece and Rome, and indeed the whole universe: vanquisher of the orators, conqueror of the philosophers, glorious victor over empires."[62] Interestingly, Gatti presents Catherine's achievements without having recourse to paradoxical arguments regarding God's capacity to enable the weak. Instead she is used in an implicitly profeminist sense as an exemplum of women's capacity for intellectual excellence. That Gatti was acquainted with the contemporary discourse on women's "nobility and excellence" may be argued from her later, unexpected reference to the legendary Assyrian queen Semiramis, frequently cited as an exemplum of female military valor: in an audacious conceit, Gatti compares her own triumphant struggle against worldliness to Semiramis's victories in the field.[63]

The number of works of didactic and polemical prose produced by women in the period that interests us here is clearly too great to allow for individual discussion of each. I shall therefore discuss a mere four, two religious and two secular, two familiar and two little touched by criticism to date. The works are chosen for their literary and intellectual interest, but their selection is obviously not intended to suggest that others of the works listed above are not equally deserving of study. Of those that have yet to become the focus of sustained critical interest, leading candidates are Grumelli's *Vita di Santa Grata*, Cervoni's *Orazione*, Erculiani's *Lettere di philosophia naturale*, and Matraini's *Considerationi sopra i sette salmi penitentiali*.

3. Preachers in Print: Religious *Institutio* in Maddalena Campiglia and Chiara Matraini

The first pair of texts under consideration here, Matraini's *Dialoghi spirituali* and Campiglia's *Discorso sopra l'annonciatione*, exemplify the distinctively Counter-Reformation phenomenon of the didactic religious text authored by a secular woman.[64] Both command interest by virtue of their literary sophistication and the modes in which they negotiate issues of authority, which were particularly sensitive in this instance, given the authors' lay status. The two works are widely dissimilar in terms of their position within the output of their respective authors. Matraini's *Dialoghi* was the product of a writer in her eighty-seventh year with a publishing career of almost half a century behind her, while Campiglia's *Discorso* was the debut publication of woman in her early thirties with a high-profile literary future ahead. While the *Discorso* was published in Campiglia's native Vicenza, Matraini's *Dialoghi* appeared in the great publishing center of Venice, where the second edition of her *Lettere* had come out five years earlier, in 1597. Until 1597 Matraini had always published in her native Lucca; her shift to Venetian publishers for the last two works of her long career may probably be taken as indicative of her increased literary fame.[65] A further token of this is her appearance, with four sonnets, in a 1601 religiously themed poetic anthology published in Bologna. Besides the Bolognese nun Febronia Pannolini, the only other female poet included was Tarquinia Molza, among the most celebrated women of the age.[66]

Both Campiglia's *Discorso* and Matraini's *Dialoghi* are dedicated to women. These dedications serve, in different ways, as initial legitimizing gestures on their authors' part. The dedicatee of Matraini's *Dialoghi* is Marfisa d'Este Cibo, Marchioness of Massa and Carrara, whom we earlier encountered as the Cellia of Leonora Bernardi's *Tragicomedia pastorale*. This was only the second time that Matraini had addressed a work to a figure of this stature, the previous instance being her *Considerationi sopra i sette salmi*, of 1586, also dedicated to an Este princess, Lucrezia d'Este della Rovere (1535–98).

Campiglia's dedicatee is the aristocratic Vicentine Dominican tertiary Vittoria Trissino, of the family that had produced Vicenza's most distinguished sixteenth-century intellectual, Giangiorgio Trissino (1478–1550), a contemporary of Castiglione and Bembo. Aside from her literary associations and her social prestige, Vittoria Trissino serves as an icon of female piety for Campiglia and, perhaps more specifically, an embodiment of a female piety capable of functioning outside the institutional constraints of the cloister. Widowed young, Trissino had refused pressures from her family to remarry and had withdrawn into a cell she had built for her in the courtyard of her family *palazzo* in Vicenza.[67] As Adriana Chemello has recently noted, Trissino's decision to live her religious vocation outside the convent reflects a wider trend among aristocratic women in Vicenza, expressed in the movement of the Dimesse, which was formalized as an order by Antonio Pagani in 1584.[68] Whether or not she was formally a Dimessa, Campiglia certainly had reasons to associate herself with any movement that served to create a social space for the uncloistered unmarried woman. As we saw in chapter 3, at the time of the publication of the *Discorso* she was living separately from her husband after the failure of their marriage, a position of social difficulty for a woman of this period, as hints in the *Discorso* suggest.[69]

Both Campiglia's *Discorso* and Matraini's *Dialoghi* display a certain formal eclecticism. Neither can be described as a straightforward treatise, although Campiglia's is closer to the norm. Matraini's *Dialoghi* is made up of three separate sections, the first and third of which are further subdivided. It opens with the four "spiritual dialogues" that lend their title to the volume as a whole. These are followed by a visionary narrative featuring the author as protagonist, addressed to an "Accademia dei Curiosi." The work concludes with a series of moral lectures *(sermoni),* again addressed to the Curiosi. These three sections are unified by the recurrent themes of sin, penitence, salvation, and the vanity of human wisdom. The four *dialoghi,* which probably rework a Boethian philosophical dialogue we know Matraini to have been at work on in the 1560s, thematically trace a moral trajectory through study and the rejection of vice (dialogues 1 and 2) to the cultivation of virtue (3) and the ascent to God through true penitence and grace (4).[70] The visionary *narratione* follows a parallel ascending trajectory, this time cast in a prophetic-allegorical idiom, narrating the author's spiritual enlightenment and progressive journey toward truth. Finally, the harangues to the Curiosi reiterate the danger of sin, warning against the lures of sensuality, worldliness, and intellectual hubris, before a closing poetic sequence, addressed to the Virgin and Matraini's name saint, Santa Chiara, leads us back into the realm of the blessed. As in all her late religious works, Matraini's prose exposition is punctuated throughout the volume by poetic interludes, here used to mark off the work's various structural segments. These also serve a unifying function, with poems to the Virgin, for example, being found at the conclusion of the first and third dialogues, as well as at the end of the work.[71] Further variety is supplied by the inclusion of lyrical prose forms, such as the oration and prayer we find inserted into the *narratione*.

Campiglia's *Discorso* lacks the formal articulation into sections that characterizes Matraini's *Dialoghi*, but it is nonetheless possible to identify quite distinct, formally and thematically differentiated phases of the work. Striking especially in this regard is the ten-page narrative near the beginning of the work, which recounts the story of the Annunciation from the moment of the arrival in heaven of Mary's parents, Saints Joachim and Anna, to the moment of Gabriel's descent, taking in a "silent speech" from Adam and Eve pleading for humanity's remission from sin; God's summoning of a council of the angels to inform them of his decision to reverse the Fall through his incarnation and sacrifice; and the departure of Gabriel, hymned on his way by the heavenly hosts.[72] As Eleonora Carinci has recently shown, Campiglia's principal source in the initial, narrative section of the *Discorso* is Pietro Aretino's *Vita di Maria Vergine*, which would also be used by Lucrezia Marinella in her 1602 prose work of the same name.[73] While Campiglia follows Aretino quite closely in some places, her imitation is stylistically more independent than Marinella's and draws on other influences, such as the Tasso of *Gerusalemme liberata*.[74] Like Marinella's later *Vita*, the narrative portion of the *Discorso* may be seen as an attempt to translate into artistic prose the aspirations of the contemporary religious verse epic, a feature of the work that inspired Gregorio Ducchi to contrast Campiglia's enterprise in the *Discorso* with the frivolousness of past secular poets who had "sung steamily of arms and love."[75] In the remainder of the *Discorso*, a continuing narrative thread competes with an increasingly dominant element of discursive meditation, while in the final quarter of the work Campiglia shifts to prescribing, specifically, the contemplations that should accompany the telling of the rosary.[76] In terms of genre, this final section of the work locates itself within the recent, principally Dominican tradition of the rosary manual, a form of religious writing that up to this point had been, as we might expect, the province of male authors, specifically clerics.[77]

Campiglia's self-authorization in this complex literary project was not easy, though it was evidently successful, given the confidence with which she emerged as a literary figure from this point. The authorial persona of the *Discorso* is notably embattled and self-deprecating. In her dedicatory letter she speaks of the work as "the first fruits of the feeblest of trees," and within the text she speaks of her fear of being condemned by the world for her audacity in undertaking a work of this kind, "unworthy, ignorant, and abject" as she is.[78] Relatively little of this self-deprecation is gender based, although the author describes herself at one point as "a negligible little woman" (minima donniciuola).[79] Rather, she presents herself as someone whose possibilities for intellectual development have been constrained by circumstances, writing in the horticultural metaphor of the dedicatory letter of "the fierce drought of others' malice, which saps all that meager potential [*virtù*] that my little terrain might otherwise have acquired from the dews of heaven."[80] Nor is Campiglia's self-abasement as author entirely consistent. Her self-consciously ornate prose style signals her literary ambition, as does her referencing of epic and other elite forms, such as the lyrical description of female beauty.[81] Campiglia also demonstrates considerable scriptural and theological erudition, hinting at one point at a greater fund of learning that she might call on if decorum permitted when she notes that it would be possible to compare the unborn infant Saviour to "many *figurae* with which scripture is replete."[82] If she refrains from regaling her readers with these typological figures, it is simply because she fears that such a disquisition might be seen by her critics as evidence of "arrogance" and "presuming to have read and seen too much."[83]

Campiglia's self-conscious allusion in this passage to the social risk of displaying excessive familiarity with "the divine pages" is interesting given the sensitivity of the whole question of access to scripture on the part of women and laypeople in her culture. Women were certainly encouraged to read devotional works and to engage in structured religious meditation of the type prescribed by such instruments as rosary manuals. Direct engagement with holy writ was, however, a different matter, especially the kind of autonomous and intense intellectual engagement attested by the *Discorso*. Along with its didactic and exhortatory pretensions, this engagement with scripture makes of the *Discorso* a remarkably audacious work for a laywoman of this age.[84] An interesting hint at Campiglia's ambitions is offered by a reference late in the text to the "sublime and rare sermons of the Most Reverend Fiamma."[85] The reference is to Gabriele Fiamma's *Sei prediche . . . in lode della beata Vergine*, a popular and much-published collection of six sermons on the Annunciation preached in Naples in 1573, which Campiglia seems to have used quite extensively as a source in the *Discorso*.[86] This allusion to Fiamma alerts us to the elements in her own work that assimilate it to preaching, notably the oratorical rhythms of its prose, its insistent use of quasi-oral devices such as exclamation and rhetorical question, and its mingling of argument and exposition with lyric, prayerlike meditational passages, and occasional passages of moral exhortation. Campiglia's preacherly ambitions are acknowledged implicitly in a number of the encomiastic poems that accompanied the *Discorso*. Vicenzo Tassello is most emphatic in this regard, congratulating Campiglia on showing those lost in the mires of the world the "salutiferous path" to heaven.[87] Gregorio Ducchi and Marco Stecchini compliment her on filling the breasts of her listeners with "burning zeal" and piercing them with a "sacred and holy spear."[88] Campiglia mitigates the audacity of constituting herself as textual preacher by addressing herself in her moral exhortations most frequently to an audience of women ("noi donne"), whom she berates sporadically throughout the treatise for their vanity and worldliness, holding up the Virgin, by contrast, as a model of female decorum.[89] These attacks on women should probably be seen as rhetorically strategic rather than expressive of a genuine circumscription of her intended audience. A less explicitly gendered exhortation contrasting the Virgin's pious taciturnity with the vapid and often ill-intentioned verbal excess that characterizes modern urban life seems rather to repropose a moral quality traditionally gendered as feminine as exemplary for both sexes.[90]

If the *Discorso* constitutes itself by stealth as didactic discourse—Campiglia's original presentation of the work stresses, rather, its character as spontaneous personal outpouring—Matraini's *Dialoghi* make fewer bones about the author's ambitions and qualifications as spiritual authority. The work's structural organization in three genre-differentiated sections enables Matraini to essay an entire sequence of authoritative poses, all by cultural tradition essentially masculine: that of rational *institutor* in the *dialoghi*, Dantean visionary sage in the *narratione*, and moral-religious orator in the *sermoni*. Of the three, only the second author type might be said to be bigendered by tradition, in that a precedent for a discourse rooting its authority in exceptional visionary experience existed in the writings of female mystics. In its specific literary form, however—an account of a dream vision in which a spiritual guide leads the pilgrim-visionary to a vantage point from which the earth and the three realms of the afterlife may be seen—Matraini's *narratione* directs the reader specifically to a Boethian-Dantean tradition in which the intrusion of a female subject was a novelty.[91] Only a *canzone* by Isotta Brembati published in 1587 may be suggested as a possible precedent in this regard, though Brembati's dream vision is secular in content.[92] Equally novel are the scenarios we encounter in the *dialoghi*, of a didactic dialogue in which a woman imparts instruction to a male interlocutor, and in the *sermoni*, where a female preacher-lecturer delivers a sequence of moral diatribes to a male audience configured as academic. A feature of Matraini's last work that differentiates it from her previous experiments in religious discursive prose is its emphasis on such quasi-oral forms of discourse. Both the *dialoghi* and the *sermoni* stage a female voice—the author's own—that we are encouraged not simply to absorb textually but to "hear." Especially given the audience's configuration as male in both cases, the work brings us up quite sharply against the Pauline injunction against women teaching. Here in a literal and quite unmitigated sense we see a woman assuming a *cathedra* in the presence of men.

A precedent for the *Dialoghi* in this respect is offered by Matraini's *Lettere* of 1595, and perhaps more particularly by the slightly expanded version of that text Matraini published in 1597. Matraini's letters are eccentric with regard to the tradition of *lettere familiari* that dominated Italian epistolographic production in the sixteenth century. Rather than the informal, candid, character-revealing epistles envisaged by that tradition, they mostly take the form of short essays, with a superscription bearing the recipient's name virtually their only concession to the epistolary form.[93] Quite a number of the *lettere*, which appear to have been composed in the 1560s but perhaps were revised later, portray Matraini in a didactic role with regard to male correspondents. One notable example is a letter to her son, Federico Cantarini, which recasts in letter form the educational material of Isocrates's oration to Demonicus, a translation of which Matraini had published in 1556.[94] Another, of particular interest for the *Dialoghi spirituali*, given its theological subject matter and apparent late date of composition, is a letter included for the first time in the 1597 *Lettere*, to an otherwise unknown and perhaps invented Teofilo Calderini, described as a "most talented youth" (virtuosissimo giovane), who had purportedly, in a letter to Matraini, proposed an opinion that she considered heretical. Matraini responds with a lengthy theological disquisition setting him right, a remarkably assertive piece of self-positioning for a female writer of this time.[95]

The dialogues that open Matraini's *Dialoghi spirituali* are close in several respects to the world of the *Lettere*, featuring as an interlocutor the young son of her friend Cangenna Lipomeni, who appears as a correspondent of Matraini's in the *Lettere*. The young man, who is given the fictional name Filocalio (Lover of Beauty), is portrayed in conversation with Matraini herself, represented as Theofila (Lover of God). This use of disguised allusive names serves to shift Matraini's dialogues toward the fictional-allegorical model of colloquy typified by works such as Leone Ebreo's *Dialoghi d'amore* (1535), in which female speakers were often accorded a role of authority that they were very rarely given in quasi-documentary works employing identifiable historical figures as speakers.[96] Matraini's *dialoghi spirituali* are almost unique in this period in figuring an identifiable female speaker in the authoritative role of *princeps sermonis* (lit. "leader of the conversation"), except in the special case of all-female dialogues, which are in any case rare. This anomalous situation is mitigated to an extent by the age discrepancy between the two speakers: Filocalio is clearly at least a generation younger than Matraini, and his submissive stance toward her is thus interpretable in a quasi-filial light. The role of mother was not commonly conceived at the time to include advanced moral-philosophical and theological instruction, however, and Filocalio is hardly a child: the first dialogue portrays him as on the point of engaging on a commercial career before the eloquence of Theofila's advocacy of learning wins him over to the life of the mind. Although her method of teaching is more dogmatic than Socrates's, Matraini seems to cast herself in her late works in the Socratic role of philosophical mentor to the male youth of her city. As Janet Smarr has noted, Matraini portrays Filocalio as at first falling into conversation with her by chance but then returning to her house by choice to seek her out as teacher.[97] Like Socrates's, her authority is portrayed as deriving not from any external, institutionalized source but from her own intrinsic wisdom and charisma.

If, in the *dialoghi*, Matraini portrays herself instructing a young man, her closing harangues to the Accademia dei Curiosi also show her addressing a series of moral lectures to a putatively male audience: how could an "academy" be conceived of otherwise at this time? The Curiosi have not been identified as an actual academic grouping, nor, if they had been, is it easy to imagine an occasion when a female speaker might be invited to address them.[98] The rather aggressive and hectoring tone in which the *sermoni* are cast also speaks against their constituting actual or imagined academic lectures, in that the etiquette of late Renaissance literary academies demanded a polite social tone. *Accademia* here is perhaps best interpreted, then, as designating a generic collective grouping rather than a real or fictional institution, something along the lines of the "congregation of the curious." Effectively, the Curiosi seem to serve as an embodiment of a certain, negatively connoted existential and intellectual model. The *sermoni* upbraid them for their enslavement to sensual love (*sermone* 1) and, more generally, for their subordination of reason to the *affetti* (*sermone* 3); they are also taken to task for their pursuit of secular knowledge, especially natural-philosophical and cosmological, at the expense of self-knowledge and piety (*sermone* 2). *Sermone* 2 is especially interesting when read in conjunction with the opening of the visionary *narratione*, also addressed to the Curiosi, in which the author portrays herself as intent on her activity within the "fair and spacious garden of the human sciences," hopeful of garnering therein some "fine and worthy fruit of wisdom," when she is confronted with the vision of a miraculous winged lady clad in purple and gold who berates her for the vanity of this ambition.[99] The lady's point is that the wisdom Matraini is vainly seeking in the mortal world can be found within herself; as in the second *sermone* to the Curiosi, a fallacious secular model of intellectual enquiry is opposed to the truer path of the spirit. Matraini opens her second *sermone* with the opening phrase of the anonymous *Meditationes piisimae de cognitione humanae conditionis,* attributed to Saint Bernard: "Many people know many things, and yet do not know themselves."[100] This intuition is fundamental to Matraini's claim to spiritual authority in this volume, which rests in narrative-autobiographical terms on the intellectual "conversion" dramatized in her dream vision. It is this that gives her the spiritual capital we see her expending in her *sermoni;* like Dante, she returns from her journey with a mission of worldly reform. The Accademia dei Curiosi simultaneously embodies the audience for this mission and evokes her previous, now successfully transcended self.

It is noteworthy that Matraini's *narratione,* the only portion of the *Dialoghi spirituali* that shows the author as being taught, rather than teaching, chooses as *institutrix* a female figure, the "miraculous lady," whom the protagonist-author refers to not only as "wise and most trusted guide" but also as "sweetest friend" and "fair and dear nurse."[101] Female guide figures are, of course, found in Boethius and Dante, Matraini's principal sources, but the gender of the guide acquires particular significance in this context, echoing as it does that of the author-protagonist. Authoritative female figures abound in the *Dialoghi spirituali,* from Theofila and the miraculous lady, to the dedicatee, Marfisa d'Este, and the Virgin, the subject of three poems. The volume concludes with a madrigal to Matraini's name saint, Clare, that richly works the seam of onomastic wordplay that Matraini had long used in her secular poetry: *chiarezza* as "clarity," "brilliance," "spiritual illumination," "fame."[102] The same punning pervades a sonnet at the beginning of the volume that speaks of Matraini's return to her studies after an illness: Matraini figures herself as the moon goddess, Diana, reflecting the light of the Apollonian sun, that is, the sciences.[103] The relation is precisely that traditionally attributed to the Virgin: that of reflector and channel of God's grace. The *Dialoghi spirituali* as a whole may be seen as an extended meditation on women's potential as illuminators, whether imparting formal instruction (the Theofila of the *dialoghi*) or acting as a moral and spiritual "example and mirror" (Saint Clare).[104] It offers a fitting culmination to the *oeuvre* of a woman who had been one of the pioneers of female-authored didactic writing in the 1550s, with her translation of Isocrates's *To Demonicus* and her *Orazione dell'arte della guerra*.

Campiglia's *Discorso*, though less consistently celebratory of the feminine than Matraini's *Dialoghi*, similarly contains elements that serve to affirm women's potential as spiritual mentors. The worldly, fashion- and gossip-obsessed women who serve as the principal target of her moral sermonizing in the work constitute one, negative model of female behavior. A countermodel is supplied, however, by Vittoria Trissino and the other "infinitely worthy" ladies of the Trissino family named in the dedicatory letter, by the "honored ladies" of the Compagnia del Rosario mentioned in the final part of the treatise, and by the Virgin and her circle of demure female companions.[105] More implicitly, as well, Campiglia as author herself represents a living exemplum of female piety and intellectuality, to which the modest author cannot call attention but her paratextual celebrants most emphatically do. This counterposition of negative and positive female models reaches something of a climax in the *Discorso* with an extended comparison between the figures of Eve and the Virgin, the first "mother of sin and author of our universal damnation," the second "mother of innocence and minister of salvation."[106] Campiglia's strategy in the work regarding gender was a well-conceived one at a time when misogynistic attitudes were beginning to be more freely articulated: she acknowledges in some of her fellow women the "Eve-like" feminine weaknesses that misogynist satirists had targeted but emphasizes that such weaknesses are a choice and correctable, rather than something to which women are inescapably condemned. The highest guarantor of this truth is, precisely, the Virgin Mary, emblematic of the highest possibilities of femininity and humanity. Campiglia thanks her in one passage of exhortation to errant women for having "aggrandized and ennobled" her sex.[107]

4. Proclaiming Women's Worth: Fonte, Marinella, and the *Querelle des femmes*

The final two works to be surveyed in this chapter have, with justice, attracted much critical attention over recent decades as the first two full-scale female-authored interventions in the *querelle des femmes* published in Italy.[108] While women's voices had not been entirely absent from the *querelle* down to the 1590s, Fonte's dialogue and Marinella's treatise were quite new in terms of scale and ambition, and their appearance within a few months of each other in 1600 made an impression within the Italian literary world. This was especially true of Marinella's *La nobiltà et l'eccellenza delle donne*, which had two further editions, in 1601 and 1621, and was read and used by all subsequent writers in the field.[109] *Il merito delle donne* had a lesser critical fortune, at least outside Fonte's native Venice, but it too won praise from a number of sources.[110]

The context for the publication of both works, as well as for the composition of Marinella's *Nobiltà*, was the storm stirred by Giuseppe Passi's 1599 treatise *I donneschi diffetti*, the most sustained and high-profile attack on women's supposed failings as a sex to have appeared for many years. Marinella's treatise appears to have been commissioned from her directly as a response to Passi by the Venetian publisher Giambattista Ciotti, possibly at the prompting of the Accademia Veneziana.[111] Fonte's treatise had been completed (or nearly completed) eight years earlier, just prior to her death in 1592, but it was clearly the new topicality afforded to its subject by the Passi controversy that led to its being dusted off for publication.[112] The dates of the dedicatory letters of Fonte's dialogue and Marinella's treatise suggest that the publication of Fonte's *Il merito* may have been spurred, not simply by the polemical atmosphere of the moment, but, more precisely, by the appearance of Marinella's treatise, published about three months earlier.[113] Further evidence for this may be offered by the long title given to *Il merito delle donne* in its printed edition, seemingly calculated to bring out the analogy between the two texts, which in English reads: "The Worth of Women: Wherein Is Clearly Revealed Their Nobility and Their Superiority to Men."[114] This describes the content of Marinella's treatise more accurately than it does Fonte's less provocative dialogue, which lays more emphasis on persuading men to treat women with the decency they deserve than on arguing the theoretical case for their superiority to men.

The different contexts in which the two works were composed, as well as their different genres, accounts for the more measured quality of Fonte's profeminism. Marinella's *Nobiltà* was written at the height of a fevered debate and bears its polemical heart on its sleeve. Merely because it was written pre-Passi, however, we should not assume that *Il merito delle donne* was not a response to misogynistic provocation. The *querelle des femmes* had been brewing anew since the mid-1580s in the literary academies of the mainland Veneto, especially Padua and Treviso, and the new misogynist discourse of these years had already provoked one female-authored response in Camilla Erculiani's *Lettere di philosophia naturale*.[115] Fonte was reasonably well connected with literary circles in the mainland Veneto: verse by her appears in collections published in Padua and Verona in, respectively, 1583 and 1586, and her literary acquaintances included the Padua-based Issicratea Monte.[116] While she makes no mention of specific antagonists in *Il merito delle donne*, speaking only of "many men who have written attacks on our sex," it is not implausible that the recent *terraferma* debates were among the motives that prompted her to write.[117]

Despite their shared thematics, Fonte's *Merito* and Marinella's *Nobiltà* are quite dissimilar works. *La nobiltà* is a formally argued academic treatise, setting out its case for the superiority of women to men through a combination of theoretical reasoning and exemplification (or "powerful arguments" and "infinite examples," to cite the title page of the revised edition of 1601).[118] *Il merito* is cast as a dialogue between seven Venetian ladies of varying age and marital status and pursues its argument in a notably unsystematic manner, successfully imitating the drift of informal conversation, even if the device of a ludic debate in the style of Castiglione's *Cortegiano* acts to a degree as a structuring force.[119]

A further difference is the thematic range of the two works. Where Marinella's treatise, in keeping with its academic character, preserves a tight focus on the material announced on its title page, Fonte's is markedly more dispersive. Indeed, after a first book centered quite closely on the theme of women's merits, men's defects, and the state of male-female relations, the second book of *Il merito* turns to a broader, encyclopedic purview, encompassing discussions of weather and its causes, the peculiarities of beasts, birds, and fish, and the curative properties of stones and herbs, as well as excursions on the glories of Venice, on the liberal arts and their practitioners, on colors, and on dress. These two disparate books are unified by the premise, stated explicitly at points in the discussion, that knowledge is empowering and that women's exclusion from "science" lies at the root of their subjection to men.[120]

In this impulse to extend the remit of women's education Fonte is close to the spirit of the Paduan *speziala* Camilla Erculiani, who had presented her natural-philosophical *Lettere* as evidence of the fact women that were "as suited to the acquisition of knowledge of all kinds [*le scienze*] as men."[121] Also relevant as a precedent is Maria Gondola's 1585 letter-treatise on women's intellectual dignity, which takes as its starting point readers' likely astonishment in seeing a treatise on Aristotle's *Meteorology* dedicated to a woman and sets out to combat the prejudice that women "lack a capacity for science [*scienze*] and the understanding of things."[122] This urge on the part of intellectual women to go beyond humanistic and literary pursuits and embrace the "sciences" more generally appears to have been something of a trend of the period, most impressively realized in Margherita Sarrocchi's participation in the early seventeenth-century disputes over Galileo's theories.[123]

Besides these obvious differences in form and content, *Il merito delle donne* and *La nobiltà et l'eccellenza delle donne* differ substantially in the character of their gender analysis and in their relation to the rhetorical traditions of the *querelle des femmes*. Marinella's work is by far the more conventional of the two works, as is only to be expected given the polemical context in which it was conceived. What was required in response to Passi was, precisely, a conventional academic treatise refuting his "libels" using similar methods of argumentation. Radical novelty of form would have been counterproductive in a discursive context of this kind; Marinella impressed readers precisely through her ability to write like a man. Her opening chapters, setting out the philosophical arguments for women's superiority to men, rehearse material already well established within the tradition, although she distances herself very clearly in her prefatory note from the paradoxical register in which those arguments had conventionally been cast.[124] She begins in chapter 1, as was conventional, with etymology, inferring women's excellence from the excellence of the words *donna, femina, Eva, Isciah,* and *mulier*.[125] She then goes on, in chapters 2 and 3, to argue for women's corporeal and spiritual superiority to men, laying particular emphasis as proof on their superiority in beauty, which she illustrates at length by reference to Neoplatonic philosophy and the Neoplatonizing lyric tradition.[126] Her third main argument, in chapter 4, is that the etiquette of social gallantry toward women reflects a lurking consciousness of their superiority, as does the convention whereby women are permitted to dress more splendidly than men.[127] Her final argument (chapter 5) is that the evidence of men's and women's actions, as revealed by the study of history, clearly demonstrates the superiority of the latter, in spite of the censorship of male historians. This is proposed as a lesson to the present day, when women are discouraged from developing their talents as a result of men's envy and fear.[128] The exemplification that follows exhaustively demonstrates this contention in a series of eleven sections exemplifying women's virtues, beginning with their capacity for intellectual activity and proceeding to their love for their families and their country. The 1601 edition, quite substantially revised, adds a polemical sixth chapter at this point, in which, in a series of separately headed subsections, Marinella "demolishes" in succession the arguments of a distinguished series of male misogynist authorities: Aristotle, Boccaccio *(Il corbaccio)*, Sperone Speroni, Torquato and Ercole Tasso, and a mysterious "Monseigneur Arrigo de Namur."[129] Following this, in both the 1600 and 1601 editions, Marinella proceeds to the second part of her treatise, "The defects and failings of Men." This is argued simply by exemplification in a series of twenty-five chapters, expanded to thirty-five in the 1601 edition, precisely the number of chapters that Passi had devoted to the defects of women.[130]

While the majority of Marinella's arguments, and much of her exemplification, were traditional, it would be unfair to represent her contribution to the *querelle* as purely an efficient rehearsal of commonplaces that readers were more used to encountering from men. The section in the 1601 edition addressing individual misogynist authors' arguments contains much that is fresh, and often pithily formulated. Important especially are her remarks on men's social dominance over women as a tyranny, rather than a just reflection of their different natures, as Aristotle had argued, and her powerful rebuttal of arguments that would condemn a virtuous woman's to her household as her proper sphere. On the contrary, Marinella argues, "the fame of women's deeds, in respect of their practice of the sciences and of virtuous action, should resonate not only in their own City, but across diverse and various provinces."[131]

Another important innovation within both the 1600 and 1601 editions of Marinella's treatise is the coupling of examples of women's excellence with examples of men's defects. While the list of examples of outstanding women from history, marshaled to prove the dignity of their sex, had been an established literary exercise since the late fourteenth century, a list of infamous men intended for this kind of gender-polemical reason was considerably more of a novelty.[132] Marinella's innovation in this regard was tacitly acknowledged by Passi when he imitated her in his 1603 *Monstruosa fucina delle sordidezze de gl'huomini*, which returns to the same material, while attempting to outshine Marinella in the quantity and quality of the erudition demonstrated.[133] The lack of precedents for this exercise in the denigration of men enabled Marinella to showcase her extensive historical erudition, doubtless assisted by access to the library of her brother Curzio, who had been active in his youth as an editor of classical and modern historical texts.[134] Among the sources cited in this section are the classical historians Livy, Plutarch, Herodian, Thucydides, Appian, Sallust, and Justin; the modern Italian historians Leandro Alberti (1479–1552), Paolo Giovio (1483–1552), Giovanni Tarcagnota (d. 1566), Giovanni Botero (1543–1617), and Scipione Ammirato (1531–1601); the Byzantine Nicetas Acominatus (c. 1155–c. 1215); and the Venetians Marcantonio Sabellico and Pietro Marcello (fl. 1502).[135] Less vaunted but probably exploited with equal or greater assiduity were popular repertories of thematically organized anecdotage, such as Valerius Maximus's *Factorum et dictorum memorabilium libri novem* and Battista Fregoso's similarly entitled compendium, first published in 1509.[136] Marinella also displays an impressive degree of mischievous ingenuity in making up the number of her examples. Petrarch features twice, once in the list of "vainglorious and boastful men," on the strength of his remarks concerning his literary fame in *canzone* 360, and once, in his lyric persona, in a list of "lachrymose men, given to weeping."[137] Wittily, as well, Marinella inserts her antagonist Giuseppe Passi in her chapter on men who have sullied themselves by the practice of the magic arts, justifying her decision by the remarkable level of detailed knowledge he displays in the chapter on female witches in *I donneschi diffetti*.[138]

As these last examples suggest, one of the pleasures of Marinella's *La nobiltà et l'eccellenza delle donne* is its quite frequent display of sarcastic wit, a feature of her writing on display especially in the "failings of men" section of the treatise though also to some extent in the combative chapter added in 1601 countering the misogynistic arguments of Aristotle and others. Her chapter on "gambling men" ("De gli huomini giucatori") contains an entertaining sketch of decrepit gambling addicts, myopic with age and "incapable of seeing an elephant in a snowfield," who may yet be seen peering over a card table with two pairs of spectacles perched on their nose.[139] The chapter on lachrymose men notes sardonically of "poor poets" that "they have no need to squirt onion juice in their eyes" to make them weep.[140] The chapter on "primped, groomed, painted, and bleached men," in particular, has much has lively material of this kind.[141] Interesting especially is the passage in which Marinella turns a critical eye on the arguments of moralists who attacked women for their vanity in dress and self-adornment, noting that a parallel could be found in men's obsessive cultivation of the outward tokens of fortitude and virility.[142]

> Gli huomini sempre si vedono con l'armi alla cintola, co' vestimenti, che hanno del soldato, e con le barbe accommodate in guisa, che paiono, che minacciano, e caminano con certi passi, che credono di porgere altrui spavento, e . . . spesso fanno in modo, che il ferro lor risoni intorno. . . . Che son tutte queste cose, se non belletti, et orpellature? E sotto queste coperte d'ardito, e di valoroso celano un vilissimo animo di coniglio o di fuggitiva lepre.[143]

> [Men can always be seen with arms at their belt, wearing military-style garments, with their beards styled in as menacing a way as possible, walking with a certain stride, with which they think to strike fear into their observers' hearts, . . . and very often accompanying their passage with a rattling of iron. . . . What are these things if not cosmetics and fripperies? And very often these bold and valorous appearances conceal the cringing mind of a rabbit or a fleeing hare.]

The sardonic outspokenness Marinella wields with such gusto in passages of this kind deserves underlining as a relative novelty in the tradition of women's writing in Italy, even if precedents may be noted in a few letters by Laura Cereta and in a few passages in Laura Terracina's *Discorso sopra tutti li primi canti d'Orlando furioso*. The social pressure on women to manifest a properly feminine decorum characterized by gravity, modesty, and "sweetness" was too powerful for most female writers to have any incentive to risk the aggressive persona of the satirist in their writings. It is notable that those who did, such as Cereta and Terracina, were not among the most socially integrated female writers of their day. Marinella's fearlessness in this regard was partly dictated by circumstance and the rhetorical requirements of polemic: Passi's jeers against women could not be effectively countered by a writer whose tongue was tied by considerations of decorum. It is remarkable, nonetheless, to see a female writer breaking through the sarcasm barrier so trenchantly. Subsequent female writers took up this genre with relish, responding to ever-increasing levels of hostility from an increasingly misogynistic environment. Marinella's finest heir in this regard, though perhaps not one she would have been happy to acknowledge, was her Venetian compatriot Arcangela Tarabotti, who picked up the theme of men's vanity in her *Antisatira*, of 1644.[144] More immediately, in 1614 Veneranda Bragadin, took Marinella's tonal innovation to new extremes in her virulent *ad hominem* invective letter against the misogynist Giovanni Battista Barbo, which concludes by advising him that as a man in his seventies, he would be better off trawling churches in search of a suitable tomb instead of offending women with his insipid satires.[145] Interestingly and unexpectedly, Bragadin makes a discreet reference in her satire to the long-banned scurrilous writings of Pietro Aretino, taunting Barbo by saying that he lacks Aretino's ability to "delight while speaking ill."[146]

The character of Marinella's innovations in *La nobiltà* raise the interesting question of whether she was acquainted with Fonte's *Il merito delle donne* when she was writing her treatise. The expectation would be that she was not, as *Il merito* was not in print, but the possibility of her having read the work in manuscript is not to be discarded: the two women seem to have had a mutual acquaintance in the medic and *letterato* Lucio Scarano, the dedicatee of *La nobiltà et l'eccellenza delle donne*, and Fonte's literary mentor Giovanni Niccolò Doglioni was a member of the Accademia Veneziana, along with Scarano and Curzio Marinelli.[147] *Il merito* offers a partial precedent for Marinella in two respects: in the detailed cataloging of men's vices that occupies a large part of the first book and moments of the second and in the sarcastic tone it adopts in these passages. Fonte's approach is very different from the erudite approach of Marinella, and her critiques of male failings are based on the behavior of contemporary Venetian husbands, fathers, brothers, and sons rather than on exempla from ancient and modern history. Balance is provided by speakers defending men, though not always with the utmost conviction, and the more outspoken satirical attacks tend to be voiced by a single speaker, Leonora, a young widow determined not to remarry. Even if Fonte's anticipation of Marinella is far from absolute, however, the parallels between them in this regard remain intriguing. Especially suggestive is Leonora's brief but withering attack on men's personal vanity, which recalls Marinella's chapter on male adornment, mentioned above; as in the case of Marinella, it is couched self-consciously as a reversal of male satirists' frequent attacks on women's overconcern with their looks.[148]

These shared points aside, Fonte's approach to the subject of sex and gender in *Il merito delle donne* differs very significantly from Marinella's and shows a far greater independence from the male-authored tradition of debate within the *querelle des femmes*. Fonte, clearly *au fait* with this tradition, provides an efficient though brief summary of traditional profeminist arguments in book 1 of her dialogue. She demonstrates women's intrinsic superiority to men through an ingenious interpretation of the creation myth in Genesis first devised by the German humanist Henricus Cornelius Agrippa (1486–1535) and argues for women's capacity for excellence in traditionally male fields with lists of classical exempla of female prowess of a type that had circulated in the works of humanists and their vernacular successors since the late fourteenth century.[149] This is not Fonte's principal emphasis, however. More than in the relation of the sexes in the abstract, *Il merito delle donne* is concerned with the relation between men and women in everyday life, or more precisely, within elite households in Venice (Fonte herself was of the *cittadinanza*, the elite class immediately below the ruling patriciate of Venice, and her speakers are defined as patricians). This concreteness and specificity represent a striking novelty within the *querelle des femmes* and serve to expose the degree to which the arguments of the majority of *querelle* texts had become ossified and purely formal by this point. Especially noteworthy in this regard is Fonte's attention to economic issues, and particularly to the functioning of the dowry system, where she points to the frequent discrepancy between women's rights under the law and the treatment they effectively received.[150] In this context the more theoretical *querelle* sections of book 1 seem to have been intended largely to undermine defenses of the status quo that relied on women's "imbecility." Women, she writes, are naturally the equals of men but are effectively infantilized socially, denied education, deprived of control over their own financial resources, and forced into a situation of dependence that offers no safeguard against abuse. Marriage is particularly indicted as an instrument of oppression; an extended passage in book 1 is given over to detailing the indignities women suffer at the hands of their husbands, ranging from unfaithfulness to profligacy with money to physical violence to a jealous surveillance that will hardly permit them to leave the house.[151] The most educated speaker in the dialogue, Corinna, expresses her determination never to marry, while the most forceful, Leonora, a widow, is just as determined not to marry again.[152]

An essential feature of the fictional dialogues Fonte dramatizes in *Il merito delle donne* is their "secret" character as conversations between women, a point underlined on several occasions in the work when the speakers speculate on what men might think if they could hear them.[153] This, again, was a rhetorical novelty, at least within the polite, noncomic tradition of dialogue.[154] Structurally, the closest parallel is offered by works like Pietro Aretino's *Dialogo* and his *Ragionamento,* in the latter of which the prostitute Nanna offers advice to her daughter on the basis of her picaresque life experience. There again the male reader is invited to eavesdrop on a feminine conversation to which he could normally never listen and to hear truths about how he and his sex are regarded that he might prefer not to know.[155]

Despite this fiction of privileged access to a hermetic female *domestica conversazione,* however, Fonte is in fact attentive throughout to her potential male readers.[156] While she has her speakers condemn male vice and exploitation of women, they are quick to point out the existence of real or potential exceptions in the form of exemplary husbands and much-loved fathers, brothers, and sons. Women's propensity to love and care for men is emphatically stressed even as it is lamented by some speakers as the cause of much grief. The most richly exemplified sections of the "virtues of women" section in book 1 are those concerning women who have sacrificed their lives for their menfolk or performed heroic deeds in order to save them from danger.[157] Women's capacity for patriotism is also emphasized, both through historical example and through the speakers' and the author's patent pride as Venetians. The book opens with a glittering description of Venice's beauty and opulence, while an extended passage in book 2 extols the virtues of the city's republican constitution and the wisdom of its governing class.[158] Rather than the "internal enemy" they might easily appear to be, the women of the Venetian elite are here portrayed as an effective and loyal support system for their men, asking from them in return only a minimum standard of decency and humanity. This implicit plea is made explicit, in a brilliant self-referential excursus in book 2, when Leonora improvises an oration addressed to men in the course of a discussion of rhetoric as an art.[159] The tone of the speech is humble and conciliatory in the extreme, offering an ironic contrast to Leonora's customary outspoken persona. It calls, not for the equality we see her elsewhere proclaiming as women's right, but merely for men to treat women with a modicum of respect and gratitude in return for the boundless tribute of love they supply. Leonora's change of tone wittily dramatizes the key rhetorical tenet of the need to accommodate to differing audiences: one tone may be permitted in a *domestica conversazione* between women, quite another in a public address to men. Leonora's disingenuously wheedling tones as *oratrix* have an element of self-parody in context, pointing up the character of Fonte's own conciliatory rhetorical strategies in the dialogue as a *captatio benevolentiae* of precisely this kind.[160]

As the incident of Leonora's oration demonstrates, *Il merito delle donne* makes full use of the literary dialogue's traditional vocation of ambiguity, brilliantly articulated in the mid-1570s by the Paduan *letterato* Sperone Speroni in his *Apologia dei dialoghi*.[161] Both the radical position Leonora sporadically assumes in the conversation and the conciliatory position she impersonates in her oration are present in the dialogue, acting as flints in a tinderbox, to use Speroni's analogy, producing sparks of truth to ignite the tinder of the receptive reader's mind.[162] Fonte's *Il merito delle donne* lies at the opposite extreme of the genre of literary dialogue from Chiara Matraini's *Dialoghi spirituali* in terms of both its didactic character and the density of its fictional realization. Matraini's dialogues are unequivocally magisterial, even catechistic, with Filocalio cast in the passive role of disciple, while Fonte's is much more open, with a more straightforwardly didactic model surfacing only in the more "scientific" portions of book 2. With respect to their fictional embodiment, Matraini's *Dialoghi* are relatively light on scene setting, while Fonte's *Il merito* opens with a quite extended narrative passage describing the setting of her conversations, in Leonora's idyllic garden, and the occasion that gives rise to them, the return of the young bride Elena to her female circles in Venice after her honeymoon on her husband's country estate. More than the sober, philosophical tradition of dialogue in which Matraini's *Dialoghi* insert themselves, Fonte's *Il merito* recalls the ludic model of works such as Girolamo Parabosco's *I diporti* (c. 1550) or Scipione Bargagli's *Trattenimenti* (1587), which are eclectic *divertissements*, rather than systematic dialogues, encompassing entertainments of various species. Besides Leonora's parodic oration, *Il merito* includes a *novella*, a riddle, and numerous lyric poems recited or sung by Corinna, as well as a thirty-six-stanza ottava rima allegorical narrative sufficiently self-contained to have been published in the eighteenth century as an independent work.[163] An early source, Pietro Paolo Ribera, also mentions a series of "trophies" of famous women that Fonte had intended to add to her dialogue had she lived.[164] Ribera also dwells in his brief appreciation on the work's "beauty and charm" and on its "delightful style," which makes it, in his opinion, the equal of the finest literary works of the day.[165] Generic though it is, Ribera's language captures something of the character of *Il merito* and its particular blend of *docere* and *delectare*.

The "cornucopian" character of *Il merito delle donne* is apparent especially in book 2 of the dialogue, where most of the verse and prose interpolations appear. This is also, of course, where we encounter Corinna's disquisitions on the wonders of the natural world, which contribute so much to the work's thematic and textural *varietas*. The dialogue's dispersiveness here risks incoherence, yet Fonte maintains a thread of unity by having Leonora sporadically intervene, with increasing exasperation, to pull the conversation back to its original remit of the relations of the sexes. Her comically treated frustration thematizes the conflict between impulses of unity and "errancy" that was the stock in trade of contemporary Aristotelian poetic theory. A recent critical essay has rightly adduced as a context for book 2 of *Il merito* the genre of popular compilations of knowledge known as *selve di varia lettione*, literally "forests of various reading."[166] Some works of this kind seem especially close to Fonte in their combination of Plinyesque encyclopedic erudition with *querelle*-derived exemplification of the "wonders of women." Luigi Contarini's *Vago e dilettevole giardino*, first published in Vicenza in 1588, lists its attractions on its title page as "marvelous *exempla* of women" and "the origin and emblems of the Amazons," along with "the excellence and powers of many natural cures," "remarkable *exempla* of the virtues and vices of men," and "the seven wonders of the world." Giovanni Felice Astolfi's *Scelta curiosa et ricca officina di varie antiche, e moderne istorie*, which includes an appreciative entry on Fonte, has selections of ancient and modern *donne letterate* and female warriors, as well as lists of the greatest armies assembled in human history and of "serpents, dragons, and beasts of all kinds that have been tamed by the power of man."[167]

One respect in which the *selva* tradition makes an illuminating comparison with *Il merito* is that it can help clarify the attitude toward "learning" that we find in Fonte's dialogue. Although the erudition conveyed in *selve* such as Contarini's and Astolfi's can appear random to the modern reader, it is presented as both useful and precious: the facts assembled are conceived of not as "trivia," as in the modern equivalent, but rather as the covetable tesserae of a mosaic of universal knowledge. A fervent drive to empowerment by learning pervades the second book of *Il merito*, conveyed through an implicit metaphor of mental journeying. If Leonora speaks wistfully at one point of the impossible fantasy of undertaking a sea voyage to see the "marvels of the world,"

Corinna's erudition virtually transports her listeners from their enclosed Venetian garden to view the wonders of the earth, sea, and sky.[168] The microcosmic ambitions of the second *giornata* lend a structure to the argument that belies its apparently spontaneous drift: we proceed from a discussion of astrology and cosmology to a discussion of the inhabitants of the ocean, the air, and the land, the latter proceeding through animal and vegetable to mineral. Learning is presented here as a means of taking possession of a universe from which women have been effectively debarred through ignorance. Disinheritance, literal and figurative, is a fundamental theme of *Il merito*. Just as individual women often find their inheritance from their mortal fathers usurped by rapacious brothers, so women are excluded by their male "brothers" from the rightful, equal place God had ordained for the sexes in the scheme of creation.[169]

Perhaps the most striking conceptual novelty of *Il merito delle donne,* by comparison with previous writings on women and their status, is the dialogue's flirtation with the notion of a secular single life as an attractive alternative to marriage for a woman. This theme is present from the beginning of the dialogue and even informs its physical setting. The garden where the women's conversations take place is presented as having been designed by Leonora's aunt, a wealthy woman who chose to remain single, and it has as its centerpiece a fountain featuring statues of women allegorizing the pleasures of liberty and the treacherousness of men.[170] Leonora announces her intention to follow in her aunt's footsteps, and not marry again now that she has been widowed, as does the learned young Corinna, protagonist of the scientific disquisitions of book 2. Corinna, indeed, announces her intent with a sonnet-manifesto for freely chosen intellectual spinsterhood, *Libero cor nel mio petto soggiorna* (A free heart dwells within my breast). On the basis of this wise decision, Lucrezia pronounces Corinna happier than any other woman that lives.[171]

To some extent, the ideal that Fonte sketches in *Il merito delle donne* of a single, intellectually active life for women may be seen as regendering a model of male secular singlehood familiar from works such as Giovanni Della Casa's *An uxor sit ducenda,* which posit marriage and the responsibilities that come with it as antithetical to the intellectual life. This hardly diminishes the novelty, however, of seeing such a position articulated by a woman, given the traditional social understanding that women's life choice was essentially between marriage and the convent.

One interesting question raised by Fonte's proposal of a single, intellectual life as a new existential ideal for women in *Il merito delle donne* is the potential influence on her thought of Maddalena Campiglia, who, as we saw in chapter 3, proposed a similar solution for the protagonist of her pastoral *Flori*, published in 1588, just before the likely date of composition of Fonte's dialogue.[172] As I have argued elsewhere in accounting for the emergence of this ideal of elective intellectual spinsterhood in female writers of the late sixteenth century, it is important to take into account socioeconomic developments in this period that lessened the possibilities of marriage for upper-class women. Secular spinsters *were* emerging as a social phenomenon in the period, whether or not this was as a matter of choice.[173] Another factor to take into account when considering the particular, heroic cast Fonte and Campiglia give to this ideal of singlehood is the existence of a prestigious precedent in the fifteenth-century figure of Isotta Nogarola, whose "praiseworthy intent" to refuse marriage and devote herself to a life of letters is given great prominence in Giuseppe Betussi's biography, published numerous times from 1545.[174] Although it is not difficult to identify developments of this kind that may have led to Fonte's and Campiglia's independently formulating their ideal of secular spinsterhood, it is also, however, far from impossible that Fonte may have been acquainted with Campiglia's play. The two women had literary contacts in common (certainly Luigi Groto and Issicratea Monte, and perhaps also Muzio Manfredi and Cesare Simonetti), and Campiglia had extensive connections in Venice, where she seems to have spent an extended period in 1591–92.[175]

Given the ludic character of Fonte's dialogue generally, it is difficult to estimate how seriously she may have intended her vision of secular spinsterhood as a potential life choice for women. When the ingénue Virginia seems inclined at the end of the dialogue to follow Corinna in her commitment to remain single, her mother, Adriana, reminds her, first, that she has no choice in the matter, since her uncles—her father is dead—are determined to marry her, and second, that if she were able to remain a spinster, social decorum would require of her a life of retirement and austerity such that she would probably regret her choice.[176] Another speaker, Lucrezia, remarks soberly on the practical difficulty for a woman of attempting to live without a man's protection.[177] The passage seems to have been inserted to counterbalance the ideal vision of an unshackled yet sociable existence embodied by Leonora's aunt, who takes as one of her symbols the sun, signifying that without a husband to control her, she was free to share her company with "every noble spirit."[178]

This textured treatment of the issue of marriage offers a good example of what is more generally a strength of Fonte's dialogue, its delicate mediation between realist and utopian discourses. On one level, *Il merito delle donne* is the only fictional work we possess from the period by an Italian woman that is set in a modern, historically identifiable context and reflects contemporary reality, even if in a stylized manner. We find mentions in it of the fashions of the day, including the "horns" (corna) of hair sported by Fonte herself in her authorial portrait, and references to topical events such as the building of the new bridge over the Rialto, completed in 1591.[179] At the same time, however, the work's "realism" is tempered by a countervailing injection of fantasy: the garden in which the dialogue is set comes straight from the idealizing tradition of Boccaccio's *Decameron* and Bembo's *Asolani*, the names of the majority of the speakers (Lucrezia, Corinna, Virginia, Cornelia, Elena) from the annals of classical history and myth.[180] This dreamlike fusion of the contemporary and the atemporal, the particular and the universal was not unusual as a feature of the *cornici* of literary dialogues. Bembo's *Asolani*, set in an idealized Asolo, was influential in this regard. What is of interest in Fonte is the way in which she uses the space opened up by this device to explore women's predicament in a manner simultaneously attentive to social and cultural constraints and alert to possibilities beyond them.

CODA

In their very different ways, Lucrezia Marinella's *La nobiltà et l'eccellenza delle donne* and Chiara Matraini's *Dialoghi spirituali*, published within two years of each other in Venice, represent something of a high point within the history of Italian women's experimentation with authoritative voices and roles. Both Matraini and Marinella represent themselves as women deserving of an audience, and one extending beyond women to men. Neither feels the least need to apologize, as so many early female writers had, for her feebleness of intellect as a woman or her audacity in speaking in public. Neither shows herself in the least apologetic for the sex she was born into. "I have never desired to be a man," Marinella states in her initial note to the reader, "do not now, and never shall, even if I outlive Nestor."[1] This assertiveness of tone was something of a trend in the period, apparent even in the work of a nun like Diodata Malvasia, who requests in the preface to her 1617 history of the Marian icon of the Bolognese Monte della Guardia that "if some imperfection is found in this work, let femininity be blamed only in my individual instance, for the female sex as a whole is possessed of the capacity for heroic greatness and may perhaps even be said to manifest the virtues required for that status in a greater degree than do men."[2]

With the hindsight of history, we can find something poignant in reading confident rhetoric of this kind from intellectual women in the early Seicento, at the beginning of a century that would prove as unpropitious for them as the previous century had been kind. Marinella herself, toward the end of her long life, would disavow the feminist arguments of *La nobiltà et l'eccellenza* quite explicitly, arguing in her *Essortationi alle donne et a gli altri se saranno loro a grado*, of 1645, that women would be happier if they renounced any ambition to intellectual recognition and remained within their "proper" domestic sphere.³ Marinella's late-life miserabilism was prophetic. In the forty years following her death in 1653 only two works by secular female authors were published in Italy, while most of the handful of works published by cloistered female authors appeared only after their death.⁴ It was only in the last decade of the Seicento, with the rise of the classicizing Arcadia movement, that the figure of the female author once again came to hold a respected place within Italian literary culture and the rich legacy of the earlier tradition of women's writing in Italy began to be eagerly recouped.⁵

In view of the twentieth-century literary-historiographical tendency to limit women's writing in Italy to a few decades in the mid-sixteenth century, it is worth underlining that this Arcadian recuperation made no distinction between the early and mid-sixteenth-century female poets we now think of as canonical and the later sixteenth- and early seventeenth-century female writers discussed in this book, who appear to us now as recent critical discoveries. The important series of re-editions of female-authored texts published by Antonio Bulifon in Naples beginning in the 1690s included Marinella's *Rime sacre*, Andreini's *Rime*, and Sarrocchi's *Scanderbeide*, as well as collections of verse by Vittoria Colonna, Veronica Gambara, Tullia d'Aragona, and Laura Battiferra. Similarly, Luisa Bergalli's important 1726 anthology of female-authored poetry, *Componimenti poetici delle più illustri rimatrici d'ogni secolo*, gives as substantial a place to late sixteenth- and early seventeenth-century female poets as to their mid-sixteenth-century predecessors, with Andreini, Marinella, Lucia Colao, Lucchesia Sbarra, and Maddalena Salvetti ranking alongside Colonna, Gambara, d'Aragona, Battiferra, Gaspara Stampa, and Olimpia Malipiero (fl. 1559–68) as the best-represented poets in the collection.⁶ The project of a monograph on Counter-Reformation Italian women's writing, which would have seemed outlandish in the late nineteenth and twentieth centuries, would have seemed far less so in the formative era of Italian literary historiography in the late seventeenth and early eighteenth centuries, when the ideological structures that would later make the notion of "Counter-Reformation women's writing" seem a virtual oxymoron were not yet in place.

Another lesson we can learn from late seventeenth- and early eighteenth-century ways of doing literary history is the desirability of considering secular and religious literary production in conjunction. Here again, Bergalli can serve as a model: her anthology freely mixes secular and religious women writers, and within the output of secular writers it makes no distinction between verse on secular and religious themes. As the present volume makes clear, secular and religious writings of this period have much in common when viewed from the perspective of gender, and religious writings frequently manifest precisely the kind of affirmative attitude toward women's capacities and potential that modern critics find exciting in the secular writings of the day. While to speak of feminism in this period is to risk anachronism, we can undoubtedly speak of a tradition of Counter-Reformation philogyny embodied in significant numbers of both male- and female-authored works of this period. This tradition had its roots both in the secular-humanistic tradition of protofeminist thought as it had developed through the fifteenth and early sixteenth centuries, and in medieval religious discourses that had valorized women in their capacity as champions of faith. These secular and religious gynephile discourses were perceived as complementary and mutually reinforcing to an extent that we struggle to recognize today, uniting to affirm woman's capacity to transcend the uninspiring moral persona Aristotelian science had endowed her with, as a poor and dysfunctional copy of man. In this book we have seen Leonora Bernardi lining up Tuccia alongside Esther and Judith as exemplars of female virtue, Francesca Turina drawing on protofeminist arguments evolved by Henricus Cornelius Agrippa in a Marian sonnet, Lucrezia Marinella moving between celebrating the fortitude of Zenobia and Artemisia in her *La nobiltà et l'eccellenza delle donne* and celebrating that of the virgins martyrs in her *Rime sacre* three years later, and Pietro Paolo Ribera cursing misogynists as heretics for their failure to acknowledge women's God-given gifts. Until we recognize the degree to which the Counter-Reformation participated in the early modern project of revalorizing women, we cannot have a true grasp of the intellectual lineage of modern feminism, despite the wealth of scholarship over the past three or four decades that has explored this lineage's secular strands.

APPENDIX
Italian Women Writers Active 1580–1635

Collected below is biographical and bibliographical material on all female writers known from the period 1580–1635 (including a few significant "ghosts," for whom no surviving writings are known). In the case of better-known writers, for whom biographical material can be easily accessed, the reader is referred to the secondary sources in the bibliography for further details. The lists of literary contacts are limited to cases in which there is some evidence of a reciprocal relationship, in the form of sonnet exchanges, letter exchanges, or inclusion of prefatory verse in published volumes. For especially well connected writers such as Isabella Andreini and Maddalena Campiglia, the lists of literary contacts are not exhaustive but illustrative. References for evidence of literary relationships are cited only in cases where this evidence is not easily available elsewhere in secondary literature or cited elsewhere in this book.

Only modern secondary literature is cited in these entries. The most comprehensive listings of earlier secondary literature on Italian female writers are found in Bandini Buti 1946; entries below for writers with an entry in that work (which lists writers alphabetically, generally giving their married name first) are marked "BB." Entries below for writers with an entry in the *Dizionario biografico degli italiani* (down to vol. 73, Meda–Messadaglia) are marked "DBI." Entries below for writers with an entry in Bergalli 1726 are marked "LB."

Acquaviva, Dorotea
Daughter of Giovanni Antonio Acquaviva, Duke of Atri, Abruzzo (1490–1554), and Isabella Spinelli of Cariati (b. 1500). Sister of Jesuit general Claudio Acquaviva (1543–1615). Does not appear to have married. No surviving works. Mentioned as writer in Ammirato 1598, 42; De' Pietri 1634, 67. Literary contact: Muzio Sforza (L. Russo 1985, 75–101). Bibliography: Guida 2008, 64–70, 171–76, 455.

Aiutamicristo, Elisabetta (d. 1580)
Palermo. Noblewoman. Verse in: *Rime* 1585. BB.

Albiosi Maggi, Ginevra (b. c. 1565)[†]
Venice(?). Verse in: Sanudo 1613; Magno, "Rime," 12v–13r (sonnet exchange with Celio Magno). LB. BB.

[†]This date is calculated on the basis of a sonnet to Ginevra Albiosi by Celio Magno in "Rime di diversi," 102,

ANDREINI, ISABELLA (1562–1604)
Born Padua (probably as Isabella Canali). Married Francesco Cerracchi (Andreini was their professional name) and joined acting company of Gelosi c. 1578. Seven children, including actor and dramatist Giovanni Battista Andreini (c. 1579–1654). Died in childbirth in Lyons following acting tour in France. Member of Accademia degli Intenti, Pavia, 1601. Published works: I. Andreini 1588 (+ 1588 *bis*, 1590, 1594, 1598×2, 1599, 1602, 1603, 1616, 1620),† [1596?], 1601, 1603. Verse in: T. Tasso 1586; *Rime* 1587a; Caporali 1589; Mausoleo 1589; *Nuova scielta* 1592; Borgogni 1594; Caraffa 1598; Spelta 1602; Petracci 1608; C. Fiamma 1611; Adriano Grandi 1620. Posthumous publications: I. Andreini 1605, 1607, 1611 (+ 1616), 1617a (+ 1620, 1625, 1627, 1652), 1617b (+ 1620 bis, 1621, 1625, 1628, 1634, 1638, 1647, 1652, 1663). Modern editions: I. Andreini 1995, 2002, 2005. Literary contacts: Gherardo Borgogni, Gabriello Chiabrera, Adriano Grandi, Laura Guidiccioni, Angelo Ingegneri, Giovanni Battista Marino, Erycius Puteanus, Antonio Maria Spelta. Bibliography: see references in Cox 2008, 323n5, 333n90. LB. BB. DBI (s.v. "Canali").

ASINARI VALPERGA, MARGHERITA
Piedmont. Daughter of playwright Federico Asinari (c. 1527–75), Count of Camerano. Married Ghiron Valperga in 1572. No surviving works. Cited in Della Chiesa 1620, 254, as a poet and said in two letters written by Muzio Manfredi, dated 1591 and 1593, to have been inspired to write a pastoral by reading Barbara Torelli's *Partenia* (Manfredi 1594, 76; Manfredi 1606, 217–18). BB.

AVOGADRO, PAOLA VIRGINIA
Verse in: Bursati 1621.

AZZALINA, MARIA
Padua(?). Verse in: Gagliardo 1584.

BARTOLI, MINERVA (1562–1602)
Urbino. Noblewoman. Daughter of Luca Bartoli and Camilla Paciotti; sister of poet Clemente Bartoli (1561–1621). Verse in: Ricciuoli 1594; Scaioli 1611. Literary contacts: Alessandro Miari (Miari 1591, 2), Roberto Poggiolini (Poggiolini 1613, 230–34), Federico Ricciuoli. Bibliography: Vecchietti 1790–96, 2:89–90. LB. BB.

---

which describes her as "a mezzo il dì de l'età vostra" (halfway through your life), conventionally 35 years old. The poem must date from between 1600, when Albiosi seems to have introduced herself to Magno by writing him a sonnet "replying" to the first sonnet of his printed *Rime* (Giustinian and Magno 1600; her sonnet is that cited in the present entry), and 1602, the year of Magno's death.
† On the editorial fortunes of Andreini 1588, see ch. 3, n. 64.

BATTIFERRA DEGLI AMMANATI, LAURA (1523–1589)
Born Urbino. Illegitimate daughter of nobleman and prelate Giovanni Antonio Battiferri (d. 1561) and Maddalena Coccapani. Married (1) Vittorio Sereni, musician (d. 1549); (2) Bartolomeo degli Ammanati, sculptor and architect, in 1550. Lived in Urbino, Rome, and then, following her second marriage, Florence. Published works: Battiferra 1560, 1564 (+ 1566, 1570). For appearances in anthologies and other verse collections, see Vecchietti 1790–96, 2:118–20; Battiferra 2006, 266–309, 360–63; and the online bibliography available on the website Cinquecento plurale.[†] Modern editions: Battiferra 1879, 2000, 2005, 2006. Literary contacts: Silvio Antoniano, Girolamo Bargagli, Lucia Bertani, Savino Bobali (Sabo Bobaljević), Agnolo Bronzino, Annibale Caro, Benvenuto Cellini, Agostino De Cupiti, Gabriele Fiamma, Antonio Galli, Antonfrancesco Grazzini ("il Lasca"), Silvano Razzi, Fiammetta Soderini, Gherardo Spini, Benedetto Varchi. Bibliography: Cox 2008, 297n22, to which should be added Guidi 2000, 2005; and Montanari 2005. LB. BB. DBI.

BENDINELLI BALDINI, SILVIA
Born Lucca. Lived in Piacenza in her adult life. Daughter of humanist Antonio Bendinelli; sister of poet Scipione Bendinelli. Published work: Silvia Bendinelli 1587. Verse in: Scipione Bendinelli 1588; Ducchi 1589; *Rime* 1589; Guazzo 1595. Literary contacts: Carlo Gatti, Giacomo Nicelli, Ippolito Piacentino (*Rime* 1589); Muzio Manfredi (Manfredi 1606, 233–34). LB. BB.

BENIGNI DELLA PENNA MANFREDI, IPPOLITA (C. 1575–AFTER 1611)
In service of Dorothea of Brunswick-Lüneburg (1546–1617). Married poet Muzio Manfredi c. 1590. Musical *virtuosa*. Member of academies of the Insensati of Perugia and the Affidati of Pavia (as "la Ferma") (Passi 1609, prefatory sonnet), possibly also of the Informi of Ravenna, as "la Riposata" (Ginanni 1739, 463). Verse in: Manfredi 1604; Passi 1609; Sanudo 1613; Ginanni 1739. Dedicatee of: Sasso 1601. Tributes in: Sasso 1601; Manfredi 1604. Literary contacts: Leandro Bovarini (Bovarini 1602, 40–44, 160–66), Giuseppe Passi, Cesare Rinaldi (Rinaldi 1608, 62), Giacomo Sasso, Tiberio Sbarra (Sasso 1601, 4r, 15v–16r, 42v–43r). Bibliography: Bronzini 1625, *giornata quinta*, 52; Bertolotti 1887, 128, 168–69; Olivieri Secchi 1998, 303–4. LB. BB.

BERNARDI BELATTI, LEONORA (1559–1616)
Born Lucca to patricians Antonio Bernardi and Lucrezia Trenta. Goddaughter of Francesco de' Medici (Saltini 1883, 158). Married Vicenzo Belatti of Garfagnana, with whom she spent time at the Este court at Ferrara in the 1580s and 1590s. At least one child, Pietro Paolo. Noted as musical performer. Went blind c. 1611 (Grillo

[†] The web address is www.nuovorinascimento.org/cinquecento/bibliografie.html, under "Laura Battiferri Ammanati" (accessed 30 December 2010). The bibliography is edited by Chiara Zaffini, with the collaboration of Antonio Corsaro.

1612b, 261, 482–83; Durante and Martellotti 1989b, 244). Verse in: Grillo 1589; *Scelta* 1591; Franciotti 1616. Lost works: pastoral drama, *Clorindo* (Lucchesini 1825– 31, 9:169); two other pastorals (Tiraboschi 1824, 1925–26); religious narrative on Saint Eustace (Grillo 1612a, 422–23, 921). Conjecturally identifiable as author of the *Tragicomedia pastorale* discussed in ch. 3. Literary contacts: Domenico Chiariti (Grillo 1612a, 649–50), Angelo Grillo, Niccolò Tucci (Grillo 1612a, 367–68, 400– 401, 411–12, 871–72, 878, 921; 1612b, 261, 482–83, 551–53). Bibliography: G. Sforza 1879, 353–55. LB. BB.

BERTANI, BARBARA (FL. 1585)
Reggio. Said to have been member of Accademia degli Elevati (Guasco 1711, 225– 26). Literary contact: Alessandro Miari. BB.

BERTOLAIO CAVALETTI (CAVALLETTI), ORSINA (D. 1592)
Ferrara. Daughter of Camillo Bertolaio. Married poet Ercole Cavaletti (1553–89). Mother of Barbara Cavaletti Lotti. Verse in: *Lieti amanti* 1586; *Rime* 1587a; *Nuova scielta* 1592; Caraffa 1598; C. Fiamma 1611; Guaccimani 1623; *Rime* 1723. Interlocutor in: T. Tasso 1991a. Literary contacts: Vittoria Galli (see her entry below), Angelo Grillo (Durante and Martellotti 1989b, 140–41), Torquato Tasso. LB. BB.

BIANCHI STANCHI, ELENA. *See* Stanchi, Elena Bianca

BRAGADIN CAVALLI, VENERANDA (C. 1566–AFTER 1619)
Venice. Daughter of Giovanni Antonio Bragadin (Venetian patrician?).[†] Married Ottavio Cavalli (1560–1618) of Verona. Mother of poet Francesco Cavalli. Published works: Bragadin 1613, 1614, 1619. Verse in: *Le muse contentiose* 1614; Viola 1618. Literary contacts: Lodovico Aleardi (Bragadin 1619, 88); Marcantonio Balcianelli (Bragadin 1619, 36); Giovanni Battista Barbo, Pietro Antonio Toniani (Bragadin 1619, 94–102), Dionisio Viola. LB. BB.

BREMBATI GRUMELLI, ISOTTA (C. 1530–1586)
Bergamo. Married (1) Elio Secco d'Aragona; (2) Count Giovanni Girolamo Grumelli, in 1561. Mother of nun writer Flavia Grumelli (see her entry below); another daughter, Virginia, married Giulio Secco Soardo. Verse in: *Tempio* 1568; *Esequie* 1572; *Rime* 1587c. Editorial role in: *Esequie* 1572. Literary contacts: Diomede Borghesi (Borghesi 1566, *seconda parte*, 8r; *terza parte*, 5r), Ercole Tasso (E. Tasso 1593, 56r, 60r–v and *tavola*). Posthumous tribute vol.: *Rime* 1587c. Bibliography: D. Calvi 1664, 340–42; Jaffe 2002, 281–310. LB. BB.

[†] Bragadin claims to be of noble birth in Bragadin 1619, 79, but I found no Giovanni Antonio Bragadin of the appropriate generation in any branch of the patrician genealogies of Marco Barbaro held in the Archivio di Stato in Venice. Her father may have been an illegitimate son of the patrician Bragadin family and used its surname.

CAMILLIARDI, CHIARA
Verse in: Borsieri 1611.

CAMPIGLIA, MADDALENA (1553–1595)
Vicenza. Noblewoman. Daughter of Carlo Campiglia (d. 1571) and Polissena Verlato (d. 1572), the latter the illegitimate daughter of a Vicentine nobleman. Born illegitimately; legitimized prior to 1565, when her parents married (they had been cohabiting since 1542). Married Dionisio Colzè in 1576; separated probably by 1577. Published works: Campiglia 1585, 1588, 1589. Verse in: Maganza, Rava, and Thiene [1583?]; Gagliardo 1584; Ducchi 1586; Zarrabini et al. 1586; Rossi 1587; Calderari 1588; Baldi 1589a; Ducchi 1589; Grillo 1589; *Mausoleo* 1589; Passero 1589; C. Gonzaga 1591b; Manfredi 1593; Morsolin 1882, 62–64. Editorial material in: C. Gonzaga 1591a, 1592. Lost works: tragedy or epic on Saint Barbara (ch. 1, at n. 143); other "worthy writings" (scritti di pregio), left unpublished at her death (Perrone 1996, 41). Literary contacts: Bernardino Baldi, Camillo Camilli (Campiglia 1589, 8r), Cortese Cortesi, Gregorio Ducchi, Claudio Forzatè, Orsatto Giustinian, Curzio Gonzaga, Angelo Grillo, Luigi Groto, Angelo Ingegneri, Giovanni Battista Maganza, Muzio Manfredi, Lucillo Martinengo (*Mausoleo* 1589, 74), Francesco Melchiori (Morsolin 1882, 61–66), Issicratea Monte (Groto 2007, 337–38), Felice Passero (Passero 1589, prefatory madrigal), Agostino Rava, Muzio Sforza, Marco Stecchini, Torquato Tasso. See also Campiglia 2004, 306; and ch. 6, at n. 58). Evidence of a planned, though unpublished, posthumous tribute volume, edited by her nephew Alessandro Campiglia, in Grillo 1612a, 735, 738. Bibliography: Morsolin 1882; Mantese 1967; M. Milani 1983; Perrone 1996; Chemello 2003; Cox and Sampson 2004; Ultsch 2005a, 2005b; Bossier 2007; Carinci 2009, 115–54; Gherardi 2009. LB. BB. DBI.

CAPECE, ISABELLA (1569–1590)
Naples. Noblewoman. Daughter of Giovanni Girolamo Capece, of the Nido branch of the Capece family, and Giovanna Castracucco. Posthumous publication: Capece 1595. LB. BB.

CAPPELLO, LAURA BEATRICE (C. 1540–1617)
Born to a father from Venetian patrician family of Cappello; mother from noble Brescian family of Martinengo. Brought up in Pavia by maternal aunt Lucrezia Martinengo; tutored by poet Filippo Binaschi. Became nun at the Augustinian convent of Santa Maria Teodote ("della Pusterla"); professed 1561; prioress from 1581. Verse in: Guazzo 1595. Literary contacts: Filippo Binaschi, Stefano Guazzo, Giovanni Battista Massarengo. Bibliography: Cappello Passarelli 1908. LB. BB.

CARRARI, INNOCENZA (1561–1618)
Treviso. Sister of Fabrizia and Silvestro Carrari (see following entry). Member of Accademia degli Erranti, Ceneda, as "la Piscatrice" (*Poesie* 1590, 18r). Verse in: *Poesie* 1590; *Poesie* 1591. LB. BB.

CARRARI VIVIANI, FABRIZIA
Treviso. Sister of Innocenza Carrari and priest and *letterato* Silvestro Carrari
(Burchelati 1609, 52–53; Binotto 1996, 151). Married by 1590. Member of
Accademia degli Erranti, Ceneda, as "la Boscareccia" (*Poesie* 1590, 16v). Verse in:
Poesie 1590; Montanaro 1587. BB.

CASTAGNA MALATESTA, GIROLAMA
Verse in: Sanudo 1613; Rosini 1621b (derivative of Sanudo 1613). LB. BB.

CAVALETTI, ORSINA. *See* Bertolaio Cavaletti, Orsina

CAVALETTI LOTTI, BARBARA (D. C. 1599)
Daughter of Orsina and Ercole Cavaletti of Ferrara. Married Paolo Lotti of Ravenna.
Returned to Ferrara after her husband died. Verse in: Guaccimani 1623; *Rime* 1723.
LB. BB.

CERVONI, ISABELLA (C. 1576–AFTER 1600)
Colle di Val d'Elsa. Daughter of poet Giovanni Cervoni (fl. 1574–1607). Member of
Accademia degli Affidati, Pavia. Published works: I. Cervoni 1592, 1597a, 1597b,
1598, 1600. Verse in: *Oratione* 1599; G. Cervoni 1600; Massini 1609. Unpublished
canzone in I. Cervoni, "Canzone." LB. BB.

COLAO, LUCIA
Born Venice (Colao, "Rime," 23r). Lived in Oderzo, near Treviso. Verse in: Colao,
"Rime"; Bergalli 1726, 2:2–16 (as *incerta*). Possibly blind (Giustinian 1600, 69).
Literary contact: Orsatto Giustinian. Bibliography: Liruti 1865. LB.

COPIO SULLAM, SARRA (C. 1600–1641)†
Venice. Daughter of Jewish merchant Simone Copio (d. 1606) and Ricca de' Grassini
(d. 1645). Married Jacob Sullam c. 1614. One daughter, Rebecca (d. 1615). Published
work: Copio 1621 (also published by Antonio Pinelli in Venice the same year). Verse
in: Cebà 1623; Zinani 1627; possibly Ferrari [1638?].‡ Modern editions: Boccato
1973, 1987; Fortis 2003; Copio 2009. Literary contacts: Baldassare Bonifaccio,
Ansaldo Cebà, Leone Modena, Numidio Paluzzi, Gabriele Zinani. Bibliography: see
Cox 2008, 360n158, to which should be added Copio 2009. LB. DBI.

COREGLIA, ISABETTA (FL. 1628–1650)
Lucca. Niece of Antonio Bendinelli, Lateran canon and prior of San Bartolomeo,
Pistoia. No evidence of marriage; probably Carmelite tertiary (Coreglia 1628, 10).
Musical *virtuosa*. Lived temporarily in Venafro, near Naples, in 1630s; associated
with Accademia degli Incauti. Published works: Coreglia 1628, 1634, 1650.

† Regarding Copio's date of birth, I follow Harrán 2009, 15–16. Previous scholarship dates her birth to c. 1590–92.
‡ Ferrari's opera libretto has a prefatory sonnet by a "Signora S.C.," who may be Copio.

Unpublished verse in: Coreglia, "Raccolta di varie composizioni." Literary contacts: Girolamo Fontanella (Coreglia 1634, a3v; Fontanella 1994, 37–41, 159–60), Desiderio Montemagni (Coreglia 1628, 6r). Bibliography: Capucci 1983; Cox 2008, 209–10, 215–16. BB. DBI.

"Costanza L."
Padua(?). Verse in: Ferro 1581.

dalla Torre, Marina
Treviso. Daughter of Giovanni dalla Torre. Verse in: *Poesie* 1590.

dalla Torre, Zanetta
Treviso(?). Verse in: *Choro delle muse* 1613. BB.

Damiana, Suor (fl. 1613)
Venice(?). Verse in: Antonazzoni 1613.

de' Ferrari, Maria
Lucca(?). Verse in: *Scelta* 1591. Literary contact: Domenico Chiariti (*Scelta* 1591, index).

Della Chiesa, Francesca Benedetta (b. c. 1595)
Born Saluzzo, Piedmont. Noblewoman. Daughter of Nicolino Della Chiesa of Cervignasco and Lucia Corva; sister of priest and *letterato* Francesco Agostino Della Chiesa. Nun in Cistercian convent of Rifreddo from 1620; later abbess. For evidence of literary activity, see ch. 1 at n. 128. BB.

Della Valle, Lisabetta
Cosenza. Probably related to Lucrezia Della Valle. Verse in: Sanudo 1613; Rosini 1621b (derivative of Sanudo 1613).

Della Valle, Lucrezia (d. 1622)[†]
Cosenza. Noblewoman. Daughter of Sebastiano Della Valle and Giulia Quattromani; niece of *letterato* Sertorio Quattromani ; sister of poet Fabrizio Della Valle. Married Giovanni Battista Sambiasi; "numerous children" (Spiriti 1750, 104). Verse in: Spiriti 1750, 103n1. Lost works: love *canzoniere* of fifty-three poems. Bibliography: Spiriti 1750, 102–4. BB (s.vv. "Della Valle," "De Valle").

di Zucco, Lucella
Daughter of Romolo di Zucco, lord of Zucco and Cuccagna, near Udine (Liruti 1865, 15). Sister of Enrico di Zucco and Giovanni di Zucco. Verse in: *Poesie* 1590; *Rime* 1590; Bratteolo 1597, 1601. LB. BB.

[†]For Della Valle's date of death, see De Frede 1999, 15n5. Earlier sources give 1602.

DONI, ANTONIA
Rome. Verse in: *Raccolta* 1589; *Tempio* 1591. LB. BB.

ERCULIANI, CAMILLA. *See* Greghetti Erculiani, Camilla

FABRA, STRATONICA
Verse in: Sanudo 1613; Rosini 1621b (derivative of Sanudo 1613). LB.

FERRO, CHERUBINA
Verse in: Sanudo 1613; Rosini 1621b (derivative of Sanudo 1613). LB.

FONTE, MODERATA (MODESTA POZZO ZORZI) (1555–1592)
Venice. Daughter of Girolamo Pozzo (*cittadino* and lawyer) and Marietta dal Moro; orphaned in infancy. Married Filippo Zorzi (1558–98), *cittadino* and lawyer. Related through the marriage of her aunt Saracino Saracini to historian Giovanni Niccolò Doglioni. Four children. Published works: Fonte 1581a, 1581b, 1582, 1585, 1592, 1600. Verse in: Monte 1578a; Zucconello 1583; *Carmina* 1586; Doglioni 1587; Caporali 1589. Unpublished verse in: "Rime e poesie," fol. 160v (sonnet to Domenico Venier). Lost works: contributions to planned verse collections in memory of Giovanni Tommaso Costanzo (c. 1582–83) and in praise of Prospero Visconti's *palazzo* in Milan;[†] published *rappresentazioni* (see ch. 3 at n. 9). Modern editions: Fonte 1988, 1995, 1997, 2006, 2009; Kolsky 1999, 11–16. Literary contacts: Domenico Chiariti (Caporali 1589, 4v–5r), Giovanni Niccolò Doglioni, Luigi Groto, Orazio Guarguanti, Bartolomeo Malombra, Issicratea Monte, Cesare Simonetti. Bibliography: see references in Cox 2008, 323n5, to which should be added Olivieri Secchi 1998, 307–11; Kolsky 1999; Datta 2003, 160–63; Carinci 2007; Quaintance 2009; Ross 2009. LB. BB (s.v. "Dal Pozzo").

FRANCO, VERONICA (1546–1591)
Venice. Daughter of Francesco Franco and Paolo Fracassa. Married Paolo Panizza; separated by 1564. Courtesan. Six children, three of whom died in infancy (Rosenthal 1992, 66). Published works: Franco 1575a, 1580. Verse in: Fratta 1575; Franco 1575b; Manfredi 1593. Editorial role in: Franco 1575b. Modern editions: Franco 1995, 1998a, 1998b. Literary contacts: Orsatto Giustinian, Celio Magno, Muzio Manfredi, Marco Stecchini, Domenico Venier, Marco Venier, Maffeo Venier. Bibliography: see Cox 2008, 317n4, 339n141, to which should be added Wojciehowski 2006 and Ray 2009c, 123–55. LB. BB. DBI.

GABRIELLI, CLIZIA
Padua(?). Verse in: Ferro 1581.

[†]For the Costanzo volume, which is well attested as a project, see Doglioni 1988, 9, and 1997, 39; Fonte 1997, 228; and Groto 2007, 334, 337. I conjecture the existence of a planned volume in praise of the Visconti *palazzo* on the basis of Manfredi 1606, 66, which mentions sonnets on the subject by Orazio Guarguante and Fonte; and Strassoldo and Strassoldo 1616, 27, where two further sonnets on the same theme are found.

GALLI AURISPI, VITTORIA
Urbino. Noblewoman. Daughter of courtier and *letterato* Antonio Galli (1510–61) and Caterina Stati; married Aurispa Aurispi. At least one son, Narciso. Verse in: Ricciuoli 1594. Dedicatee of: Lanci 1588; Baldi 1590, 307–60. Literary contacts: Bernardino Baldi, Orsina Cavaletti,[†] Cornelio Lanci, Federico Ricciuoli. LB. BB.

GATTI, BEATRICE
Vicenza. Probably the daughter of medic Teodoro Gatti (fl. 1585).[‡] Entered convent of Santa Maria di Araceli in 1604 with name of Suor Diodora. Published work: B. Gatti 1604.

GONDOLA, MARIA (MARA GUNDULIĆ)
Ragusa (Dubrovnik), Dalmatia (Croatia). Daughter of Italophile erudite Ivan Gundulić (1507–85). Married philosopher and *letterato* Niccolò Vito di Gozze (Nikola Vitov Gučetić). Published work: letter to Fiore Zuzori (Cvijeta Zuzorić) in Vito di Gozze 1585, unnumbered but *2r–**4r. Interlocutor (with Zuzori) in: Vito di Gozze 1581. Bibliography: Torbarina 1931, 73–74; Rabitti 2002, 420; Römer 2004.

GRASSI, OTTAVIA
Bologna. Verse in: Segni 1583. Literary contact: Orsina Cavaletti(?) (*Rime* 1587a, 214).[§] BB.

GREGHETTI ERCULIANI, CAMILLA
Padua. Probably the daughter of an apothecary. Married Girolamo Erculiani, apothecary at Le tre stelle.[#] Describes herself as an apothecary *(speziala)*. Published work: Herculiana 1584.

GROSSI SACCHI, LAURA
Verse in: Sanudo 1613; Rosini 1621b (derivative of Sanudo 1613). LB.

GRUMELLI, FLAVIA (D. AFTER 1609)
Bergamo. Daughter of Isotta Brembati (see her entry above) and Giovanni Girolamo Grumelli. Nun in Benedictine convent of Santa Grata; abbess by 1595. Published work: Grumelli 1596.

[†]This is based on a statement by Cristoforo Bronzini, in one of the unpublished *giornate* of his *Dialogo della dignità delle donne* (Bronzini, "Dialogo," Magl. VIII.1522, pt. 1, p. 398), where he speaks of a "dolcissima amicizia" (dearest friendship) between the two poets.
[‡]Gatti identifies her "dolcissimo padre" as a medic at B. Gatti 1604, A2v. The likelihood of his being the Teodoro Gatti discussed in Mantese 1969, 72–73, is increased by the coincidence of his name with the spiritual name adopted by Beatrice: Mantese notes that he is referred to as "Diodoro" in documents of the time.
[§]Cavaletti's madrigal *Velate i capei d'oro* mourns the death of a Bolognese female poet referred to as "la Grassi." Ottavia Grassi is one possibility, although another is Emilia Grassi (fl. 1585), mentioned in Fantuzzi 1781–94, 9:132.
[#]I am grateful to Eleonora Carinci for this information.

GUIDICCIONI LUCCHESINI, LAURA (1550–1599)
Lucca. From patrician family; daughter of Niccolò Guidiccioni, a cousin of the poet Giovanni Guidiccioni (1480–1551). Sister of *letterato* Cristoforo Guidiccioni (1538–82). Musical *virtuosa*. Married Orazio Lucchesini. Employed at Medici court in Florence from 1588. Scripted a ballet for marriage of Ferdinando de' Medici and Christine of Lorraine in 1589, and wrote three short pastoral plays (now lost), performed at various Medici events between 1590 and 1599. Verse in: T. Tasso 1587; Santi 1608; Treadwell 1997. Literary contacts: Isabella Andreini (MacNeil 2005, 6–8), Sinolfo Saracini (Santi 1608). LB. BB. DBI.

HERCULIANA, CAMILLA. *See* Greghetti Erculiani, Camilla

MALLONI, MARIA "CELIA" (1599–AFTER 1627)
Actress; daughter of actress Virginia Malloni. In Confidenti company 1618–19. Verse in: *Corona* 1621. Literary contacts (from *Corona* 1621): Giovanni Paolo Fabri, Bernardo Morandi, Andrea Salvadori. Bibliography: Megale 2007. DBI.

MALVASIA, DIODATA (VIRGINIA) (C. 1533–AFTER 1617)
Bologna. Daughter of Count Annibale Malvasia. Published work: Malvasia 1617. Verse in: Malvasia 1617. Unpublished convent history, datable to 1575, in Biblioteca Comunale dell'Archiginnasio, Bologna, MS Gozzi 189. Literary contact: Robert Poggiolini (Malvasia 1617, dedicatory sonnet). Bibliography: Fantuzzi 1781–94, 5:163–64; Callegari and McHugh 2011. BB.

MANFREDI, LAURA
Padua(?). Verse in: Ferro 1581.

MARCHESI DELLA TORRE, CATERINA (CATELLA) (C. 1585–AFTER 1623)
Udine. From wealthy mercantile and landowning family. Daughter of Antonio Marchesi and Livia Sasso. Married Count Giulio della Torre (d. 1623) c. 1600. Three children: Luigi (d. 1636), Giulio, Ginevra. Verse in: Bratteolo 1597; *Poesie* 1598; *Lagrime* 1599; Strassoldo and Strassoldo 1616. Literary contacts: Giacomo Bratteolo, Lucella di Zucco (Bratteolo 1601, 10r), Giovanni Strassoldo. LB. BB.

MARESCOTTI, MARGHERITA
Siena. Marescotti may have been her married name: *Rime* 1596 describes her as "Margherita Silvestri de' Marescotti." Verse in: *Rime* 1588; Guazzo 1595; *Rime* 1596; Sanudo 1613. LB (s.v. "Malescoti"); BB (s.v. "Malescotti," inaccurate on some details).

Italian Women Writers Active 1580–1635   263

MARINELLA VACCA, LUCREZIA (C. 1579–1653)†
Venice. Daughter of medic and *letterato* Giovanni Marinelli (d. before 1593); sister of medic and *letterato* Curzio Marinelli (d. 1624). Married Girolamo Vacca (c. 1559–1629), Paduan medic, in 1607. Moved to Padua during her marriage. Two children: Antonio (d. 1662), Paolina. Published works: Marinella 1595, 1597 (+ 1605c, 1606b [both partial]), 1600/1601 (+ 1621), 1602 (+ 1606a [partial], 1610a, 1610b, 1617), 1603 (+ 1605b [partial]), 1605a, 1618, 1624, 1635, 1643, 1645, 1648. Verse in: A. Gatti 1604; C. Fiamma 1613; Sanudo 1613; Petrelli 1616a; Colle 1621. Editorial material in: Tansillo 1606. Unpublished verse in: "Poesie dedicate" (see ch. 2 at n. 113); "Raccolta d'alcune rime" (see ch. 1, n. 84); Magno, "Rime," 8v–9r (sonnet exchange with Celio Magno).† Lost work: panegyric of Carlo de' Medici (1595–1666), early 1620s (Von Tippelskirch 2008, 141). Modern editions: Marinella 1997a, 1997b, 1998, 1999, 2007, 2008, 2009, 2011. Literary contacts: Teodoro Angelucci, Giovanni Maria Avanzi, Giacomo Bordoni ("Raccolta d'alcune rime"), Cristoforo Bronzini, Giovanni Colle, Girolamo Fontanella (Fontanella 1994, 160–63),‡ Alessandro Gatti, Orsatto Giustinian (Giustinian 1600, 69), Boncio Leoni, Celio Magno, Ascanio Persio, Giuseppe Policreti, Lucio Scarano, Tommaso Stigliani (Stigliani 1605, 52). Bibliography: see the references in Cox 2008, 323n5 to which should be added Mongini 1997; Olivieri Secchi 1998, 307–11; Datta 2003, 164–66; Kolsky 2005; Haskins 2007; Maggi 2008, 111–24; Malpezzi Price and Ristaino 2008; Zaja 2008; Carinci 2009, 156–215; Ross 2009; Stampino 2009; Lazzari 2010; and Stampino 2010. LB. BB. DBI.

MASSIMI, MADDALENA
Verse in: Bovarini 1602. LB. BB.

MATRAINI CANTARINI, CHIARA (1515–1604)
Lucca. From non-noble mercantile background. Daughter of Benedetto Matraini and Agata, or Agnese, Serantoni. Married Vicenzo Cantarini (d. 1542), in 1530; one son, Federico (b. 1533). In Genoa from c. 1562 to c. 1565; then returned to Lucca. Published works: Matraini 1555, 1556, 1581, 1586, 1590, 1595, 1597, 1602. Verse in: *Rime* 1556; Scandianese 1557; Segni 1601; Scaioli 1611. Modern editions: Matraini 1989, 2007, 2008. Literary contacts: Alessandro Bovio, Domenico Chiariti (Matraini 1602, prefatory poem), Benedetto Dell'Uva, Lodovico Domenichi, Aldo Manuzio the Younger (Manuzio 1592, 24–25), Giuseppe Mozzagrugno, Benedetto Varchi. Bibliography: see references in Cox 2008, 297n25; see also Smarr 2005, 81–97; Rabitti 2007; Marcheschi 2008; Carinci 2009, 58–113. LB. BB (s.v. "Contarini"). DBI.

†See introduction, n. 5.
†Another copy of Marinella's sonnet is found in "Rime e poesie," 59. Magno's reply, *Qual ghirlanda giamai di più bei fiori*, is available in the electronic version of Magno's *Rime* at www.bibliotecaitaliana.it.
‡While Fontanella's odes to Isabetta Coreglia (see her entry, above) make it clear that the two were acquainted, his poem to Marinella may simply be a tribute. The text was first published in 1638.

MIANI NEGRI, VALERIA (C. 1563?–AFTER 1620)†
Padua. Daughter of Vidal Miani, lawyer (d. before 1615). Married Domenico Negri (d. 1612–14) of Venice in 1593. At least one daughter, Isabella (1598–1618); four other children or stepchildren. Published works: Miani 1604, 1611. Verse in: Manzoni 1609; *Polinnia* 1609; C. Fiamma 1611; Sanudo 1613. Modern edition: Miani 2010. Literary contacts: Marcantonio Balcianelli, Arrigo Falconio, Fabio Leonida, Ercole Manzoni, Gaspare Murtola, Pietro Petracci (Petracci 1615, 251). Bibliography: Decroisette 2002, 176–82; Rees 2008, 2010; Finucci 2010. LB. BB.

MOLZA PORRINO, TARQUINIA (1542–1617)
Modena. Daughter of Camillo Molza (d. 1558), the son of poet Francesco Maria Molza (1489–1544). Married Paolo Porrino (d. 1579) in 1560; moved to Parma on her marriage. Joined *concerto delle donne*, Ferrara, as singer, 1583; retired to Modena, 1589. Made honorary citizen of Rome, 1610. Verse in: Guazzo 1595; Segni 1600; Sanudo 1613; Vandelli 1750. Interlocutor in: A. Romei 1585; Patrizi 1963; T. Tasso 1991b. Literary contacts: Bernardino Baldi, Angelo Grillo, Muzio Manfredi, Giulio Morigi, Francesco Patrizi, Antonio Querenghi (Querenghi 1616, 76), Annibale Romei, Torquato Tasso. Bibliography: Vandelli 1750; Riley 1986; Stras 1999; Stevenson 2005, 288–91, 501–2. LB. BB.

MONTE, ISSICRATEA (1564–1584/85)
Rovigo. Daughter of Giovanni Monte of Vicenza and Laura(?) Ricchieri, descendent of humanist Celio Rodigino (Lodovico Ricchieri) (1469–1525). Marriage arranged in 1582 with Giulio Mainente fell through as a result of dowry issues (Groto 2007, 298–99, 337, 362). Published works: Monte 1577, 1578a, [1578b?], 1581. Verse in: Ferro 1581; Maganza, Rava and Thiene [1583?]; Gagliardo 1584; Bonardo 1584, 1598; Cessi 1897.‡ Literary contacts: Giovanni Maria Bonardo, Maddalena Campiglia (Groto 2007, 337–38), Moderata Fonte (Monte, [1578b?], prefatory sonnet), Luigi Groto, Giovanni Battista Maganza (M. Milani 1983, 395n8). Bibliography: Tomasini 1644, 364–67; De Vit 1883; Cessi 1897; M. Milani 1983. LB. BB.

NALDI, BIANCA
Palermo. Supposed author of Naldi 1614 (perhaps apocryphal: see Cox 2008, 175, 347n47).

NIEVO ANGARAN, BIANCA (C. 1531–1588)
Vicenza. Daughter of Galeazzo Nievo and Paola Thiene. Married Count Giacomo Angaran c. 1546. Five children: Stefano, Fabrizio, Marcantonio, Beatrice, Cillenia. Accused of heresy in 1560s and again in 1587, when she was confined in the

---

†As Katie Rees notes (Rees 2010, 24), the 1563 birthdate generally ascribed to Miani on the basis of Ribera 1609, 335, is open to question. The biographical details given here are based on Rees's archival research: see Rees 2010, 24–29, 177–79.
‡In listing these editions of Bonardo, I rely on the list of Monte's published poems in Cessi 1897, 14–16. I have consulted only the later editions, Bonardo 1598 and 1600.

convent of Santa Maria di Araceli; she was executed on the orders of the Inquisition the following year. Verse in: *Rime* 1567; Gagliardo 1584. Literary contacts: Claudio Forzatè, Giuseppe Gagliardo, Giovanni Battista Maganza. Bibliography: M. Milani 1983; Gherardi 2008, 19–35, 211–14.

OMBONI LUPI, DOMENICA
Bergamo. Wife of poet Orazio Lupi (b. c. 1556); mother of at least two children, Andrea and Marta (d. before 1587). Verse in: Lupi 1587.

"A.P."
Siena. Verse in: *Poesie* 1596. Almost certainly identifiable with the Agnese Piccolomini named elsewhere in the volume (*Poesie* 1596, 6, 41–48).

PALLAVICINO LUPI, ISABELLA (C. 1545–1623)
Daughter of Girolamo Pallavicino, Marquis of Cortemaggiore and Camilla Pallavicino of Busseto; married Giovanni Paolo Meli Lupi (1550–71), Marquis of Soragna. Ruled Soragna as regent 1571–91. Two children: Camilla Meli Lupi (d. 1611), Giovanni Paolo Meli Lupi (1571–1649). Notable literary patron and founder of Accademia degli Illuminati. No surviving works. Dedicatee of: T. Tasso 1581 (by Angelo Ingegneri); Campiglia 1588; Ongaro 1600; Pallantieri 1603; Scaioli 1611. Recorded as writer of vernacular verse in Della Chiesa 1620, 201, and Campiglia 1589 (see ch. 3, n. 148).

PANNOLINI, FEBRONIA
Bologna. Nun at Dominican convent of Sant'Agnese. Verse in: Segni 1601. Bibliography: Fantuzzi 1781–94, 6:270–72; Stevenson 2005, 300–301, 525–26. BB.

PICCOLOMINI, AGNESE. *See* "A.P."

PICO SALVIATI, RENEA (RENATA) (D. 1607)
Mirandola and Florence. Daughter of Lodovico II Pico, lord of Mirandola (1527–68), and Fulvia di Correggio (d. 1590). Great-granddaughter of Veronica Gambara. Married Florentine patrician Francesco Salviati c. 1588. At least two children, Costanza (1598–1654) and Fulvia (d. 1650). No surviving works. Described as a poet in Manfredi 1580, 215 (misnumbered 115), and in Bronzini, "Dialogo," Magl. VIII.1522, pt. 1, pp. 373–74, where she is said to have written verse in the vernacular, Latin, and Greek. Filogenio 1589, 173, also praises her classical learning.

PIGAFETTA, OSANNA
Vicenza. Noblewoman. Daughter of Camillo Pigafetta (d. c. 1550) and Margherita Chiericati. Sister of Maddalena Pigafetta (d. 1581), on whom see Chemello 2003, 73–74; aunt of explorer and *letterato* Filippo Pigafetta (1533–1604). Nun in Dominican convent of San Domenico; prioress by 1579. Published works: Pigafetta 1586a, 1586b. Dedicatee of: Granada 1581 (dedicatory letter by the publisher, Giorgio Angelieri).

PIGHINI, GINEVRA
Padua(?). Verse in: Ferro 1581.

POGGI, SEMIDEA (GINEVRA) (1560S?–AFTER 1637)
Bologna. Daughter of Cristoforo Poggi, nobleman and knight of Santo Stefano, and Lodovica Pepoli. Lateran canoness; entered convent of San Lorenzo 1579 or c. 1584.† Published work: Poggi 1623. Verse in: Lodi 1632. Lost works: *Desideri di Parnaso; Poesie spirituali* (Fantuzzi 1781–94, 7:73). Literary contacts: Domenico Cavallina(?), Alessandro Pellicani(?), Roberto Poggiolini.‡ Bibliography: Fantuzzi 1781–94, 7:73; Masetti Zannini 1995. BB.

"S.R." *See* Ronchi Valentini, Silvia

RAMPONI ANDREINI, VIRGINIA (1583–?1630)
Born Genoa or Milan.§ Actress; married actor and dramatist Giovanni Battista Andreini, son of Isabella and Francesco Andreini; acted with her husband in Fedeli company. Verse in: G. Andreini 1606a, 1606b. Tributes in: *Rime* 1604. Bibliography: Wilbourne 2007. BB.

REGANELA, LIVIA
Verse in: *Giustiniano* 1614.

RICCI, FRANCESCA
Rome. Verse in: Agaccio 1598.

RONCHI VALENTINI, SILVIA
Verse in: *Carmina* 1586. Probably the "*Signora* S.R." who appears in *Compositioni* 1585.

SALAROLI ARIOSTI, MADDALENA (D. 1639)
Bologna. Noblewoman. Daughter of Giulio Cammillo Salaroli and Vittoria Mengoli. Married (1) Count Alessandro Zani (d. after 1605); (2) Count Ugo Ariosti. Lost work: *La conversione di S[anta] Maria Maddalena, poema . . . diviso in quattro canti*, dedicated to Laura Poeti of Bologna. Bibliography: Fantuzzi 1781–94, 7:267. BB.

SALVETTI ACCIAIUOLI, MADDALENA (C. 1557–1610)
Florence. Daughter of patrician Salvetto Salvetti. Married patrician Zanobi Acciaiuoli (1548–1613) in 1572. At least one son, Mario (1583–1651). Published

---

† Fantuzzi and Masetti Zannini differ on this dating, Fantuzzi giving the earlier date, Masetti Zannini preferring the later.
‡ Ten named poets and three *incerti* contributed prefatory verse to Poggi 1623. The named poets are identified only by their initials or by shortened versions of their names: "Cav. R.P.," "Sig. Al. Pell," "Sig. G.L.," "Sig. A.A.R.," "Sig. C. L.," "Sig. D. C. Acad. Operoso," "Sig. M.A.L.," "Sig. D. M. P.," "Sig. C.F.P." I have conjecturally identified Pellicani and Cavallina here on the basis of their appearance with Poggi in *Lodi* 1632.
§ On Ramponi's place of origin, see Wilbourne 2007, 62–65.

works: Salvetti 1590, 1611. Verse in: Segni 1600. Possible lost work: volume of *rime spirituali* mentioned in Lanci 1590, 205, 252. Dedicatee of: Lanci 1590, 1591. Literary contacts: Pietro Angeli da Barga (Lanci 1590, 252), Belisario Bulgarini (Salvetti 1611, prefatory verse, as "L'Aperto Academico Intronato"), Cornelio Lanci. LB. BB.

SALVIANI, LUCIA
Orvieto. Probably related to the printer Baldo Salviani, of Venetian origin. Verse in: *Rime* 1587b.

SARROCCHI BIRAGO, MARGHERITA (C. 1560–1618)
Born Naples; lived in Rome. Daughter of Giovanni Sarrocchi; ward of Cardinal Guglielmo Sirleto (1514–85). Married Carlo Birago (d. 1613). Published works: Sarrocchi 1606, 1623. Verse in: Manfredi 1575; Iasolini 1588; *Mausoleo* 1589; Marino 1602a; *Poesias* 1612. Unpublished correspondence verse and letters attested in Verdile 1989–90; and Colombo 1992. Literary contacts: Rinaldo Corso, Francesco Della Valle, Galileo Galilei, Muzio Manfredi, Aldo Manuzio the Younger, Giovanni Battista Marino, Torquato Tasso, Vincenzo Toraldo, Francesca Turina,[†] Luca Valerio. Bibliography: Favaro 1983, 1:1–24; Verdile 1989–90; Pezzini 2005, 2007; Stevenson 2005, 541; Russell 2006. LB. BB.

SBARRA CODERTA, LUCCHESIA (1576–?1662)
Conegliano. Noblewoman. Daughter of Pietro Sbarra and Tranquilla da Colle. Married (1) Monfiorito Coderta (d. before 1607); (2) Giovanni Battista Rota, after 1615. At least one child: Giovanni Battista Coderta (d. before 1607). Published work: Sbarra 1610. Verse in: Sabbadini 1615. Lost works: verse collection published by Marco Claseri mentioned in Claseri's dedication to Sbarra 1610; ottava rima poem *L'immortal compagnia di dame e d'eroi*, published by Claseri in 1621.[‡] LB. BB.

SBARRA COLLALTO, LODOVICA
Sister of Lucchesia Sbarra (see preceding entry). Married (1) Giovanni Battista Coderta; (2) Giulio Collalto.[§] Mother of Silvestra Collalto Sebanelli (d. 1674), recorded as a poet in Bergalli 1726. Verse in: Sbarra 1610. LB. BB.

SEBASTIANI SPOLVERINI, ERSILIA (C. 1572–AFTER 1597)
Verona. Daughter of silk merchant Giovanni Girolamo Sebastiani and Lavinia Verità, an illegitimate daughter of Count Michele Verità (d. 1592). Married Licurgo Spolverini (d. 1615), nobleman and lawyer. At least one child, a daughter, Adria

---

[†] A sonnet exchange between Turina and Sarrocchi is found in Turina, "Poesie," 273r–274r.
[‡] "Serie di uomini e donne illustri di Conegliano meritevoli dalle memorie dei posteri," Archivio di Stato di Conegliano, AMVC, b. 561, art. 4, fasc. 7.
[§] Archivio di Stato di Conegliano, AMVC, b. 413, art. 3, no. 9.

(b. 1591). Published works: Spolverini 1596, [Spolverini] 1596. Verse and prose in: Rime 1596; *Varie compositioni* 1596.† Bibliography: A. Smith 2009. LB. BB.

SILVI, DOMICILLA (FL. 1585)
Reggio. Sister of Silvia Silvi (see following entry). Said to have been member of Accademia degli Elevati (Guasco 1711, 225–26). Literary contact: Alessandro Miari. LB. BB.

SILVI, SILVIA (FL. 1585)
Reggio. Sister of Domicilla Silvi (see preceding entry). Said to have been member of Accademia degli Elevati (Guasco 1711, 225–26). LB. BB.

SOLZA ROTA, PAOLA
Bergamo. Noblewoman. Married *letterato* and *cavaliere* Lodovico Rota (1579–1630) in 1602. No surviving works. Dedicatee of: Grillo 1613 (see Durante and Martellotti 1989b, 245, 258). Recorded as poet in D. Calvi 1664, 456.

SORI, ISABELLA
Alessandria. Daughter of Giovanni Battista Sori, medic. Said to have been member of Accademia degli Immobili (Avalle 1853–55, 4:533). Published work: Sori 1628. Bibliography: Maestri 1993. BB.

SPANNOCCHI DE' SERGARDI, FULVIA
Siena. Daughter of Girolamo Spannocchi. Married Claudio Sergardi (1532–88). Seems to have remarried a Tuti (*Rime* 1596). Verse in: *Rime* 1579; Guazzo 1595; *Rime* 1596. Dedicatee of: Bargagli 1587. LB (as "Flavia Spanocchi"). BB.

SPINOLA, LAURA
Genoa. Probably a relative of Angelo Grillo. Verse in Grillo 1589. LB. BB.

SPINOLA, LUCIA
See note to following entry.

SPINOLA SPINOLA, LIVIA
Genoa. Daughter of Alessandro di Lorenzo Spinola (Chater 1999, 598n24). Wife of Alessandro Spinola, soldier and poet. Cousin by marriage of Angelo Grillo. Verse in: Goselini 1588; Grillo 1589; *Mausoleo* 1589; *Scelta* 1591; Guazzo 1595(?);‡ Borgogni

---

†My entry on Spolverini draws on recent biographical research by Alison Smith, which will appear in her essay on Spolverini for the forthcoming volume *Verona al femminile*, edited by Paola Lanaro for Cierre, Verona. Given the complexity of the publishing history of Spolverini's work, it may be useful to clarify the relationship of the various publications containing work by her. Her *oeuvre* consists of four vernacular poems (two sonnets, a madrigal and a *canzone*), a Latin poem, and an oration. All six works are found in *Varie compositioni* 1596, while *Rime* 1596 contains the sonnets, the madrigal, and the oration; Spolverini 1596, the *canzone* and the Latin poem; and [Spolverini] 1596, the oration.

‡The name Lucia Spinola is given in Guazzo's list of contributors, but the dialogue following her madrigal at Guazzo 1595, 349, names the poet as Livia.

1599. Literary contacts: Giuliano Goselini, Angelo Grillo, Orazio Navazzotti (Borgogni 1599, 299–300), Torquato Tasso (Durante and Martellotti 1989b, 127, 131–32, 135–36). LB. BB.

SPOLVERINI, ERSILIA. *See* Sebastiani Spolverini, Ersilia

STANCHI, ELENA BIANCA
Verse in: Guazzo 1595. LB. BB.

STROZZI, LORENZA (FRANCESCA) (1514–1591)
Born Florence. Sister of patrician Ciriaco Strozzi (1504–65). Nun in Dominican convent of Saint Niccolò, Prato. Published work: L. Strozzi 1588 (+ 1601). Bibliography: Masson 1925a, 1925b; Pierattini 1942, 1943; Stevenson 2002, 2005, 297–300, 554–56. BB.

TALEA NOCI, VITTORIA
Verse in: Scaioli 1611. LB. BB.

TORELLI BENEDETTI, BARBARA (1546–AFTER 1602)
Parma. Daughter of Gaspare Torelli, the legitimized son of Count Francesco Torelli of Montechiarugolo, and Maddalena Musacchi (d. 1592). Married Giovanni Paolo Benedetti (d. 1592). Unpublished work: pastoral drama (*Partenia*, c. 1586) in B. Torelli. Verse in: Manfredi 1593; Agaccio 1598; P. Filippi 1607. Dedicatee of: Garofani 1582. Literary contacts: Bernardino Baldi, Curzio Gonzaga, Ferrante Gonzaga, Giovanni Battista Guarini (Affò 1789–97, 4:296), Muzio Manfredi, Girolamo Pallentieri. Bibliography: Affò 1789–97, 4:292–97; Sampson 2004; Burgess-Van Aken 2007. LB. BB.

TREVISANI CONTARINI, ANDRIANA
Venice. Verse in: Manfredi 1593. LB. BB.

TURINA BUFALINI, FRANCESCA (1553–1641)
Città di Castello. Daughter of Giovanni Turrini (d. 1554) and Camilla di Carpegna; brought up by Pietro di Carpegna. Married Giulio Bufalini (1504–83) c. 1573.[†] Three children: Giulio (1576–1642), Camilla (b. 1579), Ottavio (1582–1623). Published works: Turina 1595, 1627,[‡] 1628. Verse in: Marzi 1589; Segni 1600; Alberti 1603; Sanudo 1613; Marino 1614, *parte terza*; Della Valle 1622; Guaccimani 1623; Bruni 1630; Balducci 1645. Lost work: *Il Filocopo del Boccaccio ridotto in ottava rima* (2 cantos presented in manuscript to Cardinal Cinzio Aldobrandini, 1596;

[†] Turina speaks of marrying when "almost twenty" ("toccando il fin de' quattro lustri") in an autobiographical passage in her unpublished romance "Florio" (Turina, "Il Florio," 5.48, unpaginated).
[‡] The 1627 edition of Turina's *Rime*, seemingly surviving in only a single copy, in the Biblioteca Vaticana (originally in the possession of the Barberini family), is a variant shorter version of Turina 1628, containing only 144 pages to the latter's 313 (see Costa-Zalessow 2009, 25).

Personeni 1786, 39–41). Unpublished works: Turina, "Il Florio" (ottava rima chivalric poem [see ch. 5, n. 1]); "Poesie" (occasional and religious verse); "Rime" (occasional verse [see Corbucci 1901, 57–61, for a description of the contents]). Modern editions: Turina 2005, 2009. Literary contacts: Filippo Alberti, Francesco Balducci, Antonio Bruni, Francesco Della Valle, Capoleone Ghelfucci, Ottavio Marzi, Margherita Sarrocchi (see note to her entry above). Bibliography: Corbucci 1901; Torrioli 1940; Bà 2001, 2005, 2006, 2007, 2008, 2009, 2010; Lanza 2007; Costa-Zalessow 2009. LB. BB (s.v. "Turrini").

VALIGNANI, ISABELLA
Chieti. Noblewoman. Verse in: Pansa 1596. An Orazio Valignani appears in the same volume.

VENTURELLI, CHERUBINA (D. AFTER 1650)
Born Amelia, near Terni (southern Umbria). Nun in Benedictine convent of Santa Chiara in Amelia. Published work: Venturelli 1612 (for a list of subsequent editions, see Weaver 2002, 268). Bibliography: Weaver 2002, 216–27; Bandursky 2009.

VERNAZZA, BATTISTA (TOMMASINA) (1497–1587)
Genoa. Daughter of patrician Ettore Vernazza (d. 1524), founder of the Oratorio del Divino Amore, and Bartolomea Rizzo. God-daughter of Saint Catherine of Genoa. Lateran canoness in convent of Santa Maria delle Grazie. Published work: Vernazza 1588 and 1602 (+ 1636, 1662, 1755). Verse in: Vernazza 1819. Bibliography: Solfaroli Camillocci 1999; Parisotto 2009. BB.

"VIRGINIA N." (FL. 1585)
Verse in: Rime 1585. LB. BB.

NOTES

INTRODUCTION

1. See the list in Cox 2008, 248–52, to which should be added Pigafetta 1586a, 1586b; B. Gatti 1604; and Marinella 1606a.
2. See ch. 1, n. 19.
3. Dionisotti 1999, 237–39. For a discussion of Dionisotti's thesis and its influence, see Cox 2008, xx–xxi.
4. Key early studies are Conti Odorisio 1979; and Chemello 1983. Throughout this study, I refer to Marinella's treatise by the title of the revised, 1601 edition, which is that by which it is best known. The title of the 1600 edition has *nobiltà* and *eccellenze* in the plural.
5. I suggest here an amendment of Marinella's birthdate from the usually cited 1571, which is based on a parish record giving her age at the time of her death in 1653 as 82 (Haskins 2006, 84). Evidence arguing for a birthdate of 1579 includes the 1601 portrait reproduced in Colonna, Marinella, and Matraini 2008, 121, fig. 6, which identifies her as 22 at the time of portrayal; Ribera 1609, 330, seemingly written between 1605 and 1607, which describes her as 27 at the time of writing; and the publisher's preface to Marinella 1643, which speaks of her having published *La Colomba sacra* (1595) at age 15 or 16. Less precise but still suggestive is the fact that the dedicatory letter to Marinella 1602 ascribes the author's literary ambition to "the audacity that boils within youthful hearts" (l'audacia, che bolle ne' cuori giovani), a claim that, as Laura Benedetti notes, would have read as odd for an author in her thirty-second year (Benedetti 2008, 393n12). While it is conceivable that the conflicting evidence reflects a consistent attempt on Marinella's part to misrepresent her age in order to present herself as a prodigy (Haskins 2006, 83n7), the possibility should also be countenanced that the 1653 death record is erroneous. The redating suggested here would have the advantage of placing Marinella's age at her 1607 marriage as 27 or 28—late by the standards of the age but not completely anomalous—rather than the improbably late 36. If the 1579 date is accepted, it increases the likelihood that Curzio Marinelli should be considered Lucrezia's half-brother, rather her full brother, given his distance from her in age: his first published work dates from 1580, which would place his date of birth in the early 1560s at the latest.

6. The biobibliographical section of Panizza and Wood 2000 has entries for Andreini, Campiglia, Fonte, Marinella, and Sarrocchi.

7. L'Arrotato Accademico Raffrontato, in Sarrocchi 1606, a2v: "opera certo delle maggiori che possa produrre giamai intelletto humano."

8. See ch. 6 at n. 129.

9. On these developments, see Cox 2008, 166–227.

10. A selection of Grillo's religious verse is available in Durante and Martellotti 1989b, 335–438. On a projected complete edition of the 1629 edition of his *Pietosi affetti*, see Morando 2009, 51n8. The two dates given for Tansillo's poem are those of its first, partial publication and the publication of its first complete version (on the text's complete publishing history, see ch. 1, n. 205). Subsequent instances of two publication dates separated by a slash indicate texts published in two different versions.

11. Brand and Pertile 1999, 258, 305.

12. Quondam 2005a, 127.

13. For citations of recent criticism in this area, see ch. 1, nn. 175, 191, 193, 208–9.

14. The series, edited by Alberti Rabil and Margaret King, has now transferred to the Center for Renaissance and Reformation Studies in Toronto. The volumes published so far are Fonte 1997, 2006; Marinella 1999, 2008, 2009; Campiglia 2004; Sarrocchi 2006; Matraini 2008; Copio 2009; and Miani 2010. Battiferra 2006 and Matraini 2007 also contain quite substantial amounts of material written during this period. The two volumes in progress are editions of Barbara Torelli's *Partenia* (by Barbara Burgess-Van Aken and Lisa Sampson) and Lucrezia Marinella's *Arcadia felice* (by Letizia Panizza). An edition of a 1585 "defense of women" by Maria Gondola is also forthcoming in a volume of Italophone writings by sixteenth-century Dalmatian women (by Francesca Gabrielli). Other works by women from this period available in modern editions are Campiglia 1996; Marinella 1997a, 1997b, 1998; I. Andreini 1995/2002, 2005; Turina 2005, 2009; and Fonte 2009. See also Marinella 2007.

15. A rare recent study of religious writings by Italian women in this period is Carinci 2009. See also Colonna, Matraini, and Marinella 2008; and Marcheschi 2008, which includes discussion of Matraini's late religious writings. The only overview of the female-authored literature of this period to date is Cox 2008, 149–63.

16. Murphy 2003.

17. The point is made by Quondam in Quondam 2005a, 133–34. See also the remarks of Morando 2009, 37–38.

18. Lanyer was, of course, half-Italian; on her contacts with Italian culture, see Benson 1999.

19. I know of only four comparative studies in this field relating to the period in question: J. Campbell 1997 and Jones 1998, both on English and Italian material; Gagliardi 2005, on Spanish, Italian, and English; and Jung 2008, on Italian and Spanish.

20. For brief comment, see Cox 2008, 347n44.

21. For the translations of *Mirtilla*, see Mauri 1996a, 209–16, and 1996b, 256–60; for that of the *Lettere*, Malquori Fondi 1997.
22. See Masson 1925b, 64–65.
23. De Coste 1647, 1:797–804 (Molza); 2:97–105 (Strozzi), 717–19 (Fonte), 724–27 (Sarrocchi). For the comparison of Sarrocchi with Petrarch, Ariosto, and Tasso, see 2:725.
24. I. Andreini 1603, unnumbered [28–29]. The sonnets are addressed to Catherine (under the approximative name Caterina Savelli, Vidame d'Umans), and to her mother, Giulia Savelli (under the name Marchesa Pisani). They were republished in I. Andreini 1605, 50–51, with the addition of a sonnet to Catherine's husband, Charles d'Angennes (1577–1652), Vidame du Mans.
25. See ch. 1, n. 92.
26. Della Chiesa 1620. For discussion of clerics' contributions to the *querelle des femmes*, see ch. 1, sec. 2.
27. See ch. 4 at nn. 32, 92–97.
28. For a summary of debate on the issue, see Luebke 1999, 1–7; and O'Malley 2000.
29. In the borderline case of Laura Battiferri/Battiferra, I use the archaic, or modern English-language, version, Battiferra. For further discussion of this point, see Cox 2008, xxvii–xxviii.
30. Useful critical summaries of historiographical developments in this field over the past few decades include Hudon 1996; Ditchfield 1999; and Laven 2006. For comments on the terminological issue, see Hudon 1996, 803–4; Ditchfield 1999, 387–89; and Laven 2006, 720.

CHAPTER ONE: Contexts

1. For further discussion of the context of Italian women's writing in this period, see Cox 2008, 138–49, which the present analysis is intended to complement.
2. Cox 2008, 1–120.
3. *Selve* containing mentions of modern Italian learned women include L. Contarini 1589, 384, 404 bis–405, 416; and Astolfi 1602, 109–14. Treatises on the glories of particular cities including such mentions include Alberici 1605, 19, 27, 59, 63, 69; Mini 1614, 106; Morigi 1619, 270–73; Superbi 1629, 138–41; and De' Pietri 1634, 67. See also nn. 7–8 below. "Defenses of women" besides those mentioned in the text incorporating lists of modern learned women include Lanci 1590, 204–6, 251–52; Ribera 1609, 271–335 passim; and Bursati 1621, 191–94. On the record of fifteenth-century learned women within sixteenth- and seventeenth-century encomiastic literature, see Ross 2009, 96–111.
4. On Della Chiesa, discussed in sec. 2 below, see Conti Odorisio 1979, 74–78; Santacroce 1999–2000, 18–19; Heller 2003, 41–43; and Ross 2009, 106–7. On Bronzini, see Jordan 1990, 266–69; Giochi 1993; Cusick 2005; Harness 2006, 43,

137–40; Cox 2008, 190–91; Spinelli 2008, 676–78; Cusick 2009, esp. xx, 194–95, and 340n10; and Ross 2009, 107–9. The dates given for Bronzini are those of the publication of the four published volumes of the *Dialogo*, a complete manuscript version of which survives in the Biblioteca Nazionale Centrale in Florence (Bronzini, "Dialogo"). On the date of composition, see Spinelli 2008, 678; and Cusick 2009, 105, 373n23.

5. Ribera 1609, 300: "alcuni trofei delle donne antiche e moderne." The detail is repeated in Bronzini 1625, *giornata quarta*, 117.

6. Murphy 2003, 77; Cox 2008, 342n166.

7. Bigolina appears in Scardeone 1560, Marescotti 1589, and Della Chiesa 1620; Scrovegni in Scardeone 1560 and Della Chiesa 1620.

8. Nogarola and Brenzoni appear in Boccaccio and Betussi 1545; Pellegrini 1579, 17v; Valerini 1586, 106; and Dalla Corte 1596, 2:400–401, 417–18. Querini 1597, 29, explicitly positions Spolverini as heir to Verona's fifteenth-century tradition of women's writing. It is interesting in this connection that Spolverini was one of very few sixteenth-century women writers to write in Latin as well as Italian.

9. See ch. 3 at n. 94.

10. Campiglia to Francesco Melchiori, 23 February 1588, in Morsolin 1882, 61: "la divina Vittoria." Campiglia seems to be politely declining a request for a portrait of herself, perhaps for a gallery of "female worthies."

11. Bragadin 1619, 7: "con le sue divine opere ha illustrato il sesso femminile." Bragadin misidentifies Fonte as still alive. On Marinella's dates, see introduction, n. 5.

12. Marinella 1601, 37–41; 1999, 83–93. Marinella's modern examples, mainly Latinists, are Brenzoni, Nogarola, Gambara, Colonna, Battista Sforza (1446–72), Costanza Varano (1426–47), Damigella Trivulzio (d. 1527), Cassandra Fedele (1465?–1558), and Laura Terracina (1519–c. 1577).

13. Turina 2005, 219–20, and 2009, 130–31: "dotte, angeliche parole"; "rime alte e famose." For the sequence in general, see Turina 2005, 211–20, and 2009, 108–33. For a comparison of Colonna and Turina as poets of widowhood, see Bronzini 1625, *giornata quarta*, 129. Turina's homage needs to be placed in the context of her connections with the Colonna family, on which see Torrioli 1940, 18, 26–27.

14. See ch. 2 at nn. 151 and 211.

15. Sarrocchi's Rosmonda is the daughter of a warrior woman, "fierce Almena" (Almena la fera), summoned by the sultan as a wife precisely on the grounds of her prowess (Sarrocchi 1623, 26–27, 29 [3.51–56, 75]; 2006, 126–27, 132 [3.55–60, 79]). Marinella's Meandra is the niece of the dowager queen of Argos and Corinth, said to have in the past "wielded a sword on the battlefield" (2011, 207, and 2009, 196 [9.12]; già in campo trattò il ferro). Parenthetical references to narrative poems are to canto and stanza. On the female warrior as archetype for the female writer, see Cox 1997b, 138–39.

16. T. Tasso 1980, 365–66 (12.29–31, Clorinda suckled by a tiger); Fonte 1995, 30, and 2006, 97–98 (2.31–32, Risamante raised by a wizard). Sarrocchi's second warrior woman, Silveria, is raised by a bear.

17. Cox 2008, 5–6, 91.
18. Cox 2008, 104, 146–47.
19. On women's attainments in art and music in this period, see Bowers 1986; Newcomb 1986; Riley 1986; Durante and Martellotti 1989a; Garrard 1994; Jacobs 1997; Carter 1999; and Cusick 2009. On the emergence of actresses as acclaimed and increasingly "acceptable" cultural personae, see Andrews 2000; and Henke 2002, 85–105. Several of the women discussed in the present book as writers were also lauded as actresses or musical *virtuose:* aside from the famous examples of Isabella Andreini and Tarquinia Molza, these include Leonora Bernardi, Laura Guidiccioni, and Isabetta Coreglia. A handful of poems are known by the singer Ippolita Benigni and the actresses Virginia Andreini and Maria Malloni. See the appendix for details.
20. Leoni 1602, 29r (no. 44): "Elicona è la bocca"; "carmi felici"; "dardi e saette." The poem is headed "Apollo e Parnaso nel petto e nel volto di Madonna" (Apollo and Parnassus in Madonna's breast and face). The title page credits Vincenzo Lodovici for the captions.
21. M. Sforza 1590a, 29–45. On Sforza's life and writings, see L. Russo 1985; and Nuovo 1994, 313–17.
22. M. Sforza 1590a, 32: "qual da perle, e rubini / uscendo"; "cedono a lei / nel parlar . . . / Sappho, et Aspasia, e d'African la figlia."
23. M. Sforza 1590a, 34, 45. The comparisons are found in the commentary (also by Sforza) that accompanies the text. By contrast with these icons of male eloquence, the poet compares himself to the quintessentially feminine figure of Echo (M. Sforza 1590a, 30).
24. M. Sforza 1590a, 43: "nova Minerva accorta e desta / viril, faconda, affabile, e honesta." See M. Sforza 1590a, 14, for another comparison of the lady to Minerva.
25. M. Sforza 1590a, 15: "donna maschia, detta da Hippocrate Taura, la quale (come vogliono i Platonici), incita più ad amare." Ficino speaks of the special attraction of women who display "a certain masculine character" (masculam quandam indolem) in his commentary on Plato's *Symposium* (Ficino 2002, 231 [7.9]). I have been unable to identify the Hippocratic doctrine Sforza is referring to here, unless this is a garbled reference to the description of the Amazonian race of the Sauromatae, found in Hippocrates's *Airs, Waters, Places* (see Allen 1985, 48).
26. Cox 2008, 81, 295n9; for a general discussion, see 154–55.
27. This argument is made in more detail in Cox 2008, 85–88.
28. On *cittadini* as a status group, see Grubb 2000. A detailed account of Marinella's financial standing can be found in Haskins 2006 and 2007. On Fonte's, see Rosenthal 1992, 85–86.
29. A marriage arranged for Monte in 1582, to Giulio Mainente, also a poet, seems to have fallen through on account of the insufficiency of her dowry. See Groto 2007, 298–99, 337, 362.
30. The only single-authored work of Sarrocchi's published during her lifetime was Sarrocchi 1606, seemingly unauthorized. Sbarra 1610 is prefaced by a letter from the publisher, Marco Claseri. A letter of Fonte's explains her adoption of a pseudonym

(her real name was Modesta Pozzo) by her unmarried status at the time of her early publications (Carinci 2002, 9). Earlier still, she had figured under her initials, "M.P." (Monte 1578a, A1v). Other instances of women appearing under disguised names in this period include "Signora S.R." (Compositioni 1585, D2r–v); "Virginia N." (Rime 1585), "A.P." (Poesie 1596). See the appendix.

31. See esp. Sarrocchi to Galileo, 29 July 1611 and 13 January 1612, in Galilei 1901, 163–64 and 261–62, where Sarrocchi speaks of having left unfinished the episode of a review of Italian auxiliary troops being sent to aid her Christian hero Scanderbeg at the beginning of the poem in order to "leave space to praise a few princes" (164; lasciare alcun loco [da] lodare alcun prencipe) or to "place her friends and patrons in it" (262; potervi poner dentro de' miei amici e padroni), presumably by creating fictional heroic ancestors for them.

32. Campiglia 1996, 72.

33. Tasso to Campiglia, 12 August 1589, in T. Tasso 1852–55, 4:234 (no. 1160).

34. On Turina, see the letters from Cardinals Ottavio Paravicini (1552–1611) and Domenico Pinelli (1541–1611) of, respectively, 22 July 1595 and 9 August 1595, thanking her for copies of the Rime spirituali (San Giustino, Archivio Bufalini, Inventario Azzi, busta 2, fasc. 25, recorded in Giangamboni and Mercati 2001, 32). On Fonte, see ch. 3 at n. 13.

35. For details of the dedications of Marinella's works, as well as those of other women in this period, see Cox 2008, 248–53.

36. For Marinella's receipt of a ring from Margherita Gonzaga d'Este, Duchess of Ferrara, the dedicatee of her first published work (Marinella 1595), see Lavocat 1998b, xiii. For a mention of gifts received from Eleonora de' Medici Gonzaga, Duchess of Mantua and dedicatee of Marinella 1605a, see Marinella 1618, A2r. For Marinella's correspondence with Bronzini in the 1620s, see Von Tippelskirch 2008, 140–41. I take Bronzini's date of birth, which differs from that given in the Dizionario biografico degli italiani, from Giochi 1993, 175n1.

37. Cox 2008, 154.

38. On this pattern, see Graziosi 2005, 147–48. Studies of sixteenth- and early seventeenth-century Italian convent writings include Weaver 1994, 1998, 2002, 2009; Graziosi 1996, 2005, 2009; Lowe 2003; Baernstein 2005; and Callegari and McHugh 2011.

39. Cox 2008, 213, 244–45.

40. For bibliography on Tarabotti, see Cox 2008, 360n157, to which may be added Ray 2009c, 184–213, and 2009a.

41. Marquets published a verse collection commemorating the Colloquy of Poissy in 1562 and a translation of Marcantonio Flaminio's Latin religious poetry in 1568. On Castellani, see Graziosi 2009, 166–71. Another precedent is Raffaela Sernigi's La rappresentazione di Moisè, probably published before the author's death in 1557 (see Weaver 2002, 123, 268).

42. Rasponi 1572; Calcina 1576. I would like to thank Marco Mazzotti, of the Biblioteca Manfrediana, Faenza, for supplying me with a copy of the former work.

Bandini Buti 1946, 2:168, also attributes to Rasponi a *Ragionamento sulla cognitione di Dio* (Bologna 1570). That Calcina was alive at the time of the publication of her poem is implied by the title page as well as by the madrigal by her fellow nun Claudia Dotti published at the close of the work.

43. Pigafetta 1586a; L. Strozzi 1601. Pigafetta also published an anonymous life of Saint Dominic, in a translation, presumably from the Latin, by a nun in her convent (Pigafetta 1586b). The translator is identified as Paola Almerici, sister of the early sixteenth-century *beato* Paolo da Vicenza (on whom see Serafino Razzi 1577, 236–37).

44. On Vernazza's writings, see Graziosi 1996, 314–16; Solfaroli Camillocci 1999; and Parisotto 2009.

45. Grumelli 1596; B. Gatti 1604; Malvasia 1617; Poggi 1623. On Malvasia, see Graziosi 1996, 319–20; Bohn 2004, 268–69; and Callegari and McHugh 2011. On Poggi, see Graziosi 1996, 320–22; and ch. 2 at nn. 66–70. On Grumelli, see ch. 6 between nn. 42 and 44.

46. On the evidence for a 1612 edition, see Weaver 2002, 217n5, 268.

47. On Bonanno's sonnet (a reply to the academician Antonio Alfano), see *Rime* 1726, 17; and Grassi 1900, 77. On Pannolini and Cappello, see their entries in the appendix.

48. Antonazzoni 1613, 38 (noted in Graziosi 1996, 313–14); *Lodi* 1632, 78.

49. See Graziosi 1996 and 2005. On the effects of the Counter-Reformation on nuns' public visibility as writers, see Graziosi 1996, 316, and 2009, 173.

50. The online Italian national catalog (ICCU) lists 15 copies of Malvasia 1617 in Italy, and the ICCU catalog and Edit16, the catalog of sixteenth-century works, list 14 copies of L. Strozzi 1588 and 26 of Vernazza 1588 between them. Three further copies of Malvasia are found in the United Kingdom (at the British Library, the Bodleian, and University College London); one in the United States (University of Dayton, Ohio), and two in France (at the Bibliothèque Nationale and the Bibliothèque Mazarine). The Bibliothèque Nationale also has one copy of L. Strozzi 1588 and two of L. Strozzi 1601, while the British Library has one copy of L. Strozzi 1601. Of the other single-authored works discussed here, Calcina, B. Gatti, Grumelli, Pigafetta, and Rasponi all exist in single copies (listed on both ICCU and, where appropriate, Edit16), while three copies of Poggi 1623 survive (at the Biblioteca Civica in Padua, British Library, and the library of Smith College, Northampton, MA).

51. On "autorialità debole" as characteristic of nuns' published writings, see Graziosi 2005.

52. L. Strozzi 1601, A3v ("vermis, et non homo"), A4r ("illustrium virorum consiliis precibusque"). For a useful analysis of the rhetorical uses of self-deprecating language in early modern women's spiritual writing, see Weber 1990.

53. Fantuzzi 1781–94, 7:73, citing a seventeenth-century source.

54. Besides a sonnet from her fellow nun Serafina Maioli, Rasponi 1572 contains sonnets by Marietta Leoni, seemingly a laywoman, Vincenzo Carrari, Girolamo Rossi (1539–1607), and Pomponio Spreti (1537–89). Rossi was the author's nephew and

dedicated to her his *Discorso consolatorio nelle adversità* (1572). Malvasia 1617 contains prefatory verse by Roberto Poggiolini; and Poggi 1623 contains verse by a number of mainly lay encomiasts, including Poggiolini, identified by their initials (see her entry in the appendix). Poggi's dedicatee, Onorio Capra, was in exile from Vicenza at the time of the dedication, having been placed under a death sentence by the Venetian republic after a murder in 1620 (Castellini 1783–1822, 13:192–93; Povolo 1993, 128–29). For more on the framing of Malvasia 1617, see ch. 6, n. 7.

55. Guazzo 1595, 534–35.

56. For literature on the rise of the madrigal form in this period, see ch. 2, n. 9. The first printed verse anthology exemplifying this trend is *Rime* 1587a.

57. Guazzo's love poem to Cappello, *Questa è Laura Beatrice*, is found in *Scelta* 1591, *Seconda parte*, 51, with another madrigal thanking Cappello for a medical remedy; see also *Prima parte*, 61, for further verse to her. For Massarengo, see *Rime* 1593, 151–52.

58. For more on this contrast, see Cox 2008, xxvi–xxvii.

59. If my hypothesis concerning the identity of Gatti's father is correct (see her entry in the appendix), then she came from a dynasty of physicians, some of whom also had literary interests, as was the case with Marinella's father and brother (see Mantese 1969, 71–74).

60. Marta Bonanno (d. 1595) has verse in *Rime* 1726, 1:14–16, 173, 242–43, 345; Laura in *Rime* 1726, 1:14, 306. On the sisters, whose brother Bartolomeo Bonanno (d. 1582) was a member of the Accademia degli Accesi, the collective author of the volume their verse appears in, see Grassi 1900, 75–79.

61. Pigafetta was the aunt of Campiglia's estranged husband, Dionisio Colzè (Mantese 1974, 1022n1320), and a cousin of Campiglia's, Livia Loschi, was a nun in the same convent as Pigafetta, San Domenico in Vicenza (Morsolin 1882, 67). Cappello must certainly have been aware of Torelli through their mutual acquaintance Filippo Binaschi (d. 1589), who tutored Cappello in Latin and vernacular literature as a girl and was famed as a literary celebrant of Torelli (see Guazzo 1595, 14; Cappello Passarelli 1908, 448–49, 451, 453–54; and Cox 2008, 306n106). It is possible that the two women were related, since their mothers were both from the Martinengo family.

62. The extent to which women's intellectual emergence was facilitated by their family context is stressed in Ross 2009, whose analysis embraces, among the women discussed here, Moderata Fonte, Lucrezia Marinella, and Isabella Andreini (195–226).

63. Russell 2006, 5–7. The practice of employing tutors for girls or allowing them to share in their brothers' private education was unusual at this time, but we do know of other examples: see Vandelli 1750, 5–6, and Forciroli 2007, 225, on Molza; Stevenson 2002, 111, on Lorenza Strozzi; and the text of this chapter on Laura Beatrice Cappello and Catella Marchesi. On convent schooling, the most common form of elementary education for women at this time, see Strocchia 1999.

64. On Molza's philosophical interests, see Molza 1750; on Sarrocchi, see Cox 2008, 162; and on Marinella, see ch. 5 at nn. 232–34. The level of Lucrezia Della

Valle's education may be inferred from the fact that Sertorio Quattromani made her his heir, leaving her his substantial library of primarily Latin books (De Frede 1999, 15). An eighteenth-century source records her works as including "a very learned Platonic *capitolo* on the nature of love" (Spiriti 1750, n. 1; un capitolo intorno alla natura di Amore molto dotto e platonico).

65. On Pulzio Sbarra, see D. Rhodes 1993. On Antonio Bendinelli, see Young 1860, 2:332; and Berengo 1965, 271–72. The Bendinelli family seems to have produced another, later female writer in the form of Isabetta Coreglia; see her dedicatory letter to Coreglia 1628, where she identifies the dedicatee, Antonio Bendinelli, as her uncle.

66. For the Carrari sisters, see *Poesie* 1590 (where Fabrizia appears under her married name, Viviani); and *Poesie* 1591. Their brother was the priest and letterato Silvestro Carrari (1558–92); see Burchelati 1609, 52–53, 67; and Binotto 1996, 151. For Lucella di Zucco's co-appearance with Giovanni di Zucco (identified as her brother in Liruti 1865, 15), see *Rime* 1590.

67. See Doglioni 1988, 5, 7; and 1997, 34, 36.

68. Turina 1628, 119, and 2009, 56: "fu per le mie mani eletto / il fuso e l'ago"; "spender gl'anni / ne i bei studi di Palla."

69. Sbarra 1610, A9r: "chi cantò Turno e Aiace."

70. Cox 2008, 64, 67, 77, 288n111.

71. For Cervoni's membership in the Affidati, see *Oratione* 1599, G1r; also Cervoni's sonnet to the poet Filippo Massini (1559–c. 1617) in Massini 1609, 184, thanking him for introducing her to the academy. For her works, see her entry in the appendix.

72. See I. Cervoni, "Canzone." Bronzini 1625, *giornata quarta*, 122, speaks of other, presumably unpublished works of Cervoni's written before her thirteenth year ("non havendo ancora tocco il terzodecimo anno"). For Marchesi's debut, see Bratteolo 1597.

73. Isabella is identified as Giovanni's daughter in the dedicatory letter to G. Cervoni 1600, to which she contributed a sonnet. Giovanni Cervoni's bithdate is given in most sources as 1508, but this seems hard to equate with Isabella's birthdate (which I have calculated from I. Cervoni 1598, where the author describes herself as 22 years old), and still more so with the fact that he appears to have been active as a writer as late as 1607 (Marsand 1835–38, 1:639–41).

74. See, e.g., Tomagni 1565, 146r–147v.

75. There are suggestions in the framing scenes of the dialogue that Cervoni is adopting a position for rhetorical purposes that he did not necessarily hold in life, but his arguments in the body of the work are not noticeably paradoxical in style. On the place of paradox in *querelle* texts, see Daenens 1983.

76. Tomagni 1565, 77v: "acciocche non si dicesse una donna esser stata da più dell'huomo, e la figliuola del padre." Cervoni repeats the accusation in Tomagni 1565, 146r. The same anecdote, presumably picked up from Tomagni, is found in Bronzini 1625, *giornata quarta*, 24.

77. M. Sforza 1590a, 82 ("ago obliando, e gonna"), a4v ("copiosi, scelti, e bellissimi libri").

78. Bratteolo 1597, dedicatory letter: "lettere latine e volgari." On the notable level of culture of the nuns of Santa Chiara in this period, see Paolin 1996, 81–82; Paolin also emphasizes their unorthodoxy and resistance to the spiritual oversight of the ecclesiastical authorities.

79. *Rime* 1561; Cox 2008, 103–5. For Bratteolo's allusion to Irene, see Bratteolo 1597, 134v: "Splender di par con la famosa Irene."

80. Bratteolo 1601.

81. See, e.g., Bratteolo 1601, 2v, where, in a poem by Francesco Codropio, Apollo recognizes Caterina as "she who often affixed choice and precious verses in Delos" (colei che nel mio Delo affisse / rime sovente pellegrine, e conte); and 9r and 14r, for descriptions of her by Pietro Petracci and Pietro Diana as "worthy offspring of Apollo" (degna prole d'Apollo) and "tenth Muse" (decima Musa).

82. For a discussion of this issue in relation to fifteenth-century female intellectuals, see Cox 2008, 6–7. Where Marchesi is concerned, it is possible that the remarkable sonnet in the voice of a falsely accused adulterous wife attributed to her in Bergalli 1726, 2:83, and briefly discussed in B. Croce 2003, 174–75—"S'io il feci mai, ch'io venga in odio al Cielo"—attests to a body of unpublished work available to Bergalli in manuscript, which may date from after Marchesi's marriage. The only published verse I have found by her dating from after her marriage is a sonnet in Strassoldo and Strassoldo 1616, 71.

83. Fonte 1592, 1600 (probably written between 1588 and 1591: see Chemello 1988, xviii); Marinella 1617, 1618. For details of the 1617 expansion of Marinella 1602, see Carinci 2009, 166, 169–70, 201–4; for the date of Marinella 1618, see Cox 2008, 334n94. Ross 2009, 203–4, notes Fonte's and Marinella's continuing literary activity while married but misrepresents the effect of marriage on Marinella's output by misdating her marriage to c. 1601.

84. On Fonte, see Fonte 1585 and *Carmina* 1586, 46, discussed in Kolsky 1999, which reproduces the texts at 11–16. For Marinella, see "Raccolta d'alcune rime," commemorating the sojourn in her married home of Padua in 1614 of the Venetian *podestà* Giovanni Battista Foscarini and his wife Elena. The volume, edited by the Paduan Servite Giacomo Bordoni, contains verse by six poets, including the editor and Marinella's long-term literary contact, Giuseppe Policreti. Marinella's contribution comprises two sonnets to Elena (10v–11r) and one to Giovanni Battista (14r). See also ch. 2 at n. 113. A passage on Marinella in a 1614 poem by Giovanni Battista Barbo listing notable Paduan writers gives a sense of the admiration she enjoyed in Paduan literary circles: "E sol per adornar questo emispero / una gran Marinella mandò Giove / che de le Muse havesse ella l'impero. / Onde ne mostra con mirabil prove / quanto di ciò sia degna a tutte l'hore, / ch'a far opre eccellenti ella si move" (Barbo 1614, 100 [misnumbered 88]; And to adorn this hemisphere, Jove sent us a great Marinella to preside over the Muses; and she shows her worthiness of this honor through her marvelous prowess, each time she turns her hands to new works).

85. Vito di Gozze 1585. Gundilić also features as an interlocutor in Vito di Gozze 1581, along with Fiore Zuzori (Cvijeta Zuzorić), the dedicatee of Vito di Gozze 1585.

86. See Kirkham 2002, 537; and Salvetti 1611, dedicatory letter. Battiferra's husband was the sculptor and architect Bartolomeo Ammanati (1511–92), and Salvetti's was the Florentine patrician Zanobi Acciaiuoli (1548–1613). On Battiferra and Ammanati's relationship, see Kirkham 2002.

87. On the sonnet, see Fonte 1592; and Ross 2009. On the epitaph, see Doglioni 1988, 9–10, and 1997, 39–40. The case of Francesco Andreini, who devoted much energy to memorializing Isabella Andreini after her death, is more complex, since professional and commercial motives were involved. See Ray 2009c, 161–65; and Ross 2009, 214–15, 226–28.

88. T. Tasso 1991a; Kirkendale 2001, 187. The Cavaletti appear together as poets in *Rime* 1587a.

89. For Ippolita's academic name, see Passi 1609, prefatory sonnet. Manfredi's is used on the title page of several of his books (see, e.g., Manfredi 1580).

90. Torrioli 1940, 19. The only counterexample I know of to this norm of spousal supportiveness in this period is Maddalena Campiglia, who alludes darkly in her *Discorso sopra l'Annonciatione*, of 1585, to her husband's malign impeding of her intellectual development (see ch. 6, n. 80). Although a letter by Margherita Sarrocchi's friend Luca Valerio of 31 August 1613 to Galileo announces the death of her husband with the comment that this will allow her "more liberty to philosophize" (Galilei 1901, 560; più libero spazio di filosofare), in practice Sarrocchi was already a significant protagonist in Roman literary culture during the years of her marriage.

91. A counterexample to this pattern is Francesca Turina, who had three children and was in her late eighties when she died.

92. Russell 2006, 10–12. In addition to the Umoristi, Sarrocchi may also have been a member of the Oziosi of Naples (De Miranda 2000, 61n42). There is also evidence that she hosted some kind of academy in her own home (see Verdile 1989–90, 183–84). Ottonelli 1646, 392, speaks of Sarrocchi hosting an academy "in the palace of a leading lord" (nel Palazzo di un principalissmo Signore). This may have been the Ordinati, founded in 1608 as a rival to the Umoristi. Its meetings took place in the Roman residence of Cardinal Giovanni Battista Deti (1580–1630), and Sarrocchi was closely involved in it from the start (Verdile 1989–90, 199–200 and n. 143; Russell 2006, 14–15).

93. On Molza, see Bissari 1648, 12; on Cavaletti, Solerti 1895, 1:130–31.

94. On Andreini, elected to the Intenti in 1601, see I. Andreini 1605, 2–5; on Cervoni, in the Affidati by 1599, see above at n. 71. For the Sienese case, see Cox 2008, 316n194. For information on the academies mentioned in this discussion, see Maylender 1926–30.

95. On Benigni's membership in the Affidati and the Insensati, see above at n. 89. Ginanni 1739, 463, also records her as a member of the Informi of Ravenna, under the name "la Riposata." Turina's membership in the Insensati and in the Accinti, of Città di Castello, is discussed as fact in Corbucci 1901, 32, and Torrioli 1940, 14. A sonnet in

Turina, "Rime," 22, addressed to the Insensati—"Benedetto sia 'l dì ch'apersi al canto"—seems sufficiently close in its rhetoric to other sonnets accepting academy memberships to offer supporting evidence on this point.

96. For the Carrari sisters, see their entries in the appendix. Pallavicino Lupi is described as "Principessa et institutrice" of the Accademia degli Illuminati in the dedicatory letter to Ongaro 1600, 4, the term *principessa* implying active leadership rather than simply patronage, in that the *principe* of an academy—usually a rotating elected office—was its director or chair. Maylender 1926–30, 3:142–43, mistakenly locates the academy in Rome.

97. For the Carrari sisters, see their entries in the appendix; for Monti, Pietropoli 1986, 60; for the Silvi sisters, Guasco 1711, 225–26; for Sori, Avalle 1853–55, 4:533; and for Della Valle, Spiriti 1750, 103 and n. 3.

98. On the evidence for Fontana's membership in the Accademia di San Luca, see Murphy 2003, 195–96. On Gentileschi's membership in the Accademia del Disegno, see Garrard 1989, 34, 495n37.

99. Olimpici among the *Flori* poets include Chiappino, Muzio Manfredi, Fabio Pace (1567–94), Antonmaria Angiolello (d. c. 1590), Giovanni Battista Titoni, Gherardo Bellinzona (d. after 1602), and Pietro Paolo Volpe. Volpe is identified as a member of the academy in the heading to his poem on *Flori*, and Manfredi identifies himself as an Olimpico on the frontispiece of several of his works (e.g., Manfredi 1593); for the others, see P. Calvi 1772–82, 5:12–18 (Angiolello), 123–34 (Pace), 178 (Bellinzona), 234–35 (Chiappino), and 235–37 (Titoni). Titoni and the painter-poet Giovanni Battista Maganza (1513–86), also a member, were among the contributors of encomiastic verse to Campiglia 1585 (see ch. 6, n. 58).

100. Morsolin 1882, 64: "queste cose . . . fur preparate nell'Accademia."

101. See the dedicatory letters to C. Gonzaga 1591b and 1592; for comment, see Riccò 2008, 291n46. More generally on Campiglia's relationship with Gonzaga, see Cox and Sampson 2004, 4 and n. 8.

102. Grillo 1592b, 105: "onde i suoi figli illustri [sc. "della vostra patria"] han ben per voi / onde chiamarsi Olimpici." Further evidence of Campiglia's closeness to the academy is offered by her appearance in Rossi 1587, a verse collection in memory of a member of the academy, six of whose sixteen contributing poets are identified as members. The work was published together with a funeral oration delivered by another Olimpico and addressed to the academy.

103. Morsolin 1882; Mantese 1967; Chemello 2003; Gherardi 2009.

104. See Sampson 2006, 107–8, for Torelli; Cox 2008, 146, 330n69, for Monte; and Rees 2008, 46 and Finucci 2010, 3, for Miani. On the Ricovrati's later record of admitting female members, see Cox 2008, 181. Another, later example of interest is Isabetta Coreglia's relationship with the Accademia degli Incauti of Naples, attested in the paratexts to Coreglia 1634.

105. Details of the activities of the Scolari Incamminati are found in Archivio di Stato di Conegliano, AMVC, busta 427, art. 2-A, no. 1, summarized in Vital 1902; see esp. 8r, 23v, as well as Vital 1902, 9–10, for the academy's seemingly well-attended

public lectures, held in Sbarra's home. Although Lucchesia was in her early teens at the time of the academy's operations, it does not seem unlikely that she may have received part of her education in this way. On the Aspiranti, see Archivio di Stato di Conegliano, AMVC, busta 427, art. 2-A, no. 4 (fasc. 9). D. Rhodes 1993 discusses Pulzio's cultural activities generally.

106. Marinella 1600, dedicatory letter: "da Vostra Signoria Eccellentissima in una Lettione fatta nella Libraria della Serenissima Signoria di Venetia fui con le sue lodi inalzata fino al Cielo nelle cose di Poesia" (in a lecture in the Library of the Most Serene Senate of Venice, I was raised to the heavens by your Excellency in matters of poetry). Scarano praises Marinella in print in his dialogue *Scenophylax* (Scarano 1601, 17).

107. Kolsky 2001, 976–77; see 975n11 for the evidence that Ciotti commissioned the work. On Marinella's relationship with the Accademia Veneziana, see Lavocat 1998b, xiii–xiv; on its history (1593–c. 1609), see Maylender 1926–30, 5:444–46.

108. On Tridentine convent reforms, see Hufton 1998, 370–75; Zarri 2000, 100–117; and Lowe 2003, 140–41, 191–92, 231–32, 298, 393–94; for a list of post-Tridentine papal rulings regarding the integrity of convents, see also Schutte 2006, app. 1. Further bibliography is cited in Pomata and Zarri 2005, esp. xii–xiv; and Ray and Westwater 2005, 26n4. More generally, see Cohen 2007, 336–39, for a bibliographical survey of recent work on early modern Italian convent culture.

109. On nuns' resistance to the imposition of stricter claustration, see Evangelisti 2003, esp. 688, 691–92, 694–99, and the bibliography listed in 678n3. See also Laven 2005, 100–105; and Callegari and McHugh 2011.

110. On the phenomenon of coerced claustration in this period and its social and economic causes, see the bibliography cited in Ray 2009c, 306n4. An excellent brief account is Pomata 2002.

111. The metaphor is contemporary (see Cox 1995, 540; and Laven 2005, 108n21).

112. This is underlined in Strocchia 2009, 184–90. For an interesting case from the 1480s, see Gill 1996, 179–84. The novelty of post-Tridentine regulations, by comparison with earlier reform initiatives, is brought out well in Evangelisti 2003, 681–85.

113. On Tridentine marriage regulation, see Dean and Lowe 1998, 5–6; and Hacke 2004, 31–32, 35–36, 89–90.

114. Cowan 2007, 131, notes that the Tridentine moral condemnation of extramarital relationships had a limited impact within the Venetian patriciate, at least down to the late seventeenth century. On the status of concubines and the offspring of extramarital unions in this period, see Cowan 2007, 117–34; and cf. Eisenach 2004, 134–77, on pre-Tridentine Verona.

115. This goes for Europe generally. See Hufton 1998, 363–423, for a balanced comparative overview of women's lives in Catholic and Protestant Europe; see also Laven 2006, 718–19. On Italy specifically, see Cohn 1996, 57–75. Recent studies of aspects of Counter-Reformation culture stressing the degree of agency exercised by women in this period include Valone 1992, 1994; Dunn 1994, 1997; Chojnacka 1998;

Dieffendorf 2004; Bilinkoff 2005; and Harness 2006. See also Hudon 2004 on continuities between women's place within pre- and post-Tridentine religious culture.
116. Storey 2008.
117. See De Boer 2001, esp. 97–122.
118. Antoniano 1584, 153v–154r; see also Cox 2008, 197–98. On attitudes toward women's assuming a teaching role, see ch. 6, sec. 2.
119. Ottonelli 1646, 388–439. *Accademiche* might imply, more specifically, female members of academies, although Ottonelli seems to be using the term in a more general sense.
120. For an analysis along these lines, see Sberlati 1997, which presents the Counter-Reformation as unequivocally retrogressive with regard to female intellectuality.
121. Antoniano 1584, 154r: "ogni regola può patire qualche eccezione." For Antoniano's correspondence with Battiferra, see Battiferra 2000, 88 (no. 84), 105–6 (no. 98a–b).
122. Ottonelli 1646, 392–93.
123. Cox 2008, 187, 353n94. On the history of this argument within the Renaissance *querelle des femmes*, see Cox 1995, 516–21; on an interesting instance in a dialogue of Tasso's, see McClure 2008, 758.
124. Stumpo 1998, 749.
125. Della Chiesa 1620, 1: "se bene il pensiero, e la professione mia sii più di fuggire la conversatione delle donne, che di lodarle." Della Chiesa was later cited, along with other Italian profeminist clerics, by the French Minim friar Hilarion de Coste as a justificatory precedent for his composing a "famous women" treatise (see de Coste 1647, "Au lecteur," unnumbered [1]).
126. Interesting in this regard are Della Chiesa's *Theatro* entries for the courtesans Tullia d'Aragona and Veronica Franco (Della Chiesa 1620, 292, 296), which carefully avoid any mention of their profession. On the notion of education as corrupting for women in Seicento writings, see Cox 2008, 196–202.
127. Derossi 1790, 46–47. For references to Francesco Scipione's treatise in the *Theatro*, see Della Chiesa 1620, 135, 212.
128. Della Chiesa 1620, 157: "un bellissimo discorso . . . se bene non l'habbi [sc. "l'auttore"] ancor dato alle stampe." Francesca Della Chiesa's now-vanished treatise may be seen as part of a microgenre of convent writings in praise of convent life, including such works as Rasponi 1572 and Arcangela Tarabotti's 1643 *Paradiso monacale*.
129. Genoese noble families, like Venetian ones, were much ramified, which makes these relationships hard to ascertain. For Maria Spinola's poetic activity, see Cox 2008, 333n80. For Laura and Livia Spinola, see their entries in the appendix.
130. Cox 2008, 141, 327n43. Grillo also wrote a madrigal in praise of Tarquinia Molza, published under his pseudonym, Livio Celiano (see Molza 1750, 26 [misnumbered 154], 92).
131. Durante and Martellotti 1989b, 221: "invece hanno fatto l'imagine della loro insufficienza." See also 222–23 for speculation that Grillo was responsible for secur-

ing Fontana the commission for her lost painting of the martyrdom of Saint Sebastian for San Paolo Fuori le Mura, where he was stationed in 1602–7. For Grillo's letter to Caccini, see Grillo 1616, 213; and Durante and Martellotti 1989b, 263, 462–63. For a letter to Bernardi, see Grillo 1612a, 151–52. For mentions of Bernardi in other letters, see Grillo 1612a, 367–68, 400–401, 411–12, 422–23, 649–50, 872, 878, 921; Grillo 1612b, 261, 482–83, 552; and Grillo 1616, 10.

132. Grillo 1612b, 187–90. For Bembo's letter to Clara, see Albonico 1989, 326–27. A similar letter, from Luigi Groto to Laura Peregrini Mazzarelli of Rovigo, is found in Groto 2007, 85–87.

133. Grillo 1612b, 189: "furono emule de gli eroi, e prescrissero con fatti et con scritti egregi il segno a' più nobili intelletti." The only hint we find in Grillo of reservations with regard to intellectual women is found in an undated letter to Niccolò Tucci in 1612a, 878, where he contrasts Leonora Bernardi's modesty with the self-regard to which some "singular" women (donne . . . singolari) can be subject. The reference may be to Margherita Sarrocchi, noted for her assertiveness; it is plausible that Grillo may have met her during his time in Rome from 1602 to 1607 (Durante and Martellotti 1989b, 208–26).

134. Grillo 1608a, 13. An edition of the *Rivelationes*, the first in Italy since 1557, came out in Rome in 1606, while Grillo was stationed in the city at San Paolo fuori le Mura.

135. A good sense of Baldi's intellectual range may be had from Serrai 2002; and Nenci 2005. On his verse, see Motta 2004, 261–63; and Volpi 2005.

136. Baldi 1724, 31–32.

137. Baldi 1724, 31, and 1590, 307–8; Serrai 2002, 115n163.

138. Bronzini 1625, *giornata quarta*, 83; Lanci 1590, 40.

139. Serrai 2002, 218.

140. For the poem to Coignard, see Serrai 2002, 115n163; for that to Molza, Serrai 2002, 103, 236. For Baldi's description of Campiglia's poetic talent ("Flori, / che col latte materno insieme ebbe / il nettar de le Muse"), see Ducchi 1589, 5; and Baldi 1992, 191. Campiglia contributed a sonnet to Baldi 1589a. On Torelli, see Baldi 1590, 350.

141. The letters to Giovanna Doria Colonna and Vittoria Doria Gonzaga are reproduced in Durante and Martellotti 1989b, 442–43. Other examples of collections of spiritual verse authored or edited by male religious that are dedicated to women include Pesaro 1591 (Madre Giustina Moresini, S. Maria degli Angeli, Murano); De Cupiti 1592 (Caterina d'Austria [Catalina Micaela], Duchess of Savoy [1567–97]); Tartaglia 1598 (Virginia Vitelli, Countess of Correggio); and da Poppi 1606 (Cassandra Capponi Ricasoli).

142. In addition to her association with Gregorio Ducchi, mentioned below, Campiglia was also acquainted, perhaps through Grillo or Ducchi, with the Benedictines Felice Passero and Lucillo Martinengo (see her entry in the appendix), while one of the contributors of prefatory verse to her *Flori* was an Augustinian hermit, Gherardo Bellinzona (P. Calvi 1772–82, 5:178). Campiglia's clerical contacts are also attested by the poems she contributed to a memorial collection for the Augustinian hermit

Spirito Pelo Anguisciola (1534–86) and to a posthumous work by the Lateran canon Cesare Calderari (Rossi 1587; Calderari 1588).

143. The work is attested by a sonnet in Grillo 1604, 172, which describes it as a *tragica carme* (tragic song). While the term seems to suggest a *tragedia sacra* (on which, as a genre, see text at nn. 227–29), it may have been a narrative poem whose subject matter assimilated it to tragedy.

144. Both pastorals are discussed in ch. 3, sec. 2.

145. Campiglia 1585, afterword by Gregorio Ducchi, unnumbered ("un ardentissimo spirito la cui mente conversa[ndo] sempre . . . con le cose celesti"); Campiglia 1585, M2v, *Altri d'arme e d'amor cantaro accesi* ("profani inchiostri").

146. Solfaroli Camillocci 1999; Capece 1595. Both works are discussed in ch. 6, sec. 2.

147. Cox 2008, 43–44, 91–92, 141.

148. Campiglia 1585, afterword by Gregorio Ducchi, unnumbered: "dando imitabile essempio non pure à quei dell'uno ma dell'altro sesso ancora, come si debba il tempo felicemente à propria, & ad altrui salute spendere."

149. See Grillo 1589, 5v (sonnet 19); and Ferretti 2007, 126. Recent discussions of male-female spiritual relationships in this period that offer some points of contact with my argument here include Hudon 2004 and Bilinkoff 2005.

150. For the editions of the *Vita di San Francesco*, see Marinella 1605c, 1606b. For discussion of da Poppi's anthology, see Maggi 2008. On the printing history of the *Vita di Maria Vergine*, see Marinella 2008, 120.

151. Marinella 1605a, 1606b. On the latter edition, see Carinci 2009, 163, 166. Ventura appears to have made a practice of such spin-off editions in these years (see Grillo and Talenti 1605). Poems from Marinella's *Rime sacre* were also anthologized in C. Fiamma 1613, 91, 104, 166–67, 218, 295; and Petrelli 1616b, 266.

152. Alberici 1605, 56. Baldi 1724, 31–32 (written in 1603), similarly presents Laura Battiferra as a religious poet, emphasizing her *Sette salmi spirituali* and ignoring her earlier, mainly secular *Primo libro delle opere toscane*.

153. Marinella 1998, 3: "spinta dalla verità e dall'amore che ogn'uno porta al proprio sesso." Another reading of Marinella's *Nobiltà* that sees it as compromised by its "interest" is found in Spelta 1612, 144.

154. Cox 2008, 172–73.

155. Cox 2008, 123–24 and 319n12, 176–77 and 348n53.

156. Where women's contributions are concerned, besides Marinella and Veneranda Bragadin, mentioned below, a letter by an otherwise unidentified Bianca Naldi was published in Vicenza in 1614, though there are grounds for doubting the authenticity of its attribution (Cox 2008, 175, 347n47).

157. Bronzini is referred to as "quel prete" (that priest) in a letter of 3 February 1610 from Belisario Vinta to Orazio della Rena (Minute di Lettere e Registri, Cosimo II: Vinta, 302), consulted online on the Medici Archive Project site (http://documents.medici.org). Ecclesiastical status was required for his office as train bearer (*caudatario*) to Cardinal Carlo de' Medici, assumed in 1615.

158. For discussion of Ribera, see Cox 2008, 143–44, 173. On Bursati, see Jordan 1990, 261–66; and Heller 2003, 39–41.

159. A rare exception is the Augustinian Iacopo Filippo Foresti, author of a compendium of lives of famous women published in 1497, which his coreligionist Bursati cites in his list of sources (Bursati 1621, "A Zoilo in particolare," unnumbered and 192). A further exception is Francesco Scipione Della Chiesa, mentioned above at n. 127.

160. Passi was a layman at the time of the composition of Passi 1599, although he later became a monk. For discussion of his life and works, see Mordani 1837, 150–55; Bertolotti 1887; and Rebonato 2004, 196–97. On Spelta, who later published a compensatory treatise on women's excellence (Spelta 1612), see Bollea 1906; and Rebonato 2004, 205–13. On Barbo, see Vedova 1832–36, 1:73; and for Bragadin's response to Barbo, see ch. 6 at n. 27. The only male religious writer I have come across who wrote on the nonfeminist side of the debate in these years (though his treatise cannot properly be described as misogynistic) is Cipriano Giambelli, author of Bramoso 1589.

161. Della Chiesa 1620, 2: "a guisa di rabbiosi cani . . . con bocca pieno di veleno."

162. Ribera 1609, 15 ("peggio di Beza in Ginevra, e del Rabbino in Ghetto de' Hebrei"), 195.

163. Ribera and Della Chiesa praise Marinella's *Nobiltà* in their discussions of learned women (Ribera 1609, 7, 330–31; Della Chiesa 1620, 214), while Bursati cites her in his preface in a list of *querelle* writings (Bursati 1621, "A Zoilo in particolare," unnumbered). Bursati has his feminist speaker cite also Moderata Fonte as an authority at one point (Bursati 1621, 188–89, citing the proem to the fourth canto of *Tredici canti del Floridoro*), while her *Il merito delle donne* is warmly acclaimed in Ribera 1609, 300.

164. Bursati 1621, 24: "l'onestà, le maniere, le gentilezze, i costumi delle donne, danno, cioè porgono all'huomo la vera e giusta regola, la dritta norma del vivere accostumatamente e lodevolmente nel mondo."

165. Della Chiesa 1620, 47: "la generosità, la nobiltà, la prudenza, la temperanza, la sagacità . . . di questo donnesco sesso: e dall'altra parte . . . la dapoccagine, l'ignobiltà, l'imprudenza, l'intemperanza, la pazzia, la viltà, la crudeltà, e rigidezza della più parte delli huomini di questo nostro tempo."

166. Ribera 1609, 5: "ella è più devota e servente nel divino servigio; . . . è più pietosa in tutte le fatiche, e necessità del prossimo; . . . offende meno a Dio ne' gravi peccati, come sono homicidi, bestemmie, pergiuri, sette, seditioni, tradimenti, e heresie." Similar points regarding women's superiority to men in matters of faith are made in Pellegrini 1579, 9r–v, and, more grudgingly, in Valiero 1744, 3. In a more secular context, Lucrezia Marinella speaks of woman as tempering man's innate cruelty, and rendering him capable of civil life: "[la donna] lo raffrena, l'humilia, lo fa capace delle ragione, e della vita civile" (Marinella 1601, 137).

167. The classic statement of this notion is found in Kelso 1997, 25, 36.

168. Cited in Carpanè 2005, 211: "il tipo del vero cavalier cristiano." A study of the

figure of Judith in seventeenth-century epic by Paola Cosentino is forthcoming in the proceedings of the 2009 conference "Le donne della Bibbia, la Bibbia delle donne," edited by Rosanna Gorris Camos.

169. Grillo 1612b, 552: "Che non hanno fatto le donne per la via dello spirito? Io non leggo lettione, che mi muova più, che quella delle sante donne, che dopo di loro han lasciata la via di seguirle."

170. Crashaw 1972, 334 (no. 183): "Foemina, tam fortis fidei? jam credo fidem esse / plus quam grammaticè foeminei generis." For discussion, see Sabine 1992, 115–16, and 2006, 432.

171. See Dolan 1999.

172. On the French phenomenon, see Cave 1969, 85–87; and Ferguson 1999.

173. On the effects of censorship on Italian literature in this period, see Grendler 1977; and Rozzo 2001.

174. A good recent overview of literary developments in the period 1575–1600, covering much ground omitted from previous literary histories, is now available in Da Pozzo 2007a.

175. G. Fiamma 1575, "Ai lettori." On Fiamma as a spiritual poet, see Ossola 1976, 248–63; Leri 2003; and Zaja 2009, which cites further bibliography in 235n2. For discussion of Fiamma's poetic theory, see Ussia 1999, 15–18; and Zaja 2009, 236–42. On Counter-Reformation sacred poetics more generally, see Ardissino 2009.

176. For Fiamma's use of the language of a return *ad fontes*, see, for example, G. Fiamma 1575, [A6r]: "Ho adunque ritornata, quanto piu altamente ho potuto, la poesia toscana alla religione, alla pietà, alla virtù, e a Dio, per cui fu trovata ne' primi secoli" (with as high an art as I could muster, I have returned Tuscan poetry to religion, to piety, to virtue, and to God, the ends for which poetry was originally invented).

177. On the history of this syncretic view of the ancient vatic tradition, see Falco 2007, 114.

178. G. Fiamma 1575, [A6r]: "ornamenti, figure, tropi, e vagheze."

179. G. Fiamma 1575, [A6r]. On the possible allusion to Bembo in Fiamma's formula of *grave leggiadria*, see Zaja 2009, 241–42.

180. G. Fiamma 1575, [A6r]: "gran fallo e quasi insopportabile." The description of Petrarch as "dux et magister spurcarum libidinum" derives from an anonymous report submitted to the Congregation of the Index during the pontificate of Gregory XIII (1572–85). For discussion, see Cerrón Puga 2003, 250; Avellini 2004, 140–41; and Cecchi 2005, 249.

181. G. Fiamma 1575, [A5r]: "degno di ogni lode, che si possa dare a qual si voglia raro e singolare intelletto."

182. G. Fiamma 1575, [A5v]: "a persone mature può insegnar l'amor platonico e filosofico."

183. See the example discussed in Zaja 2009, 279–82.

184. I borrow the term *poetics of conversion* from the title of Freccero 1986, though the phrase is used there in a very different sense.

185. On the metaphor in Augustine, and on Petrarch's appropriation of it in his Latin writings, see Quillen 1994.

186. Fiamma exaggerates his originality when he states in his preface that "non si trova Poeta, fin'hora in questa lingua, che [habbia] scritto altro, che amori, non solamente vani, e lascivi, ma anco furiosi" (G. Fiamma 1575, [A5v]; no poet in this language has written of anything other than vain and lascivious, not to say insane, love). "Amori furiosi" is of course a reference to Ariosto's immensely popular *Orlando furioso*.

187. Cecchi 2005.

188. G. Fiamma 1575, dedicatory letter: "la prima . . . a scrivere con dignità in rima le cose spirituali." Although this compliment is sometimes presented merely as a gesture toward the dedicatee, Colonna's nephew, Marcantonio Colonna (1535–84) (see, e.g., Ferretti 2005, 174n34), it is equally possible that Marcantonio was chosen as dedicatee in part because of his relationship with Vittoria. On Colonna as a religious poet, see the bibliography cited in Cox 2008, 291nn147, 149, to which may be added Brundin 2008. On Malipiero, see Roche 1989, 91–94; Quondam 1991, 203–62; Forni 2005, 65–69; and Zaja 2009, 237–38.

189. Colonna 1546, 2r–3r.

190. Turchi 1568. On the tradition of psalm translations in the post-Tridentine period, see Leri 2003; Quondam 2005a, 190–92; and Ferretti 2007, 131n59.

191. On Italian religious lyric in this period, see Ussia 1993, 1999; Föcking 1994; Delcorno and Doglio 2005, 2007; Quondam 2005a, 171–78; Ardissino and Selmi 2009, and the bibliography cited in Quondam 2005a, 129n2. Statistics on the print publication of volumes of religious verse in this period are available in Vassalli 1989, 95 (fig. 2).

192. On the structure of verse collections in this period, see Martini 2002.

193. On Grillo as a spiritual poet, see Besomi 1969, 154–85; Raboni 1991; Föcking 1994, esp. 155–250; Bruscagli 2007, 1608–10; Ferretti 2007; Piatti 2007, 94–99; Chiarla 2009; and Morando 2009. On Tasso, see Santarelli 1974; Ardissino 1996, 2003; T. Tasso 2001; Ferretti 2005; Piatti 2007, 78–94; and Piatti 2010. On Marino, see Besomi 1969; Guardiani 1997; and Martini 2003. A sense of the presence of these poets in the early Seicento anthology tradition may be had from the analysis of Pietro Petracci's 1607 anthology *Le muse sacre* in Ussia 1999, 25–46; see esp. the statistical breakdown at 34, which shows Grillo as the dominant figure with 64 poems, followed by Marino with 53, Petracci himself with 30, Tasso with 26, and Fiamma with 23.

194. See Powers 2001.

195. G. Fiamma 1575, [A6r]. The canticle of Miriam is mentioned in Exodus 15:20–21; that of Deborah in Judges 5:1–31; that of Judith in Judith 16:1–27; and that of Mary (the *Magnificat*) in Luke 1:46–55. In addition to David, the supreme exponent of this biblical poetic tradition, Fiamma cites five other male biblical poets—Barak, Ezechiel, Habbakuk, Zacharias, and Simeon.

196. On Moses and Miriam as the earliest poets, see also De Cupiti [c. 1599], 16r (1.55); and Francesco Cirocchi in Verucci 1627, A3v, who cites them as the second

sacred poets after Job. See also Ardissino 2009, 370 and 374, for allusions to Miriam in the poetics of Francesco Patrizi and Tommaso Campanella.

197. See Ossola 1976, 248n28, for Fiamma's comments on Colonna. For his correspondence with Battiferra, see Battiferra 2006, 158, 405.

198. G. Fiamma 1575, 489–98. Fiamma makes the connection with the canticles of Deborah and Judith in his commentary at 490 (gloss on stanza 1); see also 491 (gloss on stanza 3) for Deborah. For poems in the voice of Mary Magdalene and the Virgin Mary, see G. Fiamma 1575, 317, 356, discussed in Zaja 2009, 278–82.

199. Turina 1595, A2r–A3r, and 2005, 153–54. The letter is praised by Cristoforo Bronzini as "one of the noblest and most judicious dedications" he has ever seen (Bronzini 1625, *giornata quarta*, 128; una delle più nobili, e giudiciose dedicatorie, ch'io mi vedessi già mai).

200. Turina 2005, 153: "facilissimo filo di tessitura donnesca . . . semplicissima tela."

201. Turina 2005, 153: "obligo è d'ogni lingua, secondo la sua capacità e misura, di lodare e di magnificare il Signore, né altro parendomi tutto questo universo che un concorso di voci alla lode ordinate del [= dal] divin beneplacito."

202. Turina 2005, 153: "una inchinazione assai forte, alla piacevolezza del verso . . . o amara o insulsa."

203. Turina 2005, 153: "essendo la poesia, a giudicio mio, non tanto in terra nasciuta quanto piovuta dal cielo per beneficio d'Iddio, e perciò dovendosi le sue bellezze addobbare non con meretricii ornamenti, ma con vestimenti pietosi di matronal pudicizia."

204. G. Fiamma 1575, 356–57: "da matrona casta, e non da giovane impudica." For the context, see Zaja 2009, 280–82. Although Fiamma's *Rime spirituali* was technically banned from 1580 for its inclusion of biblical translations (Rozzo 2001, 206; Ferretti 2007, 131n59), it continued to be read and imitated. See ch. 4 at nn. 111–12 and ch. 6 at nn. 73–74 for evidence of the imitation of Pietro Aretino, banned since 1559, by Lucrezia Marinella and Maddalena Campiglia.

205. Tansillo's *Lagrime* was first published in 1560 in a 42-stanza version with a false attribution. The same version appeared in 1571, after the poet's death, under his own name. A 13-canto version was published in 1585; a competing, 15-canto version in 1606. See Toscano 1987; Milburn 2003, 61–63; and Piatti 2007, 62–74.

206. Sannazaro 2009, 2–93; Vida 2009. Both Sannazaro's and Vida's epics were translated into Italian in this period, Vida's by Alessandro Lami (1573), Sannazaro's by numerous poets, including, perhaps most notably, Giovanni Giolito de' Ferrari (1583). See Giolito de' Ferrari and Sannazaro 2001 for a modern edition.

207. Tansillo was described by one sixteenth-century editor, presumably on these grounds, as "the religious Ariosto" (spirituale Ariosto) (see Chiesa 2002, 187). For Tasso's enthusiastic response to the poem, as reported by Giulio Cesare Capaccio (1552–1634), see Serassi 1785, 483 and n. 2.

208. This literature has been relatively little studied until recently, though see

now, for the religious narrative poems of the age, the excellent overview in Doglio 2007a, 1638–48. See also Chiesa 2002; Ardissino 2005; Borsetto 2005; and Quondam 2005a, 196–204. Information on some of the religious narrative poems of this period is available at www.sursum.unito.it/archivi. On the *poema eroico* in this period, see ch. 5, n. 2.

209. For bibliographical details, see Quondam 2005c, 268, 270–71; for critical discussion, Piatti 2007, 94–99. More generally, on *lagrime* poems, see Santarelli 1974, 217–35; Imbriani 2001; T. Tasso 2001; Quondam 2005a, 192–96; Piatti 2007, esp. 59–61; Ferretti 2007, 130–39; Treherne 2007; and Fisher 2007, 186–88.

210. See, most recently, Residori 2004.

211. Valvasone 1590, 2005. For secondary literature, see Provasi 1913; and Borsetto 2005.

212. Valvasone 2005, 72: "le sottili ed oscure dispute de' filosofi."

213. Valvasone 2005, 73: "Sono letti con molto gusto i sonetti, e le canzoni di alcuni valent'huomini della nostra età, che lasciando le amorose inventioni . . . hanno elette materie religiose, e morali."

214. Valvasone 2005, 74: "se non sacra, almen pia."

215. Valvasone 2005, 72–74: "historie religiose cantate leggiadramente in versi . . . le meraviglie de' cavalieri erranti . . . le mirabili opere di Dio, e i meriti de' suoi gloriosi santi."

216. Sometimes this competition takes the form of direct *riscrittura* (see Graziano 1597; and Gallucci 1618).

217. Passero 1589. For a brief discussion of the poem, see Doglio 2007a, 1642, who gives Passero's date of birth as c. 1555.

218. Passero 1589, 2: "sacra historia . . . opre al tutto del mio nome indegne." *Opre* may simply mean "deeds" here but could also be translated as "works," i.e., secular writings.

219. The poem was inspired, along with several other literary works, by the finding and reburial of the bones of Placidus and his companions at Messina in 1588, mentioned in Passero 1589, 34–35.

220. Passero 1589, 1, 4: "saggio guerrier, non men ch'invitto e forte"; "non si potea fra giudicio intero / s'egli era miglior santo o cavaliero."

221. Passero 1589, 4–5: "sceso di vetustissima famiglia . . . ei, che 'l vero honor fin da le fasce / solo stimò."

222. For the ekphrasis, see Passero 1589, 63–66; for the predictive vision, 34–35.

223. Passero 1589, 26. A degree of ambivalence on Passero's part regarding the classicizing quality of this scene may be indicated by the episode immediately following, in which Saint Benedict destroys a temple of Apollo that had previously stood on the mount.

224. For the descriptions of Placido and Flavia, see Passero 1589, 13 and 94.

225. Cf. esp. the lines in Passero 1589, 94 ("due stelle erano gli occhi, anzi due soli"; "gli archi sottili, e neri al mondo soli") with those in Ariosto 1976, 1:129 (7.12):

"Sotto due negri e sottilissimi archi / son duo negri occhi, anzi duo chiari soli"). On similar imitations in religious narrative of the equivalent figure in Tasso's *Gerusalemme liberata*, Armida, see ch. 4, n. 94.

226. Castelletti 1594, "Tavola delle cose notabili," F1r ("destriero vagamente descritto"), F3r ("bellissimi traslati").

227. On the tradition of *tragedia spirituale* in this period, see Clubb 1964; Clubb 1989, 209–25, esp. 213–18; Cascetta 1995; Rizzo 2000; Cosentino 2004, 398–407; Cosentino 2007; and Lasagna 2009. On the parallel Latin tradition of sacred drama sponsored by the Jesuits, see Chiabò and Doglio 1994; Oldani and Yanitelli 1999; and Saulini 2002.

228. Licco 1605; C. Cortesi 1607. For details of the original production of Licco's play, see the dedicatory letter to Donia 1600.

229. Very little work has been done on the *commedia spirituale* to date, though see Eisenbichler 1983 and 2000.

230. Ercolani 1608. The work's interesting dedicatory letter by Ottavio Cinuzzi speaks of Ercolani's intent in his comedies to turn this "pagan genre of poetry to good use, as an exemplary form of diversion" (A2v; provare se questo gentilesco poema potesse rivolgersi in buon'uso ed essemplare ricreatione). No criticism seems to exist on Ercolani's four spiritual comedies, which exist only in a handful of copies. On the author, see Nardi 1984, 104; and Reardon 2002, 244n4.

231. Ercolani 1615, unnumbered: "una commedia parte spirituale e parte temporale"; "huomini troppo amici del mondo"; "persone, che aspirano al Paradiso." The play was first published in 1605.

232. For an interesting reading of the play as self-referentially staging the "redemption of the theatrical profession," see Zampelli 2002.

233. Venturelli's play is structured like a classical drama, in five acts (the author prefers the nonclassical term *parti*), and the majority of the action is located offstage and represented as narration (Weaver 2002, 218–19). For Campiglia's play, see n. 143 above.

234. For religious lyric, see n. 141 above. For narrative and dramatic works, see, e.g., Dell'Uva 1582 (Felice Orsini Colonna); Lanci 1585 (Suor Maria da Magnale of San Giovanni Evangelista di Boldrone, Florence); Brunetti 1586 (Atilia Lanzesa de' Franchia); Lanci 1588 (Vittoria Galli Aurispi); Martinengo 1590 (Leonora d'Austria Gonzaga, Duchess of Mantua [1534–94]); De Cupiti 1593 (Caterina d'Austria, Duchess of Savoy); Castelletti 1594 (Faustina Orsini Maffei [1557–94]); Ciotti 1606, vol. 1 (Suor Perpetua Soranzo of San Lorenzo, Venice) and vol. 2 (Lodovica Bon, abbess of Saints Rocco and Margherita, Venice); Ercolani 1608 (Suor Camilla della Stufa of Sant'Agata, Florence); and Campeggi 1617 (Maria de' Medici, queen of France [1575–1642]).

235. On gender and the role of women in the *Gersusalemme liberata*, see, most recently, Migiel 1993; Benedetti 1996; Zatti 1998, 163–68; Cavallo 1999; Yavneh 1999; Gough 2001; and Güntert 2007.

236. The representation of women in *Aminta* and *Pastor fido* is discussed in

J. Campbell 1997, comparing these with the female-authored pastorals of Isabella Andreini and Mary Wroth. See also, on *Aminta,* ch. 3 at n. 125.

237. Clubb 1989, 65–89.

238. Tortoletti 1628, 234–52; Carpanè 2006, 35. Tortoletti's epic offers interesting evidence of the relatively profeminist cultural attitudes of Rome during the papacy of Urban VIII (Maffeo Barberini [1568–1644]), noted in Cox 2008, 180; see Carpanè 2006, 11, on Tortoletti's Barberini connections. Tortoletti later published a vernacular version of the poem, dedicated to Anne of Austria, queen of France (Tortoletti 1648).

239. Mercurio 1621, 4–5: "Chi non scorge nelle martiri di Santa Chiesa quanto vagliano le donne nelle virtù dell'animo, e del corpo . . . è cieco più, che talpa."

240. Mercurio 1621, 5. Mercurio is careful to stipulate that although the martyrs were sustained by God's grace, this did not lessen their suffering, understood as a "human action" (azione humana), so that direct comparisons with pagan "martyrs" can be made.

241. Ciotti 1606, dedicatory letter to vol. 2, unnumbered: "se si attende con quanta constanza tante Verginelle habbino sparso il sangue per la fede, possono esser con giusta raggione ripresi i calluniatori del sesso feminile." The dedicatee is Lodovica Bon, abbess of the Augustinian convent of Saints Rocco and Margherita in Venice.

242. See ch. 4 at n. 83. On the representation of virgin martyrs in Counter-Reformation literature and drama, see Clubb 1964, esp. 107–12; Harness 2006, 62–99; and Doglio 2007a, 1639–41.

243. Passero 1589, 95.

244. See ch. 5, n. 78.

245. T. Tasso 1980, 47–58 (2.14–53). On the figure of Sofronia as prototypical for later Counter-Reformation representations of the female martyr, see Benedetti 2005, 98–100; Selmi 2005, 454; and Bruscagli 2007, 1604. More generally, on her representation in Tasso, see Yavneh 1999.

246. Passero 1589, 18: "Però d'ogni virtù, che tosto apprese, / o che che trahea da la materna cuna, / d'obedienza più la mente accese, / e sola a questa preferia ciascuna."

247. T. Tasso 1980, 13 (1.1): "Molto egli [sc. Goffredo] oprò . . . molto soffrì"; Gallucci 1618, 1 (1.1): "Molto sostenne . . . molto soffrì."

248. For the distinctions between heroics of action and heroics of endurance, see Rose 2002. The notion of "passion" replacing action as the basis of heroism in religious epic is articulated explicitly in Lodovico Verucci's preface to his 1627 *L'eremita Antonio* (see Selmi 2005, 449). Also interesting in this regard is the *canzone* by Maffio Venier in da Poppi 1606, 18v–21r, contrasting the martial epic hero of antiquity, embodied by Hannibal, with the modern Christian epic hero represented by Saint Francis.

249. De Cupiti [c. 1599]. For discussion, see Quondam 1973, 119–21; and Semola 2006.

250. For examples of poets presenting themselves as converts from a more worldly

early poetic career, see Bruscagli 2007, 1600–1605, to which might be added Passero 1589 and Montefuscoli 1593. An important precedent is the proemial sonnet to Vittoria Colonna's *Rime spirituali* (Colonna 1982, 85 [S1:1]), which De Cupiti imitates closely in the first poem he attributes to the *poeta illuminato* after his conversion (De Cupiti 1592, 78; De Cupiti [c. 1599], 133v, *Poiche sol per pietà senz'alcun merto*).

251. De Cupiti [c. 1599], 8r (1.2). These lines are attributed to an angel sent by God to reproach the poet.

252. See B. Croce 1967, 312–30; Jannaco and Capucci 1966, 162–65; and F. Croce 2002, 35–36.

253. Grillo 1612b, 530; Durante and Martellotti 1989b, 238 ("dove sotto il soave riso di molli versi si beve l'eterno pianto della perpetua dannatione"). Grillo's letters are undated in the printed edition of 1612, but their dates may be broadly ascertained, using Durante and Martellotti's biography, by the author's location at the time of writing.

254. Grillo 1612b, 559: "che [chi] sparge lascivi carmi nelle sue carte, semina semi di morte nell'altrui cuore." The addressee is a "Signor Alessandro," presumably only partially identified because this is a letter of reproach. The date can only be estimated here, since the author's location is not given; however, the letter is flanked on either side by letters from Grillo's last period in San Benedetto di Mantova (1608–11).

255. On "lasciviousness" as a motive for literary censorship in Seicento Italy, see Carminati 2008, 23, 27, 37–38, 47, 89–91, 152, 174, 255–56.

256. See Cox 2005a.

257. Passi 1599, 281: "il silentio e le poche parole è l'ornamento loro" (i.e., "delle donne").

258. Spelta 1607, 32–33; the term *scempiezza* is on p. 31.

259. Boccalini 1910–12, 1:66 (*centuria* 1, *ragguaglio* 22); Cox 2008, 198.

260. Briani 1616, 143 (*ragguaglio* 49): "in una Accademia di tanta stima e valore, ove a gran fatica havevano potuto haver luogo il famoso Ariosto et il gran Torquato Tasso, che un sesso feminile, nato per apprendere il *Priapus*, fosse stato così honorevolmente raccolto." See also Briani 1616, 133 (*ragguaglio* 42), where a group of "honored ladies and matrons" (honorate dame, e matrone) are seen begging the poet Francesco Maria Molza to indulge their taste for priapic writings. For discussion of Briani, see Firpo 1960.

261. Cox 2008, 184–95.

262. Cox 2008, 204–33 and 252–53.

263. On women's engagement with polemic in this period, see Cox 2008, 210–12; and ch. 6 at nn. 24–30.

264. Cox 2008, 183, 191–92.

CHAPTER TWO: Lyric Verse

1. On the female-authored lyric poetry of the mid-sixteenth century, see Cox 2008, 64–75, 80–91, 108–18, and the secondary literature cited there.

2. On the exceptional market conditions pertaining in the 1540s and 1550s in Italy and their implications for women's writing, see Dionisotti 1999, 227–54, esp. 237–39; and Robin 2007.

3. For Andreini's anthology appearances, see her entry in the appendix. The website http://repim.muspe.unibo.it lists musical settings for twenty-six of her poems, of which one has nine settings. Other anthology appearances by women in this period are listed in n. 7 below.

4. Further discussion and exemplification will be offered in an anthology of early modern Italian women's lyric verse that I am currently preparing for publication by the Johns Hopkins University Press.

5. The main collections are L. Strozzi 1588; Salvetti 1590; Matraini 1595/1597; Turina 1595, 1627/1628; I. Andreini 1601, 1605; Marinella 1602; Sbarra 1610; Bragadin 1613, 1614, 1619; Poggi 1623; and Coreglia 1628 (the list does not include I. Andreini 1603, which was published outside Italy). The pamphlet publications are Fonte 1585; Silvia Bendinelli 1587; Campiglia 1589; I. Cervoni 1592, 1597a, 1597b, 1600; I. Andreini [1596?]; and Spolverini 1596.

6. The complete modern editions are Matraini 1989; Campiglia 1996; and Turina 2005. See also I. Andreini 2005 for a partial edition of I. Andreini 1601 and 1605; Turina 2009 for a partial edition of Turina 1595 and 1628; and Kolsky 1999, 13–16, for a reproduction of the texts of Fonte 1585. An edition of Turina 1628, edited by Paolo Bà, is forthcoming in the journal *Letteratura italiana antica*. The only poetic works of this period that have attracted sustained critical attention are L. Strozzi 1588 (on which see Masson 1925a, 1925b; Pierattini 1942, 1943; and Stevenson 2002 and 2005, 297–300); Campiglia 1589 (on which see Perrone 1996; Cox and Sampson 2004, 27–28; and Ultsch 2005a, 87–91); Matraini 1595/1597 (on which see the bibliography cited in Cox 2008, 297n25, to which may be added Matraini 2007); and I. Andreini 1601/1605 (on which see MacNeil 2005; and Giachino 2001). See also n. 21 below for critical studies of Turina 1628.

7. The chief poetic manuscripts by female writers of this period containing lyric verse unpublished during the authors' lifetime are Battiferra, "Rime"; Colao, "Rime"; Turina, "Rime"; Turina, "Poesie"; and Coreglia, "Raccolta di varie composizioni." Anthologies and collections of verse published between 1580 and 1630 in which women appear as authors include Ferro 1581 (Clizia Gabrielli, "Costanza L.," Laura Manfredi, Issicratea Monte, Ginevra Pighini); Segni 1583 (Ottavia Grassi); Maganza, Rava, and Thiene [1583?] (Maddalena Campiglia, Monte); Zucconello 1583 (Moderata Fonte); Gagliardo 1584 (Maria Azzalina, Campiglia, Monte, Bianca Angaran [Bianca Nievo]); *Compositioni* 1585 ("Signora S.R."); *Rime* 1585 (Elisabetta Aiutamicristo, Tarquinia Molza, "Virginia N."); *Carmina* 1586 (Moderata Fonte, Silvia Ronchi); *Rime* 1586a (Vittoria Colonna, Tullia d'Aragona, Veronica Gambara); *Rime* 1586b (Lucia Salviani); Montanaro 1587 (Fabrizia Carrari); *Rime* 1587a (Isabella Andreini, Orsina Cavaletti, Isabella Andreini); *Rime* 1587b (Cavaletti); Rossi 1587 (Campiglia); *Rime* 1588 (Margherita Marescotti); Caporali 1589 (Andreini, Fonte); *Mausoleo* 1589 (Andreini, Campiglia, Margherita Sarrocchi, Livia Spinola); *Raccolta* 1589 (Antonia

Doni); *Rime* 1589 (Silvia Bendinelli); Ducchi 1589 (Bendinelli, Campiglia); *Poesie* 1590 (Fabrizia Viviani [Fabrizia Carrari], Innocenza Carrari, Marina dalla Torre); *Rime* 1590 (Lucella di Zucco); *Poesie* 1591 (Innocenza Carrari); *Scelta* 1591 (Leonora Bernardi, Maria de' Ferrari, Livia Spinola); *Tempio* 1591 (Doni); Guazzo 1595 (Bendinelli, Elena Stanchi, Laura Beatrice Cappello, Marescotti, Molza, Fulvia Spannocchi, Spinola); *Nuova scielta* 1592, revised edition of *Rime* 1587a (Andreini, Cavaletti); *Poesie* 1596 (Marescotti, A.P. [probably Agnese Piccolomini], Spannocchi); *Rime* 1596 (Ersilia Spolverini); *Varie compositioni* 1596 (Spolverini); Bratteolo 1597 (Catella Marchesi); Caraffa 1598 (Andreini, Cavaletti); *Poesie* 1598 (Marchesi); *Tromba* 1598 (Fabrizia Carrari); *Oratione* 1599 (Isabella Cervoni); *Lagrime* 1599 (Marchesi); Segni 1600 (Andreini, Molza, Febronia Pannolini, Maddalena Salvetti, Francesca Turina); Bratteolo 1601 (di Zucco); Segni 1601 (Chiara Matraini, Molza, Pannolini); Petracci 1608 (Andreini); *Polinnia* 1609 (Valeria Miani); C. Fiamma 1611 (Andreini, Cavaletti, Miani); Costantini 1611 (Andreini); Scaioli 1611 (Minerva Bartoli, Matraini, Vittoria Talea); Antonazzoni 1613 ("Suor Damiana," incerta); *Choro delle Muse* 1613 (Zanetta dalla Torre); C. Fiamma 1613 (Lucrezia Marinella); Sanudo 1613 (Ginevra Albiosi, Ippolita Benigni, Geronima Castagna, Lisabetta Della Valle, Stratonica Fabra, Cherubina Ferro, Laura Grossi, Marescotti, Marinella, Miani, Molza, Turina); *Giustiniano* 1614 (Livia Reganela); Sabbadini 1615 (Lucchesia Sbarra); Franciotti 1616, 239–94 (Bernardi); Petrelli 1616a (Marinella); *Corona* 1621 (Maria Malloni); Rosini 1621a (Colonna, Gambara); Rosini 1621b, derivative of Sanudo 1613 (Castagna, Della Valle, Fabra, Ferro, Marinella, Molza); and Guaccimani 1623 (Barbara Cavaletti, Orsina Cavaletti, Turina). See also Ussia 1999, 30, on Pietro Petracci's *La celeste lira*, of 1612, which contains three sonnets by Vittoria Colonna; Verdile 1989–90, 176, on Margherita Sarrocchi's appearance in a 1612 anthology on the death of Margaret of Austria; and ch. 1, n. 84, and below in this chapter at n. 113 for manuscript collections featuring verse by Lucrezia Marinella. The list above corrects Cox 2008, 144 and 329n59, on *Poesie* 1590 and Ferro 1581, respectively.

8. For an overview, excluding Tasso, see Bruscagli 2007. On Tasso's verse, see Da Pozzo 2007b, 1894–1900, citing further bibliography.

9. On this development, see Martini 1981; Vassalli 1988, 227–29, and 1989, 96–97; Raboni 1991, 138–46; Martini 1994; Ritrovato 2004, 122–36; and Bruscagli 2007, 1580–86.

10. Martini 2002; Bruscagli 2007, 1564–80.

11. See ch. 1, nn. 175 and 193, for secondary literature.

12. For secondary literature on Grillo as a religious poet, see ch. 1, n. 193.

13. For discussion and further exemplification, see Bruscagli 2007, 1577–78, 1614–15; and Arrullani 1911. On Giustinian, see Mammana 2001.

14. Bruscagli 2007, 1586–88.

15. Massini 1609, †3v–†4r: "sonettoni . . . a guisa di Pitonesse . . . parole sonanti . . . translationi smoderate . . . sensi così oscuri, che noi stessi non gl'intendiamo." For comment, see Volpi 2005, 39. The bibliography on the baroque trend in

poetry and poetics is immense. A recent collection of essays, useful for orientation, is F. Croce et al. 2002. On Marino, see Fulco 1997, citing earlier bibliography.

16. On the latter tendency, see, most recently and most comprehensively, Bettella 2005, 128–70.

17. Terracina 1548, 33r–46v; Stampa 2010, 252–54 (no. 220, *Di chi ti lagni, o mio diletto e fido*).

18. For Turina, see Turina 1628, 77–78, 130–64, 168–80, and 2005, 211–20; and, for selections from both works, Turina 2009, 72–132. For Della Valle, see Spiriti 1750, 103n1, where the interesting proemial sonnet of the sequence is transcribed. Another female poet of this period who seems to have written on erotic themes is Barbara Lotti (see *Rime* 1723, 234–35, for some fragments, which do not, however, make the gender of the poetic voice clear). See also below at n. 58 on Lucia Colao.

19. Durante and Martellotti 1989b; Raboni 1991; Ferretti 2007, esp. 110–20.

20. Salvetti 1590.

21. Sbarra 1610, A1r–B2v; Turina 1628, 67–81, 117–230; Turina 2009. For discussion of Turina's autobiographical verse, see Bà 2001, 2007, and 2009, 90–100; and Costa-Zalessow 2009.

22. Cox 2008, 208–10. The quotation—"Il candore, e la chiarezza dello stile del Petrarca"—is from Francesco Visdomini, cited above in n. 15.

23. Sbarra 1610, C7v, C8v–D3r, declares her discipleship to Marino in a sequence of laudatory poems addressed to him. Marino's *Rime* was published in Venice in 1602, the year before Marinella's *Rime sacre*.

24. In total, besides sonnets and madrigals, I. Andreini 1601 contains 10 *canzonette morali*, 9 *scherzi*, 9 eclogues, 6 *canzoni*, 4 blank-verse *rime funerali*, 3 *capitoli*, 2 *sestine*, 2 *epithalamia*, and 2 *centoni*. The metrical diversity of the volume is emphasized by the index, which groups the poems by metrical form.

25. Bruscagli 2007, 1595. On Andreini's poetic relations with Chiabrera, see MacNeil 2005, 4–5.

26. Matraini 1590, 1602. Matraini 1590 is especially noteworthy in this respect, containing 6 sonnets and 13 madrigals, excluding paratexts. By contrast, Matraini 1581 contains only sonnets and a *canzone*, and Matraini 1586 contains only sonnets. Matraini 1595/1597 also keeps faith with Petrarchan metrical norms.

27. Battiferra 2006, 244 (rhymed on *cielo* and *terra*). The other poem is Battiferra, "Rime," 60r, no. 90 (rhymed on *Dio* and *uomo*). For Colao, see Colao, "Rime," 48v. See also *Rime* 1596, aa4r, for a sonnet by "A.P." (probably Agnese Piccolomini), using only four rhyme words *(riso, pianto, cielo, terra)*. The more complex form, involving the recurrence of both rhyme words in each line, appears to have been invented by the Neapolitan poet Ferrante Carafa (1509–87) (see Carafa 1573, 164). Besides in Carafa, on whom see Gigante 2007, 35, 42, 46–47, *sonetti continui* are found principally in the verse of Venetian poets such as Domenico Venier and Gabriele Fiamma (Zaja 2009, 275n83). See also, from the mainland Veneto, Menichini 1597, 152v–155r.

28. Marinella 1693; L. Strozzi 1601; Poggi 1623. The only other published Latin

writings by Italian women in this period that I have come across are short poems by Febronia Pannolini and Tarquinia Molza, in Segni 1600 and 1601, and a longer one by Ersilia Spolverini, published in Spolverini 1596 and *Varie compositioni* 1596. For two unpublished Latin letters by Margherita Sarrocchi, see Verdile 1989–90, 186–88.

29. Turina 1595, 149–72, and 2005, 211–20. Further religious verse by Turina may be found in Turina 1628, 222–308; and Turina, "Poesie," 287–90, 311r–336v.

30. Religious lyrics by Campiglia are found in Campiglia 1585, N2v–N3v; Zarrabini et al. 1586, i2v–i3v; and Morsolin 1882, 63. For Spinola and Bernardi, see *Scelta* 1591, 34, 50–53. Bernardi is discussed below in the text. For Bragadin, see Bragadin 1614, 38–49; for Andreini, I. Andreini 1601, 208–14 (and for a selection, I. Andreini 2005, 140–47); and for Salvetti, Salvetti 1611, 53r–66r. Battiferra's late religious verse is found in the second half of Battiferra, "Rime," partially published in Battiferra 2006; Coreglia's, in Coreglia 1628 and Coreglia, "Raccolta di varie composizioni"; Colao's, in Colao, "Rime"; and Vernazza's, in Vernazza 1588, 1602 (esp. 19–39), and 1819.

31. Sbarra 1610, B4r–C5r; *Rime* 1587a, 211, 214. For other poems in this genre, see Salvetti 1611, 66r (misnumbered 56r); and Battiferra 2006, 232. Bronzini 1625, *giornata quarta*, 122, mentions unpublished early spiritual works by Cervoni.

32. For the statement that Colonna was "dimenticata" by the end of the sixteenth century, see Quondam 2005a, 177.

33. Colonna 1586; Patti 2002; Trinchieri Camiz 2003. Verse by Colonna also appeared in three poetic anthologies of this period: *Rime* 1586b; Petracci 1612 (see Ussia 1999, 30); and Rosini 1621a. Colonna's presence in *Rime* 1586b is considerably expanded with regard to the anthology's first publication in 1556 (as *Rime di diversi ed eccellenti autori*): while the 1556 edition contains only three of her poems, the 1586 edition has nineteen.

34. T. Tasso 1997, 69; G. Fiamma 1575, dedicatory letter; De Cupiti [c. 1599], 21r–v; Ancina 1599, c3r (also d1r).

35. Ancina 1599, c2v–c3r. See also Aurelio Alconi's preface to Bruni 1615, where Colonna is listed in the still more select company of Virgil, Ovid, Dante, Petrarch, Casa, and Bembo. For a tribute to Colonna by the Sicilian poet Tomaso Costo, see Cox 2008, 291n150; for tributes from Maddalena Campiglia and Francesca Turina, see ch. 1 at nn. 9–10 and 13.

36. Della Chiesa 1620, 298: "E dirò una cosa mirabile in questo luogo, che forse non si trova in lingua Toscana compositione d'huomo alcuno, che gli sia superiore in grandezza e bellezza di pronti concetti."

37. Colonna 1982, 85 (S1:1). For imitations of these lines by late sixteenth-century religious poets, see, e.g., Grillo 1589, 5v; and De Cupiti 1592, 78.

38. Grillo 1596, 45.

39. Grillo 1608b. For further poems in the voice of the Virgin, see G. Fiamma 1575, 356, 358; Grillo 1596, 135–38; and Marino 1602b, 164–78. For poems in the voice of Mary Magdalene, see G. Fiamma 1575, 317, 320; Grillo 1596, 28–29; and Marino 1602b, 179–85.

40. Marinella 1643, 495–96, 503–5, 509–12, 516–18, 522–25, 528–59, 534–35. The psalm versions are attributed in the text to Saint Francis, who sings them to the music of an angel in a vision.

41. Segni 1601. The letter soliciting Marinella to contribute to the new project, from the Bolognese academic Ascanio Persio (1554–1610), is in the Biblioteca Marciana, Venice (see Kolsky 2005, 326–27; and Haskins 2007, 203n2). The proposed volume was to comprise a reprint of Segni's 1601 anthology, along with a new history of the icon by Persio and additional verse from "Marino and others" (Kolsky 2005, 327n5; con rime del Marini e con altri versi).

42. Marinella 1693, 7–11. The sonnets are also published in [Persio] 1603, 81–88, the only published outcome of Persio's project.

43. Two copies of Marinella 1603, in Rome and Bologna, are listed on the Italian national online catalog (ICCU), and one, at Monash University, Melbourne, Australia, is listed on Worldcat. The dedicatory letter (to Eugenia Ceruti Scaini) is signed by Ascanio Collosini, presumably a relative of the publisher, Giovanni Battista Collosini.

44. C. Fiamma 1613, 91, 104, 166–67, 218, 295; Petrelli 1616a, 266; Marinella 1605b.

45. Baffetti 2007, 192–93.

46. Erythraeus 1645–48, 1:249–50. Almost half of Strozzi's hymns, forty-nine, are in Sapphic verse. Strozzi mentions Sappho's invention of the form in her dedicatory letter (L. Strozzi 1601, a3r), describing her as "a most learned woman" (doctissima foemina). For an earlier instance of the use of Sapphic meter by a female Italian writer, this time in a vernacular, rhymed adaptation, see Stampa 2010, 252–54 (no. 220, numbered 297 in twentieth-century editions of Stampa's verse). On Strozzi's imitation of Horace in the *Hymni*, see Pierattini 1942, 1943.

47. Masson 1925b, 61. Strozzi uses six meters for her hymns: Sapphic adonic, iambic dimeter, trochaic tetrameter catalectic, asclepiadic glyconic, iambic trimeter, and trochaic dimeter brachycatalectic. For descriptions of these meters, standard in the hymns of the Dominican liturgy, see P. Smith 2008, 14–19. For Strozzi's own metrical descriptions, see L. Strozzi 1601, 1, 4, 11, 29, 33, 38; and Masson 1925b, 59–61.

48. L. Strozzi 1601, 37–38 (Antonino), 46 (Zenobius), 70–71 (Dominic), 93–94 (Reparata), 108–9 (Nicholas). Strozzi also customizes her hymn collection at a more personal level, including acrostics in two hymns to her name saints, Lawrence and Francis (her secular given name was Francesca) (see L. Strozzi 1601, 72–74, 92–93).

49. On the *Vita*, see Masson 1925a, 9–10 and 10n1, summarizing details found in secondary sources. There is a copy of the work in the Bibliothèque Nationale, Paris, without indication of authorship.

50. Masson 1925b, esp. 64–65. See also Masson 1925a, 7–10, on Strozzi's literary *fortuna* in seventeenth-century France.

51. Battiferra, "Rime"; Colao, "Rime." See Battiferra 2006, 70n2, for a full description of the Casanatense manuscript. For a description of the Treviso manuscript, see Biblioteca Comunale di Treviso 2000, 152–56.

52. The "Rime spirituali" section is at Battiferra, "Rime," 43r–70r; see also Battiferra 2006, 220–65, for selections.

53. Kirkham 2006, 31. Battiferra's sonnet exchange with the Neapolitan religious poet Agostino De Cupiti (Battiferra 2006, 84, 368n16) probably also dates from these years. De Cupiti (1550–1618) was in Florence in the 1580s in the service of Francesco de' Medici and was admitted to the Accademia Fiorentina in 1586.

54. Bergalli 1726, 2:283–84. Bergalli notes that the manuscript was in the possession of the Amalteo family of Oderzo, near Treviso, at the time of publication of her anthology.

55. Bergalli 1726, 2:284.

56. Selva is also said to have composed a lost spiritualization of Bembo's *rime*. On the tradition, which also embraced Ariosto, see Wardropper 1958, 255–77; Cecchi 2005, 252–53; and the literature on Malipiero cited in ch. 1, n. 188. For a female-voiced (though male-authored) moral *riscrittura* of Petrarch, see Arbizzoni 1987.

57. Colao, "Rime," 49r and *carte allegate*, 1r. Bergalli 1726, 2:3, has a revised version of the latter sonnet.

58. See, e.g., Colao, "Rime," 48r–v and *carte allegate*, 8v, 10r–11v; and Bergalli 1726, 2:16.

59. On Battiferra's debt to Colonna in her religious verse, see Brundin 2008, 184–85; for local examples of influence, see Battiferra 2006, 405n163, 430n293.

60. See, e.g., Battiferra, "Rime," 52v (no. 55, *Questo tanto gelato horrido verno*), 55v (no. 73, *Qual hor ch'io miro il gran figliuol di Dio*).

61. See esp. Turina 1628, 258, and 2009, 196 (no. 139, *Sopra un testo di morte*); and Turina 1628, 242, and 2009, 192 (no. 134, *Sopra la caduta d'un dente*). For Battiferra, see *Questo tanto gelato horrido verno*, cited in the previous note.

62. Battiferra, "Rime," 56r (no. 76). The *Vorrei* incipit, also used by Battiferra in her sonnet *Vorrei teco, Gesù, pendere in croce* (Battiferra 2006, 236), is particularly characteristic of Colonna (see Colonna 1982, 99, S1:28, *Vorrei l'orecchia aver qui chiusa e sorda*, and S1:29, *Vorrei che sempre un grido alto e possente*; and 111, S1:53, *Vorrei che 'l vero Sol, cui sempre invoco*).

63. Turina 1628, 235.

64. Battiferra 2006, 220, 226; for commentary, see 426n266, 427n271.

65. See, e.g., I. Andreini 1601, 213, and 2005, 146. For Colao, see, e.g., Colao, "Rime," *carte allegate*, 10r–11v.

66. Poggi 1623, 57: "stimai carcere il chiostro . . . consumai vaneggiando i mesi e gli anni." The sonnet is reproduced in Graziosi 1996, 322.

67. Poggi 1623, 61.

68. Poggi 1623, 61: "Doppo [sic] il lungo invernar nel forte infido / fra periglio ed error, ch'io fei davanti."

69. Poggi 1623, 61: "Mentre udite intonar sacrati canti / de' bellici strumenti ecco lo strido."

70. Poggi 1623, 57: "dissi / quei sol concenti miei, ch'eran'affanni / mentre invocava abissi incontr'abissi, / voce di cataratte, horrori, e danni" (I spoke only verses

of misery, while a voice of cataracts, horrors, and doom invoked abysses against abysses).

71. Poggi 1623, 57: "sincera, e bianca."

72. See Grillo 1592b, 186v: "siami Parnaso / hoggi il Calvario"; see also the prefatory note to the 1629 edition of Grillo's *Pietosi affetti*, cited in Ferretti 2007, 109. On the tradition of Christocentric lyric in this period in general, see Ussia 1999, 47–55.

73. For the texts, see T. Tasso 2001, 13–16; and Grillo 1592b. For discussion of Tasso's *canzone*, see Ferretti 2005. For Grillo's *capitolo*, see Ferretti 2005, 176; and 2007, 112, 124, 128–29. On the relationship between meditative literature and devotional poetry in post-Tridentine Italy, see Föcking 1994, 171–99 (on Grillo's *Pietosi affetti*); Mongini 1997, 363–75 (on Marinella's *Vita del serafico e glorioso San Francesco*); Ardissino 2003, 110–13 (on Tasso's *Rime sacre*); and Fisher 2007, 172–80 (on Tansillo's *Lagrime di San Pietro* and Orlando di Lasso's 1594 madrigal settings from it). See also, for comparative material, Cave 1969, 24–93.

74. Fonte 1582, 51: "E 'l giogo altier d' una tremenda Croce, / ch' altrui dà spirto, e voce / fia 'l mio Parnaso, ove altra fonte scorre / da le sacrate vene. / Fian gli angeli pij le mie Camene" (Let the high yoke of a tremendous Cross that gives us breath and voice be my Parnassus, where a different fount flows from the sacred veins. Let the holy angels be my Muses). *Fonte* here may play on Fonte's pseudonym, though it also recalls the "lucido fonte" of Colonna's first spiritual sonnet (Colonna 1982, 85 [S1:1]).

75. Fonte 1582, 54: "limbo de' pensieri indegni."

76. For wordplay, see, e.g., the close of stanza 6 (Fonte 1582, 53): "E, perché 'l morto viva, / more il principio onde la vita è viva" (And, that the dead may live, the source must die through whom life lives). Fonte expresses admiration for Venier in both *Il Floridoro* and *Il merito delle donne* (see Fonte 1997, 217, and 2006, 283 [10.22–23]). A sonnet from her addressed to him survives in manuscript (see her entry in the appendix).

77. Battiferra's husband was in contact with Michelangelo, and there is evidence that he sent him examples of Battiferra's own early spiritual verse in 1561 (Kirkham 2002, 526). For the theme of Christ's passion in Michelangelo and Colonna, see Cambon 1985, 117–36; D'Elia 2006; Rabitti 2006, 486–87; and Brundin 2008, 86–89.

78. Battiferra 2006, 230: "m'impiagan tutta queste piaghe sante, / questa corona mi trafigge e punge, / e teco ogn'or m'inchiodan questi chiodi."

79. Battiferra 2006, 230: "questo ferro . . . / . . . // trapassa tanto il mio [core] dentro e di fuore / che per dolcezza manco a dramma a dramma"; "possente Amor, ch'al sempiterno Amante / l'anime lega con sì stretti nodi." For the *dramma-fiamma* rhyme, see Alighieri 1994, 3:518 (*Purg.* 30.44–48). Battiferra borrows a further, rich rhyme in the quatrains—*fiamma* and *infiamma*—from Petrarch (Petrarca 1996a, 1081 [no. 270, lines 17–18]).

80. Turina 1628, 254: "E tù lancia crudel, ch'al mio Signore / passasti il sen, ferite hoggi il mio core."

81. For Colonna's poems to the Virgin, see Russell 2000; Brundin 2001; and Brundin 2008, 109–14, 116–20. For Carafa's, see Gigante 2007, 35–51. For an over-

view of the place of Marian verse within the tradition of devotional lyric in this period, see Ussia 1999, 55–64.

82. Corbellini 1598; Ancina 1599. Other Marian collections by single poets down to 1600 are listed in Quondam 2005a, 206–7. See also the anthologies of Marian verse in C. Fiamma 1613 and Petrelli 1616a. On Tasso's verse to the Virgin, and particularly his important *canzone* to the Virgin of Loreto, see Santarelli 1974, 257–93.

83. Martinengo 1595; Campeggi 1617; Marinella 1602. Campeggi's cantos are labeled *pianti* (weepings). Marinella's poem (which was expanded to seven cantos in its 1617 edition), is discussed in chapter 4. Sannazaro's earlier Marian epic, *De partu virginis*, was also published frequently in the period, in Latin and in the vernacular. For one translation, see Giolito de' Ferrari and Sannazaro 2001.

84. Carafa 1573, 116v *(Chi lontan da Maria vedrà mai Cristo?)*, 119r *(Se trà Cristo, e Maria vivo, chi fia [?])*. The second sonnet rhymes on *Cristo* or *Maria* in all but the first line.

85. Vernazza 1819, 1; Turina 1628, 266: "per la sua destra eletta."

86. Matraini 1590, 3, 12, 15–16, 21–22, 31–32, 36, 41–2, 45, 50, 54–55, 58–59, 61, 63–64, 67–68, 76–77, 79–80, 83 (misnuumbered 93). See also Matraini 1989, 307–8, 193–95 (for poems first published in Matraini 1595/1597); Segni 1601, 24; and Matraini 1602, 20–24, 59–60, 108–12. For an earlier Marian sonnet by Matraini (1555), see also Matraini 1989, 788–89, and Matraini 2007, 96–98. Carinci 2009, 93–95, briefly discusses the verse in Matraini 1590.

87. Segni 1601, 23–26 (misnumbered 24); Della Chiesa 1620, 128.

88. For Marinella, see Marinella 1693, 6–8, 10, 23–24; for Bragadin, see Bragadin 1614, 38–39, 44–45, 49; for Turina, see Turina 1628, 266–69, 273, and Turina, "Poesie," 293, 321, 322v, 328v–330r, 332v–333r, 335r–336r, 340; for Battiferra, see Battiferra, "Rime," 47v (no. 38), 52r (nos. 53–54), 56v (no. 78, also in Battiferra 2006, 240), 57v (no. 82), 58v (no. 84); and for Colao, see Colao, "Rime," 17v–19r, 49r, 50v–52r (earlier version at 3r–4r). See also Graziosi 1996, 323, for a manuscript of Marian verse by an anonymous Genoese nun dating from c. 1630.

89. Grillo ends his sonnet to Bernardi *(E sì chiare, e sì belle, e sì devote)* by having the Virgin pronounce "Ah, da mie lodi impura / lingua fia lunga, e tu mia Musa sia" (Grillo 1589, 26r; Let every impure tongue remain remote from my praises, and let you be my Muse). The poem that elicited this tribute is discussed below. For the other poets mentioned, see *Scelta* 1591, 34 (for Spinola); Poggi 1623, 58; and Malvasia 1617, Cc1r–Cc2v.

90. An influential statement of this view is Warner 1976, from whose title the phrase in quotation marks is taken. On the theological notion of Mary as "second Eve" and its implications for gender thinking, see Pelikan 1996, 42–45.

91. Capece 1595, pt. 2, p. 6: "felice il sesso feminile per haver nel loro sesso una tal Imperatrice del Cielo, e della Terra."

92. See ch. 6 at n. 107.

93. Turina, "Poesie," 293 *(Il sesso femminile narra le sue prerogative e possanza— Sonetto per l'anunciatione della beatissima Vergine)*.

94. Turina, "Poesie," 293: "Io non da vil fango hebbi i natali / ma quando l'huomo assomigliossi a Dio / trassi dal gran conforto il viver mio / e spirai dal perfetto aure vitali" (I did not have my origins in base mud, but when man took on God's form, I drew my life from this great consolation and breathed the breath of life from this perfection). For the relevant argument in Agrippa, see Agrippa 1996, 50.

95. Turina, "Poesie," 293: "Morte già m'appressò l'arco e gli strali / quando uccidere il mondo hebbi in desio / e s'al huom chiusi il Ciel anco poss'io / spalancarli [i.e., "gli"] lassù gl'archi fatali" (Death proffered me the bow and the arrows when I wished to slay the world, [but] if I closed Heaven to man, I can also open those fatal arches on high). The compensatory relationship between Eve and Mary is also alluded to in two madrigals in Turina 1628, 268–69. See also Fonte 1997, 94 and n. 60.

96. Turina, "Poesie," 293: "Dall'Olimpo stellato al [sic] ime arene / piombando a volo . . . / Angiol sublime ad annunciar lo viene."

97. Turina, "Poesie," 293: "Chi crea l'impone, e chi redime il vuole; / Chi procede il consente, e quindi avviene / che dal mar di Maria sorge il mio sole."

98. *Scelta* 1591, 90–93; Franciotti 1616, 291–94; Lucchesini 1825–31, 9:169n7.

99. For Judith as "another Mary" (altra Maria), see Carpanè 2006, 9–65; and Ciletti 2010, esp. 355–67. For Esther as typological anticipation of the Virgin, see Baskins 1993, esp. 40.

100. Franciotti 1616, 292. Bernardi's description of Tuccia draws closely on that of Petrarch in his *Triumph of Chastity* (Petrarca 1996b, 254 [lines 148–51]).

101. For an example of this type of analysis applied to biblical heroines, see G. Fiamma 1575, 493–96.

102. Paoli 2003. See, as an example of literature directly relating to the 1588 miracle, Scipione Bendinelli 1588, which contains a contribution by a third female Lucchese poet of the period, Silvia Bendinelli (Scipione Bendinelli 1588, A4r).

103. See Paoli 2003, 544–45.

104. Marinella 2008, 122.

105. On Venice's traditional figuration as a "virgin city" in this sense, see Sperling 1999, 82–83.

106. Marinella published two lives of Francis (Marinella 1597 and 1643), and the *Rime sacre* contain poems to Francis himself; to his biographer, Saint Bonadventure; and to the Franciscan Capuchin order (Marinella 1693, 17, 19, 26). On Titian's altarpiece and its context, see Goffen 1986, esp. 138–54.

107. Marinella 1693, 6. The poem is anthologized in C. Fiamma 1613, 218; and Petrelli 1616a, 266. It is also present in the selection of Marinella's spiritual verse in Marinella 1606a.

108. Marinella 2011, 381, 383, and 2009, 281, 283 (16.83, 92): "il sen fecondo / figliando resti ognor vergin pudica"; "gravoso pondo / del l'Italia lo scettro, anzi del mondo."

109. Marinella 1693, 11–16, 25, 27–28, 30. Marinella's male saints, in order of appearance, are Stephen, Bonadventure, John the Baptist, Nicholas of Tolentino, Francis, Jerome, and Mark.

110. Petrelli 1616b. Petrelli coincides with Marinella on 4 of the female saints (Mary Magdalene, Lucy, and the two Catherines); the others he includes are Marcella, Candida, and Clare. Petrelli's choices are heavily dependent on Petracci 1608, which includes poems to the same 7 female saints, along with 16 male saints.

111. For Colonna, see Colonna 1982, 143–47 (S1:116–24); for Strozzi, Masson 1925a, 11–13, which gives a convenient index of Strozzi's titles. Colonna 1982, 192 (S2:30), is not counted here, as it is outside the main printed tradition of her verse. Baldi 1589a, like Strozzi's a liturgical-year collection, has 10 female saints to 70 male saints.

112. Turina, "Poesie," 341–55. The poems are part of a sequence apparently prepared for presentation to Cardinal Francesco Barberini.

113. "Poesie dedicate," 21r–22v. Beatrice d'Este retreated to a hermitage near Padua at the end of her life and hence enjoyed a special cult in the city.

114. Several of Marinella's poems in the *Rime sacre* take a formally ekphrastic form, being presented as descriptions of paintings. See, e.g., Marinella 1693, 7 *(Sopra un ritratto della madre di Christo pallido e lagrimoso)*, 15 *(Sopra il ritratto di Santa Maddalena, la quale piangendo par che miri il crocefisso)*, 27 *(Sopra un ritratto di S[anta] Caterina figliuola del Re Costo)*, and 28 *(Sopra una pittura di Santa Eufemia)*. On the vogue for this kind of ekphrastic lyric in this period, see Ussia 1993, 45; Treherne 2007; and Morando 2009. Other female-authored examples include *Scelta* 1591, 34 (Livia Spinola); and Salvetti 1611, 61r, 63r.

115. Marinella 1693, 12: "Candida rosa o bianco avorio eletto / di vivo asperso, e cristallino humore"; "Nel candor di tua neve e latte puro, / vermiglie rose e sanguignose stelle." The quotations are from two successive sonnets.

116. Marinella 1693, 14: "lucida perla," "candido giglio," "meraviglioso sol"; "Poesie dedicate," 21v: "altera rosa, / che a' primi rai del sol vaga, e pomposa / S'imperla, e indora."

117. Marinella 1693, 6: "Simil è a lei ne' più sereni albori, / Ch'esce ridente da l'aurato tetto / vermiglia aurora, e sparge con diletto, / e dal seno, e dal crin nettare e fiori."

118. Marinella 1693, 23: "Bella madre d'Amore."

119. Marinella 1601, 9–24, esp. 13–24; Marinella 1999, 52–68, esp. 57–68. See ch. 6, sec. 4, for discussion of the treatise.

120. Colonna 1982, 146 (S1:122); see also 192 (S2:30) for a sonnet to Saint Ursula from outside the main print tradition of her *Rime spirituali*. For other examples of female-authored verse on female martyrs, see Battiferra, "Rime," 61r (no. 93) (on Saint Christina); and Bragadin 1614, 47 (on Saints Catherine of Alexandria and Dorothy).

121. Turina's female saints are Judith, Mary Magdalene, Catherine of Alexandria, Theresa, Francesca Romana, and Lucy. The interest in intellectual and spiritual leadership apparent in her choice of Catherine, Theresa, and Francesca Romana is also reflected in Turina's choice of male saints, which include Augustine, Dominic, Francis, Charles Borromeo, Ignatius Loyola, Francis Xavier, and Filippo Neri.

122. Marinella 1693, 28: "O fortezza invincibile, e divina." On Marinella's treatment of the theme of female martyrdom in her narrative poem *La Colomba sacra*, see ch. 4, sec. 3.

123. Marinella 1693, 13: "Ardi in gel d'honestate, ardi d'amore."

124. Marinella 1693, 13: "porge a' sensi mesti / liete dolcezze di celeste ardore. / Con le tue fiamme sante il Cielo accendi, / che t'accende, e t'infiamma, e ardi, / arde egli, tu de' folgori soi, ei del tuo foco."

125. Marinella 1693, 28.

126. Marinella 1693, 28: "bianco latte."

127. Marinella 1693, 15: "vivi soli"; "d'alabastro i membri."

128. See ch. 4 at nn. 25–32.

129. Marinella 1693, 16: "Il crin d'oro ondeggiante a l'aura ha sciolto / la bella Maddalena . . . e 'n vestir schietto / odia sè, stratia i crin, percuote il petto." The references in the incipit are to Bembo's sonnet 5, *Crin d'oro crespo e d'ambra tersa e pura* (Bembo 1960, 510–11), and Petrarch's sonnet 90, *Erano i capei d'or a l'aura sparsi* (Petrarca 1996a, 441).

130. Marinella 1693, 25: "nido si fe' d'infernai mostri"; "la beltà pur don del Cielo." Cf. 16 for a sonnet speaking of Magdalene's "beauties dear to Christ" (bellezze a CHRISTO care).

131. On the presence of Mary Magdalene within Counter-Reformation culture in general, see B. Croce 2003, 197–206; Fabrizio-Costa 1986, 176–79; Haskins 1993, 251–76; Ussia 1993, 107–39; and Harness 2006, 55–61. On her place in devotional lyric, see Ussia 1988; and Ussia 1999, 72–73. See also, on Marino, Guardiani 1997, 348–52; and Martini 2003, 187–88.

132. For a more detailed breakdown of subthemes associated with Mary Magdalene in devotional lyric, see Ussia 1988, 400–402.

133. Colonna 1982, 145, 162 (S1:121, 155). The phrase quoted in the text, from sonnet 121 ("ond'io mi specchio e tergo") echoes Petrarch, who uses it to describe the poet's relationship with Laura in sonnet 146 (Petrarca 1996a, 701).

134. Zarrabini et al. 1586, i2v–i3r: "un'altra Maddalena."

135. Zarrabini et al. 1586, i3v *(Donna fedel, ch'un chiuso, amaro pianto)*; Morsolin 1882, 63 *(Ecco la Maddalena ai piedi santi)*; Campiglia 1585, M4r ("Sembrate vera MADDALENA in vero").

136. For Campiglia's phrase, see Zarrabini et al. 1586, i3r ("specchio d'alma penitenza").

137. In addition to the poems discussed here, see Battiferra 2006, 238 *(Son questi i pie, o Signor mio, che tanto[?])*. For a male-authored example, see the five-madrigal sequence on the subject in Marino 1602b, 182–84.

138. Morsolin 1882, 63 (lines 7–9).

139. The characterization of this overrunning of the boundary between octave and sestet as an "error," though perhaps an allowable one ("error comportabile"), is Campiglia's own (Campiglia to Francesco Melchiori, 23 February 1588, in Morsolin 1882, 63).

140. For the *Rime spirituali*, see ch. 4, sec. 2; for the ottava rima poem, see Turina 1628, 300–308.

141. Turina 1628, 240: "magnanima amorosa Maddalena."

142. Turina 1628, 240: "liquefatto il core."

143. On Turina's childhood in Gattara, home of her maternal uncle, Count Pietro di Carpegna (1514–86), see Bà 2006. The late Gattara sequence in Turina 1628 is heralded narratively in the heading on 222 ("Nel far ritorno a i boschi") and characterized internally by references to the harshness of the landscape (see, e.g., "Horride balze, inhabitati monti" [Fearful cliffs, bare mountains], on 231).

144. Turina 1628, 223, and 2009, 188 (no. 130): "diritti viaggi / al Ciel."

145. Turina 1628, 223, and 2009, 188 (no. 130): "qui svelar suol gli arcani più secreti / il divin lume con gl'immensi raggi."

146. Petrarca 1996a, 625: "alti monti"; "selve aspre."

147. Turina 1628, 234: "gl'antri fan risonar de la lor pena."

148. Turina 1628, 224.

149. Turina 1628, 232: "quel ch'altrui quasi peregrin mondano / mostrossi al'hor, che ritornò da morte."

150. Turina 1628, 232: "d'amor lagrimando"; "mille volte baciar l'amate piante."

151. D'Aragona 1547; Battiferra 1560/2000; Salvetti 1590. Salvetti's title, *Rime toscane*, may be an homage to Battiferra's *Il primo libro delle opere toscane*, although see also Angeli and Colonna 1589.

152. As printed, the sequence to Christine comprises one hundred poems, but one sonnet, *Donna gloria del Mondo alta immortale*, is repeated: Salvetti 1590, 5–6 and 32–33.

153. The discrepancy between the numerologically significant 99 or 100 poems in the Christine sequence and the less motivated 46 of the Ferdinando series may suggest that the latter was an afterthought. For Salvetti's poetic influences, see esp. her sonnets *Se nel bel colle Ideo vostra bellezza* and *In qual vago giardino colse Natura* (Salvetti 1590, 17–18), the first of which reworks famous archetypes by Bembo and Della Casa, while the second combines influences from the lyric language of Petrarch and Tasso.

154. Cox 2008, 116, 157. See also on *Calisa* ch. 3 at nn. 144–51.

155. I. Andreini 1601, 1, and 2005, 30: "finti ardori," "falsi . . . dolori," "falsi . . . diletti."

156. T. Tasso 1994, 1:3–4. Andreini also alludes in the poem to Petrarch's opening sonnet (Petrarca 1996a, 5), describing her verse as written "con vario stile" (in a varied style).

157. Andreini's proemial sonnet compares the gender flexibility of her poetic voice with that of her performance career, speaking of her happiness to act "or donne, ed ora / uom" (I. Andreini 1601, 1, and 2005, 30; now women, now a man). Andreini's posthumously published *Lettere* (1607) adopts a similar "hermaphroditic register" (see Ray 2009c, 157–59).

158. I. Andreini 1601, 178–80, and 2005, 122–26. MacNeil 2003, 135–40, discusses a musical setting of the poem.

159. I. Andreini 1601, 70, 72–73, 106, 135, 150–51, 155, 156, 175, 185–86, and 2005, 86, 98, 130.

160. See *Nuova scielta* 1592, 76, 79, 83, for Cavaletti; and Fonte 1997, 221–23, for Fonte. A sonnet to the Ferrara-based singer Laura Peverara in Fonte 1997, 153–54, and an exchange with the Ferrara-based Domenico Chiariti in Caporali 1589, 4v–5r, suggest that Fonte was familiar with the Ferrarese poetic *ambienti* in which Cavaletti moved.

161. Sbarra 1610, E6r ("aurea rete"), E4r ("Gordiani intrichi"), E7v ("amoroso tarlo").

162. The Collalto family's principal seat was at Susegana, near Sbarra's hometown of Conegliano, and they were influential figures in the town (see Rios 1896; and Passolunghi 1991, xlvii–xlviii, both of which document Pulzio Sbarra's connections with the family). The dedicatee of Sbarra 1610 is a Collalto (Count Giacomo), and Sbarra's sister, Lodovica, who contributed a sonnet to the volume (Sbarra 1610, F3r), was married to another member of the family.

163. Pulzio Sbarra's theatrical interests are explored in D. Rhodes 1993.

164. Sbarra 1610, E3v ("ferino Amante"), E3r bis ("lei, che nuda Endimion raccoglie").

165. Sbarra 1610, E7v, E3v bis.

166. Genealogies of the Coderta family record Giovanni Battista as the only son of Lucchesia Sbarra and her husband Monfiorito Coderta (Archivio di Stato di Conegliano, AMVC, busta 413, art. 3, no. 9). Giovanni Battista is recorded as having predeceased Monfiorito, who in turn predeceased his own father, another Giovanni Battista, who died in 1607.

167. For discussion, see Bruscagli 2007, 1577–78.

168. Gelmi 1588; Burchelati 1599.

169. See n. 166. Orazio Lupi, by contrast, ends the sequence in his 1587 *Rime* dedicated to the deaths of his son and daughter (Lupi 1587, 38r–62r) with a verse exchange between him and his wife, Domenica Ombona, in which she urges him to master his grief (61v–62r).

170. For examples of this kind of "public" mourning verse, see *Rime* 1561; Fonte 1585; Silvia Bendinelli 1587; *Rime* 1587c; *Mausoleo* 1589; *Rime* 1590; *Poesie* 1591; and *Lagrime* 1599.

171. Goselini's mythological references in some cases coincide with Sbarra's and may have been a source for her. See esp. Goselini 1588, 307 (no. 158) for a reference to Ganymede; 308 (no. 159) for one to Adonis, Narcissus, and Hyacinth; and 317 (no. 177) for one to the death of Adonis. Sbarra refers to Ganymede and Hyacinth in Sbarra 1610, A5v and A4r, respectively. For Adonis, see below.

172. Sbarra 1610, B1r, B2v.

173. Sbarra 1610, A8v: "E da disperation fatta sicura, / più cose fei deliberata, e

franca, / Per tor la vita a questo novo inferno" (and, made bold by my desperation, I did several things, determined and free, to take my life from this new hell). See also A1ov: "ebbi i pensier colmi / d'un funesto desìo d'uscir di vita" (my thoughts were filled with a morbid desire to leave this life).

174. Sbarra 1610, A12r ("Contra il pianto io non spero altro che il pianto"), A1ov ("Nè volsi, nè vorrò, nè voglio aita"). The former line echoes a line from Petrarch's *doppia sestina* 332 (Petrarca 1996a, 1282, line 42: "Né contra Morte spero altro che Morte").

175. Sbarra 1610, A6r (misnumbered A4r): "Temo, che quel cingial ferito l'abbia; / conoscoli il mio sangue in su le labbia."

176. Sbarra 1610, A6r (misnumbered A4r): "Ahi, che 'l mio bello Adon disteso langue, / e Morte ha gli occhi suoi di morte asperso, / e già in bianche viole il viso involve. / E queste amare lagrime, che io verso / oprato han sì, ch' io più non veggo il sangue, / ma sembra à gli occhi miei sol poca polve" (Alas, my beautiful Adonis is lying there languid. Death has strewn death on his eyes, and his face is already fading into pale anemones. These bitter tears I have shed have blinded me to his blood, which seems to me only dry dust). The concluding phrase, "poca polve," is found in Petrarca 1996b, 498 (*Triumphus temporis*, line 120); cf. also Petrarca 1996a, 1145 (no. 292): "poca polvere."

177. Bragadin 1619, 50–53. For precedents, see Matraini 1989, 256; Matraini 2007, 178–80, for a sonnet by Chiara Matraini on the death of her son, probably dating from the early 1570s (Rabitti 2007, 10); and Di Bona 1569, 36r–37v, 65v–66r), for poems by the Dalmatian poets Speranza Vittoria di Bona (Nada Bunić) and Giulia di Bona (Julija Bunić) on the death of their sister Cassandra.

178. Page references for these four segments within Turina 1628 are given in nn. 183–84.

179. Turina 1628, 137–58, and 2009, 76–98 (nos. 21–42). Turina was certainly already writing verse at this stage, since a letter from her husband, Giulio Bufalini, written during this absence, in February 1575, asks her to send him any "fine sonnet or ottava" (bel sonetto, o ottava) she has written (Torrioli 1940, 19). The context makes clear that this verse was amorous in theme. Stylistic analysis tends to confirm the marital absence poems as a distinct group within Turina's output, less fluent than the bulk of her verse and containing recurring phrases, such as "liquefatto / i argento/i" (Turina 1628, 140, 143, 145, and 2009, 80, 82, 84 [nos. 24, line 6; 27, line 1; 29, line 3]), not found elsewhere.

180. For Croce's comments, see B. Croce 2003, 165: "scriveva con schietto sentimento rime spirituali, e rievocava con commossa semplicità le immagini della vita sua di fanciulla e di sposa" (she wrote religious verse with sincere feeling and evoked the images of her life as a girl and a bride with moving simplicity). For a typical anthology appearance, see Baldacci 1968, 485–87, where her verse is described as "confined within the bounds of a simple womanly sweetness" (racchiusa nei limiti di una semplice dolcezza muliebre).

181. On Turina's period of residence with the Colonna, see Torrioli 1940, 26.

182. Turina 1628, 49–56. Particularly intimate is sonnet 56, in which the poet revisits the woods she had walked in with Lucrezia.

183. The autobiographical sequence falls at Turina 1628, 67–81 (81 misnumbered 69), following a series of poems of consolation addressed to Colonna family members. A transitional sonnet on 67 mourns the deaths of Tomacelli and Ottavio. For the details of Ottavio's murder, possibly orchestrated by Turina's other son, Giulio, see Torrioli 1940, 27; Bà and Milani 1998, 55–56; and Costa-Zalessow 2009, 18.

184. Turina 1628, 117. Turina's second encomiastic sequence is at 70 bis–116 (with a gap in page numbering between 87 and 100), and her second autobiographical sequence is at 117–230, though the thematic division between this and the section that follows, headed "Rime sacre varie" (231–313), is not absolute. Anna Colonna married Taddeo Barberini (1603–47), prefect of Rome and nephew of Pope Urban VIII, in 1627.

185. For genealogies of the family, see Bà and Milani 1998, 89; and Giangamboni and Mercati 2001, 266–67.

186. Turina 1628, 117–29, and 2009, 54–71. For discussion of these poems, see Bà 2006; and Costa-Zalessow 2009, 10–11.

187. Sbarra 1610, A9r: "A l'or vissi, a l'or seppi d'esser viva."

188. Petrarca 1996a, 958 (no. 234). On the fortunes of Turina's sonnet, praised by Croce, see Costa-Zalessow 2009, 34.

189. Turina 1628, 126–28. The figure of Camilla presumably had a particular significance for Turina, since Camilla was the name of both her mother and her daughter.

190. I differ in my reading of these poems from Costa-Zalessow 2009, 10, who interprets them as actual records of Turina's activities in youth.

191. Turina 1628, 126, and 2009, 64 (no. 10; "ardito e fiero"); Turina 1628, 127, and 2009, 66 (no. 11; "di cui più che d'ogni altro è il cor bramoso"). Although the laurel is awarded here for running, it is clear that the plant's role as a symbol of poetic immortality is also of relevance.

192. On Giovanni Turini's career, see G. Milani 1997. Turina speaks of her father in the dedication of Turina 1595 as a "celebrated captain" (Turina 2005, 154; capitano . . . di celebre memoria), and she gives a heroic account of his career in the service of Henri II of France (1519–59) in her unpublished ottava rima romance "Il Florio" (Turina, "Il Florio"); the passage is at 5.22–33.

193. Turina 1628, 166, and 2009, 106 (no. 50): "Viscere del mio sen, cara pupilla / de gli occhi miei, vezzoso pargoletto." A later poem, on the death of her second son, Ottavio, *Viscere del mio sen, figlio diletto,* poignantly echoes this incipit (Turina 1628, 206, and 2009, 176 [no. 118]).

194. Turina 1628, 208, and 2009, 180 (no. 122). The sequence on Ottavio's death is at Turina 1628, 204–7, and 2009, 176 (nos. 118–19). A poem on Giulio's son Giovanni follows one to Ottavio's son Giovanni Battista at Turina 1628, 209, and 2009, 180 (no. 123), while the next two sonnets speak of her fears for Giulio during an illness he suffered shortly after his brother's death (Turina 1628, 210–11, and 2009,

178 [nos. 120–21]; the modern edition of Turina's verse does not in all cases follow the sequence of the original).

195. See ch. 4 at nn. 52–55.

196. Turina 1628, 209: "Amoroso bambin, puro angeletto, / fai che d'amor mi sfaccia, e mi distille / qual'hor con quelle luci alme e tranquille / dolce mi vedi, e mi ti stringi al petto."

197. The breadth of Turina's literary acquaintance is best illustrated by the manuscripts of her verse in San Giustino and Città di Castello (Turina, "Poesie" and "Rime"). An indication of her principal contacts may be found in her entry in the appendix.

198. Sabbadini 1615, 77: "femina predatrice." Sbarra's use of *femina* in this context is noteworthy, as the term was generally pejorative.

199. Ducchi 1586 (proemial sonnet, unnumbered): "Donna Real, ben lodar debbo anch'io / del tuo volto divin l'almo splendore / l'heroico del magnamino tuo core / s'hor per te sola è in pregio il sesso mio." See also in the same sequence Campiglia's later sonnet *Poi ch'è del sesso nostro alma beatrice,* in which the thought of Isabella Pallavicino is said to compensate women for the misery of their subjection to men.

200. Miani 2010, 38: "il nostro sesso illustrato a meraviglia dal chiarissimo sole della serenissima sua luce."

201. For Fonte's bridal sonnets, see Fonte 1997, 210–15. For examples of female-authored poems for Venetian governors' wives, see *Rime* 1596, C4r–v, *Varie compositioni* 1596, and Spolverini 1596 (on Chiara Dolfin Cornaro, wife of the future doge Giovanni Cornaro [1551–1629], *capitanio* of Verona); *Polinnia* 1609, F2r–v (Valeria Miani on Maria Bembo Contarini, wife of Tomaso Contarini, *podestà* of Padua); "Raccolta d'alcune rime," 10v–11r (Lucrezia Marinella on Elena Foscarini, wife of Giovanni Battista Foscarini, *podestà* of Padua in 1614); Bragadin 1614, 15 (also on Elena Foscarini); *Giustiniano* 1614, 73 (Livia Reganela on Marina Giustinian, wife of Pietro Giustinian, *capitanio* of Vicenza); and Bragadin 1619, 41 (Bragadin on Samaritana Foscarini, wife of Sebastiano Foscarini, *podestà* of Verona). On the context of tributes of this kind, see A. Smith 2009. Intriguingly, Chiara Dolfin, subject of the tributes by Ersilia Spolverini cited above, is also among the Venetian ladies mentioned by Fonte, who gives the text of a sonnet composed for the marriage of her sister, Gracimana Dolfin Nani (Fonte 1997, 213–14).

202. For Cavaletti, see *Rime* 1587a, 214; for Bragadin, Bragadin 1619, 17–19. Verse addressed to women of the Colonna family is found in Turina 1628, 9–15, 24–31, 38–48. Verse addressed by her to female members of the Barberini, Peretti, and Aldobrandini families is found in Turina, "Poesie."

203. Andreini's verse for Christine is found in MacNeil 2003, 300–305; for Maria, in I. Andreini 1603, 14–19, and 1605, 32. For Cervoni, see I. Cervoni, "Canzone"; and I. Cervoni 1600. See also ch. 3, sec. 2, for discussion of Leonora Bernardi's *Tragicomedia pastorale,* which appears to have been performed before Christine and her husband, Ferdinand, and which contains praise of the couple under the pastoral

names Cristilla and Dinando ([Bernardi?], "Tragicomedia pastorale," 29v–30r [3.6] (hereafter cited as "Gentildonna lucchese"); see also 3r–4r [*prologo*]).

204. Poems to Maria de' Medici are found in Turina, "Poesie," 250r–v and 283; poems to Maria Maddalena d'Austria, Claudia de' Medici della Rovere (1604–48), Grand Duchess Vittoria della Rovere (1622–94), and Anna de' Medici (1616–76) at 253–57 of the same manuscript.

205. I. Cervoni, "Canzone." Cervoni's first published work was I. Cervoni 1592.

206. I. Cervoni 1600, D1r–v (stanzas 6 and 7 of the third *canzone*).

207. I. Cervoni 1600, D1v–D2r (stanzas 8 and 9 of the third *canzone*); also D2v (stanza 11) for Cornelia. The warning to men not to underestimate women's intelligence is found at the end of stanza 9.

208. I. Cervoni 1597a, 1597b. Cervoni's examples of Christian ruler-consorts who converted their husbands are Saint Clothilde (475–545), wife of the Frankish king Clovis I (c. 466–511), and Theodolinda (c. 570–628), wife of the Lombard king Agilulf (590–616).

209. Salvetti 1590, 28–29.

210. Salvetti 1590, 29: "schivar de le donne i vili uffici."

211. Gambara 1995, 103; Battiferra 2006, 278. Gambara's sonnet was first published in 1558, Battiferra's in 1563. Salvetti's echoes of Battiferra are discussed in the text. For Gambara, compare esp. lines 7–8 of Salvetti's sonnet, "cui tempo non potrà . . . / sveller, né pur crollar Fortuna fella" (whom time cannot uproot nor cruel Fortune destroy), with lines 6–7 of Gambara's, "Nè potrà il Tempo con la sua ruina / far del bel nome vostro empia rapina" (Nor will ruinous Time be able cruelly to pillage your name).

212. Battiferra 2006, 278: "Et io, che già lasciai l'ago e la gonna" (I, who left behind the needle and the skirt).

213. Battiferra 2006, 278: "Musa e Donna"; Salvetti 1590, 29: "sotto l'ombra real del vostro velo."

214. The rhyme *donna-s'indonna* originally derives from Dante's *Paradiso* (Alighieri 1994, 4:102 [*Par.* 7.11–13]).

215. Matraini 1602, 23: "O mirabil di Dio possente Donna / che 'l gran nemico, a noi facendo guerra / col piè dell'humiltà gettasti a terra / ond'hor (volendo) in ciel l'huomo s'indonna" (O miraculous and puissant Lady, who trampled the great enemy with the foot of humility, so that now, if he wishes, man transcends himself in heaven).

CHAPTER THREE: Drama

1. For the tradition of female-authored convent drama, see Weaver 2002; and for instances of sacred drama by a laywoman, see Pulci 1996. For an overview of Italian laywomen's narrative and dramatic production to 1580, see Cox 2008, 12–13, 113–14. For Bigolina, see Bigolina 2002, 2004, 2005.

2. The surviving plays are, in chronological order (insofar as this can be established), Fonte 1581a; B. Torelli, "Partenia"; I. Andreini 1588; Campiglia 1588;

"Gentildonna lucchese"; Miani 1604; and Miani 1611. A sacred play by Cherubina Venturelli may also date from this period (see ch. 1 at n. 46). The narrative works are Fonte 1581b, 1582, 1592; Marinella 1595, 1597, 1602, 1605a, 1618, 1624, 1635; Sarrocchi 1606/1623; and Salvetti 1611. Works documented but lost include a tragedy or narrative poem on Saint Barbara by Maddalena Campiglia (see ch. 1, n. 143); a hagiographic poem on Saint Eustace by Leonora Bernardi (Grillo 1612a, 422–43, 921); and a four-canto ottava rima poem on the conversion of Mary Magdalene by Maddalena Salaroli Ariosti of Bologna (see Fantuzzi 1781–94, 7:267). See also Battiferra 2006, 256–65, for a fragment of religious epic by Laura Battiferra; and Cox 2008, 334n98, for evidence of other lost narrative works.

3. The identification of "Hélisenne" with Marguerite Briet, accepted for most of the twentieth century, has recently been called into question; see, e.g., Chang 2009, 140.

4. Three of these works (Sidney's, Tyler's, and Dowriche's) are translations of various levels of fidelity. With the exception of Wroth's *Love's Victory*, all were published.

5. Erythraeus 1645–48, 1:259–60, emphasizes the novelty of Margherita Sarrocchi's engagement with epic on precisely these grounds, noting Proba and the Greek epigrammist Erinna as the only classical precedents but dismissing any claims that either should be considered a true epic poet.

6. Cox 2008, 164.

7. Fonte 1581a/2009.

8. For documentation on this tradition, see Solerti 1902b. On the performance context, see Shiff 1993, 5–12; and Quaintance 2009, 196–203.

9. Doglioni 1988, 7; 1997, 36. The early seventeenth-century literary historian Alessandro Zilioli, in his biography of Fonte in Zilioli, "Istoria delle vite," 145, speaks of "those dramatic pieces of hers that have been acted many times in Venice" (quelle rappresentazioni sceniche le quali molte volte in Venezia sono state recitate). Details of surviving anonymous plays written before Fonte's death in 1592 are found at Solerti 1902b, 513–16, 517–19. The texts may be found in a collection in the Biblioteca Marciana, Venice (Misc. 2615.9).

10. Magno's sonnet is found at ms. Venice Biblioteca Marciana It. IX.171 (6092), 38 and 81. The text (*Schiera gentil, ch'i nudi incolti carmi* [no. 202]) may be found in the electronic edition of Magno's *Rime* on the Biblioteca Italiana site (www.bibliotecaitaliana.it).

11. Monte 1578a. The performance information is on the title page of the printed edition: "da lei propria recitata nell'Illustriss[imo] et Eccellentiss[imo] Collegio a Sua Serenità" (performed by her in person in the Most Illustrious and Excellent Collegio before the Most Serene Doge). The Collegio was the highest Venetian council of state. See also Tomasini 1644, 366, for an account of Monte's performance of an oration before da Ponte that so amazed the doge that he subjected her to an interrogation on the principles of the art of oratory to verify her authorship of the speech. Tomasini's source is the Rovigo-born cleric Baldassare Bonifaccio, or Bonifacio (1584–1659). The oration in question is presumably that printed as Monte [1578b?].

12. Monte 1578a, A1v: "nova Minerva." Fonte features as "Mad[onna] M[odesta] P[ozzo]."

13. Groto 2007, 337. Groto refers to the play, using a curious term, as "una plenipedia recitata al doge il giorno di S. Stefano" (a *plenipedia* acted before the Doge on Saint Stephen's Day).

14. See Weaver 2002, 64, for comment.

15. For critical discussion, see esp. Quaintance 2009; see also Malpezzi Price 2003b, 30–31.

16. Fonte 2009, 214 (lines 40 and 43): "i diletti e' piaceri"; "la felicità somma, e 'l sommo bene." The Epicurean's speech as a whole is at lines 37–45.

17. Fonte 2009, 224 (lines 269–80). Fonte has the Erythraean sibyl speak of having addressed her Christian prediction to the emperor, Augustus, seemingly confusing her with the Tiburtine sibyl, to whom this prophecy is generally attributed.

18. Petrarca 1996a, 1362–66. Quaintance 2009, 203–10, speculates that Fonte may have been influenced by Lorenzo Valla's philosophical dialogue *De voluptate*, which features a debate between two speakers, identified with the Epicurean and Stoic schools. Although this is possible, it would require a better knowledge of Latin on Fonte's part than her other works attest, as Valla's dialogue had not been translated when Fonte composed *Le feste* (see Fonte 1997, 35 and n. 12, on the probable level of her acquaintance with the language).

19. The fullest discussion of the commission is Jaffe 2002, 114–25. See also Rabitti 1981, 148; Smarr 2005, 93; and Marcheschi 2008, 59–62.

20. Fonte 1988, 62; Marinella 1600, 15r–v.

21. Fonte 1988, 117; 1997, 172–73. See also Fonte 1988, 88–90, and 1997, 139–40, on the pleasures of hunting (also alluded to in Fonte 2009, 218 [lines 120–25]); and Fonte 1988, 123–24, and 1997, 179–80, on those of the villa (also alluded to in Fonte 2009, 218 [see n. 24 below]).

22. Marinella 1997a, 446: "Fa adunque di mestieri che tu sprezzi e che tu odî questo corpo, come . . . fracido cadavero e oscura tomba dell'anima."

23. Fonte 2009, 216 (lines 99–104).

24. See esp. the joint song of the two choruses in Fonte 2009, 222 (lines 201–10), condoning pleasure as a legitimate repose for virtuous souls; see also the first chorus's intervention on 218 (lines 131–41), echoing the Epicurean's speech on pleasure by recalling to the doge and the other noble spectators their own pleasures in their country retreats on the river Brenta, west of Venice.

25. See Fonte 1988, 137–39, and 1997, 196–97.

26. The two earliest editions of *Aminta*, published by Aldo Manuzio in Venice and Cristoforo Draconi in Cremona, seem to have been completed by December 1580, although Manuzio's bears the date 1581 (Sozzi 1954, 14, 24–25). On the status of the *Aminta* and its influence on subsequent pastoral production, see Sampson 2006, 98–102.

27. Studies of Italian pastoral drama include Pieri 1983; Clubb 1989, 91–187; Chiabò and Doglio 1992; Di Benedetto 1999; Riccò 2004; Sampson 2006; Ariani

2007b, 1746–57; and F. Schneider 2010. On the pastoral mode more generally in sixteenth-century Italian culture, see Gerbino 2009.

28. Ingegneri 1989, 25.

29. Barish 1994; Riccò 2008.

30. Costa 1641; Salvi 2004.

31. B. Torelli, "Partenia." A critical edition, edited by Lisa Sampson and Barbara Burgess-Van Aken, is forthcoming in the Other Voice in Early Modern Europe series from the Center for Reformation and Renaissance Studies, Toronto.

32. I. Andreini 1995/2002; Campiglia 2004. Andreini's play may date from earlier in the 1580s (see Vazzoler 1992, 284).

33. "Gentildonna lucchese"; Miani 1604. For evidence that *Amorosa speranza* was completed by 1598, see Finucci 2010, 9.

34. See Solerti 1902a; Kirkendale 2001, 185–212; Fenlon 2001, 217–29; and Megale 2003, 330. Guidiccioni also scripted a danced *intermezzo* performed at the 1589 wedding of Christine of Lorraine and Ferdinando de' Medici (see Treadwell 1997, 66, for the text). In addition to the plays listed here, a possible further lost pastoral by the Piedmontese Margherita Asinari Valperga is recorded (see her entry in the appendix).

35. Belatta, or Belatti, was Bernardi's married name, and she appears as "Leonora Belatta di Bernardi" in Franciotti 1616, 289. The surname on the Marciana manuscript first appears to read "Hqxmhhm," but on closer inspection the double consonant reads as *ll* written over an original *m*, suggesting that the scribe had anticipated the final *m* and then corrected it by overwriting. Tiraboschi 1824, 1925–26, records Bernardi as having written three pastoral dramas, while Lucchesini 1825–31, 9:169, gives the title of one, *Clorindo*. For further evidence of her authorship, see below, n. 108.

36. See Roberts 1997, esp. 162–63, 173; Decroisette 2002, 149–55; Sampson 2006, 42, 103–6; Riccò 2008, 287–89; and Gerbino 2009, esp. 202–3.

37. Ingegneri 1989, 7: "admettendo le vergini in palco e le donne oneste, quello che alle comedie non lice, [pastorals] danno luoco a nobili affetti, non disdicevoli alle tragedie stesse." For a contrast between the "pure and modest loves" (amori puri e modesti) of pastoral and the more shameless ones of comedy, see Zuccolo 1613, 21r.

38. T. Tasso 1977a, 670–73 (1.2); Guarini 1977, 893–95 (4.9). Parenthetical references to narrative plays are to act and scene.

39. Manfredi 1602, a4v–a5r: "più di una di quelle cose, le quali alle donne honorate e nobili e di palazzo [dirò così] e parimente alle Principesse, vostre pari, piacere e dilettare sogliono: e tutte modeste e tutte honeste e tendenti tutte al pudico costume, ed alla instruttione di donne caste, e savie e di virgini buone e prudenti." Manfredi's use of the term *donne di palazzo* alludes to the ideal of feminine conduct sketched by Castiglione in his *Cortegiano* (1528), combining modesty with social ease (*affabilità*).

40. Manfredi 1602, a5r–v. The *Contrasto* is unusual within Italian pastoral drama for its virtually all–female cast. For discussion, see Sampson 2006, 106, 221–22; Pignatti 2007, 723; and Gerbino 2009, 206–14.

41. See Ingegneri 2002, 20–21, 57–58; Riccò 2004, 264n62; Sampson 2006, 105; and Gerbino 2009, 205. For further examples of Italian court women's participation in private dramatic and balletic performances, see Tizzoni 1995, 224; Fenlon 2001, 215; Treadwell 2002; Bosi 2005; Sampson 2006, 105–6; McClure 2008, 766; and Gerbino 2009, 202, 204–7, 231–33.

42. Battiferra 2000, 154–64.

43. For the text and a translation of the second eclogue, see Kirkham 2001, 164–73; and Battiferra 2006, 206–17. For identification of the setting and the figures depicted, see Battiferra 2006, 424nn255–56 (correcting Kirkham 2001, 152–61). On Striggio's setting, see Gerbino 2009, 221–29. On a third, lost eclogue by Battiferra, see Battiferra 2006, 424n255.

44. D'Aragona 1547, 24v–25r. For another pastoral eclogue praising d'Aragona's poetic talents and portraying her crowned as the tenth Muse, see Muzio 1550, 10v–13v. D'Aragona herself occasionally uses pastoral language and imagery in her verse (see, e.g., d'Aragona 1547, 3r, *Se gli antichi pastor di rose e fiori*).

45. See below at n. 115, and see also n. 119.

46. On Stampa's verse as crafted for performance, see Smarr 1991. On continuities between the figures of courtesan *virtuose* and actresses, see Gerbino 2009, 200.

47. Valerini 1991, 36: "Che dirò delle pastorali da lei prima introdotte in scena?" For comment, see Gerbino 2009, 195–201.

48. See Gerbino 2009, 194–95, 198. Valerini 1991, 36, speaks evocatively of Armani's costume in her nymph roles: "Andava in abito di ninfa sì vezzoso che si poteva a Diana assimigliare, quando per piacer all'amato Endimione sen già più del consueto adorna e lasciva" (She dressed in a nymph costume so charming that one might compare her to Diana when, to please her beloved Endymion, she was dressed in more than her usual finery and seductiveness).

49. Riccò 2004, 326–36. The four Innominati who contributed verse to *Partenia* were Muzio Manfredi, Bernardino Baldi, Girolamo Pallentieri (1510?–91), and Camillo Malaspina. For a complete list of Torelli's poets, see Riccò 2004, 326; and Sampson 2006, 126n44.

50. On the continuing place of manuscript in the circulation of literary works in sixteenth-century Italy, see Richardson 2009, 18, which cites *Partenia* as an example. A print publication of Torelli's play appears to have been contemplated in the early 1590s (see Sampson 2004, 100 and n. 11).

51. Manfredi 1587, 43: "la più bella che fino a qui in lingua nostra si sia veduta."

52. On the proposed Guastalla performance and Manfredi's role in advocating it, see Sampson 2004, 108; 2006, 108; and Riccò 2004, 102n145. For the letter to Carlo Emmanuele, see Manfredi 1606, 214. Although the letters in Manfredi 1606 cannot be taken as a record of letters actually sent (Pignatti 2007, 724, describes them as "fittizie" [fictional]), the substantive content of the work seems consistent with external evidence where this exists.

53. Ingegneri 1989, 25; Riccò 2004, 20. *Partenia* is also praised in L. Contarini 1589, 469; and Astolfi 1602, 112.

54. Grillo 1589, 52r; C. Gonzaga 1591b, 165; T. Tasso 1852–55, 4:234 (no. 1160, 12 August 1589). Grillo's sonnet was republished in successive editions of his *Rime* and his *Pietosi affetti* (see, e.g., Grillo 1592b, 123, and 1599, 142r).

55. On the publishing details of *Mirtilla*, see I. Andreini 1995, 28. For the French translations, see Mauri 1996a, 256–60; 1996b, 209–16. The first of these, by Roland du Jardin, remains in manuscript, while the second, whose translator is unknown, was published.

56. For evidence of the performance, see Rees 2008, 43–44; and Finucci 2010, 24–25.

57. The prologue to the play, spoken by a *fata*, Linfadusa, at one point directly addresses Ferdinand and Christine, who are portrayed as accompanied by their infant son, Cosimo II ("Gentildonna lucchese," 2v). The fact that only one child is mentioned, and that he is described as a "regal infante," makes it likely that the performance took place sometime between 12 May 1590, when Cosimo was born, and 10 November 1591, when the couple's next child, Eleonora, was born. References in the text suggest that it was performed in the spring. For evidence of a tradition of amateur performance at the Florentine court in the 1590s, see Fenlon 2001, 215.

58. See her entry in the appendix.

59. See above at n. 34. For the term *pastorella per musica* as a description of such works, see Gerbino 2009, 237n69; for *pastorale per musica* used in a similar sense, see Bosi 2005, 10. There is some evidence for a performance of Tasso's *Aminta* in 1590, when the author himself was visiting Florence (see Fenlon 2001, 213–15).

60. Tirsi's trick, based on the story of Acontius and Cydippe in Greek myth, involves his writing a vow to marry him on an apple and throwing into the temple of Diana, where Partenia finds it and reads it aloud. For critical discussion of the play, which was rediscovered in the early twentieth century (Zonta 1906), see Riccò 2004, 326–36; Sampson 2004 and 2006, 106–12; and Burgess-Van Aken 2007.

61. To date there is no secondary literature on the *Tragicomedia* beyond a mention in Rees 2010, 18n62.

62. Bernardi's play signals the importance of this Ariostan subtext by drawing the name of her second heroine, Dalinda, from a character in the story (see Ariosto 1976, 1:82–109 [5.5–6.16]).

63. For critical discussion of *Flori*, see Cox 2000a, 56–57; Chemello 2003, 91–99; Cox and Sampson 2004; Ultsch 2005a, 76–87; Sampson 2006, 112–18; and Riccò 2008, 287–98.

64. *Mirtilla* exists in two redactions, I. Andreini 1588 and 1594, both with numerous reprints. For a discussion of the revisions, see Mauri 1996b, 200–202; for a list of variants, I. Andreini 1995, 24–28. I. Andreini 1995 reproduces the 1588 edition. For critical discussion of the play, see Vazzoler 1992; Doglio 1995; Mauri 1996b, 199–209 (also in Mauri 1996a, 243–55); J. Campbell 1997 and 2002; Decroisette 2001, 211–15; Decroisette 2002, 161–69; MacNeil 2003, 37–46, 122–25; Sampson 2006, 118–23; and Riccò 2008, 287–98.

65. On the Narcissus theme in *Mirtilla*, see Mauri 1996b, 204–5; 1997. The same

motif is found in Campiglia's *Flori* in the figure of Urania (Campiglia 2004, 200–202 [4.3]) and in Isabetta Coreglia's *Erindo* in the figure of Rosalba. On developments of this motif in the writings of Andreini's husband, Francesco, and her son Giovanni Battista, see Riccò 2008, 298 and n. 57.

66. For a list of such set-piece scenes, see J. Campbell 2002, xxiii. Studies considering the *Mirtilla* in the context of the *commedia dell'arte* include G. Romei 1992, 189–90; and Vazzoler 1992.

67. The fullest critical discussion of Miani's pastoral is Rees 2010, 74–125. See also Decroisette 2002, 176–82; Rees 2008, 48–55; and Finucci 2010, 21–25.

68. Miani 1604, 12v (1.3): "poi ch'hebbe colto / il virginal mio fiore." Venelia's marital status is somewhat unclear in the play; while she refers to Damone at 13r as her husband ("marito," "sposo"), her rival Tirenia later (16r [1.4]) gives the impression that the two were not married, and the final scene sees him returning, humbled, to marry her ("goder gl'himenei dolci e soavi" [4.6]). It is possible that the initial marriage is to be understood as of the informally agreed type permitted prior to the Council of Trent (see ch. 1 between nn. 113 and 114), the second as a formalization of the initial vows.

69. The scene between Filemone and Clorilli is at "Gentildonna lucchese," 41r–44r (3.6). For the satyr scene, see below, n. 134.

70. On the essentially undramatic character of *Flori*, see Cox and Sampson 2004, 29–31.

71. I. Andreini 1995, 120–22, and 2002, 72–74 (4.2).

72. I. Andreini 1995, 120, and 2002, 72 (4.2): "chi fugge [la donna], ancora fugge / di sé la più pregiata e nobil parte"; "Tanto l'uomo / può viver senza lei, quant'ella puote / senza l'uom sostener sua fragil vita."

73. I. Andreini 1995, 124, and 2002, 75 (4.2): "sopra umana dolcezza"; "focosi sospir."

74. Mauri 1996a, 259. For the omitted passage, see I. Andreini 1995, 122: "[vaga ninfa . . . che] ti levi i panni" (subjunctive). I. Andreini 2002, 73, translates this as "take off your clothes."

75. B. Torelli, "Partenia," 50r (4.2), cited in Sampson 2004, 113n23. See also B. Torelli, "Partenia," 44r (3.5), where Partenia laments to Diana: "Dunque sovrana Dea l'intatta, e cara / virginitate mia sarà rapita?" (So, then, supreme Goddess, is my intact and dear virginity to be seized from me?).

76. The phrase in the text, "virginale in tutto e per tutto," is from Riccò 2004, 333.

77. B. Torelli, "Partenia," 68v: "Non già perche Partenia / si trovi accesa del'amor di Tirsi; / ma sol per haver fatto un giuramento."

78. B. Torelli, "Partenia," 50v: "gentil, leggiadro, e bello."

79. B. Torelli, "Partenia," 50v: "Sian benedette . . . le fatiche, / c'ho per te fatte."

80. Sampson 2004, 103, 113n23; 2006, 110.

81. B. Torelli, "Partenia," 3v (1.1); for a description of Ottinio as "[il] gran Pastor di questi colli," see 7r (1.2). This kind of geographically specific setting is found in a number of Italian pastorals (see Riccò 2004, 144n47). Other female-authored exam-

ples are Bernardi's *Tragicomedia*, which is set in the countryside near Fiesole, and Isabetta Coreglia's *Dori* and *Erindo*, both set near Lucca.

82. Riccò 2004, 335–36. On the Christian emphases of the Innominati's output, see also Denarosi 2003, 399–400.

83. See above at n. 53. Ingegneri's prefatory sonnet to *Partenia*, reproduced in Riccò 2004, 330, highlights the play's advocacy of celibacy as a particular merit: "quinci sanno / le donne esser pudiche e non amanti" (here women learn to be chaste and not lovers).

84. Ariosto 1976, 1:635–40 (25.26–46); Finucci 1992, 199–225; Shemek 1998, 111–16; DeCoste 2004 and 2009, 76–99; Bateman 2007, 12–17; Mac Carthy 2007, 146–51; Giannetti 2009, 85–86. The story echoes that of Ovid's Iphis and Ianthe.

85. Bigolina 2002, 128–36, 169–87; 2005, 120–27, 156–71. On the theme of same-sex love between women in Campiglia, see Perrone 1996; and Cox and Sampson 2004, 23–26. More generally, on the representation of lesbian desire in Italy in this period, see DeCoste 2009; and Giannetti 2009; Giannetti cites earlier bibliography at 252n58. For early modern England, see Traub 2002.

86. See the instances discussed in Giannetti 2009, 90–110.

87. Riccò 2008, 298: "puro amore di bellezza disincarnata e divina."

88. Campiglia 2004, 68 (1.2): "Giovane sfortunata, troppo, troppo / di terrena beltà ti compiacesti."

89. *Revolutionary* is Lori Ultsch's term (see Ultsch 2005a, 77, 83).

90. See, e.g., Campiglia 1585, 6: "Viveano questo animi felici di casti desiri, e di virginal unione, che niun'altro matrimonio giamai fu più vero, più sinciero, o più santo" (These souls lived happily in their chaste desires and virginal union, so that no other marriage was ever more true, more pure, or more holy). For discussion, see Ultsch 2005a, 75–76; and Rees 2008, 53, which relates the Flori-Alessi story to hagiographic tradition. On celibate marriage as an ideal in medieval Europe, see Elliott 1993.

91. Campiglia 1585, afterword by Gregorio Ducchi, unnumbered: "vivendo al tutto diversamente, con gran stupore altrui, dal costume donnesco." Ducchi's remark ostensibly concerns Campiglia's devotion to intellectual activity, but it is hard not to suspect a veiled allusion to her lifestyle. On the failure of Campiglia's marriage, see Mantese 1967, 104–6, summarized in Cox and Sampson 2004, 3, but also now Gherardi 2009, 12–22, which provides evidence that relations between the spouses had broken down by September 1577, earlier than previously thought. See also Gherardi 2009, 8–11, for evidence that Campiglia's mother, Polissena Verlato, was also separated from her husband, whom she appears to have left c. 1542, about twenty years prior to his death.

92. Cox and Sampson 2004, 9, 27.

93. Campiglia 2004, 322n92.

94. Campiglia 2004, 64–65 (1.1). For discussion, see Cox 2005b, 21–22. Campiglia's citing of Colonna as a literary role model may reflect the impact of the recent republication of Colonna's *Rime spirituali* in Verona in 1586.

95. Campiglia 2004, 268 (5.3): "Sian nostri figli le cose create / dal divino nostro pelegrino ingegno." Flori speaks here in the first-person plural ("nostri . . . nostro"), referring to herself and Licori, who is implied here to have shared in her poetic ambitions at one time.

96. Campiglia 2004, 248: "correr dietro a l'impossibil sempre."

97. Venelia describes Alliseo in Miani 1604, 65r (5.1) as "quel ch'a le volte con suoi dolci preghi / mi fa restar, che non sò quel che voglia" (he who sometimes with his sweet wooing leaves me unsure of what I wish); see also her declaration of love at 68v–69r (5.2). For Lucrino, see esp. 76v–77v (5.4), where Venelia is seen gazing adoringly at his portrait, and the following scene, for their reencounter on his return from Argos, where he has been training for the priesthood.

98. Further exceptions are found in Miani's *Celinda,* discussed below in this chapter, and in episodes in Moderata Fonte's *Floridoro* and the first redaction of Margherita Sarrocchi's *Scanderbeide.* See ch. 5 at nn. 89 and 135–38.

99. Miani 1604, 42r (3.6): "bipartito core." See also 15r (1.4), where Tirenia exclaims to the absent Alliseo, "Do you not know, poor wretch, that your lover Venelia's heart is divided a thousand ways?" (Non sai misero forse / che Venelia tua amante / in più di mille lochi hà 'l cor partito[?]).

100. Miani 1604, A6r: "travagliati pensieri . . . moleste cure dell'animo"; Decroisette 2002, 178–79.

101. For Lucrino's identification as a Venetian patrician, see Miani 1604, 15v (1.4): "Questo pastore è di pregiata stirpe, / da la bella città del mar reina." For Carrari's reference to her abandonment by "Damone," see *Poesie* 1590, 17r: "Perché à le cure tue Damon non torni? / Vedi com'ho di pianto gli occhi molli / poi che dal camin dritto errando vai" (Damone, why do you not return to your duties? You can see how my eyes have been drenched in tears ever since you went wandering from the true path).

102. On the preference for "polygonal" love plots within early Seicento literature, see Godard 1984, 175–79; Sampson 2006, 206 (with reference to pastoral); and Getto 1969, 327, 360 (with reference to *novella* and romance).

103. See "Gentildonna lucchese," 56r (4.4): "Di furioso Amore folle consiglio / fu questo tuo[,] Dalinda."

104. "Gentildonna lucchese," 9r (1.1): "in ogni altra cosa al padre i figli / soggetti sono; in questo libertade / ha lor concesso la Natura e Dio / d'unirsi come all'hor [a lor] diletta, e piace." Alfisbeo's position is consistent with post-Tridentine canon law, which insisted on the free consent to marriage of both spouses, although in practice this was frequently overridden by family interests (see Hacke 2004, 89–92).

105. "Gentildonna lucchese," 16r (1.4): "Che poteva il voler del vecchio padre, / se 'l tuo cieco volere / non consentiva all'altrui voglia?"

106. Cellia is identified in "Gentildonna lucchese," 25r (2.5) as "quella . . . / che 'l Pò più ch'altra ninfa honora e 'nchina / Quella che, per bear i Toschi lidi / si giunse in matrimonio / al generoso Aldranio" (she whom the Po honors and reverences more than any other nymph, she who, to make blessed the shores of Tuscany, joined herself

in matrimony to the noble Aldranio). The legitimized daughter of Francesco d'Este (1516–78) and hence a cousin of the Duke of Ferrara, Marfisa d'Este married Alderano Cibo (1552–1606), heir to the marquisate of Massa and Carrara, in 1580. The device of a reported set-piece speech by an *à clef* character may have been suggested by a passage in act 1, scene 2, of *Aminta,* in which Tirsi reports a speech by the negatively portrayed figure of Mopso, variously identified by critics as Sperone Speroni (1500–1588) and Antonio Montecatini (1537–99).

107. "Gentildonna lucchese," 25r, 27r (2.5): "Proteo novello"; "fermi e costanti / solo nell'incostanza loro." For Cellia's *paragone* as a whole, see 26r–27r.

108. Bosi 2005; Gerbino 2009, 231–34. The presence of Marfisa d'Este in the *Tragicomedia* may be taken as contributory evidence for Bernardi's authorship, in that Bernardi's husband, Vincenzo Belatti, as a native of the Garfagnana, was a subject of the Este and the two spent time at the Este court in the 1580s (G. Sforza 1879, 353–54). A letter of 1581 from Marfisa d'Este recommends a "Vincenzo Bellati" to her cousin, Cardinal Luigi d'Este (Masetti Zannini 2008, 108–9); it is probably the same man, since Marfisa mentions his "considerable wealth" (considerevole ricchezza), a detail that coincides with what we know of Bernardi's husband from other sources (see Forciroli 2007, 223).

109. Campiglia 2004, 58–66 (1.1), 170–86 (3.6), 244–56 (5.1).

110. The phrase *duel between friendship and love* is taken from the title of a popular comedy of the period, Sforza degli Oddi's *L'erofilomachia, overo il duello d'amore, et d'amicitia* (1572). On the popularity of this motif in pastoral drama, see Riccò 2004, 172–87.

111. Campiglia 2004, 112–14 (2.1): "Che colui / mal del nome d'amico allor si vanta / ch'altrui servendo al proprio ben sol mira." See also Licori's opening lines in the play, on 58 (1.1): "verace amico / stimar sempre commune il bene e 'l male / deve del caro amico" (a true friend should always hold in common what befalls his dear friend, good or ill). For Serrano's contrasting willingness to sacrifice his friend, see 124 (2.3). On the theme of female friendship in Italian early modern female-authored literature, see Graziosi 2005, 168–73; Fonte 1997, 123–24 and 123n4; and Cox 2008, 313n177, 370n235. For comparative material, see Fox 2008, 141–93.

112. Cabani 1995, 55–68.

113. C. Gonzaga 2000, 276 (19.61): "Tacciano pur Pilade, Oreste, Achille / et Patroclo, et con Niso Eurialo ancora" (Let Pilades and Orestes, Achilles and Patroclus, Nisus and Eurylus be silent).

114. I. Andreini 1995, 104–5, and 2002, 59–60 (3.5).

115. Sampson 2004, 113n22; Cox and Sampson 2004, 34. On Talia's characterization in *Partenia*, see Sampson 2004, 103, and 2006, 111.

116. See the description of Talia in B. Torelli, "Partenia," 69v (5.4), as "dotta in saper d'ogni virtute / de le pietre, e de l'erbe" (knowledgable about the [curative] virtues of all minerals and herbs). For Erminia as "medica," see T. Tasso 1980, 607 (19.114).

117. Coreglia 1634, 73 (4.3): "la cara libertade . . . / a l'ombra dell'alloro"; see also

99 (5.1). Like Campiglia and Torelli, Coreglia encourages identification between Nerina and herself as poet by using a pastoral pseudonym she adopted in other contexts (see Cox 2008, 209–10). Coreglia seems never to have married, and a poem in Coreglia 1628, 10, suggests that she may have been a Carmelite tertiary.

118. Campiglia 2004, 182, 320n74, 284–86. Campiglia's own musical interests are attested in her letters to Francesco Melchiori (see Morsolin 1882, 61–66).

119. See MacNeil 2003, 38–46, 296–300. "Filli" was Andreini's own pastoral name.

120. This conjectural reconstruction of the distribution of roles in performances of *Mirtilla* originated in Taviani 1984 and has subsequently been generally accepted. On its implications for the play, see G. Romei 1992, 189; and Vazzoler 1992, 285.

121. I. Andreini 1995, 65–80, and 2002, 43 50 (3.2). For discussion, see J. Campbell 1997, 113–14, and 2002, xviii–xx; Ray 1998; Decroisette 2002, 161–69; and Sampson 2006, 121–22. On the satyr's place generally within the social and erotic economy of Renaissance pastoral drama, see Garraffo 1985; Ray 1998; and Decroisette 2002, 155–61.

122. Miani 1604, 20r–26v (2.2), 48v–50r (4.5), 50r–55v (4.6).

123. On the darker tone of Miani's punishment scene, which is conducted in a quasi-judicial manner after the satyr's "arrest" by Isandro, see Decroisette 2002, 182.

124. For analysis of Andreini's nymph-satyr scene in relation to its sources, see Ray 1998. See also Vazzoler 1992, 295; Riccò 2004, 151; and Sampson 2006, 122. For Miani, see Decroisette 2002, 179–82; and Rees 2008, 50–51, and 2010, 119–23.

125. For the phrase in the text, see T. Tasso 1977a, 652 (1.1): "'l mio trastullo / è . . . / seguir le fere fugaci, e le forti / atterrar combattendo."

126. Riccò 2004, 57–69.

127. Beccari 1785, 311–16 (4.7), 323–29 (5.2–3). An earlier episode, on 273–76 (2.4), shows another nymph, Melidia, tricking the same satyr.

128. See F. Contarini 1599, 76–77 (3.3), for Lirida's trapping of the satyr in company with Dorina; 77–80 (3.4) for the satyr's rescue by his wife (cf. Miani 1604, 26v–28v [2.3]); 118–19 (4.4) for the satyr's revenge trapping of Dorina; and 120–22 (4.5) for her rescue by Florindo.

129. Decroisette 2002, 162n53, 163n54.

130. See Decroisette 2002, 165–66.

131. On the episode in Ariosto, see Benson 1992, 139–48. On Flaminia Romana's dramatization, see Nicholson 1999, 246–48, 259–62; and Henke 2002, 89–91.

132. See Miani 1604, 50v (4.6), for a description of the satyr as a "vecchio impazzito, disdentato, e fiacco" (mad, toothless, feeble old creature); see also 57v (4.8), where the goatherd who unties him after Tirenia's tortures advises him that nymphs are best left to "giovanetti" (youths) rather than toothless old men like himself.

133. B. Torelli, "Partenia," 25v–26v (2.5), 45r–v (3.5).

134. "Gentildonna lucchese," 33r–v (2.7): "Hor questa / non è virtù da grande?" The actual attack is at 36r–37r (3.2–3). For the equivalent scene in *Flori*, see Campiglia 2004, 106–10 (1.6), discussed in Decroisette 2002, 174–76.

135. Cox and Sampson 2004, 16–17.

136. Androgeo is presented in act 5, scene 3, as having voluntarily submitted to Flori's "impero" (Campiglia 2004, 264; jurisdiction). He describes himself as her "servo," (266; servant). On Flori's autonomy from male authorities in the play, see Cox and Sampson 2004, 26 and n. 68.

137. Campiglia 2004, 274 (5.3).

138. T. Tasso 1977a, 686 (2.3): "fa d'uopo / d'esser un uom, Aminta, un uom ardito." "Gentildonna lucchese," 15v, 16v (1.5): "Inutil pianto ad huom viril non lice / sempre versar"; "E se haver non può luogo quella legge / che ogni amato riami, habbila quella / che l'odiato riodij, e tu qual prima / torna viril, e forte." See also 22v (2.4), where Armilla urges Filemone to put aside his tears and show himself a "bold and valorous lover" (ardito e valoroso Amante).

139. "Gentildonna lucchese," 11r, 17r: "ricovrai la libertà primiera" (Clorilli, 1.2); "Ricovra homai la libertà primiera" (Coribante to Filemone, 2.4).

140. Chater 1999, 578–79; Schuetze 1990; Lieti amanti 1990.

141. Lieti amanti 1990, 44: "lieto fuor de l'amoroso impaccio." The quotation is from the principal female-authored contribution to this microgenre, Orsina Cavaletti's male-voiced Sdegno la fiamma estinse, on which see Lieti amanti 1990, 23–24; and Newcomb 1992, 84.

142. See Urania's speech in Bracciolini 1597, 44v–45r (4.2); for Acrisio's display of anger and its effect, see 48r–51v (4.3–4). For discussion of the play, see Barbi 1897, 13–21, and Rees 2010, 89–90, which relates Bracciolini's play to Miani's *Amorosa speranza*. On the date of composition of Bracciolini's *Amoroso sdegno*, see Bracciolini 1597, A4r (Giovanni Battista Ciotti, "Ai lettori"), where it is described as having been written "six or seven years ago" (già sei, o sette anni sono); but cf. Barbi 1897, 7n1, for a document that speaks of the play as composed during the author's adolescence ("età più tosto fanciullesca che giovenile"), hence presumably in the early 1580s, since he was born in 1566. Since Bracciolini was based in Florence in the late 1580s, Bernardi may have been acquainted with his play.

143. "Gentildonna lucchese," 41r–44r (3.6).

144. Campiglia 1589 and 1996; Ducchi 1589, 45–53. The Vicenza edition contains an extended passage in praise of Tasso's friend and patron Cardinal Scipione Gonzaga (1542–93) that is not present in the version in Ducchi's anthology (Campiglia 1996, 84–85 [lines 197–223]). For critical discussion of the poem, see Perrone 1996; Cox and Sampson 2004, 26–27; and Ultsch 2005a, 87–91.

145. Campiglia 1996, 79 (lines 35–36): "con mie ragioni et arti lei ritrarre / da questi vani et infelici amori."

146. Campiglia 1996, 80 (line 104): "so che donna amo donna." For Flori's "confession" and self-defense generally, see lines 101–17.

147. The only example of Campiglia's verse for Calisa is a madrigal of 1588 reproduced in Morsolin 1882, 65. On the tradition of female-authored verse addressed to female patrons using the language of Petrarchan love, see ch. 2 at n. 154.

148. See Campiglia 1996, 81 (lines 139–41), where Calisa is said to have inscribed

the phrase "Your pain pleases me" (Il tuo dolor mi piace) on the bark of a laurel tree. The mention of laurel makes it likely that the reference is to a poetic, rather than an epistolary, exchange. Della Chiesa 1620, 201, attests to Pallavicino's having written verse.

149. "Diversi componimenti in lode dell'opera," in Campiglia 1588, K7r, lines 10–11 ("O di Natura / strano, contrario, inusitato effetto"); and K4r, lines 7–8 ("Sai che donna per donna alfin non sente / quel che sentì per Amaranta Flori"). Manfredi also seems to have disapproved of *Flori*'s other innovation in the treatment of erotic love in pastoral, namely, its idealization in Flori and Alessi of a sublimated Neoplatonic love. See Manfredi 1606, 195 (nominal letter to Campiglia of 29 August 1591, probably invented or reworked): "pregai il canchero ad Alessi et a tutte le ninfe che amino così fatti pastori" (I wished a cancer on Alessi and all nymphs who love shepherds of this kind).

150. For Campiglia's dialect verse, see Gagliardo 1584; and M. Milani 1983.

151. For the phoenix image and its accompanying sonnet, see Cox and Sampson 2004, 308–9. For Campiglia's and others' sense of her singularity, see Cox and Sampson 2004, 8; and Campiglia 2004, 308–10.

152. See I. Andreini 1601, 236–37 for Amaranta's speech, 233–40 for the poem in general.

153. I. Andreini 1601, 272–80. The speaker, Mirtillo, is identified as a "learned shepherd" (dotto pastor).

154. I. Andreini 1601, 281–92 (eclogue 9), 241–47; 2005, 149–59 (eclogue 3). *Galatea* in particular may offer some indication of the character of Laura Guidiccioni's lost *pastorelle* for the Florentine court. The two writers were friends (see I. Andreini 1601, 123–25, and 2005, 106–15, for a series of poems by Andreini mourning Guidiccioni's death).

155. *Poesie* 1590, 16v–18r. Viviani's incipit echoes the opening of Petrarch's sonnet 310 (Petrarca 1996a, 1190).

156. *Poesie* 1590, 17v: "su la sinistra sponda / di questo rio."

157. For the mention of the Cospiranti, see *Poesie* 1590, 17r; for "Coridone," 16v. Silvestro Carrari's membership in the Cospiranti is attested in Burchelati 1591, to which he contributes prefatory verse under the academic name "il Rinverdito."

158. On the mainland Veneto as a locus for women's writing, see Cox and Sampson 2004, 6–7, 10; and Cox 2008, 145–46.

159. See above at n. 101. If this conjecture is correct and Miani was an acquaintance of Carrari's, she may be a possible candidate for identification as one of the poet-nymphs portrayed in the eclogue. Other possibilities include the other two female poets of the Collalto volume, Innocenza Carrari (Fabrizia's sister) and Marina dalla Torre, as well as Lucia Colao, active in nearby Oderzo. Another possibility, especially given her connections with the circles of the Collalto (on which see ch. 2, n. 162), is Lucchesia Sbarra. Despite her youth—Sbarra was about 14 at the time—contemporary cultural patterns of precocious literary activity (see ch. 1 at n. 72) make the possibility that she may have been active as a poet by this age difficult to preclude.

160. E. Russo 2008, 27. The attack on Marino took place in early 1609. Miani's dedication of *Amorosa speranza* to Descalzi is discussed in Rees 2010, 57–59, and the connections between the two women are examined on 29–33. I refer to the dedicatee here as Descalzi Uberti for consistency with usual early modern naming practice, which places a woman's natal surname before her marital name. Miani 1604 gives her name as Uberti Descalzi.

161. On Leonida and Falconio, see Erythraeus 1647–48, 1:49–50 and 53–54.

162. Rodinò 2010. Since both Vanni and Murtola were in Rome in the jubilee year of 1600, it is possible that the contributions of Vanni, Murtola, Leonida, and Falconio to *Celinda* all derive from a particular contact or journey of Miani's. For evidence that Miani was already working on a tragedy, perhaps *Celinda*, in the late 1590s, see Finucci 2010, 9. Miani's other encomiasts in *Celinda* are more local: Ercole Manzoni, a poet from Este, near Padua, on whom see Miani 2010, 371n11; and Marcantonio Balcianelli, a Marinist poet from Verona, also in contact with Veneranda Bragadin (Bragadin 1619, 36). Miani 2010, 372n19, conflates Balcianelli with an earlier figure with the same surname, the medic Giovanni Balcianelli (b. 1526). A seventh poet, Gratiadio Conservi, has not been identified.

163. See ch. 1, n. 143.

164. See Haskins 2007, which includes previously unpublished documentation of Marinella's married life. On Marinella's contacts with Paduan literary circles, see ch. 1, n. 84, and ch. 2 at n. 113.

165. Verdile 1989–90, 185, lists Leonida among Sarrocchi's literary acquaintants but does not cite evidence.

166. Studies of early modern Italian tragedy have tended to concentrate on the first period of the genre's development, down to about the 1560s (Bergel 1965; Ariani 1974; Di Maria 2002). Overviews of the tragic production of the period covered in this book are available in Ariani 2007b, 1736–46; and Jannaco and Capucci 1966, 336–43. See also the more comprehensive but dated surveys in Bertana 1904, 84–168; and Herrick 1965.

167. The count is based on titles containing the word *tragedia* in the ICCU catalog during the period in question, excluding reprints of pre-1590 titles and *dramme per musica*. On *tragedia spirituale* as a genre, see ch. 1 at nn. 227–28.

168. On Forzatè's *Recinda* (among the most successful tragedies of the era in performance terms, with two recorded performances), see Neri 1904, 149–51; and Mangini 1983, 304, 326 and n. 151. On tragedy in Padua and in the Veneto more generally in this period, see Crovato 1975, 45–77; Mangini 1983, 298–311; and Finucci 2010, 32–35.

169. Ingegneri 1989, 7: "l'occhio disioso di dilettazione." On the expense of staging tragedies in this period, see Bertana 1904, 108–9. On tragedy as preponderantly a written genre, see Barish 1994, esp. 4–5. Documented performances of tragedies in the Veneto in the later sixteenth and early seventeenth centuries are listed in Mangini 1983, 322–36.

170. Ingegneri 1607, a4r–v.

171. See, e.g., in this period, Gabriele Zinani, *Almerigo* (1590), set in Constantinople; Claudio Forzatè, *Recinda* (1590), Algiers; Alessandro Miari, *Il Prencipe Tigridoro* (1592), and Muzio Manfredi, *Semiramis* (1593), ancient Assyria; and Maffeo Venier, *Hidalba* (1496), Friesland.

172. On the prominence of female characters within Italian Renaissance tragedy, see Di Maria 2002, 101–25; as well as Clubb 1964, 110; Herrick 1965, 116; and Finucci 2010, 28–30. On tragedy as a "feminized genre" in an English Renaissance context, see Purkiss 1998, xxvii.

173. Detailed discussions of *Celinda* and its sources may be found in Finucci 2010, 30–46; and Rees 2010, 126–76. See also, more briefly, Bertana 1904, 132–35 (little more than a detailed plot summary); Mangini 1983, 307; and Rees 2008, 55–60.

174. The device of the "prologue ghost," first used by Euripides and Seneca, had been incorporated into Italian drama by Giraldi Cinzio and Speroni in the 1540s. See Bertana 1904, 111; and Moorman 1906, 85–88.

175. The conventionality of this pair of figures is implicitly acknowledged by their lack of names outside their role descriptions, "Nutrice" and "Consigliere."

176. Miani 2010, 80–110 (1.3).

177. See Herrick 1965, 222–25; and Crovato 1975, 52–57.

178. On Zinani's play, see Bertana 1904, 96–101, and Herrick 1965, 235–38; on Angeli's, see Herrick 1965, 245–48. On Giraldi's *Arrenopia*, see Bertini 2008, 161–257.

179. Firenzuola 1971, 106–19 (1.2); Zanrè 2003, 165–66; Giannetti 2009, 87–89, 124–25. The plot motif of the cross-dressing boy who seduces the daughter of his hosts derives ultimately from the story of Achilles and Deidamia, told by Statius and Ovid (see Callen King 1987, 174–82; and Heslin 2005). The same plot device is used by the Spanish writer Maria de Zayas in her *Amor solo per vencer*, of 1647 (see Velasco 2000, 24–29).

180. But see Giannetti 2009, 90–110, for other instances, mainly from comedy, where the desire in question is not based on one protagonist's having mistaken the other for a man. Giannetti underlines the importance of the Firenzuola novel in establishing a discourse of female-female desire not resting on the Ovidian-Ariostan topos of "impossibility" (see Giannetti 2009, 87).

181. Miani 2010, 228 (4.7): "tra gli horrori di Marte, il suo bel volto / le vaghezze di Venere scopriva."

182. Miani 2010, 216 (4.4): "fallo amoroso." Autilio uses the phrase "amoroso fallo" to describe his own "crime" on 66 (1.1). The couple's pledge to marry is mentioned in Celinda's original confession to her nurse on 104 (1.3).

183. See esp. Miani 2010, 66 (1.1), where Autilio rehearses his reasons for maintaining secrecy despite the potentially grave consequences for his father and his subjects.

184. Sixteenth-century dramatic adaptations of the Ghismonda-Guiscardo story are discussed in Herrick 1965, 188–95. For Luigi Groto's *Hadriana*, based on the story of Romeo and Juliet, see Herrick 1965, 213–17. Besides the Ghismonda-based plays,

affairs or secret marriages on the part of royal daughters punished harshly by their fathers are found in Giraldi Cinzio's famous *Orbecche* (1541), as well as in later works such as Giacomo Guidoccio's *Mathilda* (1592) and Verlato's *Rodopeia*.

185. For Autilio's dying plea to Celinda to remain alive for the sake of their child, see Miani 2010, 282 (5.5). Katie Rees's statement that "Celinda makes it clear that her death is motivated by the impossibility of giving birth to a 'successor bastardo' [bastard heir]" (Rees 2008, 60) is misleading in that the phrase, though uttered by Celinda, occurs in a very different context: Celinda is speaking of her distaste at the idea of marrying another royal suitor while pregnant with Autilio's child (Miani 2010, 106 [1.3]).

186. On this character type in mid-sixteenth-century Italian tragedy, see Di Maria 2002, 114–19. For later sixteenth-century instances, see Herrick 1965, 215–17 (Groto's *Hadriana*), 224–25 (Verlato's *Rodopeia*), 191–94 (Federico Asinari's *Tancredi* [1588] and Pomponio Torelli's play of the same name [1597]); see also Neri 1904, 151 (Forzatè's *Recinda*).

187. See, e.g., Miani 2010, 106 (1.3), Nurse; 144 (2.3), Cubo; 206 (4.4), Nurse; 282 (5.5), Autilio, quoted in n. 189 below.

188. Cox 2008, 168–72.

189. For Celinda's allusion to her "debil cor," see Miani 2010, 214 (4.4). For Autilio's speech, see 282 (5.5), esp. lines 172–77: ". . . in tante alte sciagure / mostrar vogliate quell'ardir che solo / d'alme regali e generose è dote, / e sopportando di Fortuna i colpi / che ne i sublimi più mostran sua forza, / vogliate star in vita" (In such dire misfortunes, show that courage that resides alone in royal and noble souls, and braving the blows of Fortune, which fall hardest on the highest, resolve to remain in life).

190. More explicit religious concerns about suicide are expressed in Pomponio Torelli's *Tancredi* (1597), which has a Christian, medieval setting. In a significant amendment to his Boccaccian source, Torelli has a priest minister spiritually to Ghismonda after her self-poisoning, persuading her to confess and seek absolution for her sin prior to her death (see Torelli 2004, 130–31, lines 2499–2541; for similar scruples in Francesco Bracciolini's epic *La croce racquistata* [1611], see Cabani 1995, 75–76).

191. See esp. Alcandro's heroic narration in Miani 2010, 226–34 (4.7), of Lucinia's defeat of two Persian warriors, one of whom is said to have considered defeat at a woman's hands worse than death (234, lines 164–65); see also 168 (3.1), where the overconfident Attamante, certain of his victory over this "woman accustomed to the distaff and spindle" (donna avezza a la connocchia, al fuso), finds himself unseated by Lucinia.

192. See ch. 5 at nn. 76–78.

193. For further examples, see Cox 2008, 214–15, 365n195, 369n228.

194. Torelli 2004, 127, line 2417: "donnesco valor." See also 63, line 289, for a description by Ghismonda of her heart as "dauntless" (invitto), and cf. above, n. 189, for Celinda's reference to her own "weak heart."

195. Miani 2010, 106 (1.3): "Perdei con la virtù l'animo regio / a l'hor, che di donzella / mi conobbi esser donna."

196. Miani 2010, 212 (4.4).

197. Miani 2010, 212 (4.4), line 117. Cf. T. Tasso 1977a, 671; and Alighieri 1994, 2:83 (*Inf.* 5.56). In his moralizing revision of Tasso's chorus (see above at n. 38), Guarino had proposed the counterformula "Piaccia, se lice" (Let only what is licit please).

198. For the term *hypothetical stageability*, see Barish 1994, 24. For evidence that Miani's *Amorosa speranza* was performed, see Rees 2008, 43–44; and Finucci 2010, 24–25.

199. The former scene, in Miani 2010, 256 (5.3), contains a quite detailed description of the litter, enhancing the visual effect: "questa intricata bara / d'intessuti tronconi e rotti" (this litter of closely woven snapped branches). See also 170 (3.1) for a similarly detailed description of a boy herald dressed "in barbaro vestir d'oro contesto / cui pende al fianco una ritorta spada" (in barbarous dress of woven gold, with a curved sword at his side).

CHAPTER FOUR: Sacred Narrative

1. Secondary literature on religious narrative production in this period is cited in ch. 1, n. 208.

2. Examples of this belated circulation are the *Passione di Christo*, of Niccolò Cicerchia (1335–76) (Varanini 1965, 309–79), republished in Florence in 1591, for the first time since 1551, and in 1600; and the *Vita di nostra Donna*, of Antonio Cornazzano (c. 1432–84), republished in 1591 in Treviso, for the first time since 1533.

3. For mention of Tornabuoni's narrative poems, see Serdonati 1596, 586, reproduced in Della Chiesa 1620, 204.

4. For the unfinished work, see below at n. 140. The lost works are a life of the second-century martyr Saint Eustace by Leonora Bellati (which may, however, have been a tragedy rather than a narrative poem) and a poem on Mary Magdalene by Maddalena Salaroli Ariosti (see ch. 3, n. 2). Another female-authored hagiographic narrative from the period, which I have not been able to consult, is the 1630 version of Margherita Costa's *Santa Cecilia*, of which only a single copy appears to exist, at the Biblioteca Giovardiana, Veroli (a revised version was published in 1644). See also Grumelli 1596, discussed below in ch. 6.

5. Muzi 1844, 188; Gamurrini 1909, 328. On Turina's poetic relationship with Ghelfucci, who authored an extensive love *canzoniere* addressed to her, now in the Biblioteca Comunale of Arezzo, see, most comprehensively, Bà 2010; also Torrioli 1940, 15–18, and Bà and Milani 1998, 61–64. On Ghelfucci's *Rosario della Madonna* and its contemporary reception, see Torrioli 1940, 20–25; and Martini 2003, 184.

6. See ch. 1, n. 204.

7. On the 1596 ban and its subsequent retraction, see Fragnito 1997, 204–10, 302–3; and 2005, 117–31. On the effects of ecclesiastical censorship on narrative poetry drawing on biblical subject matter, see Chiesa 2002, 173–83.

8. Fonte 1582, 19–20, 31–32, 43. The text of both poems may be found on the Italian Women Writers site, www.lib.uchicago.edu/efts/IWW/. There has been no sustained critical discussion of these works to date, though see the brief remarks in Malpezzi Price 2003a, 34–35; and Doglio 2007a, 1647–48.

9. Luke 23:27–31, John 19:26–27; all biblical references are to the King James version. While Fonte describes her work in her dedicatory letter (to Doge Niccolò da Ponte) as "estratta da i quattro Evangelisti" (taken from the four Gospels), it is possible that she also made use of "premixed" synthesizing accounts of Christ's passion and resurrection, such as that in Cicerchia (see above, n. 2), or Amulio 1556, 236v–244v and 245v–250r. In the case of *La passione*, another possible source is Pietro Aretino's *Passione di Giesu* (1534), on whose own eclectic use of source materials see Boillet 2007, 143–49. On the use of Aretino, officially banned in this period, by Lucrezia Marinella and Maddalena Campiglia, see the text of this chapter at nn. 111–12 and ch. 6 at nn. 73–74.

10. Fonte 1582, 33–34, 40–41, 47–48.

11. Fonte 1592, A2v–A4r, B3r–B4v (stanzas 10–20, 38–45).

12. Fonte 1582, 10–12, 47–48. For the relevant passages in Fonte 1592, see the previous note.

13. Malpezzi Price 2003a, 34, misleadingly describes Langosca as Savoy ambassador to Venice in her own right. Fonte's letter suggests that Langosca was proposed as dedicatee by her Cremonese literary contact Orazio Guarguanti (1554–1611), on whom see Fonte 1997, 182, 217–18; see also Manfredi 1606, 66.

14. Fonte 1592, †4r.

15. Colonna 1557, 2008. For a discussion of Fonte's *canzone*, see ch. 2 at nn. 74–76.

16. See nn. 11–12 for references.

17. Fonte 1592, A2v: "in solitaria cella."

18. See n. 10 for Fonte 1582; for Fonte 1592, see C1v–D2r (stanzas 53–79). This episode is the longest in *La resurrettione*, comprising 26 stanzas.

19. For the Virgin's waiting for Christ's resurrection "armed with faith" (armata di fè), see Fonte 1592, A4r (stanza 18); for Magdalene's "new love," D1v (stanza 76); for Cleopas as "poor in faith" (povero di fede), D3v (stanza 87).

20. Fonte 1592, B4v (stanza 47): "Donne . . . sciocche, e leggiere"). An interesting point of comparison for Fonte, in respect of the philogynistic emphases of her account of Christ's passion and death, is offered by the prose meditations on the same theme by the German Lutheran religious writer Catharina Regina von Grieffenberg (1633–94) (see Tatlock 2009, 28, 31).

21. Fonte 1582, 31–32. On anti-Semitism in Fonte, and its context, see Fonte 1997, 75 and n. 41. Jews are described in the *Passione* as "vermi vilissimi," "stuol superbo e schivo," "popol rio" (Fonte 1582, 21, 22, 36; vilest worms, proud and contemptuous horde, evil race). At the same time, however, Fonte underlines Christ's forgiveness of his tormentors while on the Cross (Luke 23:34–35) and has the grieving Virgin later recall it when refusing to blame the Jews for her son's death (Fonte

1582, 38, 47). The *canzone* that ends the *Passione*, following a commonplace of penitential literature, blames the Christian sinner's soul as worse than the Jews in the metaphorical torment it inflicts on Christ through sin (Fonte 1582, 53 [stanza 5]: "Hor non fur mai gli Hebrei / nel tuo mortal sì rei / come ne l'alma noi" [The Jews were never so cruel to you in your mortal self as we are in the spirit]).

22. Fonte 1582, 41: "quel corpo, ahimè, vergine e casto."

23. Fonte 1582, 40 ("le belle chiome innanellate e d'oro"; "[il] viso suo più candido, che latte"), 41–42 ("empio crin"; "occhi vani, insidiosi"). For comparable treatment of the same theme in Lucrezia Marinella's *Rime sacre*, see ch. 2 at n. 130.

24. Camilli 1592, 80. More nuanced is Valvasone's *Lagrime di Santa Maria Maddalena*, first published in 1586, which excuses Magdalene's transgressions as the result of possession by a Fury (Valvasone 1592, 167r, 168r). Here her beauty is presented in positive terms, said to have grown following her encounter with Christ (171r).

25. Fonte 1592, C1v–C3r (stanzas 53–62).

26. Fonte 1592, C3r–v (stanzas 62–63): "dolce Amata"; "dolci accenti." Earlier in the poem, in stanza 15 (A3v), the Virgin too is portrayed as spectacle, with the internal audience this time made up of "wonder-struck angels" (angeli stupefatti).

27. Fonte 1592, C1v (stanza 53): "quasi un bel fior"; cf. Petrarca 1996a, 739 (sonnet 160): "Qual miracol è quel, quando tra l'erba / quasi un fior siede."

28. Petrarca 1996a, 725–34.

29. Fonte 1592, C1v–C2r (stanzas 53–54).

30. Where Fonte's Petrarchan subtexts are concerned, aside from that noted in n. 27, above, see, for the topos of the grass and flowers springing up beneath the lady's feet as she walks, Petrarca 1996a, 751 (sonnet 165, lines 1–4); and for the motif of the loosed golden hair, 441 (sonnet 90, lines 1–2).

31. Ariosto 1976, 1:202 (10.34): "Or si ferma s'un sasso, e guarda il mare; / né men d'un vero sasso, un sasso pare" (Now she sits on a stone and gazes at the sea; and, as much as a real stone, she seems a stone herself).

32. Fonte 1592, C2r (stanza 55); cf. Ariosto 1976, 1:218 (10.96). The same Ariostan motif is used in the same narrative context in Marinella 1610a, 211–12, in a passage that may reflect Fonte's influence. For another example of the use of an erotic episode from Ariosto in a sacred context in this period, see Cave 1969, 283–84.

33. Javitch 1978, 98–101.

34. On Laura's hair as "net" or "snare," see Petrarca 1996a, 796 (sonnet 181). For use of this Petrarchan metaphor, in a similarly negative sense, in Counter-Reformation descriptions of Mary Magdalene, see Ussia 1988, 413–14, 417; and 1993, 129.

35. See Fonte 1988, 167–68; and 1997, 235–36.

36. For discussion, see, most comprehensively, Bà 2009, 102–25. See also Torrioli 1940, 19; Bà 2007, 490–93; Lanza 2007, 109–18; and Costa-Zalessow 2009, 21–24. For a modern edition, see Turina 2005.

37. Rosary-themed verse collections flourished in the later sixteenth century, stimulated in part by the institution in 1573 by Gregory XIII of the feast of Santa

Maria del Rosario (see Quondam 2005a, 208, listing 13 works within this "thematic microsegment" of religious poetry published between 1581 and 1600; see also Martini 2003, 183–84). Another rosary-themed sonnet sequence by a female author, on a much smaller scale than Turina's (17 sonnets), is found in Bragadin 1614, 38–45.

38. Turina 1595, 1, and 2005, 155: "Svegliati e surgi, o pigra anima mia." Henceforth, page references are to the 1595 edition. The 2005 edition gives the page number from the 1595 edition before each sonnet.

39. Turina 1595, 62: "Anima, hor non è tempo di dormire: / vien con Christo ne l'orto a vigilare."

40. Turina 1595, 12, 17, 23. Similar calls to participate are found in medieval works such as the *Meditations on the Life of Christ* (e.g., *Meditations* 1961, 68, 81).

41. See, e.g., Turina 1595, 75, 85. For discussion and further exemplification of Turina's first-person interjections in the *Rime spirituali*, see Bà 2007, 492–93.

42. The "Gaudioso" section has 50 sonnets; the "Doloroso," 37; and the "Glorioso," 40. Turina's collection is substantial by the standards of rosary-themed verse collections if we omit epics such as Montefuscoli's *Grandezze del verbo ristrette ne' misteri del rosario* (1593) and Ghelfucci's *Rosario della Madonna* (1603). Ancarano 1588 contains 15 sonnets and 15 ten-stanza ottava rima poems (1,410 lines in total, to Turina's 2,108), while some rosary texts are much shorter: Bonello 1583 contains a mere three *canzoni*; Della Porta 1584, 30 *ottave*; and Tartaglia 1598, 15 sonnets.

43. On the dedicatory letter, see ch. 1 at nn. 199–204. Turina also addresses two madrigals to Clement, preceding the "Doloroso" and "Glorioso" sections. The following year, she dedicated a secular work to his nephew, Cinzio Aldobrandini (see ch. 5, n. 1).

44. Turina 1595, 34: "segni di stupendissimo valore."

45. Turina 1595, 104–5. On the tradition of this rare scene, see Breckenridge 1957, 28–32; Snyder 1985; and L. Campbell 1998, 262.

46. A precedent for Turina's use of a sonnet sequence as a vehicle for sacred narrative is Carafa 1573; see also, later, Morone 1621, 347–67.

47. Although she starts with more complex and conventional rhyme schemes, Turina introduces *cdcdcd* rhymes in her tercets and *ababbaba* rhymes in her quatrains beginning on Turina 1595, 7 and 11, respectively. Subsequently, these alternating forms recur quite frequently, sometimes combined in the same poem (see, e.g., Turina 1595, 20–21, 34–36, 44, 59–60, 105–6, 109, 111, 121, 125–26, 133, 136–37).

48. Turina 1595, 36–37: "Giace il mio servo"; "Miserere di me! la mia figliuola / spirito ancide iniquitoso, e rio."

49. Turina 1595, 102, 64. For other examples of such lyric interludes, see 34, evoking the innumerable multitude of Christ's miracles; and 49, describing Christ's tears at the death of Lazarus.

50. See ch. 1 at n. 203.

51. The quotation in the text ("una santa, e devota semplicità") derives from the prefatory letter to Montefuscoli 1593. See also Ancina 1599, a1v–a2v; and, for discussion, Selmi 2005, 427–28, 440–41, 464.

52. Turina 1595, 16, 19–20: "tremanti braccia"; "dolcezza e . . . affezione." The story of Simeon derives from Luke, 2:25–35. Turina's emotionalism here may be contrasted with the gravity of Vittoria Colonna's sonnets on the same theme (Colonna 1982, 142 [S1:114–15]).

53. Turina 1595, 23: "Servi la Madre, e 'l suo Figliuol divino; / scoti la cuna, accendi 'l piccol foco; / scalda le fasce, e gli prepara i bagni."

54. Turina 1595, 14, 16; see also 19, where the child's eyes are described as "amorosette e belle." For examples of comparable language in the 1628 *Rime*, see ch. 2 at nn. 193–96. Especially in her use of diminutives, Turina's verse in the nativity portions of the *Rime spirituali* may be compared to spiritual lyrics on the same theme by Grillo, marked by their taste for *mignardise* (see Martini 1994, 371–74). Gabrielle Coignard's treatment of the same narrative also offers some analogies with Turina's (see Ferguson 1999, 203–4).

55. Turina 1595, 16: "feminea cetra."

56. Marinella 1610b, 28 (2.15): "L'ama Figlio, Dio il prega, e Padre honora." Marinella's phrasing recalls that of a sonnet of Colonna's addressing the Virgin: "L'adorasti Signor, Figlio il nudristi, / L'amasti Sposo, e L'onorasti Padre" (Colonna 1982, 135 [S1:100]).

57. Marinella 1610a, 107: "con riverenza di Figlia, con charità di Sposa, e con humiltà di Serva."

58. Turina 1595, 147.

59. De Cupiti 1593, 311 (12.13), 406 (15.28), 529–30 (19.26–29).

60. Montefuscoli 1593, unnumbered. The text is briefly discussed in Quondam 1973, 126–27.

61. This calculation relies on the new birthdate of 1579 proposed in this book for Marinella (see introduction, n. 5). As a precedent for this kind of precocious debut, it should be recalled that Tasso began his first epic, the fragmentary *La Gierusalemme*, when he was 16 and published his *Rinaldo* at 18. See also ch. 1 at n. 72.

62. Marinella 1595 is 253 stanzas long; Marinella 1597, 239 stanzas. Malpezzi Price and Ristaino 2008, 64–65, misleadingly cite as the number of stanzas in the two poems the total number of lines (respectively, 2024 and 1912).

63. Martinengo 1590 is discussed in Selmi 2005, 455–61; Passero 1589 and Martinengo 1590, in Doglio 2007a, 1641–42.

64. Marinella's knowledge of Filippi's poem is attested in Marinella 1601, 43; and 1999, 92.

65. Dell'Uva 1982. For discussion, see Doglio 2007a, 1639–41.

66. Passero 1589 has 288 stanzas; Castelletti 1594, 204. Dell'Uva's *Le vergini prudenti* is the longest of these small-scale works, with 571 stanzas.

67. Examples of lay male authors of religious works are cited in Doglio 2007a, 1643. See also Donia 1600, by a Sicilian medic and *letterato*.

68. Cataudella 2001.

69. See ch. 1, n. 234.

70. The choice of dedicatee for the first work may reflect the Modenese origins of

Marinella's father (the Este ruled Modena, as well as Ferrara). On women's dedicatory practices in the later Cinquecento, see Cox 2008, 154–57.

71. Marinella 1595, though less decorative, has friezes marking the opening of cantos 2–4.

72. The contributors of prefatory verse to Marinella 1595 are Teodoro Angelucci (d. c. 1600), Boncio Leoni, Giovanni Maria Avanzi (1549–1622), and Giuseppe Policreti. For identification, see Lavocat 1998b, xiii. Leoni was also the second contributor to Marinella 1597.

73. Marinella 1595, dedicatory letter, 2r ("rozzo e basso stile"); 1597, A2r ("la bassezza e debolezza dell'ingegno mio").

74. Marinella 1597, A2r–v: "provincie, e cittadi, ove nascono e sono nati divinissimi e nobilissimi poeti."

75. For the *Rime*, see ch. 2, n. 106.

76. Columba's story was well known through its inclusion in the popular and much-published anonymous hagiographic compendium *Legendario delle santissime vergini* (the first word sometimes spelled *Leggendario*), which Laura Benedetti has identified as Marinella's source (Benedetti 2005, 97).

77. The only comparative discussion of the two poems to date is found in Malpezzi Price and Ristaino 2008, 61–79. For *La Colomba sacra*, see also Santacroce 1999–2000, 54–55; and Benedetti 2005, 95–101. For *La vita di San Francesco*, see Doglio 1989, 437–38; Mongini 1997; Kolsky 2005, 329; Selmi 2005, 434–40, 468–69; and Maggi 2008, 111–24.

78. The episode of Francis's voyage to Egypt (here "Babilonia") is found at Marinella 1997b, 419–22 [2.1–24]). The account is largely taken up by a verbatim account of Francis's preaching (419–20 [2, 10–17]) and includes little descriptive detail.

79. Marinella 1997b, 410–11 (1.35–45). Francis's later struggles with the devil are briefly described on 424 (2.36).

80. The phrase quoted in the text, "descrittioni delle devotioni, delle contemplationi," is from Giovanni Battista Bonelli's preface to Martinengo 1590, unnumbered.

81. For discussion, see below in the text. Most of the properly epic business of *La vita di San Francesco* is concentrated in its opening canto. See, e.g., Marinella 1997b, 410 (1.35–37) for a scene in hell recalling in miniature Tasso's scene of the council in hell at the beginning of canto 4 of the *Gerusalemme liberata*; 410 (1.38) for an instance of the epic topos of the disguised supernatural agent; and 413–14 (1.58–62) for Francis's epically treated journey to Rome to seek papal approval of his order.

82. Marinella 1997b, 405 (1.2): "Te non chiam'io, che canti al suon de l'armi / del crudo Marte i paventosi aspetti, / ma te Francesco d'invocar sol parmi / che la tua vita e 'l tuo morir mi detti." For context, see Selmi 2005, 462–63.

83. Marinella 1997b, 405 (1.3), 406 (1.9), 411 (1.45). See also 412 (1.51) for a reference to Francis as "il chiaro eroe" (the glorious hero); 407 (1.17), 417 (1.83), and 422 (2.23), where he is termed or compared in simile to a military leader ("il capitano eletto"; "il gran capitano"; "capitan generoso"); and 425 (2.45) for a reference to Francis's followers as a militia of "guerrieri." In militarizing the figure of Francis,

Marinella was consistent with a general trend of the period (see, e.g., Maggi 2008, 91, 93, 97–98, 104–7).

84. Marinella 1595, 8v (1.23): "in purpureo color di regio ornato / venerando più ch'huom assai riluce." On Marinella's ambiguous representation of Aureliano, mainly condemnatory but partly admiring, see Lavocat 1998b, xxxix.

85. For Columba as "guerriera di Christo," see Marinella 1595, 9r (1.24). For comment, see Benedetti 2005, 101.

86. Marinella 1595, 31r (2.43): "femina vil . . . cui la conocchia è troppo grande somma."

87. Marinella 1595, 43v.

88. In medieval bestiary lore, eagles were famed for their ability to look directly into the sun. For Columba's defeat of the Roman "eagle," see Marinella 1595, 44r (4.54): "O potenza romana, ove hora sono / di tante guerre l'honorate palme? / . . . / . . . a Colomba humil / Aquila altera / cede" (O Roman potency, where now are the honored palms of your many victories? . . . To the humble dove, the haughty eagle yields).

89. On Aurelian's victory over Zenobia, see Marinella 1595, 6r (1.6–8).

90. See ch. 1 at n. 245; and Benedetti 2005, 98–100.

91. Marinella 1595, 9r (1.24), 39r (4.24–25).

92. Marinella 1595, 7r (1.14).

93. T. Tasso 1980, 108 (4.30).

94. For scenes in religious epics modeled on Tasso's account of Armida's embassy to the Christian camp in canto 4 of the *Gerusalemme liberata*, see Gallucci 1618, 263–64 (13.3–11); and Carpanè 2005, 236–37. Moderata Fonte appropriates a phrase from a description of Armida—"nativi gigli" (native lilies)—for her description of Mary Magdalene in *La resurrettione di Giesu Christo*, while Sebastiano Castelletti, in his *La trionfatrice Cecilia*, appropriates a phrase of Tasso's describing Armida's aspirations to material victory over the crusaders—"in treccia, e in gonna" (in tresses and skirt)—to describe Saint Cecilia's spiritual victory over her tormentors. See, for Fonte, text above at n. 29, and cf. T. Tasso 1980, 481 (16.23); for Castelletti, see Castelletti 1594, 2 (1.3), and cf. T. Tasso 1980, 108 (4.27). See also Cosentino 2007, 67–69, on allusions to the figure of Armida in Federico Della Valle's tragedy *Iudit* (1627); and Carpanè 2006, 22–23, for echoes of Virgil's Dido in the descriptions of Judith in Bartolomeo Tortoletti's *Iuditha vindex et vindicata* (1628). A similar poetic "conversion" of the figure of Ariosto's Alcina is discussed in ch. 1 at n. 225.

95. T. Tasso 1980, 107 (4.23).

96. Marinella 1595, 37v, 39v (4.16, 17).

97. For the phrase *frail warrior* (fral guerriera), used of Mary Magdalene in Paolo Silvio's *Maddalena penitente* (1602), see Selmi 2005, 444–45. For Columba as anti-Armida, note Tasso's comparison of Armida to a "timid swan" (timido cigno) fleeing the crusading army's "eagle" in the final canto of his poem (T. Tasso 1980, 638 [20.68]); and see above, n. 88, for Marinella's reversal of this imagery.

98. See, e.g., the opening cantos of Martinengo 1590 and Castelletti 1594, which

give much space to the beauty of their female saint-protagonists and the love they inspire in their admirers.

99. Marinella 1997b, 437 (3.39).

100. The borrowing is noted in Malpezzi Price and Ristaino 2008, 65–66.

101. Marinella 1693, 19, contains a madrigal "to the most reverend Capuchin fathers, true imitators of the seraphic Francis" *(Alli molto reverendi padri Capuccini veri imitatori del serafico San Francesco)*. The Capuchin order, established in Venice in the 1530s, had assumed an especially high profile since the votive church of the Redentore was entrusted to them in 1592.

102. Marinella 1997b, 422–23 (1.25–33), 426–31 (2.50–88). Images of Francis in meditation, sometimes equipped with a skull and a crucifix, were popular in this period (see *Immagine* 1982, 91–93).

103. For Francis as latter-day martyr, see Marinella 1997b, 437 (3.36–38).

104. The philosophical connections between the *Discorso* and the poem it accompanies are examined, with different emphases, in Mongini 1997, esp. 386–403; Selmi 2005, 434–40; and Maggi 2008, 117–18. See also Zaja 2008, 399–400. I take the title *Discorso del rivolgimento amoroso, verso la somma bellezza* from the title page of Marinella 1597: Marinella 1997a gives a variant title.

105. For a reading of the *Vita di San Francesco* as embodying, specifically, the model of "spiritual exercise" prescribed by Ignatius Loyola, see Mongini 1997, 363–75.

106. Marinella 1997b, 440 (3.56–58). On Angelico and Diamantina, see Haskins 2006, 92–93.

107. Marinella 1617, 37v–46v.

108. On the 1617 revision, see Carinci 2009, 166, 169–70, 201–4. The 1610 edition was also revised, though much less extensively (see 200–201).

109. For the Magdalene digression, see Marinella 1617, 36v–47v (verse version) (5.7–6.40). For discussion, see Carinci 2009, 169–70, 201–3.

110. Marinella 1610a, 252–53; 2008, 244. The most likely source is the Golden Legend (Marinella 2008, 244n253).

111. Carinci 2009, 181–97; see also, 177–78, where Carinci notes that Marinella's list of sources is largely drawn from Razzi. For discussion of Marinella 1602, see, most fully, Carinci 2009, 163–215; see also Kolsky 2005, 329, 331; Marinella 2008, 119–28; and Piantoni 2009.

112. Marinella 1998, 2–3.

113. Marinella 1610b, 2 (1.2). The emphatic presence of the poetic *io* here should be noted as a counterexample to Serena Pezzini's contention that female authors of epic tend to prefer more self-effacing styles of incipit (Pezzini 2005, 193–97).

114. On the fortunes of Sannazaro's epic in this period, see ch. 1, n. 206. For the comparison of Martinengo's epic to Tasso's *Liberata*, see Andrea Chiocchi, dedicatory letter, unnumbered, in Martinengo 1595.

115. Marinella 1610b, 37 (2.40): "Da la Vergine pia, dal nato Duce / preser congedo i gloriosi Heroi." For Mary as "Diva" or "Dea," see, e.g., 24 (2.2), 27 (2.11), and 62

(4.27); for heaven as "Olimpo," 31 (2.24); and for the angels as "Numi," 60 (4.21). Marinella's use of such classicizing language in Christian contexts is reminiscent of that of Lorenza Strozzi in L. Strozzi 1588 (see Stevenson 2002, 113).

116. Marinella 1610b, 3 (1.3): "'l mele / stillar ruvidi tronchi"; "'l tosco, e 'l fele / deposer l'hidre"; "Il fero Re de' sempiterni horrori." Marinella's description of the Golden Age echoes the opening lines of the chorus at the end of the first act of Tasso's *Aminta* but "upgrades" Tasso's diction to a more epic register (*idre* in place of *serpi* for "snakes"). Classicizing descriptions of dawn and night are found on 11 (1.30), 25 (2.5), 32 (2.26), 60 (4.19), and 64 (4.32). Epic similes occupying half an octave may be found on 20 (1.55), 62 (4.25), and 68 (4.43), and one occupying an entire octave on 59 (4.18).

117. The text of the letter is found in Marinella 1998, 199–201. For discussion, see Piantoni 2009, 435–38.

118. Marinella 1998, 200.

119. Marinella 1998, 199: "la grandezza di questo modo di scrivere ora da me usato, il quale, s'io non m'inganno, tiene il sommo dell'altezza dell'eloquenza."

120. Maggi 2008, 117–18. Marinella's list of *auctores* may be found in Marinella 1998, 199–200. As Eleonora Carinci notes, for understandable reasons, Marinella's declared sources omit her actual principal stylistic model, Aretino (Carinci 2009, 173–74).

121. The only critical discussion in print to date of Marinella's *De' gesti heroici* is Kolsky 2005, 334–36. An abridged edition is currently being prepared under the direction of Armando Maggi, to be published by Longo (Ravenna).

122. Marinella's conduit to the Medici at this point was Cristoforo Bronzini, whom she acknowledges in Marinella 1624, 260; see Von Tippelskirch 2008, 140–41, which notes that Marinella wrote an encomium of Carlo de' Medici in the early 1620s on Bronzini's advice.

123. Marinella 1624, 248: "spoglie, archi, carri trionfali, imprese, trofei"; for the Medicean procession, see 249–60. The only previous work of Marinella's to include dynastic praise within the texture of the fiction is her 1605 *Arcadia felice* (Marinella 1998, 160–63).

124. Marinella 1624, 307: "giustissimi duci, e sovrani heroi"; "reggere con pietà, et amore non pur la bella Firenze e l'Etruria, ma il mondo tutto."

125. Marinella 1610b, 224–25; 1603, 13r–14v.

126. For examples, see Marinella 1617, 40v (5.41–42) (verse version) ("E l'aureo crin . . . / . . . / spruzzato alquanto del bel sangue humano, / onde in piu parti rosseggiando splende; / cosi fiammeggia l'or cui dotta mano / di porporini smalti adorno rende"); and 1624, 40 ("la cui bianchezza aspersa del suo sangue, pareva avorio, sparso di purpurine rose, overo spruzzato d'ostro"). The first passage quoted echoes a passage in Tasso describing Clorinda's golden hair scattered with blood after she is wounded in battle (T. Tasso 1980, 83 [3.30]).

127. On this motif in Marinella, see ch. 5 at n. 236.

128. *Amore innamorato, et impazzato* is discussed in ch. 5, sec. 4. See also ch. 2

at nn. 166–76 and 193–96 for maternal verse by Lucchesia Sbarra and Francesca Turina; and Marinella 1635, 363, 364, 373–76, and 2009, 254, 257, 265–67 (15.23, 36–37, 74–85), for an episode in her epic *L'Enrico* foregrounding the mutual devotion between a young soldier, Ernesto, and his mother.

129. See ch. 2 at n. 185.

130. The fiend Hapalo, sent by the devil, first appears to goad Lapa at Marinella 1624, 37. The same name is used for a demon who fulfills a similar role of worldly temptation in Marinella 1997b, 410 (1.37).

131. For comparisons between Lapa's maternal love and erotic obsession, see, e.g., Marinella 1624, 7, 74.

132. See, e.g., Lapa's attempts to dissuade Catherine from self-mortification in Marinella 1624, 56 and 63–65.

133. See Marinella 1610a, 41–42 for the description of the Virgin's convent school, 49–51 for her brilliance as an interpreter of scripture. For discussion, see Carinci 2009, 206–7, which notes sources for Marinella's account in Aretino.

134. See Marinella 1610a, 50–51, and 2008, 150, for Mary's childhood teaching; Marinella 1610a, 230–31, and 2008, 234, for her activity as a proselytizer after Christ's death. For discussion, see Carinci 2009, 208–9. For Catherine's childhood teaching role, see Marinella 1624, 15–18; for her later activity as a teacher in the convent to which Marinella unhistorically consigns her, 164–86; for God's directive to her to preach publicly, leaving her "solitude," 194; and for her preaching, 198–99, 240–41.

135. For Catherine's miraculously granted literacy, see Marinella 1624, 132. For discussion of this episode in early biographies of Catherine, see Tylus 2009, 11–14. More generally, we see God assuring Catherine that he will infuse her with the wisdom and knowledge necessary for preaching at Marinella 1624, 156 and 194.

136. Marinella 1624, 199: "sembrava un Paolo, un Dionisio, un Giovanni, un Domenico." For Catherine as "fisher of souls" (pescatrice), see 241.

137. Brundin 2008, 150–51.

138. The first two books had already been published in 1600. For other poems within this tradition, which flourished particularly in the early Seicento, in the wake of Tasso, see Quondam 2005a, 199–200.

139. For Cebà's date of death, often given as 1623, see Harrán 2009, 39n239. For discussion of his *La Reina Ester*, see Belloni 1893, 141–45; Jannaco and Capucci 1966, 453–55; Cavarocchi Arbib 1999, 148–51; and Fortis 2003, 44–45. Listings of narrative poems in ottava rima using Old Testament material are found in Belloni 1893, 147 (16th–17th centuries); Quondam 2005a, 198 (16th century). See also Carpanè 2006.

140. Battiferra 2006, 256–65. Battiferra describes the intended subject of her poem as "the valor of the first, ancient kings, descended from the lofty and great Hebrew lineage" (il valor de' primi antichi regi / scesi dall'alto, e gran lignaggio hebreo).

141. Accaiuoli speaks of Salvetti's having intended to publish the three cantos prior to the onset of the illness that killed her (Salvetti 1611, §2r), a claim borne out by

Salvetti's own dedicatory letter (§3r–v). Publishing the opening segment of a poem before the poem was completed was not uncommon in the period (see Beer 1999, 60–62). A certain local stylistic unevenness in the published version of Salvetti's *David* may attest to the lack of a final revision.

142. Salvetti 1611, §3r: "seguitando insino che, per la morte di detto suo persecutore, vien assunto alla dignità reale."

143. For Pantasilea's relation to Marpesia, see Salvetti 1611, 22r. Salvetti departs from the conventional mythological account that has her the granddaughter, not the daughter, of Marpesia.

144. Salvetti 1611, §3r: "intessendo nell'opera alcuni episodi: ma derivanti, e aderenti (come membra, e da capo) dalla primiera attione"; "fondati su qualche verace storia."

145. Cebà 1615, "A color che leggeranno," unnumbered: "la quale [poesia] perderebbe il suo nome se non favoleggiasse su l'historia."

146. Harrán 2009, 38–39. The poem was provisionally banned in 1621, definitively in 1624.

147. See Salvetti 1611, 35v–36r, for an initial description of the sculpted panels and their context; 36r–51v for a detailed description of their contents. The episode occupies the entire third canto of the poem.

148. Fonte's poem is discussed in ch. 5. A treatise by Cornelio Lanci dedicated to Salvetti mentions "Moderata Fontana" in a list of female poets, praising her for her "very beautiful epic poem" (Lanci 1590, 251; poema eroico molto bello).

149. On the figure of Erinta, see Quint 2004, 66–67. More generally on Bracciolini's poem, see Baldassari 2005.

150. Baldassari 2005, 67 and n. 16. Bracciolini speaks of Maria Maddalena's directive in a letter to Maffeo Barberini. The evidence should be handled with some caution, since Bracciolini uses Maddalena's request to justify his decision to dedicate the work to the Medici rather than to Barberini, to whom it had originally been promised.

151. Harness 2006, 43; Cusick 2009, 194.

152. Harness 2006, 51–53.

153. Cox-Rearick 1993, esp. 282–314. On the linguistic thesis of Tuscan's descent from Aramaic, see Simoncelli 1984, esp. 22–27. The most comprehensive study of the Etruscan myth and its political uses in Renaissance Florence is Cipriani 1980; see also, on the origins of the myth, Schoonhoven 2010.

154. For the legend of Atlas's founding of Fiesole, see Rubinstein 2004, 15–18. A likely source for Salvetti is the chronicle of Giovanni Villani (c. 1280–1348), which was printed quite frequently in the sixteenth century, down to 1587. Salvetti attributes the foundation of Fiesole not to Atlas but to Italo, who in the medieval sources had been Atlas's successor, conflating this figure with the Italus of Aristotle's *Politics* 7.10 (Salvetti 1611, 32v; see also 32r, which expands on Aristotle's description of Italus's role in bringing civilization to his land). The only "Annian" detail that Salvetti retains is the story of Hercules's sojourn in Tuscany (38r–39r; cf. Gelli 1979,

116–18, and Cipriani 1980, 34–35). She modifies the story, however, to have Hercules marry the daughter of King Italus, adding his heroic blood to what will ultimately be the Medici line. Leonora Bernardi refers to the same Etrscan foundation myths in the prologue to her *Tragicomedia pastorale*, discussed in ch. 3 (see "Gentildonna lucchese," 2r–3r).

155. See Salvetti 1611, 33v for the sybil's prophecy of Italo's dynastic future, 35v for an allusion to her prophecy to Augustus.

156. In addition to Fonte's and Salvetti's epics, female-authored works between 1580 and 1630 dedicated to women born into the Medici family or to Medici consorts include Salvetti 1590 and Marinella 1597 (Christine of Lorraine); Marinella 1605a and Miani 1611 (Eleonora de' Medici Gonzaga); Marinella 1618 and Bragadin 1619 (Caterina de' Medici Gonzaga); I. Cervoni 1600, L. Strozzi 1601, and I. Andreini 1603 (Maria de' Medici); and Marinella 1624 (Maria Maddalena d'Austria). To these may be added Lucia Colao's manuscript "Rime," dedicated to Bianca Cappello (see the appendix), and Leonora Bernardi's *Tragicomedia pastorale*, written for performance before Christine of Lorraine and Ferdinando I de' Medici (see ch. 3 at n. 57); see also Sarrocchi 1623, dedicated to Giulia d'Este, a Medici through her maternal line. For discussion and later examples, see Cox 2008, 185–86, 207.

157. Salvetti 1611, 32v, 22r–24r.

158. The comparison of the Amazons to Diana's nymphs is traditional (see Freeman 1996, 436–37, for classical sources). Salvetti's glamorizing decription of her Amazonian troops contrasts with the dourer portrayal of an Amazon army in Ascanio Grandi 1636, 310 (8.65), as "aspre donzelle / dura progenie, martial famiglia" (cruel damsels, a hard breed, a martial family); only the leader, Tigrina, is beautified (310 [8.66]).

159. Tomalin 1982, 47–48, 142–43; Benson 1992, 133–34; Piéjus 2009, 35, 37. On the more general tendency for narratives of Amazonian communities to end in defeat or suppression at male hands, see Kleinbaum 1983, esp. 11–12; Freeman 1996, 435; Schwarz 2000, 14–15; and Heller 2003, 220–21. On Greek attitudes toward Amazons as representative of a more general fear of the "manly woman," perceived as a threat to social order, see McIrnerney 2003, 324.

160. See Bastogi 2008, 599, 603–4; also, on the political capital represented by Christine's paternal descent from the crusader and early king of Jerusalem—and hero of Tasso's *Gerusalemme liberata*—Godfrey of Bouillon (c. 1060–1100), see 599, 606–7, 609. Ferdinando had a more tenuous connection with the principal Medici line— again, matrilineal in character—through his paternal grandmother, Maria Salviati (1499–1543), whose mother was a daughter of Lorenzo il Magnifico (1449–92).

161. Fonte 1995, 55–58, and Fonte 2006, 134–40 (3.49–64); Bracciolini 1611, 176–78 (20.36–60). To an extent, Fonte balances the male bias for her Medici dynasty with the patriotically inspired praises of the Venetian Bianca Cappello that follow (Fonte 1995, 58, and 2006, 140 [3.65–66]). Praises of dynastic women are not uncommon in epic of the period, but these are generally segregated from the encomia of their husbands (for a classic example, see Ariosto 1976, 1:282–85 [13.57–73], and

for a more contemporary one, see Udine 2004 [originally published in 1599], 13–14, 46–50). What is distinctive in Salvetti is the amount of space accorded to women within a bigendered dynastic encomium.

162. By contrast, Bracciolini 1611 omits Eleonora from the list and mentions Giovanna d'Austria only in passing for bringing imperial blood into the family (177 [20.48]). Only the living and powerful Christine of Lorraine (177 [20.50–51]) and Maria Maddalena d'Austria (178 [20.60]) are given a little more space, and only Christine is praised for her personal moral attributes, rather than simply for her bloodline. Gabriello Chiabrera, in a similar encomiastic genealogy of the Medici, praises the two "regal brides" Christine and Maria Maddalena for their "superhuman blood" (sangue, che de l'human passa il confine) without even mentioning them by name (Chiabrera 1615, 59).

163. Salvetti 1611, 46r: "d'alta prudenza mar vasto, e profondo"; "alma viril sotto feminil gonna."

164. Salvetti 1611, 46v. Cf. Bracciolini 1611, 177 (20.54), which mentions Isabella only in passing, as the mother of Virginio Orsini, to whom Bracciolini devotes an octave; Leonora is not mentioned.

CHAPTER FIVE: Secular Narrative

1. For mentions of Franco and Andreini engaged in the writing of epic, see Manfredi 1594, 100; and Belloni 1893, 286n4. The text of Turina's "Florio," an ottava rima version of Boccaccio's *Filocolo*, is found in Turina, "Il Florio." Turina began work on this poem in the 1590s and presented a two-canto sample in manuscript to Cardinal Cinzio Aldobrandini in 1596 (Personeni 1786, 39–41). It was completed at the end of her life, in 1640 (Torrioli 1940, 17, 30–31).

2. Critical literature on the three works is listed in Cox 2008, 333–34, nn. 89 and 96–97. On *L'Enrico*, see also Cabani 1995, 91–100; Kolsky 2005, 336–40; Malpezzi Price and Ristaino 2008, 80–104; Stampino 2009 and 2011; and Lazzari 2010. On *La Scanderbeide*, see also Pezzini 2007. On epic poetry after Tasso, the surveys in Belloni 1893 and 1912 remain useful. See also, more briefly, Jannaco and Capucci 1966, 444–49; B. Croce 1967, 283–96; and Arbizzoni 1997, 727–35. Important recent contributions are Foltran 2004 and 2005; Quint 2004; Zatti 2004; Arbizzoni, Faini, and Mattioli 2005; and Carpanè 2006.

3. For Terracina, see Shemek 1998, 126–57; for the dramatic piece, see ch. 3 at n. 131.

4. On d'Aragona, see Cox 2008, 312n167. On Bernal, see Park 1981; and Gagliardi 2003 and 2005, 49–58. On Tyler, see Bistué and Uman 2007 and the bibliography cited there on 322n1. Bernal's romance appeared twice in Italian translation (1558 and 1609), though without any indication of female authorship (Gagliardi 2003, 162–73). Works by Italian women in the related genres of historically based Latin epic and ottava rima war narrative are discussed in Cox 2008, 12–13, 113.

5. Vives 1996, 42, c3r: "non facile animus est pudicus, quem ferri et lacertorum et

virilis roboris cogitatio occupavit." On Vives's treatise on female education, influential throughout Europe, see Fantazzi and Matheeussen 1996; and Fantazzi 2000. Margaret Tyler wittily tackles the question of the supposed inappropriateness of arms as a subject for women in the preface to her *Mirrour of Princely Deedes and Knighthood* (see Bistué and Uman 2007, 305).

6. On Gonzaga's treatment of love, see Varini 2008, 137–40. On the poem generally, see Razzoli Roio 2000. For a plot summary, see C. Gonzaga 2000, 662–69. The modern edition of the poem uses the variant title adopted in C. Gonzaga 1591a, *Il Fidamante*.

7. C. Gonzaga 1591a; Marinella 1601, 81–82.

8. Fonte 1581b, 4r: "non esperta verginella, / stando rinchiusa in fra l'anguste mura."

9. Sarrocchi 1606, †2r. The author of the letter is an otherwise unidentified "Arrotato Accademico Raffrontato." On the "titanic" challenge represented by the epic poem, see Beer 1999, esp. 56, 64.

10. Capaccio 1608, 203.

11. Erythraeus 1645–48, 259–60, cited in Cox 2008, 358n142.

12. Cox 2008, 164. For Marino's and Stigliani's attacks on Sarrocchi, see also Verdile 1989–90, 196–98, which reproduces Stigliani's poems; and Russell 2006, 12–13.

13. Fonte speaks in her dedicatory letter (Carinci 2002, 9; Fonte 2006, 49) of the poem's original planned length being "more than fifty cantos" (meglio di cinquanta canti). Doglioni 1988, 7, and 1997, 36, confirms that Fonte wrote more of the work than is found in the 1581 printed edition.

14. For the Raggiadora plot, see Fonte 1995, 35–43, 46, 71–74, and 2006, 106–17, 120–21, 160–65 (2.58–97, 3.7–8, 4.49–66). For the Lucimena plot, see Fonte 1995, 87–88, 91–108, and 2006, 184–85, 190–214 (5.62–64, 6.3–85). Also left in suspense is a narrative featuring an enchanted pyramid of glass encasing two conspirators against a lady's virtue, who may be rescued only by someone prepared to take on her husband's ghost (see Fonte 1995, 21–22, and 2006, 83–86 [1.89–97]).

15. Fonte 1995, 47, and 2006, 121 (3.9). For comment, see Weaver 1997, 115–16. Later in the poem, Fonte uses Ariosto's tapestry metaphor, but in a manner that emphasizes the quality of her materials—here, the history of Venice—rather than her skill as a weaver (see Fonte 1995, 213, and 2006, 368–69 [13.1–2]).

16. For Tasso's theoretical position on this issue, see T. Tasso 1977b, 1:12; see also, more diffusely, 2:195–96. Sarrocchi's choice of subject is more problematic than Marinella's in this regard, being too recent happily to permit of fictional invention; note, for example, her incongruous inclusion of a well-documented fifteenth-century figure such as Borso d'Este (1413–71) in a fictionalized heroic role (Russell 2006, 30, 64).

17. Summaries of the plot of *L'Enrico* may be found in Belloni 1893, 285–98; and Malpezzi Price and Ristaino 2008, 171n5. On the historical events described in the

poem, see Madden and Queller 1997; and Madden 2003. For summaries, see Malpezzi Price and Ristaino 2008, 81–83; and Lazzari 2010, 41–45. The Fourth Crusade was in fact formally under the leadership of Bonifazio di Monferrato (c. 1150–1207), who figures as a minor character in Marinella's poem. On Marinella's tendency in general (consistent with Venetian historiography generally) to overstate Venice's role in the crusade, see Pertusi 2004, 66nn170, 172. See also, more generally, Stampino 2009, 25–28, on Marinella's divergences from the historical record.

18. For a modern account of Scanderbeg's life and campaigns, see Hodgkinson 1999; for a summary, see Russell 2006, 22–24.

19. Scaramelli 1585. On de' Monti's poem, see Dolla 1987. Russelll 2006, 24n54, citing Quadrio, mentions a fourth, lost poem on the subject by Francesco Bardi. Pezzini 2005, 220, notes that the 1593–1606 war between the Hapsburgs and the Ottoman Empire, fought mainly in the Balkans, gave new resonance to Scanderbeg's story in the years that Sarrocchi was writing. See also, on the contemporary appeal of the poem's subject, Russell 2006, 21.

20. Di Manzano 1594; F. Contarini 1615. The Fourth Crusade was also the subject of a pictorial cycle in the Ducal Palace in Venice, painted after the fire of 1577, featuring work by Jacopo and Domenico Tintoretto.

21. Pancetti 1622, 153–57 (14.28–64). Marinella may also have been inspired by Strozzi's reference to the taking of Byzantium in his poem as "an illustrious subject for a mind not vulgar, fit to make the Aonian trumpet clearly sound" (G. Strozzi 1624, 109 [11.43]; materia illustre a non volgar'ingegno / da far chiara sonar l'Aonia Tromba). The plots of Pancetti's and Strozzi's poems, both essentially fanciful rather than historical, are summarized in Belloni 1893, 189–210; see also Doglio 1983, 176–78. For evidence that Marinella was already planning an epic by 1624, see Marinella 1624, A3v.

22. Critics have generally assumed that the edition was published with Sarrocchi's connivance, despite its presenting itself as unauthorized, though see Russell 2006, 16–17. Besides the two printed editions of the poem, a damaged partial manuscript in the Biblioteca Nazionale Universitaria of Turin (N.V.32) attests to Sarrocchi's revisions: it contains fragments of cantos 13 and 14 that include some octaves not present in the 1623 edition (Verdile 1989–90, 201).

23. Sarrocchi's relationships with Valerio and with Galileo are detailed in Favaro 1983, 1:1–24; and Verdile 1989–90, 189–94. Valerio also refers, in a letter to Galileo of 31 August 1613, to other expert readers: "altri uomini assai dotti in quest'arte" (quoted in Favaro 1983, 1:21).

24. Galilei 1901, 164 (letter of 29 July 1611: "con occhio inimico"), 261 (letter of 13 January 1612: "lo darò più tosto a Vulcano ch'al Sole").

25. One of the principal structural changes Sarrocchi introduced between the 1606 and 1623 versions of the poem was the addition of an Italian dimension to the poem, in the form of two Italian contingents sent to Albania in response to Scanderbeg's pleas for assistance, one by Alfonso the Magnanimous of Naples (1396–

1458), the other by Pope Pius II (1405–64). Both expeditions are fictional (Russell 2006, 23, 29–30). For Sarrocchi's deliberations on the encomiastic possibilities offered by these episodes, see ch. 1, n. 31.

26. Foltran 2004, 48; see also on this figure, named Bessana, 46, 51–54.

27. Marinella 2011, 56, and 2009, 98 (1.68): "questa infida gente / al Ciel nemica, al l'uomo infesta e grave, / che di Cristo il pastor sprezza." For discussion, see Stampino 2011, 14–15. For further instances of Marinella's negative characterization of the Greeks in her poem, see Stampino 2009, 21n76. On Italian attitudes toward the Greeks of Byzantium, see Bisaha 2004, 118–34 (focused, however, on an earlier period).

28. For the episode of Esone's proposed sacrifice of Idilia, thwarted by the Christian warrior Giacinto, see Marinella 2011, 230–48 (10.15–11.17). For the statue of Minerva, see Marinella 2011, 212–13, 201–2 (9.34–35); for discussion, see Stampino 2009, 22. For the appearance of the Nikopeia in the Greeks' procession, see Marinella 2011, 328 (14.62); for its capture by the Latins, see 341 (14.126). On the central place assumed by the icon in Venetian religious culture of the 1620s and 1630s, see Moore 1984. For discussion of the episode in Marinella, see Stampino 2011, 16–18.

29. For discussion, see Stampino 2009, 44–46 (Meandra), 51–56 (Emilia), 35–40 (Areta).

30. See Stampino 2009, 31 (Alessio), 29–31 (Oronte), 32–33 (Esone).

31. Marinella's initial description of Mirtillo is at Marinella 2011, 74 (2.74–75). The phrase quoted in the text, "micidiale e crudele," is in stanza 75. For discussion of the characters of Mirtillo and Eudocia, see Stampino 2009, 31–32, 62–65. The curiously romance name Mirtillo is already used for this character in Di Manzano 1594.

32. See Pezzini 2005; and Russell 2006, 38–39.

33. The legend of Scanderbeg's upbringing at the Ottoman court is found in the standard sixteenth-century biographical account of Marinus Barletius. Modern historians question the story (see Hodgkinson 1999, 52–61).

34. The Christian woman married to a "pagan" is Calidora (see text at nn. 135–38 below).

35. Summaries of the actions of the principal characters of the poem may be found in Sarrocchi 2006, 64–71. Mauro's treacheries are concentrated in cantos 10–12 of the poem, only the first of which appears in Sarrocchi 2006.

36. Sarrocchi 1623, 128 (12.96).

37. Sarrocchi 1623, 198–204, and 2006, 313–20 (19.1–59). On the absence of a supernatural element in the 1623 version of the poem, see Pezzini 2005, 215–18; the 1606 edition has more of a sustained supernatural presence through the figure of Calidora, discussed below in the text.

38. On the relation between the two redactions of the poem, see Cox 2000a, 61–62; and Russell 2006, 25–26.

39. Barlezio 1580, 14v. Barletius had been available in a vernacular version since

1554, in a much-reprinted translation by Pietro Rocca. For later Italian vernacular works possibly among Sarrocchi's sources, see Russell 2006, 24n54.

40. The seizure of Comite is narrated in canto 3 of Sarrocchi 1606; his death and that of his followers, in canto 4, stanza 26 (p. 31). Sarrocchi omits all mention of the massacres and forced conversions that Barletius says took place in Krujë after the city's capture by Scanderbeg.

41. Sarrocchi 1606, 88 (12.30): "mentre hor notte gli copre, hor tradimento."

42. Tommaso Stigliani, probably basing his judgment on the 1606 redaction, accused Sarrocchi of having written a supposedly heroic poem without a hero (Stigliani 1625, 455: "s'appella eroico, e non contien eroi").

43. Sarrocchi 1623, 16, and 2006, 108 (2.37–38).

44. Russell 2006, 38–39.

45. Sarrocchi 1623, 262, and 2006, 201 (7.104): "sciocca e vil turba."

46. Sarrocchi 1623, 80 (8.10–11). The phrase "mad zeal" (zelo folle) is at 7.97 (1623, 77; 2006, 199).

47. Stampino 2009, 19–20.

48. Zorzi 2004–5, 416 and 418–19, notes that Marinella was following an established tradition within Venetian historiography of the period on this point.

49. Marinella 2011, 317 (14.9): "sazi di posa ed avidi di preda . . . quanta richezza accoglia / Bisanzio antico entro la nobil soglia." See also 528 (24.54), where the Latin invaders of the city are once again described as "senza pietà, di preda avidi, e d'oro" (pitiless and avid for booty and gold).

50. Marinella 2011, 457 (20.40): "vasta ingordigia e sete ria / del l'oro."

51. Madden 2003.

52. See Stampino 2009, 34–40; and Lazzari 2010, 139–43.

53. Marinella 2011, 122, and 2009, 121 (4.85): "d'onor . . . ambitiosa brama."

54. Marinella 2011, 467, and 2009, 308 (21.12): "sprezza / ciò, ch'a salute sua buon si discopre."

55. On the likelihood that the character of Venier in L'Enrico is intended as an ideal "ancestor" of Sebastiano, see Marinella 2009, 113n13.

56. For a reading of L'Enrico as programmatically antiheroic in this sense, see Kolsky 2005, 336–40.

57. A brief, rather oblique reference to the siege of Mantua is found in Marinella 2011, 176 (7.66).

58. Marinella 2011, 161–76 (7.2–66). The first set of images described seem to be sculptural reliefs carved in crystal (144 [7.2]); the second, paintings (173 [7.52]).

59. On Marinella's account of Venetian history, see Stampino 2009, 17–18.

60. Fonte's account of Lepanto and the celebrations that followed in Venice is at Fonte 1995, 214–18, and 2006, 369–77 (13.5–28). Marinella's is at Marinella 2011, 173–74, and 2009, 177–79, 401–2 (7.50–56). For a self-referential description of the *enargeia* of the painted scenes of Lepanto, see Marinella 2011, 173, and 2009, 178, 401 (7.52).

61. Fonte 1995, 201, and 2006, 345 (12.31): "ingegni pellegrini."
62. Fonte 1995, 200, and 2006, 343–44 (12.24–28).
63. Marinella's ekphrasis begins with an account of Venice's earliest doges, from Paolo Lucio Anafesto (d. 717?) to Obelerio Antenori (d. 811) (Marinella 2011, 165–66, and 2009, 169–71, 394–95 [7.18–24]). She then leaps to the thirteenth and fourteenth centuries for a brief sequence climaxing in Antonio Venier, doge from 1382 to 1400 (2011, 166–67, and 2009, 171, 396 [7.25–26]) before returning to the ninth through twelfth centuries for the remainder (2011, 167–71, and 2009, 173–76, 396–400 [7.27–44]). For the device of the mysterious cloud, see 2011, 172–73, and 2009, 177, 400–401 (7.48–49).
64. For descriptions of the Venetians at the time of Orso Ipato as a "popolo feroce" and of "animo atroce" (atrocious spirit), see Marinella 2011, 165, and 2009, 169–70, 394 (7.19). For the snake image, relating to Venice's turning against Oblerio Antenori, see 2011, 166, and 2009, 170–71, 395 (7.23).
65. On Pietro I (canonized in the 18th century), see Marinella 2011, 168–69, and 2009, 173–74, 397–98 (7.33–34). On Pietro II, see 2011, 170–71, and 2009, 175, 399 (7.40–41). Marinella's account of Pietro I Orseolo's rejection of political power is especially emphatic in its "antiworldliness": he is said to leave behind "the hated throne and the black world" (7.33; il seggio odiato, e 'l mondo tetro).
66. Marinella 2011, 174–75, and 2009, 179, 403 (7.57–59): "immobile e cheto soffre e tace, / invitissimo Heroe tra pene e doglie"; "novella stella."
67. A more consistently celebratory prediction of Venice's future glories is found in canto 16 in the form of a divine vision recounted by a hermit to Enrico's son Raniero. See Stampino 2009, 17, for discussion; see also, on Marinella's and Fonte's encomia of a feminized Venice in their works, Lazzari 2010, 120–24. On the "myth of Venice" and its literary expression in this period, see Doglio 1983.
68. Marinella 2011, 153, and 2009, 156, 383 (6.38). Marinella's language in the whole account of Candiano's story is ambiguous: while initially he is condemned for his "voracious desire to rule" (2011, 131, and 2009, 152, 380 [6.22]; di regnar . . . desio vorace), ultimately he is said, after the fire incident, to leave Venice "to the voracity of others' desires" (1635, 153, and 2009, 155, 383 [6.36]; alla voracità del l'altrui voglie). This seems to place Candiano and his political opponents on the same moral plane.
69. See Cox 2008, 372n250, for the context.
70. Generallly on the figure of the female knight in Italian chivalric fiction in this period, see the critically naive but usefully comprehensive overview in Tomalin 1982. On Ariosto's *guerriere* in particular, see Benson 1992, 123–55; Shemek 1998, 77–125; Bateman 2007; and Mac Carthy 2007, 73–94, 135–64. More generally on gender in Ariosto, see Bryce 1992.
71. Benson 1992, 134–39; Cox 2005b, 17–18; Mac Carthy 2007, 2–11. The first of these proems, to canto 20, was present in earlier versions of the poem; that to canto 37, mentioning Colonna, was added in 1532.
72. On the figure of Clorinda, see Benedetti 1996, 33–58. On Gildippe, see Stephens 1989, 178–83. An overview of the treatment of gender in Italian epic after

Tasso, stressing its misogyny, is available in Pezzini 2005, 198–202. For further exemplification, see Belloni 1893; and Tomalin 1982.

73. On Bracciolini, see ch. 4 at n. 149; on Sempronio, see Foltran 2005, 192–93, 206, 213–14.

74. Belloni 1893, 85–86; Foltran 2005, 72–75.

75. On the figure of the female knight in Fonte, see Finucci 1995, xxvii–xxxiv; and Malpezzi Price 2003a, 106–10. On the female knight in Sarrocchi, see Pezzini 2005, 204–10; and Russell 2006, 32–36. On the figure in Marinella, see Benedetti 2005, 104–7; Stampino 2009, 42–51; and Lazzari 2010, 61–93 and (comparatively with Fonte) 93–97. As comparative material, the figure of the *guerriera* Minerva in Beatriz Bernal's *Don Cristalián* is of interest (see Gagliardi 2003, 137–38, 147–54).

76. Fonte 1995, 61–62 (4.1–4); also in 1997, 261–63. The passage enjoyed a notable *fortuna*, being quoted or referred to in Marinella 1601, 11, 32, and 1999, 55, 78–80; Bursati 1621, 189; and Bronzini 1624, *giornata seconda*, 37–38. See also Bergalli 1726, vol. 1, "A chi legge," unnumbered.

77. Marinella 2011, 65 (2.29): "l'uso e non natura ha messo / timor nell'un, valor nell'altro sesso." Maddalena Campiglia points up the ideological implications of the figure of the female knight with similar explicitness in her *argomenti* to C. Gonzaga 1591a (see Cox 1997b, 138).

78. One common species of taunt recommends the *guerriera* to abandon warfare for feminine pursuits such as the "needle and the spindle," while another, less common, employs sexual double entendre to cast doubt on women's capacity to bear arms. For examples of the first type, see T. Tasso 1980, 648 (20.95); and Marinella 2011, 90 (3.51). For an example of the second, see Marinella 2011, 522–23, and 2009, 337 (24.28). For discussion of this last passage, see Stampino 2011, 24–25.

79. Claudia and Meandra die of wounds incurred in a duel between the two of them, while Silveria is crushed by an elephant. See Stampino 2009, 51; and Russell 2006, 36, for comment. A precedent for the Claudia-Meandra solution is offered by a scene in Ascanio Grandi's *Il Tancredi* (1632), in which two female warriors fight one another and are fatally wounded (Tomalin 1982, 189–91; Lazzari 2010, 63n9). However, Grandi's female protagonists, unlike Marinella's, are love rivals fighting out of jealousy, and the episode has misogynistic overtones quite remote from Marinella's development of the equivalent scenario.

80. Sarrocchi 1623, 155–57, and 2006, 276–80 (15.8–29). For comment, see Cox 2008, 163–65.

81. The king of Cyprus is named as Risamante's future husband in Fonte 1995, 54 (3.44), and he is mentioned again, along with the king of Crete, as a notable absence at the joust in which Floridoro makes his combat debut (Fonte 1995, 87, 145, and 2006, 184, 265 [5.59, 9.37]). It seems likely that they are the two unnamed *guerrieri* we see arriving in Armenia in the final canto in time to see Risamante's triumph over Biondaura's armies there (Fonte 1995, 221–22, and 2006, 43–44 [13.43–44]).

82. Fonte's interest in the Ariostan figure of Marfisa is apparent in her *Il merito delle donne* (see Cox 1995, 564–65, and 1997a, 139–40).

83. For a skeptical view of Bradamante's war record in the *Furioso*, see Bateman 2007, 3–4.
84. Fonte 1995, 52, and 2006, 130 (3.38).
85. Ariosto 1976, 1:48 (3.24): "del seme di Ruggiero in te concetto." On the Aristotelian view that regarded the male seed as the active power in conception, see Allen 1985, 95–100. For Renaissance debates on this issue, see Maclean 1980, 35–37.
86. Fonte 1995, 54 (3.44): "del re di Cipri sia da te concetta / unica figlia."
87. Fonte 1995, 124, and 2006, 236 (8.13): "e dell'uno e dell'altra io fui concetta."
88. Fonte 1995, 49, and 2006, 124 (3.19). For Risamante's battle with the serpent/dragon, see 1995, 47–48, and 2006, 122–24 (3.13–17). The creature is referred to in the episode as both *serpe* and *drago* (the latter term in itself meaning interchangeably "serpent" and "dragon"), and Fonte uses as points of comparison both the jaculus and the amphisbaena, poisonous snakes described by Pliny and Lucan (3.13), and the dragon fought by the hero Cadmus in Greek mythology (3.16).
89. Fonte 1995, 52, and 2006, 130 (3.36).
90. Fonte 1995, 48, and 2006, 123 (3.16); Ovid 1977, 128–30 (3.50–94). Ovid's work was widely available in translation by Fonte's time, notably through Lodovico Dolce's ottava rima version, *Le trasformationi*, first published in 1553.
91. For discussion of the Rosmonda-Vaconte story, see Pezzini 2005, 205–9. On the figure of Rosmonda, see also Russell 2006, 32–36.
92. On Erminia as literal and metaphorical prisoner of Tancredi, see T. Tasso 1980, 80 (3.20), 176 (6.56–58), 597 (19.82), 600–601 (19.93–95).
93. Vaconte reproaches himself in one speech soon after his first meeting with Rosmonda for his attraction to an "enemy to my king, and a rebel against God" (Sarrocchi 1623, 143 [13.127]; inimica al mio Re, rubella a Dio). By the end of the speech, however, he is already predicting the eventual happy outcome of their story, with her conversion and their marriage.
94. Fonte 1995, 79–80, and 2006, 172–74 (5.22–27). For discussion of the figure of Circetta, see Finucci 1995, xxxiv–xxxv; Cox 1997b, 142–43; and Malpezzi Price and Ristaino 2008, 88–90.
95. Fonte 1995, 127–28, and 2006, 240–41 (8.26–30).
96. Fonte 1995, 129, 192, 220, and 2006, 242–43, 332, 380 (8.34, 11.93, 13.36).
97. Fonte 1995, 125–26, and 2006, 236–38 (8.14–19). Fonte anticipates Circetta's fate prior to her introduction into the story in the proem to canto 5, which warns young women against the erotic deceptions of men.
98. Another possible contrastive model for Fonte is the Erina of Lodovico Dolce's *Sacripante* (1536), a *maga* on the Alcina model, like Circetta presented as a daughter of Circe (see Terpening 1997, 40–41).
99. For Circetta's agelessness, see Fonte 1995, 127, and 2006, 240 (8.27).
100. See, however, Cavallo 1999 and Gough 2001 on Tasso's departures from the Ariostan archetype. The possibility that Fonte was acquainted with portions of Tasso's *Gerusalemme liberata* when she composed *Il Floridoro* cannot be excluded, even though a complete edition did not appear until February 1581, three months after

Fonte sent the *Tredici canti* to its dedicatees, Bianca Cappello and Francesco de' Medici, on 10 November 1580 (Carinci 2002, 9). A pirated partial edition of the poem had appeared in Venice in August 1580 (T. Tasso 1580), and the circulation of individual cantos in Venice from the 1570s in circles not remote from Fonte's is attested. See, e.g., Carpanè 2001–2, 298–99, on a letter of 1579 written by the Friulian medic and *letterato* Ottavio Amalteo [1543–1626] about two cantos of the poem he had read in Venice, one of which he had copied and was circulating. Amalteo is mentioned in a list of famous doctors in Fonte 1988, 126, and 1997, 182. The 1580 edition of the *Goffredo*, as Tasso's poem was titled in early printings, contains the episode set in Armida's magic kingdom, 16.1–62 (T. Tasso 1580, 59r–62r).

101. The Erina episode is at Marinella 2011, 136–77, 465–96, and 2009, 137–83, 305–36, 375–406, 414–28 (5.62–7.72; 21–22). For discussion, see Cox 1997b, 142–43; Panizza 1999, 14; Stampino 2009, 57–62; and Lazzari 2010, 98–119.

102. Marinella 2011, 148 (6.15): "consanguineo amore." For Erina's attraction to Venier and her insomnia, see Marinella 2001, 141, 143–44, and 2009, 143, 146 (5.88, 98–99).

103. For the intellectual character of the pleasures of Erina's island, see, e.g., Marinella 2011, 141–42 (5.89–93), where a female bard, Altea, sings of the wonders of the terrestrial and celestial worlds.

104. Marinella 2011, 440 (19.75): "Sotto angeliche faccie d'Acheronte / immagin strane." Marinella's imitation of Tasso is especially close at 443–44 (19.88–91), where a disembodied song urges the philosophical case for hedonistic indulgence (cf. T. Tasso 1980, 440–41 [14.62–65], 467 [15.57], 478 [16.14–15]). See also Marinella 2011, 440 (19.74) for an image of seductive *donzelle* frolicking in a fountain, and cf. T. Tasso 1980, 468–70 (15.58–64).

105. Marinella 2011, 447 (19.105–6). For the scene of Catherine's temptation by the devil in the form of a beautiful youth, see Marinella 1624, 137–38. For a differing interpretation of this episode, arguing that Marinella uses the misogynistic discourse analyzed here to critical and ultimately profeminist ends, see Lazzari 2010, 127–32.

106. For Costanzo's speech, see Marinella 1635, 420–22 (18.63–71); for Aristides's, 422–24 (18.72–79).

107. Marinella 2011, 420 (18.63: "amator delle donne, amico agli agi"); 422 (18.72: "dotto e grave"). See also 424 (18.80), where Aristides's speech is said to have been listened to with approval only by those "guided and instructed by right reason" (da vera ragion retti ed instrutti).

108. Marinella 2011, 423(18.75): "E dirò che quel sesso lento e molle / con risi, sguardi, e con lusinghe e vezzi / inferma l'armi e 'l coraggioso tolle / da quel fervor che fa che gloria apprezzi" (I say that that slow and soft sex, with smiles, glances, flattery, and charming ways, disables arms and distracts the courageous man from that fervor that leads him to prize glory).

109. For the later scenes of the Byzantine women's valor, see Marinella 2011, 515 (23.83). For a differing reading of the episode of the Aristide-Costanzo debate, see Lazzari 2010, 192–95.

110. Cox 2008, 214, 216, 365n195, 369n228. Within Marinella's own trajectory, *L'Enrico* may perhaps be regarded as anticipating Marinella's later *Essortationi alle donne* (1645), which reads, at least superficially, as a retraction of the profeminism of her youth (see Benedetti 2008; and Cox 2008, 223–25).

111. For a different perspective, see Lazzari 2010, 155–74, which argues that Marinella departs from the heroizing traditions of epic in her portrayal of male characters in order to give emphasis to female warriors.

112. For references, see above, n. 14.

113. Fonte 1995, 43, and 2006, 117 (2.96): "Or poi che la natura ingiusta e avara / non mi diè forza all'animo conforme." See also 1995, 39, and 2006, 111 (2.76), for the Pygmy king's confession of his inability to win his beloved's love through "valore."

114. For Nicobaldo's forced-marriage ordeal, see Fonte 1995, 95–100, and 2006, 194–201 (6.20–44); for his kidnap by the *maga*, see 1995, 101–4, and 2006, 204–8 (6.53–65). For another representation in a female-authored text of a male figure forced into an unwelcome marriage by his family, see ch. 3 at n. 105.

115. On the beauty of the king of the pygmies, see Fonte 1995, 36, and 2006, 106 (2.59); for his "angelic and divine voice" (voce angelica e divina), see 1995, 38, and 2006, 110 (2.72); for his difficulty in speaking, see 1995, 36, and 2006, 106 (2.59–60). Fonte's characterization of the Pygmy king as a paradigm of beauty is unexpected in context, given the tendency in chivalric poems to represent pygmies as ugly. Boiardo's Brunello, seemingly a pygmy, is described at Boiardo 1999, 1355 (2.22.20) as having "the foulest face ever seen" (più soza fronte mai non fiè Natura); see also 882–83 (2.3.40) for a description. Fonte's modern editors assume that her Pygmy king is envisaged as Caucasian (Fonte 2006, 110n21), but there seems no particular reason to assume this, given the generic character of his description, especially since representations of beautiful young male figures of African descent were not unknown in the art of the period (see Bestor 2003, 658 and nn. 99–100).

116. Fonte 1995, 44–46, and 2006, 118–20 (3.1–6).

117. Fonte 1995, 166, and 2006, 295 (10.61): "Ben parve . . . ai gesti, al movimento / superbo, al grave, eroico, e fier sembiante / esser il fior degli altri." Fonte's characterization of Floridoro is discussed in Finucci 1995, xxii–xxvi; and Weaver 1997, 115.

118. Fonte 1995, 84, and 2006, 180 (5.46): "Ogni sua parte fuor che la favella / par d'una giovenetta illustre e bella." For his physical description, see 5.45–46.

119. For Floridoro's white armor, see Fonte 1995, 116, 118, and 2006, 223–24, 226 (7.30, 40); for his assumed name, which recalls that of the heroine of Boccaccio's *Filocolo*, Biancofiore, see 1995, 170, and 2006, 300 (10.79). His horse at the joust is also pure white (1995, 115, and 2006, 223 [7.28]).

120. T. Tasso 1980, 31 (1.58): "se 'l miri fulminar ne l'arme avolto / Marte lo stimi; Amor, se scopre il volto." Cf. Fonte 1995, 84, and 2006, 180 (5.46): "parea d'Amor la propria imago."

121. T. Tasso 1980, 31–32 (1.59–60): "nobilissima fuga."

122. Fonte 1995, 113–14, and 2006, 220–21 (7.18–23).

123. Fonte 1995, 114, and 2006, 221 (7.23): "con voce dolcissima e soave." Floridoro's relative passivity is effectively brought out through the contrast between his character and that of his resourceful foster brother Filardo, who turns out to have orchestrated the report of their mother's death to serve Floridoro's ends. See also Fonte 1995, 142–44, and 2006, 259–63 (9.19–30), for a scene in which Filardo invigorates Floridoro when he despairs of his love.

124. For Silano, see above at nn. 96–97. The story of Amandriano, left unfinished, is at Fonte 1995, 14–22, and 2006, 74–85 (1.56–96); that of Acreonte's attempted assault on Celsidea is at 1995, 184–89, and 2006, 320–27 (11.49–76), with a preamble at 1995, 177, and 2006, 310–11 (11. 14–17); and that of Lideo is at 1995, 71–74, and 2006, 160–65 (4.49–66).

125. C. Gonzaga 2000, 44 (4.12 14).

126. Sarrocchi's treatment of her hero in this respect diverges from the general tendency in epic after Tasso toward an ever more rigidly exemplary characterization of the leader (Zatti 2004, 45).

127. The irony is macabrely reinforced when the sultan has Ferratte's flayed corpse put on display identified as Scanderbeg's to demoralize his troops.

128. Sarrocchi 1623, 123–27 (12.48–89).

129. Dianora is first introduced at Sarrocchi 1623, 143 (14.6–13). On the figure of Dori (Donica in the 1606 version), loosely based on Scanderbeg's actual wife, Marina Andronika, or Donika, see 2006, 66. For Scanderbeg's defense of the women of Krujë, see 1623, 127 (12.90–91).

130. For Scanderbeg's incipient Christian sentiments during his freeing of Dori, see Sarrocchi 1623, 8, and 2006, 93–94 (1.70). For Dianora's prayers to the Virgin and their consequences, see 1623, 144–45 (14.22–31). See also 1623, 36 (4.41), for Sofia's conversion of Ariodeno.

131. Marinella 2011, 549–57, and 2009, 344–51 (25.42–74). We learn at 25.46, unexpectedly, that Eudocia is a disciple of the wizard Esone. For discussion of the episode, which echoes Virgil's treatment of Dido following Aeneas's abandonment, see Lazzari 2010, 151–53.

132. For Giacinto's beauty, see Marinella 2011, 98, 111–12 (3.91, 4.37); the latter passage is also in 2009, 109–10. For his rescue of Idilia and their immediate separation, see 2011, 245–52, and 2009, 229–32 (11.1–33). For her reappearance as a simulacrum in the scene of demonic enchantment discussed above in the text, see 2011, 441–42(19.78–83). For discussion of the Giacinto-Idilia plot, see Lazzari 2010, 143–48; and Stampino 2011, 28–31.

133. Tronsarelli 1643; Foltran 2004, 43. For Marinella's insistence on her fidelity to classical models, see Marinella 2011, 39, and 2009, 77.

134. Sarrocchi 1606, 80 (9.90–92).

135. Scanderbeg forbids Serano to marry Calidora after her husband's death (which occurs during the capture of the city), arguing that although a moral act in itself, it would compromise the relations between his occupying troops and the inhabitants of Krujë by encouraging a perception of the captors of the city as motivated

by "ambition and sinful lust" (ambition . . . libidin ria) rather than by pure religious zeal (Sarrocchi 1606, 51 [6.37]). He also encourages his lieutenant to mitigate his guilt by the sophistic consideration that he was still a pagan at the time of his seduction of Calidora (51 [6.36]).

136. The importance of the episode is emphasized by Giuliana Morandini, who includes extracts from it in her anthology (2001, 39–47). See also Cox 1997b, 143–44; and Russell 2006, 25–26. Sarrocchi underlines the centrality of Virgil's episode of Dido and Aeneas as a subtext for the Calidora-Serano episode by a prominent imitation of Virgil's famous comparison of Dido to a wounded deer (Sarrocchi 1606, 54 [6.72]; Virgil 1999, 1:426 [Aen. 4.68–73]).

137. Sarrocchi 1606, 25 (3.50–51): "le scorre per l'ossa un sottil fuoco / . . . / D'un gelido sudor bagnata, e molle / a l'orecchie, a la lingua il vigor manca."

138. Sarrocchi 1606, 63 (8.5): "infocata man di ferro ardente."

139. Sarrocchi 1623, 69, and 2006, 182 (7.15).

140. See Sarrocchi 1623, 139 (13.91); cf. T. Tasso 1980, 109 (4.31–32). The sense of the passage is lost in the translation in Sarrocchi 2006, 260.

141. Sarrocchi 1623, 88, and 2006, 205–6 (9.5–7): "ampie spalle," "colmo petto," "fianco stretto," "moscoloso e schietto / braccio," and "nerbosa man."

142. Sofia's philosophical training and poetic talent are outlined at Sarrocchi 1623, 33 (4.7).

143. Sarrocchi 1623, 34 (4.17): "di sudor molle." See also 4.8, on the same page, for a description of Ariodeno's "long hand" and "muscular arm" (lunga mano; braccio nerboruto). Ariodeno responds to Sofia's confession with a seduction speech of notably libertine inflection (34–35 [4.24–29]), to which she responds in turn with a chaste speech of reproach.

144. Campiglia 2004, 98–101 (1.5).

145. The episode is at Sarrocchi 1606, 57–58 (7.25–31).

146. T. Tasso 1980, 291 (9.85). The episode as a whole is at 9.81–88.

147. Sarrocchi 1606, 57 (7.25): "eburneo petto."

148. Sarrocchi 1623, 43–44, and 2006, 144–46 (5.16–30). The only hint of moral disapprobation in the 1606 episode is found in the narrator's comment that Sinano acted brutally in killing a youth of such beauty that he should have inspired him with pity, if not "obscene love" (1606, 57 [7.27]; laido amor).

149. Sarrocchi 1623, 69, and 2006, 183 (7.19). Sabalio and Saladino are said to share a "chaste common bed" (commun letto pudico) now that "cold age has extinguished the ardent age in them" (che l'età fredda in lor la calda ha spenta).

150. Sarrocchi 1606, 93 (14.65): "non donna, belva." The phrase quoted is from the 1606 version, where the two characters are called Rosana and Clori. At 1623, 131, and 2006, 241 (13.4), it is stylistically elevated to read "donna . . . che di fierezza avanza ogn'altra belva." For a critical discussion of the episode of Rosmonda's encounter with Silveria, see Pezzini 2007, 103–11.

151. The description of Silveria is at Sarrocchi 1623, 132, and 2006, 243–44 (13.14–16). The passage is also quoted in Pezzini 2007, 106.

152. Sarrocchi 1623, 132, and 2006, 243 (13.15, line 5).
153. See ch. 2 at n. 16.
154. Sarrocchi 2006, 244–45, 413 (13.20): "bellezza, ardir non più veduto"; "con venustà viril, donnesco volto."
155. Sarrocchi 1623, 133–34, and 2006, 247–49 (13.30–37). For the literary antecedents of the scene, see 2006, 247n14. A difference between Silveria's garden and those of seductresses such as Alcina and Armida is that, as Sarrocchi underlines (13.30), its beauty is the product of honest industry ("industria") rather than magic.
156. See ch. 3 at n. 176.
157. Sarrocchi 1623, 241, and 2006, 383–86 (23.87–100).
158. Marinella 2011, 485, and 2009, 328, 420 (22.28): "vaga sirena." Marinella does not name herself in the passage, but her identity is clear, and she refers to two of her works, *La vita di Maria Vergine* and *L'Enrico*.
159. Marinella 2011, 485, and 2009, 328, 420 (22.29): "Stupirà il mondo de' suoi detti al suono; / . . . / Le sacre muse a corteggiarla sono; / a quella Febo la sua gloria assegna."
160. Marinella 2011, 485, and 2009, 328, 420 (22.29): "E fia d'onor forse più ch'altra degna."
161. Fonte 1995, 161, and 2006, 288 (10.36–37).
162. The evidence for Bronzini's contacts with Marinella in this period is summarized in Von Tippelskirch 2008, 140–41. For Bronzini's praise of Sarrocchi, see Bronzini 1625, 130–38.
163. See n. 167 below.
164. Russell 2006, 40–41. See also, on the relation between the two poems, Stampino 2009, 24–25.
165. Lanci 1590, 251; Della Chiesa 1620, 243; Bronzini 1625, *giornata quarta*, 116; Zilioli, "Istoria delle vite," 144–45.
166. See Verdile 1989–90, 201–3; see also the introduction at n. 23 for a further encomium.
167. Marinella 1624, A3v (publisher's preface): "un lungo, e sommo honore."
168. Cox 2008, 225.
169. See Marinella 1645; and, for discussion, Cox 2008, 223–25, and Benedetti 2008.
170. On Marinella's limited literary activity in the first decade of her marriage, see ch. 1 at nn. 83–84. For discussion of the publication date of *Amore innamorato, et impazzato*, which is sometimes listed as first published in 1598, see Cox 2008, 334n94.
171. Caterina, daughter of Ferdinando de' Medici and Christine of Lorraine, was Eleonora's niece. On Medici women's salient role as dedicatees of female-authored literature in this period, see ch. 4, n. 156.
172. Marinella 1624, a3v: "quasi mille Stanze." It seems safe to assume that Marinella had some hand in composing the fulsome publishers' prefaces that accompany several of her works (Marinella 1605a, 1624, 1643).
173. On Marinella's prose style, see ch. 4 at nn. 117–20. The publisher of *Arcadia*

felice, Giambattista Ciotti, calls attention to the work's ornate style ("ornato modo di parlare") in his prefatory note. The interpolated poems in the work are listed in a prefatory *tavola* in Marinella 1605a.

174. In fact, Diocletian retired to Split in Dalmatia. The only sustained critical discussions of *Arcadia felice* to date are Lavocat 1998b; Kolsky 2005, 332–34; and Malpezzi Price and Ristaino 2008, 25–37. See also Lavocat 1998a, 84–87.

175. The term *novella-romanzo* derives from Baratto 1984. On the combination of romance and pastoral elements in Renaissance pastoral novels, see R. Schneider 2002; cf. E. Rhodes 1989, esp. 354–55.

176. Lavocat notes as a partial counterexample Giulio Cesare Capaccio's "piscatorial romance" *La Merghellina*, of 1598 (Lavocat 1998b, xli, n. 157). On the Italian editions of the *Diana*, see Montemayor 1996, 26–28, 39–40, 42, 47–48; and Burke 2000, 402, 412, which, however, omits the 1585 edition. On the likelihood that Marinella was acquainted with this work, see Lavocat 1998b, xliv, as well as 27n136 and 102n445.

177. Lavocat 1998b, viii, xli. The principal pastoral romances of the period were Antonio Droghi's *Leucadia* (1598), dedicated to Isabella Pallavicino Lupi, and Giovanni Maria Bernaudi's *La zotica*, apparently also published in 1598, though only surviving in later, Seicento editions. For discussion of the former work, see Ariani 2007a, 1706.

178. See Lavocat 1998b, xliv; more generally, on the romance elements in *Arcadia felice*, see vii–ix, xli–li. The literary sources for the individual romance episodes are identified by Lavocat in her notes.

179. Lavocat 1998b, xlii–xliii.

180. The episode of Ersilia's accusation is at Lavocat 1998a, 80. Montemayor's *Diana* contains two stories of female-female attraction, using the motif of gender miscognition through disguise: Selvagia-Ismenia (book 1) and Felismena-Celia (book 2).

181. Marinella 1998, 177–78. Iele's announcement is made to her mother, Amaranta, who first protests, arguing the case for love using the *carpe diem* arguments of the Dafne of Tasso's *Aminta*, before unexpectedly capitulating and professing herself happy with any life her daughter may choose.

182. Marinella 1998, 200: "Apuleio dolcissimo ed eloquentissimo dicitore." The only sustained critical discussions to date of *Amore innamorato, et impazzato* are Ussia 2001, 31–37, 155–56; and Malpezzi Price and Ristaino 2008, 38–60. For briefer mention, see also Panizza 1999, 8–9; and Kolsky 2005, 328–29.

183. On Minturno's poem, which anticipates Marinella in having Cupid fall in love with an invented figure rather than Psyche (in Minturno's case "Eroina"), see Ussia 2001, 21–31; and Minturno 2008.

184. Ussia 2001. On the literary and artistic reception of the Cupid-Psyche myth in Renaissance Italy, see also Guthmüller 1999, which cites earlier bibliography at 27n11.

185. Udine 2004. For discussion, see also Guthmüller 1999; and Ussia 2001, 86–

97. Marinella must have read Udine's poem shortly after its publication, as she mentions it in Marinella 1601, 87–88.

186. Marinella 1624, A3v: "poema di assai più bella inventione, che la Psiche di Apulegio [sic]." See also, as evidence of Marinella's competitive attitude toward her male forebears, Marinella 1618, 183 (8.41), where, in a rare case of a woman employing the topos of the epic "outdoing," she announces the superiority of her version of literary madness to those of Euripides (*Orestes*) and Ariosto.

187. Marinella 1618, 136 (6.37–38). The story of Cupid's theft of Jove's thunderbolt may have been inspired by Plutarch's description of Alcibiades's shield device of Eros holding a thunderbolt. On this iconographic motif in classical art, see Hallett 2005, 231.

188. Marinella 1618, 242–44 (10.61–67).

189. The Latin word for sources, *fontes*, literally means "springs."

190. On the tradition of allegorical readings of the Cupid-Psyche myth between late antiquity and the seventeenth century, see Guthmüller 1999, 39–40; and Ussia 2001, 141–58.

191. Tansillo 1606, A5v.

192. See T. Tasso 1977b, 1:49, 59–64. Specifically, Tasso defines the core of lyric style as lying in the pleasingness and charm of its *concetti* ("la soavità, la venustà e . . . la amenità de' concetti") and characterizes it as possessing "a certain smiling, florid, sensual quality" (1:60; un non so che di ridente, di fiorito, e di lascivo).

193. See, e.g., for Cupid, Marinella 1618, 22 (1.59), 48 (1.60), and 56 (3.11), in the last of which he is said to risk falling in love with his image as Narcissus did; for Ersilia, 9 (1.18–19); and for Venus, 23–25 (1.61–67), a passage unusual within the female-authored literature of the period as an extended description of a female nude.

194. Marinella 1618, 52: "Ersilia, che spogliata da' suoi panni stanca per molte fatiche si lava nel fiume, ci potrà significare l'anima christiana, che gittati da parte li panni de' piaceri mondani, lava il nero della coscienza sua nel puro e nell'ampio del fiume della penitenza perfetta."

195. Marino 1975. Marino retells the story of Cupid and Psyche in canto 4 of the poem; see Ussia 2001, 113–26, for discussion.

196. Petrarca 1996b, 248 (lines 118–26). A *canzone* in Salvetti 1590, 50–60, inspired by the same Petrarchan episode, portrays Christine of Lorraine similarly disabling and humiliating Cupid (see esp. 55).

197. Ersilia's initial interest in Cupid is described at Marinella 1618, 48 (1.60).

198. Marinella 1618, 64 (3.35). For this imagery in *La Colomba sacra*, see ch. 4 at n. 88. A similar power relationship is found between the devil and Saint Catherine in Marinella 1624.

199. On the Bragadin-Barbo dispute and on Naldi's letter, see ch. 6 at nn. 27–28.

200. Apuleius 1989, 1:226 (5.12): "sexus infestus."

201. Marinella 1618, 103–5 (5.13–20).

202. Ariosto 1976, 2:885–94 (34.9–44).

203. Barbo n.d., 7–27.

204. Lavocat 1998b, xlv–xlvi; see also, more generally, R. Schneider 2002, 274n15.

205. After an initial mention at Marinella 1998, 36, Ersilia's story proceeds at 55–58, 68–69, 77, 79–91.

206. On games in the pastoral novel and their significance in general, see Lavocat 2006. The games episode in Marinella is in Marinella 1998, 54–70; see Lavocat's notes to this edition for her relation to her sources.

207. Marinella 1998, 22–25.

208. Marinella 1998, 69–70: "coro di vergini ninfe." On the dance episode, see Lavocat 1998a, 85–86. Diocletian's reception of the event underlines its implied gender values: he praises the youth of Arcadia after the games for their "strength, worth, and prowess" and the girls for their "grace, beauty, and virtue" (Marinella 1998, 70; gagliardia, valore, e prodezza . . . leggiadria, bellezze, e virtù).

209. We first meet Ersilio in part 1, where he and Alfisbeo are introduced as a pair of "young shepherds" (Marinella 1998, 36; ambedue pastori giovani). Boccaccio similarly deceives the reader in *novella* 3 of Day 2 of his *Decameron*, describing the cross-dressing princess of England, disguised as a monk, as though she were actually a man (Boccaccio 1992, 157–61).

210. Licori-Canente is first introduced at Marinella 1998, 14. We hear of her writing verses for Diocletian at 16 and see her perform, along with other nymphs, at 25–28.

211. The principal evidence of Marinella's musical talents is found in Ribera 1609, 330, who praises both her singing and her instrumental skills, especially on the lute. Bronzini's testimony, cited by Lavocat 1998b, xxiv, n. 86, is taken from Ribera.

212. Cox 2008, 149.

213. Marinella 2011, 141–42 (5.89–93).

214. On Wroth's figure of Melissea, seen as a reworking of Montemayor's Felicia, see Roberts 1995, xxvi; and Yang 2003. A further influence on Marinella in her depiction of Erato is Virgil's representation of the Cumaean sibyl in book 6 of the *Aeneid* (see Marinella 1998, 163; cf. Virgil 1999, 1:534–36 [6.48–53]).

215. Sannazaro 1990, 149 (ninth prose): "attraere dal cielo le offuscate stelle tutte stillante di vivo sangue." Sannazaro's imitator Droghi in the ninth prose of his *Leucadia* (Droghi 1598, 292–311) similarly pairs a sinister old female witch, Lena, with a more benign male *mago*, in this case her son, Lidio.

216. Marinella 1998, 148–49. Ismaele is acting on instructions from Emireno at Marinella 1998, 124–26. The depiction of Ismaele's conduct during the black rite has a markedly orientalist cast; see esp. 148, where he is described as carrying out the task "with a barbarous aspect" (con barbaresca sembianza). His ethnicity is also recalled in the description of him as "l'Indiano" on the same page.

217. The description of the approach to Erato's kingdom is at Marinella 1998, 153–54, the allusion to the herb moly at 151.

218. Marinella 1998, 169.

219. Marinella 1998, 169. The zither appears to be of the same breed of marvels as

the mechanical hydraulic organs described among the wonders of Emireno's palace in part 3 (126; see also below in the text at nn. 232–33).

220. Mary Wroth similarly places the domain of her *maga* Melissea on Delos, traditionally sacred to Apollo. See Yang 2003, 10.

221. Marinella 1998, 168–69: "quivi vide i ciembali, il dorato arco della casta figliuola di Giove, i risonanti timpani della gran Madre Berecintia, e le sacre facelle di Cerere (there she saw the cymbals and the golden arch of the chaste daughter of Jove [Diana], the resonant drums of the great mother Berecynthia [Cybele], and the sacred sparks of Ceres). For the reference to Erato as "wise vates" (savia vate), see 166.

222. On the displacement of Pan from *Arcadia felice*, see Lavocat 1998b, xvi–xviii.

223. Marinella 1998, 106–7. For the episode with Albino, see Marinella 172–75; for the priest of Diana in part 2, 79–80. The reference to this last figure as "High Priest" (Sacerdote Sommo) is on 80.

224. For the suggestion that the cult of Diana in *Arcadia felice* represents contemporary Marian worship, see Marinella 1998, 173n731. For the nun figure of the Entello story (the protagonist's aunt, Teselide), see 106.

225. Marinella 1605a, 173: "ministro de gli honori della Triforme Diana." See also Coreglia 1634, 70 (4.2), where Diana is referred to as the "chaste triform goddess" (casta triforme dea).

226. Another female-authored pastoral work of the period that represents Arcadian religious culture as matriarchal is Isabetta Coreglia's *La Dori*, of 1634. Aside from Diana, the principal deity featuring in the play is Fauna, a version of the Roman goddess Opi, or Bona Dea. Leonora Bernardi's *Tragicomedia pastorale*, discussed in chapter 3, portrays a religious landscape that seems to feature cults of both Jove and Diana, as well as both male and female priests. See esp. "Gentildonna lucchese," 64v, for a reference to a female character, Lidia, as "de la gran Dea Ministra" (minister to the great goddess).

227. On the political themes of the work, see Lavocat 1998b, xxx–xli.

228. Marinella 1998, 83–85; the phrase "cupido desiderio di reggere" is at 84. The emptiness of worldly ambition is a common theme in Marinella's writings. See, e.g., the sermon of Saint Francis on the theme in Marinella 1997b, 415–16 (1.72–74); see also above at n. 65 for her praise in *L'Enrico* of Venetian doges who voluntarily retired from rule.

229. Marinella 1998, 175: "colui che raffrenò con potente e moderata mano l'indomiti popoli."

230. Marinella 1998, 81–82, 89–90, 187–88. The episode of Diocletian's refusing the offer of governance of Arcadia is at 21.

231. Marinella 1998, 157–59. See also 18–19 for an episode in which a satyr, Sileno, alludes to Diocletian's vanity in allowing himself to be worshipped as a god in Rome. On Marinella's ambivalent portrayal of Diocletian, Lavocat 1998b, xxviii–xl.

232. For discussion of Emireno's *wunderkammer*, see Lavocat 1998b, xlix–l. Besides the artifacts mentioned in the text here, Emireno's marvels include a type of camera obscura, perhaps conceived on the basis of the description in Giambattista

della Porta's *Magia naturalis*, which had been translated into Italian in 1582 (Marinella 1998, 121–22; Lavocat 1998b, xlix, n. 199).

233. On the reception of Hero's *Pneumatics* in Italy, see Marr 2004, 209n22, 211n33, 213, 216, and 2006, 154–55. By the time Marinella was writing *Arcadia felice*, hydraulically operated automata were on view in Italian gardens such as Buontalenti's at Pratolino (see the bibliography cited in Marr 2004, 216nn59–60).

234. Marinella 1998, 170–71. The reference is to Aristotle's *Meterology*. The view that Marinella maintains here, associated with Democritus in antiquity, was soon after the publication of the work to be verified empirically by Galileo, using the recently invented telescope.

235. Herculiana 1584; Cox 2008, 161–62.

236. For this suggestion in the case of Erina and Fileno, see Panizza 1999, 4, 14n33.

237. Marinella 1618, 101 (5.8): "soavi cure, ed amorosi affetti." For the Megaera episode, see 102 (5.9–11).

238. For Eurinia's *innamoramento* with Caronte, see Marinella 1618, 91, 93–96 (4.45, 52–61).

239. Marinella 1998, 137–42. On the use of *sdruccioli* in this period, see Gerbino 2004.

240. Marinella 1998, 137: "Non c'era in tutta l'Arcadia un più deforme volto del suo ancor che si riputasse in bellezza un Amore e un Adone." See also 31, where Dameta is introduced in similar terms. On the literary tradition of the topos, see Sampson 2006, 79, 95n70.

241. See ch. 6 at nn. 141–43.

CHAPTER SIX: Discursive Prose

1. See Cox 2008, 16, 235.
2. On these writers and their output, see Cox 2008, 8–12.
3. See on these works Cox 2008, 112–13.
4. Nogarola 1563; [L. Gonzaga] 1552 and 2008. The issue of the authorship of Gonzaga's letters has been discussed most recently in Bragantini 2008; Ray 2009b; and Ray 2009c, 87–94.
5. Vernazza is included here on the grounds that she had consented to publication of her work during her lifetime, although she was dead by the time the first three volumes of her *Opere* appeared.
6. See Solfaroli Camillocci 1999 for details. The members of the committee included Borromeo's confessor, Francesco Adorno (1533–86), and the theologian and spiritual writer Achille Gagliardi (1536–1607).
7. The verse, by Marco da Crema (described as a reader in theology at the Convento della Misericordia), an *anonimo* (perhaps Crema), Malvasia herself, and a lay poet, Roberto Poggiolini, is at Malvasia 1617, a3r–b4v; the preface, "Al divoto Let-

tore," is at c1r–c3v. Plautus is cited as "il Comico," the other authorities by name. The engraved frontispiece to the volume shows the Madonna of the San Luca icon hovering over the city of Bologna, with a text uniting the two, seemingly envisaged as spoken by Bologna and addressed to the Virgin (though with a pun on Malvasia's own religious name): "Da Dio data me difendi, e honori" (God-given one, defend and protect me).

8. It is quite likely that these three works were known to Matraini, given that Colonna was a powerful influence on Matraini as a poet (Rabitti 1981, 159–60; 2000, 484–85) and Matraini and Battiferra had a mutual acquaintance in Benedetto Varchi (1503–65).

9. Matraini 1581, 1586, 1590, 1602. Matraini's late religious works have been little studied until recently, though see Carinci 2009, 73–87. See also Bullock and Palange 1980, 253–61; Rabitti 2007, 15–17; and Marcheschi 2008. Marcheschi and Carinci emphasize reformist thought as a context for Matraini's religious writings. More detailed studies of Matraini 1590 may be found in Paoli 2003, 538–45; and Carinci 2009, 89–113. For Matraini 1602, see below, n. 64. There are no modern editions in Italian of any of these works, but selections in translation from all four are found in Matraini 2007, 107–31, 204–15; see also Matraini 2008, 67–118, for a partial translation of Matraini 1590.

10. Bullock and Palange 1980, 258–59. Matraini's life of the Virgin is included in this chapter rather than in chapter 4, with Marinella's 1602 *Vita*, because of the different character of the works: while Marinella's is essentially a straight narrative, Matraini's *Vita* combines narrative with meditative discursuses.

11. See ch. 1, n. 61.

12. Marinella 1597. For secondary literature, see ch. 4, n. 104.

13. Franco 1998a; 1998b, 23–46. For critical discussion, see the literature cited in Cox 2008, 339n141, to which may be added Ray 2009c, 123–55.

14. Matraini 1989, 121–95, 303–8. For a sample letter in English translation, see Matraini 2007, 135–38. For discussion, see Rabitti 1999, 215–25; Rabitti 2007, 18–22; and Marcheschi 2008, 137–41.

15. Vernazza 1602, 436–588; I. Andreini 1607. On the authorship issue, see Taviani 1984, 11–15; and Ray 2009c, 161–65.

16. Herculiana 1584; Vito di Gozze 1585, 2r–4r. See also the dedicatory letter to Vito di Gozze 1581 for a defense of women's intellectual capacity by the author himself. Erculiani's text is discussed briefly in Cox 2008, 162, while an edition of Gondola's is forthcoming in a volume of Dalmatian women's writing for the Other Voice in Early Modern Europe series, to be edited by Francesca Maria Gabrieli.

17. Sori 1628; Maestri 1993.

18. See Cox 2008, 149. On the earlier, fifteenth-century tradition of Latin oratory by women, see Cox 2008, 9–10, and 2009, 77–78, 87.

19. Monte 1577, 1578a, [1578b?], 1581; *Varie compositioni* 1596, E1r–G4v. On Monte's orations, see ch. 3 at nn. 11–12; on Spolverini's, see A. Smith 2009. Valeria Miani,

on the evidence of Ribera 1609, 335, is sometimes also said to have delivered an oration on the occasion of Empress Maria's visit. See, however, Rees 2010, 24, for a skeptical examination of the evidence.

20. The evidence for Spolverini's delivery of the oration is found in a dialect poem by "Picegaton di Memorosi da San Lazaro" (Giovanni Fratta), in *Varie compositioni* 1596, 228. The poem talks of the speech having been commissioned by the ladies of Verona ("de comession / delle compagne ghe fe l'oracion"). For Monte, see ch. 3, n. 11.

21. That Gatti delivered the oration may be inferred from internal evidence. See, e.g., B. Gatti, A6r, where the author enjoins her father and her brothers and sisters "here present" (che mi sete attorno) not to weep at losing her to a cloistered life.

22. It is possible that Issicratea Monte also practiced this form of quasi-deliberative political oratory, in addition to the demonstrative oratory that survives by her. Della Chiesa 1620, 196–97, records lost orations by her addressed to Pope Gregory XIII, Emperor Rudolf II, Henri III of France, Philip II of Spain, the Consistory of Cardinals, and "the Christian Princes" (li Principi Christiani), as well as moral and religious orations in praise of poverty, against worldly vanity, and for the Compagnia dello Spirito Santo.

23. Fonte 1600, 1988, 1997; Marinella 1600, 1601, 1999, 2007. For critical bibliography, see below, n. 108.

24. Jones and Rosenthal 1998, 18–21; Shemek 1998, 126–57; Cox 2008, 25, 121. Outside Italy, full-scale defenses of women had been produced before this point by Christine de Pizan (1365–c. 1434) and Marie de Romieu (c. 1545–90).

25. On the relation between *La nobiltà* and Passi's treatise, see Panizza 1999, 15–18; and Kolsky 2001, 974, 977. On Marinella's "demolitions" of Aristotle et al., see below, n. 129.

26. Franco's principal polemic is with the Venetian poet Maffio Venier (1550–86), author of a series of abusive poems addressed to her. See Wojciehowski 2006 for a recent analysis.

27. The sonnet, *capitolo*, and *discorso* appear in *Muse contentiose* 1614 and in Bragadin 1619, 68–82. Bragadin's sonnet had appeared earlier, in Bragadin 1613, 87. The term *discorso* seems to be that of the editor of the 1614 volume; in Bragadin 1619 the text is presented simply as a letter, with the heading "Eccellente Accademico Fecondo." I discuss the Bragadin-Barbo polemic in detail in an essay to be published in the forthcoming volume *Verona al femminile*, edited by Paola Lanaro for Cierre, Verona.

28. Cox 2008, 175.

29. Copio 1621. The text is available in Copio 2009, 524–33, a translation at 311–32. For discussion, see Boccato 1973; Fortis 2003, 61–81; and Harrán 2009, 45–56. More generally, on Copio, see the literature cited in Cox 2008, 360n158, as well as Harrán 2009. For evidence of a lost *querelle* text by Copio, see Cox 2008, 346.

30. Maestri 1993.

31. 1 Timothy 2:12; see also 1 Corinthians 34–35 on the inappropriateness of women speaking in church.

32. *Corpus Iuris Canonici* 1879–81, 1:86 (*Decreti prima pars, distinctio* 23, *capitulum* 29): "Mulier, quamvis docta et sancta, viros in conventu docere non presumat."

33. Ottonelli 1646, 400: "Dall'hora in poi, se qualche donna s'è posta ad insegnare, è stata per ordinario strumento del diavolo, architetta di frodi, fabra d'inganni, maestra di falsità e d'errori."

34. Spelta 1607, 313: "come se fossero tanti Platoni et Aristoteli, o per dir meglio Thomasi et Agostini." For further exemplification, see ch. 1 at nn. 257–58.

35. Ottonelli 1646, 406: "Le parole delle donne sono vive fiamme di lascivo ardore con che molte volte . . . consumano i cuori degli uditori." See also, generally, 404–39.

36. Silvano Razzi 1595–1606, 6:90r–91v: "facendo tutto il contrario di Eva." Even Ottonelli 1646, 403, allows women who convert their husbands or instruct them in the Christian faith as counterexamples to the general rule that women should not teach men.

37. See ch. 3 at nn. 17–20.

38. Ribera 1609, 307–11. See also on Bocchi, Della Chiesa 1620, 141, and Bronzini 1625, *giornata quinta*, 26–27; and on Novella Bolognese, Bronzini 1625, *giornata quinta*, 24–25.

39. Della Chiesa 1620, 203; Boccaccio 2001, 250: "aut invidia . . . aut muliebri temeritate inpulsa." Neither Della Chiesa nor Marinella, who cites Leontion along with Diotima and Catherine of Alexandria as examples of women who taught or debated with men, mentions the sexual promiscuity Boccaccio accuses her of (Marinella 1601, 38, 39, 42, and 1999, 84, 86, 92; Boccaccio 2001, 252).

40. Della Chiesa 1620, 46: "non meno sanamente, e dottamente insegnerebbero di quello, ch'habbino fatto i maggiori, e più eloquenti Oratori del mondo." Bursati 1621, 177–78, takes a similar line.

41. Della Chiesa 1620, 46: "hanno havuto ardire [le donne] di legger nelle pubbliche università alla presenza d'eccellentissimi dottori, e di predicare nelle più frequentate chiese di Roma, e d'altre principali città d'Europa alla presenza di prencipi, cardinali, e del Papa istesso." See also 95, where Battista Vernazza's scriptural learning is compared to that of "a very great preacher" (un grandissimo predicatore), and 159, where Fulvia Colonna's is judged the equal of "any great theologian or preacher" (ogni gran teologo, o predicatore).

42. Bronzini 1625, *giornata quarta*, 136.

43. Grumelli 1596, 12r–13r; Fonte 1988, 132–35, and 1997, 189–92. For discussion of the episode in Fonte, see below at nn. 159–60.

44. Grumelli 1596, 14v: "la quale [religione christiana] era insegnata, e mostrata da lei, e con le parole, e con i veri effetti." Grumelli's portrayal of Santa Grata is of interest as a representation by a cloistered late sixteenth-century woman of a saintly woman living in and engaging with the world; Grata is even potayed as briefly ruling Bergamo after the death of her father, Lupo. Grata was also the subject of a published biography by an eighteenth-century nun in the same convent (Tassis 1723); on her legend, see M. Cortesi 2002.

45. Capece 1595, A4r: "spirito et energia."
46. Vernazza 1588, 1:A2r: "[che] esse più con lume sopranaturale, e con uso continuo d'oratione, che con industria humana o con altro studio siano state composte."
47. Vernazza 1602, dedicatory letter, unnumbered: "Ma molto più illustre, & ammirabile pare si sia mostrata l'infinita sapientia, & providentia divina in oprar sì, che non pur huomini, ma etiandio donne, che sono & di sesso più fragile, & di scientie di sua natura meno capaci, habbiano . . . altamente filosofato nella Christiana scuola." Da Piacenza's examples, apart from Vernazza, are Saint Catherine of Genoa and Catherine's cousin and follower Tommasina Fieschi (c. 1448–1534).
48. Matraini 1586, A2r: "degne e dottissime persone"; "una tanto e sì dificile impresa . . . più tosto da grandi, e elevati intelletti, che d'una semplice Donna, poco prattica de' Misteri della Sacra Scrittura."
49. Matraini 1586, A2r–v: "forse inspirata da Dio"; "con l'ingegno mio ascendere a quell'altezza, alla quale assai rare e specolativi intelletti già s'erano alzati."
50. Cervoni may have been inspired to this feat by recollection of Catherine of Siena's letters to Gregory XI (c. 1331–78), on which see Tylus 2009, 28–30. Cervoni's hometown, Colle di Val d'Elsa, is only about twelve miles from Siena, although it was ruled by Florence from the fourteenth century.
51. I. Cervoni 1598, 4: "Ma che dirà il mondo, quando sentirà le mie parole in sì alta materia? In materia tutta diversa da la natura e qualità d'una semplice verginella? . . . Non resterà stupefatto che io . . . ardisca hora d'entrar'a parlare . . . nel genere deliberativo . . . dinanzi a un Sommo Pontefice?"
52. I. Cervoni 1598, 4. Cervoni cites the phrase, from Psalms 8:2 and Matthew 21:16, in Latin: "Ex ore infantium et lactantium perfecisti laudem." A further claim to divine inspiration is found in the *congedo* to the *canzone* to "the rulers of Christendom" (i Prencipi Christiani), which follows the oration (I. Cervoni 1598, 41–42); see also the first stanza of the *canzone* (29–30), where Cervoni compares herself to Cassandra in her prophetic insight.
53. See esp. I. Cervoni 1598, 28: "non si maravigli la Santità Vostra, se una semplice Verginella ha detto tante, e così diverse cose . . . poi che la Natura m'inclina a lo studio e che tanto mi diletta il leggere e osservar parte di quello, ch'io leggo" (Your Holiness should not wonder that a simple young girl should have spoken of so many and diverse things . . . for Nature inclines me to study, and I take great pleasure in reading and taking note of a portion of what I read).
54. I. Cervoni 1598, 98: "Et ardirò di dire con debita riverenza, che se, come la Natura m'è stata benigna in generarmi con tale inclinazione e facilità d'ingegno, mi fosse così la fortuna favorevole nel procacciarmi un Mecenate, e foste Voi quegli, spererei far tal progresso ne le lettere che forse non sarebbe stato in me collocato il talento in vano."
55. Capece 1595, A4v (preface by Francesco di Pietri): "ha procurato . . . arrichirla [sc. "quest'opera"] et ornarla di molti e nuovi concetti"; "rendere chiaro il suo parto ed immortale." See also, on the same page, di Pietri's remark that one of Pagano's intentions in publishing the work was "to leave for posterity some monument to

himself and his fruits" (per lasciar a' posteri alcuno monumento di sé e de' suoi frutti). Useful as context for the relationship between Pagano and Capece is Bilinkoff 2005.

56. Matraini 1581, 1, 3, 89–108; Paoli 2003, 542–44. Mozzagrugno was based in Lucca at the church of Santa Maria Forisportam, for which Matraini had commissioned an altarpiece (see ch. 3, at n. 19; and Paoli 2003, 542–43).

57. Paoli 2003, 542: "Né . . . le fu consentito di sottrarsi del tutto ad una mediazione maschile al momento della pubblicazione dell'opera" (nor was [Matraini] able to escape a male intervention at the moment of the work's publication).

58. Aside from those named in the text, the other contributors are Ducchi, Antonio Frizzimellega, Cortese Cortesi, Iseppe Gagliardia, Vincenzo Tassello, Giovanni Battista Maganza, Fantino Fantini, Marco Stecchini, Fabrizio Pasqualigo, and Giovanni Battista Titoni. All but Maganza, Fantini, Stecchini, Ingegneri, Barbo, and Groto also contributed verse to Campiglia 1588.

59. Campiglia 1585, unnumbered: "cibo spirituale"; "da sì benigna madre allettato."

60. Campiglia 1585, unnumbered: "utile del prossimo et honor della patria."

61. Campiglia 1585, M4r: "nova del secolo nostro / Safo [sic], e Sibilla"; "secretaria."

62. B. Gatti 1604, A2r: "dotata di quanta eloquenza, di quanta scienza, e di quanta prudenza fusse giamai sparsa non solo frà tutti i savij della Grecia, e di Roma; ma di tutto l'universo mondo; vincitrice delli oratori, superatrice de' filosofi, e trionfante gloriosa dell'imperii." Gatti goes on to augur (A2v) that Catherine's spirit will inspire her to speak "a gloria di Dio, e maraviglia forsi di chi mi ascolta" (to the glory of God, and perhaps to the wonderment of my listeners).

63. B. Gatti 1604, A3v: "Se tanto fù lodata l'invitta Reina di Babilonia, movendosi senza dimora con una treccia sciolta, solo per riscattar la sua Città, che già era presa dalle nemiche squadre; maggiore honore mi debbo recar io, tagliandomi le chiome, per salvarmi dal mondo così pericoloso; per farmi acquisto non di una Città, ò di una Provintia, ma si ben del Paradiso" (If the dauntless queen of Babylonia was so praised when she set off with one braid loose merely to rescue her city, which was in prey to the enemy troops, I deserve greater honor for cutting my hair to save me from this so perilous world, acquiring in the process not a city or a province but Paradise itself). For the episode in Semiramis's legend referred to here, see Fonte 1997, 102 and n. 71.

64. Neither work has been much studied until recently, though see now Carinci 2009, 125–54, on Campiglia's *Discorso;* see also Cox and Sampson 2004, 7–8, and Ultsch 2005a, 74–76. On Matraini's *Dialoghi,* see Smarr 2005, 81–97; Marcheschi 2008, 85–89; and Carinci 2009, 83–87.

65. Matraini seems already to have been pursuing Venetian publishing contacts in the 1580s. A letter of 1585 to her from Aldo Manuzio (1547–97), of the great publishing family, indicates that she wrote to him at this time, enclosing verse (Manuzio 1592, 24–25).

66. Segni 1601, 24–26. One of Matraini's sonnets is addressed to a Giorgio Terriciuoli, who presumably approached her to ask for a contribution to the volume.

67. Chemello 2003, 77–78.
68. Chemello 2003, esp. 73–75. Campiglia's relationship with the Dimesse movement is examined in Chemello 2003; and Ultsch 2005b.
69. See, e.g., Campiglia 1585, 83, where the author speaks of unspecified "travails," "tribulations," and "rancors" (travagli, tribulationi, rancori mondani).
70. Matraini 1989, 177–81. For evidence of the 1560s dialogue, see Cox 2008, 112, 311n159.
71. The distribution of poems in the initial, *dialoghi* section of the work is discussed in Smarr 2005, 82.
72. Campiglia 1585, 8–18. Adam and Eve's speech is introduced with the phrase "Ben penso io che . . . nel silentio, in questo modo ragionassero a Dio" (9).
73. Carinci 2009, 130–40. For Marinella, see ch. 4 at nn. 111–12.
74. See, e.g., Campiglia 1585, 11, where Satan is described "hissing and roaring like a poisonous snake or a fierce lion" (a guisa d'avvelenato Serpe, e fiero Leone, fischiava, & ruggiva); cf. T. Tasso 1980, 399 (13.21.5; 13.23.8). The equivalent passage in Aretino is at Aretino 1552, 38v, quoted in Carinci 2009, 134.
75. Campiglia 1585, appendix of laudatory verse, M2v: "Altri d'arme e d'amor cantar accesi."
76. The rather abrupt shift occurs at Campiglia 1585, 70.
77. Quondam 2005a, 207–8. A rosary-themed poetic sequence by Francesca Turina is discussed in chapter 4.
78. Campiglia 1585, unnumbered and 24: "primitia di debolissima pianta"; "indegna, ignorante, et abietta."
79. Campiglia 1585, 8.
80. Campiglia 1585, unnumbered: "l'ardente siccità della malignità altrui, che strugge, e dilegua quanta poca virtù potesse havere il picciolo terreno mio, acquistato dalle rugiade celesti." *Altrui* here is likely to refer to Campiglia's estranged husband. See p. 5 for an allusion to the misery of marriage to a person of "savage and venemous heart" (cor . . . ferigno e pieno di tosco), and 23 for a description of unhappily married women as "often hat[ing] the very air that breathes round them" (bene spesso odiano quest'aria, che li spira d'intorno).
81. See, e.g., the elaborate physical description of the Virgin at Campiglia 1585, 37–38.
82. Campiglia 1585, 77: "Potrei assimigliar questo signor mio, salvator nostro rinchiuso nel ventre della Beatissima Madre sua a mille figure, di che sono piene le divine carte."
83. Campiglia 1585, 77 (following directly on from the previous passage): "ma forsi che ad'arroganza mi sarebbe ascritto, e detto che prossumer [sic] troppo mi voglio d'haver veduto, e letto."
84. Nervousness about women and the "vulgar" getting direct access to scripture was notoriously one of the reasons for the church's disapproval of vernacular translations of the Bible in this period (on which see Fragnito 1997 and 2005).

85. Campiglia 1585, 80: "il Reverendiss[imo] Fiamma nelle sublime, & rare prediche sue."

86. The collection was reprinted six times between 1576 and 1591. Campiglia cites Fiamma on the point that Mary's domain extends throughout the universe, to hell as well as heaven, and consists in the exercise of mercy. The reference is to a passage in the final sermon of the book (G. Fiamma 1576, 277–78 [sermon 6, pt. 1]). Further on Campiglia's use of Fiamma in the *Discorso,* see below, nn. 89, 90, and 106; see also Carinci 2009, 141, 143–44, 146, 148–49.

87. Campiglia 1585, M3v: "salutifero sentiero."

88. Campiglia 1585, M2v ("ravviva i petti d'infiammato zelo"), N1v ("pungi i cor di sacro santo telo").

89. See esp. Campiglia 1585, 40–41, 46–50. Compare G. Fiamma 1576, 138–39 (sermon 3, pt. 2), 172–73 (sermon 4, pt. 1), although, in the second passage cited Fiamma goes on to broaden his point to include men.

90. Campiglia 1585, 59–60; cf. G. Fiamma 1576, 173 (sermon 4, pt. 1). Campiglia's emphasis on malicious talk *(maldicenze)* may reflect her own precarious social situation.

91. Matraini reinforces the parallel with Dante by quite frequent textual echoes of the *Commedia.* See Matraini 1602, 97 ("Voi che in così frale e piccioletta barca" [cf. Alighieri 1994, 4:21 *(Par.* 2.1)]) and 88 ("e caddi come corpo morto cade" [cf. Alighieri 1994, 2:94 *(Inf.* 5.142)]).

92. *Rime* 1587c, 87–93; Jaffe 2002, 300–303. Brembati's *canzone* portrays the poet being guided to Parnassus by a mysterious female figure, perhaps allegorizing Poetry or Immortality. See also ch. 5 at n. 221 for an otherworldly journey undertaken by a female sage in Lucrezia Marinella's *Arcadia felice.*

93. On the anomalousness of Matraini's *Lettere,* see Quondam 1981, 123; and Rabitti 1999, 219–20. For a description of the collection, see Rabitti 2007, 20–22.

94. Matraini 1989, 156–66; Rabitti 1999, 216.

95. Matraini 1989, 147–52 (letter 8). For a discussion of the letter and its theological contents, see Marcheschi 2008, 121–30.

96. Cox 2000b.

97. Smarr 2005, 85.

98. Maylender 1926–30, 2:148–50, records various Accademie dei Curiosi in Italy, but none securely documented before the late eighteenth century.

99. Matraini 1602, 73: "vago e spatioso giardino dell'humane scienze"; "bel frutto e degno di sapienza." The precise allegorical significance of the lady is not given in the text, although a possible candidate is Immortality, seen figured in the *Lettere* as a "celeste donna, vestita d'aurea e purpurea veste" (Matraini 1989, 133; heavenly lady dressed in golden and purple raiments).

100. *Meditationes* 1587, 298: "Multi multa sciunt, & seipsos nesciunt." The text was published frequently throughout the sixteenth century in Italy, in Latin down to the 1550s, afterwards mainly in vernacular translation.

101. Matraini 1602, 87, 76, 88: "saggia e fidatissima duce"; "dolcissima amica"; "alma nutrice, e cara."

102. Matraini 1602, 113, *Chiara fiamma d'amor divino ardente.*

103. Matraini 1602, 7, *All'ombra dell'oscura horrida morte.* Matraini supplies the significance of the poem in an explanatory note. See 8, where the sun is said to represent "lo studio delle buone scienze" (the study of the sciences).

104. Matraini 1602, 113: "un chiaro essempio e speglio."

105. Campiglia 1585, dedicatory letter, unnumbered ("donne d'infinito valore, e preggio [sic]"), 85 ("honorate signore"), 19. Campiglia's source for the detail of the Virgin's *donzelle*, named in the text as Abel, Susanna, Rebecca, Abigea, and Siphora, is likely to have been Aretino (see Carinci 2009, 137n61).

106. Campiglia 1585, 36: "Quella madre del peccato, & autora della universal dannatione nostra; questa madre dell'innocenza, & ministra della salute eterna dell'anime nostre." The whole passage comparing Eve and Mary is at 35–37. Campiglia's model is probably G. Fiamma 1576, 77 (sermon 2, pt. 2); see also 171 (sermon 4, pt. 1). See also, for Mary as a corrective to Eve, Fonte 1988, 56; Fonte 1997, 94 and n. 60; and ch. 2 at nn. 90–97.

107. Campiglia 1585, 50: "aggrandito e nobilitato."

108. For Italian female-authored interventions in the *querelle* down to the 1590s, see text above at n. 24. Secondary literature on Fonte's *Il merito delle donne* is listed in Cox 2008, 333n91, to which should be added Olivieri Secchi 1998, 307–11; Datta 2003, 160–63; Jung 2008; and Ross 2009, 278–84. Secondary literature on *La nobiltà et l'eccellenza delle donne* is listed at Cox 2008, 339n140, to which should be added Olivieri Secchi 1998, 307–11; Benedetti 1999, 454–56; Datta 2003, 164–66; Malpezzi Price and Ristaino 2008, 105–19; Traninger 2008, 194–98; Ross 2009, 286–91; and Lazzari 2010, 175–212 (comparatively with *L'Enrico*).

109. For citations of Marinella's treatise, see Ribera 1609, 330; Spelta 1612, 144; Della Chiesa 1620, 214; Bursati 1621, A6r, 315–16; and Bronzini 1625, *giornata quarta*, 112–13 (echoing Ribera). For discussion of Marinella's reputation in the seventeenth century, see Panizza 1999, 5n10, 29–30; and Ross 2009, 291–94. Spelta remarks of *La nobiltà*: "I do not know which polished pen of a most subtle philosopher could have written better on the subject" (non sò qual forbita penna d'ingegnoso filosofo havesse potuto meglio a sì fatto proposito scrivere).

110. A particularly fulsome appreciation is found in Ribera 1609, 300 (see below, n. 165). Mentions of *Il merito* are also found in Astolfi 1602, 114; Goldioni 1603, 187 (a much reprinted work); Bronzini 1624, *giornata prima*, 30, and 1625, *giornata quarta*, 117 (echoing Ribera); Superbi 1629, 141; Tomasini 1644, 372; de Coste 1647, 2:718; and Palazzi 1681, 91.

111. See ch. 1, at n. 107. On the controversy engendered by Passi's treatise, and on the various profeminist responses to it, see Cox 2008, 173–76.

112. Doglioni 1988, 8. According to Doglioni 1997, 38, Fonte completed the dialogue the night before her death in childbirth. Chemello 1988, xviii, dates the composition of the text by internal references to the period 1588–91.

113. The date of Marinella's dedicatory letter for *La nobiltà* is 9 August 1600, that of Fonte's daughter Cecilia Zorzi for *Il merito delle donne*, 10 November.

114. Fonte 1600: *ove chiaramente si scuopre quanti siano elle [le donne] degne, e più perfette de gli huomini.*

115. Herculiana 1584, a3v–a4r ("Ai lettori"), refers defensively to recent attacks on women and to the author's desire to vindicate "the worthy spirit of the women of our day" (il buon'animo delle donne de nostri tempi). See also the similar remarks in her dedicatory letter, cited at Cox 2008, 162, 342n162. On polemics on women in the academies of the Veneto in the 1580s and 1590s, see Cox 2008, 172.

116. For Fonte's acquaintance with Groto and Monte, see ch. 3 at nn. 12–13. The mainland verse collections in which Fonte appears are Zucconello 1583 and *Carmina* 1586.

117. Fonte 1588, 43, and 1997, 97: "tanti c'hanno scritto in nostro biasimo." See also 1988, 71, and 1997, 116, for a further reference to the tradition of antifeminist writings.

118. Marinella 1601, title page: "forti ragioni"; "infiniti esempi."

119. The debate concerns the merits of men. Its regulator (or "queen"), terms, and sides (Elena, Virginia, and Lucrezia arguing for men; Corinna, Leonora, and Cornelia arguing against them) are decided at Fonte 1988, 23–24, and 1997, 56–57.

120. On the theme of education as empowerment in Fonte, see Collina 1989, 155–56; and Cox 1997a, 10. On the thematic continuities between books 1 and 2 of *Il merito*, see Cox 1997a, 9–12.

121. Herculiana 1584, a2v: "far conoscere al mondo, che noi siamo atte a tutte le scientie, come gli huomini."

122. See text above at n. 16. Vito di Gozze 1585, where the letter appears, is dedicated to the Dalmatian *letterata* Fiore Zuzori (Cvijeta Zuzorić). For the quotation given here in the text, see 3r: "prive della capacità delle scienze, e cognitione delle cose."

123. Cox 2008, 162, 342n163. See also ch. 5 at nn. 232–34 for Marinella's display of scientific learning in her fictional works. Also interesting in this regard is the incidence of prefatory sonnets by women in scientific treatises: see Bonardo 1600, first published in 1584 (Issicratea Monte); Doglioni 1587 (Fonte); and Iasolini 1588 (Sarrocchi).

124. Marinella 1601, 1–2; 1999, 35. On the element of rhetorical paradox within the *querelle* tradition, see Daenens 1983. On Marinella's (and Fonte's) exceptionality in this regard, see Cox 1995, 521. A useful critical overview of scholarship on the *querelle* is Zimmerman 2003.

125. Marinella 1601, 3–8; 1999, 45–51. For the equivalent section in Passi, see Passi 1599, 1–11. For discussion, see Chemello 1983, 155–56; Panizza 1999, 20; and Chemello 2000, 466–68. For a summary of Marinella's arguments in the treatise in general, see Panizza 1999, 19–29. For more detail, see Chemello 1983, 150–64; and Allen and Salvatore 1992, 16–29.

126. Marinella 1601, 9–24, esp. 13–24, and 1999, 52–68, esp. 57–68. Cf. Passi

1599, 196–207 (discourse 18), where Passi speaks at length of the deceptiveness of women's beauty and the moral dangers it represents to men.

127. Marinella 1601, 24–26, and 1999, 69–71. Chapter 4 also contains a critique of Aristotle's views on women, anticipating that in chapter 6 of the expanded 1601 edition.

128. Marinella 1601, 32, and 1999, 79: "Ma poche sono quelle, che dieno opera à gli studi, overo all'arte militare in questi nostri tempi; percioche gli huomini, temendo di non perdere la signoria, et di divenir servi delle donne, vietano à quelle ben spesso ancho il sapere leggere, e scrivere" (Few women today give themselves to study, or to the military arts, because men, fearing to lose their dominion and to become subject to women, often prevent them even from learning to read or write). Chapter 5 is at 1601, 30–36, and 1999, 77–83.

129. My word *demolish* translates the verb *si distrugge* used on the title page of Marinella 1601 ("... non solo si distrugge l'opinione del Boccaccio, d'ambedue i Tassi, dello Sperone, di Monsig[nor] di Namur, e del Passi, ma d'Aristotile il grande ancora"). For the section in question, see 1601, 108–34, and 1999, 119–45. For discussion, see Panizza 1999, 25–29.

130. The section "I difetti et i mancamenti de gli huomini" occupies 192 pages in the 1601 edition (Marinella 1601, 135–326), by comparison with the 132 pages of "Della nobiltà et eccellenza delle donne" section (3–134). The two sections are termed *parti*, or "parts."

131. Marinella 1601, 130, and 1999 110–11: "il grido dell'operationi donnesche, parlo in materia di scientie, e d'attioni virtuose, deve risonare non solo nella propria Città: ma in diverse, e varie provincie." For the context of the remark, see Cox 2008, 171, 196. On male rule as tyranny in Marinella and Fonte, see Cox 1995, 520–21, 525.

132. On the humanistic origins of the catalog of famous women, see Cox 2008, 18–26.

133. Passi 1603. The work was followed by a sequel four years later (Passi 1609). An important literary context for the work of both Marinella and Passi is the protobaroque encyclopedism of the Venice-based Lateran canon Tommaso Garzoni (1549–89). On Passi as an imitator (and occasionally plagiarist) of Garzoni, see Rebonato 2004, 196–205. Marinella also seems occasionally to borrow directly from Garzoni. See, e.g., Marinella 1601, 277–78, for an anecdote concerning a Spartan ambassador who refused to treat with the Corinthians, having seen that their leaders gambled, which reprises verbatim a passage in Garzoni 1591, 65v.

134. Curzio contributed an essay to an edition of Guicciardini in 1580 and notes to editions of Giovio and Livy in 1581.

135. The notes and index in Marinella 1999 are useful in identifying Marinella's sources, although that edition is not complete.

136. Fregoso's compendium was available only in Latin, while Valerius's had been available in vernacular translation since the 1530s. On the widespread plagiaristic use of such compendia by sixteenth-century vernacular writers, see Cherchi 1998. In the most thorough examination of Marinella's sources to date, Chemello 1983,

166–68, notes a greater reliance on vernacular and translated sources than is found in Passi.

137. Marinella 1601, 188, 273: "Delli vanagloriosi e vantatori"; "De gli huomini lagrimosi, e teneri al pianto." Marinella's active and creative role as reader and citer of texts is stressed in Chemello 2000, 470–72.

138. Marinella 1601, 253. Marinella dryly remarks, "I believe that in our own day Passi is a great man in matters of magic and necromancy, as he speaks of these things with great learning" (credo che a' nostri tempi nella magia e negromantia sia un grande huomo il Passi, perciochè dottissimamente ne' suoi scritti ne ragiona). For the relevant chapter in Passi, see Passi 1599, 123–60 (discourse 15). Later, in 1614, Passi published a treatise on natural magic.

139. Marinella 1601, 277: "Onde più volte si sono veduti vecchi decrepiti, paralitici, con gli occhi scarpellini, che non havrebbono veduto uno elefante in uno campo di neve, con dua paia di occhiali al naso, mettere al punto, perche non potevano giucare altrimenti."

140. Marinella 1601, 275: "i poveri poeti"; "non accade, che si spremano ne gli occhi succhi di cipolla per lagrimare."

141. Marinella 1601, 262–69, and 1999, 166–75: "De gli huomini ornati, politi, bellettati, e biondati."

142. Critiques of female vanity in dress and of the use of cosmetics and hair dye, were quite prevalent in the period. Besides Passi 1599, 161–95, see, e.g., Agnelli 1592.

143. Marinella 1601, 263; 1999, 167. Marinella perceptively notes that this bravado is constitutive of masculinity, in that those men who do not affect it are accused of being "of a feminine spirit" (d'animo feminile).

144. On Marinella's difficult relationship with Tarabotti, see Cox 2008, 372n252.

145. Bragadin 1619, 82: "Hor per concluder vi consieglio, che deponiate il compor fraperie, e visitando spesso le chiese, vi provediate di qualche avello per posar le membra."

146. Bragadin 1619, 74: "non essendo il tuo stile simile a quello di P . . . A . . . , tutto che dica male, diletta." Another *ad hominem* female-authored polemical work of the period that resembles Bragadin's somewhat in its caustic style is Sara Copio's 1621 *Manifesto* (see above, n. 29, for references).

147. On Scarano's relationship with Marinella and her father and brother, see Panizza 1999, 4–5. On Fonte's mention of him in *Il merito delle donne*, see Fonte 1997, 134 and n. 30.

148. Fonte 1588, 169; 1997, 237.

149. For the Genesis arguments, see Fonte 1588, 26, and 1997, 60 and n. 24. For the exemplification of women's excellence in letters and arms, see 1588, 62, and 1997, 100–102.

150. Cox 1995, 526–27, 558–61.

151. See Fonte 1988, 33–38, and 1997, 68–72.

152. For Corinna's decision, see Fonte 1988, 17–19; for Leonora's, 21.

153. See, e.g., Fonte 1988, 17, 71, 169, and 1997, 47, 116, 238. On the structural

importance to the text of men's absence from the discussions, see Chemello 1983, 108; Malpezzi Price 1989a, 178; and Malpezzi Price, 2003a, 146–47.

154. For previous examples of Italian dialogues featuring all-female groups of speakers, see Cox 2000b, 394–97. One close to Fonte's in structural terms, and a possible source for her, is Zabata 1583, on which see Cox 1995, 569–75.

155. Aretino 1969. For discussion of this genre of dialogue, see Grantham Turner 2003. Carini 2007, 97–100, conjectures a possible direct influence of Aretino's *Dialogo* and *Ragionamento* on Fonte.

156. The phrase *domestica conversazione* (domestic conversation or gathering) is found at Fonte 1988, 14, and 1997, 45. For comment on the term, see Collina 1989, 149.

157. Fonte 1988, 63, 65–67; 1997, 103–4, 106–11. On Fonte's conciliatory attitude toward men, by comparison with Marinella, see Smarr 2005, 217–18, 220–21.

158. For historical exempla of female patriotism, see Fonte 1988, 63, 67, and 1997, 102–3, 111. For praises of Venice, see 1988, 13–14, 140–43, and 1997, 43–44, 200–204. On Fonte's Venetian patriotism in *Il Floridoro*, see ch. 5 at nn. 61–62. For critical discussions of Fonte's attitude toward Venice in *Il merito*, see Rosenthal 1993, 123–30; Jones 1998, 165–66; and Malpezzi Price 2003b, 25–26, all of which, however, emphasize her occasional criticisms of Venice rather than her praise.

159. For discussion of the episode, see Chemello 1983, 140–42, and 1988, xliv–xlviii; Jones 1998, 169–72; and Smarr 2005, 221–22.

160. As an example of Leonora's conciliatory tone, note the forms of address used throughout: "Carissimi ed amatissimi uomini" (Fonte 1988, 132, and 1997, 189; Dearest and most cherished menfolk); "carissimi ed inseparabili amici" (1988, 134, and 1997, 191; dearest and inseparable friends); "giustissimi e prudentissimi uomini" (1988, 134, and 1997, 192; supremely just and wise men).

161. The *Apologia* appeared in print only in 1596, after Fonte's death, although it is possible that she read it in manuscript. For a consideration of Speroni's precepts in conjunction with Fonte, see Malpezzi Price 2003a, 123–28.

162. See Cox 1992, 72, 177n16.

163. For the riddle, see Fonte 1988, 31–32, and 1997, 65–67; for the *novella*, 1988, 107–11, and 1997, 161–68; and for the narrative poem, 1988, 173–81, and 1997, 241–58. The eighteenth-century edition of the poem is Fonte 1797. Doglioni's description of Fonte's composition of this last work suggests that it was written independently and inserted into the text of *Il merito delle donne* by its editors in the published edition. He writes that it "is to be published at the end of *Il merito delle donne*" (Doglioni 1988, 9; pur deve con *Il Merito delle Donne* stamparsi nel fine). Lyric poetry is distributed throughout the volume, but see esp. Fonte 1588, 146–59, and 1997, 208–25.

164. See ch. 1 at n. 5.

165. Ribera 1609, 300: "sì bello e vago per l'intentione e tessitura del dilettevole stile che, a giudicio de' intendenti, può stare al bilancio di qualunque compositione che in luce uscita sia a' nostri giorni."

166. Magnanini 2003. See also on the genre Cherchi 1998, 74–77, 211–33; and Cherchi 2004.

167. L. Contarini 1589 ("i meravigliosi essempi delle donne"; "L'origine & l'imprese delle Amazone"; "L'eccellenza & virtù di molti naturali"; "I varij, & mirabili eseempi di virtù, & vitij degli huomini"; "Le sette meraviglie del mondo"); Astolfi 1602 ("Serpenti, dragoni, & fiere di ogni sorte, dall'ingegno dell'huomo rese manusuete"). On Contarini, see Cherchi 1998, 283–94; on Astolfi, Cherchi 2004. Astolfi's entry on Fonte is at Astolfi 1602, 113–14.

168. For Leonora's desire to travel and see "le maraviglie del mondo," see Fonte 1588, 97, and 1997, 149.

169. On these themes in Fonte, see Cox 1995, 527, and 1997a, 10–12.

170. On the garden setting of Fonte's dialogue and its significance, see Chemello 1983, 109–12; Malpezzi Price 1989a, 169–71; Jordan 1990, 254–55, and 1996, 58–59; Jones 1998, 165, 167–68; Malpezzi Price 2003a, 136–38; and Smarr 2005, 222–23.

171. Fonte 1588, 17–19; 1997, 48–50. There is some suggestion in the text that Corinna may be a member of the tertiary order of the Dimesse (see Fonte 1997, 45 and n. 5; Zarri 2000 [first published 1987], 477–78; and Smarr 2005, 216).

172. On the similarity between the ideals figured by Fonte in Corinna and by Campiglia in Flori, see Cox 2008, 158–59; and Carinci 2009, 150–53.

173. See on these developments, Cox 1995, esp. 543n80, 544–50; and Ambrosini 2000, 424–27.

174. See Boccaccio, Betussi, and Serdonati 1596, 348: "lodevole . . . proposito."

175. For evidence of Fonte's acquaintance with Monte and Groto, see ch. 3 at nn. 12–13; and for Campiglia's with the same figures, Cox 2008, 203. Manfredi, a key figure in Campiglia's circle, mentions Fonte in a letter to Orazio Guarguante of 26 March 1591 (Manfredi 1606, 66). Simonetti, who contributed a sonnet to Fonte 1581b, was a member of the Accademia Olimpica of Vicenza and contributed to a collection orchestrated by the Olimpici in which Campiglia also appeared (Rossi 1587). Campiglia speaks of having spent the winter of 1591/92 in Venice in her dedicatory letter to the 1592 edition of Curzio Gonzaga's *Inganni* (C. Gonzaga 2003, 35: "buona parte del verno passato io lo dispensai in Venetia").

176. Fonte 1988, 171, also 17; 1997, 238–39, also 48.

177. Fonte 1988, 171–72; 1997, 240.

178. Fonte 1988, 22, and 1997, 55: "ogni gentile spirito."

179. On the fashion for *corna*, see Fonte 1988, 167, and 1997, 235. Fonte's authorial portrait is reproduced in 1988, facing p. 3, and 1997, facing p. 43. For the mention of the Rialto bridge, see 1988, 142, and 1997, 201–2.

180. On the significance of the speakers' names, see Chemello 1983, 109.

CODA

1. Marinella 1601, 2, and 1999, 40: "Io non ho desiderato, ne desidero, ne mai desidrerò, anchor ch'io vivessi più tempo di Nestore, di essere maschio."

2. Malvasia 1617, "Al divoto lettore": "ritrovando qualch'imperfettione, iscusi il sesso femminile nel mio particolare, certo che nell'universale v'è la virtù heroicha, e forsi in miglior conditione vi son tutte quelle virtù, che ne' maschi."

3. Marinella 1645; Cox 2008, 223–25; Benedetti 2008. The extent to which the highly ambiguous *Essortationi* represents a genuine shift in Marinella's views is difficult to gauge.

4. See Cox 2008, 242–45, to which should be added Dorigista [Maria Isabella Dosi Grati], *Le fortune non conosciute del dottore* (Bologna, 1688). See also, for discussion, Cox 2008, 213, 221, 226–27.

5. See on this development Cox 2008, 228–33, and the bibliography cited there.

6. In descending order, the best-represented poets in the collection are Stampa, with 35 poems; Colonna and Colao (identified as *incerta*), with 26; Laura Battiferra, with 23; Andreini and Gambara, with 18; Salvetti, with 15; and Sbarra, Marinella, Malipiero, and d'Aragona, with 14. Geocultural factors influenced Bergalli in her choice to some degree: of the eleven poets just named, six (Stampa, Colao, Andreini, Sbarra, Marinella, and Malipiero) were Venetian or from the mainland Veneto.

BIBLIOGRAPHY

For reasons of space, short titles are given for manuscripts and early printed texts except in cases where the long title contains important information. Titles of modern volumes of conference proceedings are also abbreviated. Long titles of primary texts may be consulted at the website of the Istituto Centrale per il Catalogo Unico (ICCU), http://www.sbn.it/opacsbn/opac/iccu/antico.jsp, or, in the case of sixteenth-century works, at the website of the Census of Italian 16th Century Editions (EDIT16), http://edit16.iccu.sbn.it/web_iccu/ihome.htm. At the time of writing, the following primary texts included in this bibliography are not listed in either of these catalogs: Barbo 1616, which I consulted in the Codrington Library, All Souls College, Oxford; Barbo n.d., Bragadin 1614, Camilli 1592; Grandi 1620, and Tartaglia 1598, all of which I consulted in the British Library; Bratteolo 1601 and Sabbadini 1615, which I consulted in the Biblioteca Civica Comunale V. Joppi, Udine; B. Gatti 1604, which I consulted in the Biblioteca Civica Bertoliana, Vicenza; Spelta 1612, which I consulted in the Biblioteca Civica, Pavia; and Turina 1627, of which a single copy exists, in the Biblioteca Vaticana, Vatican City.

Female authors' works are sometimes listed in library catalogs under their married surname rather than their natal surname (e.g., Veneranda Cavalli in place of Veneranda Bragadin). The married names of all female authors cited in the bibliography are available in the appendix to this volume.

Manuscripts

Battiferra, Laura. "Rime." MS 3229. Biblioteca Casanatense, Rome.
Bronzini, Cristoforo. "Dialogo della dignità e nobiltà delle donne." 25 vols. Magl. VIII.1513–38. Biblioteca Nazionale Centrale, Florence.
Cervoni, Isabella. "Canzone . . . sopra 'l felicissimo Natale del Ser[enissi]mo Prencipe di Toscana." Magl. VII.138. Biblioteca Nazionale Centrale, Florence.
Colao, Lucia. "Rime." MS 3125. Biblioteca Comunale, Treviso.
Coreglia, Elisabetta. "Raccolta di varie composizioni." MS 205. Biblioteca Statale, Lucca.
"Gentildonna lucchese" [Leonora Bernardi?]. "Tragicomedia pastorale." MS It. IX.239 (6999). Biblioteca Marciana, Venice.
Magno, Celio. "Rime di Celio Magno et di vari autori allo stesso." Ms. It. IX.162 (6310). Biblioteca Marciana, Venice.

"Poesie dedicate alla beata Beatrice d'Este." MS B.P. 367. Biblioteca Civica, Padua.
"Raccolta d'alcune rime intorno alle lodi dell'Illustrissimo S[igno]r Giovan Battista Foscarini dignissimo podestà di Padova." MS Correr 160. Biblioteca Correr, Venice.
"Rime e poesie di varii a Celio Magno." MS It. IX.172 (6903). Biblioteca Marciana, Venice.
Torelli, Barbara. "Partenia, favola boschereccia." MS a.a.1.33. Biblioteca Statale, Cremona.
Turina, Francesca. "Il Florio." Inventario Azzi, busta 185 bis. Archivio Bufalini, San Giustino.
———. "Poesie di Francesca Turina Bufalini in parte autografe, e di vari a lei." Inventario Azzi, busta 185, sec. 4. Archivio Bufalini, San Giustino.
———. "Rime." MS Quaderno Corbucci. Biblioteca Comunale Giosuè Carducci, Città di Castello.
Zilioli, Alessandro. "Istoria delle vite de' poeti italiani." MS It. X.1 (6394). Biblioteca Marciana, Venice.

Printed Primary Sources

Affò, Ireneo. 1789–97. *Memorie degli scrittori e letterati parmigiani*. 5 vols. Parma: Stamperia Reale.
Agaccio, Giovanni Maria. 1598. *Rime*. Parma: Erasmo Viotti.
Agnelli, Cosimo. 1592. *Amorevole aviso alle donne circa alcuni loro abusi*. Ferrara: Benedetto Mammarello.
Agrippa, Henricus Cornelius. 1996. *Declamation on the Nobility and Preeminence of the Female Sex*. Edited and translated by Albert Rabil. Chicago: University of Chicago Press.
Alberici, Giacomo. 1605. *Catalogo breve de gl'illustri et famosi scrittori venetiani*. Bologna: Eredi di Giovanni Rossi.
Alberti, Filippo. 1603. *Rime*. Venice: Giovanni Battista Ciotti.
Alighieri, Dante. 1994. *La commedia, secondo l'antica vulgata*. Edited by Giorgio Petrocchi. 2nd ed. 4 vols. Florence: Casa Editrice Le Lettere.
Ammirato, Scipione. 1598. *Il Rota, overo delle imprese, dialogo*. Florence: Filippo Giunti.
Amulio, Natalino. 1556. *Adunatione de i quattro evangelisti in uno, cioè vita, passione, e resurrettione, di Iesu Christo nostro Salvatore*. Venice: Al Segno de la Speranza.
Ancarano, Gasparo. 1588. *Novo rosario della gloriosissima Vergine Maria*. Venice: Bernardo Giunti.
Ancina, Giovanni Giovenale. 1599. *Tempio armonico della beatissima Vergine N[ostra] S[ignora]*. Rome: Niccolò Muzi.
Andreini, Giovanni Battista. 1606a. *La Florinda*. Milan: Girolamo Bordone.
———. 1606b. *Il pianto d'Apollo. Rime funebri in morte d'Isabella Andreini*. Milan: Girolamo Bordone & Pietromartire Locarni.
Andreini, Isabella. 1588. *Mirtilla, pastorale*. Verona: Girolamo Discepolo.

———. 1594. *La Mirtilla, pastorale . . . di nuovo . . . riveduta, ed in molti luoghi abbellita.* Bergamo: Comin Ventura.

———. [1596?]. *Epitalamio nelle nozze dell'illust[rissi]mi . . . don Michele Peretti et . . . donna Margherita Somaglia.* N.p. [The couple were married twice, the first time secretly in 1588, the second time publicly in 1596 (Hill 1997, 1:239–30); the latter seems the more likely date of publication.]

———. 1601. *Rime.* Milan: Girolamo Bordone & Pietromartire Locarni.

———. 1603. *Rime.* Paris: Claudio de Monstr'oeil.

———. 1605. *Rime.* Milan: Girolamo Bordone & Pietromartire Locarni.

———. 1607. *Lettere.* Venice: Marcantonio Zaltieri.

———. 1611. *Lettere et ragionamenti.* Turin.

———. 1617a. *Fragmenti di alcune scritture.* Venice: Giovani Battista Combi.

———. 1617b. *Lettere . . . aggiuntovi di nuovo li ragionamenti piacevoli.* Venice: Giovanni Battista Combi.

———. 1995. *Mirtilla.* Edited by Maria Luisa Doglio. Lucca: Pacini Fazzi.

———. 2002. *La Mirtilla: A Pastoral.* Edited and translated by Julie D. Campbell. Tempe, AZ: Medieval and Renaissance Texts and Studies.

———. 2005. *Selected Poems of Isabella Andreini.* Edited by Anne MacNeil. Translated by James Wyatt Cook. Lanham, MD: Scarecrow.

Angeli, Pietro, and Mario Colonna. 1589. *Poesie toscane.* Florence: Bartolomeo Sermartelli.

Antonazzoni, Francesco, ed. 1613. *Le funebri rime di diversi eccellentissimi autori, nella morte della signora Camilla Rocha Nobili, comica Confidente, detta Delia.* Venice: Ambrosio Dei.

Antoniano, Silvio. 1584. *Tre libri dell'educatione christiana dei figliuoli.* Verona: Sebastiano dalle Donne & Girolamo Stringari.

Apuleius. 1989. *Metamorphoses.* Edited and translated by J. Arthur Hanson. 2 vols. Cambridge, MA: Harvard University Press.

Aretino, Pietro. 1552. *Vita di Maria Vergine, di Caterina Santa, e di Tomaso Aquinate, beato.* Venice: Eredi di Aldo Manuzio.

———. 1969. *Sei giornate.* Edited by Giovanni Aquilecchia. Bari: Laterza.

Ariosto, Ludovico. 1976. *Orlando furioso.* Edited by Cesare Segre. 2nd ed. 2 vols. Milan: Mondadori.

Astolfi, Giovanni Felice. 1602. *Scelta curiosa et ricca officina di varie antiche, e moderne istorie.* Venice: Eredi di Marchiò Sessa.

Baldi, Bernardino. 1589a. *La corona dell'anno.* Vicenza: Agostino dalla Noce.

———. 1589b. "Discorso di chi traduce sopra le machine semoventi." In *De gli automati, overo machine semoventi*, by Hero of Alexandria, translated by Bernardino Baldi, 4r–14r. Venice: Girolamo Porro.

———. 1590. *Rime varie.* In *Versi e prose*, 307–60. Venice: Francesco de' Franceschi Senese.

———. 1724. *Encomio della patria.* In *Memorie concernenti la città di Urbino*, 1–36. Rome: Giovanni Maria Salvioni.

———. 1992. *Ecloghe miste*. Turin: Res.
Balducci, Francesco. 1645. *Rime*. Rome: Francesco Moneta.
Barbo, Giovanni Battista. 1614. *Rime piacevoli*. Vicenza: Giovanni Domenico Rizzardi.
———. 1616. *L'oracolo, overo invettiva contra le donne, con l'aggiunta d'alcune stanze contra una donna di mala vita*. Vicenza: Giovanni Domenico Rizzardi.
———. N.d. *L'oracolo, overo invettiva contra le donne*. Vicenza: Francesco Grossi.
Bargagli, Scipione. 1587. *I trattenimenti . . . dove da vaghe donne e da giovani huomini rappresentati sono honesti, e dilettevoli giuochi*. Venice: Bernardo Giunti.
Barletius, Marinus. See Barlezio, Marino.
Barlezio, Marino [Marinus Barletius]. 1580. *Historia del magnanimo et valoroso signor Georgio Castrioto, detto Scanderbego*. Translated by Pietro Rocca. Venice: Fabio & Agostino Zoppini.
Battiferra, Laura. 1560. *Il primo libro delle opere toscane*. Florence: Giunti.
———. 1564. *I sette salmi penitentiali del santissimo profeta Davit . . . con alcuni . . . sonetti spirituali*. Florence: Giunti.
———. 1879. *Lettere di Laura Battiferri Ammanati a Benedetto Varchi*, edited by Carlo Gargiolli. Bologna: Gaetano Romagnoli. [Reprinted Bologna: Commissione per i Testi di Lingua, 1968.]
———. 2000. *Il primo libro delle opere toscane*. Edited by Enrico Maria Guidi. Urbino: Accademia Raffaello.
———. 2005. *I sette salmi penitenziali del santissimo profeta David con alcuni sonetti spirituali*. Edited by Enrico Maria Guidi. Urbino: Accademia Raffaello.
———. 2006. *Laura Battiferra and Her Literary Circle*. Edited and translated by Victoria Kirkham. Chicago: University of Chicago Press.
Beccari, Agostino. 1785. *Il sacrificio, favola pastorale*. Vol. 17 of *Parnaso italiano*, edited by Andrea Rubbi. Venice: Antonio Zatta.
Bembo, Pietro. 1960. *Prose e rime*. Edited by Carlo Dionisotti. Turin: UTET.
Bendinelli, Scipione. 1588. *L'ode alla Madonna de' Miracoli di Lucca*. Translated by Massinissa Bendinelli. Lucca: Vincenzo Busdraghi.
Bendinelli, Silvia. 1587. *Corona in morte del serenissimo sig[nor] Ottavio Farnese*. Piacenza: Anteo Conti.
Bergalli, Luisa, ed. 1726. *Componimenti poetici delle più illustri rimatrici d'ogni secolo*. 2 vols. Venice: Antonio Mora.
Bigolina, Giulia. 2002. *Urania*. Edited by Valeria Finucci. Rome: Bulzoni.
———. 2004. *Urania, the Story of a Young Women's Love: The Novella of Giulia Camposanpiero and Thesibaldo Vitaliani*. Edited and translated by Christopher Nissen. Tempe, AZ: Medieval and Renaissance Texts and Studies.
———. 2005. *Urania, a Romance*. Edited and translated by Valeria Finucci. Chicago: University of Chicago Press.
Bissari, Pietro Paolo. 1648. *Le scorse olimpiche*. Venice: Francesco Valvasense.
Boccaccio, Giovanni. 1992. *Decameron*. Edited by Vittore Branca. Turin: Einaudi.
———. 2001. *Famous Women*. Edited and translated by Virginia Brown. Cambridge, MA: Harvard University Press.

Boccaccio, Giovanni, and Giuseppe Betussi. 1545. *Libro di Messer Giovanni Boccaccio delle donne illustri . . . con una additione fatta . . . delle donne famose dal tempo di M[esser] Giovanni fino a i giorni nostri.* Venice: Comin di Trino.

Boccaccio, Giovanni, Giuseppe Betussi, and Francesco Serdonati. 1596. *Libro di M[esser] Giovanni Boccaccio delle donne illustri, tradoto di latino in volgare per M[esser] Giuseppe Betussi, con una giunta fatta dal medesimo d'altre donne famose, e un'altra giunta fatta per M[esser] Francesco Serdonati, d'altre donne illustri antiche e moderne.* Florence: Filippo Giunti.

Boccalini, Traiano. 1910–12. *Ragguagli di Parnaso, e Pietra del paragone politico.* Edited by Giuseppe Rua. 2 vols. Bari: Laterza.

Boiardo, Matteo Maria. 1999. *L'inamoramento d'Orlando.* Edited by Antonia Tissoni Benvenuti and Cristina Montagnani. Milan: Ricciardi.

Bonardo, Giovanni Maria. 1584. *La grandezza, larghezza, e distanza di tutte le sfere, ridotte à nostre miglia, cominciando dall'inferno, fino alla sfera, dove stanno i beati.* Venice: Fabio & Agostino Zoppino.

———. 1598. *Madrigali.* Venice: Agostino Zoppino & Nepoti.

———. 1600. *La grandezza, larghezza, e distanza di tutte le sfere, ridotte a nostre miglia.* Venice: Giacomo Zoppini e Fratelli.

Bonello, Raffaele. 1583. *I quindici misterii del santissimo rosario . . . con altre rime spirituali.* Venice: Domenico & Giovanni Battista Guerra.

Borghesi, Diomede. 1566. *Delle rime . . . parti prima-sesta.* Padua: Lorenzo Pasquato.

Borgogni, Gherardo. 1592. *Nuova scielta di rime.* Bergamo: Comin Ventura.

———, ed. 1594. *Le muse toscane di diversi nobilissimi ingegni.* Bergamo: Comin Ventura.

———, ed. 1599. *Rime di diversi illust[rissimi] poeti de' nostri tempi, di nuovo poste in luce.* Venice: Minima Compagnia.

Borsieri, Girolamo. 1611. *L'amorosa prudenza, favola pastorale . . . con un discorso allegorico d'Hettore Capriolo . . . e l'aggiunta di due libri di madrigali, raccolti da Girolamo Rezzani.* Milan: Erede di Pacifico Ponzio e Giovanni Battista Picaglia.

Bovarini, Leandro. 1602. *Rime.* Perugia: Vincenzo Colombara.

Bracciolini, Francesco. 1597. *L'amoroso sdegno, favola pastorale.* Venice: Giovanni Battista Ciotti.

———. 1611. *La croce racquistata, poema heroico.* Venice: Bernardo Giunti, Giovanni Battista Ciotti & Compagni.

Bragadin, Veneranda. 1613. *Rime diverse.* Padua: Gasparo Crivellari.

———. 1614. *Varie rime.* Verona: Bartolomeo Merlo.

———. 1619. *Rime.* Verona: Angelo Tamo.

Bramoso, Accademico Sollecito [Cipriano Giambelli]. 1589. *Discorso intorno alla maggioranza dell'huomo e della donna.* Treviso: Angelo Mazzolini.

Bratteolo, Giacomo, ed. 1597. *Rime di diversi elevati ingegni de la città di Udine.* Udine: Giovanni Battista Natolini.

———, ed. 1601. *Rime di varii autori nelle nozze de i molto illustri e felicissimi sposi il signor Giulio de la Torre et la sig[no]ra Caterina Marchesi.* Udine: Giovanni Battista Natolini.

Briani, Girolamo. 1616. *Aggiunta a' ragguagli di Parnaso del sig[nor] Traino Boccalini, intitolata parte terza.* Venice: Giovanni Guerigli.

Bronzini, Cristoforo. 1624. *Della dignità, e nobilità delle donne, dialogo . . . settimana prima, e giornata prima.* Florence: Zanobi Pignoni.

———. 1625. *Della dignità, e nobilità delle donne, dialogo . . . settimana prima e giornata quarta.* Florence: Zanobi Pignoni.

Brunetti, Pier Giovanni. 1586. *David sconsolato, tragedia spirituale.* Florence: Giorgio Marescotti.

Bruni, Antonio. 1615. *Selva di Parnaso.* Venice: Ambrogio & Bartolommeo Dei.

———. 1630. *Le tre gratie.* Rome: Ottavio Ingrillani.

Burchelati, Bartolomeo. 1591. *Ragionamento di rapina.* Treviso: Domenico Amici.

———. 1599. *Il funerale del signor Giovanbattista Burchelati Amiconi. Celebrato, e pianto dall'eccell[ente] sig[nor] Bartolomeo Burchelati, lo addolorato padre.* Treviso: Evangelista Deuchino.

———. 1609. *Commentariorum memorabilium multiplicis hystoriae Tarvisinae locuples promptuarium libris quatuor distributum.* Treviso: Angelo Regattini.

Bursati, Lucrezio. 1621. *La vittoria delle donne.* Venice: Evangelista Deuchino.

Calcina, Eugenia. 1576. *Priego alla Vergine beatissima.* Bologna: Giovanni Rossi.

Calderari, Cesare. 1588. *Il trofeo della Croce di n[ostro] sig[nor] Giesu Christo.* Vicenza: Agostino dalla Noce.

Calvi, Donato. 1664. *Scena letteraria de gli scrittori bergamaschi aperta alla curiosità de' suoi concittadini.* Bergamo: Eredi di Marc'Antonio Rossi.

Calvi, Paolo. 1772–82. *Biblioteca e storia di quei scrittori così della città come del territorio di Vicenza che pervennero fin'ad ora a notizia.* 6 vols. Vicenza: Giovanni Battista Vendramin Mosca.

Camilli, Camillo. 1592. *Le lagrime di s[anta] Maria Maddalena.* In *Vita della serafica, e ferventissima amatrice di Giesu Christo Salvatore s[anta] Maria Maddalena . . . con le lagrime della medesima*, by Salvestro da Prierio and Camillo Camilli, edited by Serafino Razzi, 69–86. Florence: Sermartelli. Venice: Giorgio Angelieri.

Campeggi, Ridolfo. 1617. *Le lagrime di Maria Vergine, poema heroico.* Bologna: Sebastiano Bonomi.

Campiglia, Maddalena. 1585. *Discorso sopra l'annonciatione della beata Vergine, et la incarnatione del s[ignor] n[ostro] Giesu Christo.* Vicenza: Perin Libraro.

———. 1588. *Flori, favola boscareccia.* Vicenza: Eredi di Perin Libraro & Tomaso Brunelli.

———. 1589. *Calisa, ecloga.* Vicenza: Giorgio Greco.

———. 1996. *Calisa.* In Perrone 1996, 75–88.

———. 2004. *Flori, a Pastoral Drama.* Edited by Virginia Cox and Lisa Sampson. Translated by Virginia Cox. Chicago: University of Chicago Press.

Canoniero, Pietro Andrea. 1606. *Della eccellenza delle donne.* Florence: ad istanza di Simon Grenier & Iacopo Fabeni.

Capaccio, Giulio Cesare. 1608. *Illustrium mulierum et illustrium litteris virorum elogia.* Naples: Giovanni Giacomo Carlino & Costantino Vitale.

Capece, Isabella. 1595. *Consolatione dell'anima*. Naples: Giovanni Giacomo Carlino & Antonio Pace.
Caporali, Cesare. 1589. *Le piacevoli rime . . . Con un'aggiunta di molte altre rime, fatte da diversi eccellentissimi ingegni*. Venice: Giorgio Angelieri.
Carafa, Ferrante. 1573. *Dell'Austria . . . dove si contiene la vittoria della Santa Lega all'Echinadi, divisa in cinque parti*. Naples: Giuseppe Cacchi.
Caraffa, Ercole, ed. 1598. *Fiori di madrigali di diversi autori illustri*. Venice: Giacomo Vincenti.
Carmina. 1586. *In illustriss[imos] adolescentes Philippum et Albertum Fucheros frates diversorum carmina*. Verona: Sebastiano dalle Donne.
Caruso, Francesco. 1592. *Dialogo della nobiltà delle donne*. Naples: Giuseppe Cacchi.
Castelletti, Sebastiano. 1594. *La trionfatrice Cecilia, vergine e martire romana*. Florence: Filippo Giunti.
Castellini, Silvestro. 1783–1822. *Storia della città di Vicenza*. 13 vols. Vicenza: Francesco Vendramini Mosca.
Castiglione, Baldassare. 1960. *Il libro del Cortegiano*. In *Opere di Baldassare Castiglione, Giovanni della Casa, Benvenuto Cellini*, edited by Carlo Cordiè, 5–361. Milan: Ricciardi.
Cebà, Ansaldo. 1615. *La reina Esther*. Genoa: Giuseppe Pavoni.
———. 1623. *Lettere . . . scritte a Sarra Copia*. Genoa: Giuseppe Pavoni.
Cervoni, Giovanni. 1600. *Discorso in laude de la christianissima madama Maria de' Medici*. Florence: Giorgio Marescotti.
Cervoni, Isabella. 1592. *Canzone . . . sopra il battesimo del serenissimo gran prencipe di Toscana*. Florence: Sermartelli.
———. 1597a. *Canzone . . . al christianissimo Enrico Quarto, re di Francia . . . sopra la sua conversione*. Florence: Giorgio Marescotti.
———. 1597b. *Canzone . . . al santissimo padre e signor nostro, Papa Clemente VIII, sopra la beneditione del christianissimo Enrico Quarto, Re di Francia*. Florence: Giorgio Marescotti.
———. 1598. *Orazione . . . al santissimo, e beatissimo padre, e signor nostro Papa Clemente ottavo, sopra l'impresa di Ferrara. Con una canzone . . . a' prencipi christiani*. Bologna: Giovanni Battista Bellagamba.
———. 1600. *Tre canzoni . . . in laude de' Christianiss[imi] Re, e Regina di Francia, e di Navarra, Enrico Quarto, e Madama Maria de' Medici*. Florence: Giorgio Marescotti.
Chiabrera, Gabriello. 1615. *Firenze, poema*. Florence: Zanobi Pignoni.
Choro delle Muse. Rime nella partenza dell'illustrissimo sig[nor] Giovanni Zeno, podestà meritissimo di Vicenza. 1613. Edited by Giacomo Natalini. Vicenza: Francesco Grosso.
Cieco d'Adria, Alvise Groto. See Groto, Luigi.
Ciotti, Giovanni Battista, ed. 1606. *Corona overo ghirlanda di candidi gigli di virginità, e di sanguigne rose di martirii di diversi santi, e sante*. 3 vols. Venice: Giovanni Battista Ciotti.
Colle, Giovanni. 1621. *Accademia Colle bellunese de ragionamenti accademici, poe-*

tici, morali, astrologici, naturali & varij diletteuoli, & eruditi. Venice: Evangelista Deuchino.
Colonna, Vittoria. 1546. *Le rime spirituali*. Venice: Vincenzo Valgrisi.
———. 1548. *Le rime spirituali*. Venice: Vincenzo Valgrisi.
———. 1557. *Pianto . . . sopra la passione di Christo*. Bologna: Antonio Manutio.
———. 1586. *Rime spirituali*. Verona: Girolamo Discepoli.
———. 1982. *Rime*. Edited by Alan Bullock. Bari: Laterza.
———. 2005. *Sonnets for Michelangelo: A Bilingual Edition*. Edited and translated by Abigail Brundin. Chicago: University of Chicago Press.
———. 2008. *The Plaint of the Marchesa di Pescara on the Passion of Christ*. In Colonna, Marinella, and Matraini 2008, 47–65.
Colonna, Vittoria, Lucrezia Marinella, and Chiara Matraini. 2008. *Who Is Mary? Three Early Modern Women on the Idea of the Virgin Mary*. Edited and translated by Susan Haskins. Chicago: University of Chicago Press.
Compositioni volgari, et latine, in lode del clariss[imo] sig[nor] Luigi Mocenico, capitano di Vicenza, fatte nella partenza. 1585. Vicenza: Agostino dalla Noce.
Contarini, Francesco. 1599. *La fida ninfa, favola pastorale*. Vicenza: ad istanza di Francesco Bolzetta.
———. 1615. *Isaccio, tragedia*. Venice: Giovanni Battista Ciotti.
Contarini, Luigi. 1589. *Il vago e dilettevole giardino*. Vicenza: Eredi di Perin Libraro.
Copio, Sara. 1621. *Manifesto . . . nel quale è da lei riprovata e detestata l'opinione negante l'immortalità dell'anima, falsamente attribuitale dal Sig. Baldassare Bonifaccio*. Venezia: Giovanni Alberti.
———. 2009. *Jewish Poet and Intellectual in Seventeenth-Century Venice: The Works of Sarra Copia Sulam in Verse and Prose along with Writings of Her Contemporaries*. Edited and translated by Don Harrán. Chicago: University of Chicago Press.
Corbellini, Aurelio. 1598. *Componimenti poetici in lode della gloriosa vergine Maria*. Pavia: Andrea Viani.
Coreglia, Isabetta. 1628. *Rime spirituali e morali*. Pistoia: Pierantonio Fortunati.
———. 1634. *La Dori, favola pastorale*. Naples: Giovanni Domenico Montanaro.
———. 1650. *Erindo il fido, favola pastorale*. Pistoia: Fortunati.
Corona di lodi alla signora Maria Malloni detta Celia comica. 1621. Edited by Giovanni Pietro Pinelli. Venice: Antonio Pinelli.
Corpus Iuris Canonici. 1879–81. 2 vols. Edited by Emil Albert Friedberg. Leipzig: Bernhard Tauchnitz.
Cortesi, Cortese. 1607. *Giustina, reina di Padova*. Vicenza: Pietro Greco & Giacomo Cescato, ad istanza di Francesco Bolzetta.
Costa, Margherita. 1641. *Li buffoni, commedia ridicola*. Florence: Amadore Massi & Lorenzo Landi.
Costantini, Antonio, ed. 1611. *Rime . . . in lode del gloriosissimo Papa Sisto Quinto, et altre da lui raccolte di diversi famosi poeti de l' età nostra*. Mantua: Aurelio & Lodovico Osanni.

Crashaw, Richard. 1972. *The Complete Poetry of Richard Crashaw*. Edited by George Walton Williams. New York: New York University Press.

Dalla Corte, Girolamo. 1596. *L'istoria di Verona*. 2 vols. Verona: Girolamo Discepolo.

da Poppi, Silvestro, ed. 1606. *Rime spirituali di diversi autori in lode del serafico padre S[an] Francesco, e del sacro Monte della Verna*. Florence: Volcmar Timan.

d'Aragona, Tullia. 1547. *Rime della Signora Tullia di Aragona et di diversi a lei*. Venice: Giolito.

de Coste, Hilarion. 1647. *Les eloges et les vies des reynes, des princesses, et des dames illustres en pieté, en courage, et en doctrine, qui ont fleury de nostre temps, et du temps de nos pères*. 2 vols. Paris: Sebastien Cramoisy.

De Cupiti, Agostino. 1592. *Rime spirituali*. Vico Equense: Giuseppe Cacchi.

———. 1593. *Caterina martirizzata, poema sacro*. Naples: Giovanni Giacomo Carlino & Antonio Pace.

———. [c. 1599]. *Il poeta illuminato*. Vico Equense: Giovanni Giacomo Carlino & Antonio Pace. [The printers give the date of this work twice, once as 1598 and once as 1599.]

Della Casa, Giovanni. 2001. *Rime*. Edited by Giuliano Tanturli. Parma: Ugo Guanda.

Della Chiesa, Francesco Agostino. 1620. *Theatro delle donne letterate con un breve discorso della preminenza e perfettione del sesso donnesco*. Mondovi: Giovanni Gislandi & Giovanni Tommaso Rossi.

Della Porta, Cesare. 1584. *Stanze sopra i quindeci misteri del s[antissi]mo rosario*. Cremona: Cristoforo Draconi.

Della Valle, Francesco. 1622. *Rime*. Rome: Alessandro Zannetti.

Dell'Uva, Benedetto. 1582. *Le vergini prudenti*. Florence: Bartolomeo Sermartelli.

De' Pietri, Francesco. 1634. *Dell'historia napoletana, libri due*. Naples: Giovanni Domenico Montanaro.

Di Bona, Speranza Vittoria. 1569. *Difesa de le rime et prose*. N.p.

Di Manzano, Scipione. 1594. *I tre primi canti del Dandolo, poema heroico*. Venice: Francesco Bariletti.

Doglioni, Giovanni Niccolò. 1587. *L'Anno*. Venice: Giovanni Antonio Rampazetto.

———. *See* Goldioni, Leonico.

———. 1988. "Vita della signora Modesta Pozzo de' Zorzi nominata Moderata Fonte." In Fonte 1988, 3–10.

———. 1997. "Life of Moderata Fonte." In Fonte 1997, 31–40.

Dolce, Lodovico. 1561. *La vita di Giuseppe, discritta in ottava rima*. Venice: Giolito.

Donia, Matteo. 1600. *Il Giorgio, poema sacro et heroico*. Palermo: Giovanni Battista Maringo.

Droghi, Antonio. 1598. *Leucadia*. Bologna: Eredi di Giovanni Rossi.

Ducchi, Gregorio. 1586. *La Scacheide*. Vicenza: Perin Libraro & Giorgio Greco.

———, ed. 1589. *Rime diversi di molti illustri compositori per le nozze dell'illustrissimi signori Gio[vanni] Paolo Lupi marchese di Soragna e Beatrice Obici*. Piacenza: Giovanni Bazachi.

Ercolani, Ercolano. 1608. *Rappresentazione eremitica spirituale.* Siena: Matteo Florimi.

———. 1615. *Eliodoro, commedia spirituale.* Siena: Matteo Florimi.

Erculiani, Camilla. *See* Herculiana, Camilla.

Erythraeus, Janus Nicius [Giovanni Vittorio Rossi]. 1645–48. *Pinacotheca.* 3 vols. Amsterdam: Willem Jansz Blaeu.

Esequie. 1572. *Le suntuosissime esequie celebrate nella mag[nifi]ca città di Bergamo, in morte dello ill[ustrissim]o signor Astorre Baglioni, con alcuni legiadri componimenti latini, e volgari.* Perugia: Valente Panizza.

Ferrari, Benedetto. [1638?]. *La maga fulminata.* Venice: Antonio Bariletti.

Ferro, Livio, ed. 1581. *Corone et altre rime in tutte le lingue principali del mondo in lode dell'illustre s[ign]or Luigi Ancarano di Spoleto, cavaliere.* Padua: Lorenzo Pasquati.

Fiamma, Carlo, ed. 1611. *Il gareggiamento poetico.* Venice: Barezzo Barezzi.

———, ed. 1613. *Il sacro tempio dell'imperatrice de' cieli Maria Vergine santissima.* Vicenza: Francesco Grossi.

Fiamma, Gabriele. 1575. *Rime spirituali.* Venice: Francesco de' Franceschi Senese.

———. 1576. *Sei prediche . . . in lode della beata Vergine, sopra l'evangelio di S[an] Luca, "Missus est Angelus Gabriel."* Venice: Francesco de' Franceschi Senese.

Ficino, Marsilio. 2002. *Commentaire sur "Le Banquet" de Platon, De l'Amour.* Edited and translated by Pierre Laurens. Paris: Les Belles Lettres.

Filippi, Marco. 1592. *Vita di Santa Caterina vergine e martire.* Venice: Domenico & Giovanni Battista Guerra.

Filippi, Paolo. 1607. *Rime.* Venice: Giovanni Zenaro.

Filogenio, Hercole [Ercole Marescotti]. 1589. *Dell'eccellenza delle donne, discorso.* Fermo: Sertorio de' Monti.

Firenzuola, Agnolo. 1971. *Le novelle.* Edited by Eugenio Ragni. Rome: Salerno.

Fontanella, Girolamo. 1994. *Ode.* Edited by Rosario Contarino. Turin: Res.

Fonte, Moderata. 1581a. *Le feste. Rappresentatione avanti il serenissimo prencipe di Venetia Nicolo da Ponte, il giorno di S[anto] Stefano 1581.* Venice: Domenico & Giovanni Battista Guerra.

———. 1581b. *Tredici canti del Floridoro.* Venice: Francesco Rampazetto.

———. 1582. *La passione di Christo descritta in ottava rima.* Venice: Domenico & Giovanni Battista Guerra.

———. 1585. *Canzon nella morte del ser[enissi]mo principe di Venetia Nicolò da Ponte.* Venice: Sigismondo Bordogna.

———. 1588. *Il merito delle donne.* Venice: Domenico Imberti.

———. 1592. *La resurrettione di Giesu Christo nostro signore, che segue alla Santissima Passione descritta in ottava rima.* Venice: Giovanni Domenico Imberti.

———. 1600. *Il merito delle donne . . . ove chiaramente si scuopre quanto siano elle degne, e piu perfette de gli huomini.* Venice: Domenico Imberti.

———. 1797. "Amore disarmato." In *Poemetti italiani,* 10:12–24. Turin: Società letteraria di Torino & Michelangelo Morano.

———. 1988. *Il merito delle donne: ove chiaramente si scuopre quanto siano elle degne e piu perfette de gli uomini.* Edited by Adriana Chemello. Venice: Eidos.

---. 1995. *Tredici canti del Floridoro.* Edited by Valeria Finucci. Modena: Mucchi.
---. 1997. *The Worth of Women.* Edited and translated by Virginia Cox. Chicago: University of Chicago Press.
---. 2006. *Floridoro: A Chivalric Romance.* Edited by Valeria Finucci and Julia Kisacky. Translated by Julia Kisacky. Chicago: University of Chicago Press.
---. 2009. *Le feste.* In Quaintance 2009, 211–31.
Franciotti, Cesare. 1616. *Viaggio alla [Santa] Casa di Loreto, distinto in dodici giornate.* Venice: Giovanni Battista Combi.
Franco, Veronica. 1575a. *Rime.* [Venice?].
---, ed. 1575b. *Rime di diversi eccellentissimi autori nella morte dell'illustre sign[or] Estore Martinengo conte di Malpaga.* [Venice?].
---. 1580. *Lettere.* [Venice?].
---. 1995. *Rime.* Edited by Stefano Bianchi. Milan: Mursia.
---. 1998a. *Lettere.* Edited by Stefano Bianchi. Rome: Salerno.
---. 1998b. *Selected Poems and Letters.* Edited and translated by Ann Rosalind Jones and Margaret Rosenthal. Chicago: University of Chicago Press.
Fratta, Giovanni, ed. 1575. *Panegirico nel felice dottorato dell'illustre et eccellentissimo sig[nor] Giuseppe Spinelli.* Padua: Lorenzo Pasquati.
Gagliardo, Giuseppe, ed. 1584. *Sonagitti, spataffi, smaregale e canzon, arcogisti in lo xiequio e morte de quel gran zaramella barba Menon Rava.* Padua: Paolo Meitti.
Galilei, Galileo. 1901. *Carteggio, 1611–13.* Vol. 11 of *Le opere: Edizione nazionale.* Florence: G. Barbera.
Gallucci, Agostino. 1618. *San Francesco, overo Gierusalemme celeste acquistata, poema sacro.* Venice: Barezzo Barezzi.
Gambara, Veronica. 1995. *Le rime.* Edited by Alan Bullock. Florence: Olschki; Perth: University of Western Australia.
Garofani, Antonio Maria. 1582. *Sommario dell'indulgenze di Parma et di Gerusalemme.* Parma: Eredi di Seth Viotti.
Garzoni, Tommaso. 1591. *Il theatro de' vari, e diversi cervelli mondani.* Venice: Giovanni Battista Somasco.
Gatti, Alessandro. 1604. *Madrigali.* Venice: Giovanni Battista Ciotti.
Gatti, Beatrice. 1604. *Oratione di Madonna Beatrice Gatti, nel suo entrar nel Monasterio d'Araceli; detta poi Suor Diodora.* Vicenza: Giovanni Pietro Gioannini & Francesco Grossi.
Gelli, Giovanni Battista. 1979. *Dell'origine di Firenze,* edited by Alessandro D'Alessandro. *Atti e Memorie dell'Accademia Toscana di Scienze e Lettere La Colombaria* 44:59–122.
Gelmi, Giovanni Antonio. 1588. *Rime . . . nella morte del figliuolo, con altri componimenti volgari et latini di diversi nell'istessa materia.* Verona: Sebastiano dalle Donne.
Ghelfucci, Capoleone. 1603. *Il rosario della Madonna, poema eroico.* Venice: Nicolo Polo.
Giambelli, Cipriano. *See* Bramoso, Accademico Sollecito.

Ginanni, Pietro Paolo, ed. 1739. *Rime scelte de poeti ravennati antichi e moderni defunti.* Ravenna: Antonmaria Landi.
Giolito de' Ferrari, Giovanni, and Iacopo Sannazaro. 2001. *De partu Virginis: Il parto della Vergine.* Rome: Città Nuova.
Giustinian, Orsatto. 1600. *Rime.* In Giustinian and Magno 1600.
Giustinian, Orsatto, and Celio Magno. 1600. *Rime.* Venice: Andrea Muschio.
Giustiniano. 1614. *Per l'illustrissimo signor Pietro Giustiniano, capitanio di Vicenza.* Vicenza: Francesco Grossi.
Goldioni, Leonico [Giovanni Niccolò Doglioni]. 1603. *Delle cose maravigliose e notabili della città di Venetia.* Venice: Domenico Imberti.
Gonzaga, Curzio. 1591a. *Il Fidamante, poema eroico.* Venice: Eredi di Curzio Troiano Navo, al segno del Leone.
———. 1591b. *Rime.* Venice: Eredi di Curzio Troiano Navo [al segno del Leone].
———. 1592. *Gli inganni, commedia.* Venice: Giovanni Antonio Rampazetto.
———. 2000. *Il Fidamante.* Edited by Ester Varini and Ilenia Rocchi. Rome: Verso l'Arte.
———. 2003. *Gli inganni.* Edited by Anna Maria Razzoli Roio. Rome: Verso l'Arte.
[Gonzaga, Lucrezia]. 1552. *Lettere.* Venice: Gualtiero Scotto.
———. 2008. *Lettere.* Edited by Renzo Bragantini and Primo Griguolo. Rovigo: Minelliana.
Goselini, Giuliano. 1588. *Rime.* Venice: Francesco Franceschi.
Granada, Luis de. 1581. *Del memoriale della vita christiana . . . parte prima.* Vicenza: Giorgio Angelieri.
Grandi, Adriano. 1620. *Rime, prima parte.* Verona: Bartolomeo Merlo.
Grandi, Ascanio. 1636. *Il Tancredi, poema eroico.* Lecce: Pietro Micheli.
Graziano, Giulio Cornelio. 1597. *Di Orlando santo vita, et morte.* Treviso: Evangelista Deuchino.
Grillo, Angelo. 1589. *Parte prima–seconda delle rime.* Bergamo: Comino Ventura.
———. 1592a. *Capitolo al Crocifisso nel venerdì santo.* In Guarguanti, Tansillo, and Valvasone 1592, 186r–190v.
———. 1592b. *Nuova scielta delle rime morali.* Edited by Giulio Guastavino. Bergamo: Comino Ventura.
———. 1596. *Pietosi affetti.* Vicenza: Eredi di Perin Libraro.
———. 1599. *Rime.* Venice: Giovanni Battista Ciotti.
———. 1604. *Pietosi affetti.* Vicenza: Eredi di Perin Libraro.
———. 1608a. *Christo flagellato.* Venice: Giovanni Battista Ciotti.
———. 1608b. *Essequie di Giesu Christo Nazareno . . . celebrate co 'l pianto di Maria Vergine.* Venice: Giovanni Battista Ciotti.
———. 1612a. *Lettere.* Edited by Pietro Petracci. Venice: Bernardo Giunti & Giovanni Battista Ciotti.
———. 1612b. *Delle lettere . . . volume secondo.* Edited by Pietro Petracci. Venice: Evangelista Deuchino.
———. 1613. *Pietosi affetti.* Venice: Giovanni Battista Ciotti.

———. 1616. *Delle lettere . . . volume terzo.* Edited by Pietro Petracci. Venice: Evangelista Deuchino.
Grillo, Angelo, and Christoforo Talenti. 1605. *Scielta d'alcuni pii . . . componimenti per eccitar gli animi divoti alla contemplatione delle cose celesti.* Bergamo: Comin Ventura.
Groto, Luigi [Alvise Groto, Cieco d'Adria]. 1601. *Rime . . . nuovamente ristampate, e ricorrette.* Venice: Giacomo Zoppini.
———. 2007. *Le famigliari del Cieco d'Adria.* Edited by Marco de Poli, Luisa Servadei, and Antonella Turri, with an introductory essay by Mario Nanni. Treviso: Antilia.
Grumelli, Flavia. 1596. *Vita di Santa Grata . . . con alcuni discorsi . . . sopra l'istessa vita.* Bergamo: Comin Ventura.
Guaccimani, Giacomo, ed. 1623. *Raccolta di sonetti d'autori diversi et eccellenti dell'età nostra.* Ravenna: Pietro de' Paoli & Giovanni Battista Giovannelli.
Guarguanti, Orazio, Luigi Tansillo, and Erasmo da Valvasone. 1592. *Le lagrime di San Pietro del signor Luigi Tansillo, con le Lagrime della Maddalena del signor Erasmo da Valvasone . . . aggiuntovi l'Eccellenza della Gloriosa Vergine Maria, del signor Horatio Guarguante.* Venice: Simon Cornetti e Fratelli.
Guarini, Giovanni Battista. 1977. *Il pastor fido.* In *Il teatro italiano,* 729–947.
Guazzo, Stefano. 1595. *La ghirlanda della contessa Angela Bianca Beccaria.* Genoa: Eredi di Girolamo Bartoli.
Gučetić, Nikola Vitov. *See* Vito di Gozze, Niccolò.
Herculiana, Camilla [Camilla Erculiani]. 1584. *Lettere di philosophia naturale.* Krakow: Stamperia di Lazaro [Jan Januszowski].
Iasolini, Giulio. 1588. *De rimedi naturali che sono nell'isola di Pithecusa, hoggi detta Ischia, libri due.* Naples: Giuseppe Cacchi.
Ingegneri, Angelo. 1607. *Tomiri, tragedia.* Naples: Giovanni Giacomo Carlino & Costantino Vitale.
———. 1989. *Della poesia rappresentativa e del modo di rappresentare le favole sceniche.* Edited by Maria Luisa Doglio. Modena: Panini.
———. 2002. *Danza di Venere.* Edited by Roberto Puggioni. Rome: Bulzoni.
Lagrime di diversi nobilissimi spiriti in morte de la molto illustre signora Lucina Savorgnana Marchesi. 1599. Udine: Giovanni Battista Natolini.
Lanci, Cornelio. 1585. *Rappresentazione di S[an] Bastiano.* Florence: Sermartelli.
———. 1588. *Rappresentatione di S[an] Basilio Magno.* Urbino: Bartolomeo Ragusi.
———. 1590. *Esempi della virtù delle donne.* Florence: Francesco Tosi.
———. 1591. *La Niccolosa, commedia.* Florence: Bartolomeo Sermartelli.
Leoni, Giovanni Battista. 1602. *Madrigali.* Venice: Giovanni Battista Ciotti.
Licco, Gasparo. 1605. *La trionfatrice Christina.* Serravalle di Vinetia: Marco Claseri.
Lieti amanti. 1586. *I lieti amanti, primo libro de madrigali a cinque voci.* Venice: Giacomo Vincenzi & Riccardo Amadini.
Lieti amanti. 1990. *I lieti amanti: Madrigali di venti musicisti ferraresi e non.* Edited by Marco Giuliani. Florence: Olschki.

Lodi al Signor Guido Reni, raccolte dall'Imperfetto Accad[emico] Conf[uso]. 1632. Bologna: Nicolo Tebaldini.
Lupi, Orazio. 1587. *Delle rime*. Milan: Pacifico Pontio.
Maganza, Giovanni Battista, Agostino Rava, and Marco Thiene. [1583?]. *La quarta parte delle rime alla rustica di Menon, Magagno, e Begotto*. Venice: Giorgio Angelieri.
Magno, Celio. 1600. *Rime*. In Giustinian and Magno 1600.
Malipiero, Girolamo. 1536. *Il Petrarca spirituale*. Venice: Francesco Marcolini.
Malvasia, Diodata. 1617. *La venuta et i progressi miracolosi della s[antissi]ma Madonna dipinta da S[an] Luca posta sul Monte della Guardia dall'anno che ci venne 1160 sin all'anno 1617*. Bologna: Eredi di Giovanni Rossi.
Manfredi, Muzio, ed. 1575. *Per donne romane*. Bologna: Alessandro Benacci.
———. 1580. *Cento donne cantate*. Parma: Erasmo Viotti.
———. 1587. *Cento madrigali*. Mantua: Francesco Osanna.
———. 1593. *La Semiramis, tragedia*. Bergamo: Comin Ventura.
———. 1594. *Cento lettere*. Pavia: Andrea Viano.
———. 1602. *Il contrasto amoroso*. Venice: Giacomo Antonio Somasco.
———. 1604. *Cento artificiosi madrigali*. Venice: Roberto Meietti.
———. 1606. *Lettere brevissime*. Venice: Roberto Megietti.
Manuzio, Aldo. 1592. *Lettere volgari*. Rome: Santi.
Manzoni, Ercole. 1609. *Amorosi spiriti. Seconda parte de' madrigali*. Padua: Lorenzo Pasquati.
Marescotti, Ercole. *See* Filogenio, Hercole.
Marinella, Lucrezia. 1595. *La Colomba sacra, poema heroico*. Venice: Giovanni Battista Ciotti.
———. 1597. *Vita del serafico, et glorioso S[an] Francesco . . . Con un discorso del rivolgimento amoroso, verso la somma bellezza*. Venice: Pietro Maria Bertano e Fratelli.
———. 1600. *Le nobiltà et eccellenze delle donne, et i diffetti, e mancamenti de gli huomini*. Venice: Giovanni Battista Ciotti.
———. 1601. *La nobiltà et l'eccellenza delle donne, co' diffetti et mancamenti de gli huomini*. Rev. ed. Venice: Giovanni Battista Ciotti.
———. 1602. *La vita di Maria Vergine imperatrice dell'universo, descritta in prosa, et in ottava rima*. Venice: Barezzo Barezzi.
———. 1603. *Rime sacre*. Venice: ad istanza di [Giovanni Battista?] Collosini.
———. 1605a. *Arcadia felice*. Venice: Giovanni Battista Ciotti.
———. 1605b. *Scielta d'alcune rime sacre*. Bergamo: Comin Ventura.
———. 1605c. *Vita del serafico et glorioso S[an] Francesco, descritta in ottava rima*. Venice: Barezzo Barezzi.
———. 1606a. *L'imperatrice dell'universo*. Bergamo: Comin Ventura.
———. 1606b. *Vita del serafico e glorioso S[an] Francesco, descritta in ottava rima*. In *Sette canzoni di sette famosi autori in lode del serafico p[adre] s[an] Francesco, e del sacro Monte della Verna*, edited by Silvestro Poppi. Florence: Giovanni Antonio Caneo & Raffaello Grossi.

―――. 1610a. *La vita di Maria Vergine imperatrice dell'universo . . . descritta in prosa.* Venice: Barezzo Barezzi. [Published with 1610b.]

―――. 1610b. *La vita di Maria Vergine imperatrice dell'universo . . . poema heroico.* Venice: Barezzo Barezzi. [Published with 1610a.]

―――. 1617. *La vita di Maria Vergine imperatrice dell'universo, descritta in prosa, et in ottava rima . . . aggiuntevi le vite de' dodici heroi di Christo, e de' quattro evangelisti.* Venice: Barezzo Barezzi.

―――. 1618. *Amore innamorato, et impazzato, poema . . . con gli argomenti, et allegorie a ciascun canto.* Venice: Giovanni Battista Combi.

―――. 1624. *De' gesti heroici e della vita meravigliosa della serafica S[anta] Caterina da Siena libri sei.* Venice: Barezzo Barezzi.

―――. 1635. *L'Enrico, overo Bisanzio acquistato, poema heroico.* Venice: Ghirardo Imberti.

―――. 1643. *Le vittorie di Francesco il serafico, li passi gloriosi della diva Chiara.* Padua: Giulio Crivellari.

―――. 1645. *Essortationi alle donne et a gli altri se saranno loro a grado.* Venice: Francesco Valvasense.

―――. 1648. *Holocausto d'amore della vergine Santa Giustina.* Venice: Matteo Leni.

―――. 1693. *Rime sacre.* In *Rime delle signore Lucrezia Marinella, Veronica Gambara, ed Isabella Della Morra . . . con una giunta di quelle . . . della signora Maria Selvaggia Borghini*, 1–63. Naples: Antonio Bulifon.

―――. 1997a. *Rivolgimento amoroso dell'uomo verso la divina bellezza.* In Mongini 1997, 441–53.

―――. 1997b. *Vita del glorioso e serafico S[an] Francesco.* In Mongini 1997, 405–40.

―――. 1998. *Arcadia felice.* Edited by Françoise Lavocat. Florence: Olschki.

―――. 1999. *The Nobility and Excellence of Women and the Defects and Vices of Men.* Edited and translated by Anne Dunhill, with an introduction by Letizia Panizza. Chicago: University of Chicago Press.

―――. 2007. *Le nobiltà, et eccellenze delle donne et i diffetti e mancamenti de gli huomini.* Reprint of Marinella 1600. In *Nouvelles de la république des lettres* 1–2:7–201.

―――. 2008. *The Life of the Virgin Mary, Empress of the Universe.* In Colonna, Marinella, and Matraini 2008, 119–246.

―――. 2009. *Enrico, or Byzantium Conquered: A Heroic Poem.* Edited and translated by Maria Galli Stampino. Chicago: University of Chicago Press.

―――. 2011. *L'Enrico, overo Bisanzio acquistato.* Edited by Maria Galli Stampino. Modena: Mucchi.

Marino, Giovanni Battista. 1602a. *Rime . . . parte prima.* Venice: Giovanni Battista Ciotti.

―――. 1602b. *Rime. . . . Parte seconda.* Venice: Giovanni Battista Ciotti.

―――. 1614. *La lira.* Venice: Giovanni Battista Ciotti.

―――. 1629. *La lira. . . . Parte prima[–terza]. Poesie di diversi al Cavalier Marino.* Venice: Ciotti.

———. 1975. *Adone*. Edited by Marzio Pieri. 2 vols. Bari: Laterza.
Marquets, Anne de. 1997. *Sonets spirituels*. Edited by Gary Ferguson. Geneva: Droz.
Martinengo, Lucillo. 1590. *Vita di Santa Margherita detta Pelagia, ridotta nell'ottava rima*. Brescia: Policreto Turlini, ad istanza di Giovanni Battista Borelli.
———. 1595. *Della vita di nostra signora, la gloriosa vergine Maria, in sacro poema ridotta*. Brescia: Policreto Turlini.
Marzi, Giovanni Battista. 1589. *Ottavia furiosa*. Florence: Filippo Giunti.
Massini, Filippo. 1609. *Rime*. Pavia: Andrea Viani.
Matraini, Chiara. 1555. *Rime et prose*. Lucca: Vincenzo Busdraghi.
———. 1556. *Oratione d'Isocrate a Demonico*. Translated by Chiara Matraini. Florence: Lorenzo Torrentino.
———. 1581. *Meditationi spirituali*. Lucca: Vincenzo Busdraghi.
———. 1586. *Considerationi sopra i sette salmi penitentiali del gran re e profeta Davit*. Lucca: Vincenzo Busdraghi.
———. 1590. *Breve discorso sopra la vita e laude della beatissima Vergine e madre del figiuol di Dio*. Lucca: Vincenzo Busdraghi.
———. 1595. *Lettere . . . con la prima, e seconda parte delle . . . rime*. Lucca: Vincenzo Busdraghi, ad istanza di Ottaviano Guidoboni.
———. 1597. *Lettere . . . con la prima e seconda parte delle . . . rime, con una lettera in difesa delle lettere, e delle armi*. Venice: Nicolò Moretti.
———. 1602. *Dialoghi spirituali . . . con una notabile narratione alla grande Accademia de' Curiosi, et alcune rime, e sermoni*. Venice: Fioravante Prati.
———. 1989. *Rime e lettere*. Edited by Giovanna Rabitti. Bologna: Commissione per i Testi di Lingua.
———. 2007. *Collected Poetry and Prose*. Translated and edited by Eleanor Maclachlan, with an introduction by Giovanna Rabitti. Chicago: University of Chicago Press.
———. 2008. *Brief Discourse on the Life and Praises of the Most Blessed Virgin and Mother of the Son of God*. In Colonna, Marinella, and Matraini 2008, 67–118.
Mausoleo di poesie volgari, et latine in morte del sig[nor] Giuliano Gosellini, fabricato da diversi poeti de' nostri tempi. 1589. Milan: Paolo Gottardo Pontio.
Meditationes. 1587. *Divi Bernardi abbatis ad humanae conditionis cognitionem meditationes devotissimae*. In *Meditationes S[ancti] Augustini, et S[ancti] Bernardi, aliorumque sanctorum antiquorum patrum*, 298–350. Lyons: Antoine Gryphius.
Meditations on the Life of Christ: An Illustrated Manuscript of the Fourteenth Century, Paris, Bibliothèque nationale, Ms. Ital. 115. 1961. Translated by Isa Ragusa. Edited by Isa Ragusa and Rosalie B. Green. Princeton, NJ: Princeton University Press.
Menichini, Andrea. 1597. *Rime . . . a' prencipi christiani, et altri personaggi per l'universal crociata contra gl'inimici di Santa Chiesa*. Treviso: Evangelista Deuchino.
Mercurio, Scipione. 1621. *La commare o riccoglitrice*. Venice: Giovanni Battista Ciotti.
Miani, Valeria. 1604. *Amorosa speranza, favola pastorale*. Venice: Francecso Bolzetta.
———. 1611. *Celinda, tragedia*. Vicenza: Francesco Bolzetta & Domenico Amadio.

———. 2010. *Celinda, a Tragedy*. Edited by Valeria Finucci. Translated by Julie Kinsacky. Toronto: Centre for Reformation and Renaissance Studies.
Miari, Alessandro. 1591. *Il prencipe Tigridoro, tragedia . . . con un'aggiunta di rime a diversi*. Reggio: Ercoliano Bartoli.
Mini, Paolo. 1614. *Discorso della nobiltà di Firenze e de' fiorentini*. Florence: Volcmar Timan.
Minturno, Antonio [Antonio Sebastiani]. 2008. *Amore innamorato*. Edited by Gennaro Tallini. Rome: Aracne.
Molza, Tarquinia. 1750. *Opuscoli inediti . . . con alcune poesie*. Bergamo: Pietro Lancellotti.
Montanaro, Pomponio, ed. 1587. *Rime di varii auttori per lo molto illustre Signor Giacopo Prainer, libero barone in Stiibing, Fladmiz, e Kabenstan*. Verona: Girolamo Discepolo.
Monte, Issicratea. 1577. *Oratione . . . nella congratulatione del sereniss[imo] principe Sebastiano Veniero*. Venice: Domenico & Giovanni Battista Guerra.
———. 1578a. *Seconda oratione . . . nella congratulatione dell'invitiss[imo] et sereniss[imo] principe di Venetia Sebastiano Veniero*. Venice: Domenico & Giovanni Battista Guerra.
———. [1578b?]. *Oratione . . . nella congratulatione del serenissimo principe di Venetia, Nicolò da Ponte*. Venice: Domenico & Giovanni Battista Guerra.
———. 1581. *Oratione . . . alla sacra maestà di Maria d'Austria . . . nella venuta di s[ua] maestà a Padova*. Padua: Paolo Meietti.
Montefuscoli, Giovanni Domenico. 1593. *Grandezze del verbo ristrette ne' misteri del rosario*. Naples: Orazio Salviani appresso Giovanni Giacomo Carlino & Antonio Pace.
Montemayor, Jorge de. 1996. *Los siete libros de la Diana*. Edited by Julian Arribas. London: Tamesis.
Morigi, Paolo. 1619. *La nobiltà di Milano*. Milan: Giovanni Battista Bidelli.
Morone, Bonaventura. 1621. *Rime sacre*. Venice: Santo Grillo e Fratelli.
Morosini, Andrea. 1627. *L'imprese et espeditioni di Terra Santa, et l'acquisto fatto dell'Imperio di Costantinopoli dalla Serenissima Republica di Venetia*. Venice: Antonio Pinelli.
Le muse contentiose. 1614. Vicenza: ad istanza di Battista di Martini.
Muzio, Girolamo. 1550. *Ecloghe . . . divise in cinque libri*. Venice: Giolito.
Naldi, Bianca. 1614. *Risposta . . . ad una lettera di Giacomo Violati libraro in Venetia, scritta per occasione di ringratiamento, per haverle mandato i "Donneschi Diffetti" di Giuseppe Passi*. Vicenza: Giacomo Violati.
Nogarola, Isotta. 1563. *Dialogus, quo utrum Adam vel Eva magis peccaverit, quaestio satis nota, sed non adeo explicata, continetur*. Edited by Francesco Nogarola. Venice: Paolo Manuzio.
Nuova scielta di rime di diversi illustri poeti. 1592. Bergamo: Comin Ventura.
Ongaro, Antonio. 1600. *Rime*. Farnese: Niccolò Mariani.

Oratione, e poemi de gli Affidati nella morte del catolico Filippo II, re di Spagna. 1599. Pavia: Eredi di Girolamo Bartoli.

Orlandini, Leonardo. 1600. "A i lettori." In Donia 1600, †2r–†4r.

Ottonelli, Giovanni Domenico. 1646. *La pericolosa conversatione con le donne, o poco modeste, o ritirate, o cantatrici, o accademiche*. Florence: Luca Franceschini & Alessandro Logi.

Ovid. 1977. *Metamorphoses: Books I–VIII*. 3rd ed. Translated by Frank Justus Miller. Revised by G. P. Goold. Cambridge, MA: Harvard University Press.

Palazzi, Giovanni. 1681. *La virtu in giocco, overo dame patritie di Venetia famose per nascita, per lettere, per armi, per costumi*. Venice: Giovanni Parè.

Pallantieri, Girolamo. 1603. *La Bucolica di Virgilio, tradotto verso per verso*. Bologna: Vittorio Bennacci.

Pancetti, Camillo. 1622. *Venetia libera, poema heroico*. Venice: Andrea Muschio.

Pansa, Muzio. 1596. *Rime*. Chieti: Isidoro Faci, Pasquale Gallo, & Carlo Vullietti.

Passero, Felice. 1589. *La vita di San Placido e suo martirio*. Venice: Giolito.

Passi, Giuseppe. 1599. *I donneschi diffetti*. Venice: Giacomo Antonio Somasco.

———. 1602. *Dello stato maritale*. Venice: Giacomo Antonio Somasco.

———. 1603. *La monstruosa fucina delle sordidezze de gl'huomini*. Venice: Giacomo Antonio Somasco.

———. 1609. *Continuatione della monstruosa fucina delle sordidezze de gl'huomini*. Venice: Evangelista Deuchino & Giovanni Battista Pulciani.

Patrizi, Francesco. 1963. *L'amorosa filosofia*. Edited by John Charles Nelson. Florence: Le Monnier.

Pellegrini, Tommaso. 1579. *Discorso del Costante Academico Occulto in laude delle donne*. Venice: Domenico Nicolini.

[Persio, Ascanio]. 1603. *Historia della santa imagine della gloriosa Vergine, la qual si conserva sul Monte della Guardia vicino a Bologna*. Bologna: Vittorio Benacci.

Pesaro, Giovanni Battista da. 1591. *Rime spirituali*. Venice: Paolo Ugolino.

Petracci, Pietro, ed. 1607. *Le muse sacre, scelta di rime spirituali de' più eccellenti autori d'Italia*. Venice: Evangelista Deuchino & Giovanni Battista Pulciano.

———, ed. 1608. *Ghilranda [sic] dell'aurora, scelta di madrigali de' più famosi autori di questo secolo*. Venice: Bernardo Giunti & Giovanni Battista Ciotti.

———, ed. 1612. *La celeste lira. Componimenti di diversi eccellentissimi autori sopra il santissimo sacramento della eucaristia*. Venice: Evangelista Deuchino.

———. 1615. *Rime diverse*. Venice.

Petrarca, Francesco. 1996a. *Canzoniere*. Edited by Marco Santagata. Milan: Mondadori.

———. 1996b. *Trionfi, rime estravaganti, codice degli abbozzi*. Edited by Vincio Pacca and Laura Paolino, with an introduction by Marco Santagata. Milan: Mondadori.

Petrelli, Eugenio, ed. 1616a. *Nuovo concerto di rime sacre . . . composte da' più eccellenti poeti d'Italia sopra i principali misteri della vita, e morte di Christo nostro signore e della regina de' cieli*. Venice: Antonio Pinelli.

———, ed. 1616b. *Nuovo concerto di rime sacre, composte in lode de' santi, et in varii soggetti spirituali, e morali, da' più eccellenti poeti d'Italia . . . parte seconda.* Venice: Antonio Pinelli.

Pigafetta, Osanna. 1586a. *Trattato detto direttorio delle hore canoniche.* Vicenza: Stamperia del Convento di San Domenico.

———, ed. 1586b. *Vita, gesti e costumi del beatissimo padre nostro s[anto] Domenico, con alcuni essempi e fioretti de' padri e frati dell'ordine nostro, ne i principii della nostra Religione.* Translated by Paolina Almerici. Vicenza: Stamperia del Convento di San Domenico.

Poccianti, Michele. 1589. *Catalogus scriptorum florentinorum omnis generis.* Florence: Filippo Giunta.

Poesias diversas compuestas en deferentes lenguas en las honoras che hizo a Roma la nación de los españoles a la magestad catolica de la reyna D[oña] Margarita de Austria nuestra senora. 1612. Rome: Giacomo Mascardi.

Poesie. 1590. *Poesie di diversi eccellenti ingegni trivigiani al conte Antonio Collalto per la sua elezione a collateral generale della Serenissima Repubblica Veneta.* Edited by Giovanni dalla Torre. Treviso: Eredi di Angelo Mazzolini & Domenico Amici.

Poesie. 1591. *Poesie funebri di diversi nobili ingegni trivigiani per la morte dell'illustr[e] s[ignor] Francesco Brescia.* Treviso: Domenico Amici.

Poesie. 1596. *Poesie toscane e latine da diversi autori composte nell'essequie dell'illustre sig[nora] Isabella Marescotti de' Ballati, gentildonna sanese.* Edited by Salvestro Marchetti. Siena: Bonetti.

Poesie. 1598. *Poesie latine et volgari composte da diversi nobilissimi ingegni in lode dell'illustrissimo signor Nicolo Contarini.* Udine: Giovanni Battista Natolini.

Poggi, Semidea. 1623. *La Calliope religiosa.* Vicenza: Francesco Grossi.

Poggiolini, Roberto. 1613. *La cetra.* Venice: Ambrosio Dei.

Policreti, Giuseppe. 1587. *La conversione della Maddalena.* Vicenza: Perin Libraro.

Polinnia per l'illustrissimo signor Tomaso Contarini, cavaliere . . . e podestà di Padova. D'autori diversi. 1609. Padua: Francesco Bolzetta.

Pulci, Antonia. 1996. *Florentine Drama for Convent and Festival: Seven Sacred Plays.* Edited by James Wyatt Cook and Barbara Collier Cook. Translated by James Wyatt Cook. Chicago: University of Chicago Press.

Querenghi, Antonio. 1616. *Poesie volgari.* Rome: Guglielmo Facciotti.

Querini, Carlo. 1597. *Orazione in laude della mag[nifica] città di Verona.* Verona: Girolamo Discepolo.

Raccolta d'orationi e di rime di diversi . . . nella morte dell'illustriss[imo] e reverendiss[imo] Cardinal Farnese. 1589. Rome: Francesco Coattini.

Rasponi, Felicia. 1572. *Dialogo dell'eccellenza dello stato monacale, et alcuni essercitii di esso.* Bologna: Pellegrino Bonardo.

Razzi, Serafino. 1577. *Vite dei santi e beati, cosi huomini come donne del sacro ordine de' frati predicatori.* Florence: Bartolomeo Sermartelli.

Razzi, Silvano. 1595–1606. *Delle vite delle donne illustri per santità.* 6 vols. Florence: Eredi di Iacopo Giunti.

Ribera, Pietro Paolo. 1609. *Le glorie immortali de' trionfi et heroiche imprese d'ottocento quarantacinque donne illustri antiche e moderne dotate di conditioni e scienze segnalate*. Venice: Evangelista Deuchino.

Ricciuoli, Federico. 1594. *Ecloghe et rime*. Urbino: Bartolomeo & Simone Ragusi.

Rime. 1556. *Rime di diversi signori napolitani, e d'altri*. Edited by Lodovico Dolce. Venice: Gabriele Giolito.

Rime. 1561. *Rime di diversi nobilissimi et eccellentissimi autori in morte della signora Irene delle signore [sic] di Spilimbergo*. Venice: Domenico & Giovanni Battista Guerra.

Rime. 1567. *Rime di diversi illustri autori in lode della s[ignora] Cintia Tiene Bracciadura*. Padua: Lorenzo Pasquati.

Rime. 1579. *Rime et versi nella morte del reverend[issi]mo mons[igno]r Alessandro Piccolomini archivescovo di Patrasso*. Siena: Luca Bonetti.

Rime. 1585. *Rime et versi in lode della ill[ustrissi]ma et ecc[ellentissi]ma s[igno]ra d[on]na Giovanna Castriota*. Edited by Scipione de Monti. Vico Equense: Gioseppe Cacchi.

Rime. 1586a. *Il primo volume delle rime scelte di diversi autori, di nuovo corrette e ristampate*. Venice: Giovanni & Giovanni Paolo Giolito de' Ferrari.

Rime. 1586b. *Rime di vari autori novamente raccolte e date in luce*. Orvieto: Baldo Salviani.

Rime. 1587a. *Rime di diversi celebri poeti dell'età nostra, nuovamente raccolte e poste in luce*. Bergamo: Comino Ventura.

Rime. 1587b. *Rime di diversi eccellenti auttori, fatte nelle nozze felicissime de gli illustriss[imi] sig[nori] il sig[nor] Marco Pij di Savoia, sig[nore] di Sassuolo, e la sig[nora] d[onna] Clelia Farnese*. Edited by Alfonso Caraffa. Ferrara.

Rime. 1587c. *Rime funerali di diversi illustri ingegni, composte nella volgare, e latina favella, in morte della molto ill[ustre] sig[nora] Isotta Brembata Grumella*. Bergamo: Comino Ventura.

Rime. 1588. *Rime de diversi alla illustrissima signora la signora Felice Maldenti de' Theodoli, contessa di Cicigliano*. Ferrara: Vittorio Baldini.

Rime. 1589. *Rime nelle nozze dell'illustriss[i]mo et eccell[entissi]mo signor . . . Alessandro Carretti . . . et dell'illustrissima sign[ora] . . . donna Faustina Sforza*. Piacenza: Giovanni Bazachi.

Rime. 1590. *Rime di diversi nobilissimi spiriti de la patria del Friuli, in morte de l'ill[ustrissi]mo signor Giorgio Gradenico*. Udine: Giovanni Battista Natolini.

Rime. 1593. *Rime di diversi autori nelle quali si veggono molti concetti d'amore felicemente spiegati, et nel fine alcuni piacevoli ennimi*. Pavia: Eredi di Hieronimo Bartoli.

Rime. 1596. *Rime di diversi in lode dell'illustrissima signora Chiara Cornara, degnissima capitania di Verona, con una orazione in fine*. Verona: Girolamo Discepoli.

Rime. 1604. *Rime in lode della Signora Verginia Andreini comica Fedele*. Florence: Volcmar Timan.

Rime. 1723. *Rime scelte de' poeti ferraresi antichi, e moderni*. Ferrara: Eredi di Bernardino Pomatelli.

Rime. 1726. *Rime degli Accademici Accesi di Palermo*. Edited by Giovanni Battista Caruso. 2 vols. Palermo: Antonino Cortese.
Rinaldi, Cesare. 1608. *Rime*. Venice: Bernardo Giunti & Giovanni Battista Ciotti.
Romei, Annibale. 1585. *Discorsi*. Venice: Francesco Ziletti.
Rosini, Celso, ed. 1621a. *Il sacro museo poetico . . . Prima parte*. Venice: Evangelista Deuchino.
———, ed. 1621b. *Il sacro museo poetico . . . Seconda parte*. Venice: Evangelista Deuchino.
Rossi, Armonio, ed. 1587. *Diverse compositioni di poesia toscane e latine. In Oratione funerale. . . . in morte del reverendissimo p[adre] maestro Spirito Pelo Angusciola . . .*, by Gherardo Bellinzona. Vicenza: Agostino dalla Noce.
Rossi, Giovanni Vittorio. *See* Erythraeus, Janus Nicius.
Ruscelli, Girolamo. 1553. *Tre discorsi a M[esser] Lodovico Dolce*. Venice: Plinio Pietrasanta.
———. 1559. *Del modo di comporre in versi nella lingua italiana*. Venice: Giovanni Battista & Melchiorre Sessa.
Sabbadini, Goffredo, ed. 1615. *Componimenti volgari, et latini di diversi illustri autori in lode de l'illustrissimo sig[no]r Vicenzo Capello degnissimo luogotenente generale de la patria del Friuli*. Udine: Pietro Lorio.
Salvetti, Maddalena. 1590. *Rime toscane . . . in lode della serenissima signora Cristina di Loreno, gran duchessa di Toscana*. Florence: Francesco Tosi.
———. 1611. *Il David perseguitato o vero fuggitivo, poema eroico*. Florence: Giovanni Antonio Caneo.
Sannazaro, Iacopo. 1990. *Arcadia*. Edited by Francesco Erspamer. Milan: Mursia.
———. 2009. *Latin Poetry*. Edited by Michael C. J. Putnam. Cambridge, MA: Harvard University Press.
Santi, Gismondo, ed. 1608. *Sonetti di diversi accademici sanesi*. Siena: Salvestro Marchetti.
Sanudo, Leonardo, ed. 1613. *Vita, attioni, miracoli, morte, resurrettione, et ascensione di Dio humanato, raccolti . . . in versi lirici da' più famosi autori di questo secolo*. Venice: Santo Grillo e Fratelli.
Sarrocchi, Margherita. 1606. *La Scanderbeide, poema heroico*. Rome: Lepido Faci.
———. 1623. *La Scanderbeide, poema heroico*. Rome: Andrea Fei.
———. 2006. *Scanderbeide: The Heroic Deeds of George Scanderbeg, King of Epirus*. Edited and translated by Rinaldina Russell. Chicago: University of Chicago Press.
Sasso, Giacomo. 1601. *Lettura . . . sopra il sonetto di Bernardo Tasso, "Poi che la parte men perfetta, e bella."* Venice: Giacomo Antonio Somasco.
Sbarra, Lucchesia. 1610. *Rime*. Conegliano: Marco Claseri.
Scaioli, Alessandro, ed. 1611. *Parnaso de poetici ingegni*. Parma: Erasmo Viotti.
Scandianese, Tito Giovanni. 1557. *La fenice . . . di nuovo ristampata con nuove aggiunte*. Venice: Giolito.
Scaramelli, Baldassare. 1585. *Dui canti del poema heroico di Scanderbec . . . con altre rime e prose*. Carmagnola: Marcantonio Belloni.
Scarano, Lucio. 1601. *Scenophylax*. Venice: Giovanni Battista Ciotti.

Scardeone, Bartolomeo. 1560. *De antiquitate urbis patavii, et claris civibus patavinis, libri tres.* Basel: Nicolaus Episcopius.

Scelta di rime di diversi moderni autori non più stampate, parte prima. 1591. Genoa: Eredi di Gierolamo Bartoli.

Segni, Giulio, ed. 1583. *Scelta di varii poemi volgari et latini composti nella partenza dell'eccellentiss[imo] sig[nor] Gio[vanni] Angelo Papio dalla città di Bologna.* Bologna: Giovanni Rossi.

———, ed. 1600. *Tempio all'illustrissimo et reverendissimo signor Cinthio Aldobrandini, cardinale San Giorgio.* Bologna: Eredi di Giovanni Rossi.

———, ed. 1601. *Componimenti poetici volgari, latini, e greci di diversi, sopra la s[anta] imagine della beata Vergine dipinta da San Luca, la quale si serba nel Monte della Guardia presso Bologna.* Bologna: Vittoria Benacci.

Serassi, Pierantonio. 1785. *La vita di Torquato Tasso.* Rome: Pagliarini.

Serdonati, Francesco. 1596. *Giunta d'altre donne illustri antiche e moderne.* In Boccaccio, Betussi, and Serdonati 1596.

Sforza, Muzio. 1590a. *Delle rime . . . parte prima.* Venice: Domenico & Giovanni Battista Guerra.

———. 1590b. *Delle rime . . . parte seconda.* Venice: Altobello Salicato.

Silvio, Paolo. 1605. *La Madalena penitente, poema sacro.* Rimini: Giovanni Simbeni, ad istanza di Matteo Cappello.

Sori, Isabella. 1628. *Ammaestramenti e ricordi circa a' buoni costumi, che deve insegnare una ben creata madre ad una figlia . . . divisa in dodeci lettere, con una particolare aggionta di dodeci difese, fatte contro alcuni sinistri giudicii, fatti sopra de gli medemi ammaestramenti, e del sesso donnesco: e nel fine un panegirico delle cose più degne dell'illustrissima città d'Alessandria, et di molti pellegrini ingegni usciti da essa.* Pavia: Giovanni Maria Magro.

Spelta, Antonio Maria. 1602. *La curiosa et dilettevole aggionta del sig[nor] Ant[onio] Maria Spelta, cittadino pavese all'historia sua.* Pavia: Pietro Bartoli.

———. 1607. *La saggia pazzia, fonte d'allegrezze, madre de' piaceri, regina de' bell'humori. Libro primo-secondo.* Pavia: Pietro Bartoli.

———. 1612. *Donneschi trofei.* Pavia: Pietro Bartoli.

Spolverini, Ersilia. 1596. *Ad illustrissimam Claram Corneliam poemata duo.* Verona: Girolamo Discepolo.

[Spolverini, Ersilia]. 1596. *Oratione in lode dell'Illustr[issi]ma Signora Chiara Cornara.* Verona: Girolamo Discepolo. Published anonymously.

Stampa, Gaspara. 2010. *The Complete Poems: The 1554 Edition of the "Rime."* Edited by Jane Tylus. Chicago: University of Chicago Press.

Stigliani, Tommaso. 1605. *Delle rime.* Venice: Giovanni Battista Ciotti.

———. 1625. *Il canzoniero.* Venice: Evangelista Deuchino.

Strassoldo, Giovanni, and Giulio Strassoldo. 1616. *Dei componimenti volgari e latini.* Venice: Giovanni Battista Ciotti.

Strozzi, Giulio. 1624. *Venetia edificata, poema eroico.* Venice: Pinelli.

Strozzi, Lorenza. 1588. *In singula totius anni solennia hymni.* Florence: Filippo Giunta.

———. 1601. *In singula totius anni solennia hymni*. Paris: Denis Binet.
Superbi, Agostino. 1629. *Trionfo glorioso d'heroi illustri et eminenti dell'inclita, e maravigliosa città di Venetia . . . diviso in tre libri*. Venice: Evangelista Deuchino.
Tansillo, Luigi. 1606. *Le lagrime di San Pietro del sig[nor] Luigi Tansillo, cavate dal suo proprio originale, poema sacro et heroico*. Venice: Barezzo Barezzi.
Tarabotti, Arcangela. 2005. *Lettere familiari e di complimento*. Edited by Meredith Ray and Lynn Westwater, with an introduction by Gabriella Zarri. Turin: Rosenberg & Sellier.
Tartaglia, Ortensio. 1598. *Rime spirituali sopra il rosario della gloriosa Maria Vergine, santissima madre d'Iddio*. Aquila: Lepido Faci.
Tassis, Maria Aurelia. 1723. *La vita di Santa Grata, vergine regina nella Germania, poi principessa di Bergamo*. Padua: Giuseppe Comino.
Tasso, Ercole. 1593. *Poesie . . . composte da lui in sua giovanile età*. Bergamo: Comin Ventura.
Tasso, Torquato. 1580. *Il Goffredo*. Venice: Domenico Cavalcalupo.
———. 1581. *Gerusalemme liberata*. Parma: Erasmo Viotti.
———. 1586. *Discorso in lode del matrimonio, et un dialogo d'amore . . . con una lettera intorno alla revisione, alla correttione, et all'accrescimento della sua "Gerusalemme."* Milan: Pietro Tini.
———. 1587. *Il re Torrismondo*. Bologna: Giovanni Rossi.
———. 1852–55. *Le lettere*. Edited by Cesare Guasti. 5 vols. Florence: Le Monnier.
———. 1977a. *Aminta*. In *Il teatro italiano*, 648–721.
———. 1977b. *Scritti sull'arte poetica*. Edited by Ettore Mazzali. 2nd ed. 2 vols. Turin: Einaudi.
———. 1980. *Gerusalemme liberata*. Edited by Lanfranco Caretti. 2nd ed. Turin: Einaudi.
———. 1991a. *La Cavaletta overo de la poesia toscana*. In *Dialoghi*, edited by Bruno Basile, 183–244. Milan: Mursia.
———. 1991b. *La Molza overo de l'amore*. In *Dialoghi*, edited by Bruno Basile, 245–62. Milan: Mursia.
———. 1994. *Le rime*. Edited by Bruno Basile. 2 vols. Rome: Salerno.
———. 1997. *Discorso della virtù feminile e donnesca*. Edited by Maria Luisa Doglio. Palermo: Sellerio.
———. 2001. *Lagrime*. Edited by Maria Pia Mussini Sacchi. Novara: Interlinea.
Il teatro italiano. Vol. 2, *La tragedia del Cinquecento*. 1977. Edited by Marco Ariani. Turin: Einaudi.
Il tempio della divina signora Donna Geronima Colonna d'Aragona. 1568. Padua: Lorenzo Pasquati.
Tempio fabricato da diversi coltissimi, e nobilissimi ingegni in lode dell'illustr[issima], et ecc[ellentissi]ma donna Flavia Peretta Orsina, duchessa di Bracciano. 1591. Rome: Giovanni Martinelli.
Terracina, Laura. 1548. *Rime*. Venice: Gabriel Giolito de' Ferrari.

Tiraboschi, Girolamo. 1824. *Poesia italiana*. Vol. 7, pt. 3, of *Storia della letteratura italiana*. Milan: Società Tipografica de' Classici Italiani.
Tomagni, Giovanni David. 1565. *Dell'eccellentia de l'huomo sopra quella de la donna, libri tre*. Venice: Giovanni Varisco.
Tomasini, Giacomo Filippo. 1644. *Elogia virorum literis et sapientia illustrium*. Padua: Sebastiano Sardi.
Torelli, Pomponio. 2004. *"Il Tancredi": Modello ed evoluzione nella tragedia del Cinquecento*. Edited by Sabrina Morini. Milan: Unicopli.
Tornabuoni, Lucrezia. 1978. *I poemetti sacri di Lucrezia Tornabuoni*. Edited by Fulvio Pezzarossa. Florence: Olschki.
———. 2001. *Sacred Narratives*. Edited and translated by Jane Tylus. Chicago: University of Chicago Press.
Tortoletti, Bartolomeo. 1628. *Iuditha vindex et vindicata*. Rome: Typis Vaticanis.
———. 1648. *Giuditta vittoriosa, poema eroico*. Rome: Lodovico Grignani.
La tromba dell'illustriss[imo] sig[nor] Benedetto Corraro podestà di Vicenza, formata di poesie diverse. 1598. Vicenza: Giorgio Greco.
Tronsarelli, Ottavio. 1643. *L'honestà del poema eroico, discorso*. In *La vittoria navale*, 500–537. Rome: Andrea Fei.
Turchi, Francesco, ed. 1568. *Salmi penitenziali di diversi eccellenti autori. Con alcune rime spirituali, di diversi cardinali*. Venice: Giolito.
Turina, Francesca. 1595. *Rime spirituali sopra i misterii del santissimo rosario*. Rome: Domenico Gigliotti.
———. 1627. *Rime*. Città di Castello: Santi Molinelli.
———. 1628. *Rime*. Città di Castello: Santi Molinelli.
———. 2005. *Rime spirituali sopra i misteri del santissimo rosario*. Edited by Paolo Bà. *Letteratura italiana antica* 6:153–220.
———. 2009. *Autobiographical Poems: A Bilingual Edition*. Edited by Natalia Costa-Zalessow. Translated by Joan E. Borrelli with Natalia Costa-Zalessow. New York: Bordighiera.
Udine, Ercole. 2004. *La Psiche*. Edited by Salvatore Ussia. Vercelli: Mercurio.
Valerini, Adriano. 1586. *Le bellezze di Verona*. Verona: Girolamo Discepoli.
———. 1991. "Orazione in morte della divina signora Vincenza Armani, comica eccellentissima." In *La commedia dell'arte: Storia, testi, documenti; La professione del teatro*, edited by Ferruccio Marotti and Giovanna Romei, 27–41. Roma: Bulzoni.
Valiero, Agostino. 1744. *Modo di vivere proposto alle vergini che si chiamano dimesse* (1577). In *La istituzione d'ogni stato lodevole delle donne christiane*, edited by Gaetano Volpi. Padua: Giuseppe Comino.
Valvasone, Erasmo di. 1590. *Angeleida*. Venice: Giovanni Battista Somasco.
———. 1592. *Le lagrime di Santa Maria Maddalena*. In Guarguanti, Tansillo, and Valvasone 1592, 165–78.
———. 2005. *Angeleida*. Edited by Luciana Borsetto. Alessandria: Edizioni dell'Orso.
Vandelli, Domenico. 1750. "Vita di Tarquinia Molza, detta l'Unica." In Molza 1750, 3–25.

Varanini, Giorgio, ed. 1965. *Cantari religiosi senesi del Trecento. Neri Pagliaresi. Fra Felice Tancredi da Massa. Niccolò Cicerchia.* Edited by Giorgio Varanini. Bari: Laterza.
Varchi, Benedetto. 1555. *I sonetti . . . novellamente messi in luce.* Venice: Plinio Pietrasanta.
Varie compositioni scritte in lode de l'illustrissimo sig[nor] Giovanni Cornaro, capitanio di Verona; e de l'illustrissima sig[nora] Chiara Delfina sua consorte. 1596. Verona: Girolamo Discepoli.
Vedova, Giuseppe. 1832–36. *Biografia degli scrittori padovani.* 2 vols. Padua: Tipografia della Minerva.
Vernazza, Battista. 1588. *Opere spirituali.* 3 vols. Venice: Eredi di Francesco Ziletti.
———. 1602. *Delle opere . . . tomo quarto.* Verona: Angelo Tamo.
———. 1819. *Sonetti inediti della Venerabile Battista Vernazza.* Edited by Giuseppe Ronco. 2nd ed. Genoa: Stamperia Pagano.
Verucci, Lodovico. 1627. *L'eremita Antonio, poema sacro.* Foligno: Agostino Alteri.
Vida, Marco Girolamo. 2009. *Christiad.* Edited and translated by James Gardner. Cambridge, MA: Harvard University Press.
Viola, Dionisio. 1618. *Il museo d'amore.* Vicenza: Domenico Amadio.
Virgil. 1999. *Eclogues, Georgics, Aeneid.* 2 vols. Translated by H. Fairclough. Revised by G. P. Goold. Cambridge, MA: Harvard University Press.
Vito di Gozze, Niccolò [Nikola Vitov Gučetić]. 1581. *Dialogo dell'Amore . . . Dialogo della bellezza.* Venice: Francesco Ziletti.
———. 1585. *Discorsi sopra le metheore d'Aristotile.* Venice: Francesco Ziletti.
Vives, Juan Luis. 1996. *"De institutione feminae christianae, Liber primus," Introduction, Critical Edition, Translation, and Notes.* Edited by Charles Fantazzi and Constantinus Matheeussen. Translated by Charles Fantazzi. Leiden: Brill.
Zabata, Cristoforo. 1583. *Ragionamento di sei nobili fanciulle genovesi, le quali . . . discorrono di molte cose allo stato loro appartenenti.* Pavia: Girolamo Bartoli.
Zarrabini, Onofrio, et al. 1586. *Rime di d[on] Onofrio Zarrabbini . . . e d'altri huomini illustri.* Edited by Giulio Morigi. Venice: Niccolò Moretti.
Zinani, Gabriele. 1627. *Rime diverse.* Venice: Evangelista Deuchino.
Zuccolo, Lodovico. 1613. *L'Alessandro overo della pastorale, dialogo.* Venice: Andrea Baba.
Zucconello, Ippolito, ed. 1583. *Del giardino de' poeti in lode del serenissimo re di Polonia . . . libro secondo.* Venice: Fratelli Guerra. [Published with *Viridiarium poetarum . . . in laudes serenissimi atque potentissimi d[omini] Stephani regis Poloniae . . . in duos libros divisum* (Venice: Luigi Valvassori, 1583).]

Secondary Sources

Afribo, Andrea. 2001. *Teoria e prassi della* gravitas *nel Cinquecento.* Introduction by Pier Vincenzo Mengaldo. Florence: Franco Cesati.
Agnes, R. 1964. "La *Gerusalemme liberata* e il poema del secondo Cinquecento." *Lettere italiane* 16:117–43.

Albonico, Simone. 1989. "Ippolita Clara." In *Veronica Gambara e la poesia del suo tempo nell'Italia settentrionale,* edited by Cesare Bozzetti, Pietro Gibellini, and Ennio Sandal, 323–83. Florence: Olschki.

Alemanno, Laura. 1995. "L'Accademia degli Umoristi." *Roma moderna e contemporanea* 3 (1): 97–120.

Allen, Prudence. 1985. *The Concept of Woman.* Vol. 1, *The Aristotelian Revolution, 750 B.C.–A.D. 1250.* Grand Rapids, MI: Eerdmans.

Allen, Prudence, and Filippo Salvatore. 1992. "Lucrezia Marinella and Woman's Identity in Late Italian Renaissance." *Renaissance and Reformation* 28 (4): 5–39.

Amaturo, Raffaele. 1963. "Baldi, Bernardino." In *Dizionario biografico degli italiani,* 5:461–64.

Ambrosini, Federica. 2000. "Toward a Social History of Women in Venice: From the Renaissance to the Enlightenment." In Martin and Romano 2000, 420–53.

Andrews, Richard. 2000. "Isabella Andreini and Others: Women on Stage in the Late Cinquecento." In Panizza 2000, 316–33.

Appendini, F. M. 1802–3. *Notizie istorico-critiche sulle antichità storia e letteratura de' Ragusei.* 2 vols. Ragusa: A. Martecchini.

Arbizzoni, Guido. 1987. "Una riscrittura cinquecentesca del Petrarca: *I sonetti, le canzoni et i trionfi di M. Laura.*" In *Scritture di scritture: Testi, generi, modelli,* 539–47. Rome: Bulzoni.

———. 1997. "Poesia epica, eroicomica, satirica, burlesca: La poesia rusticale toscana; La 'poesia figurata.'" In *Storia della letteratura italiana,* edited by Enrico Malato, vol. 5, *La fine del Cinquecento e il Seicento,* 727–70. Rome: Salerno.

Arbizzoni, Guido, Marco Faini, and Tiziana Mattioli, eds. 2005. *Dopo Tasso: Percorsi del poema eroico.* Padua: Antenore.

Ardissino, Erminia. 1996. *"L'aspra tragedia": Poesia e sacro in Torquato Tasso.* Florence: Olschki.

———. 2003. "'Scolpisci prego in me devota imago': Torquato Tasso e i predicatori." In *Letteratura in forma di sermone: I rapporti tra predicazione e letteratura nei secoli XIII–XVI,* edited by Ginetta Auzzas, Giovanni Baffetti, and Carlo Delcorno, 97–121. Florence: Olschki.

———. 2005. Introduction to *Poemi biblici del Seicento,* edited by Erminia Ardissino, 1–10. Alessandria: Edizioni dell'Orso.

———. 2009. "Poetiche sacre tra Cinquecento e Seicento." In Ardissino and Selmi 2009, 367–81.

Ardissino, Erminia, and Elisabetta Selmi, eds. 2009. *Poetica e retorica del sacro tra Cinque e Seicento.* Alessandria: Edizioni dell'Orso.

Ariani, Marco. 1974. *Tra classicismo e manierismo: Il teatro tragico del Cinquecento.* Florence: Olschki.

———. 2007a. "La diegesi breve della prosa." In Da Pozzo 2007a, 1699–1718.

———. 2007b. "Il teatro." In Da Pozzo 2007a, 1719–62.

Arrullani, Vittorio Amedeo. 1911. "Il sentimento e la poesia della famiglia nel Borgogni." In *Nuovi studi intorno a Gherardo Borgogni,* 3–21. Alba: Sansoldi.

Avalle, Carlo. 1853–55. *Storia di Alessandria dall'origine ai nostri giorni*. 4 vols. Turin: Falletti.
Avellini, Luisa. 2004. "Proposte per il Petrarca all'*Indice* negli anni del papato Boncompagni." *Italianistica* 23 (2): 133–41.
Bà, Paolo. 2001. "Francesca Turina sposa Giulio I Bufalini." *Pagine altotiberine* 5 (14): 113–30.
———. 2005. "Le *Rime spirituali* di Francesca Turina Bufalini." *Letteratura italiana antica* 6:147–52.
———. 2006. "Gattara e il Marecchia nella poesia di Francesca Turina Bufalini." *Studi montefeltrani* 27:35–50.
———. 2007. "Il mondo di Francesca Turina Bufalini e le sue *Rime spirituali*." *Letteratura italiana antica* 8:485–94.
———. 2008. "'Ritratti' in versi rivolti a Francesca Turina Bufalini: 'Autoritratti' e composizioni burlesche della poetessa." *Pagine altotiberine* 12 (36): 157–69.
———. 2009. "Testimonianza poetica di Francesca Turrini Bufalini." *Campi immaginabili* 40–41:85–125.
———. 2010. "Capoleone Ghelfucci e le 'amorose poesie' a Francesca Turrini Bufalini." *Pagine altotiberine* 19 (40): 117–56.
Bà, Paolo, and Giuseppe Milani. 1998. *I Bufalini di San Giustino: Origine e ascesa di una casata. Francesca Turina Bufalini, poetessa, 1553–1641: Una donna che ha dato lustro a una famiglia*. San Giustino: Comune di San Giustino.
Baernstein, P. Renée. 2002. *A Convent Tale: A Century of Sisterhood in Spanish Milan*. London: Routledge.
———. 2005. "Vita pubblica, vita familiare, e memoria storica nel monastero di San Paolo a Milano." In Pomata and Zarri 2005, 297–311.
Baffetti, Giovanni. 2007. "Poesia e poetica sacra nel circolo barberiniano." In Delcorno and Doglio 2007, 187–204.
Baldacci, Luigi, ed. 1968. *Lirici del Cinquecento*. 2nd ed. Milan: Longanesi.
Baldassari, Guido. 2005. "Sulla *Croce racquistata*." In Arbizzoni, Faini, and Mattioli 2005, 63–94.
Balsano, Maria Antonella. 1988. Introduction to Giandomenico Martoretta, *Il secondo libro di madrigali cromatici a quattro voci 1552*, edited by Maria Antonella Balsano, i–xxii. Florence: Olschki.
Bandini Buti, Maria. 1946. *Donne d'Italia: Poetesse e scrittrici*. 2 vols. Rome: Tosi.
Bandursky, Karolina. 2009. "The *Rappresentazione di Santa Cecilia vergine e martire*, Written by Suor Cherubina Venturelli." In Weaver 2009, 37–51.
Baratto, Mario. 1984. *Realtà e stile nel "Decameron*." Rome: Editori Riuniti.
Barbi, Michele. 1897. *Notizia della vita e delle opere di Francesco Bracciolini*. Florence: G. C. Sansoni.
Barish, Jonas. 1994. "The Problem of Closet Drama in the Italian Renaissance." *Italica* 71 (1): 4–30.
Baskins, Cristelle L. 1993. "Typology, Sexuality, and the Renaissance Esther." In *Sex-

uality and Gender in Early Modern Europe: Institutions, Texts, Images, edited by James Grantham Turner, 31–54. Cambridge: Cambridge University Press.

Bastogi, Nadia. 2008. "L'iconografia celebrativa della sposa negli ingressi trionfali delle principesse straniere a Firenze." In Calvi and Spinelli 2008, 2:591–613.

Bateman, J. Chimène. 2007. "Amazonian Knots: Gender, Genre, and Ariosto's Female Warriors." MLN 122 (1): 1–23.

Battistini, Andrea. 1997. "La cultura del Barocco." In Storia della letteratura italiana, edited by Enrico Malato, vol. 5, La fine del Cinquecento e il Seicento, 463–559. Rome: Salerno.

———. 2000. Il barocco: Cultura, miti, immagini. Rome: Salerno.

Beer, Marina. 1999. "Poemi cavallereschi, poemi epici e poemi eroici negli anni di elaborazione della Gerusalemme liberata (1559–1581): Gli orizzonti della scrittura." In Venturi 1999, 1:55–65.

Belloni, Antonio. 1893. Gli epigoni della "Gerusalemme liberata," con un'appendice bibliografica. Padua: Angelo Draghi.

———. 1912. Il poem epico e mitologico. Milan: Francesco Vallardi.

Benedetti, Laura. 1996. La sconfitta di Diana: Un percorso per la "Gerusalemme liberata." Ravenna: Longo.

———. 1999. "Virtù feminile o virtù donnesca? Torquato Tasso, Lucrezia Marinella ed una polemica rinascimentale." In Venturi 1999, 2:449–56.

———. 2005. "Saintes et guerrières: L'héroisme féminin dans l'oeuvre de Lucrezia Marinella." In Les femmes et l'écriture: L'amour profane et l'amour sacré, edited by Claude Cazalé Bérard, 93–109. Paris: Presses Universitaires de Paris X.

———. 2008. "Le Essortationi di Lucrezia Marinella: L'ultimo messaggio di una misteriosa veneziana." Italica 85 (4): 381–95.

Benson, Pamela J. 1992. The Invention of the Renaissance Woman: The Challenge of Female Independence in the Literature and Thought of Italy and England. Philadelphia: Penn State University Press.

———. 1999. "To Play the Man: Aemilia Lanyer and the Acquisition of Patronage." In Opening the Borders: Inclusivity in Early Modern Europe; Essays in Honor of James V. Mirollo, 243–64. Newark: University of Delaware Press.

Benson, Pamela J., and Victoria Kirkham, eds. 2005. Strong Voices, Weak History: Early Women Writers and Canons in England, France, and Italy. Ann Arbor: University of Michigan Press.

Berengo, Marino. 1965. Nobili e mercanti nella Lucca del Cinquecento. Turin: Einaudi.

Bergel, Lienhard. 1965. "The Rise of Cinquecento Tragedy." Renaissance Drama 8:197–217.

Bertana, Emilio. 1904. La tragedia. Milan: Francesco Vallardi.

Bertini, Fabio. 2008. "Havere a la giustitia sodisfatto": Tragedie giustiziarie di Giovan Battista Giraldi Cinzio nel ventennio conciliare. Florence: Società Editrice Fiorentina.

Bertolotti, Antonio. 1887. "Muzio Manfredi e Passi Giuseppe, letterati in relazione col Duca di Mantova." Il Buonarroti, 3rd ser., 3:118–37, 155–69, 181–86.

Bertoni, Giulio. 1925. "Intorno a tre letterati cinquecenteschi modenesi." *Giornale storico della letteratura italiana* 85:376–80.
Besomi, Ottavio. 1969. *Ricerche intorno alla "Lira" di G. B. Marino*. Padua: Antenore.
Bestor, Janet Fair. 2003. "Titian's Portrait of Laura Eustochia: The Decorum of Female Beauty and the Motif of the Black Page." *Renaissance Studies* 17 (4): 628–73.
Bettella, Patrizia. 2005. *The Ugly Woman: Transgressive Aesthetic Models in Italian Poetry from the Middle Ages to the Baroque*. Toronto: University of Toronto Press.
Biblioteca Comunale di Treviso. 2000. *Catalogo dei manoscritti (nn. 2901–3105)*. Edited by Emilio Lippi. Entries by Giorgio Barbirato, Monica Donaggio, Raffaella Stauble, and Piermaria Vescovo. Treviso: Comune di Treviso.
Bilinkoff, Jodi. 2005. *Related Lives: Confessors and Their Female Penitents, 1450–1750*. Ithaca, NY: Cornell University Press.
Binotto, Roberto. 1996. *Personaggi illustri della Marca Trevigiana: Dizionario biobibliografico dalle origini al 1996*. Treviso: Fondazione Cassamarca & Cassamarca.
Bisaha, Nancy. 2004. *Creating East and West: Renaissance Humanists and the Ottoman Turks*. Philadelphia: University of Pennsylvania Press.
Bistué, Belén, and Deborah Uman. 2007. "Translation as Collaborative Authorship: Margaret Tyler's *The Mirrour of Princely Deedes and Knighthood*." *Comparative Literature Studies* 44 (3): 298–323.
Boccato, Carla. 1973. "Un episodio della vita di Sara Copio Sullam: Il *Manifesto sull'immortalità dell'anima*." *La rassegna mensile di Israel* 39:633–46.
———. 1987. "Sara Copio Sullam: La poetessa del Ghetto di Venezia; Episodi della sua vita in un manoscritto del secolo XVII." *Italia* 6 (1–2): 104–218.
Bohn, Barbara. 2004. "Female Self-Portraiture in Early Modern Bologna." *Renaissance Studies* 18 (2): 239–86.
Boillet, Élise. 2007. *L'Arétin et la Bible*. Geneva: Droz.
Bollea, Luigi Cesare. 1906. "Antonio Maria Spelta e la sua *Storia della guerra per la successione di Monferrato (1613–1618)*." *Bollettino della Società Pavese di Storia Patria* 93:409–52.
Borsetto, Luciana. 2005. Introduction to Valvasone 2005.
Bosi, Kathryn. 2003. "Accolade for an Actress: On Some Literary and Musical Tributes for Isabella Andreini." *Recercare* 15:73–117.
———. 2005. "Leone Tolosa and *Martel d'amore*: A *balletto della duchessa* Discovered." *Recercare* 17:5–70.
Bossier, Philiep. 2007. "'Non si è fermato il desiderio che nacque in me': Maddalena Campiglia e la ribellione alle convenzioni poetiche." In Corsaro, Hendrix, and Procaccioli 2007, 55–63.
Bowers, Jane. 1986. "The Emergence of Women Composers in Italy, 1566–1700." In Bowers and Tick 1986, 116–67.
Bowers, Jane, and Judith Tick, eds. 1986. *Women Making Music: The Western Art Tradition, 1150–1950*. Urbana: University of Illinois Press.
Bragantini, Renzo. 2008. Introduction to [L. Gonzaga] 2008, xiii–xvii.

Brand, C. P., and Lino Pertile, eds. 1999. *Cambridge History of Italian Literature.* Cambridge: Cambridge University Press.
Breckenridge, James. D. 1957. "'Et prima vidit': The Iconography of the Appearance of Christ to His Mother." *Art Bulletin* 39 (1): 9–32.
Brundin, Abigail. 2001. "Vittoria Colonna and the Virgin Mary." *Modern Language Review* 96:61–81.
———. 2008. *Vittoria Colonna and the Spiritual Poetics of the Italian Reformation.* Aldershot, UK: Ashgate.
Bruscagli, Riccardo. 2007. "La preponderanza petrarchesca." In Da Pozzo 2007a, 1559–1615.
Bryce, Judith. 1992. "Gender and Myth in the *Orlando Furioso.*" *Italian Studies* 47:41–50.
Bullock, Alan, and Gabriella Palange. 1980. "Per una edizione critica delle opere di Chiara Matraini." In *Studi in onore di Raffaele Spongano,* 235–62. Bologna: Massimilano Boni.
Burgess–Van Aken, Barbara. 2007. "Barbara Torelli's *Partenia:* A Bilingual Critical Edition." PhD diss., Case Western Reserve University.
Burke, Peter. 2000. "Early Modern Venice as a Center of Information and Communication." In Martin and Romano 2000, 389–419.
Cabani, Maria Cristina. 1995. *Gli amici amanti: Coppie eroiche e sortite notturne nell'epica italiana.* Naples: Liguori.
Callegari, Danielle, and Shannon McHugh. 2011. "'Se fossimo tante meretrici': The Rhetoric of Resistance in Diodata Malvasia's 1570s Convent Narrative." *Italian Studies* 65 (3): 21–39.
Callen King, Katherine. 1987. *Achilles: Paradigms of the War Hero from Homer to the Middle Ages.* Berkeley and Los Angeles: University of California Press.
Calore, Marina. 1985. "Muzio Manfredi tra polemiche teatrali e crisi del mecenatismo." *Studi romagnoli* 36:27–54.
Calvi, Giulia, and Riccardo Spinelli, eds. 2008. *Le donne Medici nel sistema europeo delle corti: XVI–XVIII secolo.* 2 vols. Florence: Edizioni Polistampa.
Cambon, Glauco. 1985. *Michelangelo's Poetry: Fury of Form.* Princeton, NJ: Princeton University Press.
Campbell, Julie D. 1997. "*Love's Victory* and *La Mirtilla* in the Canon of Renaissance Tragicomedy: An Examination of Salon and Social Debates." *Women's Writing* 4 (1): 103–25.
———. 2002. Introduction to I. Andreini 2002, xi–xxvii.
Campbell, Lorne. 1998. *The Fifteenth-Century Netherlandish Schools.* London: National Gallery Publications.
Cappello Passarelli, Egloge. 1908. "Una patrizia veneta: Donna Laura Beatrice Cappello." *La rassegna nazionale* 30 (163): 447–59.
Capucci, Martino. 1983. "Coreglia, Isabetta." In *Dizionario biografico degli italiani,* 29:41–42.

Carinci, Eleonora. 2002. "Una lettera autografa inedita di Moderata Fonte (al granduca di Toscana Francesco I)." *Critica del testo* 5 (3): 1–11.

———. 2007. "Canone, *gender*, genere letterario: *Il merito delle donne* di Moderata Fonte." In Ronchetti and Sapegno 2007, 93–100.

———. 2009. "Lives of the Virgin Mary by Women Writers in Post-Tridentine Italy." PhD thesis, University of Cambridge.

Carminati, Clizia. 2008. *Giovan Battista Marino tra Inquisizione e censura*. Padua: Antenore.

Carpanè, Lorenzo. 2001–2. "Altre testimonianze della *Liberata*." *Studi tassiani* 49–50:297–305.

———. 2005. "La *Giuditta trionfante* di Giacinto Branchi." In Arbizzoni, Faini, and Mattioli 2005, 211–48.

———. 2006. *Da Giuditta a Giuditta: L'epopea dell'eroina sacra nel Barocco*. Alessandria: Edizioni dell'Orso.

Carpani, Roberto, and Annamaria Cascetta, eds. 1995. *La scena della gloria: Drammaturgia e spettacolo a Milano in età spagnola*. Milan: Vita e Pensiero.

Carter, Tim. 1999. "Finding a Voice: Vittoria Archilei and the Florentine 'New Music.'" In *Feminism and Renaissance Studies*, edited by Lorna Hutson, 450–67. Oxford: Oxford University Press.

Cascetta, Annamaria. 1995. "La 'spiritual tragedia' e l' 'azione devota': Gli ambienti e la forma." In Carpani and Casetta 1995, 116–218.

Cataudella, Michele. 2001. "Le *Sette stanze sulla vita di San Benedetto* di T. Tasso." *Esperienze letterarie* 26:41–50.

Cavallo, Jo Ann. 1999. "Armida: La funzione della donna-maga nell'epica tassiana." In Venturi 1999, 1:99–114.

Cavarocchi Arbib, Marina. 1999. "Rivisitando la biblica Ester: Implicazioni sottese all'immagine femminile ebraica nell'Italia del Seicento." In *Le donne delle minoranze: Le ebree e le protestanti d'Italia*, edited by Claire Honess and Verina R. Jones, 143–57. Turin: Claudiana.

Cave, Terence C. 1969. *Devotional Poetry in France, c. 1570–1613*. Cambridge: Cambridge University Press.

Cecchi, Paolo. 2005. "La fortuna musicale della 'canzone alla Vergine' petrarchesca e il primo madrigale spirituale." In *Petrarca in musica*, edited by Andrea Chegai and Cecilia Luzzi, 245–91. Lucca: Libreria Musicale Italiana.

Cerrón Puga, Maria Luisa. 2003. "Censure incrociate fra Italia e Spagna: Il caso Petrarca (1559–1747)." *Critica del testo* 6 (1): 221–56.

Cessi, Camillo. 1897. *Quattro sonetti di Issicratea Monte rodigiana*. Padua: Tipografia all'Università—Fratelli Gallina.

Chang, Leah L. 2009. *Into Print: The Production of Female Authorship in Early Modern France*. Newark: University of Delaware Press.

Chater, James. 1999. "'Such Sweet Sorrow': The *Dialogo di partenza* in the Italian Madrigal." *Early Music* 27 (4): 577–99.

Chemello, Adriana. 1983. "La donna, il modello, l'immaginario: Moderata Fonte e Lucrezia Marinella." In *Nel cerchio della luna: Figure di donna in alcuni testi del XVI secolo*, edited by Marina Zancan, 95–170. Venice: Marsilio.

———. 1988. "Gioco e dissimulazione in Moderata Fonte." In Fonte 1988, ix–lxiii.

———. 2000. "The Rhetoric of Eulogy in Lucrezia Marinella's *La nobiltà et l'eccellenza delle donne*." In Panizza 2000, 463–77.

———. 2003. "'Donne a poetar esperte': La 'rimatrice dimessa' Maddalena Campiglia." *Versants*, n.s., 46:65–101.

Cherchi, Paolo. 1998. *Polimatia di riuso: Mezzo secolo di plagio (1539–89)*. Rome: Bulzoni.

———. 2004. "G. F. Astolfi: Un volgarizzatore da ricordare." *Studi secenteschi* 45:3–27.

Chiabò, Maria, and Federico Doglio, eds. 1992. *Sviluppi della drammaturgia pastorale nell'Europa del Cinque-Seicento*. Viterbo: Centro Studi sul Teatro Medioevale e Rinascimentale.

———, eds. 1994. *I gesuiti e i primordi del teatro barocco in Europa*. Viterbo: Centro Studi sul Teatro Medioevale e Rinascimentale.

Chiarla, Myriam. 2009. "La modernità degli affetti nella poesia di Angelo Grillo." In *Moderno e modernità: La letteratura italiana*, edited by Clizia Gurreri, Angela Maria Jacopino, and Amedeo Quondam. Rome: Università di Roma La Sapienza, Dipartimento d'Italianistica e Spettacolo.

Chiesa, Mario. 2002. "Poemi biblici fra Quattrocento e Cinquecento." *Giornale storico della letteratura italiana* 179 (586): 161–92.

———. 2005. "Il poema sacro secentesco: Uno sguardo ai frontespizi." In Arbizzoni, Faini, and Mattioli 2005, 285–309.

Chisi, Giovanni. 1986a. "A Conegliano le *Rime* di Luchesia Sbarra." *Il quindicinale* 5 (15): 2.

———. 1986b. "Luchesia Sbarra, poetessa gentile." *Il quindicinale* 5 (14): 3.

Chojnacka, Monica. 1998. "Women, Charity and Community in Early Modern Venice: The Casa delle Zitelle." *Renaissance Quarterly* 51 (1): 68–91.

Ciletti, Elena. 2010. "Judith Imagery as Catholic Orthodoxy in Counter-Reformation Italy". In *The Sword of Judith: Judith Studies across the Disciplines*, edited by Kevin R. Brine, Elena Ciletti, and Henricke Lähnemann, 345–68. Cambridge: Open Book.

Cipriani, Giovanni. 1980. *Il mito etrusco nel rinascimento fiorentino*. Florence: Olschki.

Clubb, Louise George. 1964. "The *Virgin Martyr* and the *tragedia sacra*." *Renaissance Drama* 7:103–26.

———. 1989. *Italian Drama in Shakespeare's Time*. New Haven, CT: Yale University Press.

Cohen, Elizabeth S. 2007. "Evolving the History of Women in Early Modern Italy: Subordination and Agency." In *Spain in Italy: Politics, Society, and Religion, 1500–1700*, edited by Thomas James Dandelet and John A. Marino, 325–54. Leiden: Brill.

Cohn, Samuel K., Jr. 1996. *Women in the Streets: Essays on Sex and Power in Renaissance Italy.* Baltimore: Johns Hopkins University Press.

Coller, Alexandra. 2007. "Ladies and Courtesans in Late Sixteenth-Century *Commedia Grave*: Vernacular Antecedents of Early Opera's *Prime Donne.*" *Italian Studies* 62 (1): 27–44.

Collina, Beatrice. 1989. "Moderata Fonte e *Il merito delle donne.*" *Annali d'italianistica* 7:142–64.

Colombo, Angelo. 1992. "Il principe celebrato: Autografi poetici di Tomaso Stigliani e Margherita Sarrocchi." *Philo-logica: Rassegna di analisi linguistica e di ironia culturale* 1 (1): 7–29.

Conti Odorisio, Ginevra. 1979. *Donna e società nel Seicento: Lucrezia Marinelli e Arcangela Tarabotti.* Introduction by Ida Magli. Rome: Bulzoni.

Corbucci, Vittorio. 1901. *Una poetessa umbra: Francesca Turina Bufalini, contessa di Stupinigi [1544–1641].* Città di Castello: S. Lapi.

Corsaro, Antonio, Harald Hendrix, and Paolo Procaccioli, eds. 2007. *Autorità, modelli, e antimodelli nella cultura artistica e letteraria tra riforma e antiriforma.* Rome: Vecchiarelli.

Cortesi, Mariarosa. 2002. "Memorie di S. Grata: Per un cammino verso la santità." In *Il legendario di Santa Grata tra scrittura agiografica e arte*, by Giordana Maria Canova and Mariarosa Cortesi, 3–73. Bergamo: Litostampa.

Cosentino, Paola. 2004. "L'ambiguo potere della *virago*: Giuditta fra trattatistica e tragedia nel Cinquecento italiano." In *Rome donne libri tra medioevo e Rinascimento: In ricordo di Pino Lombardi*, 385–407. Rome: Roma nel Rinascimento.

———. 2007. " 'Belle, caste e magnanime': Le eroine bibliche di Federico Della Valle." In *Il mito nel testo: Gli antichi e la Bibbia nella letteratura italiana*, edited by Katia Cappellini and Lorenzo Geri, 63–77. Rome: Bulzoni.

Costa-Zalessow, Natalia. 2009. Introduction to Turina 2009, 7–36.

Cowan, Alexander. 2007. *Marriage, Manners, and Mobility in Early Modern Venice.* Aldershot, UK: Ashgate.

Cox, Virginia. 1992. *The Renaissance Dialogue: Literary Dialogue in its Social and Political Contexts, Castiglione to Galileo.* Cambridge: Cambridge University Press.

———. 1995. "The Single Self: Feminist Thought and the Marriage Market in Early Modern Venice." *Renaissance Quarterly* 48 (3): 513–81.

———. 1997a. "Moderata Fonte and *The Worth of Women.*" In Fonte 1997, 1–23.

———. 1997b. "Women as Readers and Writers of Chivalric Literature." In *Sguardi sull'Italia: Miscellanea dedicata a Francesco Villari*, edited by Gino Bedani et al., 134–45. Leeds, UK: Society for Italian Studies.

———. 2000a. "Fiction, 1560–1650." In Panizza and Wood 2000, 52–64.

———. 2000b. "Seen but Not Heard: The Role of Women Speakers in Cinquecento Literary Dialogue." In Panizza 2000, 385–400.

———. 2005a. "Sixteenth-Century Women Petrarchists and the Legacy of Laura." *Journal of Medieval and Early Modern Studies* 35 (3): 583–606.

———. 2005b. "Women Writers and the Canon in Sixteenth-Century Italy: The Case of Vittoria Colonna." In Benson and Kirkham 2005, 14–31.
———. 2008. *Women's Writing in Italy, 1400–1650*. Baltimore: Johns Hopkins University Press.
———. 2009. "Gender and Eloquence in Ercole de' Roberti's *Portia and Brutus*." *Renaissance Quarterly* 62 (1): 61–101.
Cox, Virginia, and Lisa Sampson. 2004. Introduction to Campiglia 2004, 1–35.
Cox-Rearick, Janet. 1993. *Bronzino's Chapel of Eleonora in the Palazzo Vecchio*. Berkeley and Los Angeles: University of California Press.
Croce, Benedetto. 1967. *Storia dell'età barocca in Italia*. 5th ed. Bari: Laterza.
———. 2003. *Nuovi saggi sulla letteratura italiana del Seicento*. Reprint of 2nd ed., edited by Angelo Fabrizi. 2 vols. Naples: Bibliopolis.
Croce, Franco. 2002. "Introduzione al barocco." In F. Croce et al. 2002, 25–40.
Croce, Franco, et al., eds. 2002. *I capricci di Proteo: Percorsi e linguaggi del Barocco*. Rome: Salerno.
Crovato, Giambattista. 1975. *La drammatica a Vicenza nel Cinquecento*. Sala Bolognese: Arnaldo Forni. First published 1894.
Cusick, Suzanne G. 2005. "Epilogue: Francesca among Women, a '600 Gynecentric View." In *Musical Voices of Early Modern Women: Many-Headed Melodies*, edited by Thomasin LaMay, 425–43. Aldershot, UK: Ashgate.
———. 2009. *Francesca Caccini at the Medici Court: Music and the Circulation of Power*. Chicago: University of Chicago Press.
Daenens, Francine. 1983. "Superiore perché inferiore: Il paradosso della superiorità della donna in alcuni trattati italiani del Cinquecento." In *Trasgressione tragica e norma domestica: Esemplari di tipologie femminili dalla letteratura europea*, edited by Vanna Gentili, 11–50. Rome: Edizioni di Storia e Letteratura.
Da Pozzo, Giovanni, ed. 2007a. *La letteratura tra l'eroico e il quotidiano: La nuova religione dell'utopia e della scienza (1573–1600)*. Pt. 3 of *Storia letteraria d'Italia—Il Cinquecento*, edited by Giovanni Da Pozzo. Padua: Piccin-Nuova Libraria.
———. 2007b. "Lo squilibrio armonico: Torquato Tasso." In Da Pozzo 2007a, 1867–2008.
Datta, Satya. 2003. *Women and Men in Early Modern Venice*. Aldershot, UK: Ashgate.
Dean, Trevor, and K. J. P. Lowe, eds. 1998. *Marriage in Italy, 1300–1650*. Cambridge: Cambridge University Press.
De Boer, Wietse. 2001. *The Conquest of the Soul: Confession, Discipline, and Public Order in Counter-Reformation Milan*. Brill: Leiden.
DeCoste, Marie-Michelle. 2004. "Knots of Desire: Female Homoeroticism in *Orlando Furioso*." In *Queer Italia: Same-Sex Desire in Italian Literature and Film*, edited by Gary P. Cestaro, 55–69. New York: Palgrave Macmillan.
———. 2009. *Hopeless Love: Boiardo, Ariosto, and Narratives of Queer Female Desire*. Toronto: University of Toronto Press.
Decroisette, Françoise. 2001. "La première 'divine': Isabella Andreini ou l'invention

d'un rôle." In *Au théâtre, au cinéma, au féminin*, edited by Mireille Calle-Gruber and Hélène Cixous, 193–215. Paris: L'Harmattan.

———. 2002. "Satyres au feminine dans la pastorale italienne de la fin du XVIe siècle." In *La campagna e la città: Letteratura e ideologia nel Rinascimento; Scritti in onore di Michel Plaisance*, edited by Giuditta Isotti Rosowsky, 149–82. Florence: Franco Cesati.

De Frede, Carlo. 1999. *I libri di un letterato calabrese del Cinquecento: Sertorio Quattromani (1541–1603)*. Naples: Accademia Pontaniana.

Delcorno, Carlo, and Maria Luisa Doglio, eds. 2005. *Rime sacre dal Petrarca al Tasso*. Bologna: Il Mulino.

———, eds. 2007. *Rime sacre tra Cinquecento e Seicento*. Bologna: Il Mulino.

D'Elia, Una Roman. 2006. "Drawing Christ's Blood: Michelangelo, Vittoria Colonna and the Aesthetics of Reform." *Renaissance Quarterly* 59 (1): 90–129.

De Miranda, Girolamo. 2000. *Una quiete oziosa: Forma e pratiche dell'Accademia napoletana degli Oziosi, 1611–1645*. Naples: Fridericiana Editrice Universitaria.

Denarosi, Laura. 1997. "Il principe e il letterato: Due carteggi inediti di Muzio Manfredi." *Studi italiani* 17:151–76.

———. 2003. *L'Accademia degli Innominati di Parma: Teorie letterarie e progetti di scrittura (1574–1608)*. Florence: Società Editrice Fiorentina.

Derossi, Onorato. 1790. *Scrittori piemontesi savoiardi nizzardi registrati nei cataloghi del vescovo Francesco Agostino della Chiesa e del monaco Andrea Rossotto*. Turin: Stamperia Reale.

De Vit, Vincenzo. 1883. "Dell'illustre donzella Issicratea Monti." In *Opuscoli letterari editi e inediti*, 7–25. Milan: Borniardi-Pogliani.

Di Benedetto, Arnaldo. 1999. "L'*Aminta* e la pastorale cinquecentesca in Italia." In Venturi 1999, 3:1121–49.

Di Carpegna Falconieri, Tommaso, ed. 2000. *Terra e memoria: I libri di famiglia dei conti di Carpegna-Scavolino (secoli XVI–XVII)*. Introduction by Armando Petrucci. San Leo: Società di Studi Storici per il Montefeltro.

Dieffendorf, Barbara B. 2004. *From Penitence to Charity: Pious Women and the Catholic Reformation in Paris*. Oxford: Oxford University Press.

Di Maria, Salvatore. 2002. *The Italian Tragedy in the Renaissance: Cultural Realities and Theatrical Innovation*. Lewisburg, PA: Bucknell University Press; London: Associated University Presses.

Dionisotti, Carlo. 1999. *Geografia e storia della letteratura italiana*. Turin: Einaudi.

Ditchfield, Simon. 1999. "Of Dancing Cardinals and Mestizo Madonnas: Reconfiguring the History of Roman Catholicism in the Early Modern Period." *Journal of Early Modern History* 8:386–408.

Dizionario biografico degli italiani. 1960–. 73 vols. to date. Rome: Istituto dell'Enciclopedia Italiana.

Doglio, Maria Luisa. 1983. "La letteratura ufficiale e l'oratoria celebrativa." In *Storia della cultura veneta*, edited by Girolamo Arnaldi and Manlio Pastore Stocchi, vol. 4, *Il Seicento*, pt. 1: 163–87. Vicenza: Neri Pozza.

———. 1989. "Immagini di San Francesco nella letteratura del Seicento." *Rivista di storia e letteratura religiosa* 25:423–43.
———. 1995. Introduction to I. Andreini 1995, 5–16.
———. 2007a. "Il gusto encomiastico e didascalico." In Da Pozzo 2007a, 1616–52.
———. 2007b. Foreword to Delcorno and Doglio 2007, 7–11.
Dolan, Frances E. 1999. *Whores of Babylon: Catholicism, Gender, and Seventeenth-Century Print Culture*. Ithaca, NY: Cornell University Press.
Dolla, Vincenzo. 1987. "Scipione de' Monti, lo 'Scanderbego,' e la celebrazione 'Castriota.'" In *Rinascimento meridionale e altri studi in onore di Mario Santoro*, edited by Maria Cristina Cafisse et al., 49–70. Naples: Società Editrice Napoletana.
Dunn, Marilyn R. 1994. "Piety and Patronage in Seicento Rome: Two Noblewomen and Their Convents." *Art Bulletin* 76 (4): 644–63.
———. 1997. "Spiritual Philanthropists: Women as Convent Patrons in Seicento Rome." In *Women and Art in Early Modern Europe: Patrons, Collectors, and Connoisseurs*, edited by Cynthia Lawrence, 154–88. University Park: Pennsylvania State University Press.
Durante, Elio, and Anna Martellotti. 1989a. *Cronistoria del concerto delle dame principalissime di Margherita Gonzaga d'Este*. 2nd ed. Florence: Studio per Edizioni Scelte.
———. 1989b. *Don Angelo Grillo, O.S.B. alias Livio Celiano, poeta per musica del secolo decimosesto*. Florence: Studio per Edizioni Scelte.
Eisenach, Emlyn. 2004. *Husbands, Wives, and Concubines: Marriage, Family, and the Social Order in Sixteenth-Century Verona*. Kirksville, MI: Truman State University Press.
Eisenbichler, Konrad. 1983. "From *sacra rappresentazione* to *commedia spirituale*: Three 'Prodigal Son' Plays." *Bibliothèque d'humanisme et renaissance* 95 (1): 107–13.
———. 2000. "Da 'commedia erudita' a 'dramma spirituale': Innovazione nel teatro di Giovanni Maria Cecchi a metà Cinquecento." In *Teatro, scena, rappresentazione dal Quattrocento al Settecento*, edited by Paola Andrioli et al., 139–51. Galatina: Congedo.
Elliott, Dyan. 1993. *Spiritual Marriage: Sexual Abstinence in Medieval Wedlock*. Princeton, NJ: Princeton University Press.
Evangelisti, Silvia. 2003. "'We do not Have It, and We do not Want It': Women, Power, and Convent Reform in Florence." *Sixteenth-Century Journal* 34:677–700.
Fabrizio-Costa, Silvia. 1986. "Édification et érotisme: Le personage de Marie Madeleine dans la *Galeria* di F. Pona." In *Au pays d'Éros: Littérature et érotisme en Italie de la Renaissance a l'age baroque*, by the Centre Interuniversitaire de Recherche sur la Renaissance Italienne, 173–203. Paris: Université de la Sorbonne Nouvelle.
Fahy, Conor. 2000. "Women and Italian Cinquecento Literary Academies." In Panizza 2000, 438–52.
Falco, Raphael. 2007. "Marsilio Ficino and Vatic Myth." *MLN* 122 (1): 101–22.
Fantazzi, Charles. 2000. "Introduction: Prelude to the Other Voice in Vives." In *The Education of a Christian Women: A Sixteenth-Century Manual*, by Juan Luis Vives,

edited and translated by Charles Fantazzi, 1–42. Chicago: University of Chicago Press.
Fantazzi, Charles, and Constantinus Matheeussen. 1996. Introduction to Vives 1996, ix–xxviii.
Fantuzzi, Giovanni. 1781–94. *Notizie degli scrittori bolognesi.* 9 vols. Bologna: Stamperia di San Tommaso d'Aquino.
Favaro, Antonio. 1983. *Amici e correspondenti di Galileo.* Edited with an introduction by Paolo Galluzzi. 2nd ed. 3 vols. Florence: Libreria Editrice Salimbeni.
Fenlon, Iain. 2001. "Pastoral Pastimes at the Pitti Palace." In Rosa and Superbi 2004, 2:199–229.
Ferguson, Gary. 1999. "The Feminisation of Devotion: Gabrielle de Coignard, Anne de Marquets, and François de Sales." In *Women's Writing in the French Renaissance,* edited by Philip Ford and Gillian Jondorf, 186–206. Cambridge: Cambridge French Colloquia.
Ferretti, Francesco. 2005. "Fuggendo Saturno: Note sulla canzone *Alma inferma e dolente* di Torquato Tasso." In Delcorno and Doglio 2005, 157–204.
———. 2007. "Gli esordi dello 'stile pietoso' di Angelo Grillo." In Delcorno and Doglio 2007, 107–39.
Ferroni, Giulio, and Amedeo Quondam. 1973. *La locuzione artificiosa: Teoria ed esperienza della lirica a Napoli nell'età del Manierismo.* Rome: Bulzoni.
Finucci, Valeria. 1992. *The Lady Vanishes: Subjectivity and Representation in Castiglione and Ariosto.* Stanford, CA: Stanford University Press.
———. 1995. "Moderata Fonte e il romanzo cavalleresco al femminile." In Fonte 1995, ix–xxxix.
———. 2010. "Valeria Miani and the Tragic Genre." In Miani 2010, 1–53.
Firpo, Luigi. 1960. *Il più antico imitatore del Boccalini: Girolamo Briani.* Florence: Edizioni Sansoni Antiquariato.
Fisher, Alexander J. 2007. "'Per mia particolare devotione': Orlando di Lasso's *Lagrime di San Pietro* and Catholic Spirituality in Counter-Reformation Munich." *Journal of the Royal Musical Association* 132 (2): 167–220.
Föcking, Marc. 1994. Rime sacre *und die Genese des barocken Stils: Untersuchungen zur Stilgeschichte geistlicher Lyrik in Italien, 1536–1614.* Stuttgart: Franz Steiner.
Foltran, Daniela. 2004. "Calliope ed Erato: Stile e struttura nella *Babilonia distrutta* di Scipione Errico." *Schifanoia* 26–27:39–99.
———. 2005. *Per un ciclo tassiano: Imitazione, invenzione e "correzione" in quattro proposte epiche fra Cinque e Seicento.* Alessandria: Edizioni dell'Orso.
Forciroli, Francesco. 2007. *Vite dei modenesi illustri.* Edited by Sonia Cavicchioli. Transcribed by Giorgia Mancini. Modena: Aedes Muratoriana.
Forni, Giorgio. 2005. "Vittoria Colonna, la *canzone alla Vergine,* e la poesia spirituale." In Delcorno and Doglio 2005, 63–94.
———. 2007. "Florilegi fiorentini del primo Seicento in lode di San Francesco." In Delcorno and Doglio 2007, 141–85.

Fortis, Umberto. 2003. La "bella ebrea": Sara Copio Sullam, poetessa nel ghetto di Venezia del '600. Turin: Silvio Zamorani.
Fox, Gwyn. 2008. Subtle Subversions: Reading Golden Age Sonnets by Iberian Women. Washington, DC: Catholic University of America Press.
Fragnito, Gigliola. 1997. La bibbia al rogo: La censura ecclesiastica e i volgarizzameni della Scrittura (1471–1605). Bologna: Il Mulino.
———. 2005. Proibito capire: La Chiesa e il volgare nella prima età moderna. Bologna: Il Mulino.
Freccero, John. 1986. Dante: The Poetics of Conversion. Edited by Rachel Jacoff. Cambridge, MA: Harvard University Press.
Freeman, Daniel E. 1996. "'La guerriera amante': Representations of Amazons and Warrior Queens in Venetian Baroque Opera." Musical Quarterly 80 (3): 431–60.
Fulco, Giorgio. 1997. "Giovan Battista Marino." In Storia della letteratura italiana, edited by Enrico Malato, vol. 5, La fine del Cinquecento e il Seicento, 597–652. Rome: Salerno.
Gagliardi, Donatella. 2003. "'Quid puellae cum armis?' Una aproximación a Doña Beatriz Bernal y a su Cristalián de España." PhD diss., Universitat Autonoma de Barcelona. http://www.tesienxarxa.net (accessed 2 May 2010).
———. 2005. "Femina composuit: Ficciones caballerescas de autoría femenina, del Palmerín de Olivia al Cristalián de Espana." Rivista di filologia e letteratura ispaniche 8:33–58.
Gamurrini, G. F. 1909. "Delle amorose poesie di Capoleone Ghelfucci." Bollettino della Reale Deputazione di Storia Patria per l'Umbria 15:321–33.
Garraffo, Ornella. 1985. "Il satiro nella pastorale ferrarese del Cinquecento." Italianistica 14 (2): 185–201.
Garrard, Mary D. 1989. Artemisia Gentileschi: The Image of the Female Hero in Italian Baroque Art. Princeton, NJ: Princeton University Press.
———. 1994. "Here's Looking at Me: Sofonisba Anguissola and the Problem of the Woman Artist." Renaissance Quarterly 47 (3): 556–622.
Gerbino, Giuseppe. 2004. "The Madrigal and Its Outcasts: Marenzio, Giovannelli, and the Revival of Sannazaro's Arcadia." Journal of Musicology 21 (1): 3–45.
———. 2009. Music and the Myth of Arcadia in Renaissance Italy. Cambridge: Cambridge University Press.
Gherardi, Sergio. 2008. Gli Angaran del Sole: Violenza ed eresia nella Vicenza del '500. Vicenza: La Serenissima.
———. 2009. Maddalena Campiglia nei testamenti del padre. Vicenza: La Serenissima.
Giachino, Luisella. 2001. "Dall'effimero teatrale alla quête dell'immortalità, le Rime di Isabella Andreini." Giornale storico della letteratura italiana 178 (584): 530–53.
Giangamboni, Laura, and Enrico Mercati. 2001. L'archivio e la biblioteca della famiglia Bufalini di San Giustino. Città di Castello: Soprintendenza Archivistica per l'Umbria.
Giannetti, Laura. 2009. Lelia's Kiss: Imagining Gender, Sex, and Marriage in Italian Renaissance Comedy. Toronto: University of Toronto Press.

Gigante, Claudio. 2007. "'Maria, madre della vittoria': Ferrante Carafa e l'epopea di Lepanto." In Delcorno and Doglio 2007, 19–51.

Gill, Katherine. 1996. "*Scandala:* Controversies Concerning *Clausura* and Women's Religious Communities in Late Medieval Italy." In *Christendom and its Discontents: Exclusion, Persecution, and Rebellion, 1000–1500,* edited by Peter D. Diehl and Scott L. Waugh, 177–203. Cambridge: Cambridge University Press.

Giochi, Filippo M. 1993. "Un femminista *ante litteram* del XVII secolo: Cristoforo Bronzini anconitano." *Atti e memorie della Deputazione di Storia Patria delle Marche* 98:175–97.

Godard, Alain. 1984. "La *Filli di Sciro* de Guidubaldo Bonarelli: Précédents littéraires et nouveaux impératifs idéologiques." In *Réécritures 2: Commentaires, parodies, variations dans la littérature italienne de la Renaissance,* 141–225. Paris: Université de la Sorbonne Nouvelle.

Goffen, Rona. 1986. *Piety and Patronage in Renaissance Venice: Bellini, Titian, and the Franciscans.* New Haven, CT: Yale University Press.

Gough, Melinda J. 2001. "Tasso's Enchantress, Tasso's Captive Woman." *Renaissance Quarterly* 54 (2): 523–52.

Grantham Turner, James. 2003. *Schooling Sex: Libertine Literature and Erotic Education in Italy, France, and England, 1534–1685.* Oxford: Oxford University Press.

Grassi, Giovanni Battista. 1900. *Il primo volume delle rime de gli Accesi di Palermo, studio bibliografo-letterario.* Palermo: A. Giannitrapani.

Graziosi, Elisabetta. 1996. "Scrivere in convento: Devozione, encomio, persuasione nelle rime delle monache fra Cinque e Seicento." In Zarri 1996, 313–31.

———. 2005. "Archipelago sommerso: Le rime delle monache tra obedienza e trasgressione." In Pomata and Zarri 2005, 145–73.

———. 2009. "Due monache domenicane poetesse: una nota, una ignota e molte sullo sfondo." In *Il velo, la penna e la parola: Le domenicane; Storia, istituzioni e scritture,* edited by Gianni Festa and Gabriella Zarri, 163–76. Florence: Nerbini.

Grendler, Paul F. 1977. *The Roman Inquisition and the Venetian Press.* Princeton, NJ: Princeton University Press.

Grubb, James S. 2000. "Elite Citizens." In Martin and Romano 2000, 339–64.

Guardiani, Francesco. 1997. "Dieci pezzi sacri del Marino: Per un'edizione della *Lira* II." In *"Feconde vennero le carte": Studi in onore di Ottavio Besomi,* edited by Tatiana Crivelli, 348–70. Bellinzona: Casagrande.

Guasco, Giovanni. 1711. *Storia letteraria del principio e progresso dell'Accademia di belle lettere in Reggio.* Reggio: Ippolito Vedrotti.

Guida, Patrizia. 2008. *Scrittrici di Puglia: Percorsi storiografici femminili dal XVI al XX secolo.* Galatina: Congedo.

Guidi, Enrico Maria. 2000. Introduction to Battiferra 2000, 5–26.

———. 2005. Introduction to Battiferri 2005, 5–27.

Güntert, Georges. 2007. "Clorinda e la sofferta modernità del Tasso." In *Selvagge e angeliche: Personaggi femminili della tradizione letteraria italiana,* edited by Tatiana Crivelli, 109–23. Leonforte: Insula.

Guthmüller, Bodo. 1999. "Amore e Psiche a Mantova: Sulla *Psiche* di Ercole Udine." *Rassegna europea di letteratura italiana* 14:25–40.
Hacke, Daniela. 2004. *Women, Sex and Marriage in Early Modern Venice*. Aldershot, UK: Ashgate.
Hallett, Christopher H. 2005. *The Roman Nude: Heroic Portrait Statuary, 200 BC–AD 300*. Oxford: Oxford University Press.
Harness, Kelley. 2006. *Echoes of Women's Voices: Music, Art, and Female Patronage in Early Modern Florence*. Chicago: University of Chicago Press.
Harrán, Don. 2009. Introduction to Copio 2009, 1–90.
Haskins, Susan. 1993. *Mary Magdalen: Myth and Metaphor*. London: HarperCollins.
———. 2006. "Vexatious Litigant, or the Case of Lucrezia Marinella?" *Nouvelles de la république des lettres* 1:81–128.
———. 2007. "Vexatious Litigant, or the Case of Lucrezia Marinella? (Part II)." *Nouvelles de la république des lettres* 1–2:203–30.
Hassauer, Friederike, et al., eds. 2008. *Heißer Streit und kalte Ordnung: Epochen der Querelle des femmes zwischen Mittelalter und Gegenwart*. Göttingen: Wallstein.
Heller, Wendy. 2003. *Emblems of Eloquence: Opera and Women's Voices in Seventeenth-Century Venice*. Berkeley and Los Angeles: University of California Press.
Henke, Robert. 2002. *Performance and Literature in the* Commedia dell'Arte. Cambridge: Cambridge University Press.
Herrick, Marvin T. 1965. *Italian Tragedy in the Renaissance*. Urbana: University of Illinois Press.
Heslin, P. J. 2005. *The Transvestite Achilles: Gender and Genre in Statius's "Achilleid."* Cambridge: Cambridge University Press.
Hill, John Walter. 1997. *Roman Monody, Cantata, and Opera from the Circles around Cardinal Montalto*. 2 vols. Oxford: Clarendon.
Hodgkinson, Harry. 1999. *Scanderbeg: From Ottoman Captive to Albanian Hero*. London: Centre for Albanian Studies.
Hudon, William V. 1996. "Religion and Society in Early Modern Italy: New Insights." *American Historical Review* 101–3:783–804.
———. 2004. "A Bridge between Renaissance and Counter-Reformation: Some Sources of Theatine Spirituality." In *A Renaissance of Conflicts: Law, Religion and Culture in Late Medieval, Renaissance and Early Modern History*, edited by Thomas Kuehn and John Marino, 337–63. Toronto: University of Toronto Press.
Hufton, Olwen. 1998. *The Prospect before Her: A History of Women in Western Europe, 1500–1800*. New York: Vintage.
Imbriani, Maria Teresa. 2001. "Intertestualità tra le *Lagrime* di Luigi Tansillo e di Torquato Tasso." *Critica letteraria* 29:15–32.
L'immagine di San Francesco nella Controriforma. 1982. Rome: Edizioni Quasar.
Jacobs, Frederika H. 1997. *Defining the Renaissance Virtuosa: Women Artists and the Language of Art History and Criticism*. Cambridge: Cambridge University Press.
Jaffe, Irma B. 2002. *Shining Eyes, Cruel Fortune: The Lives and Loves of Italian Renaissance Women Poets*. New York: Fordham University Press.

Jannaco, Carmine, and Martino Capucci. 1966. *Il Seicento*. 2nd ed. Milan: Vallardi.
Javitch, Daniel. 1978. "Rescuing Ovid from the Allegorizers." *Comparative Literature* 30 (2): 97–107.
Jones, Ann Rosalind. 1998. "Apostrophes to Cities: Urban Rhetorics in Isabella Whitney and Moderata Fonte." In *Attending to Early Modern Women*, edited by Susan D. Amussen and Adele Seeff, 155–75. Newark: University of Delaware Press; London: Associated University Presses.
Jones, Ann Rosalind, and Margaret Rosenthal. 1998. "Introduction: The Honored Courtesan." In Franco 1998b, 1–22.
Jordan, Constance. 1990. *Renaissance Feminism: Literary Texts and Political Models*. Ithaca, NY: Cornell University Press.
———. 1996. "Renaissance Women Defending Women: Arguments against Patriarchy." In *Italian Women Writers from the Renaissance to the Present: Revising the Canon*, edited with an introduction by Maria Ornella Marotti, 55–67. University Park: Pennsylvania State University Press.
Jung, Ursula. 2008. "Ingenium und Tradition: Moderata Fontes *Il merito delle donne* (1600) und Maria de Zayas' *Desengaños amorosos* (1647)." In Hassauer et al. 2008, 230–55.
Kelso, Ruth. 1997. *Doctrine for the Lady of the Renaissance*. 2nd ed., with a foreword by Katherine M. Rogers. Champaign: University of Illinois Press.
Kirkendale, Warren. 2001. *Emilio de' Cavalieri "Gentiluomo Romano": His Life and Letters, His Role as Superintendent of all the Arts at the Medici Court, and His Musical Compositions*. Florence: Olschki.
Kirkham, Victoria. 2001. "Cosimo and Eleonora in Shepherdland: A lost Eclogue by Laura Battiferra degli Ammanati." In *The Cultural Politics of Duke Cosimo I de' Medici*, edited by Konrad Eisenbichler, 149–75. Aldershot, UK: Ashgate.
———. 2002. "Creative Partners: The Marriage of Laura Battiferra and Bartolomeo Ammanati." *Renaissance Quarterly* 55 (2): 498–558.
———. 2006. Introduction to Battiferra 2006.
Kleinbaum, Abby Wettan. 1983. *The War against the Amazons*. New York: New Press.
Kolsky, Stephen. 1999. "Per la carriera poetica di Moderata Fonte: Alcuni documenti poco conosciuti." *Esperienze letterarie* 24:3–17.
———. 2001. "Moderata Fonte, Lucrezia Marinella, Giuseppe Passi: An Early Seventeenth-Century Feminist Controversy." *Modern Language Review* 96:973–89.
———. 2005. "The Literary Career of Lucrezia Marinella (1571–53): The Constraints of Gender and the Writing Woman." In *Rituals, Images and Words: Varieties of Cultural Expression in Late Medieval and Early Modern Europe*, edited by F. W. Kent and Charles Zika, 325–42. Turnhout, Belgium: Brepols.
Lanza, Antonio. 2007. "L'ispirazione sacra ed elegaica della poesia di Francesca Turina Bufalini." *Pagine altotiberine* 11 (33): 105–18.
Lasagna, Paola. 2009. "Forme di tragedia sacra nel Seicento benacense." In Ardissino and Selmi 2009, 175–204.

Laven, Mary. 2005. "Cast Out and Shut In: The Experience of Nuns in Counter-Reformation Venice." In *At the Margins: Minority Groups in Premodern Italy*, edited by Stephen J. Milner, 93–110. Minneapolis: University of Minnesota Press.

———. 2006. "Encountering the Counter-Reformation." *Renaissance Quarterly* 59 (3): 706–20.

Lavocat, Françoise. 1998a. "*La chaîne mystérieuse:* Danser en arcadie et en utopie." In *Sociopoétique de la danse*, edited by Alain Montandon, 81–97. Paris: Anthropos.

———. 1998b. Introduction to Marinella 1998, vii–lx.

———. 2006. "Playing Shepherd: Allegory, Fiction, Reality." In *Pastoral and the Humanities: Arcadia Re-inscribed*, edited by Mathilde Skoie and Sonia Bjørnstad Velásquez, 65–77. Bristol: Phoenix.

Lazzari, Laura. 2010. *Poesia epica e scrittura femminile nel Seicento: "L'Enrico" di Lucrezia Marinelli*. With a preface by Virginia Cox. Leonforte: Insula.

Leri, Clara. 2003. "Esercizi metrici sui *Salmi*: La poesia di Gabriele Fiamma." In *Scrittura religiosa: Forme letterarie dal Trecento al Cinquecento*, edited by Carlo Delcorno and Maria Luisa Doglio, 127–59. Bologna: Il Mulino.

Liruti, Gian Giuseppe. 1865. *Delle donne di Friuli illustri per lettere*. Udine: Giuseppe Seitz.

Lowe, K. J. P. 2003. *Nuns' Chronicles and Convent Culture in Renaissance and Counter-Reformation Italy*. Cambridge: Cambridge University Press.

Lucchesini, Cesare. 1825–31. *Storia letteraria del ducato lucchese, libri sette*. 2 vols. Lucca: Francesco Bertini.

Luebke, David M., ed. 1999. *The Counter-Reformation*. Oxford: Blackwell.

Mac Carthy, Ita. 2007. *Women and the Making of Poetry in Ariosto's "Orlando Furioso."* Leicester: Troubadour.

Maclean, Ian. 1980. *The Renaissance Notion of Woman*. Cambridge: Cambridge University Press.

MacNeil, Anne. 2003. *Music and Women in the* Commedia dell'arte. Oxford: Oxford University Press.

———. 2005. Introduction to *Selected Poems of Isabella Andreini*, edited by Anne MacNeil, translated by James Wyatt Cook, 1–21. Lanham, MD: Scarecrow.

Madden, Thomas F. 2003. *Enrico Dandolo and the Rise of Venice*. Baltimore: Johns Hopkins University Press.

Madden, Thomas F., and Donald E. Queller. 1997. *The Fourth Crusade: The Conquest of Constantinople*. 2nd ed. Philadelphia: University of Pennsylvania Press.

Maestri, Delmo. 1993. "Isabella Sori: Una scrittrice alessandrina del Seicento." *Critica letteraria* 21–22 (79): 225–41.

Maggi, Armando. 2008. "Francesco d'Assisi e le stimmate alla luce del Barocco: *Sette canzoni di sette famosi autori* (1606) e *Rime spirituali di diversi autori* (1606) raccolte da F. Silvestro da Poppi Minore Osservante." *Studi secenteschi* 49:79–130.

Magnanini, Suzanne. 2003. "'Una selva luminosa': The Second Day of Moderata Fonte's *Il merito delle donne*." *Modern Philology* 101 (2): 278–96.

Malpezzi Price, Paola. 2003a. *Moderata Fonte: Women and Life in Sixteenth-Century*

Venice. Madison, NJ: Fairleigh Dickinson Press; London: Associated University Presses.

———. 2003b. "*Venezia Figurata* and Women in Sixteenth-Century Venice: Moderata Fonte's Writings." In *Italian Women and the City: Essays*, edited by Janet Levarie Smarr and Daria Valentini, 18–34. Madison, NJ: Fairleigh Dickinson University Press; London: Associated University Presses.

Malpezzi Price, Paola, and Christine Ristaino. 2008. *Lucrezia Marinella and the Querelle des Femmes in Seventeenth-Century Italy*. Madison, NJ: Fairleigh Dickinson Press.

Malquori Fondi, Giovanna. 1997. "De la lettre-canevas à la 'pièce de cabinet': Les *Lettere* d'Isabella Andreini, traduites par François de Grenaille." In *Contacts culturels et échanges linguistiques au XVIIe siècle en France,* edited by Yves Giraud, 125–45. Paris: Papers in Seventeenth-Century Literature.

Mammana, Simona. 2001. "Orsatto Giustinian, poeta coniugale." In *Sonetti alla moglie*, by Orsatto Giustinian, edited by Simona Mammana. Florence: Le Càriti.

Mangini, Nicola. 1983. "La tragedia e la commedia." In *Storia della cultura veneta*, edited by Girolamo Arnaldi and Manlio Pastore Stocchi, vol. 4, *Il Seicento*, pt. 1: 297–326. Vicenza: Neri Pozza.

Mantese, Giovanni. 1967. "Per un profilo storico della poetessa vicentina Maddalena Campiglia: Aggiunte e rettifiche." *Archivio veneto* 81:89–123.

———. 1969. *Per una storia dell'arte medica in Vicenza alla fine del secolo XVI. Con un dizionarietto di antichi farmachi a cura di Franco Brunello*. Vicenza: Accademia Olimpica.

———. 1974. *Memorie storiche della chiesa vicentina*. Vol. 4, *Dal 1563 al 1700*. Vicenza: Accademia Olimpica.

Marcheschi, Daniela. 2008. *Chiara Matraini poetessa lucchese e la letteratura delle donne nei nuovi fermenti religiosi del 500*. Lucca: M. Pacini Fazzi.

Marr, Alexander. 2004. "Understanding Automata in the Late Renaissance." *Journal de la Renaissance* 2:205–22.

———. 2006. "Gentille curiosité: Wonder-working and the Culture of Automata in the Late Renaissance." In *Curiosity and Wonder from the Renaissance to the Enlightenment*, edited by R. J. W. Evans and Alexander Marr, 149–70. Aldershot, UK: Ashgate.

Marsand, Antonio. 1835–38. *I manoscritti italiani della Regia Biblioteca Parigina*. 2 vols. Paris: Imprimerie Royale.

Martin, John, and Dennis Romano, eds. 2000. *Reconsidering Venice: The History and Civilization of an Italian City State, 1297–1797*. Baltimore: Johns Hopkins University Press.

Martini, Alessandro. 1981. "Ritratto del madrigale poetico fra Cinque e Seicento." *Lettere italiane* 33 (4): 529–48.

———. 1994. "Marino e il madrigale attorno al 1602." In *The Sense of Marino*, edited by Francesco Guardiani, 361–92. New York: Legas.

———. 2002. "Le nuove forme del canzoniere." In F. Croce et al. 2002, 199–226.

———. 2003. "Le Divozioni del Marino." In "Parlar l'idioma soave": Studi di filologia, letteratura e storia della lingua offerti a Gianni A. Papini, edited by Matteo M. Pedoni, 181–95. Novara: Interlinea.
Marx, Barbara. 2008. "Politica culturale al femminile e identità medicea." In Calvi and Spinelli 2008, 1:146–67.
Masetti Zannini, Gian Ludovico. 1995. "Una canonichessa erborista: Semidea Poggi (sec. 16–17)." Strenna storica bolognese 45:383–401.
———. 2008. Marfisa d'Este Cybo: "Gentil fu da che nacque." Edited by Alessandro Vincenzo Masetti Zannini. Ferrara: Este Edition.
Masson, Paul-Marie. 1925a. "Jacques Mauduit et les hymnes latines de Laurence Strozzi." Revue de musicologie 6 (13): 6–14.
———. 1925b. "Jacques Mauduit et les hymnes latines de Laurence Strozzi (suite)." Revue de musicologie 6 (14): 59–69.
Mauri, Danielle. 1996a. "La Mirtilla di Isabella Andreini e la sua seconda traduzione francese." In "Il n'est nul si beau passetemps / que se jouer a sa pensee" (Charles d'Orléans): Studi di filologia e letteratura francese in onore di Anna Maria Finoli, edited by Maria Colombo, Marina Fumagalli, and Anna Maria Raugei, 243–60. Pisa: Edizioni ETS.
———. 1996b. Voyage en Arcadie: Sur les origines italiennes du théâtre pastoral français à l'âge baroque. Paris: Honoré Champion; Florence: Edizioni Cadmo.
———. 1997. "Il mito di Narciso in tre testi di Isabella, Francesco, e Giambattista Andreini." In La commedia dell'arte tra Cinque e Seicento in Francia e in Europa, edited by Elio Mosele, 207–21. Fasano: Schena.
Maylender, Michele. 1926–30. Storia delle Accademie d'Italia. 5 vols. Bologna: L. Cappelli.
Mazzotta, Giuseppe. 2000. "Le lagrime della Beata Vergine di Torquato Tasso." In Maria Vergine nella letteratura italiana, edited by Florinda M. Iannace, 39–42. Stony Brook, NY: Forum Italicum.
McClure, George W. 2008. "Women and the Politics of Play in Sixteenth-Century Italy: Torquato Tasso's Theory of Games." Renaissance Quarterly 61 (3): 750–91.
McIrnerney, Jeremy. 2003. "Plutarch's Manly Women." In Andreia: Studies in Manliness and Courage in Classical Antiquity, edited by Ralph M. Rosen and Ineke Sluiter, 319–44. Leiden: Brill.
Megale, Teresa. 2003. "Guidiccioni, Laura." In Dizionario biografico degli italiani, 61:329–30.
———. 2007. "Malloni, Maria." In Dizionario biografico degli italiani, 68:237–38.
Migiel, Marilyn. 1993. Gender and Genealogy in Tasso's "Gerusalemme Liberata." Lewiston, NY: Edwin Mellon.
Milani, Giuseppe. 1997. "Il colonello Giovanni Turini." Pagine altotiberine 1, fasc. 2: 105–8.
Milani, Marisa, ed. 1983. "Quattro donne fra i pavani." Museum patavinum 1 (2):387–412.

Milburn, Erika. 2003. *Luigi Tansillo and Lyric Poetry in Sixteenth-Century Naples*. Leeds, UK: Maney.
Mongini, Guido. 1997. "'Nel cor ch'è pur di Cristo il tempio': La *Vita del serafico e glorioso San Francesco* di Lucrezia Marinella tra influssi ignaziani, spiritualismo, e prisca teologia." *Archivio italiano per la storia della pietà* 10:359–453.
Montanari, Luciana. 2005. "Le rime edite ed inedite di Laura Battiferri degli Ammanati". *Italianistica* 34 (3): 11–27.
Moore, James H. 1984. "'Venezia favorita da Maria': Music for the Madonna Nicopeia and Santa Maria della Salute." *Journal of the American Musicological Society* 37 (2): 299–355.
Moorman, F. W. 1906. "The Pre-Shakespearean Ghost." *Modern Language Review* 1 (2): 85–95.
Morandini, Giuliana, ed. 2001. *Sospiri e palpiti: Scrittrici italiane del Seicento*. Genoa: Marietti.
Morando, Simona. 2009. "'O che spettacol miro / di sangue, e di martiro': I *Pietosi affetti* di Angelo Grillo nell'opera dei pittori." In *Il sacro nell'arte: La conoscenza del divino attraverso i sensi tra XV e XVIII secolo*, edited by Laura Stagno, 37–54. Genoa: Università degli Studi di Genova.
Mordani, Filippo. 1837. *Vite di ravegnati illustri*. Ravenna: de' Roveri.
Morsolin, Bernardo. 1882. *Maddalena Campiglia, poetessa vicentina del secolo XVI: Episodio biografico*. Vicenza: Paroni.
Motta, Uberto. 2004. "Petrarca a Milano al principio del Seicento." In *Petrarca in barocco: Cantieri petrarcheschi; Due seminari romani*, edited by Amedeo Quondam, 227–73. Rome: Bulzoni.
Murphy, Caroline P. 2003. *Lavinia Fontana*. New Haven, CT: Yale University Press.
Muzi, Giovanni. 1844. *Memorie civili di Città di Castello*. 2 vols. Città di Castello: Francesco Donati.
Nardi, Franco Daniele. 1984. "Matteo Guerra e la Congregazione dei Sacri Chiodi (secc. XVI–XVII): Aspetti della religiosità senese nell'età della Controriforma." *Bullettino senese di storia patria* 91:12–148.
Nenci, Elio, ed. 2005. *Bernardino Baldi (1553–1617), studioso rinascimentale: Poesia, storia, linguistica, meccanica, architettura*. Milan: Franco Angeli.
Neri, Ferdinando. 1904. *La tragedia italiana del Cinquecento*. Florence: Galletti & Cocci.
Newcomb, Anthony. 1986. "Courtesans, Muses, or Musicians? Professional Women Musicians in Sixteenth-Century Italy." In Bowers and Tick 1986, 90–115.
———. 1992. Review of Licco 1990. *Notes*, 2nd ser., 49 (1): 83–86.
Nicholson, Eric. 1999. "Romance as Role Model: Early Female Performances of *Orlando Furioso* and *Gerusalemme Liberata*." In *Renaissance Transactions: Ariosto and Tasso*, edited by Valeria Finucci, 246–69. Durham, NC: Duke University Press.
Nuovo, Isabella. 1994. "Muzio Sforza." In *Puglia neo-latina: Un itinerario del Rinasci-*

mento fra autori e testi, edited by Francesco Tateo, Mauro de Nichilo, and Pietro Sisto, 311–31. Bari: Cacucci.

Oldani, Louis J., and Victor R. Yanitelli. 1999. "Jesuit Theater in Italy: Its Entrances and Exit." *Italica* 76 (1): 18–32.

Olivieri Secchi, Sandra. 1998. "Libelli contro e a favore della donna a Venezia e in Romagna." In *Il libro in Romagna: Produzione, commercio e consumo dalla fine del XV secolo all'età contemporanea*, edited by Lorenzo Baldacchini and Anna Manfron, 1:285–325. Florence: Olschki.

O'Malley, John. W. 2000. *Trent and All That: Renaming Catholicism in the Early Modern Era*. Cambridge, MA: Harvard University Press.

Ossola, Carlo. 1976. "Il 'queto travaglio' di Gabriele Fiamma." *Letteratura e critica: Studi in onore di Natalino Sapegno*, edited by Walter Binni et al., 3:239–86. Rome: Bulzoni.

Ossola, Carlo, and Cesare Segre, eds. 2001. *Antologia della poesia italiana: Il Cinquecento*. 2nd ed. Turin: Einaudi.

Panizza, Letizia. 1999. "Introduction to the Translation." In Marinella 1999, 1–34.

———, ed. 2000. *Women in Italian Renaissance Culture and Society*. Oxford: European Humanities Research Association.

Panizza, Letizia, and Sharon Wood, eds. 2000. *A History of Women's Writing in Italy*. Cambridge: Cambridge University Press.

Paoli, Maria Pia. 2003. "Nell'Italia delle 'Vergini belle': A proposito di Chiara Matraini e di pietà mariana nella Lucca di fine Cinquecento." In *Religione cultura e politica nell'Europa dell'età moderna*, edited by Carlo Ossola, Marcello Verga, and Maria Antonietta Visceglia, 521–45. Florence: Olschki.

Paolin, Giovanna. 1996. *Lo spazio de silenzio: Monacazioni forzate: Clausura, e proposte di vita religiosa femminile nell'età moderna*. Pordenone: Biblioteca dell'Immagine.

Parisotto, Edoardo. 2009. *La Venerabile Battista Vernazza*. Genova: De Ferrari.

Park, Sidney Stuart. 1981. Introduction to "*Don Cristalián de España* de Beatriz Bernal: Edición modernizada con introducción critica," 1–51. PhD diss., Temple University.

Passolunghi, Pier Angelo. 1991. *La barriera fatta nel Castello di S. Salvatore, descritta per Giovanni dalla Torre nell'anno 1599*. Susegana: Amministrazione Culturale / Biblioteca Comunale.

Patti, Gloria. 2002. "Le due Vittorie: Tra Michelangelo Buonarroti e Pietro Vinci." In *Quattordici sonetti spirituali della Illustrissima et Eccellentissima Divina Vittoria Colonna . . . messi in canto a cinque voci (1580)*, by Pietro Vinci, edited by Gloria Patti, vii–xxiii. Florence: Olschki.

Pelikan, Jaroslav. 1996. *Mary through the Centuries: Her Place in the History of Culture*. New Haven, CT: Yale University Press.

Perrone, Carlachiara. 1996. *"So che donna ama donna": La "Calisa" di Maddalena Campiglia*. Galatina: Congedo.

Personeni, Angelo. 1786. *Notizie genealogiche, storiche, critiche e letterarie del Cardinale*

Cinzio Personeni da Ca Passero Aldobrandini, nipote di Clemente VIII. Bergamo: Francesco Locatelli.
Pertusi, Agostino. 2004. *Bisanzio e i Turchi nella cultura del Rinascimento e del Barocco: Tre saggi di Agostino Pertusi*. Milan: Vita e Pensiero.
Pezzini, Serena. 2005. "Ideologia della conquista, ideologia dell'accoglienza: *La Scanderbeide* di Margherita Sarrocchi (1623)." *MLN* 120 (1): 190–222.
———. 2007. "La scoperta dell'identico: Ideologia dell'accoglienza ne *La Scanderbeide* (1623), poema eroico di Margherita Sarrocchi." In Ronchetti and Sapegno 2007, 101–11.
Piantoni, Luca. 2009. "Mirabile cristiano ed eloquenza sacra in Lucrezia Marinelli." In Ardissino and Selmi 2009, 435–45.
Piatti, Angelo Alberto. 2007. "'E l'uom pietà da Dio, piangendo, impari': Lacrime e pianto nelle rime sacre nell'età del Tasso." In Delcorno and Doglio 2007, 53–106.
———. *"Su nel sereno de' lucenti giri": Le "Rime sacre" di Torquato Tasso*. Alessandria: Edizioni dell'Orso.
Piéjus, Marie-Françoise. 2009. "Le pays des femmes homicides: Utopie et monde à l'envers." In *Visages et paroles de femmes dans la literature italienne de la Renaissance*, 19–49. Paris: Université de la Sorbonne Nouvelle.
Pierattini, Giovanna. 1942. "Suor Lorenza Strozzi, poetessa domenicana (1514–91)." *Memorie domenicane* 59 (3): 113–15, (4): 142–45, (5): 177–83.
———. 1943. "Suor Lorenza Strozzi, poetessa domenicana (1514–91)." *Memorie domenicane* 60 (1): 19–25.
Pieri, Marzia. 1983. *La scena boschereccia nel Rinascimento italiano*. Padua: Liviana.
Pietropoli, Giuseppe. 1986. *L'Accademia dei Concordi nella vita rodigiana dalla seconda metà del sedicesimo secolo alla fine della dominazione austriaca*. Padua: Signum.
Pignatti, Franco. 2007. "Manfredi, Muzio." In *Dizionario biografico degli italiani*, 68:720–25.
Pomata, Gianna. 2002. "Family and Gender." In *Early Modern Italy*, edited by John A. Marino, 69–86. Oxford: Oxford University Press.
Pomata, Gianna, and Gabriella Zarri, eds. 2005. *I monasteri femminili come centri di cultura fra Rinascimento e Barocco*. Rome: Edizioni di Storia e Letteratura.
Povolo, Claudio. 1993. "La conflittualità nobiliare in Italia nella seconda metà del Cinquecento. Il caso della Repubblica di Venezia: alcune ipotesi e possibili interpretazioni." *Atti dell'Istituto Veneto di Scienze, Lettere, ed Arti: Classe di Scienze Morali, Lettere, ed Arti* 151 (1): 89–139.
Powers, Katherine. 2001. Introduction to *Musica spirituale, libro primo (Venice, 1563)*, edited by Katherine Powers, vii–xxix. Middleton, WI: A-R Editions.
Provasi, Pacifico. 1913. *L' "Angeleida" di Erasmo di Valvasone e i poeti italiani sulla caduta di Lucifero*. Udine: Giuseppe Vetri.
Purkiss, Diane. 1998. Introduction to *Three Tragedies by Renaissance Women*, edited by Diane Purkiss, xi–xxxix. Harmondsworth, UK: Penguin.

Quaintance, Courtney. 2009. "*Le feste*, written by Moderata Fonte." In Weaver 2009, 193–231.

Quillen, Carol. 1994. "Plundering the Egyptians: Petrarch and Augustine's *De doctrina christiana*." In *Reading and Wisdom: The "De doctrina christiana" of Augustine in the Middle Ages*, edited by Edward D. English, 153–71. Notre Dame, IN: University of Notre Dame Press.

Quint, David. 2004. "Francesco Bracciolini as a Reader of Ariosto and Tasso in *La Croce Racquistata*." In Rosa and Superbi 2004, 1:59–77.

Quondam, Amedeo. 1973. *La locuzione artificiosa: Teoria ed esperienza della lirica a Napoli nell'eta del manierismo*. Rome: Bulzoni.

———. 1981. "*Le carte messaggiere*": *Retorica e modelli di comunicazione epistolare*. Rome: Bulzoni.

———. 1991. *Il naso di Laura: Lingua e poesia lirica nella tradizione del classicismo*. Modena: Panini.

———. 2005a. "Note sulla poesia spirituale e religiosa (prima parte)." In Quondam 2005b, 127–211.

———, ed. 2005b. *Paradigmi e tradizioni*. Rome: Bulzoni.

———. 2005c. "Saggio di bibliografia della poesia religiosa." In Quondam 2005b, 213–82.

Rabitti, Giovanna. 1981. "Linee per il ritratto di Chiara Matraini." *Studi e problemi di critica testuale* 22: 141–65.

———. 1999. "Le lettere di Chiara Matraini tra privato e pubblico." In Zarri 1999, 209–34.

———. 2000. "Vittoria Colonna as Role Model for Cinquecento Women Poets." In Panizza 2000, 478–97.

———. 2002. "La letteratura femminile e l'Europa." In *Storia della letteratura italiana*, edited by Enrico Malato, vol. 12, *La letteratura italiana fuori d'Italia*, edited by Luciano Formisano, 399–433. Rome: Salerno.

———. 2006. "Vittoria Colonna tra la Francia e la Spagna." In *Il Petrarchismo: Un modello di poesia per l'Europa*, edited by Floriana Calitti, Loredana Chines, and Roberto Gigliucci, 2:481–98. Rome: Bulzoni.

———. 2007. Introduction to Matraini 2007, 1–36.

Raboni, Giulia. 1991. "Il madrigalista Livio Celiano e il benedettino Angelo Grillo." *Studi secenteschi* 32:137–88.

Ray, Meredith Kennedy. 1998. "*La castità conquistata*: The Function of the Satyr in Pastoral Drama." *Romance Languages Annual* 9:312–21.

———. 2009a. "Letters and Lace: Arcangela Tarabotti and Convent Culture in Seicento Venice." In *Early Modern Women and Transnational Communities of Letters*, edited by Julie D. Campbell and Anne R. Larsen, 45–73. Aldershot, UK: Ashgate.

———. 2009b. "Textual Collaboration and Spiritual Partnership in Sixteenth-Century Italy: The Case of Ortensio Lando and Lucrezia Gonzaga." *Renaissance Quarterly* 62 (3): 694–747.

———. 2009c. *Writing Gender in Women's Letter Collections of the Italian Renaissance.* Toronto: University of Toronto Press.

Ray, Meredith, and Lynn Westwater. 2005. Introduction to Tarabotti 2005, 25–39.

Razzoli Roio, Anna Maria. 2000. Introduction to C. Gonzaga 2000, iii–xii.

———, ed. 2008. *Cavalieri ed eroi alla corte di Mantova: Il "Fido amante" di Curzio Gonzaga.* Rome: Verso l'Arte.

Reardon, Colleen. 2002. *Holy Concord within Sacred Walls: Nuns and Music in Siena, 1575–1700.* Oxford: Oxford University Press.

Rebonato, Alessandro. 2004. "Di alcuni imitatori di Tommaso Garzoni." *Studi secenteschi* 45:195–215.

Rees, Katie. 2008. "Female-Authored Drama in Early Modern Padua: Valeria Miani Negri." *Italian Studies* 63 (1): 41–61.

———. 2010. "Women Writers for the Theatre in Early Modern Italy: Valeria Miani Negri." PhD thesis, University of Cambridge.

Residori, Matteo. 2004. *L'idea del poema: Studio sulla "Gerusalemme conquistata" di Torquato Tasso.* Pisa: Scuola Normale Superiore.

Rhodes, Dennis E. 1993. "Una biblioteca privata a Conegliano intorno all'anno 1600." *Ateneo veneto,* n.s., 31:101–9.

Rhodes, Elizabeth. 1989. "Sixteenth-Century Pastoral Books, Narrative Structure and *La Galatea* of Cervantes." *Bulletin of Hispanic Studies* 66:351–60.

Riccò, Laura. 2004. *"Ben mille pastorali": L'itinerario dell'Ingegneri da Tasso a Guarini e oltre.* Rome: Bulzoni.

———. 2008. *"Su le carte e fra le scene": Teatro in forma di libro nel Cinquecento italiano.* Rome: Bulzoni.

Richardson, Brian. 2009. *Manuscript Culture in Renaissance Italy.* Cambridge: Cambridge University Press.

Riley, Joanne Marie. 1986. "Tarquinia Molza (1542–1617): A Case Study of Women, Music, and Society in the Renaissance." In *The Musical Woman: An International Perspective,* edited by Judith Lang Zaimont, 470–93. New York: Greenwood.

Rios, Antonio. 1896. "Giostre a Conegliano nel carnevale del 1604." *Nuovo archivio veneto,* 1st ser., 12:79–94.

Ritrovato, Salvatore. 2004. "Antologie e canoni del madrigale (1545–1611)." *Studi e problemi di critica testuale* 69:115–36.

Rizzo, Gino. 2000. "Per la tragedia spirituale secentesca (Bonaventura Morone e Girolamo Pipini)." In *Teatro, scena, rappresentazione dal Quattrocento al Seicento,* edited by Paola Andrioli et al., 217–35. Galatina: Congedo.

Roberts, Josephine A. 1995. Introduction to *The First Part of the Countess of Montgomery's Urania,* by Lady Mary Wroth, edited by Josephine A. Roberts, xv–xcviii. Binghamton, NY: Medieval and Renaissance Texts & Studies.

———. 1997. "Deciphering Women's Pastoral: Coded Language in Wroth's *Love's Victory.*" In *Representing Women in Renaissance England,* edited by Claude J. Summers and Ted-Larry Pebworth, 163–74. Columbia: University of Missouri Press.

Robin, Diana. 2007. *Publishing Women: Salons, the Presses, and the Counter-Reformation in Sixteenth-Century Italy.* Chicago: University of Chicago Press.
Roche, Thomas P. 1989. *Petrarch and the English Sonnet Sequences.* New York: AMS.
Rodinò, Simonetta Prosperi Valenti. 2010. "Vanni: (1) Francesco Vanni." In "Grove Art Online," *Oxford Art Online,* http://www.oxfordartonline.com/subscriber/article/grove/art/T087883pg1 (accessed 25 March 2010).
Romei, Giovanna. 1992. "La commedia dell'arte e la favola pastorale." In Chiabò and Doglio 1992, 181–99.
Römer, Zdenka Janeković. 2004. "Marija Gondola Gozze: *La querelle des femmes* u renesansnom Dubrovniku." In *Žene u Hrvatskoj: Ženska i kulturna povijest,* edited by Andrea Feldman, 105–23. Zagreb: Ženska infoteka.
Ronchetti, Alessia, and Maria Serena Sapegno, eds. 2007. *Dentro/fuori: Critica femminista e canone letterario negli studi di italianistica.* Ravenna: Longo.
Rosa, Massimilano, and Fiorella Gioffredi Superbi, eds. 2004. *L'arme e gli amori: Ariosto, Tasso, and Guarini in Late Renaissance Florence.* 2 vols. Florence: Olschki.
Rose, Mary Beth. 2002. *Gender and Heroism in Early Modern England.* Chicago: University of Chicago Press.
Rosenthal, Margaret F. 1992. *The Honest Courtesan: Veronica Franco, Citizen and Writer in Sixteenth-Century Venice.* Chicago: University of Chicago Press.
———. 1993. "Venetian Women and their Discontents." In *Sexuality and Gender in Early Modern Europe: Institutions, Texts, Images,* edited by James Granthan Turner, 107–32. Cambridge: Cambridge University Press.
Ross, Sarah Gwyneth. 2009. *The Birth of Feminism: Woman as Intellect in Renaissance Italy and England.* Cambridge, MA: Harvard University Press.
Rozzo, Ugo. 2001. "Italian Literature on the Index." In *Church, Censorship and Culture in Early Modern Italy,* edited by Gigliola Fragnito, 194–222. Cambridge: Cambridge University Press.
Rubinstein, Nicolai. 2004. "The Beginnings of Political Thought in Florence: A Study in Medieval Historiography." In *Studies in Italian History in the Middle Ages and the Renaissance,* edited by Giovanni Ciappelli and Nicolai Rubinstein, 1–42. Rome: Edizioni di Storia e Letteratura.
Russell, Rinaldina, ed. 1994. *Italian Women Writers: A Bio-Bibliographical Sourcebook.* Westport, CT: Greenwood.
———. 2000. "Vittoria Colonna's Sonnets on the Virgin Mary." In *Maria Vergine nella Letteratura Italiana,* edited by Florinda M. Iannace, 125–37. Stony Brook, NY: Forum Italicum.
———. 2006. "Margherita Sarrocchi and the Writing of the *Scanderbeide.*" In Sarrocchi 2006, 1–57.
Russo, Emilio. 2008. *Marino.* Rome: Salerno.
Russo, Luigi. 1985. *Muzio Sforza, poeta monopolitano tra rinascenza e controriforma (1541–1597).* Bari: Puglia Grafica.
Sabine, Maureen. 1992. *Feminine Engendered Faith: The Poetry of John Donne and Richard Crashaw.* London: Macmillan.

———. 2006. "Crashaw and Abjection: Reading the Unthinkable in His Devotional Verse." *American Imago* 63 (4): 423–43.
Sacchi, Guido. 2006. *Fra Ariosto e Tasso: Vicende del poema narrativo; Con un'appendice di studi cinque-secenteschi.* Pisa: Edizioni della Normale.
Saltini, Guglielmo Enrico. 1883. "L'educazione del principe Francesco de' Medici: Documenti." *Archivio storico italiano* 11 (134): 157–72.
Salvi, Marcella. 2004. "'Il solito è sempre quello; l'insolito è più nuovo': *Li buffoni* e le prostitute di Margherita Costa fra tradizione e innovazione." *Forum italicum* 38 (2): 376–99.
Sampson, Lisa. 2004. "'Drammatica secreta': Barbara Torelli's *Partenia* (c. 1587) and Women in Late Sixteenth-Century Theatre." In *Theatre, Opera, and Performance in Italy from the Fifteenth Century to the Present: Essays in Honour of Richard Andrews*, edited by Brian Richardson, Simon Gilson, and Catherine Keen, 99–115. Leeds, UK: Society of Italian Studies.
———. 2006. *Pastoral Drama in Early Modern Italy: The Making of a New Genre.* London: Legenda.
Santacroce, Maria Chiara. 1999–2000. "Aristotele misogino: La difesa delle donne negli scritti di Lucrezia Marinella." Tesi di laurea, Università degli Studi di Milano, Facoltà di Lettere e Filosofia.
Santarelli, Giuseppe. 1974. *Studi sulle rime sacre del Tasso.* Bergamo: Centro Tassiano.
Saulini, Mirella. 2002. *Il teatro di un gesuita siciliano: Stefano Tuccio, S.J.* Rome: Bulzoni.
Sberlati, Francesco. 1997. "Dalla donna di palazzo alla donna di famiglia: Cultura e pedagogia femminile tra Rinascimento e Controriforma." *I Tatti Studies* 7:119–74.
Schneider, Federico. 2010. *Pastoral Drama and Healing in Early Modern Italy.* Aldershot, UK: Ashgate.
Schneider, Regina. 2002. "Of Oaten Flutes and Magic Potions: Montemayor's *Diana* as Pastoral Romance." *Narrative* 10 (3): 262–76.
Schoonhoven, Erik. 2010. "A Literary Invention: The Etruscan Myth in Early Renaissance Florence." *Renaissance Studies* 24 (4), 459–71.
Schuetze, George C. 1990. *Settings of "Ardo Sì" and Its Related Texts.* Madison, WI: A-R Editions.
Schutte, Anne Jacobsen. 2006. "The Permeable Cloister?" In *Arcangela Tarabotti: A Literary Nun in Baroque Venice*, edited by Elissa B. Weaver, 19–36. Ravenna: Longo.
Schwarz, Kathryn. 2000. *Tough Love: Amazon Encounters in the English Renaissance.* Durham, NC: Duke University Press.
Selmi, Elisabetta. 2005. "'Inchiostri purgati' e il 'Parnaso in pulpito' (memoria e riscrittura tassesca nell'epica sacra del Seicento)." In Arbizzoni, Faini, and Mattioli 2005, 423–75.
Semola, Mariangela. 2006. "Il *Poeta illuminato* di Agostino de Cupiti: Una visione della aldilà di fine Cinquecento." *Annali dell'Istituto Universitario Orientale di Napoli, Sezione Romanza* 48 (2): 505–28.

Serrai, Alfredo. 2002. *Bernardino Baldi: La vita, le opere, la biblioteca.* Milan: Edizioni Sylvestre Bonnard.
Sforza, Giovanni. 1879. *F. M. Fiorentini ed i suoi contemporanei lucchesi: Saggio di storia letteraria del secolo XVII.* Florence: F. Menozzi.
Shemek, Deanna. 1998. *Ladies Errant: Wayward Women and the Social Order in Early Modern Italy.* Durham, NC: Duke University Press.
Shiff, Jonathan. 1993. *Venetian State Theater and the Games of Siena, 1595–1605: The Grimani Banquet Plays.* Lewiston, NY: Edwin Mellen.
Simoncelli, Paolo. 1984. *La lingua di Adamo: Guillaume Postel tra Accademici e fuorusciti fiorentini.* Florence: Olschki.
Simons, Patricia. 1994. "Lesbian (In)visibility in Italian Renaissance Culture: Diana and Other Cases of *Donna con Donna.*" *Journal of Homosexuality* 27:81–123.
Smarr, Janet Levarie. 1991. "Gaspara Stampa's Poetry for Performance." *Journal of the Rocky Mountain Medieval and Renaissance Association* 12:61–84.
———. 2005. *Joining the Conversation: Dialogues by Renaissance Women.* Ann Arbor: University of Michigan Press.
Smith, Alison A. 2009. "Women and Political Sociability in Late Renaissance Verona: Ersilia Spolverini's *Elogio* of Chiara Cornaro." In *Donne di potere nel Rinascimento*, edited by Letizia Arcangeli and Susanna Peyronel, 405–15. Rome: Viella.
Smith, Philip Carl. 2008. "The Hymns of the Medieval Dominican Liturgy, 1250–1369." BA thesis, University of Notre Dame. http://musicasacra.com/dominican/Studies/smith-medieval_hymnal-2008.pdf.
Snyder, James. 1985. "'The Joyous Appearance of Christ with a Multitude of Angels and Holy Fathers to His Dearest Mother': A Mystical Devotional Diptych by Jan Mostaert." In *Tribute to Lotte Brand Philip: Art Historian and Detective*, edited by William W. Clark et al., 175–84. New York: Abaris Books.
Solerti, Angelo. 1895. *Vita di Torquato Tasso.* 2 vols. Turin: Ernesto Loescher.
———. 1902a. "Laura Guidiccioni ed Emilio de' Cavalieri (i primi tentativi di melodramma)." *Rivista musicale italiana* 9:797–829.
———. 1902b. "Le rappresentazioni musicali di Venezia dal 1571 al 1605." *Rivista musicale italiana* 9:503–58.
Solfaroli Camillocci, Daniela. 1999. "La monaca esemplare: Lettere spirituali di Battista Vernazza (1497–1587)." In Zarri 1999, 235–61.
Sozzi, Bortolo Tomaso. 1954. *Studi su Tasso.* Pisa: Nistri-Lischi.
Sperling, Jutta Gisela. 1999. *Convents and the Body Politic in Late Renaissance Venice.* Chicago: University of Chicago Press.
Spinelli, Riccardo. 2008. "Simbologia dinastica e legittimazione del potere: Maria Maddalena d'Austria e gli affreschi del Poggio Imperiale." In Calvi and Spinelli 2008, 2:645–79.
Spiriti, Salvatore. 1750. *Memorie degli scrittori cosentini.* Naples: Stamperia de' Muzi.
Stampino, Maria Galli. 2009. "A Singular Venetian Epic Poem." In Marinella 2009, 1–66.
———. 2011. Introduction to Marinella 2011, 5–33.

Stephens, Walter. 1989. "Saint Paul among the Amazons: Gender and Authority in *Gerusalemme Liberata*." In *Discourses of Authority in Medieval and Renaissance Literature*, edited by Kevin Brownlee and Walter Stephens, 169–200. Hanover, NH: University Press of New England.
Stevenson, Jane. 2002. "Conventual Life in Renaissance Italy: The Latin Poetry of Suor Laurentia Strozzi (1514–91)." In *Women Writing Latin, from Roman Antiquity to Early Modern Europe*, edited by Laurie J. Churchill, Phyllis R. Brown, and Jane E. Jeffrey, vol. 3, *Early Modern Women Writing Latin*, 109–31. New York: Routledge.
———. 2005. *Women Latin Poets: Language, Gender, and Authority from Antiquity to the Eighteenth Century*. Oxford: Oxford University Press.
Storey, Tessa. 2008. *Carnal Commerce in Counter-Reformation Rome*. Cambridge: Cambridge University Press.
Stras, Laurie. 1999. "Recording Tarquinia: Imitation, Parody and Reportage in Ingegneri's 'Hor che 'l ciel e la terra e 'l vento tace.'" *Early Music* 27 (3): 358–77.
Strocchia, Sharon T. 1999. "Learning the Virtues: Convent Schools and Female Culture in Renaissance Florence." In *Women's Education in Early Modern Europe: A History, 1500–1800*, edited by Barbara J. Whitehead, 3–46. New York: Garland.
———. 2009. *Nuns and Nunneries in Renaissance Florence*. Baltimore: Johns Hopkins University Press.
Stumpo, Enrico. 1998. "Della Chiesa, Francesco Agostino." In *Dizionario biografico degli italiani*, 36:748–51.
Tatlock, Lynne. 2009. Introduction to *Meditations on the Incarnation, Passion, and Death of Jesus Christ*, by Catharina Regina von Greiffenberg, translated and edited by Lynne Tatlock, 1–38. Chicago: University of Chicago Press.
Taviani, Ferdinando. 1984. "Bella d'Asia: Torquato Tasso, gli attori e l'immortalità." *Paragone letteratura* 36 (408–10): 3–76.
Terpening, Ronnie H. 1997. *Lodovico Dolce, Renaissance Man of Letters*. Toronto: University of Toronto Press.
Tizzoni, Monica. 1995. "L'istanza tragicomica tra diletto di corte e moralità: La rappresentazione dell'*Arminia* di Giovan Battista Visconti." In Carpani and Cascetta 1995, 219–64.
Tomalin, Margaret. 1982. *The Fortunes of the Warrior Heroine in Italian Literature: An Index of Emancipation*. Ravenna: Longo.
Toppi, Niccolò. 1678. *Biblioteca napoletana*. Naples: Bulifon.
Torbarina, Josip. 1931. *Italian Influence on the Poets of the Ragusan Republic*. London: Williams & Norgate.
Torrioli, Igea. 1940. "Francesca Turina Bufalini e la società colta tifernate nel sec. XVI." *L'Alta Valle del Tevere* 8:1–36.
Toscano, Tobia R. 1987. "Note sulla composizione e la pubblicazione de *Le lagrime di San Pietro* di Luigi Tansillo." In *Rinascimento meridionale e altri studi in onore di Mario Santoro*, edited by Maria Cristina Cafisse et al., 437–61. Naples: Società Editrice Napoletana.
Traninger, Anita. 2008. "Wandelbare Orte: Zur Rhetorizität und 'Toposhaftigkeit' der

Querelle des femmes bei Cornelius Agrippa (1486–1535) und Lucrezia Marinella (1571–1653)." In Hassauer et al. 2008, 183–205.

Traub, Valerie. 2002. *The Renaissance of Lesbianism in Early Modern England*. Cambridge: Cambridge University Press.

Treadwell, Nina. 1997. "The Performance of Gender in Cavalieri/Guidiccioni's *ballo* 'O che nuovo miracolo.'" *Women and Music* 1:55–70.

———. 2002. "'Simil combattimento fatto da Dame': The Musico-Theatrical Entertainments of Margherita Gonzaga's *Balletto delle donne* and the Female Warrior in Ferrarese Cultural History." In *Gender, Sexuality, and Early Music*, edited by Todd. C. Borgerding, 27–40. New York: Routledge.

Treherne, Matthew. 2007. "Pictorial Space and Sacred Time: Tasso's *Le lagrime della beata Vergine* and the Experience of Religious Art in the Counter-Reformation." *Italian Studies* 62 (1): 5–25.

Trinchieri Camiz, Franca. 2003. "Music Settings to Poems by Michelangelo and Vittoria Colonna." In *Art and Music in the Early Modern Period: Essays in Honor of Franca Trinchieri Camiz*, edited by Katherine A. McIver, 377–88. Aldershot, UK: Ashgate.

Tylus, Jane. 2009. *Reclaiming Catherine of Siena: Literacy, Literature, and the Signs of Others*. Chicago: University of Chicago Press.

Ultsch, Lori J. 2005a. "*Epithalamium interruptum:* Maddalena Campiglia's New Arcadia." *MLN* 120 (1): 70–92.

———. 2005b. "Maddalena Campiglia, dimessa nel mondano cospetto? Secular Celibacy, Devotional Communities, and Social Identity in Early Modern Vicenza." *Forum italicum* 39 (2): 350–77.

Ussia, Salvatore. 1988. "Il tema letterario della Maddalena nell'età della Controriforma." *Rivista di storia e letteratura religiosa* 24 (3): 385–424.

———. 1993. *Il sacro Parnaso: Il lauro e la croce*. Catanzaro: Pullano.

———. 1999. *Le sacre muse: Poesia religiosa dei secoli XVI e XVII*. Borgomanero: Fondazione Achille Marazza.

———. 2001. *Amore innamorato: Riscritture poetiche della novella di Amore e Psiche, secoli XV–XVII*. Vercelli: Mercurio.

Valone, Carolyn. 1992. "Roman Matrons as Patrons: Various Views of the Cloister Wall." In *The Crannied Wall: Women, Religion, and the Arts in Early Modern Europe*, edited by Craig Monson, 49–72. Ann Arbor: University of Michigan Press.

———. 1994. "Women on the Quirinal Hill: Patronage in Rome, 1560–1630." *Art Bulletin* 76 (1): 129–46.

Varini, Ester. 2008. "Tra imitazione e variazione: Il *Fido Amante* di Curzio Gonzaga." In Razzoli Roio 2008, 137–49.

Vassalli, Antonio. 1988. "Sull'edizione delle *Rime* di B. Guarini: Una riflessione." In *Forme e vicende, per Giovanni Pozzi*, edited by Ottavio Besomi, Giulia Gianella, Alessandro Martini, and Guido Pedrojetta, 225–38. Padua: Antenore.

———. 1989. "Editoria del petrarchismo cinquecentesco: Alcune cifre." In *Il libro di*

poesia dal copista al tipografo, edited by Marco Santagata and Amedeo Quondam, 91–102. Modena: Panini.
Vazzoler, Franco. 1992. "Le pastorali dei comici dell'arte: La *Mirtilla* di Isabella Andreini." In Chiabò and Doglio 1992, 281–99.
Vecchietti, Filippo. 1790–96. *Biblioteca picena*. 4 vols. Osimo: Domenicantonio Quercetti.
Velasco, Sherry M. 2000. "María de Zayas and Lesbian Desire in Early Modern Spain." In *Reading and Writing the Ambiente: Queer Sexualities in Latino, Latin American, and Spanish Culture*, edited by Susana Chávez-Silverman and Librada Hernández, 21–42. Madison: University of Wisconsin Press.
Venturi, Gianni, ed. 1999. *Torquato Tasso e la cultura estense*. 3 vols. Florence: Olschki.
Verdile, Nadia. 1989–90. "Contributi alla biografia di Margherita Sarrocchi." *Rendiconti dell'Accademia di Archeologia, Lettere e Belle Arti* 61:165–206.
Vital, Adolfo. 1902. *Un'accademia coneglianese del secolo XVI*. Conegliano: G. Nardi.
Volpi, Mirko. 2005. "Bernardino Baldi lirico." In Nenci 2005, 25–53.
Von Tippelskirch, Xenia. 2008. "Letture e conversazioni a corte durante la reggenza di Maria Maddalena d'Austria e di Cristina di Lorena." In Calvi and Spinelli 2008, 1:131–43.
Wardropper, Bruce W. 1958. *Historia de la poesia lirica a lo divino en la Cristiandad occidental*. Madrid: Revista de Occidente.
Warner, Marina. 1976. *Alone of All Her Sex: The Myth and the Cult of the Virgin Mary*. New York: Random House.
Weaver, Elissa B. 1994. "Le muse in convento: La scrittura profana delle monache italiane (1450–1650)." In *Donna e fede: Santità e vita religiosa in Italia*, edited by Lucetta Scaraffia and Gabriella Zarri, 253–76. Rome: Laterza.
———. 1997. Review of Fonte 1995. *MLN* 112 (1): 114–16.
———. 1998. Introduction to *Satira e antisatira*, by Francesco Buoninsegni and Arcangela Tarabotti, edited by Elissa Weaver. Rome: Salerno.
———. 2002. *Convent Theatre in Early Modern Italy: Spiritual Fun and Learning for Women*. Cambridge: Cambridge University Press.
———, ed. 2009. *Scenes from Italian Convent Life: An Anthology of Convent Theatrical Texts and Contexts*. Ravenna: Longo.
Weber, Alison. 1990. *Teresa of Avila and the Rhetoric of Femininity*. Princeton, NJ: Princeton University Press.
Wilbourne, Emily. 2007. "'Isabella ringiovinita': Virginia Ramponi Andreini before Arianna." *Recercare* 19:47–71.
Wilson, Katharina M., ed. 1991. *An Encyclopedia of Continental Women Writers*. 2 vols. New York: Garland.
Wojciehowski, Dolora Chappelle. 2006. "Veronica Franco vs. Maffio Venier: Sex, Death, and Poetry in Cinquecento Venice." *Italica* 83:367–90.
Yang, Sharon Rose. 2003. "The Sage Felicia and the Grave Melissea: *Diana* of George of Montemayor, an Inspiration for Wroth's Defense of Women in *Urania*." *ANQ* 16 (2): 5–13.

Yavneh, Naomi. 1999. " 'Dal rogo alle nozze': Tasso's Sofronia as Martyr Manqué." In *Renaissance Transactions: Ariosto and Tasso*, edited by Valeria Finucci, 270–94. Durham, NC: Duke University Press.

Young, M[ary]. 1860. *The Life and Times of Aonio Paleario*. 2 vols. London: Bell & Daldry.

Zaja, Paolo. 2008. "Marinelli (Marinella), Lucrezia." In *Dizionario biografico degli italiani*, 70:399–402.

———. 2009. " 'Perch'arda meco del tuo amore il mondo': Lettura delle *Rime spirituali* di Gabriele Fiamma." In Ardissino and Selmi 2009, 235–92.

Zampelli, Michael A. 2002. "Giovanni Battista Andreini's *Maddalena* of 1617: Staging the Redemption of the Theatrical Profession." In *From Rome to Eternity: Catholicism and the Arts in Italy, c. 1550–1650*, edited by Pamela M. Jones and Thomas Worcester, 63–85. Leiden: Brill.

Zanrè, Domenico. 2003. "Alterity and Sexual Transgression in the Sixteenth-Century Tuscan Novella." In *The Italian Novella: A Book of Essays*, edited by Gloria Allaire, 159–68. New York: Routledge.

Zarri, Gabriella, ed. 1996. *Donna, disciplina, creanza Cristi dal XV al XVII secolo: Studi e testi a stampa*. Rome: Edizioni di Storia e Letteratura.

———, ed. 1999. *Per lettera: Scrittura epistolare femminile tra archivio e tipografia, secoli XV–XVII*. Rome: Viella.

———. 2000. *Recinti: Donne, clausura, e matrimonio nella prima età moderna*. Bologna: Il Mulino.

Zatti, Sergio. 1998. "Dalla parte di Satana: Sull'imperialismo cristiano nella *Gerusalemme Liberata*." In *La rappresentazione dell'altro nei testi del Rinascimento*, edited by Sergio Zatti, 146–81. Lucca: Pacini Fazzi.

———. 2004. "Epigoni del Tasso nella Firenze granducale." In Rosa and Superbi 2004, 1:39–58.

Zimmerman, Margarete. 2003. "The Old Quarrel: More Than Just Rhetoric?" In *The Querelle des femmes in the Romania: Studies in Honour of Friedericke Hassauer*, edited by Wolfram Aichinger et al., 27–42. Vienna: Turia & Kant.

Zonta, Giuseppe. 1906. "La *Partenia* di Barbara Torelli-Benedetti." *Rassegna bibliografica della letteratura italiana* 14:206–10.

Zorzi, Niccolò. 2004–5. "Niceta Coniata fonte dell'*Enrico, ovvero Bisanzio acquistato* (1635) di Lucrezia Marinella." *Incontri triestini di filologia classica* 4:415–28.

INDEX

academies: artistic, 17, 282n98; literary, 13, 15–18, 48, 50, 95–96, 118, 228, 233, 256–58, 282n104
Acciaiuoli, Zanobi, 158, 281n86
Acquaviva, Claudio, 60, 253
Acquaviva, Dorotea, 253
actresses, 4, 8, 48, 95, 111, 113, 275n19. *See also* performers, noblewomen as
Adonis (mythological figure), 40, 79–80, 212
Agnes, Saint, 69, 71, 142
Agrippa, Henricus Cornelius, 67, 243
Aiutamicristo, Elisabetta, 253
Alberici, Giacomo, 28
Alberti, Filippo, 270
Albiosi, Ginevra, 253, 296n7
Alcina (in Ariosto), 40, 42, 183–85, 212
Aldobrandini, Cinzio, 8, 339n1
Aleardi, Lodovico, 256
Alessandria (Piedmont), 17, 268
Alighieri, Dante, 62, 64, 127, 205, 231, 234, 298n35, 363n91
allegory: as critical paratext, 7, 201–3; as literary device/mode, 137, 175, 184–85, 204–5, 245, 247, 363n92
Almerici, Paola, 277n43
Amazons, 3, 43, 123, 146, 158–59, 161–62, 275n25, 338nn158–59
Ammanati, Bartolomeo, 59, 281n86
Ancina, Giovanni Giovenale, 56, 65
Andreini, Francesco, 216, 254, 281n87, 317n65
Andreini, Giovanni Battista, 41, 254, 266, 317n65
Andreini, Isabella, xiii, 6–7, 17, 164, 216, 254, 262, 281n87, 323n154; as actress, xvii, 4, 77, 95, 100–101, 111–12, 306n157; critical work on, 292–93n236, 295n6, 316n64, 357n15; as lyric poet, xvii, 51–52, 54–56, 62, 76–78, 84, 295–96nn5–7; marriage/domestic life of, 15–16, 281n87; *Mirtilla*, 92, 94–103, 106, 110–13; pastoral eclogues of, 115, 117–18; translations of works by, xvii, 97, 102, 316n55
Andreini, Virginia, 266
Angaran, Bianca, 264, 295n7
Angeli, Niccolò degli, 123
Angelica (in Ariosto), 137, 182, 201, 204
Angeli da Barga, Pietro, 267
Angelucci, Teodoro, 263, 332n72
Angiolello, Antonmaria, 282n99
Anguissola, Sofonisba, 23–24
anthologies, lyric, 8–9, 52, 251, 295–96n7; religious, 28, 35, 65–66, 70, 227, 289n193
Antoniano, Silvio, 21–22, 254
"A.P.," 265, 296n7, 297n27
Apollo (mythological figure), 48, 62–63, 153, 209, 211, 235, 275n20, 280n81, 291n223
Apuleius, 154, 200–201, 205
Aquinas, Saint Thomas, 214, 220
Arcadia (literary movement), 251
Aretino, Pietro, 242, 244; as model/source, 152, 229, 328n9, 335n120, 364n105, 368n155
Ariosto, Lodovico, 37, 49, 132, 159, 165–66, 168, 289n186, 290n207; 'converted' to religious uses, 39–40, 136–37; as model/source, 99, 171, 174, 179–81, 183–84, 201–2, 204, 212; sex and gender in, 42, 45, 104, 113, 177–78, 180, 212. *See also* Alcina; Angelica
Aristotle, 160, 220–21, 238, 337n154, 356n234; as gender theorist, xiii, 204, 239–40, 346n85; as poetic/rhetorical theorist, 154, 167, 246

Armani, Vincenza, 95
Armida (in Tasso), 147–48, 183–85, 193, 207–8, 333n94
art (visual). *See* ekphrasis
artists, female, xvi, 2, 17, 23–24, 275n19, 284–85n131
Asinari, Federico, 254, 326n186
Asinari, Margherita, 254
Astolfi, Giovanni Felice, 246
Augustine of Hippo (Saint Augustine), 25, 34, 220, 304n121
Avanzi, Giovanni Maria, 263, 332n72
Avogadro, Paola Virginia, 254
Azzalina, Maria, 254, 295n7

Balcianelli, Marcantonio, 256, 264, 324n162
Baldi, Bernardino, 24–26, 46, 257, 261, 264, 269, 286n152, 304n111
Balducci, Francesco, 270
Barbo, Giovanni Battista, 29, 49, 205, 218, 225, 242, 280n84
Bardi, Francesco, 341n19
Barezzi, Barezzo, 7
Bargagli, Girolamo, 255
Bargagli, Scipione, 245, 268
Barletius, Marinus, 172, 342n33, 342n39
Baroque literary movement, xiv, 47–48, 52–55, 78, 149, 195, 203
Bartoli, Clemente, 254
Bartoli, Minerva, 25, 254
Battiferra, Laura, 5, 15–17, 25, 52, 215, 251, 255, 273n29, 281n86; literary contacts of, 22, 36, 300n53; 301n77; as religious poet, 35, 55–56, 59–62, 64–65, 158, 286n152, 304n120, 312n2; as secular poet, 3, 76, 86, 94, 116–18
beauty: female, 46, 53, 70–72, 185, 194–95, 238; male, 124, 187–88, 193–94, 348n115; saintly, 40, 70–72, 147–49, 155. *See also* Adonis; Narcissus; Neoplatonism
Beccari, Agostino, 113
Beccaria, Angela Bianca, 9–10
Bellinzona, Gherardo, 282n99
Bembo, Pietro, 24, 33, 46, 52, 72, 77, 249, 298n35, 300n56
Bendinelli, Antonio, 12, 255
Bendinelli, Scipione, 12, 255, 303n102
Bendinelli, Silvia, 2, 12, 255, 296n7, 303n102

Benedict, Saint, 39, 44, 143, 291n223
Benigni, Ippolita, 15, 17, 255, 295n7
Bergalli, Luisa, 60, 251, 300n54, 370n6
Bergamo, 8, 256, 261, 265, 268
Bernal, Beatriz, 87, 165, 339n4, 345n75
Bernardi, Leonora, 2, 24, 31, 255–56, 275n19, 285n131, 296n7, 312n2; as lyric poet, 56, 66–68, 252; *Tragicomedia pastorale*, 93, 97–99, 101, 107–9, 113–15, 310–11n203, 318n81, 338n154, 355n226
Bertani, Barbara, 256
Bertani, Lucia, 255
Betussi, Giuseppe, 1, 248
Bible: as source/inspiration for literature, 33–35, 37–38, 62–64, 131–41, 151–54, 157–60, 229–30. *See also* canticles; censorship; psalms/psalm translations
Bigolina, Giulia, 2, 87, 104, 218, 274n7
Binaschi, Filippo, 257, 278n61
Bobali, Savino, 255
Boccaccio, Giovanni, 32, 125–26, 154, 199, 218, 221, 239, 249, 339n1, 348n119
Boccalini, Traiano, 48
Boethius, 228, 231, 234
Boiardo, Matteo Maria, 159, 167, 177, 201, 204, 348n115
Bologna, 8, 58, 222, 227, 261–62, 265–66, 357n7. *See also* Monte della Guardia, Sanctuary of
Bolzetta, Francesco, 120
Bona, Giulia di, 308n177
Bona, Speranza Vittoria di, 308n177
Bonanno, Laura, 10
Bonanno, Marta, 10
Bonanno, Onofria, 8, 10
Bonardo, Giovanni Maria, 264, 365n123
Bonarelli, Guidobaldo, 107
Bonifaccio, Baldassare, 49, 219, 258, 312n11
Bordoni, Giacomo, 280n84
Borghesi, Diomede, 256
Borgogni, Gherardo, 254
Borromeo, Saint Carlo, 21, 214, 304n121
Bovarini, Leandro, 255
Bovio, Alessandro, 27, 263
Bracciolini, Francesco: *Amoroso sdegno*, 115, 322n142; *La croce racquistata*, 159, 162, 178, 339n162, 339n164

Bragadin, Marcantonio, 176
Bragadin, Veneranda, 3, 15, 197–98, 256; as poet, 56, 66, 80, 84, 304n120, 330n37; as polemicist, 29, 205, 218–19, 225, 242, 358n27
Branchi, Giacinto, 31
Bratteolo, Giacomo, 13–14
Brembati, Isotta, 10, 231, 256
Brenzoni, Laura, 2, 274n12
Briani, Girolamo, 48
Bridget of Sweden, Saint, 24
Briet, Marguerite, 312n3
Bronzini, Cristoforo, 2, 29, 159, 197, 222, 286n157, 290n199; as contact of Lucrezia Marinella, 7, 196, 263, 276n36, 335n122, 351n162
Bronzino, Agnolo, 160, 255
Bruni, Antonio, 270
Bruno, Giordano, xiv
Bufalini, Giulio (1504–83), 81, 269
Bufalini, Giulio (1576–1642), 83, 269
Bufalini, Ottavio, 83, 269
Bulgarini, Belisario, 267
Bulifon, Antonio, 215, 251
Buonarroti, Michelangelo, 64
Burchelati, Bartolomeo, 79
Bursati, Lucrezio, 29–30

Caccini, Francesca, 24
Calcina, Eugenia, 8, 277n50
Camilli, Camillo, 135, 178, 257
Camilliardi, Chiara, 257
Camillo, Giulio, 154
Campanella, Tommaso, xiv, 290n196
Campeggi, Ridolfo, 65
Campiglia, Maddalena, 2–3, 5–7, 257, 278n61, 321n118; and Accademia Olimpica, 17–18, 95–96, 111, 282n99, 282n102; *Calisa*, 77, 116–17; critical work on, 316n63, 322n144, 361n64; *Discorso*, 26–27, 66, 105, 215, 225–31, 235; *Flori*, 17, 26, 92–106, 109–18, 123, 127, 194, 219, 248, 323n149; lost works by, 41, 257, 286n143; as lyric poet, 56, 73–74, 116, 295–96n7, 310n199; personal/domestic life of, 16, 105–6, 248, 281n90, 318n91, 362n80; verse in praise of, 17–18, 25, 225, 282n99, 361n58

canticles (biblical), 33, 35–36, 289–90nn195–96, 290n198
Capaccio, Giulio Cesare, 166–67, 352n176
Capece, Isabella, 27, 66, 215, 223–24, 257
Caponsacchi, Pietro, 34
Cappello, Bianca, 60, 159, 161, 169, 338n161
Cappello, Laura Beatrice, 8–10, 257
Carafa, Ferrante, 65, 297n27
Caro, Annibale, 255
Carrari, Fabrizia, 12, 17, 107, 118, 258, 295–96n7
Carrari, Innocenza, 12, 17, 257, 296n7, 323n159
Carrari, Silvestro, 118, 258
Caruso, Francesco, 29
Cary, Elizabeth, 87
Castagna, Girolama, 258, 296n7
Castellani, Girolama, 7
Castelletti, Sebastiano, 40, 142–43, 333n94, 333–34n98
Castiglione, Baldassare, 227, 237, 314n39
Catherine of Alexandria, Saint, 31, 42–43, 221, 226; as subject of literature, 69, 71, 141–42, 304n114, 304nn120–21
Catherine of Bologna, Saint, 213
Catherine of Genoa, Saint, 23–24, 213, 270, 360n47
Catherine of Siena, Saint, 150, 213, 221, 360n50; as subject of literature, 69–70, 72, 151–57, 185
Cavaletti, Ercole, 15, 256, 258
Cavaletti, Orsina, xxiii, 15–16, 256, 258, 261, 295–96n7; as lyric poet, 24, 55–56, 78, 84, 322n141
Cavaletti Lotti, Barbara, 258, 296n7, 297n18
Cavalieri, Emilio de', 93
Cavalli, Francesco, 256
Cavallina, Domenico, 266
Cebà, Ansaldo, 157–58, 258
Cecilia, Saint, 8, 41–42, 142, 327n4, 333n94
Cellini, Benvenuto, 255
censorship, 32, 131, 152, 158, 288n173, 290n204, 294n255
Cereta, Laura, 218, 241
Cervoni, Giovanni, 13, 279n73
Cervoni, Isabella, 13, 17, 56, 84–85, 258, 297n7, 298n31; *Orazione*, 217, 224, 226

Chiabrera, Gabriello, xiv, 55, 254, 339n162
Chiappino, Paolo, 17, 282n99
Chiariti, Domenico, 256, 260, 263, 307n160
chivalric romance. *See* Fonte, Moderata: *Il Floridoro*
Christ, Jesus, as literary subject, 57, 61, 63–65, 72–76, 131–41
Christina, Saint, 40, 142, 304n120
Christine of Lorraine, 76, 262, 314n34, 338n160, 339n162; and Bernardi, 97, 310n203; and Isabella Cervoni, 13, 84; and Marinella, 143, 154; and Salvetti, 3, 54, 85–86, 162–63
Cibo, Leonora, 94
Cicerchia, Niccolò, 327n2
Ciotti, Giambattista: as editor of religious texts, 40, 43; as publisher of Marinella, 7, 18, 28, 152, 201, 236, 352n173
Cittadini, Celso, 34
Clara, Ippolita, 24
Clare of Assisi, Saint, 149, 234, 304n110
Clement VIII (pope; Ippolito Aldobrandini), 36, 68, 119, 138, 141, 217, 224
Coignard, Gabrielle, 25, 331n54
Colao, Lucia, 55–56, 60–62, 251, 258, 323n159, 338n156, 360n6
Collalto, Antonio da, 118
Collalto, Collaltino da, 78
Colle, Giovanni, 263
Colonna, Anna, 81
Colonna, Vittoria, xii, 5–6, 12, 16, 51, 157, 251, 274n12, 296n7; critical work on, 289n188; *Litere*, 213, 215; as model/icon for female poets, 3, 53, 61, 86, 106, 301n74; *Pianto*, 133, 213, 215; as religious poet, 34, 36, 56–57, 61, 63, 65, 70–71, 73, 294n250
Colzè, Dionisio, 105, 278n61, 362n80
comedy (genre), 40–42, 92–93, 199, 212. See also *commedia dell'arte*
commedia dell'arte, 95, 100
Contarini, Francesco, 113, 168
Contarini, Luigi, 246
convents: cultural life of, 20, 25, 87, 89, 280n78; educational role of, 14, 89, 156, 278n63; literary production in, 7–10, 23, 214–15, 222–23, 226, 251, 276n38, 284n128, 302n88; Tridentine regulation of,

19–20, 283n108. *See also* Poggi, Semidea; Strozzi, Lorenza; Vernazza, Battista
Copio, Sara, 49, 157, 219, 258, 358n29, 367n146
Corbellini, Aurelio, 65
Coreglia, Isabetta, xxii, 2, 56, 258–59, 275n19, 279n65, 282n104; as authors of pastoral plays, 93, 97, 110–11, 317n65, 318n81, 321n117, 355n226
Corinna (classical poet), 88
Cornaro, Chiara, 216, 310n201
Cornazzano, Antonio, 327n2
Corso, Rinaldo, 11
Cortese, Isabella, 216
Cortesi, Cortese, 40, 120, 124, 257, 361n58
Costa, Margherita, xxiii, 92, 186, 327n4
"Costanza L.," 259
Coste, Hilarion de, xvii, 284n125
Counter-Reformation, xii, xxiii–xxiv; and gender attitudes, xviii–xix, 19–32, 35–37, 41–45, 49–50, 225–26; and literature, xx, 32–45, 46–47, 54, 103, 129, 141–43, 150. *See also* censorship; convents; religious orders
Crashaw, Richard, 31
Crema, Marco da, 356n7
Crenne, Hélisenne de, 87
cross-dressing, as literary motif, 69–70, 104, 123, 200, 206–7, 325n179
Cupid (mythological figure), 200–205, 212, 353n190, 353n196

dalla Torre, Marina, 259, 323n159
dalla Torre, Zanetta, 259
"Damiana, Suor," 8–9, 259, 296n7
Dandolo, Enrico, 168
d'Aragona, Tullia, 3, 5, 76, 94–95, 165–66, 213, 217, 251, 284n126
d'Austria, Caterina, 141
d'Austria, Giovanna, 339n162
d'Austria, Maria Maddalena, 84, 154, 158–59, 160–62, 339n162
d'Austria Gonzaga, Leonora, 292n234
David (biblical figure), 4, 33, 62, 158, 161
Deborah (biblical figure), 35–36
De Cupiti, Agostino, 45–46, 56, 141–43, 255, 294n250, 300n53
dedications, of religious books to women: lyric

poetry, 25, 285n141; narrative, 41, 130, 133, 143, 158, 227–28, 292n234
dedicatory practices, of women writers, 6–7, 119, 133, 138, 143, 154, 158–59, 169, 177, 197–98, 332n70. *See also* letters, as literary genre: dedicatory
"defenses of women," 23, 29–30, 43, 49, 197, 216–19, 273n3, 358n24. See also *querelle des femmes*
de' Ferrari, Maria, 259
Della Casa, Giovanni, 56, 77, 247, 298n35
Della Chiesa, Francesca Benedetta, 23, 259, 284n128
Della Chiesa, Francesco Agostino, 2, 22–23, 29–30, 57, 66, 197, 221–22
Della Chiesa, Francesco Scipione, 23
della Porta, Giambattista, 356n232
della Rovere, Livia Feltria, 25
della Rovere, Vittoria, 161, 311n204
Della Valle, Fabrizio, 259
Della Valle, Federico, 333n94
Della Valle, Francesco, 267, 270
Della Valle, Lisabetta, 259, 296n7
Della Valle, Lucrezia, 11, 17, 54, 259, 278–79n64
Dell'Uva, Benedetto, xx, 142–43, 263
de Marquets, Anne, 7, 276n41
dialogue, as literary genre, 91, 213, 215, 217, 227–29, 232–33, 236–38, 243–49
Diana (mythological figure), 78, 235, 315n48; as Arcadian deity, 98, 106, 209–10, 355n226; as goddess of chastity, 100, 105, 161, 189, 200–201, 204; as huntress, 82, 161. *See also* Montemayor, Jorge de
Dido (in Virgil), 185, 192, 205, 333n94, 349n131, 350n136
di Zucco, Lucella, 12, 259, 262, 296n7
Doglioni, Giovanni Niccolò, 12, 88, 166, 242, 260, 365n123
Dolce, Lodovico, 121, 157, 346n90, 346n98
Dolfin, Chiara. *See* Cornaro, Chiara
Domenichi, Lodovico, 10, 263
Dominic, Saint, 59, 157, 277n43, 304n121. *See also* religious orders: Dominicans
Doni, Antonia, 260, 295–96n7
Doria Colonna, Giovanna, 25
Doria Gonzaga, Vittoria, 25, 93–94

Dotti, Claudia, 277n42
Dowriche, Anne, 87
Droghi, Antonio, 352n177, 354n215
Ducchi, Gregorio, 26–27, 225, 229, 231, 257, 361n58
d'Urfé, Honoré, 199

Ebreo, Leone (Abravanel, Judah), 233
education, of women, 11–14, 21–23, 48, 238, 243, 278n63, 284n126, 365n120. *See also* convents: educational role of; Latin: studied by women; teachers, women as
ekphrasis: in lyric verse, 70, 304n114; in narrative literature, 159, 175–76, 184, 202, 210–11
eloquence, as virtue in women, 4, 21, 56, 221, 226. *See also* orations; rhetoric
enchantress, as literary type, 40, 42, 147–48, 170, 183–85, 192–93, 207–210, 291–92n225. *See also* Alcina; Armida
England, women's writing in, xvi–xvii, 87, 165
epic, 87, 165–79, 182–86, 189–97, 200–205, 339n2; 'converted' to religious uses, 37–40, 141–54, 157–63, 229, 333n94; and gender, 30–31, 42–45, 146–49, 177–96, 292n235, 344n72
Ercolani, Ercolano, 40–41
Erculiani, Camilla, 211, 216, 226, 237–38, 261
Erizzo, Francesco, 169
Errico, Scipione, 170
Erythraeus, Janus Nicius, 59, 167, 197
Este, Alfonso II d', 217
Este, Beatrice d', 70
Este, Giulia d', 169
Este, Lucrezia d', 227
Este, Marfisa d', 109, 227, 234, 320n108
Esther (biblical figure), 42, 68, 157–58, 303n99
Eudocia (classical poet), 88, 130
Euripides, 214, 325n174, 353n186
Eve (biblical figure), 67–68, 203, 220, 235, 238, 302n90, 303n95

Fabra, Stratonica, 260, 296n7
Fabri, Giovanni Paolo, 263
Falconio, Arrigo, 119–20
family affection, as theme in lyric, 53, 78–84
family backgrounds, of women writers, 10–16

family relationships, as theme in literature: brother-sister, 40–41, 98, 190–93; father-daughter, 82, 102–3, 108, 155–56, 212, 222, 309n192; father-son, 108, 187; husband-wife, 53, 81, 85, 105, 174, 181–82, 308n179, 318n90; mother-daughter, 3, 80, 155–56, 183, 274n15; mother-son, 78–80, 82–83, 156, 181, 188, 205, 308n177; sister-sister, 308n177

"famous women" discourse, xvii, 1–2, 68, 90, 213, 287n159, 366n132

Fantini, Fantino, 361n58

Fedele, Cassandra, 216, 274n12

Ferrara, 15, 109, 255–56, 258, 264, 307n60

Ferri, Pentisilea, 24

Ferro, Cherubina, 260, 296n7

Fiamma, Gabriele, xiv, xx, 32–36, 45–46, 56, 62, 131, 230, 255, 297n27

Ficino, Marsilio, 33, 35, 275n25

Filicaia, Lodovico da, 144

Filippi, Marco, 142–43

Firenzuola, Agnolo, 123, 325n180

Florence, 6, 15, 76–77, 158–60, 265–66, 337n153. *See also* Medici women, as dedicatees of women's writing

Fontana, Lavinia, xvi, 2, 17, 24

Fontanella, Girolamo, 259, 263

Fonte, Moderata (Modesta da Pozzo): xii–xiii, 2–3, 6, 126, 260, 264, 275–76n30, 287n163; background / domestic life of, 5, 12, 14–16, 133; *Le feste*, 88–91, 221, 313n15; *Il Floridoro*, 60, 127, 132, 162, 164–68, 175–76, 179–84, 186–89, 191, 196–97; as lyric poet, 56, 63–64, 78, 84, 295n7, 307n160, 365n123; *Il merito delle donne*, 29, 91, 109, 137, 200, 212, 217, 222, 236–49, 364n108; *La passione di Christo*, 35, 130–35; *La resurrettione di Giesu Christo*, 72, 130–38, 142, 333n94

Foresti, Iacopo Filippo, 287n159

Forteguerri, Laudomia, 77

Forzatè, Claudio, 120, 257, 265, 325n171

France, women's writing in, xvii, 7, 87

Franciotti, Cesare, 67

Francis of Assisi, Saint, as literary subject, 44, 142–45, 149–51, 293n248, 299n40, 299n48, 303n106, 304n121, 355n228. *See also* religious orders: Franciscans

Franco, Veronica, 16, 164, 215, 218, 260, 284n126

François de Sales, Saint, 31

Fratta, Giovanni, 358n20

friendship, as theme in literature, 109–10

Frizzimellega, Antonio, 361n58

Gabrielli, Clizia, 260, 295n7

Gagliardia, Iseppe, 361n58

Gagliardo, Giuseppe, 265

Galilei, Galileo, 169, 211, 238, 267

Galli, Antonio, 11, 255, 261

Galli Aurispi, Vittoria, 11, 25, 256, 261

Gallucci, Agostino, 44, 144, 333n94

Gambara, Veronica, 3, 12, 16, 85–86, 251, 265, 274n12

Garibbi, Giacomo, 144

Garzoni, Candiana de', 53

Garzoni, Tommaso, 366n133

Gatti, Alessandro, 263

Gatti, Beatrice, 8, 10, 214, 216, 226, 261

Gatti, Carlo, 255

Gelli, Giovanni Battista, 160

Gelmi, Giovanni Antonio, 79

Genoa, 8, 22–23, 268, 270

Gentileschi, Artemisia, 17

Ghelfucci, Capoleone, 130, 327n5, 330n42

Giambelli, Cipriano, 287n160

Giambullari, Pierfrancesco, 160

Giraldi Cinzio, Giambattista, 121, 123

Giuliani, Vespasiano, 225

Giustinian, Orsatto, 53, 143, 257–58, 260, 263

Goffredo (in Tasso), 30, 44, 145, 147–48, 178, 189–90, 338n160

Gondola, Maria (Mara Gundilić), 15, 216, 238, 261

Gonzaga, Curzio, 18, 96, 110, 117, 166, 177–78, 189, 257, 269

Gonzaga, Eleonora de' Medici, 84, 119, 120, 197, 201, 276n36, 338n156

Gonzaga, Ferdinando, 41

Gonzaga, Ferrante II (of Guastalla), 25, 96, 269

Gonzaga, Lucrezia, 213, 356n4

Gonzaga d'Este, Margherita, 109, 143, 276n36

Gorgias, 154

Goselini, Giuliano, 53, 78–79, 269

Gozze, Niccolò Vito di (Nikola Vitov Gučetić), 15, 216
Granada, Luis de, 63
Grandi, Adriano, 254
Grandi, Ascanio, 338n158, 345n79
Grassi, Ottavia, 261, 295n7
Gregory XIII (pope; Ugo Boncompagni), 60
Grillo, Angelo, 46, 54, 201; as religious lyricist, 27–28, 31, 35, 38–39, 52, 57, 63, 65, 201, 331n54; and women writers, xix, 18, 23–26, 66–67, 96, 119, 256–57, 264, 268–69
Grimani, Marino (doge), 88
Grossi Sacchi, Laura, 261, 296n7
Groto, Luigi, 53, 89, 225, 248, 257, 260, 264; as playwright, 120, 325n184, 326n186
Grumelli, Flavia, 8, 214, 222–23, 226, 261, 277n50, 359n44
Guarguanti, Orazio, 260, 328n13, 369n175
Guarini, Giovanni Battista, xiv, 42, 52, 92–93, 96, 103, 109, 113, 115, 269
Guazzo, Stefano, 8–10
guerriera. See woman warrior, as literary type
Guidiccioni, Cristoforo, 11, 262
Guidiccioni, Giovanni, 11, 56, 262
Guidiccioni, Laura, 2, 11, 15, 93, 97, 254, 262, 275n19, 323n154

hagiography. *See* saints, as literary subjects
Henri IV, xvii, 84–85
Herculiana, Camilla. *See* Erculiani, Camilla
Hero of Alexandria, 211, 356n233
Homer, 12, 38, 130, 146, 166, 183–84, 190–92, 208
Hypatia of Alexandria, 221

Ingegneri, Angelo, 92, 94, 96, 103, 120–21, 225, 254, 257, 318n83
Innocent III (pope; Lotario dei Conti di Segni), 173
Isocrates, 154, 232

Jerome, Saint, 25, 150, 303n109
Judith (biblical figure), 35–36, 42, 68, 288n168, 304n121, 333n94
Justina of Padua, Saint, 40, 120, 124, 142

Kastrioti, Gjergj (Scanderbeg), 168, 341n18, 342n33; in Sarrocchi, 172–73, 189–91

lagrime poems, 38, 129, 131, 135, 150. *See also* Tansillo, Luigi
Lanci, Cornelio, 25, 197, 261, 267, 292n234, 337n148
Lando, Ortensio, 213
Lanyer, Aemilia, xvii, 272n18
Latin: studied by women, 11, 14, 25, 278n61, 279n64; works by women in, 56, 58–59, 265, 274n8, 274n12, 297–98n28
Lattanzi, Lattanzio, 59
Laura (in Petrarch), 4, 34, 47, 135–37, 204
Leoni, Boncio, 18, 263, 332n72
Leoni, Giovanni Battista, 4
Leonida, Fabio, 119–20, 324n165
letters, as literary genre, 213, 215–16, 227, 232, 238; dedicatory, 36–37, 133, 143, 158, 166, 223–24, 229–30, 235, 290n199
Licco, Gaspare, 40
Lottini, Angelo, 34
love, as literary theme, 33–34, 45–47, 52–54, 76–78, 93, 101–9, 165–66, 191–94, 199–203; same-sex, 104, 116–17, 123–24, 194–96, 318n85. *See also* Petrarchism; sex, as theme in literature
Loyola, Saint Ignatius, 63, 304n121
Lucca, 2, 68, 90, 93, 215, 227, 255, 258–59, 262–63
Lucchesini, Orazio, 15
Lucy, Saint, 31, 69, 142, 304n110, 304n121
Lupi, Orazio, 78, 265, 307n169
Lurago, Angela, 24
lyric poetry, 51–55, 88, 195; female-voiced (by male poets), 36, 57, 290n198; male-voiced (by female poets), 53–54, 77–78; religious, xx, 32–38, 52, 55–76, 131, 155, 289n191, 289n193; secular, 4, 45–48, 76–86, 195. *See also* occasional verse

madrigal, as musical form, 35; as poetic form, 52, 55, 58, 76, 214, 234
maga. See enchantress, as literary type
Maganza, Giovanni Battista, 257, 264–265, 282n99, 361n58
Magno, Celio, 89, 253, 260, 263

Malaspina, Vittoria, 28
Malfitani, Lodovico, 142
Malipiero, Girolamo, 34, 60
Malipiero, Olimpia, 251
Malloni, Maria ("Celia"), 8, 263, 275n19
Malombra, Bartolomeo, 260
Malvasia, Diodata, 8–10, 66, 214, 250, 262, 277n50, 278n54
Manfredi, Laura, 263
Manfredi, Muzio, 15, 93–94, 96, 116, 282n99, 325n171; and Campiglia's *Flori*, 105, 116, 323n149; as literary contact of women, 248, 253–54, 257, 260, 264, 267, 269
Manuzio, Aldo (the Younger), 263, 267, 361n65
Manzano, Scipione di, 168
Manzoni, Ercole, 264, 324n162
Marchesi, Antonio, 14, 262
Marchesi, Caterina (Catella), 13–14, 262, 280n82, 296n7
Marchesi, Lidia Sasso, 14, 262
Marescotti, Margherita, 262, 295–96n7
Margaret of Austria (later of Parma), 36, 77
Marguerite de Navarre, 87
Maria of Austria, Empress, 216
Marinella, Lucrezia, xii–xiii, xxiii, 3–7, 18–19, 250–52, 262–63, 271n5, 283nn106–7, 295–96n7; *Amore innamorato, et impazzato*, 156, 164, 197–98, 200–205, 212, 351n170, 352n182; *Arcadia felice*, 28, 120, 154, 164, 179, 197–200, 206–12, 335n123, 351–52nn173–74; background/domestic life of, 10–11, 14–16, 151, 212, 271n5; *Discorso del rivolgimento amoroso*, 155, 157, 215, 220, 334n104; *L'Enrico*, 69, 164–65, 168–79, 183–86, 191–92, 196–97, 209, 211–12, 336n128, 339n2; *Essortationi*, 197, 250, 348n110, 370n3; hagiographic writings of, 28, 130–31, 141–57, 160, 177, 185, 204, 332n77, 335n121; as lyric poet, 28, 54–58, 68–73, 144, 155, 280n84, 286n151; male vanity as theme in, 212, 241; *La nobiltà et eccellenza delle donne*, 3, 18–19, 28–30, 90, 166, 217–18, 236–42, 250, 287n166, 364nn108–9; politics/civic life as theme in, 173–77, 210–11
Marinelli, Curzio, 11, 18, 240, 242, 262, 271n5
Marinelli, Giovanni, 11, 212, 262

Marino, Giovanni Battista, xiv, 119, 167, 203, 254, 267; as lyric poet, 35, 46–50, 53–54, 65, 298n39, 305n131, 305n137
marriage, 14–15, 19–20; as theme in women's writing, 81, 100, 102–3, 108, 182, 242–43, 247–48, 317n68, 362n80. *See also* single life, as choice for women
Martinengo, Lucillo, 65, 142–143, 152, 257, 333–34n98
Mary (biblical figure). *See* Virgin Mary
Mary Magdalene (biblical figure), 27, 127, 305n131; in dramatic/narrative writings, 38, 41–42, 129, 133–37, 149, 151, 154–55, 327n4; in lyric poetry, 57, 69, 72–76, 290n198, 304n121
Marzi, Ottavio, 270
masculinity, 30–31, 44, 50, 57, 349n126; in women's writing, 114–15, 123–24, 145, 186–91, 193–94, 367n143
Massarengo, Giovanni Battista, 10, 257
Massimi, Maddalena, 263
Massini, Filippo, 279n71
Matilda, Countess of Tuscany, 188
Matraini, Chiara, 2, 16, 90, 213; late religious writings of, 27, 55, 65, 68, 86, 214–15, 223–25, 227–29, 231–35, 250; *Lettere*, 215, 227, 232, 357n14, 363n93; as lyric poet, 52, 55, 58, 65–66, 215, 296n6
matriarchy. *See* Amazons; religion, matriarchal
Mauduit, Jacques, 59
Medici, Caterina de', queen of France, 162–63
Medici, Cosimo I de', 160, 162–63
Medici, Cosimo II de', 84, 154, 159, 162, 316n57
Medici, Ferdinando I de', 76, 97, 162, 262, 314n34, 316n57
Medici, Francesco I de', Grand Duke of Tuscany, 60, 97, 161–62, 169, 255, 300n53
Medici, Isabella de', 163, 339n164
Medici, Maria de', queen of France, xvii, 59, 84–85, 292n234
Medici della Rovere, Claudia de', 311n204
Medici Gonzaga, Caterina de', 41, 197–98, 338n156
Medici Gonzaga, Eleonora de', 120, 197, 276n36, 338n156
Medici women, as dedicatees of women's writing, 338n156

Melania the Younger, Saint, 221
Melchiori, Francesco, 17, 257, 274n10, 305n139
Mercurio, Scipione, 43
Miani, Valeria, 2, 5, 18, 84, 264, 296n7; *Amorosa speranza*, 93, 97–98, 100, 106–7, 110, 112–13, 118–19, 317n67; *Celinda*, 119–28, 325n173
Miari, Alessandro, 254, 256, 268, 325n171
Minerva/Pallas (mythological figure), 4, 12, 89, 170, 182
Minturno, Antonio, 35, 201
Miriam (biblical figure), 35–36, 289–90nn195–96
misogyny, 20–22, 29–30, 42, 48–50, 113, 115, 218–19, 225, 237, 239; in women's writing, 126, 185–86. *See also* Counter-Reformation: and gender attitudes
Modena, Leone, 258
Molza, Francesco Maria, 11, 56, 264, 294n260
Molza, Tarquinia, xvii, 11, 16, 25, 264, 275n19, 284n130; as poet, 58, 295–96n7, 298n28
Monferrato, Bonifazio di, 340–41n17
Montanari Baldi, Virginia, 25
Monte, Issicratea, 5, 17–18, 237, 248, 257, 260, 264, 275n29; as orator, 89, 216, 219, 312n11, 358n22; as poet, 295n7, 365n123
Monte della Guardia, Sanctuary of (Bologna), 8, 58, 66, 250
Montefuscoli, Giovanni Domenico, 142, 330n42
Montemayor, Jorge de, 199, 208, 352n176, 352n180
Monti, Scipione de', 168
Monti, Zaccaria, 59
Morandi, Bernardo, 263
Morigi, Giulio, 264
Mozzagrugno, Giuseppe, 27, 224–25
Murtola, Gaspare, 119
music, as creative activity for women, 4, 111, 185, 207, 275n19. *See also* Caccini, Francesca; Peverara, Laura
musical settings of verse, 18, 34, 51, 56, 59, 94, 295n3, 301n73, 307n158
Muzio, Girolamo, 94

Naldi, Bianca, 49, 205, 219, 264
Naples, 46, 168, 257, 267

Narcissus (mythological figure), 40, 100, 307n171, 316–17n65
natural philosophy. *See* science, as theme in women's writing
Navazzotti, Orazio, 269
Neoplatonic love, 26, 34, 46–47, 52, 54, 85, 105, 135, 192
Neoplatonism, 33, 35, 71–72, 137, 215, 220, 238. *See also* Neoplatonic love
Nicelli, Giacomo, 255
Nogarola, Isotta, 2, 213, 216, 248, 274n12
nuns: as addressees of lyric poetry, 10, 56; as dedicatees of literary works, 277–78n54, 285n141, 292n234, 293n241; as writers (*see* convents: literary production in)

occasional verse, 53–54, 81, 84–86, 295–96n7, 310–11nn201–4
Omboni Lupi, Domenica, 265
orations, 89, 207, 213, 216–17, 222, 224, 226, 228, 233–34, 244
Orsini, Virginio, 163, 339n164
Orsini Colonna, Felice, 292n234
Orsini Sforza, Leonora, 163, 339n164
Ottonelli, Giovanni Domenico, 21–22, 220, 222
Ovid, 137, 174, 182, 201, 325n179

Pace, Fabio, 282n99
Padua, 2, 97, 119–20, 211, 237, 254, 259–61, 263–64, 266, 280n84
Pagani, Antonio, 228
Pagano, Pietro Cola, 27, 224
Palermo, 8, 219, 222, 253, 264
Palestrina, Giovanni Pierluigi da, 34
Pallavicino Lupi, Isabella, 17–18, 77, 84, 94, 105, 116, 265, 282n96, 310n199
Pallentieri, Girolamo, 269
Paluzzi, Numidio, 49, 258
Pancetti, Camillo, 168, 341n21
Pannolini, Febronia, 8, 58, 265, 298n28
Parabosco, Girolamo, 245
Parma, 15–16, 18, 95–96, 269
Pasqualigo, Fabrizio, 361n58
Passero, Felice, xx, 39–40, 44, 142–43, 257
Passi, Giuseppe, 29, 48, 205, 218–20, 236–41, 255, 287n160, 366n133

pastoral literature, 25–26, 42, 92–118, 189, 197–200, 206–12
Patrizi, Francesco, 264, 290n196
patrons, women as literary, 22, 77, 85–86, 116, 141, 161
Paul, Saint, 21, 157, 220
Pavia, 8, 10, 17, 216, 257
Pellicani, Alessandro, 266
Peregrini Mazzarelli, Laura 285n132
Peretti Sforza, Orsina, 25
performers, noblewomen as, 94, 109, 315n41
Persio, Ascanio, 263, 299n41
Peter, Saint, 37, 132, 134, 141
Petracci, Pietro, 264, 280n81, 289n193, 296n7
Petrarca, Francesco, 56, 240, 298n35; 'converted' to spiritual uses, 33–34, 60–62, 75, 135–37, 305n133; as model/source, 4, 90, 204, 301n79, 306n153, 306n156, 308n176, 323n155
Petrarchism, 46–47, 49, 52–55, 57, 115, 129, 135–36, 155
Petrelli, Eugenio, 70, 304n110
Peverara, Laura, 24, 307n160
Piacentino, Ippolito, 255
Piccolomini, Agnese. *See* "A.P."
Pico, Renea, 265
Piedmont, 22, 53, 133, 168, 216, 254, 259. *See also* Alessandria
Pietri, Francesco de', 223
Pigafetta, Filippo, 265
Pigafetta, Osanna, 8, 11, 214–15, 265, 277n50
Pighini, Ginevra, 266
Piissimi, Vittoria, 95, 111
Pizan, Christine de, 358n24
Plato, 154, 220. *See also* Neoplatonism
Pliny, 246, 346n88
Plutarch, 214, 240
"poetics of conversion," 32–41, 45, 60–61, 288n184
Poggi, Semidea, 8–10, 56, 62–63, 66, 266, 277n50, 278n54
Poggiolini, Roberto, 254, 262, 278n54, 356n7
polemical writings, 49, 218–19, 236–42, 358n24, 365n115, 367n146
Policreti, Giuseppe, 35, 263, 280n84

Ponte, Niccolò da (doge), 88–89, 133, 216
Poppi, Fra Silvestro da, 28
Porto, Luigi da, 125
Proba, 88, 130
psalms / psalm translations, 33–35, 38, 58, 62, 131, 215, 223–24, 289n190
Puteanus, Erycius, 254

Quattromani, Sertorio, 11, 259, 279n64
querelle des femmes, xix, 28–30, 68, 85–86, 217–18, 236–49, 365n124. *See also* "defenses of women"; misogyny
Querenghi, Antonio, 264

Rasponi, Felicia, 8–10, 277n54
Rava, Agostino, 257
Razzi, Serafino, 221
Razzi, Silvano, 152, 255
Reganela, Livia, 266, 296n7, 310n201
Reggio Emilia, 17, 256, 268
religion, matriarchal, 209–10, 355n226
religious orders: Augustinians, 8, 27–29, 285n142; Benedictines, xix, 7–8, 23, 39, 143, 261, 270, 285n142; Capuchins, 150, 334n101; Carmelites, 258, 321n117; Cistercians, 23, 259; Clarissans, 8; Dimesse, 228, 369n171; Dominicans, 7–8, 59, 143, 227, 265, 269; Franciscans, 28, 143, 150; Jesuits, 21, 60, 220, 253, 292n227 (*see also* Loyola, Saint Ignatius); Lateran Canons, 8, 23, 29, 214, 258, 266, 286n142, 366n133; Servites, 151, 280n84
Reni, Guido, 9
rhetoric, 21, 91, 244. *See also* eloquence, as virtue in women; orations
Ribera, Pietro Paolo, 2, 29–30, 68, 221–22, 245, 271n5
Ricci, Francesca, 266
Ricciuoli, Federico, 254, 261
Rinaldi, Cesare, 255
Rome, 20, 119, 173, 175, 222; women's writing in, xvii, 16, 22, 84, 255, 260, 266–67
Romei, Annibale, 264
Romieu, Marie de, 358n24
Ronchi, Silvia ("S.R."), 266
rosary texts, 130, 138–41, 229, 329–30n37, 330n42

saints, as literary subjects, 39–40, 42–43, 69–72, 129–31, 222–23, 277n43, 327n4. *See also* Francis of Assisi, Saint
Salaroli, Maddalena, 266, 312n2, 327n4
Salvadori, Andrea, 263
Salvetti, Maddalena, 6, 15, 266–67, 296n7; as epic poet, 131, 157–63, 178; as lyric poet, 3, 52, 76–77, 84–86, 251, 298nn30–31, 304n114
Salvi, Virginia, 17
Salviani, Lucia, 267
Sannazaro, Jacopo, 56; *Arcadia*, 199–200, 206, 208; *De partu virginis*, 37, 39, 152, 290n206
Sappho, 4, 58, 88, 226, 299n46
Sarrocchi, Margherita, xvii, 3, 6–7, 16, 48, 222, 267, 270, 281n92, 365n123; background / education of, 11–12, 22, 173, 298n28; and Galileo, 169, 238, 341n23; hostility of male writers toward, xiii, 16, 49, 88, 167, 285n133; marriage / domestic life of, 15–16, 281n90; *La Scanderbeide*, 120, 164–73, 178–79, 182–83, 189–90, 192–97, 251, 274nn15–16, 312n5, 340n16; sex and gender in, 182–83, 189–90, 192–96
Sasso, Giacomo, 255
satyrs (in pastoral literature), 112–14, 355n231
Sbarra, Lodovica, 267, 307n162
Sbarra, Lucchesia, xiii, 5–6, 12, 16, 18, 251, 267; as lyric poet, 52, 54–55, 76, 78–80, 82, 296n7, 323n159
Sbarra, Pulzio, 12, 18, 307n162
Sbarra, Tiberio, 255
Scala, Alessandra, 13
Scala, Bartolomeo, 13
Scanderbeg. *See* Kastrioti, Gjergj
Scaramelli, Baldassare, 168
Scarano, Lucio, 18, 242, 263
science, as theme in women's writing, 211–12, 237–38
Scrovegni, Maddalena, 2
selva (literary genre), 1, 246
Selva, Crisippo, 60
Semiramis (mythological figure), 43, 127, 159, 226, 361n63
Sempronio, Giovanni Leone, 178
Seneca, 214
Sernigi, Raffaela, 276n41

sex, as theme in literature, 46, 50, 102, 106, 112–13, 123–24, 126–27, 184, 192–94
Sforza, Battista, 274n12
Sforza, Muzio, 4, 14, 73, 226, 253, 257
sibyls (mythological figures), 90, 160, 221, 354n214
Sidney, Mary, xvii, 87
Siena, 13, 17, 48, 262, 265, 268. *See also* Catherine of Siena, Saint
Silvi, Domicilla, 17, 268
Silvi, Silvia, 17, 268
Simonetti, Cesare, 248, 369n175
single life, as choice for women, 105–6, 200, 247–49
Sirleto, Guglielmo, 11–12, 22
Socrates, 233
Soderini, Fiammetta, 255
Solza Rota, Paola, 25, 268
Sommi, Leone de', 113
Sori, Isabella, 17, 49, 216, 219, 268
Spain, women's writing in, 87, 165, 325n179
Spannocchi, Fulvia, 268, 296n7
Spelta, Anton Maria, 29, 48–49, 220, 254, 286n153, 364n109
Speroni, Sperone, 120–21, 239, 245, 320n106
Spilimbergo, Irene di, 14
Spini, Gherardo, 255
Spinola, Alessandro, 23, 268
Spinola, Laura, 23, 268
Spinola, Livia, 23, 56, 66, 268–69, 295–96n7, 304n114
Spinola, Lucia, 268
Spinola, Maria, 23
Spolverini, Ersilia, 2, 216, 219, 267–68, 274n8, 296n7, 298n28
Stampa, Gaspara, xii, 53, 78, 94–95, 251, 299n46
Stanchi, Elena Bianca, 269, 296n7
Stecchini, Marco, 231, 257, 260, 361n58
Stigliani, Tommaso, 167, 197, 263, 343n42
Strassoldo, Giovanni, 262
Striggio, Alessandro, 94
Strozzi, Ciriaco, 11
Strozzi, Giulio, 168, 341n21
Strozzi, Lorenza, xvii, 6, 8–11, 52, 56, 58–59, 70, 269, 277n50, 335n115

Swetnam, Joseph, xvii
Sydney, Philip, 199

Talea, Vittoria, 269, 296n7
Tansillo, Luigi, xiv, 7, 37–38, 56, 129, 132, 202, 290n205
Tarabotti, Arcangela, xxiii, 7, 9, 49, 63, 218, 242
Tassello, Vicenzo, 231, 361n58
Tasso, Bernardo, 35
Tasso, Ercole, 239, 256
Tasso, Torquato, xiv, 49, 120, 125–26, 143, 157, 169, 203, 290n207; *Aminta*, 42, 92–93, 96, 112–15, 127, 189, 313n26, 316n59; as contact of women writers, 6, 15–16, 256–57, 264, 267, 269; 'converted' to spiritual uses, 147–48, 333n94, 333n97; *Gerusalemme liberata*, 30, 37–38, 42–44, 152, 165–66, 170–71, 178, 189–90, 346–47n100; as lyric poet, 35, 46, 52, 60, 63, 65, 77, 115, 289n193; as model/source, 97–102, 108–9, 132, 165, 168, 185, 202, 320n106, 335n126; sex and gender in, 42–44, 112–13, 148, 178, 184–85, 188–90, 218, 239, 292–93nn235–36. *See also* Armida; Goffredo
teachers, women as, 156–57, 220–26, 231–35
Terracina, Laura, 5, 51, 53, 165, 215, 218, 241, 274n12
Tigliamocchi, Barbara, 161
Titian (Tiziano Vecellio), 69
Titoni, Giovanni Battista, 282n99, 361n58
Toledo, Eleonora de, Duchess of Tuscany, 3, 76, 86, 97, 160, 162–63
Tomacelli Colonna, Lucrezia, 81
Tomagni, Giovanni David, 13
Toniani, Pietro Antonio, 256
Toraldo, Vincenzo, 267
Torelli, Alda, 10, 278n61
Torelli, Barbara, 15, 18, 269; *Partenia*, 25–26, 92, 94–98, 102–3, 105, 108, 110–11, 113, 219, 254
Torelli, Pomponio, 121, 126–27, 326n186, 326n190, 326n194
Tornabuoni, Lucrezia, 130
Tortoletti, Bartolomeo, 42, 293n238, 333n94
tragedy (genre), 40–41, 87, 92, 119–28, 168, 324nn166–67
Trevisani, Andriana, 269

Treviso, 79, 118, 257–59
Trissino, Giangiorgo, 227
Trissino, Vittoria, 225, 227–28, 235
Trivulzio, Damigella, 274n12
Tucci, Niccolò, 256
Turina, Francesca, 6, 12, 15, 17, 164, 267, 269–70, 281n91, 327n5, 339n1; as lyric poet, 3, 53–54, 61, 65–67, 70, 74–76, 80–84, 156, 304n121; as occasional poet, 48, 81, 84, 281–82n95; *Rime spirituali*, 6, 36–37, 56, 130, 138–41, 150
Turini, Giovanni, 82, 269, 309n192
Tuscany, 143, 154–55. *See also* Florence; Lucca; Siena
Tyler, Margaret, 87, 165, 340n5

Uberti, Marietta, 119, 324n160
Udine, 12–14, 259, 262
Udine, Ercole, 201
Umbria, 8, 270. *See also* Turina, Francesca
Urban VIII (pope; Maffeo Barberini), 58, 119, 177, 293n238, 337n150
Urbino, 11, 24–25, 254–55, 261
Ursula, Saint, 69–70, 72, 304n120

Valerini, Adriano, 95
Valerio, Luca, 11, 169
Valerius Maximus, 240
Valgrisi, Vincenzo, 34
Valignani, Isabella, 270
Valvasone, Erasmo di, 38–39, 41, 329n24
Vanni, Francesco, 119
Varano, Costanza, 274n12
Varchi, Benedetto, xix, 255, 263, 357n8
Veneto, 5, 84, 118, 216, 218–19, 237, 267, 323n158, 370n6. *See also* Padua; Treviso; Udine; Verona; Vicenza
Venice, 46, 50, 53, 182, 207, 216, 248; as theme in women's writing, 69, 168, 175–77, 244, 310n201, 368n158; women's writing in, 3–4, 7, 84, 219, 253, 258–60, 262–63, 269. *See also* Fonte, Moderata; Franco, Veronica; Marinella, Lucrezia
Venier, Domenico, 53, 64, 89, 260, 297n27, 301n76
Venier, Maffeo, 260, 293n248, 325n171, 358n26
Venier, Marco, 260

Venier, Sebastiano (doge), 89, 174, 216
Ventura, Comin, 28, 58
Venturelli, Cherubina, 8, 41, 270
Venus (mythological figure), 70, 78–80, 102, 124, 161, 195, 203, 205, 209, 353n193
Verlato, Leonoro, 123
Vernazza, Battista, 8–9, 23–24, 27, 56, 65, 214, 223, 225, 270
Verona, 2, 216, 218, 256, 267–68
Vicenza, 8, 17–18, 95–96, 219, 225–28, 257, 261, 264–65, 277n43
Vida, Girolamo, 37, 39
Virgil, 12, 110, 159, 166, 178, 180; as model/source, 111, 130, 145–46, 350n136, 354n214. *See also* Dido
"Virginia N.," 270
virgin martyr, as literary type, 31, 40, 42–44, 71–72, 124, 142, 144–48
Virgin Mary (biblical figure), 8, 35, 210; as corrective to Eve, 66, 68, 235, 302n90; in lyric poetry, 57, 65–69, 228, 290n198, 298n39; in narrative/meditative writings, 65, 129, 131–34, 138–41, 151–54, 215, 224–25, 229, 231, 235
Visdomini, Francesco, 53
Viterbo, Annius of, 159–60
Vives, Juan Luis, 165
Vivonne, Catherine de (Marquise de Rambouillet), xvii
von Grieffenberg, Catharina Regina, 328n20

woman warrior, as literary type, 42–44, 146, 177–83, 274n15, 344n70. *See also* Amazons
Wroth, Mary, xvii, 87, 208, 355n220

Xenophon, 214

Zenobia, Queen of Palmyra, 146
Zilioli, Alessandro, 197
Zinani, Gabriele, 123, 258, 325n171
Zorzi, Filippo, 15, 133
Zuzori, Fiore, 261, 281n85, 365n122